FIELDS OF
PSYCHOLOGY

~~◇~~

Edited by

J. P. GUILFORD

Professor of Psychology, University of Southern California

~~◇~~

In Association with

ANNE ANASTASI	C. M. LOUTTIT
HORACE B. ENGLISH	MILTON METFESSEL
G. L. FREEMAN	LAURANCE F. SHAFFER
DOUGLAS FRYER	MARY SHIRLEY
KATE HEVNER	MORRIS S. VITELES
DANIEL KATZ	C. J. WARDEN

TENTH PRINTING

NEW YORK

D. VAN NOSTRAND COMPANY, INC.

250 FOURTH AVENUE

First Published, February 1940
Reprinted, September 1940; February 1941
November 1941; December 1943; August 1944
February 1945; February 1946; November 1946
July 1947

PRINTED IN THE UNITED STATES OF AMERICA
BY GEORGE S. FERGUSON COMPANY
PHILADELPHIA, PA.

~~◇~~

AUTHORS

Anne Anastasi,

Horace B. English,
The Ohio State University.
G. L. Freeman,
Northwestern University.
Douglas Fryer,
New York University.
J. P. Guilford,
University of Nebraska.
Kate Hevner,
Indiana University.
Daniel Katz,
Princeton University.
C. M. Louttit,
Indiana University.
Milton Metfessel,
University of Southern California.
Laurance F. Shaffer,
Carnegie Institute of Technology.
Mary Shirley,
University of California, Berkeley.
Morris S. Viteles,
University of Pennsylvania.
C. J. Warden,
Columbia University.

~~◇~~

PREFACE

Frequently the second course in psychology for students in colleges of liberal arts is in the nature of a survey of the fields of psychology. This seems very appropriate, especially for those students who will complete only two semesters of psychology, and for whom it is important to learn of the varied role that psychology is playing in shaping modern thinking, and how its applications ramify throughout the whole range of human endeavor. There is no better way in which an enlightened appreciation of a subject can be imparted. Such a course is appropriate also for those students who are undecided as to a possible concentration in psychology, in that it should give them a better basis for making a decision. For those who may have decided upon psychology as their field of concentration, it should serve to guide them into the special fields that are most appealing to their temperaments and purposes. A recent study of opinion among industrial psychologists revealed a very general agreement that a course on the several fields would serve as an excellent orientation for the graduate student.

While there have been several textbooks written by single authors for such a course, the editor feels that psychology is now so specialized that it is difficult for one writer to survey adequately the significant developments in all the fields. The interpretation of a field to the student can best be accomplished by a writer who is himself immersed in that field. He then writes as an intimate insider rather than as an appraising outsider. His feeling for the right emphases, unless he is a one-sided worker in that field, can seldom be matched by that of an outsider. For these and other reasons, the editor believes that the textbook for this course should be in the nature of a symposium, written by contributors who have shown by their previous writings that they are very much at home in their respective fields.

The order of the chapters in this volume is somewhat arbitrary. They may be taught in almost any preferred sequence. The adopted sequence places the main theoretical fields first, beginning with the developmental approach. The chapters on differential psychology end this first section, since individual differences emerge from developmental causes, from social factors, and from causes that tend to induce abnormalities. The transition from differential to educational and clinical problems is very direct. The divisions of other applied fields and their order were agreed upon after much exchange of ideas on the part of the contributors. The more special fields of physiological psychology and aesthetics do not fit readily into the sequence of the first section on theoretical fields. The somewhat abstruse subject of points of view comes appropriately after the more concrete material, when the student is more ready to appreciate the reasons for divergent systematic approaches to psychology. The omission of a chapter on experimental psychology may seem a serious oversight to some readers. The term "experimental psychology" is losing its traditional meaning, however, as a separate and distinct field. All fields are becoming more and more experimental, and so the term is coming to refer to a method rather than a field.

Concerning the eminence of the writers who have contributed to this volume nothing need be said. To these contributors the editor is most grateful for taking the time out of their unusually busy lives to labor for a project that they believed to be worthy of their best efforts. All of them very readily caught the spirit of the volume and its purposes as the editor had originally conceived it, and have come forward with the fruits of their unique experiences in psychology. Not only the editor, but the profession of psychology is indebted to them for this devotion to their science. The editor wishes to express his personal gratitude also to his wife, Ruth B. Guilford, without whose constant encouragement and aid the volume could not have been brought to completion.

J. P. GUILFORD.

Los Angeles, California
August, 1939

CONTENTS

CHAPTER I

INTRODUCTION

By J. P. GUILFORD, *University of Nebraska*

When the history of science is written a hundred years from now, the twentieth century will probably be known as the psychological century, just as the one before it is regarded as the biological century and the ones preceding that as the physical and chemical centuries. The reason will be that in this century psychology made its greatest early advance and came of age, just as in the preceding century biology made a lasting place for itself among the sciences and came of age. Biology had its Darwin, its Huxley, and its Mendel. Psychology has had its Watson, its Binet, and its Freud, and still greater names may be added to its roster before the close of the present century.

Human Behavior on the World Stage.—The impact of psychology and its consequences are now beginning to make themselves felt in our everyday life and in the culture of this generation. Freud is almost a household word in some quarters, and the child psychologist comes in for his share of good-natured "banter" in our current plays and literature. We are beginning to realize that from the cradle to the grave our actions are very much determined by stimuli that impinge on our sense organs day after day. We realize, also, that most important among such stimuli are those of speech, either the spoken or printed word. We literally live in an environment of verbal stimuli. We know, further, that the avenues of communication throughout the world are now so wide open that we are continually subjected to stimulation from the far corners of the earth. What we do or decide to do, what we feel or think at breakfast tomorrow morning may be determined to some extent by what has happened in London or in Paris only a few moments before. Moreover, what the masses of other people do or say or think is similarly determined by the same type of stimuli.

1

These facts have made possible an art of propaganda such as the world has never known. Psychology is being applied as never before, to the management of other people through the medium of propaganda and otherwise. International wars are now often fought with cunning barrages of words as much as with swords or bullets or poison gas. The futility of bloodshed is generally recognized and most nations turn to it only as a last resort. The battle of wits, the strategy in administering verbal attacks, and the art of persuasion go merrily on. The refinement of methods in human control depends especially upon the discovery of psychological principles of mass reactions and mass thinking. Many of these principles, it must be admitted, are as yet only vaguely understood. Many of them are applied without a conscious realization that they are being utilized. And many of them are clearly and definitely established on a scientific basis.

The Control of Human Destiny.—The control of human actions on the grand scale of the present international stage setting comes to mind first because of the critical world situation of our time. The management of other human beings and of ourselves in the smaller setting of our workaday lives also depends no less upon the knowledge and use of psychological principles.

Imagine a Utopia in which children are born perfectly formed with normal sensory and motor powers. One can think of those babes as being trained, or "conditioned" to do the right thing at the right time, which means they have acquired the right kind of responses in connection with the stimuli and situations they will later meet. Such children, after training, would rarely if ever make mistakes, would adjust themselves to new life situations with a minimum of difficulty and conflict. There would be no crime, no mental defect, and no insanity. Probably half of the present cases of physical illness would be missing from the professional files of the medical men. There would be cooperation and peace instead of bickering and war. Impossible? Under present circumstances, yes. But by proper eugenic control of the generations yet to be born and by proper training of the young of our species, these ideal conditions could conceivably be approached. Perhaps we do not know one tenth of the biology and psychology we should need to know in order to bring about this proposed race of supermen. Nevertheless, it can be said with greater assurance that we now apply only a small fraction of what we do know.

PSYCHOLOGY AND MODERN CIVILIZATION

Why There Are Fields of Psychology.—While the practical aims of psychology are to make better human beings and to make human beings better, the science reaches into every corner of the animal kingdom. In its broadest conception it is the study of the things that all living organisms do as species and as individuals. And in the study of man in particular, it is led to examine *homo sapiens* in all his forms and in all his relationships, lest some significant fact about him escape. Examining the lives of all organisms, high or low, as it does, and embracing man in all his many-sided connections, psychology naturally tends to break up into definite fields. This is true not only in its attempts to discover facts and principles, but also in the application of those facts and principles to human problems. The walks of life, and the many problems of life that draw upon psychological knowledge are even more numerous and varied than the sources of information from which that psychological knowledge is drawn.

There are, in brief, many fields of applied psychology, as well as numerous fields of theoretical and experimental psychology. In the chapters to follow we shall be interested in both kinds of fields; those involved in the search for psychological knowledge, and those for the application of that knowledge. We shall see what kinds of things the psychologist does as a scientist in his laboratory and in his field research, and we shall also see what he does in his clinic and office where he functions as a new kind of human engineer. We shall see how his discoveries are leading to changes in human thinking and in human attitudes, touching the lives of millions of people who do not even come in direct contact with him.

How Psychology Changes Ways of Thinking.—As an example of how a new science can turn the ways of thinking of people into new directions, we may cite the teachings of Darwin concerning the evolution of species. As an example from earlier history, the teaching of Copernicus that the earth is not the center of the universe will serve. Such revolutionary ideas not only change human thinking, but also people's ways of living and acting as well. The teachings of psychology now have, and will likely continue to have, probably an even more important influence upon people's ways of looking at life, particularly with respect to themselves and their associates. The science has wrought no sudden revolution, such as that provoked by Darwin, possibly because we are now more prepared for the changes that it is bringing about. But the changes are none the less real, and doubtless just as profound.

Attitudes toward Misbehavior.—It is one of the aims of the chapters that follow to suggest what some of those important changes are. Even when not pointed out explicitly, those changes may be seen by implication by one who is alert to read between the lines. As an example, consider the general attitude of parents and others toward misbehavior. The traditional causes to which misbehavior has been attributed include such things as "temptations of Satan," "animal instincts," "bad heredity," or to "sparing the rod and spoiling the child." Naming one of these "causes" often excused the parent or teacher of any blame or led to drastic efforts to counteract the "bad" influence by measures that may have left the child in an even less desirable condition than before. Psychology, on the other hand, considers misbehavior, like all behavior, as the outcome of natural forces working in more or less well-known ways. The solution is to discover what forces are operating in any particular child and to apply the necessary remedial measures. The psychologist's attitude toward misconduct is much like that of the medical doctor toward a physical disease or defect. It must be carefully diagnosed and then treated.

The Clinical versus the Personal Attitude.—As another example, consider a very closely related problem, that of the relative seriousness of different kinds of misconduct. Parents, and many teachers, too, who are questioned on this point will almost invariably place at the head of the list of serious misdemeanors such things as stealing, cheating, lying, disobedience, obscene talk, swearing, smoking, and the like. Psychologists, on the other hand, are more inclined to place among the more serious types of behavior such things as fits of depression, unusual fears, cruelty, constant whining, withdrawing from social contacts, sulkiness, and the like.

The difference is one of fundamental point of view. Parents, and many teachers, regard as most serious that behavior which transgresses conventional moral standards, or is in opposition to parental control, or is disrupting to the comfortable routine of home or school. Psychologists, on the other hand, look for the symptoms of graver maladjustments to come. They are disturbed at any signs of extreme withdrawal from life situations, nervousness, and unusual ways of getting what the child wants. They know that certain habits, if persisted in, will later make the individual ineffective and unhappy. No one, of course, not even the psychologist, condones infractions of the moral code such as lying, stealing, and the like. The psychologist, however, feels that such infractions are less prophetic of a bad future than are the other kind of symptoms that he takes more seriously. He knows, too, that adult crime often grows out of childhood maladjustment as indicated by those symptoms, and that a child who breaks the commandments because of deeper-lying emotional disturbances is more to be watched than the one who does so in the manner of a prank or a lark.

We might summarize these two different outlooks on misbehavior by saying that the parent exhibits a more personal, moral attitude, in that he is concerned about behavior that disturbs him or will reflect upon him personally, whereas the psychologist takes a more impersonal, clinical attitude, in that he cares less about the immediate consequences of the child's act than he does about the child's future development into an effective, useful, happy adult. The time will undoubtedly come when parents and teachers will also catch more of the clinical spirit in dealing with troublesome behavior in their young charges. When they do, we will see a virtual revolution in the way in which the young are brought up and a marked decrease in wastage among adults.

Other Ways in Which Psychology Touches Modern Life. —These examples are only two of many that show how psychology is changing modern life. They have to do with the rearing of children.

Other phases of life could readily be mentioned here as examples, but these must be left to later chapters. Suffice it to say that the field of education, for example, is literally being made over, from the kindergarten to the graduate college, largely because of psychological discoveries and practices, and we have seen only the beginning as yet. A careful comparison of textbooks, examinations, and other aids to teaching with those employed a hundred years ago—or even thirty years ago—will show most radical changes. The innovation of psychological tests has given to education certain indispensable tools for adjusting the child to the school and the school to the child, for vocational guidance, and for other important purposes.

The psychologist has also found applications for his science in the market place, the industrial plant, the penal institution, the medical clinic and hospital, and in political affairs. In fact, wherever human beings must be dealt with, wherever their selection, their training, their attitudes, preferences, and interests are concerned, there is a place for the use of psychological knowledge and methods. For a fuller survey of the role of psychology in all these spheres of life, the student is referred to later chapters. It is not the purpose of this survey, however, to make of the student a practicing psychologist. The aim of this volume is merely to give him a better understanding than he now has of the varied role of psychology in helping to shape the thought and the practices of modern life. If the reader should feel at this point that the case for psychology has been grossly overstated, he is invited to read further, particularly in the chapters on applications. If he is then still of the same opinion, he is begged to indulge the author's optimistic faith in the future of this young science.

REFERENCES

Dexter, E. S., and Omwake, K. T. *An Introduction to the Fields of Psychology.* New York: Prentice-Hall, Inc., 1938.

Griffith, C. R. *General Introduction to Psychology,* Revised Edition. New York: The Macmillan Company, 1928.

Higginson, G. D. *Fields of Psychology.* New York: Henry Holt and Company, 1931.

Hulin, W. S. *A Short History of Psychology.* New York: Henry Holt and Company, 1934.

CHAPTER II

ANIMAL PSYCHOLOGY (VIEWPOINT AND PROGRAM)

By C. J. WARDEN, *Columbia University*

INTRODUCTION

Animal Psychology Began with Aristotle.—Animal psychology is as old as human psychology and the other biological sciences. It was founded by Aristotle, under the patronage of Alexander the Great, in connection with his pioneer attempt to systematize the field of natural science. Many years were spent in collecting, classifying, and interpreting all the available facts and folklore of the times, relating to the mental life and behavior of animals. First-hand observations were made, also, by Aristotle and his coworkers, on a wide variety of animal types. This material was finally brought together in the *Historia Animalium* and *De Anima,* the latter volume being a comparative treatment of man and animal.

It is easy enough to criticize these works in the light of our modern knowledge. For example, when observational facts were lacking, Aristotle often filled in the account with anecdotes and hearsay. Moreover, he was a thorough-going vitalist and hence his interpretation of animal activities was teleological and anthropomorphic. Nevertheless, his contribution toward the development of animal psychology was greater than that of any other writer up to the time of Darwin. A brief account of the more important findings and theoretical viewpoint of Aristotle will be found in a recent volume by Warden.[1]

Animal Psychology during the Middle Ages.—After Aristotle, animal psychology shared the common fate of the natural sciences for two millenia or more. As is well known, this was a period of general decadence in science. The later Greeks turned their attention from science to speculative philosophy and ethics. The center of

---

[1] Numbers like this [1] throughout the volume indicate references listed separately for each chapter beginning on page 647.

interest for the Romans was politics and imperialistic ambitions.
During the early part of the Christian era, the normal interest of mankind in natural science was largely displaced by zealous religious activities. The works of Aristotle on animal psychology were either
ignored or proscribed, along with many other pagan treatises on
science. This condition continued well through the Middle Ages, the
ban being finally lifted about the beginning of the thirteenth century.
Once this occurred, the works of Aristotle soon became the source of
final authority in the field of natural history. This attitude tended to
prevent the development of direct methods of investigation. As a
matter of fact, little or no genuine advance took place until the revival of natural science in the sixteenth century.

Animal Psychology Revived by the Naturalists.—From this
time forward, rapid strides were made in the development of most
biological fields. Numerous books on natural history appeared, based
upon new observations, in which considerable attention was given
to the behavior of animals. Somewhat later, special treatises were
published dealing separately and more intensively with fishes, birds,
insects, and other animal groups. The microscope was invented near
the beginning of the seventeenth century and this soon led to the
discovery of the unicellular organisms. The published reports of
naturalists and explorers supplied important information concerning
the behavior of animals in distant lands. As the author has shown
elsewhere,[2] the accumulation of knowledge was favored by refinements in observation and by the opening up of new lines of approach.

This great advance in knowledge tended to stimulate new speculations concerning the nature of the animal mind. Some naturalists
adopted the view of Aristotle and ascribed human-like qualities to
the higher animals. Others made a sharp dichotomy between the
mental life of animals and man. They argued that animal activities
are guided by divinely implanted instincts which vary from species
to species. Man alone possesses reason and the capacity for voluntary
activity involving moral and spiritual responsibility. This view was
fostered by the theological demand that the primacy of man should
rest on a definite, qualitative basis. In contrast to these older theories,
the position of Descartes reflected the developing thought of the seven-

teenth century. He held that even the higher animals are merely living machines and possess no mental life. Their activities are simply the automatic functioning of the natural body structure. Thus all the behavior of infrahuman organisms can be explained, so he insisted, in terms of mechanistic, physiological principles. Such a radical view at this time indicates very clearly that leaders in the field of animal psychology no longer felt bound by authority and tradition.

The Influence of Darwin.—The rate of development was greatly increased by the publication of Darwin's *Origin of Species* in 1859. Previous to this time, there had been no central problem around which the interest in animal psychology might crystallize. The theory of evolution, as proposed by Darwin, offered a problem both urgent and broad in scope. The concept of mental continuity in all living organisms aroused a new and widespread interest in the mental and behavioral life of animals. It ushered in the modern epoch in comparative psychology. The movement thus begun led in time to the establishment of the science as a separate biological discipline. Perhaps there is no better way to come to an understanding of the present-day viewpoint and program of the science than by tracing briefly the major developments that have occurred since that time. In making such a survey, it will be convenient to treat in order the two following periods of the modern epoch:

The Anecdotal Period (1859-1890).
The Experimental Period (1890-   ).

The Anecdotal Period

The Question of Mental Evolution.—According to Darwin's theory, all living organisms fall into a natural phylogenetic sequence. The thread of causal continuity begins with the simplest animals and ends with man, the highest and most complex type. This continuity is not only structural but also functional and mental. It involves the type and the series of types as a whole. He sought to explain this evolutionary sequence in terms of the principles of variation and natural selection. When variants from an existing type possessed new characters that had survival value, they were likely to become new types in time under proper conditions of segregation and inbreeding. Darwin had collected considerable evidence for structural evolution before he proposed his theory. Within a few years, a large body of interested workers supplied enough additional evidence to convince the scientific world on this point. It was necessary, however, to demonstrate mental evolution in order to establish Darwin's proposal as a general theory. It is small wonder, therefore, that a large part of the writings of Darwin was given over to speculation and argument concerning the evolution of mind and behavior.

But here the evolutionary school ran into a number of serious difficulties. In the first place, very little accurate information was at hand bearing upon the mental capacities of even the more common animal types. Systematic observation and experimental methods did not emerge until several decades later. In the second place, many leading thinkers of the day were strongly opposed to a theory which linked human mentality with that of the animals. They were willing to admit that man's body might very well be a heritage from lower ape-like creatures. Nor did they object to the notion of mental evolution as applied to infrahuman organisms. They insisted, however, that there was a wide chasm between the mentality of the higher animals and that of man which the theory of evolution could not bridge. The intellectual, moral, and spiritual aspects of the human mind were special gifts from the gods and had no connection with the evolutionary process. This view was held at first even by such ardent evolutionists as Wallace and Huxley.

The Development of Instincts and Intelligence.—The first task of Darwin was to show that simple instincts tend to become complex as animal types increase in structural complexity. This should be true, according to his theory, because functional complexity would be likely to possess survival value in such a case. Thus structural and behavioral elaboration arose together naturally through the operation of the same evolutionary mechanism. The second task of Darwin was to show that a rudimentary intelligence arose from time to time out of a matrix of complex instincts. Once a connection between instinct and intelligence could be demonstrated, the further evolution of the latter might be taken for granted because of its survival value. However, the notion that instinct and intelligence are continuous phases of mental evolution was contrary to current opinion. For centuries the view had prevailed that instinct and intelligence are antithetical in nature, the one characterizing animal and the other human activities. It was only after long years of controversy that Darwin's conception was accorded general acceptance.

According to Darwin, intelligence is common to both the higher animals and man, although it has reached its most complex elaboration in the latter. One should expect, therefore, to find that animals most closely akin to man possess a rudimentary intelligence of the human sort. In the last analysis, the crucial problem for Darwin was to demonstrate that this was really true. If this gap could be bridged, complete mental continuity would be demonstrated and the general position of the evolutionary school would carry the day.

The Development of Human Morals and Spiritual Life.—As noted above, the supposedly distinctive human traits are those comprising the intellectual, moral, and spiritual life of the race. With keen insight, Darwin saw that these capacities rested upon a highly developed social life. In such a situation, so he argued, sympathy, mutual aid, parental and filial affection, and the like would possess group survival value. He further insisted that "any animal endowed with well-marked social instincts, would inevitably acquire a moral sense or conscience" as soon as its "intellectual powers" evolved up to or near the human level. He realized, however, that mere argument was not enough. The search of Darwin and his followers for concrete evidences of rudimentary human-like traits in the higher animals ushered in the anecdotal movement.

Anecdotalism.—The only evidence readily available at this time consisted of anecdotes describing the unusual exploits of animals. These were collected by the protagonists of evolution from published sources, private correspondence, and mere hearsay. Scores of such collections appeared during the three decades following the announcement of Darwin's theory. The dog, cat, horse, elephant, and monkey were the general favorites, although the social insects were often included. Some of these anecdotes were taken from unreliable sources, but most of them were dependable enough as mere stories. In any case, the exploits reported were so interpreted as to eulogize and humanize the animal's conduct. Even the more commonplace acts of the higher animals were made to appear "almost human" in their absurd anecdotal setting. One can hardly expect to capture the real spirit of the times without reading selections from Romanes [3] or similar collections.

Anecdotes Usually Humanized the Higher Animals.—In general, these anecdotes were intended to exemplify such human-like capacities as the following in the higher animals: (1) Reasoning ability, (2) social cooperation, (3) primary emotions and sentiments, and (4) a rudimentary moral sense. Reasoning ability was presumably indicated by the fact that animals are able to learn tricks, avoid capture by traps, outwit man at times, and the like. Stories purporting to show the use of signs or sounds by two animals in planning together the capture of prey were offered as evidence of social cooperation. The domestic animals provided the source of numerous anecdotes illustrating sympathy, curiosity, jealousy, emulation, and other emotions. The anthropomorphic tendency reached the ridiculous, however, in the attempt to show that the higher animals exhibit a sense of shame, a sense of justice, and other moral sentiments. The underlying assumption seemed to be that in so far as an animal behaves like man it must also feel like man.

Criticisms of the Anecdote.—The following criticisms may be urged against the anecdote as a source of scientific information regarding the mental life and behavior of animals:

(1) That the observer is likely to be untrained and unable to give an accurate account of the happening, even if his intentions are of the best; (2) that interpretative elements are likely to be confused in the report with factual elements, making it impossible for the scientist later to separate the two; (3) that the happening even when adequately reported is usually an incident cut off from the essential genetic antecedents (both individual and phyletic) which would explain it and give it proper significance; (4) that the happening, in the nature of the case, represents highly selected and atypical behavior that can have little or no statistical validity; (5) that even if the tendency of

mankind to humanize the animal—whether in a scientific or a literary mood—is restrained, errors of memory and of transmission (if verbal) are likely to enter; and (6) there is the difficulty of selecting reliable, authentic material from the various available sources. It is evident that the method, even when guardedly employed, which usually was not the case, hardly deserves to be considered scientific in the strict sense.

The Value of the Anecdote.—The anecdotal collections were widely read and the popular imagination was deeply stirred. The use of such evidence by the sober scientists of the day is to be explained in large part by the bitter controversy that raged over the doctrine of mental continuity. Although such evidence possessed little or no real value, it was an important influence in the final establishment of the evolutionary theory. Moreover, the tendency to humanize, while an error, was effective in breaking down the traditional distinction between the mental life of man and animal. The chief value of the anecdotal movement, however, was in keeping alive the broad interest that had been aroused in the field of animal psychology. In time, this interest was divorced from the controversy over mental continuity and turned in the direction of scientific investigation. This transition occurred about 1890 and ushered in the experimental period which has continued up to the present.

THE EXPERIMENTAL PERIOD

The new movement began as a revolt against the method and viewpoint of the early post-Darwinian school. The doctrine of mental continuity had been generally accepted, hence there was no further need to use anecdotal material. For the same reason, the urge to humanize animal behavior had become less pressing. There was a growing tendency to study animal activities for their own sake, quite apart from the earlier controversial setting. At first, the anecdote was replaced by careful and systematic observations of behavior. Somewhat later, simple experiments of the laboratory type were introduced. This required the invention of special methods and techniques in a hitherto unworked field. During the past half-century, the experimental approach has gradually come to play an increasingly dominant role in the science. This expansion has been paralleled by a remarkable development in the elaboration and refinement of laboratory methods. As might be expected, this shift in content and emphasis was accompanied by important changes in theoretical viewpoint. In order to understand the present position of the science, a brief review of the major developments of the period will be necessary.

The Pioneers.—The new movement arose about 1890 from the pioneer work of four great leaders: Lubbock, Morgan, Loeb, and Verworn. Sir John Lubbock was an English naturalist and statesman whose interest in the behavior of insects can be traced back to the personal influence of Darwin. Lloyd Morgan was an English biologist and thinker who studied extensively the behavior of the higher vertebrates. Jacques Loeb and Max Verworn were both physiologists of the German school who sought to analyze the activities of the lower organisms along rigidly scientific lines. For quite a time, each of these leaders worked independently of the other in his chosen field. Each devised and applied experimental methods and each developed his own particular point of view. When these four lines of work converged into a single movement, the success of a truly scientific animal psychology was assured.

Lubbock was the first of this group to make use of experimental methods, his collected studies on insect behavior appearing in 1882. He invented the maze method and the problem method for use in this field. He devised the technique of marking individuals so that their movements could be accurately traced. He was the first to present the results of behavioral investigations in tabular form showing individual variations and group averages. He formulated the principle now utilized in most experimentation that animal intelligence should be tested by placing between the organism and some natural incentive an obstacle "which a little ingenuity will enable them to overcome." After years of research, he published a volume on the *Senses, Instincts, and Intelligence of Animals* without including a single anecdote. Lubbock was far ahead of his time both in method and in viewpoint.

Morgan was the first to apply experimental methods to the study of behavior in the higher vertebrates. He compared the instinctive repertory of numerous species of birds and mammals and devised simple tests to determine their mode of learning. He originated the incubator technique, in order to eliminate the possibility of early parental influences on the unfolding of instincts in birds. In 1896, he delivered a course of lectures at Harvard and Chicago Universities which were later published as *Instinct and Habit*. As we have shown elsewhere,[4] these lectures stimulated directly the rise of experimental work in America. Previous to this time he had developed the concept of "trial and error" learning which has since played a prominent role in general psychological theory. Perhaps he is best known, however, in connection with the canon which he formulated in his *Comparative Psychology* in 1894. Morgan's canon runs as follows: "In no case may we interpret an action as the outcome of the exercise of a higher psychical faculty if it can be interpreted as the outcome of one which stands lower in the psychological scale." This is merely the law of parsimony, long accepted in the natural sciences, applied to the field of animal psychology. This canon eventually gained wide acceptance and was most effective in substituting a saner interpretation of animal behavior for the humanizing of the anecdotal period.

The early work of Loeb was confined to the plant-like, sessile co-elenterates. He found that these lowly organisms bend directly toward or away from light, gravity, and other stimuli. Such orientational responses, or tropisms, in plants had long been regarded as unconscious, physicochemical processes. Loeb's findings led him to believe that the behavior of lower animals, like that of plants, is tropistic in character. In time, he extended this concept to cover practically all instinctive behavior. He denied mental life to all but the higher animals in which the ability to learn could be demonstrated. This position was similar in general to that of Descartes mentioned in an earlier section, although somewhat less radical. It was much more extreme than the viewpoint represented by Morgan's canon. While it was rejected by many, it was an important influence in turning the tide away from the anthropomorphism of the previous period. In time, it became the fashion to believe, with Loeb, that the insect is forced to fly into a candle flame, and to treat as old-fashioned the notion of Romanes that it does so out of innate "curiosity."

Verworn extended experimental methods to the motile unicellular organisms, or Protista. His extensive researches in this field were published in 1889 as the *Protistenstudien*. His pioneer work on the lower organisms was extended and elaborated later by Jennings,[5] one of his foremost pupils. Verworn developed a tropism theory much less radical than that of Loeb. He held that the reactions of lower organisms are determined to a large extent by internal factors, or physiological states. Such motile types as he studied did not, so he found, orient directly to external stimuli after the manner of sessile animals and plants. Nevertheless, he regarded the internal determining factors as physiological rather than mental. He did not attempt, however, to extend this viewpoint to the more complex multicellular types. His main contribution was in opening a new field to experimental analysis. As we shall see, the findings of Verworn and his students on the behavior of the lower organisms assumed considerable theoretical importance at a later time.

Later Developments.—The work of the pioneers, while of outstanding importance, represented the mere beginnings of the science as we know it today. They had done little more than point the way by devising a few simple methods and applying these to a relatively small number of animal types. There still remained the task of broadening the experimental approach by the invention of new and more adequate methods and the adapting of these to many divergent types of animals. Obviously, the gradual building up of a large body of systematic facts worthy of the name of a science depended upon later developments in this direction. It will be of interest to note a few of the more important lines of advance that occurred later in the extension of experimental methods. A more complete survey of this period of rapid growth will be found in other connections.[6]

The decade centering around 1900 witnessed a remarkable outburst of animal experimentation among psychologists and biologists. Jennings [7] had begun his extensive work on the unicellular organisms, and had demonstrated "trial and error" activities and simple habit-formation in these lowly types. Studies on learning in the more complex invertebrates were carried out by various workers in Germany, France, and America. Yerkes adapted the maze method to the crab and the crayfish, and Thorndike devised the compartment maze for fishes. Many investigations were made, during this decade, on the behavior of the social insects—a continuation of Lubbock's line of research. The work of Morgan on birds was considerably extended by Thorndike, Kline, and other American psychologists.

Experiments Extended to Mammals.—The most important advance of the decade by far was the extension, for the first time, of experimental methods to the mammals. Up to this time only observational studies had been made on this group. In fact, it was commonly believed that these higher animals could not be tested profitably under artificial laboratory conditions. This new line of experimentation was initiated, about the turn of the century, by Thorndike at Harvard, by Kline and Small at Clark University, and by Pavlov in Russia. Thorndike carried out an extensive series of experiments on dogs, cats, and monkeys by means of numerous problem-boxes which he invented for the purpose. His analysis of learning and imitation in these animals excited wide interest and stimulated further research. Kline and Small studied learning in the white rat on specially devised problem-boxes and mazes. As is well known, this animal soon became the favorite type for laboratory use. The Russian physiologist, Pavlov, discovered the conditioned-reflex in the dog and thus opened up a new and important line of research. The work of these several leaders has served as a model for much of the later experimentation on the mammals.

Methods of Animal Psychology Extended to the Study of Man.— The extension of experimental methods to the higher animals was effective in stimulating the broad movement that has continued to the present time. It meant to the psychologist that many of the problems relating to learning and intelligence in man could now be approached from the genetic angle by utilizing animal studies. Once this was realized, laboratories were set up in the leading American universities, and periodicals devoted to animal research were established. This led in turn to the development of new and improved methods and to the gradual accumulation of a body of systematic facts concerning the behavioral life of animals. The steady growth of the experimental movement, during the past three decades, has been reviewed at some length in a recent paper by the present author.[8]

The Objective Viewpoint.—As we have seen, the tendency to humanize animal behavior without restraint had been discarded by the pioneers at the beginning of the experimental period. This did not mean, however, that the principle of anthropomorphic interpretation had been wholly abandoned. As a matter of fact, Morgan's canon merely insisted that such interpretation be made with reasonable sanity and caution. It was still the common belief that animal studies could hardly be classed as psychological unless inferences were drawn regarding the mental states involved. It is clear that such inferences must be based, in the last analysis, upon comparison by analogy with the mental states of man in corresponding situations. Several decades passed before this principle of anthropomorphic analogy was rejected in favor of a definite objective viewpoint. During this time, a number of speculative problems regarding the nature of the animal mind were widely discussed. Certain of these will be briefly noted here, in as much as they had a direct bearing upon the final emancipation of animal psychology from mentalistic influences.

The Question of Consciousness in Lower Animals.—The question of the proper criterion to be used to determine the presence or absence of consciousness in animals occasioned no little controversy. Loeb held that the ability to learn was the only dependable evidence of consciousness. Lubbock and Morgan argued that such a criterion was purely arbitrary, since an animal might be conscious while performing reflex and instinctive acts. They believed that all living organisms possessed at least a vague consciousness of some sort. To deny this was to raise the problem as to when and how consciousness first appeared in the evolution of animal types. In any case, the criterion of Loeb lost its meaning as soon as Jennings had demonstrated that even unicellular organisms are able to learn. These new facts seemed to support the opinion of Lubbock and Morgan that life and consciousness are coextensive. Such a view fitted in perfectly well with the prevailing doctrine of mental continuity.

Levels of Mental Activity.—The speculative emphasis then shifted to the problem of establishing a scale of psychic levels to be used in classifying animals. Morgan proposed a scale of three levels as follows: (a) *Sentience*—a dim awareness, probably possessed by the simplest organisms; (b) *effective consciousness*—associated with the use of past experience in guiding later activities; and (c) *self-consciousness*—associated with analytical reasoning ability. The latter level, so he held, presupposed a complex central nervous system and the use of language and is possessed only by man. A number of similar scales were developed by others. In all cases, the placement of a species in the psychic scale was to be made after noting the complexity of its bodily structure and behavior. It is obvious, therefore, that the assigned mental status would be a mere inference rather than a directly observed fact. Moreover, even if such a scale were acceptable its application might well be regarded as of doubtful value. What would be gained, indeed, by bringing the animal world under such a simple, three-level, psychological classification?

Behaviorism Appears.—About 1912, Watson [9] made a vigorous attack against all such speculations regarding the nature of the animal mind. He pointed out the fact that these attempts to delve into the mental life of animals had done nothing more than arouse futile controversies. These can never be settled, because the mental life of animals cannot be directly observed by man. He insisted that to try to infer their mental life from structural and behavioral complexity is merely to fall back on the principle of anthropomorphic analogy. But this principle is not logically sound; it is merely reasoning in a circle. The inner life of animals, if such they have, is forever hidden from human observation. Clearly then, it lies outside the field of scientific investigation. All attempts to interpret animal mentality turn out to be pretentious and useless speculations. In order to be truly scientific, animal psychology must reject the principle of inference by analogy and thus rid itself of the last vestige of anthropomorphism. In the final analysis, Watson had simply followed to their logical conclusion the arguments raised by the pioneers against humanizing animal behavior.

On the positive side, Watson proposed that the animal psychologist investigate stimulus-response relationships, as observed in the laboratory and the natural environment. Since the terms involved are both objective, such a treatment would bring animal psychology definitely into the field of the natural sciences. As he pointed out, the prediction and control of behavior would thus become possible without dragging mental analogues into the description at all. The behavior of the organism as a whole is to be regarded as a self-explanatory system, since complex activities may be analyzed into simple acts. The concept of behavioral levels thus supplants the older notion of psychic levels. Animal activities may even be rated as to the degree of intelligence exhibited, without recourse to mentalistic terms. For intelligent behavior is characterized by successful adjustment to environmental situations, and this factor can be checked objectively. Whatever one may think of the extension of Watson's position to the human field, it would seem to be entirely proper and adequate for animal psychology. Although there was some opposition at first, this objective principle has now become the settled viewpoint in the science.

As noted in this brief survey, a remarkable series of advances have occurred during the period which began about 1890. At the very beginning, anecdotal content and the more extreme humanizing interpretation were both thrown overboard. The gradual development of observational and experimental methods made possible the building up of a sketchy factual content. The invention of new methods and the extension and refinement of experimental techniques have been effective in rounding out this body of knowledge along systematic lines. Finally, animal psychology has adopted the objective viewpoint and thus discarded entirely the principle of anthropomorphic interpretation. Having settled these fundamental problems, it is now possible to lay out a comprehensive program of investigation as a guide to future developments. The broad outlines of such a program will be presented in the following section.

The Program of Animal Psychology

The proper program of any science is to develop its field of possible knowledge along systematic lines. Such a program is best indicated by a division of the field, from a broad perspective, into major and minor problems and lines of research. It is impossible, at the present time, to offer more than a tentative program for animal psychology because the science is still in the early formative stage. Nevertheless, this should be of some value in orienting the student with reference to the nature and scope of the field as now envisaged. Our first task will be to classify the types of behavior that are open to analysis and to point out the problems that fall naturally under each type. This will serve to indicate roughly the scope of possible knowledge relative to a given individual or a species. Our second task will be to compare and contrast the several major lines of approach which are now utilized in the analysis of behavior.

Classification of Behavior.—It has long been the tradition to divide animal activities into two main classes: Native and acquired. The first class would include reflexes, tropisms, and instincts, whereas the latter would comprise habits or learned reactions. This two-way classification rests upon the old notion that a clear-cut dichotomy exists between hereditary and environmental factors in the field of behavior. This notion has now been discarded on the basis of extensive genetic studies in the animal field. The evidence shows that hereditary and environmental factors operate together throughout the whole course of development. They are interpenetrated, rather than independent, from the moment of fertilization onward. This means that all types of behavior are partly native and partly acquired. It is doubtless true that many of the early and simpler forms of behavior are dominantly hereditary, since they appear before environmental factors can play much of a role. However, the relative dominance of the two factors can hardly be demonstrated in connection with many types of complex behavior that appear later in the life cycle. In any case, a two-way classification is of little value in formulating the multitudinous kinds of reactions to be found in the animal world. It seems best, therefore, to offer a new and more elaborate classification that does not involve the native-acquired distinction. The question as to the genetic origins of each type of behavior will thus be left open, as it should be, for independent investigation.

Receptive and Reactive Capacities.—In the following outline, an attempt has been made to divide behavior into classes that correspond to fairly definite biopsychological functions. As will be noted, two main groups of activities are here recognized: (a) Receptive capacities, and (b) reactive capacities. The one includes the sensory and perceptual processes, whereas the other comprises the behavioral reactions which occur in laboratory and habitat situations. The numerous sub-types, under each main division, follow roughly the natural lines of functional cleavage. For example, the categories under receptive capacities correspond to the sensory systems commonly found in living organisms. Moreover, the types of behavior, listed under reactive capacities, refer to important and fairly definite life activities. On the whole, the classification here offered is in agreement with the general program of research now followed in animal psychology.

General Classification of Behavior

I. *Receptive Capacities*

Chemoreception: taste, smell, common chemical sense
Thermoreception: temperature sense
Contact Reception: pressure sense
Phonoreception: hearing
Photoreception: vision
Electric Reception: sensitivity to electrical stimuli
Statoreception: equilibratory sense
Internal Reception: kinesthetic and organic senses

II. *Reactive Capacities*

Simple Movements: motor coordination, grasping, and locomotion—walking, swimming, flying, crawling, etc.
Feeding Behavior: activities associated with the securing and ingestion of food, water, etc.
Protective Behavior: autotomy-regeneration, avoiding and defense reactions, modes of attack, fighting, etc.
Reproductive Behavior: primary sexual activities, courtship, mating, care of the young, etc.

Special Types of Behavior: limited to certain animal types
  Inactive States: hibernation, sleep, hypnosis, etc.
  Sound Production and Communication, etc.

Group Behavior—Intraspecies: aggregation, migration, leadership, domestic and familiar relationships, play, etc.

Group Behavior—Interspecies: parasitism, symbiosis, commensalism, biotic community life, etc.

Orienting Behavior: positive and negative orientation to various sorts of stimuli, homing, etc.

Temperament and Emotional Expression

Motivation Factors in Behavior: incentive-drive indices and the relative importance of these factors in typical life activities

Modifiability of Behavior: learning-retention indices showing range of capacity to form new patterns of adjustment

General Intelligence: general level of behavioral capacity based on an evaluation of all indices of receptive and reactive capacities

Problems Opened by the Classification.—As might be expected, the several types of behavior listed in the outline involve different problems calling for special methods of attack. A few examples may be cited in passing. In the analysis of each receptive capacity, the most common problems are as follows: (a) Range of sensitivity to effective stimuli, (b) discrimination limens, (c) importance of the modality in normal perceptual life. The organs of hearing and vision are often elaborate enough to suggest further analysis within these fields. Can an animal make use of pitch, timbre, and intensity cues as single dimensions? How accurately can a given species localize sounds in space? Is color vision present? How does brightness vision compare with size, form, and pattern discrimination? It should be clear that the problems of sensory analysis are much the same here as in the human field. Naturally the methods of testing are quite different and introspective reports cannot be obtained on the animal subjects. In the case of many of the reactive capacities, the chief problem is to secure an adequate knowledge of the animal's mode of life in its natural habitat. Such a descriptive background is necessary in order to arrange suitable laboratory conditions for measuring motivation, learning, and intelligence. Some of the problems and methods relating to these three experimental fields will be described and illustrated in the following chapter.

Major Lines of Approach.—Before dealing with specific methods, it seems desirable to discuss very briefly the three major lines of approach which properly belong to the science. These are as follows: (a) Observation and experimentation, (b) genetic analysis, and (c) comparative synthesis. In actual practice, these several modes of investigation are not altogether distinct. There is considerable overlapping both in methodology and in content. In spite of this fact, essential differences are involved in so far as general perspective or mode of approach is concerned. Moreover, they are markedly divergent in aim and in breadth of scope. Each major line of approach fills an important place in the comprehensive program of animal psychology.

Observation and Experimentation.—Observation and experimentation play the dominant role here as in the other natural sciences. This general and basic line of approach must be utilized in all studies of animal behavior, since it is the only way to secure new concrete facts. Experimentation differs from observation mainly in the utilization of laboratory controls which insure greater specificity and accuracy of results. The stimulus is better defined, distractions of all sorts are excluded, and the response to the stimulus is more precise and definite. Such control is made possible by the use of dark rooms, soundproof rooms, automatic presentation of stimuli, apparatus limiting the freedom of the test animal, and numerous other laboratory devices. Moreover, specific problems can be set, which might never occur in nature, and these can be repeated until statistically dependable results are secured. Nevertheless, observational studies in the field are important and should always precede attempts at experimental analysis. Suitable living conditions in the laboratory and appropriate experimental settings presuppose a broad knowledge of the activities of the species in its natural habitat. Moreover, most of the reactive capacities listed in the outline above must be studied, in part at least, by systematic field work. This is particularly true of protective behavior, group behavior, reproductive behavior, homing, and the like. In the last analysis, observation and experimentation differ only in degree and tend to supplement each other in a well-rounded program of research.

The Genetic Approach.—Genetic analysis represents the developmental approach to the behavior of a given species. The interest here is in the series of changes which occur in the behavior repertory of the type during the complete life cycle. This involves the timing of the initial appearance of each activity and a record of the variations which it undergoes through the periods of maturity and decline. In actual practice, genetic analysis in animals is seldom carried beyond adolescence, largely because early development is more interesting and convenient to study. It is here, indeed, that the best evidence concerning the relative dominance of hereditary and environmental factors is to be found. Nevertheless, a complete genetic study would cover the entire life cycle of the species. It is true, of course, that genetic analysis involves observation and, at times, simple experimentation. However, the problems and perspective differ essentially from the usual cross-section studies in which observation and experimentation are employed. In seeking to build up a generalized, life-cycle pattern of behavior for the species, genetic analysis must take into account such variant factors as strain, sex, and age differences.

The Comparative Approach.—Comparative synthesis represents the broad evolutionary approach to the behavior of the animal world as a whole. It is phylogenetic in scope and perspective, whereas genetic analysis is limited to ontogenetic problems. It involves the comparison as to behavioral level of species, genera, orders, classes, phyla, and other related groups. Such comparison may be limited to a few allied species or orders or it may be extended to the larger groupings, as the evidence at hand seems to warrant. It may be restricted to a single type of activity, such as vision, or be broadened to include the complete synthesis of behavior which we have termed "General Intelligence" in the outline of the preceding section. In brief, comparative synthesis takes into account all intergroup differences in behavioral capacities.

The central aim of the comparative approach is to trace the rise in behavioral complexity which has taken place as the structural complexity of animal types has increased from age to age. This would lead, in the end, to a broad synthesis covering the evolution of general intelligence from the simplest living organism to man, the highest of the Primate order. Such a synthesis would require a comprehensive and intensive program of research on representative animal types at all levels of behavioral complexity. This suggests a task of such magnitude that it may well be regarded as the final, and perhaps ideal, goal of animal psychology. In any case, it must be admitted that up to the present little has been done toward the attainment of this end. Nevertheless, it should be realized that the facts and interpretations of animal psychology find their most interesting and meaningful place within the framework of a broad comparative synthesis.

The comparative approach presents certain fundamental difficulties that tend to hinder systematic advance. Perhaps the most important of these grows out of the wide diversity in structure and function that exists among animal types. Some notion of the scope of such divergence may be had by a cursory examination of the chapter, in a recent volume,[10] on the comparative morphology and physiology of organisms. The differences here are most marked in connection with the reactive mechanisms on which all activities depend. For example, some animals crawl, some walk, some swim, while others fly. It is difficult, indeed, to plan an apparatus which can be used to test such variant types. It is obvious, however, that the same problem must be presented to the animal types to be compared, if legitimate conclusions are to be drawn regarding differences in behavioral level. The test situations must be equally fair to all. The development of standardized apparatus suitable for testing a reasonable variety of types will be necessary before genuine advance can be made by the comparative approach.

The Present Emphasis.—The main emphasis of psychologists up to the present has been on laboratory studies rather than field work. The reasons for this should be fairly apparent. In the first place, the primary impetus behind the present movement was the development of experimental methods. The feeling still prevails, in some quarters, that field studies are of second-rate importance, and may well be left to the naturalist. In the second place, the topics that yield best to laboratory study have seemed to be more definitely psychological and more closely allied to the human field. These topics are largely confined to the following three classes of behavior: (a) Receptive capacities, (b) motivation, and (c) learning and intelligence. Most of the contributions relating to the other classes of activities, listed in the outline of the preceding section, have been made by biologists. There are some indications, however, that this narrow emphasis on laboratory work is beginning to give way to a broader systematic outlook. This is suggested by an increase in the number of comprehensive and extremely valuable field studies on primates and other animal types.

A further narrowing influence has been the continued emphasis in research on the behavior of the higher vertebrates—birds and mammals. This is due, no doubt, to the widespread feeling that the greatest contribution can be made to human psychology by work on these groups. In any case, the study of the activities of the invertebrates and the lower vertebrates has been left, very largely, to biologists with a special interest in the problems of behavior. So far as present indications go this situation seems likely to continue into the indefinite future. Another trend in emphasis is represented by the extensive interest in the learning process, as exhibited by the white rat in various test situations. A large part of the present laboratory output is concerned with some phase of this general problem. The aim here is to analyze the learning process in detail in the hope of developing a general theory applying to all organisms. It seems logical to believe, however, that the study of such higher mammals as dogs, cats, raccoons, monkeys, and apes would throw more light on the nature of the learning process in man. There is some reason to believe that this undue emphasis on the behavior of the rat is now being corrected by the recent emphasis upon primate research.

These several trends have determined, in an important way, the selection of methods and results to be presented in the chapter that follows, for our interest there will be to illustrate the more advanced developments in the field to date. This means that we shall limit the brief survey to the three topics, mentioned above, on which laboratory work has been largely concentrated. In like manner, the treatment will be restricted to the higher animals since the most refined methods have been devised for these types. Furthermore, the white rat will be given greater prominence than it properly deserves, because it has been tested so much more extensively than any other types in the animal laboratory.

REFERENCES

Jennings, H. S. *Behavior of the Lower Organisms.* New York: Columbia University Press, 1906.

Morgan, C. L. *Introduction to Comparative Psychology.* New York: Charles Scribner's Sons, 1894.

Romanes, G. J. *Animal Intelligence.* London: K. Paul, 1881.

Thorndike, E. L. *Animal Intelligence.* New York: The Macmillan Company, 1911. (Col. papers, 1898-1901.)

Warden, C. J. *A Short Outline of Comparative Psychology.* New York: W. W. Norton and Company, 1927.

Warden, C. J., Jenkins, T. N., and Warner, L. H. *Comparative Psychology. Vol. I, Principles and Methods.* New York: The Ronald Press Company, 1935.

Warden, C. J., and Warner, L. H. The development of animal psychology in the United States during the past three decades, *Psychol. Rev.*, 1927, 34, 196-205.

Watson, J. B. *Behavior: An Introduction to Comparative Psychology.* New York: Henry Holt and Company, 1914.

CHAPTER III

ANIMAL PSYCHOLOGY (METHODS AND RESULTS) *

By C. J. WARDEN, *Columbia University*

INTRODUCTION

As indicated in the preceding chapter, this brief survey will be limited in scope to the following three topics: (1) receptive capacities, (2) motivation, and (3) learning and intelligence. As a matter of fact, most of the laboratory studies that have been made, up to the present, fall within these fields. This is partly because the problems here are likely to be definite and open to ready experimental analysis. Moreover, these three fields correspond rather closely to certain major topics in human psychology, and this gives them special interest and significance. The student may refer to more comprehensive surveys of animal psychology [1] for a treatment of such other types of behavior as we have listed in the outline of the preceding chapter.

It will be impossible, in the brief space permitted, to cover even sketchily the three topics mentioned above for the animal kingdom as a whole. It seems desirable, therefore, to restrict the treatment to the methods and results relating to the behavior of the vertebrates. Even as thus limited, only a few of the better standardized methods in each field can be described and illustrated. The samples of apparatus included will be those adapted for testing the more common laboratory animals. Our primary aim will be merely to illustrate the kinds of methods and results which characterize these three major fields of investigation.

RECEPTIVE CAPACITIES

The primary aim of sensory analysis is to determine the role of taste, smell, hearing, vision, and other modes of reception in the

* Thanks are due to the Ronald Press for permission to copy the ten figures used in this chapter from Warden, Jenkins, and Warner, *Comparative Psychology,* Volumes 1 and 3.

life-activities of animal types. This end is best attained by securing precise indices in the laboratory of the receptive functions which can be checked later against the complex behavior of the natural habitat. Until this has been done, it is hardly possible to set up appropriate problems in the fields of motivation, learning, and intelligence, for such problems must be arranged to harmonize with the sensory contacts of the particular species. For example, most birds possess little or no sense of smell, hence it would be absurd to set a task for them which required the use of this function. Such a task would be proper enough for dogs since they possess a very keen sense of smell. It is clear, therefore, that sensory analysis should precede experimentation on the more complex forms of behavior. Before passing to the treatment of the concrete methods of testing the receptive capacities, it will be advisable to discuss certain concepts and principles that possess general significance for this field. As we shall see, the methodology utilized in measuring discrimination ability in animals differs in several important respects from that commonly employed in the human field.

Principles of Analysis.—An objective criterion of discrimination has long since been adopted for use in animal work. This became necessary when it was realized that any "sensations" which may arise from stimulating animals are beyond human knowledge. Moreover, verbal report is impossible in as much as there is no common language for communication between man and animal. The objective criterion which has been adopted is the well-known principle of differential response. If an animal does react positively to one stimulus cue of a setting and negatively to all other cues of the setting, we say that it is making a discrimination. Of course, this selective response must occur consistently and under conditions which insure that the decisive factor is the specific cue supplied by the positive stimulus. It is obvious, for example, that an animal can distinguish between white and black if it is able to respond to the white card of a white-black pair regularly, provided care is taken to equalize all stimulus dimensions in the setting except brightness. The same principle would apply when pairs of stimuli from any of the other sensory modalities are presented to the animal. In most instances, both stimuli of the pair are presented simultaneously in the test, although this need not be the case. It should be pointed out that the principle of differential response is sometimes used in the human field. In testing for color blindness, for example, the subject may be asked to sort out yarns according to their colors instead of making a verbal report by naming the colors. However, in most human discrimination studies the method of verbal report is used because it is more convenient and less time-consuming.

Requirements of a Test of Discrimination.—Although the differential response principle is simple enough, it is often very difficult to apply it in concrete test situations. This is especially true in connection with the determination of limens or other precise measures to be used in the comparison of different species. These difficulties center around the three basic requirements of the discrimination experiment: (1) Sufficiently specific stimulus conditions, (2) optimum motivation of the animal during the testing period, and (3) the use of a suitable response to serve as the indicator of discrimination. These several major aspects of the testing set-up will now be briefly discussed in order. The student may refer to a recent volume [2] for a more comprehensive treatment of the methodological principles involved.

(1) *Rigid Control of Stimuli.*—It is obvious that, unless the stimulus conditions are definite, it will be impossible to specify the nature of any discrimination habit established by the test procedure. The first step here is to provide for use qualitatively pure stimuli of known intensity value from which proper selections may be made. The latest methods of producing and calibrating stimuli for the several sensory domains are fully described in suitable handbooks on physics and physiology. The next step is to select stimuli for the test which are equal in all dimensions except the one that is to be systematically varied for study. Then pairs of such stimuli are presented to the animal under an appropriate training routine. If the animal possesses the ability to make the required discrimination, a differential response should be set up after a sufficient amount of training.

In some instances, it is impossible to secure pairs of stimuli that are equated in all but a single dimension. This is notably true in connection with tests for color vision and pitch discrimination. The difficulty here arises from the fact that the eye and ear do not respond to the physical intensity of stimuli after the manner of a physical instrument. To equate the stimuli in physical intensity is, therefore, to leave them unequal in sensory value to the animal. Moreover, the sensory values vary considerably from species to species. The general procedure that must be followed in such cases may be illustrated by that used in the color vision test. Let us suppose, for example, that the positive stimulus is red and the negative stimulus is green. We select monochromatic bands from the spectrum, so that the stimuli are pure as to the wave-length factor, but they vary in intensity and hence in brightness value to the animal. For the moment we ignore the latter variant and establish a differential response to the pair of stimuli. It might very well be, however, that the habit rested on the brightness rather than the color cue, since the two stimuli differ in both dimensions. A control test is then run to rule out the use of the brightness cue. This is done by varying the intensity of the stimuli through a wide range, while keeping the wave-length factor constant. Since the brightness factor is eventually reversed in the two stimuli, the differential response will break down unless the animal makes use of the color cues present. If the discrimination habit remains stable, under such conditions, color vision is clearly indicated provided the experiment has been carefully done. This method of training to a two-dimensional set of stimuli and then ruling out one dimension later by control tests is to be used only when a pair of stimuli cannot be equated sufficiently by physical means.

Furthermore, it is also necessary to eliminate possible secondary cues from all the other stimulus domains in order to specify the nature of a discrimination accurately. As a rule, such secondary cues are excluded by making the tests in a dark, soundproof room in which the temperature is kept constant. The odors which arise from the presence of the food-incentive are rendered ineffective as cues by diffusing the room with the food-odor, unless the sense of smell itself is being investigated. As a further precaution, a one-way light screen is usually placed between the test set-up and the experimenter in order to eliminate possible directive cues from the latter. In some cases, one or more of the sensory fields may be excluded by cutting the nerve which supplies the sense organ or by removing the latter entirely. Thus the auditory and optic nerves might be cut in order to isolate better the sense of smell for testing, and this would make unnecessary the use of a dark, soundproof room. Perhaps the chief advantage of the operative method of control is that exclusion is absolute provided the surgery has been properly done. However, unless the operation is very simple there is always the danger that it may lower the general level of reactivity of the animal. This in turn may tend to decrease the discrimination ability of the animal, under the test conditions, in the sensory systems that remain. In most instances, this difficulty is solved by allowing a long post-operational recovery period before making the tests. In any case, some method of control—either normal or operational—must be used to eliminate secondary cues from the other modalities, if a specific discrimination habit is to be established.

(2) *Optimum Motivation Must Be Provided.*—When suitable stimulus conditions have been arranged, the experimenter turns to the problem of providing optimum motivation to activate the animal during the test. It is now well established that most animals set up a differential response most readily when both reward and punishment are used. It is common, therefore, to give the animal a bit of choice food when it responds to the positive stimulus and to give it an electric shock, or other punishment, when it makes an error. The food-incentive varies in kind from species to species and the degree of shock to be used varies with the type of animal, its body weight, the difficulty of the discrimination that is required, and numerous other factors. The set of optimum food and shock conditions must be determined, therefore, by preliminary tests before the regular training is begun. Such conditions insure us that the animal is stimulated to do its best during the tests. Clearly this is an important consideration, especially if the experimenter is seeking to determine limens representing the limits of the capacity to discriminate for a given species.

(3) *A Suitable Response Indicator.*—There remains the problem of selecting the most suitable response to require of the animal as the objective evidence of discrimination. The aim here is to adopt a response that has no natural connection with the stimuli to be employed, and thus force the animal to make the necessary connection under the training routine. This may seem somewhat arbitrary, but only such a learned reaction can be regarded as definite and dependable. On the other hand, the indicator response should be simple in itself and easy for the animal to connect with the stimuli as presented. There are two general types of responses commonly utilized in refined laboratory work. These are associated with the two main types of discrimination test—the Discrimination-Response method and the Conditioned-Reflex method. In the first method, the animal is required to turn toward the side of the positive stimulus, pull in the positive stimulus by a cord, or reach for food concealed beneath the positive stimulus. The specific response varies with the locomotor and manual capacities of the species. In the second method, the activity of the salivary glands, or some simple motor reflex is utilized. As we shall see, these two methods differ also in certain other important respects.

Description of Methods.—A brief description of some of the apparatus and procedures employed in sensory analysis will serve to make concrete the principles set forth above. Our purpose will be merely to demonstrate the application of the two main laboratory methods — Discrimination-Response and Conditioned-Reflex — to specific problems. The apparatus here shown is limited to a single modality and to a narrow range of species. For information concerning the extension of these methods to other modalities and to other animal types, the student may consult the more comprehensive treatment of the author.[3] As a matter of fact, the basic principles of sensory analysis are much the same for the field as a whole.

The Discrimination-Response Method.—The apparatus shown in Fig. 1 for testing vision in birds and small mammals will serve to illustrate the Discrimination-Response method. The stimuli (S, S_1) in the front of the box are used in testing form discrimina-

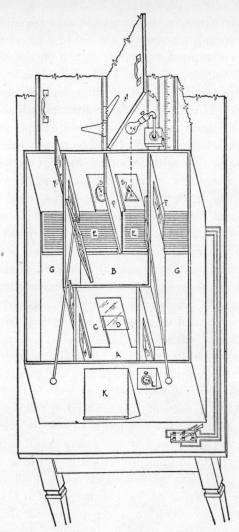

FIG. 1.—YERKES-WATSON VISION APPARATUS (BRIGHTNESS, SIZE, FORM).

A, entrance box ; *B*, reaction compartment ; *E*, *E*, electric grids ; *S*, *S*, stimuli ; *G*, *G*, passages to food and to entrance box ; *N*, light in dark box which illuminates the stimulus, the door *M* being closed during the test.   The two dark boxes are similarly equipped and are about 6 feet long.   Experimenter stands in front of apparatus, hidden from animal by one-way light screen (not shown), operates switch for applying shock to either grid, and records performance at *K*.   The stimuli shown are for testing form discrimination and can be shifted from side to side by a sliding device (not shown).   (From Warden, Jenkins, and Warner, "Comparative Psychology," Vol. I, by permission of The Ronald Press Company.)

tion, the circle and triangle being equal in area and differing only in shape. Pairs of stimuli for testing size and brightness discrimination may readily be substituted for those shown in the diagram. Size stimuli are usually selected from a closely graded series of circles, the largest one of the series (6 cm. in diameter) being taken as the positive stimulus. The limen for size discrimination can be determined by gradually increasing the diameter of the negative stimulus until the habit established earlier for larger size differences breaks down. In testing brightness discrimination, two circles of the same size are used. Differences in brightness between the two circles are regulated by placing the lights, in the long boxes (6 ft.) behind, close to one stimulus and far away from the other. After the brightness habit has been established, the limen can be determined by decreasing the difference in illumination until the break-down point is reached. In all work of this sort, the right-left positions of the two stimuli must be shifted in an irregular order to prevent the animal from forming a mere right-turn or left-turn habit. Numerous other details covering the control of stimulus factors will be found in the general reference cited above.

The procedure of testing is itself fairly simple, provided the animal is docile and the experimenter is patient and careful. The animal is brought into the dark, soundproof room and placed in the entrance compartment. After a moment, it is released by raising the door (D) and then, after observing the stimuli, it moves forward toward one of them and the door operated by the rod is closed behind it. If the response is correct, the animal finds food in a dish at G; if it is an error it is given a properly graded shock on the grid at E. In order to equalize odor cues, a dish of food is also placed at G on the "error" side, but here it is covered by a screen to prevent the animal from taking it. The experimenter stands in front of the apparatus, hidden from the reacting animal by a one-way light screen which is not shown in the drawing. This apparatus is commonly used for testing chicks, doves, white rats, guinea pigs, kittens, and other small animals. The same stimulus section may be used in testing brightness, size, and form in any animal, including man, by supplying a reaction section suitable to these several types of organisms.

The Conditioned-Reflex Method.—The Conditioned-Reflex method as utilized by Pavlov in testing tactual discrimination in the dog is shown in Fig. 2. The same general procedure is employed in testing vision, hearing, and other sensory domains. The stimuli are presented to the animal by automatic devices operated by the experimenter in the adjacent room. As a rule, the salivary reflex is used as the indicator response, although simple motor reflexes have been utilized on occasion. As will be noted, the flow of saliva is automatically measured and registered. The first step in applying this

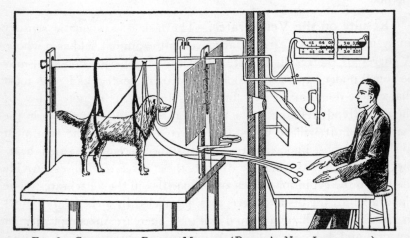

FIG. 2.—CONDITIONED REFLEX METHOD (PAVLOV'S NEW LABORATORY).

Pneumatic devices are used in applying tactual stimuli and the amount of the salivary flow is automatically measured. (From Pavlov, "Lectures on Conditioned Reflexes," by permission of International Publishers.)

method is to set up a conditioned response to the positive stimulus. This is done by associating it with the flow of saliva by giving a series of double-stimulations (stimulus-food). After this has been well established, the so-called method of contrast, involving the negative stimulus and punishment, is introduced in order to secure limens. For example, the dog in Fig. 2 is being positively conditioned to contact stimuli at a point on the right hip. Later on, tactile stimuli-shock combinations, which induce inhibition, will be applied to nearby points on the same member. By moving the negative stimulus gradually closer to the locus of the positive stimulus, the two-point threshold for touch can be determined—at the point where the inhibition breaks down. Frequent reinforcement of the positive response by giving stimulus-food combinations is usually necessary during the contrast series, in order to insure the stability of this reaction. As will be seen, this general method differs from the one described above in the following important ways: (1) The positive and negative stimuli are presented in successive series rather than simultaneously, and (2) the indicator response is somewhat simpler than the turning or reaching reactions required in connection with the Discrimination-Response method.

Results on the Vertebrates.—The task of systematic sensory analysis has not been carried far as yet in the animal field as a whole. A survey of the results to date, in each of the major domains, may be found under appropriate topics in available textbooks.[4] The most that can be done, in the present brief summary, is to note a few of the main trends relating to the evolution of sensory capacities in the vertebrates. It will be necessary, moreover, to limit the treatment to the three most important types of distance reception—smell, hearing, and vision. As a matter of fact, these three modalities provide the key to the evolution of sensory capacities in the vertebrates. The elaboration of the distance receptors, paralleled by structural changes in the brain, go hand in hand with an increase in complexity of sensory and behavioral life. A general interpretation of results, rather than a detailed citation of specific findings, will now be offered within the limitations indicated above. In most instances, the conclusions drawn are based upon scores of experimental studies.

The Sense of Smell.—The sense of smell is highly developed in the fishes and, in most types at least, it is the dominant modality utilized in food-searching and numerous other activities. The same is true of the amphibians during the early or aquatic stage of the life cycle. In the adult or terrestrial stage, however, such amphibians as frogs and toads show a reduction in olfactory acuity associated with an advance in the use of vision. A similar distinction seems to hold between the aquatic and the terrestrial reptiles. The primitive birds, like their reptilian ancestors, possessed a fair degree of olfactory acuity. This was lost, for the most part, in the evolution of the beak and the parallel elaboration of complex visual functions. The olfactory capacity is entirely absent in most of the higher, modern birds. The mammals, like their reptilian ancestors, possess at least a fair degree of olfactory acuity. There is reason to believe, moreover, that a further evolution of this sense occurred among many of the ground-living types. This is known to be true in the case of such carnivorous forms as the dogs and their allies. The ability of dogs to trail and to identify objects by odor cues is far superior to that of man or of mammals and vertebrates in general. This fact has been confirmed by a large body of experimental evidence. It seems likely, moreover, that smell is the dominant type of distance reception in most, if not all, of the ground-living mammals.

The Sense of Hearing.—Hearing is poorly developed in fishes and is entirely absent in all but the higher orders. The key to the evolution of hearing in the vertebrates is the lagena, or primitive cochlea, which gradually evolved from the labyrinth or equilibratory organ. The lagena first appears among the higher fishes and, at this stage of development, is sensitive only to a low range of pitch. The range for the goldfish, which is the longest reported to date, is 43 to 2,752 d.v. The comparable range for man is 16 to 20,000 d.v. Among the amphibians, the salamanders appear to lack the auditory sense entirely. Frogs and probably toads, on the other hand, appear to be able to hear sounds up to about 10,000 d.v. Hearing among the reptiles varies considerably from order to order. Some of the lizards can hear up to 12,500 d.v. The auditory sense seems to be lacking in turtles and in the common snakes, including the rattler. Crocodiles and alligators possess hearing, but the possible range here has not been determined. The range of hearing in birds, where a true cochlea first appears, seems to be about the same as in the lizard. The sense of hearing is well developed in all classes of mammals. Strangely enough, the auditory range is greater in some of the common mammals than in such primates as the monkey, chimpanzee, and man. Also some of them are much more sensitive to sounds of low intensity than are the primates. This is true, for example, of the guinea pig and the dog. It is only fair to say that the above conclusions, relating to the presence or absence of hearing in groups, is based on a sampling of the species of each order. The same is true of the group ranges indicated. In either case, it is possible that tests on other species might give very different results. Nevertheless, the positive indices as reported may be accepted with complete confidence.

The Sense of Sight.—Vision is an extremely complex sensory function, involving such distinct dimensions as brightness, size, form, pattern, and color. In a broad sense, color vision may be taken as the key to evolutionary advance in all of these visual fields. This is true because color vision presupposes a retina well enough developed to support a relatively high degree of efficiency in these non-chromatic dimensions. It will be sufficient, therefore, to indicate merely the evolution of color vision in the vertebrates. Apparently a few of the fresh-water fishes possess limited color vision but make little use of it in ordinary life activities. This function is much more definite and important in amphibians and reptiles. It is tetrachromatic as in man and, in some turtles at least, extends over the same spectral range as in man. The work on birds seems to indicate that many of them can distinguish approximately as many different colors as we can. The same is probably true as well for such mammalian types as the monkeys and the great apes. There is clear evidence, however, that most ground-living mammals are color blind. This has been demonstrated on the rat, rabbit, cat, dog, cow, etc. It has also been shown that it is the movement of the cape, and not its color, that excites the bull in the fighting arena. These facts support the evidence from other sources which shows that vision is of secondary importance in the life activities of all the mammals except the tree-living primates and man, who evolved from arboreal stock.

Some General Conclusions.—A number of conclusions of general significance may be drawn from the survey of trends presented above. In the first place, it is obvious that man is not the superior animal in every respect. His sense of smell is probably not above that of the average vertebrate and is far below that of the dog. His hearing is superior to that of most vertebrates, but here again his acuity is below that of the dog. His visual powers are much better developed than those of most vertebrates, but probably no better than those of his primate cousins. Another important conclusion is that superiority in one sensory field is likely to be associated with inferiority in some other. Dominance of smell, for example, goes along with poor vision with fair consistency. It is interesting to note, moreover, that the two most important types of distance reception—hearing and complex vision—were the latest to evolve in the vertebrate series. Finally, if space permitted, it would be easy to show that the relative dominance of these several sensory systems exhibits a close correlation with habitat and life activities.

MOTIVATION

Animal Drives.—An animal is a "going concern" and not a mere passive machine for the reception of stimuli from its environment. It possesses a specific internal organization, which is evolutionary and hereditary, and which follows a fairly definite species pattern. This explains, in part at least, why a dog, a cat, and an elephant respond differently to the same stimulus. The primary function of stimuli is merely to set off the internal mechanisms or systems of the animal. It is the latter which largely determine the pattern of activity which follows. They represent the inner springs of action —the innate and persistent cores of all behavior. They are definitely related, in most cases at least, to important biological needs and wants. These dynamic components of behavior have long been called instincts, but the more modern term is drives. Each of the primary drives, such as hunger, thirst, sex, and the like, can be normally satisfied by an appropriate incentive, or class of incentives. The purpose of analysis in this field is to measure the strength and persistence of the several drives which characterize various species. The indices thus obtained afford a basis for the objective interpretation of the fundamental needs and wants of the animal world.

The Isolation of Drives Is Difficult.—The work on animal motivation is much more limited in scope than is true of either of the other two fields under review. This is due to the fact that, until fairly recently, suitable methods for the study of drives had not been devised. The task of analysis is especially difficult here because the various drives are likely to be closely interrelated. In many cases, it is almost impossible to isolate them one at a time for measurement. Moreover, an adequate study of motivation presupposes a good background of knowledge regarding the behavioral potential of the type to be tested. These facts probably explain why the work in this field has been so largely limited to the white rat. A description of the methods that have been developed for testing motivation will be found in a recent textbook.[5] The Columbia Obstruction method will be emphasized in the present treatment because it is especially well standardized and offers considerable promise for future systematic work. The results obtained in an extensive project on the white rat, by the use of this method, will be supplemented by other findings of importance in this field.

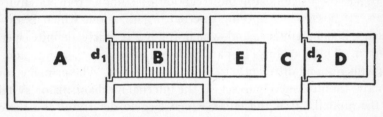

FIG. 3.—COLUMBIA OBSTRUCTION APPARATUS (GROUND PLAN).

A, entrance compartment; *B*, obstruction compartment with electric grid; *C*, incentive compartment; *D*, position of incentive; *E*, release plate; d_1, manually operated door of entrance compartment; d_2, automatic door operated by release plate. (Reproduced from Warden, "Animal Motivation," by permission of Columbia University Press.)

The Columbia Obstruction Method.—The ground plan of the Columbia Obstruction Apparatus is illustrated in Fig. 3. It consists essentially of an entrance compartment, an electric grid section, and an incentive compartment, with a small box attached to hold the actual incentive. When the aroused animal is in the entrance compartment, the electrified grid serves as an obstruction to the securing of food in the incentive compartment on the other side. Of course, the degree of shock used must be properly graded to suit the type and size of the animal being tested. The best plan here is to use a medium or optimum shock—one that will cause the animal to hesitate without inducing refusal to cross altogether. This hesitation will be less for a strong drive than for a weak one. Naturally, this will be true only if the degree of shock utilized is the same for each of the drives to be measured and compared. The general principle here is the same as that which underlies the human intelligence test—individuals and drives become directly comparable in terms of performance scores on an identical task. The apparatus itself is of small ·value, however, unless the procedure of testing is kept the same from drive to drive. Moreover, numerous controls are necessary in order to isolate a given drive and to arouse it to maximum strength for measurement.

Perhaps the best way to explain the method will be to describe, as briefly as possible, its use in the Columbia University laboratory in connection with a comprehensive project on the white rat. The broader aim of this project was to analyze the basic drive-complex of this typical rodent. The following drives were selected for investigation: (1) Hunger—male and female, (2) thirst—male and female, (3) sex—male and female, (4) maternal, and (5) exploratory. As will be seen, these are all dynamic functions which serve basic biological needs and wants. The first step was to secure mature animals of the same strain, age, and past experience. These conditions are fulfilled by the Wistar Institute rats, a closely inbred strain, and these were supplied to us at the same age (185 days) as required, over a period of years. The white rat becomes sexually mature at about sixty days, hence these animals were young adults in which the drives to be tested were fully developed.

The next step was to devise a means of arousing each drive in definite degrees, ranging from the zero point to well beyond the maximum point, so that each of these levels could be measured. The plan adopted for hunger will serve as an illustration of the way this can be done. The zero hunger group was tested without being deprived of food in their living cages at all. Other groups were tested after 2, 3, 4, 6, and 8 days of food deprivation, hence the tests were carried well beyond the maximum point. In much the same way, the maximum score was determined for thirst and for the male sex drive. The female sex drive is dependent upon the oestrus cycle, which recurs at about four-day intervals, and which is associated with marked cellular changes in the organs of reproduction. The maximum point here was determined by testing the female when in oestrum proper, as indicated by the histological picture of vaginal smears. The maternal drive was tested a few hours after the mother rat had given birth to a litter. The tendency to explore within a network of runways attached to compartment C was measured after confining the animals in small living cages. In order to cover all these conditions adequately, more than 500 animals had to be used.

Another important step was to arrange a set of standard conditions for keeping four drives quiescent whenever the other one was aroused for testing. The plan adopted here may be illustrated by noting the series of controls employed when the sex drive was to be measured. Hunger and thirst were allayed by allowing the animal access to food and water in the living cage up to the moment of the test; the maternal drive was eliminated by using only males and non-pregnant females; the exploratory drive was kept quiescent by allowing the animals to be normally active in their cages up to the time of the test. Further details concerning these controls will be found in the volume [6] covering this project as a whole.

Before the regular test began, the animal was permitted to cross to the incentive four times without shock and then once with shock. This procedure permitted it to be aroused by the incentive and to locate the position of the shock. During the test proper, which followed immediately, the animal was allowed to cross the grid with shock as often as it would within the 20 minute test period. It was, of course, replaced in the entrance compartment immediately after each crossing. The incentives employed were equally appropriate for the several drives, and the degree of shock and the length of the test period were the same throughout. The conclusion seems to be warranted, therefore, that the greater the number of crossings the stronger the drive. If this be true, then the scores obtained for the maximum strength of each drive may be taken as the general index of the particular dynamic function. On this basis, the several drives of the white rat could then be rated as to relative strength.

Some Typical Results.—The results of this investigation are shown in the graph of Fig. 4. When the maximum scores are compared, the drives fall into the following rank order: (1) Maternal,

(2) thirst, (3) hunger, (4) sex, and (5) exploratory. In a control group in which no incentive was used, the number of crossings was only 3.5 per animal. The maternal drive was even stronger than is indicated in the graph for young females having their first litter, the score for this group being 28.33 crossings. As will be seen the sex drive for the two sexes is about equal in strength. The same is true of hunger and thirst, hence the scores for both sexes were combined in drawing the curves shown in the diagram. As may be seen, there

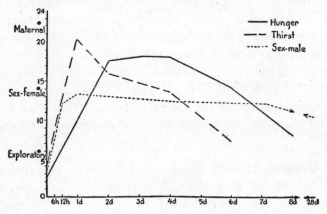

FIG. 4.—ANALYSIS OF DRIVES IN THE WHITE RAT.

Strength of drive, in terms of the number of crossings of the grid, is shown in the ordinate. The periods of deprivation for hunger, thirst, and sex (male) are indicated on the abscissa. The hunger and thirst scores for males and females are combined. (Reproduced from Warden, "Animal Motivation," by permission of Columbia University Press.)

is a greater difference between some of the drives than between others. The maternal drive is clearly the highest and the exploratory drive the lowest. Also both thirst and hunger appear to be definitely higher than sex. It has been shown elsewhere [7] that the rank order cited above is statistically reliable when computed by the method of combining averages, which stresses the ordinal factor in the results as a whole. It is impossible to say, however, whether or not this order would hold for mammals in general without further work on other representative types.

The Obstruction method has been successfully employed in testing disturbed as well as normal drives. In one case, the hunger drive was disturbed by requiring the animal to wait in compartment C, after crossing the grid, before getting the food. It was found that a delay, even as short as 15 seconds, weakened the drive, the number of crossings in the test period being decreased about 43 per cent. In another instance, the males and females were reared apart to see if this would disturb the normal development of the sex drive. This was found to be the case when the sexes were segregated before the onset of puberty, since they crossed more often then to one of their own sex than to one of the opposite sex. In still another case, the sex drive was eliminated by gonadectomy, in prepubertal animals, and then restored temporarily by injections of the appropriate sex hormone into them as adults. These and other drive disturbances were consistently reflected in the crossings score, when comparisons were made with the records of normal animals. The student may refer to the relevant sections of the author's *Animal Motivation* for a full account of these several studies of drive disturbances in the white rat.

The General-Activity Method.—Important contributions to the analysis of the physiological mechanisms underlying animal drives have been made by means of the General-Activity method. A review of the various types of apparatus employed, and of the results to date, will be found in a recent article by Richter.[8] The primary aim here is to record by automatic devices the spontaneous activity of the animal under different drive conditions. It has been demonstrated, for example, that the hunger drive is due to the rhythmic contractions of the stomach. These contractions, which arouse and activate the animal, differ greatly in periodicity and strength from species to species, and are doubtless related to natural feeding requirements. It has also been demonstrated that the sex drive is due to the gonadal hormones. The activity record is very markedly lowered in both male and female rats by the removal of the gonads. The activity of the female also drops during the sexually inactive period known as diosterum. It seems likely, moreover, that this general method of analysis should throw considerable light upon the physiological mechanism underlying the maternal drive.

Animal Drives in Man.—The study of animal motivation should make a genuine contribution to human psychology when it has been broadened in scope to include the primates. The primary drives are as deep-seated in man as they are in infrahuman organisms and play an important role in the dynamics of behavior. It is true that these drives are well overlaid by cultural factors, especially in the human adult, but even culture itself must rest upon biological needs and wants. Some of the facts already discovered by the work on the mammals can be carried over to the human field. For example, it is now known that the feeling of hunger arises from periodic stomach contractions, not unlike those of the white rat. The sex and maternal impulses in man obviously rest upon the same general types of mechanism as those found in the mammals generally. Nothing is more certain than that the basic biosocial complex of human nature evolved from that of the anthropoid level. Doubtless the study of the primary drives in the higher animals and man will enable us to understand better the relationship of culture to this fundamental biological heritage.

LEARNING AND INTELLIGENCE

The problems commonly included under this general heading have held a special interest for the animal psychologist from the very beginning of the experimental movement. This emphasis has extended down to the present, as would be indicated by a topical analysis of the research output of our laboratories. In the strict sense, learning and intelligence represent fairly distinct lines of investigation. Each field has its own particular problems and its own methods and procedures. It seems desirable, therefore, to treat the topics separately. The distinction between the two fields will become clear as we proceed with the description of concrete methods and results.

The Learning Process.—A vast array of studies dealing with the nature of the learning-retention process fall within this general field of research. By far the larger portion of the work has been done on the white rat by means of simple mazes and problem boxes. The primary interest here is not in the behavior of this species, but in an analysis of the learning process itself. The rat is used by the psychologist to study learning just as the frog is used by the physiologist to determine the essential nature of reflex action. As we shall see, there is hardly a problem in the field of human learning that has not been tried out on the white rat. In general it has been found that the conditions that make for efficient learning are much the same in rat and man. This suggests the possibility of generalizing such basic factors in learning to all living organisms. It will be desirable, at this point, to illustrate the two methods commonly employed in this major field of investigation.

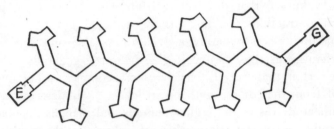

FIG. 5.—WARNER-WARDEN MAZE (LINEAR PATTERN).

This shows a 10 cul-de-sac linear pattern of the unit maze suitable for the analysis of serial learning problems. The pathway is tortuous and at the same time symmetrical. (From Warden, in "J. Genet. Psychol.", by permission of The Journal Press.)

Maze Learning.—The maze method has been chiefly utilized in this work. Many types of mazes have been devised,[9] but only a few of these are widely used at present.[10] The pattern shown in Fig. 5 is linear in design and hence is especially well suited for the study of serial learning tasks. As will be seen, it consists of a central pathway connecting the entrance box (E) with the goal box (G) and a number of blind alleys, or culs-de-sac. The maze habit is a behavior pattern corresponding to the true pathway, or the shortest distance to the food at the goal end. At first the animal enters the blind alleys along the pathway, but such errors are gradually eliminated as learning proceeds. The scores usually obtained are the number of errors per trial, and the time per trial as taken by means of a stop watch. The order in which the several blinds are eliminated may be determined by numbering them and checking the specific errors from trial to trial. The rate of progress in the formation of the maze habit can be shown graphically by plotting learning curves, based on error or time scores. The degree of permanency, or retention, of such a habit may be tested by having the animals relearn the maze after a few weeks or months, during which no further practice is allowed. Maze learning is commonly regarded as motor habit formation, similar in many respects to the development of motor skills in man. An analysis of the work on the white rat has been found to throw considerable light upon the process of trial and error learning in general.

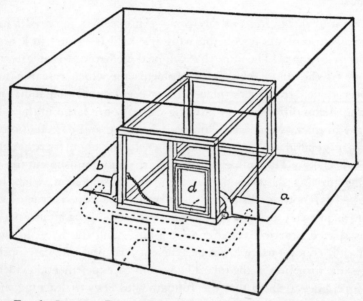

FIG. 6.—LASHLEY DOUBLE-PLATFORM APPARATUS FOR WHITE RATS.

The platforms *a, b,* must be pressed down in the order *a-b* in order to release the door, *d,* which opens inward by pressure of a spring. The weight required to depress platforms is regulated by adjustable springs underneath. The outer cage, made of wire mesh, is intended to limit the range of activity during the test. (From Lashly, "Psychobiology," by permission of The Williams and Wilkins Company.)

The Problem Method.—The problem method is also suitable for use in this field of investigation. An illustration of one of the better standardized problem boxes for the white rat is shown in Fig. 6. The animal must learn to press down the two platforms, in a set order, before the food in the inner cage becomes available. This requires some measure of ingenuity as well as skill in nose or foot manipulation. In fact, a problem apparatus differs from a maze primarily in that the animal must operate a puzzle device instead of merely running directly to a place (goal box). Performance is scored in terms of time per trial and the number and kind of useless movements which occur. The time scores are usually used in plotting learning curves, since a speedy response is likely to mean that useless movements have been dropped out. The retention of a problem-box habit can be measured in the same manner as has been indicated above for the maze.

Learning in the Rat and in Man.—An excellent survey of maze and problem-box studies on the white rat will be found in a recent volume by Munn.[11] The most that can be done here is to call attention to some of the major classes of problems on which research work has been done. In the first place, it has been found that individual, age, and strain differences in learning capacity are large in the rat as they are in man. Moreover, curves of learning and of retention are similar in general, in both species, when based upon corresponding types of tasks. The influence of reward and punishment on the learning process shows a similar trend in rat and man, when both are tested on motor tasks of the maze type. The same is true of such factors as primacy and recency, whole-part methods of attack, massed versus spaced practice, transfer of training, and the like. In brief, the major conditions that favor efficient learning in man operate in the same direction in the rat. The wealth of experimental evidence, therefore, goes to show that the fundamental laws of learning apply with equal force to man and animals. Naturally this conclusion must be restricted to such types of learning as are common to both fields.

Other Uses of Learning Experiments.—The research on animal learning often goes far beyond the point of a mere check-up on the results secured in human work. This is especially true in connection with problems that call for the use of extreme conditions or operative techniques. The following lines of research may be taken as examples of this type of investigation: (1) The evaluation of sensory functions in learning, (2) the analysis of brain and neural functions in learning, and (3) the study of physiological conditions, such as those induced by drugs, fatigue, etc., and learning. In each of these fields, extensive work on human subjects is impossible for obvious reasons.

In animals, on the other hand, the proper conditions for systematic research in these several fields can, as a rule, be readily arranged. Many of the results secured, while not directly applicable to man, provide definite clues to the understanding of less extreme conditions in man. Moreover, in some cases at least, it has been possible to check such findings directly on human subjects who have suffered accidental injuries of various kinds.

Intelligence Levels.—The methods employed in this connection differ in several essentials from those described above. In the first place, each method provides a series of tasks so graded in difficulty as to go beyond the capacity of the species being tested. In the second place, the animal is given practically unlimited opportunity to go as far as it possibly can on this graded series of tasks. The primary aim here is to determine the limits of capacity, in a given function, for various species of animals so that they can be directly compared as to intelligence level. This is surely quite different from the typical learning experiment in which a single task is employed under varying conditions of efficiency. In fact, these levels tests are similar in many respects to "power" intelligence tests in the human field, since speed is ignored in favor of utter limits of capacity. They have been devised to measure such complex behavioral functions as reasoning, imitation, symbolic, and relational responses. As might be expected, therefore, these methods have been utilized mainly in testing the higher animals and especially the primates. The following four methods have been selected to represent this general field: (1) Multiple-Plate method, (2) Delayed-Response test, (3) Multiple-Choice method, and (4) Imitation test. A general description of these and related methods will be found in a recent textbook.[12]

Multiple-Plate Method.—The general plan of the apparatus used in this test is shown in Fig. 7. The main features are as follows: (1) An entrance box leading into the large outer reaction cage, (2) an inner cage containing the food, and (3) plates in the floor, to be depressed by the animal in order to open the door of the inner cage and obtain the food. The basic response of stepping on a plate was utilized here because it is a simple and natural response for such a large number of species. The plates are wired so that, if desired, a light electric shock can be given as a signal to the animal that the wrong plate has been depressed. The outer cage is made of heavy wire mesh, and covered with a one-way light screen to eliminate the experimenter from the test situation. The apparatus can be readily adapted to both large and small animals by varying the size as required.

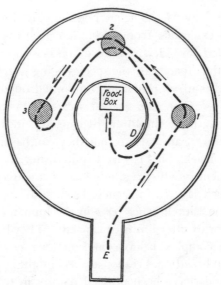

FIG. 7.—JENKINS PROBLEM APPARATUS (GROUND PLAN).

The three plates (1, 2, 3) are built with inlaid metal strips to permit the use of electric shock as desired. The door, *D*, is automatically closed when a set series of plates has been depressed. Door leading from entrance compartment to the main cage not shown in this diagram. The broken line indicates the route to be taken in step four in which plates are depressed in the order 1, 2, 3, 2, before door to food compartment opens. (From Warden, Jenkins, and Warner. "Comparative Psychology," Vol. I, by permission of The Ronald Press Company.)

The first task involves merely learning to step on plate 1. After this has been mastered, the later patterns are made increasingly complex by adding one plate each time as the animal advances from stage to stage. A new plate is added, of course, only after the simpler, preceding pattern has been thoroughly established by trainiing. When the basic series of three plates has been mastered, the animal is required to reverse its direction thereafter at plates 1 and 3. For example, the order of plates in the eight-step pattern would be: 1,2,3,2, 1,2,3,2, food box. The steps here seem to be fairly well graded in difficulty, except that the initial setting up of the plate habit (step 1) and the first reversal (step 4) require longer training as a rule. These exceptions do not invalidate the results to be reported, since the final failure point usually falls at other positions in the pattern series.

This method seems to be one of the best so far devised for the determination of levels of capacity in widely divergent species. This fact will appear from an analysis of the results that have been secured to date. The following scores represent the highest point reached by any individual of each species, when groups of 20 to 35 of the several types were tested:

Guinea pigs .... Step 1
White rats .... Step 2
Cats .... Step 7
Monkeys .... Step 22

Pre-adolescent animals of approximately the same relative age were used in all cases, and the motivation conditions were arranged in harmony with species requirements. The results would seem, there-fore, to reflect genuine species differences in levels of capacity to form such complex ordinal patterns of behavior. It is interesting to note that the two rodent types (guinea pig, rat) stand much lower than the carnivorous type (cat). There is an abundance of evidence from other lines of experimental work to support this evaluation of the two mammalian orders. The high level reached by the monkeys on this task is also in harmony with measures of primate capacity secured on various other kinds of tests.

This method was designed to test the capacity of various species to form serial habits in an ascending order of complexity. Neverthe-less, it provides an opportunity for the occurrence of a simple type of reasoning. This is especially true in the case of the animals which advance far in the series before reaching the limit. The only change in pattern, from stage to stage, is the addition of the next plate in the major sequence. After this shift has occurred a number of times, a simple inference might well develop, with respect to this constant factor, as new patterns were set for solution. This would not involve the ability to count but merely the vague notion that man might express in the phrase: "Now I go on one move further." Clearly, such "insight" would have enabled an animal to continue through the simple linear series indefinitely. But nothing of this sort occurred, even in the monkeys that advanced farthest in the series and hence had the best opportunity to develop an inference. In fact, the results seem to show that progress from step to step was pretty much a matter of trial and error for all species tested. When a new problem was set, the animal persisted in trying out the old pattern for a time. The resulting failures eventually brought about a partial disintegration of the old pattern and a renewal of exploratory activities. Finally the new and more inclusive pattern, representing the next stage, might then emerge. As a matter of fact, there seems to be no consistent transfer of training effects running through the series of patterns as a whole. It is interesting to note that some of the monkeys became greatly confused, after prolonged training, at the final failure point, and appeared to lose entirely the pattern already learned. On being retrained on the old pattern, they always failed again at the same point as before. These facts support the conclusions that the limits scores, indicated above, actually represent the true level of capacity in the function tested.

Delayed-Response Test.—The general plan of the apparatus commonly used in testing the white rat is shown in Fig. 8. It consists essentially of an entrance box, a large reaction compartment, and three small adjoining food boxes which can be lighted as required. Grids for giving electric shock can be placed in front of each of the food boxes, when punishment for errors is to be given. The apparatus may be readily adapted for animals of different size, and the number of food boxes may vary from two to four as desired. The method is used to investigate the capacity of animals to utilize memory cues in responding to food situations to which they have been trained. A further problem here bears on the nature of such cues, once their presence has been demonstrated. This means of analyzing the representative aspect of animal behavior will become clearer after the application of the method has been discussed.

At first the animal is trained to go for food to whichever one of the boxes happens to be illuminated, the order being varied irregularly from trial to trial. When this habit has been firmly established, the training is continued under the following conditions: (1) The light is turned off just as the animal is released from the entrance compartment, (2) an interval of delay—perhaps only a second at first —is interpolated between the turning off of the light and the release of the animal, (3) the interval of delay is increased in length until a limit is found beyond which the animal consistently fails to locate

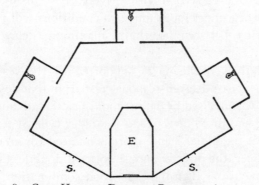

Fig. 8.—Carr-Hunter Delayed Reaction Apparatus.

Ground plan of three-compartment apparatus. *E*, entrance and restraining compartment fastened by hinges so that when raised the three faces are raised some distance from the floor. Lights in the three compartments controlled by switches at *S, S*. Runways leading from exit doors to entrance compartment not shown. (Modified from Hunter.) (From "Behav. Monog.," by permission of The Johns Hopkins Press.)

the correct food box. In order to demonstrate that the response is due to the revival of a true memory cue, it is necessary to disorient the animal during the delay interval in some manner. This precaution is based on the fact that white rats tend to preserve bodily orientation, and dogs head orientation, unless it is prevented. Obviously, if the animal orients toward the proper box before the light is turned off, and holds this position during the interval, there is no reason to suppose that its final reaction involves a memory revival.

Interesting results have been obtained on the rat, cat, dog, and raccoon by this method, which seeks to probe into the memory function of animals. The trend of the findings favors the notion that probably the birds and mammals make some use of simple symbolic processes, although the precise nature of these is not clear as yet. One might reasonably expect that the maximum delay period would be longer for the cat, dog, and raccoon than for the rat. But the results to date do not support this assumption, although it is only fair to say that the technique employed has varied considerably from one type of animal to another. Delays as long as 45 seconds have been reported on the white rat, when tested on a three-box apparatus, with bodily orientation eliminated. Corresponding indices for the dog and raccoon are 15 seconds and 25 seconds respectively. It seems likely, however, that further work under more uniform conditions will reveal a fairly high correlation between length of maximum delay and general intelligence level.

This tentative conclusion is supported by the results obtained on a different type of delayed-response test from that described above. This method was devised by Hunter and has the advantage of being less arbitrary and more direct than the older type of test. The food itself is used as the signal, hence there is no need for an early training stage. Moreover, the direct response to food doubtless insures better motivation conditions than the light-food combination. In any case, the period of maximum delay is much longer, for the same species, when this type of test is used. Delays as long as 16 hours have been reported for cats, even when a 4-box apparatus was employed. Chimpanzees are able to react successfully after an interval of 48 hours, when tested on a single-box set-up. In this case, the box is usually buried in the ground after the animal has seen the food put into it. On the whole, it would seem that this direct method offers more promise than the indirect method previously described in helping us to understand the use of memory by animals in their natural habitat.

Multiple-Choice Method.—This method was devised by Yerkes to bring into play ideational behavior, if present, in animals. The general plan of the apparatus, which can be modified for organisms of any size, is shown in Fig. 9. The number of test compartments may be reduced, if desired, in order to make the problems easier to solve. It is necessary for the animal to make use of some sort of relational cue here, since the correct box to be entered varies from trial to trial, in harmony with a specific relational pattern. Let us suppose, for example, that the problem is to select the middle box in any series of compartments presented. The series is indicated, from trial to trial, by raising the front doors of some of the boxes, and the animal is supposed to react only to these. If the three doors to the right are open, the correct box is No. 2; if the 5 doors to the

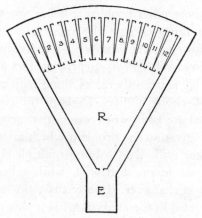

FIG. 9.—YERKES MULTIPLE-CHOICE APPARATUS (LOCOMOTOR).

Ground plan of apparatus with twelve test compartments. E, entrance compartment; R, reaction compartment. Note runways leading from exit doors at rear to the entrance compartment. (Modified from Yerkes.) (From "J. Anim. Behav.", by permission of The Johns Hopkins Press.)

left are open, the correct box is No. 10; if doors 4,5,6,7,8,9,10 are open, the correct box is No. 7. Clearly then the animal cannot solve the problem—middle box—unless it makes use of this specific relational cue. The problems that have been used most often in testing various species are: (1) Box at the left (or right) end of the series, (2) second box from the left (or right) end, (3) middle box, and (4) alternately left end and right end. A list of more difficult problems will be found in another connection,[13] together with a description of an apparatus designed for primates, in which the response is reaching toward the correct box instead of going into it bodily.

In applying this method, the general plan is to begin with Problem No. 1 and then to pass the animal along until its limit is reached on the more difficult tasks. The rating of species might depend either upon the total number of problems solved or on the difficulty of the problem which marked the limit of ability. The following records have been reported to date on various species tested on a 9-box apparatus, the numbers given here corresponding to the problems as listed above: Ring-dove, 1; crow, 1 at both left and right positions; white rat, 1; pig, 1,2,4; monkey, 1,2,4; orang-utan, 1; chimpanzee, 1 at both left and right positions, and 4. In all cases, the animals failed on one or more other problems, hence the record here would seem to represent fairly enough the relative ability of the several species tested. However, the number of individuals was relatively small in most cases. The most surprising fact indicated by these results is that the pig apparently ranks along with monkeys and chimpanzees in multiple-choice ability. Perhaps the record for the great apes will be raised by later work on larger groups. Considerable attention has been given to the problem which arises as to the nature of the relational cue utilized in solving multiple-choice tasks. Some hold that it is symbolic, or ideational, while others insist that it is merely perceptual in character. In any case, this method has proved to be extremely useful in the analysis of complex relational behavior in the higher animals.

Imitation Test.—One of the first questions raised in animal psychology was whether or not the higher animals can learn by imitating one another, as well as by the slower process of trial and error. These early workers held that imitation involved the drawing of a simple inference, such as that expressed by the phrase: "I see that monkey pulls a string and gets food; if I pull the same string I will also get food." This conception may be true but it would be most difficult to prove. At present, imitation is regarded simply as learning by observation. In order to demonstrate imitation in animals, it is necessary to plan the test in harmony with the following criteria: (1) The task must be something that is novel enough to require genuine learning; (2) the act must be performed immediately from observation, without recourse to trial and error activities; and (3) the pattern of the response in the imitator must be similar to that made originally by the imitatee. If learning occurs promptly, under these conditions, the ability of the individual or species to imitate has been demonstrated. The limits of imitative capacity can then be determined by testing the animal on a graded series of tasks of increasing difficulty.

The Observation-Cage method, devised by Thorndike, was long used in imitation studies. The apparatus consisted of a work cage for the imitatee to which was attached an observation cage for the observing animal. After the latter had been given sufficient opportunity to observe the trained imitatee solve the problem, it was placed in the work cage to see if it would then repeat the act. Of course, the imitatee was removed from the work cage before the imitator was placed within it. This shifting of the animals required time, hence the response demanded was, in reality, a delayed reaction based on imitative cues. Moreover, it seems likely that the shift would bring about emotional disturbances and a change in mental set in the imitator. These difficulties in the method itself probably explain, in large part at least, why no evidence for imitation was found in such animals as the dog, cat, and monkey. Strangely enough, these animals can be readily trained to be good observers, and hence should be able to learn simple tasks by imitation.

A new method of testing imitation was recently devised by the writer in a size suitable for monkeys. The apparatus is shown in Fig. 10. The essential feature here is the use of two work cages, separated by a mesh partition, instead of a single work cage and an observation cage as in the method described above. This plan makes it unnecessary to shift either of the animals during the test, so that both delay and disturbances are avoided. Any number of tasks can be arranged by constructing duplicate sets of panels, which can then be inserted conveniently in the back wall of the two cages. For example, the task shown in the illustration is to push down two levers with the hand and then pull open the door and take the food from the small box behind. The procedure of testing is very simple. The imitatee, which has been trained to perform the act beforehand, is placed in one of the cages and restrained by a cord. The imitator is then placed in the other cage to observe, under similar restraint. After the imitatee has performed the act five times in rapid succession, the imitator is released and thus given an opportunity to copy the act. At the same time, the imitatee is drawn back into the corner of its cage by means of the cord. The time required for each imitative act can be taken by means of a stop watch.

Up to the present, this method has been used only in testing rhesus and cebus monkeys. The following tasks, arranged in order

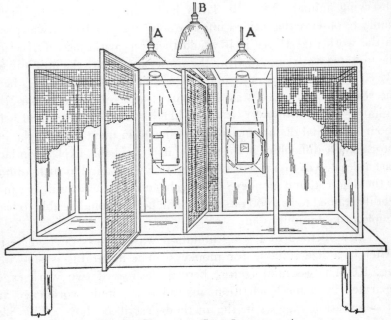

FIG. 10.—WARDEN DUPLICATE-CAGE IMITATION APPARATUS.

A part of the mesh forming the front wall has been removed in order to make the interior of the apparatus more visible. The cages for the imitator and imitatee are similar in every respect. The double-latch device is shown open in one cage and closed in the other. The light at *B* supplies general illumination to the apparatus. The two lights, *A, A*, enhance the value of the latch devices as stimuli by flooding them with light. New devices can be substituted for those shown by changing panels. The two cages are separated by a wire mesh partition. (From Warden, Jenkins, and Warner. "Comparative Psychology," Vol. I, by permission of The Ronald Press Company.)

of difficulty, were employed: (1) Pulling a chain hanging down in front of the panel, (2) opening a door in the panel by the knob, (3) pushing down one latch and then opening the door, (4) pushing down two latches and opening the door. In each case, the animal was rewarded by food placed in the small box behind the door. Several hundred tests were made on some 21 monkeys by repeating the series from time to time. If we exclude the records of six animals that refused to observe, on account of sexual or pugnacious attention to the imitatee, the results indicate a high degree of imitative behavior in these types. In fact, in over 70 per cent of the tests, the act was copied successfully within the one-minute period allowed, and often within a few seconds. In some cases, the imitator was straining at the leash to get to the mechanism and operate it before the period of observation was over. A careful check of the performance indicates clearly that fumbling and other trial-and-error activities did not occur, when the act was copied in 30 seconds or less. In some instances, rated as unsuccessful, the imitator copied the act but not with sufficient precision or force to operate the mechanism. This type of behavior might well be termed partial imitation rather than failure. The best record made by an individual monkey was immediate imitation in 23 out of the 24 tests given to it. Although some of the problems used were fairly complex, as imitation tests go, the series of tasks was not difficult enough to determine the limits of capacity in monkeys. Until this method has been extended to birds and the common mammals, the question as to whether or not the imitative function is limited to the primates must remain unanswered.

There are a number of other tests of intelligence level which have already been standardized for use, but these cannot be described here for lack of space. A brief treatment of the Quadruple-Choice method and the Box-Stacking test is given in the volume cited as a general reference at the beginning of this section. More recently a method of testing manual instrumentation, or tool-using, in primates has been developed and applied successfully to monkeys and chimpanzees. The results to date show clearly that both of these types possess the capacity to solve fairly complex problems involving the use of sticks and rakes in continuous and broken sequences.

As we have seen, the several tests of intelligence level, described in this section, have made possible the analysis of various complex behavioral functions in the higher animals. Any final rating of species must, of course, be based upon the records made in all of these functions, rather than upon the results of a single test. It would seem hardly necessary to point out here the important bearings of such investigations on a sound interpretation of the basic structure of human behavior.

REFERENCES

Klüver, H. *Behavior Mechanisms in Monkeys*.   Chicago: University of Chicago Press, 1933.

Köhler, W. *The Mentality of Apes*. New York: Harcourt, Brace and Company, 1926.

Munn, N. L. *An Introduction to Animal Psychology*. Boston: Houghton Mifflin Company, 1933.

Razran, H. S., and Warden, C. J. The sensory capacities of the dog as studied by the conditioned-reflex method (Russian Schools), *Psychol. Bull.*, 1929, 26, 202-222.

Stone, C. P., in Allen's *Sex and Internal Secretions*. Baltimore: Williams and Wilkins Company, 1934, Ch. 18.

Warden, C. J. *Animal Motivation: Experimental Studies on the Albino Rat*. New York: Columbia University Press, 1931.

Warden, C. J., Jenkins, T. N., and Warner, L. H. *Introduction to Comparative Psychology*. New York: The Ronald Press Company, 1934.

Warden, C. J., Jenkins, T. N., and Warner, L. H. *Comparative Psychology*, 3 Vol. *Vol. I, Principles and Methods*, 1935; *Vol. III, Vertebrates*, 1936. New York: The Ronald Press Company.

Yerkes, R. M., and Yerkes, A. W. *The Great Apes*. New Haven: Yale University Press, 1929.

CHAPTER IV

THE FIELD OF CHILD PSYCHOLOGY

By MARY SHIRLEY, *University of California at Berkeley*

If child psychology were a single field of ripened facts through which a scientific combine were cutting wide swaths and threshing out whole-grain truths about childhood, we should need only to examine the crop. But it is not. The field of child psychology is divided into several small patches, each tilled by different workers who plant different postulates, cultivate with different tools, harvest different crops and market them to different groups of consumers. Therefore we must get a bird's-eye view of the field before we sample the varieties of produce. Fig. 11 (p. 71) attempts graphically to do this.

Nature-Nurture Wall.—The stout wall through the middle of the field is the nature-nurture division line. South of the wall facts about the natural unfolding of growth processes ripen in the warm sun of heredity; north of it truths about the cultural patterning of behavior grow in the fertile soil of environment. The results are equally sound; but a great many gardeners cannot see over the wall. In some places, however, the wall has crumbled, and here workers are experimenting to discover the relative contributions of sun and soil to the child's development.

Generic Child-Individual Child Fence.—At right angles to the nature-nurture wall runs the generic child-individual child fence. West of the fence the workers are interested only in harvesting facts about children in general. In their research they deal with many children all at once. The child they talk about is a statistical abstraction and they consider facts about development as not very useful unless they hold for the entire child population or for a measured portion of it. East of the fence the workers are concerned about the individual John and Mary. Their children are flesh-and-blood realities which they study one at a time. They believe that a fact or a relationship established on an individual case is as scientifically valid

63

as one established on large groups; and that useful generalizations about childhood can be built up through the intensive study of many individual children.

A historical resumé will help us to understand why these division lines were built; and why small divisions of child psychology still flourish when modern economy would dictate a more systematically planned and larger scale production.

Historic Gateways to Child Psychology

Building the Wall on the Nature Side.—*Academic Experimental Psychology.*—Nineteenth century experimental psychology opened no gate to the child. In this field Wilhelm Wundt and his students were intent upon raising facts about sensory experience, and the tools they used were introspective observation and report. They would have liked to explore the sensory life of infants because they believed that only the newborn was capable of having "pure sensations,"—sensations uncolored by previous experience and wholly devoid of meaning. But obviously babies were incapable of introspecting and reporting upon their sensations. Besides, the early experimental psychologists were so busy making psychology a discipline worthy to be recognized by the scientific aristocracy,—mathematics, physics, and chemistry,—that they could not bother with children.

Something of this attitude persists in academic psychology even today. The experimental psychologist cares not a fig about the individual child; or about the generic child either, for that matter. His interest is entirely in problems,—such as learning, emotion, motivation, intelligence. He considers the child, along with the monkey, the dog, and the cat, as a useful laboratory animal, but on the whole he finds it less suitable than the rat and the college sophomore for the solution of his problems.

Biological Sciences.—The child really crept into psychology through the fields of biology and education. Nineteenth century evolutionists, eager for any and all sorts of evidence to support their hypothesis, welcomed the baby as the "missing link" between animal and man. "Ontogeny recapitulates phylogeny" they said, and when they looked at the infant they saw atavistic signs both in his anatomical structure and in his activities. Darwin pointed to the grasp reflex of the newborn as a survival from prehuman days when it was necessary for the anthropoid infant to cling to the limb of a tree or to its mother's fur. Less critical writers carried over this idea into analogy and to absurdity. To them the six-months-old baby worming along on the rug, using his arms as flippers, was recapitulating fishhood; the creeper was reliving the quadrupedal stage of mammals; and the run-about child was repeating the savage stage of human social evolution. To the biologists human growth and development provided just another illustration of the upward and onward evolutionary trend. Thus they helped to build up the nature-nurture wall. But they set to work observing and describing the course of this developmental process in babies.

Baby Biographies.—Darwin himself kept notes on the development of his own son during infancy. His was not the first biographical record to be published, but the interest of so great a man in the life processes of babies must have stimulated others to keep similar records.

William Preyer, whose book, *The Mind of the Child* published in Germany in 1881, was based on a biographical record of his son's first three years, is often called the father of child psychology. Preyer was an anatomist and embryologist, and from his experiments on fetal rabbits, chicks, and guinea pigs, and his observations on his son he saw that development of activity and sensitivity of the growing child was a continuous process extending far back into fetal life, and that in the main, animal and human infants followed the same course in acquiring control over their muscles. Preyer's influence is strong today, for many biologists and psychologists are still engaged in charting the course of motor development and seeking its anatomical and neural correlates on all sorts of animals, from salamanders to man. Modern research utilizes far more elaborate techniques— the cinema for one—than those available to a poor German scientist in the eighties; but its results tend only to confirm Preyer's wisdom in his conception of the problems and the fundamental soundness of his findings.

Following Preyer, many psychologists kept diaries of their off-spring, and several baby biographies were published in the late nine-teenth and early twentieth centuries. Shinn's biography of her neice is one of the most complete and well-organized accounts of babyhood. William Stern based his *Psychology of Early Childhood,* first pub-lished in German in 1914, upon notes kept by him and his wife on their three children. Baby biographies have been justly criticized on the grounds that the babies observed were a selected and probably superior group; that the accounts were anecdotal and perhaps prejudiced by the fact that the biographer was a near relative of the child; and that the techniques were not completely described and not comparable from one author to another. Nevertheless these careful and lengthy accounts of individual babies have contributed a great deal toward our knowledge of the course of development. They have also helped to establish the usefulness of the *longitudinal approach* * to child study, that is, the observation of the same child or the same group of children over a long period of time with a wait-and-see policy in the interpretation of data.

Building the Wall on the Nurture Side.—*Education.*— Nineteenth century education, faced with the problem of getting all children to climb the path to ideal citizenship, naturally built up the wall on the nurture side. The educators were quite aware of the crop the evolutionists were raising, and their first thought was that if the child was first a little animal, then a little savage, they must begin all the earlier to start him on the road to worthy manhood. So kinder-gartens were established as a step toward moving the school age downward. Very soon educators had a second thought; if the function of childhood was to relive the life history of the race, then these necessary recapitulatory stages must be turned to account in education. So schools began to provide materials and encourage pursuits that would help the child to progress more easily through the pastoral and tribal stages of social evolution toward education's ideal manhood.

---

* Words having a somewhat technical meaning in child psychology have been italicized. Most of these are briefly explained in the text, but the instructor may find it necessary to amplify some of them.

Mental Testing.—Because not all children reached the goal set for them by a formal educational system, school administrators turned to psychologists for a solution to their practical problems. Alfred Binet was given the task of finding out why all Paris school children did not profit equally well from instruction. His answer was the first successful scale of mental tests for use with children. These tests have been revised time after time until very few of his original test items remain in use; nevertheless Binet is still the most frequent surname of the family of mental tests for children.

Mental testing almost at once became an indispensable tool of educational and clinical psychologists; progressive educators abandoned the single goal of formal education for individualized goals more in keeping with the child's potentialities. But Binet contributed more to child psychology than a useful device for testing an abstract ability. His demonstration that intelligence was measureable added to the growing belief that all traits were measureable if only proper scales could be devised. His concept of mental age enlarged the whole concept of age until now we recognize many types of age—anatomical age, social age, educational age—in addition to chronological age and mental age. Binet did not invent the intelligence quotient, but it grew out of relating the mental to the chronological age. The theory that the IQ remains constant throughout the dynamic years of physical and mental growth has stimulated much research on the nature-nurture boundary.

The age-by-age grouping of the Binet tests is a good illustration of the *cross-sectional approach* to the study of child development. In the cross-sectional approach, laws or standards of physical or mental growth are derived by measuring different groups of children at successive ages. This differs from the wait-and-see longitudinal approach by assuming that what the four-year-olds are today, the three-year-olds will become a year from today. The cross-sectional approach is much more economical of time than the longitudinal approach, since the observer does not have to wait for the children to grow older in order to obtain measures on the next age group. Consequently in the time saved he can observe many more children and obtain results that are more representative of the entire child population.

Builders of the Generic-Individual Fence.—*Statistics.*—In the nineties Sir Francis Galton opened the statistical gate to the study of biological phenomena and particularly of human abilities. Individuals varied over a wide range in every trait that was measured; and the entire group distributed themselves according to the *normal curve of probability*. If one wished to study a given trait or the relationship between two traits it became apparent that he must observe the trait in a large group of individuals. From the point that all generalizations in order to be applicable to the population as a whole must be based on a representative sampling of that population, it became easy, but false, to reason that observations based on a single case were not scientifically valuable. Thus the fence between generic-individual child was built.

While Galton was building the statistical fence with one hand he was tearing down a section of the nature-nurture wall with the other. He made the point that twins who had been reared apart would provide the crucial test of the relative influence of heredity and environment, and he made observations on such a pair of twins. Thus he started a long line of research on twins that has produced both statistical studies and *co-twin control* studies on individual pairs, wherein one twin is systematically trained and the other left to develop at his own rate. These co-twin studies have helped us to discover what types of activities develop automatically with the maturing of body structures and what types come only from practice.

Psychoanalysis.—In the nineties, also, Sigmund Freud began to publish his psychoanalytic theories, which led to greater cultivation of child psychology on the individual child side of the fence. From his work with neurotic patients Freud observed that many *complexes* of adult patients could be traced to unfortunate experiences or shocks in early childhood. These shocks were forgotten or repressed to a subconscious level by the child, but later they intruded in symbolic form to plague him as a grown-up. The *psychoanalytic approach* to child study is one of long continued case-history analysis of the individual. From his analyses of many individuals Freud developed the theoretical framework of psychoanalysis. Some of his theories important for child psychology are that the shock of birth is the source and prototype of the emotion fear; that nursing the mother's breast is the source of the emotion love; that erotic development takes place in three stages, the oral, the anal, and the genital; and that the *Oedipus complex,* the strong emotional bond between mother and son, and the *Electra complex,* a similar strong tie between father and daughter, are the forerunners of adult heterosexual love.

After half a century psychoanalytic theory has little enough acceptance by academic psychologists; but Freud's emphasis on the lasting effects of childhood emotional experiences did much to foster child psychology. Partly to this influence must be attributed the widespread growth of child guidance clinics, wherein both the clinical approach of Freud and the testing approach of Binet are employed in straightening out the problems of difficult children.

Behaviorism.—In America John B. Watson was influential in giving child psychology a place in the field of general psychology. When in 1913 he eschewed introspection as an appropriate method for psychological research and set up objectively observed behavior as the only legitimate datum of psychology, the baby became as good a laboratory animal as the rat. Watson took a cue from Pavlov, the Russian physiologist who had developed the conditioned reflex technique, and concluded that complex behavior was built up through the conditioning of the reflex and random activities of infancy. He therefore attempted to list and describe all the reflexes of newborns, and to discover the adequate or original stimuli that produced these native responses. He took another cue from Freud about the importance of early childhood emotions, and set out to discover what the primary emotions were and to demonstrate how they could be conditioned. His observation that babies display only three primary emotions, rage, fear, and love, the adequate stimuli for which are, respectively, restriction of movement, loud sounds or loss of support, and stroking or patting the erogenous zones, has become classic. More recent investigators, however, have failed to obtain such clear-cut responses in young babies, and find instead a more diffuse emotional reaction that might be called distress. Watson did successfully show that the baby's emotions could become conditioned, setting up in year-old baby Albert a fear of animals and furry objects by striking a loud gong just as he presented the baby with a tame white rat.

Though Watson's own apparatus for the objective observation of behavior in children was very simple—a rat from the laboratory, a stick of candy, a piece of string as stimuli, and an ordinary notebook for recording—the *behavioristic approach* to the study of children has now become one of elaborate apparatus for presenting stimuli and controlling external conditions, and mechanical devices for recording the baby's reactions. This is largely because the behaviorist is concerned lest he become anthropomorphic and read into the antics of babies his own adult thoughts and feelings. Hence such problems as the child's thought and fantasy life get little attention from the behaviorists. Their most important contributions to child psychology have been made through the minute analysis of the activities and capacities of babies in the newborn nursery and through the conditioned response technique.

PRESENT LAY-OUT OF THE FIELD

In the foregoing section we have seen how attitudes toward heredity and environment, group and individual, divide the field of child psychology into four quadrants and how an interest in children themselves, in contrast to an interest in functions, capacities, abilities, and reactions, separates the field of child psychology from that of general psychology. But the field as it is today is further subdivided.

Views of the Child from Each Quadrant.—*Generic Child Side.*—The field as it is at present is schematized in the accompanying chart. Psychologists in each quadrant study the same aspects of the child—his physical and mental growth, his social reactions, his emotions—but they view the child in different ways. Those in the *nature-generic* quadrant view children against a time or age line, and see them swept along toward maturity by the dynamic forces of growth. Consequently the facts about childhood that workers in this section have gathered are: Descriptions of the growth or developmental processes; age norms or standards in development; and individual differences in the rates and limits of growth.

In the borderline plot between the *nature* and *nurture* quadrants, workers are subjecting children to environments different from those in which they presumably would have grown up, and are meas-

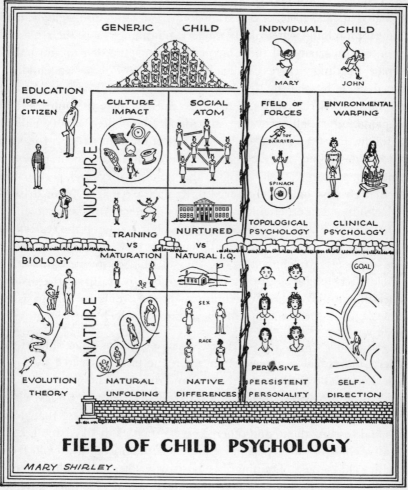

FIG. 11.—THE FIELD OF CHILD PSYCHOLOGY, A.D. 1939.

uring their development under the altered conditions. Co-twin control studies, which were mentioned above, and comparisons of foster children with their true and foster parents or their true and foster siblings represent crops from this portion of the field.

Psychologists in the *nurture-generic* quadrant view children as caught in the swirl of environmental forces, and see them reaching adulthood pox-marked by the *impact of culture*. They see that American children, subjected to a barrage of sky-scraper homes, clock-regulated meals, mechanized transportation, radio propaganda, and modern plumbing, particularly modern plumbing, have their natural appetites thwarted and their normal rhythms speeded up until they become hustling, aggressive leaders; whereas Polynesian children, rained upon by the gentler blows of grass houses, accessible and well-filled food calabashes, out-rigger canoes, distant tomtoms, and no plumbing at all, grow up into docile, contented adults willing to follow the leadership of others. Therefore the workers in this plot are describing more completely the culture pattern or code for American children; are studying the emotionality and personality of children who have been reared in it; and are making comparisons with childhood in other cultures so far as those cultures are known.

Alongside the *culture-impact* plot and bordering on the *individual child* fence is a patch wherein the child is viewed as the center or focus of social attachments. Workers in this section recognize that the child's behavior is greatly influenced by his status in the group; hence the study of the individual can proceed only on the basis of knowledge of the structure of the group to which he belongs.

Individual Child Side.—When we move to the other side of the generic-individual fence we come upon the plot cultivated by topological psychologists. Kurt Lewin and his students view the individual child as moving about in a complex field of forces where some objects, such as toys and candy, have *"plus valences"* that draw the child toward them, and other objects, such as disliked food, have negative charges that repel him. Barriers often prevent the child from reaching his goal, obtaining his positively attractive object; frequently he must move away from his goal; or he may have to approach one or the other of two negative valences—he must eat his negative spinach or be punished by doing without his positive ice cream. Workers in this section of the field describe the child's reactions to frustrating situations; and they map out the child's *life space*. Their observations are made on one child at a time, and the principles they derive apply to the dynamics of the individual rather than to those of the group.

Another section of this quadrant is that of *clinical child psychology*. Clinicians see the child as driven by basic physical and emotional needs. If environmental pressure hinders the satisfaction of these needs, the child is warped out of the normal or desirable course of development. The clinician's practical problem is that of altering conditions under which the individual child lives so that he will have a better chance for wholesome development; or of getting the child to adjust satisfactorily to an unalterable environment. Along with their practical work, clinicians are amassing facts about what types of problems are curable and what environmental changes effect the most permanent changes in the child.

In the fourth quadrant we find workers on child *personality* who view each child as stamped with his own individuality from birth and as retaining that imprint in spite of the dynamic forces of growth and the pressures of environment. They attempt to discover the child's *life style* and to observe how it permeates and pervades all his activities, and how it is consistent and persistent over a long time span.

Like the six blind men's views of the elephant, these different views of the child are each true and each inadequate. Of course the schema just outlined is oversimplified and does an equal injustice to all points of view. But it helps us to understand why so many different types of facts are gathered in child psychology; and why the same facts are interpreted in different ways by workers in different sections of the field.

If we ask whether there are not attempts to unify the field or at least to get workers to see the child from all angles, the answer is yes. In the 1920's wealthy foundations began to turn over considerable funds for the cultivation of the field of child development. The stipulation was that the "whole child" should be the object of study and that the research projects should be cooperative enterprises in which anatomists, pediatricians, psychologists, nutritionists, sociologists should collaborate both in the collection and in the interpretation of data. A number of research institutes for the study of children were organized in connection with large universities. In most of them a nursery school was established where children from two to five years became available for observation and study. Thus much of our current child psychology is the psychology of the nursery school child, and may or may not be applicable to the child in the home. Longitudinal or *growth studies* also were started in most of these centers, and several groups of children have undergone periodic observations and examinations over several years.

Nevertheless the four major divisions of the field of child psychology still exist in spite of the wall-smashing done by the "tractor" of child development institutes. We shall therefore utilize this schema in moving clockwise about the field from the lower left quadrant, taking a closer look at the tools and methods of cultivation and sampling a few products from each plot.

REFERENCES

Goodenough, F. L.　*Development Psychology*.　New York: D. Appleton-Century Company, Inc., 1934.

CHAPTER V

SOME PRODUCTS OF CHILD PSYCHOLOGY

By MARY SHIRLEY, *University of California at Berkeley*

PRINCIPLES OF DEVELOPMENT

(*Nature-Generic Quadrant*)

Human growth and development is an orderly process. The baby acquires new skills and activities in a definite sequence that varies little from child to child, although the rate of progression through the sequence shows wide individual variations. *Developmental sequences* have been quite clearly worked out for babies' assumption of motor control, their acquisition of speech, their social progress, their intellectual development, and their emotional growth.

The Motor Sequence.—The fetus becomes active long before birth, kicking and shifting its position inside the uterus. Before birth a number of complex reflexes have developed that enable the newborn to suck and swallow food, to eliminate waste products, and to make a few adaptive or protective gestures. Most of the activities of arms and legs represent random or mass activity that does not get the newborn very far toward the satisfaction of his needs or the control of his environment. But even within the hospital period the infant begins to gain control over the muscles of his eyes and neck. He focuses his eyes, fleetingly at first, then more steadfastly, on a bright object or on his mother's face; he turns his head to seek the breast; if prone, he twists enough to free his nose for breathing. In a few weeks he rears his head, until first his chin and later his chest is off the table. His eyes now move in coordinated fashion instead of going off at amusing but not alarming tangents; and his gaze follows persons as they move about the room. By three months the muscles of eyes and neck are fairly well under control, and the baby has begun to look at his hands and to catch his own fingers.

Eye-hand coordination proceeds apace during the next three months. The baby's earliest reaching is a whole-arm waving in the

75

direction of the object. Often his fists are closed, but he sometimes succeeds in batting the toy. Excited kicking accompanies his efforts; the act of reaching is first a generalized activity involving the entire body. The extra movements gradually drop out, and soon upper arm, fore-arm, and hand work together in curling the fingers around the rattle and drawing it toward the mouth. For a baby's first way of exploring and exploiting toys is with his lips and tongue. By six months the baby grasps objects that are in motion, transfers them from hand to hand, scratches, pats, and shakes them. He also squirms vigorously and "swims" when lying on a flat surface, and he sits quite comfortably in his carriage or high-chair. He has, in short, taken command of the muscles of trunk and arm.

During the next quarter year he makes more successful efforts toward creeping, first rolling, then pushing himself to a sitting position. About the time he begins to roll he discovers his toes are diverting playthings; and when he has achieved the act of sitting alone on the floor he tests his growing security by bouncing, swaying, and rocking in this position. Now when his mother holds him erect he plants his feet firmly and makes two neat footprints; whereas he formerly bent his knees and dangled his feet, or made prancing, pawing steps on his toes. A little later he stands with the less personal help of furniture. Next he begins to get about over the floor, either by hitching in the sitting position, or by creeping on hands and knees. At about the same time he divorces his index finger from the other digits and uses it to point and to poke into holes. When this stage is reached his muscular control has extended down to the pelvic region and out to the fingers.

Hoisting himself to standing position by the help of furniture, stepping along clinging to the edge of his crib or play-pen, and toddling when led by a friendly hand follow shortly. Finally he gains enough confidence to relinquish his hold and stand alone in the middle of the room. Sometimes he does this for the first time in a moment of excitement or absorption over a new toy, and when he recognizes that he is unsupported he promptly sits down. But before long he does it again and he even takes a few steps alone. The interval between the first steps and the period of walking freely about the house is sometimes only a few days, and sometimes months.

But once free walking is established the baby is soon running about, climbing steps and scrambling onto chairs, tables, and shelves. When babies achieve this degree of locomotion, which most of them do by 18 months, their motor control has migrated down to the end of their toes.

Motor progress does not stop with the achievement of walking, running, and climbing. Jumping, hopping, and skipping are further motor developments during the preschool years; and the circular pedaling of cycle tops is achieved by children who have the opportunity for using such equipment.

The motor sequence, which is practically the same for all babies, and which is similar in general for animal infants—the chimpanzee, the monkey, the cat, the rabbit, and the guinea pig—follows the anatomical law of *developmental direction.* This law states that the wave of growth sweeps over the body *cephalo-cuadad* and *proximodistally,* or downward from head toward tail, and outward from the spinal column toward the extremities of hands and feet. The fact that progress toward locomotion in human infants is consistent with that in animals, and that the motor sequence in both humans and animals follows this fundamental growth law is strong evidence that motor functions represent a natural unfolding of growth processes.

Language Development.—It is not surprising that so important a biological function as locomotion should follow an orderly sequence; but how is it with that strictly human function, the development of speech? Children of different nations acquire their own mother tongue, to be sure, but progress toward language development is similar from baby to baby. The first utterance is the birth cry, and during the first few weeks vocalizations are limited to crying, coughing, and sneezing. Usually the sounds *nga-nga* or *nwa-nwa* can be detected in the early cry. At about six weeks the baby begins to utter grunts of contentment when he is comfortably warm and fed, and by three months he coos and gurgles with pleasure when his mother bends over him and smiles and talks to him. In the next quarter year he turns his head toward a voice and seems to listen to speech and to music. He also shouts and calls for attention in pleasant tones, instead of making his wants known only by crying. At about seven or eight months he babbles in syllables, repeating *mum-mum-mum, da-da-da,* and other simple vowel-consonant combinations several times in a series.

At about nine months the baby gives evidence of comprehending a little simple speech. He responds when his name is called, and he shows that he knows the name of his sibling or his pet by looking in the proper direction when asked, "Where is Sister?" and "Where is the kitty?" Parents usually try to make some of the baby's own syllables into words at this time by attaching them to objects or persons. When the baby says "Da-da" the mother says "Yes, there is Daddy," pointing to the father and thus in due course the baby's spontaneous utterance becomes a meaningful word.

A year-old baby usually has a vocabulary of a few words that apply to members of the family, familiar playthings, or to important babyhood needs. During the second year the child discovers that every object has a name, and he learns many nouns and a few adjectives and goes about describing things,—*pri' f'ower, nice dolly, good boy.* Then he acquires a few verbs and uses them as single word sentences. "Hurt," rubbing the head does the service of four or five words, "I bumped my head and it hurts." Pronouns are the most difficult part of speech for the child to acquire and he has little command of them before the third year.

The function of children's speech also shows a rather consistent development from babyhood on. The first cries and gurgles express merely physical needs or satisfactions. Early syllabic utterances probably represent vocal play; the baby spontaneously exercises the muscles of larynx and throat just as he exercises those of his arms and legs. By six months, vocalization has taken on a social character; and the baby calls, scolds, complains, approves in the appropriate tones. The inflections of adult speech—the questioning lift of the voice, the imperious command, and the statement of fact—are often heard in the meaningless jargon of the year-old baby. Comprehensible speech first concerns the child's immediate activities and surroundings. Later he talks about events in the recent past, gives information about things he has seen or heard, and finally voices his fantasies and states his reasoning about events or natural phenomena.

Social Development.—The baby's growing interest in other persons also progresses in orderly fashion. The infant's first social response is to focus his gaze on the face and eyes of the person who cares for him; soon he smiles in response to a smile; when he begins to reach he touches the mother's hand, and with progressive control of his muscles he catches her fingers, entangles his fingers in her hair, snatches off spectacles, pokes into eyes and nostrils, and exploits adults for his pleasure. At about nine months he can be taught social games such as "peek" and "pat-a-cake." Throughout his first year his playmates are mostly adults, and older children.

During the second year the baby's play is largely solitary, although he often watches and sometimes interferes with the play of older children. At about three years this on-looker behavior develops into parallel play; two children play side by side in the sand, for example, but each uses his own toys and plays in his own fashion. Associative play in which two or more children borrow toys from one another, work on similar projects, and offer suggestions to one another comes later; and highly organized or cooperative play in which children collaborate on a common enterprise or assign definite roles and carry these out appropriately comes still later in the pre-school period.

Intellectual Development.—Intellectual responses of babies are somewhat harder to detect than motor, language, and social reactions; but even in the first year the baby discovers a few principles of cause and effect and makes some generalizations upon which he acts. Perhaps his first one is "Crying brings help." A little later his reactions suggest the generalization "Mother always helps; strangers cannot be depended upon." Still later he discovers the law of gravity: "Objects fall down, not up."

Examples of the sequence of intellectual development at later ages are to be found in the age-by-age groupings of intelligence test items. Indeed if intellectual growth did not follow an orderly pattern, it would be impossible to have intelligence tests at all.

Emotional Development.—Emotional growth also follows a rather systematic course. The earliest emotional expression is the kicking, threshing, and crying of discomfort; and the second develop·

ment is the gentler movements and pleasanter sounds of contentment. Distrust or fear of strange persons and new situations is often noticed in the fourth month. Timidity or self-consciousness develops in some children—not in all—toward the end of the first year. Stubbornness or negativism and tantrums are common in children between 18 months and 2½ years—the period at which they are learning to express themselves in speech.

The emotion of anger is first expressed in undirected kicking and screaming, but by his first birthday the baby has begun to direct his hitting and biting toward the person who thwarts him. When the child can talk he adds verbal protests to his physical objections, first the negative "No!" "I won't!" "I don't want to!" Later he threatens his adversary and calls names. Emotional development, in short, proceeds from a purely overt toward a verbal or symbolic expression, although the physiological accompaniments of emotion—glandular activity, circulatory changes, and altered tension in the smooth and striped muscles—continue from infancy to old age.

Individual Differences.—Although development of motor, lingual, social, intellectual, and emotional behavior unfolds in orderly sequences during early childhood, nevertheless there is wide variation among children in the rates at which they progress through the sequences, in the quality of their responses at the beginning of each new phase of the sequence, and in the upper limit to which each act can be perfected. The sequence is accordian-plaited; in some babies it is stretched out over a long time span; in others condensed into a short one; and in still others one portion of a sequence is extended and another contracted.

Furthermore each of these functions may be regarded as a talent, possessed in different degrees by each child even in infancy. All babies walk, but some walk gracefully almost from the first, while others lumber clumsily along throughout life; all talk, but some jabber all the time, and others utter their thoughts in the fewest possible words; all associate with people, but some seek social contacts from the cradle, while others withdraw from all but the most familiar persons; all have some degree of intelligence, but some are bright and others dull; all have emotional reactions, but some babies cry at the slightest provocation, whereas others are even-tempered day in and day out. Individual differences appear so early in babyhood that they cannot be attributed entirely to training.

Sex Differences.—As a rule girl babies pass through motor, language, and social sequences a little more rapidly than boys. They walk and jump and skip a few weeks earlier; they talk a little earlier, and in longer and more complicated sentences age for age; and they take on the socially approved reactions a little earlier. Whatever advancement girls show in motor accomplishments is readily accounted for by the fact that the growth of their bony structures is several weeks in advance of boys. Their superiority in language and social development is less clearly attributable to native or physical factors; for from the moment of birth, boy and girl babies are subjected to differences in handling and training that might affect their development of speech and of sociality.

Maturation versus Training

(Nature-Nurture Border)

Although many functions unfold in a regular order during childhood, none of them emerges at a high level of skill. All activities improve with practice or spontaneous exercise. The baby that has just discovered a new motor stunt or learned a new word repeats it tirelessly; his spontaneous practice is far more assiduous than the training adults give him. It is important, both from the theoretical standpoint of understanding the nature of development and from the practical viewpoint of education, to know how far maturation alone takes the child on the road to adulthood, and how much of the ground must be traversed by training.

Maturation of Motor Functions.—Gesell and Thompson first used the co-twin control method in studying the maturation of a motor skill, stair-climbing. The babies, a pair of identical (one-egg) twin girls, had been studied from birth and had been given repeated tests in which their performances were almost identical. Beginning at 46 weeks Twin T (for trained) was given six weeks of daily practice in climbing a short flight of stairs. During the first two weeks of training T made little progress, but later she climbed with interest and by 52 weeks she could scale the stairs in less than half a minute. Twin C (for control) was kept away from steps until 53 weeks, but on her first trial she reached the top in 45 seconds. She was then trained for two weeks, and at the end of this time she could scramble up the steps in 10 seconds. Two weeks of training at the more advanced age had enabled C to break sister T's record at the close of her six weeks of practice. But the longer training period gave T a greater interest in motor pursuits and higher confidence in her activities that could be noticed for the next six months.

McGraw also has used the twin-control method in studying the efficacy of training in motor skills. Johnny and Jimmy, a pair of like-sex, but perhaps not one-egg twins, spent their days at the laboratory until they were well over two years old. The twins were given tests in a variety of motor skills at regular intervals, and between times Johnny was subjected to intensive daily training in these skills, while Jimmy was isolated in a crib behind a screen. Johnny was given practice in hanging from a rod, crawling, creeping, sitting, and walking—phylogenetic functions (functions common to the race) that all babies achieve sooner or later. He also was trained in swimming, scaling inclines, roller skating, jumping from pedestals, riding a tricycle, arranging boxes so that he might reach a toy, all of which are ontogenetic activities (specific to the individual) that entailed the mastery of special equipment—a pool, slides, skates— activities with which the baby is not natively endowed. McGraw began training Johnny in these ontogenetic functions as soon as his phylogenetic activities had reached an appropriate stage of development. When Johnny wormed about on his abdomen she started his swimming lessons; when he began to creep she started him up inclines, gradually increasing their steepness; and when he began to balance himself on his legs she put roller skates on him.

Johnny's training in phylogenetic functions gave him little or no advantage over Jimmy. The two boys sat alone, crept, walked, and ran at almost the same ages; occasionally Jimmy was even a little ahead of his much-trained brother. In the ontogenetic functions, however, Johnny's early and continued training was more effective.

After Johnny had acquired considerable proficiency in a skill, Jimmy was given a shorter period of practice. He learned to do some of the stunts; others he refused to try. In general he did not achieve Johnny's skill and interest in the pursuits, with the single exception of tricycle riding, to which Johnny had been introduced a little too early and had consistently resisted after his early failure. That Johnny was able to master such unusual skills as swimming and roller skating before he was two years old shows what latent capacities for motor coordination the baby possesses and how they can be brought out by systematic training.

With older children studies of maturation and training in motor skills give less clear-cut results. One worker found that three months of training contributed less than maturation toward the skills of buttoning, cutting with scissors, and ladder climbing at about two-and-a-half years. Another gave twins, inferior in rolling or throwing balls at targets, a semester of practice, whereupon the trained group caught up with and surpassed their control twins whose skill was allowed to improve only through maturation in the interval. The advantage given by training does not always last, particularly if the skill is a simple one, such as speed of tapping. The practiced group surpasses the control group at the end of the training period, but after an interval of six months or so the two groups of children differ little.

The general conclusion about maturation and training in motor control seems to be that phylogenetic functions will be developed by all babies without any specific practice; even the hampering effects of being strapped to a cradle board or bundled in cumbersome clothing retards walking only a few weeks. If given freedom, safety, and encouragement, babies will spontaneously exercise in ways appropriate to their level of motor development. Ontogenetic motor accomplishments, however, are acquired more easily if systematic training is begun as soon as the basic motor coordinations involved have made their appearance.

Maturation in Language.—Since production of vowel and consonant sounds and their articulation into words require fine motor coordinations, we should expect maturation to play some part in the development of speech. But since speech is essentially a social function, we cannot expect growth alone to take care of talking as it apparently does of walking. Another co-twin study confirms this point. When the stair-climbing twins were twenty months old, T was given a period of stimulation and training in speech; meanwhile C was cared for in complete silence and her spontaneous babblings went unpraised. After two months C's language training was begun and carried on in the same manner as T's had been. C learned much more rapidly than T had done in the early weeks of training, but T's head start enabled her to keep the lead in vocabulary and speech fluency for several months.

Maturation is also important in learning to read and write. Educators and clinicians are aware that a child should not be started to school until his neuromuscular system is mature enough to enable him to make the fine motor adjustments required in reading and writing. Since chronological age is a very poor index to intellectual and physical maturity, teachers are relying more and more upon tests of intelligence and of reading readiness to determine whether the child is mature enough to enter the first grade.

Social and Emotional Maturation.—Specific training directed toward speeding up social and emotional maturity has not been tested on co-twin pairs. Authors of co-twin studies agree, however, that much of the trained twin's advantage over the untrained twin lies in his development of self-confidence and willingness to attempt new activities. Johnny became intrepid and fearlessly attempted any motor task the examiner set him, with apparent faith that she would see him through it safely. Jimmy lacked courage, and was mistrustful of the examiner and often was negativistic toward training.

Maturation's Limits.—Thus far we have not paused to define maturation or to consider what it is that matures. Child psychologists cannot answer that question; anatomists, physiologists, neurologists, and physiological psychologists must tell us what maturation is. They have offered many different answers. Some have emphasized the importance of the growth of the myelin sheath about the nerve fiber; some the growth of more dendrites about the nerve cells in the spinal cord, thus allowing for more complicated nerve connections; some have stressed the shifting of the body's center of gravity and the gradual change of body size and body mechanics; some the increasing strength of body framework through the laying down of calcium in the bones. The child psychologist cannot decide which of these processes is more important, if, indeed, any are more important than others; he must think of maturation as including all the factors commonly included under the term of physical growth.

But the child psychologist can make a general statement about what types of functions mature. Phylogenetic functions, those common not only to man but also to animals, develop along with the growth in body structure, and the age at which new skills appear is relatively little influenced by previous training. Functions never appear at the level of perfection, however, and can always be improved both through systematic training and through spontaneous exercise. The farther we move toward social and toward individualized skills the more important specific practice becomes. But for every skill an irreducible minimum of maturity must be attained before training can be effective.

Natural versus Nurtured Intelligence

In another plot on the nature-nurture boundary child psychologists are producing evidence concerning the relative influence of heredity and environment on intelligence. The tools used in this field are statistical analyses of differences in IQ between different strata of society, or differences within the same group after environmental enrichment or impoverishment.

Educational and Occupational Status of Parents.—The intelligence of children is positively related to the education of their parents, and to the father's occupational status. Average IQ's for both preschool and school ages are lowest for children of unskilled laborers and rise consistently at each step in the occupational hierarchy to the professional group whose children are, on the average, brightest. This relationship between intelligence and parents' socio-economic status may be interpreted on the nature side as indicating that intellectually superior parents breed intellectually superior children; and on the nurture side as showing that economic pressure and insecurity deprive children of the social and environmental stimulants to intellectual growth. Regardless of the interpretation, it is useful to know that for children under three years the easily obtained records of the parents' education and the father's occupation furnish as good an index to intellectual capacity as an "intelligence" test rating.

Intelligence of Foster Children.—Comparison in intelligence of foster children to foster parents and foster siblings does not render a decisive answer on the nature-nurture question because foster-home placement is selective. So far as possible each child is fitted into a home that will give him the intellectual and educational advantages appropriate for his level of ability. When there is a discrepancy between the true home and the foster home the child's IQ tends to shift slightly toward the intellectual level of the new home. But the changes are not great enough to convert a feebleminded child into a bright one or to reduce a near-genius to a dullard.

Nursery School Education and Intelligence.—Whether enrichment or impoverishment of the child's environment in the early years effects a permanent change in the child's mental ability is much disputed at present. More than one investigator has found that children show somewhat higher IQ's after a few months of attendance at nursery school. This is readily understandable, for through nursery school experience the child gains experience with adults as well as with children, and his increasing social poise makes him more at ease in the examining situation and better able to do his best. Currently, however, one research center [1] reports that children who have had the benefits of preschool training in their nursery school manifest an improvement in intellectual level that persists at least until the children enter college. The rest of the story is not yet written, for the oldest children have just reached college age. To test further the efficacy of preschool training in improving intelligence the same workers set up a "model" preschool program in the rather unprogressive and limited environment of an orphanage. One group of little orphans had the benefit of this schooling; another was kept as controls; and again the preschool children showed gains in IQ's.

Other research centers that conduct nursery schools vigorously deny that their pupils show a lasting rise in IQ. Although no one questions the sincerity of the IQ-raisers, many of the most eminent mental-test authorities in the country doubt the validity of the results, and the interpretations placed upon them. Certainly the findings of this single center need to be confirmed and verified—if they can be— by several other centers before we as a nation try to lift ourselves toward supermanhood by the bootstraps of nursery school education. To a mere onlooker it would seem that if there were a dependable way of screwing up the IQ to a higher pitch and getting it to stay there, some great people—the ancient Greeks, perhaps, or the Hebrews—would have discovered it long ago and would have incorporated it into their educational and cultural pattern.

Nature-Nurture and Intelligence.—The most workable hypothesis for the child psychologist is that heredity sets an upper and a lower limit to the child's intellectual capacity, and that environment determines where he stands within that range. Favorable environment enables the child to approximate the upper limit of his mental range and adverse environment depresses his intelligence toward his lower limit. There is plenty of room for education and social forces to work within the range, but probably little they can do toward making a permanent expansion of it. The probable effect of most environments is to stabilize the individual around some point in his range, and thus to contract his native intellectual span.

SOCIAL STRUCTURALIZATION OF THE CHILD

(Nurture-Generic Quadrant)

The Impact of Culture.—Now we cross to the nurture side of the wall and enter the culture-impact patch where the child's social and emotional behavior is seen as the logical outgrowth of the restrictions and taboos society places upon him. Obviously the critical test of this hypothesis would require that children born in one culture be reared in a very different one—New Yorkers in Samoa, for example. Since no one is willing to subject children to such radical experimentation, child psychologists are pretty well limited to observing and describing the behavior of children within their own culture. The culture-impact idea originated in anthropology and sociology and came into psychology only recently. Hence experimental methods are not yet well formulated and results are somewhat scanty; but "environmental influence," a term not too far different from culture-impact, has long been the object of psychological studies.

Ten years ago the psychologists' most used tool for studying environmental influences on children was the occupational scale, which separated the population into six or seven socio-economic strata. Careful statistical studies have revealed that occupational level of the parents is reflected in every phase of child care, from whether the child has a bed to himself and enjoys a daily bath to whether he munches on cabbage or celery and whether he is spanked or not spanked. Almost every feature of children's behavior likewise reflects the fathers' occupational status; children from the upper economic strata use richer vocabularies, possess more information, offer less sympathy, for example. But the device of economic sampling enables us to study only the statistics of cultural differences, and our present need is for methods that will enable us to get at the dynamics of cultural impact.

Cultural Patterning of the Child's Physical Needs.—The newborn baby of whatever race has a few biological needs for food, elimination, activity, and rest; and he is nicely equipped with reflex mechanisms that take care of these needs provided the environment is at all favorable. But at once his rhythmic body processes are taken in hand by society and tailored to fit the local mores. In our culture *habit training* begins at birth; the baby is put on a clock-regulated schedule of feeding and sleeping, and his daily care is little short of ritualistic. By two years the successfully habit-trained child has capitulated to society on every point; he eats when and what it dictates, exercises and rests when and where told, and eliminates waste at appropriate intervals into socially approved vessels accompanied by a certain amount of "mumbo-jumbo" called cleanliness by mothers, hygienic measures by physicians, and sanitation by civic engineers.

Cultural child psychologists, particularly those with psycho-analytic leanings, believe that if the cultural pattern in feeding or in cleanliness is imposed too early or too severely the child is likely to retaliate to society's aggression on his appetites with aggression toward society. Psychoanalysts construe the stubbornness, nega-tivism, and reversion to infantile levels of gratification such as thumb sucking or soiling, so common in two-year-olds, as the result of de-priving the child of the normal satiation of his desire to nurse the breast and to eliminate excreta at the slightest urge.

This view that babies need to satiate or to *work through* infantile response patterns before being pushed on to more adult levels of response to body needs has a good deal of support from case analyses of children showing habit problems. It also gains credence from anthropological reports that primitive children, who in general are less deprived and thwarted in the matters of feeding and elimination, are more contented and carefree than American children, and that they almost never suck their thumbs! Nevertheless the thesis that the impact of our exacting culture results in the development of ag-gressiveness, nervous mannerisms, or other undesirable emotional manifestations is far from proved. Much depends upon the manner in which the restrictions are imposed. Until the course of the train-ing processes has been carefully followed in a large number of babies, the question as to how the cultural pattern can be imposed most effectively and with least damage to the child cannot be answered.

Cultural Patterning of the Child's Social Behavior.—Most of the observations in the child's social behavior have been made in nursery schools, which impose upon children a rather specialized culture pat-tern. In the American nursery school self-sufficiency in emotions, self-help and independence in physical care, social participation, and sharing are virtues; dependence on adults, solitude, and selfishness are vices. Children who do not conform with this culture pattern are misfits in most nursery schools.

Children reach nursery school, however, with many social attitudes already formed. The child of three, for example, is conscious of his own sex; he knows what type of behavior is appropriate for boys and what is allowable only for girls or babies. "Boys don't cry" he will boast, though boys actually do cry more often and vociferously than girls at this age. By the time he reaches school age he has been imbued with attitudes toward race and class, so that he prefers as companions his own racial and social equals. The mechanism whereby these rather complex attitudes of adults are transferred to pre-school age children is an important problem for the cultural child psychologist.

Although nursery schools attempt to inculcate the socialistic principles of cooperation and sharing, the children exhibit considerable aggression, rivalry, and competition. Property rights and possessions are the most common causes of quarrels and conflicts among nursery school children as they are among nations; but long-lived enmity is not the end result of children's conflicts. At the nursery school age, aggression and sympathy are positively related; and the most frequent quarrelers are also the firmest friends. Thus the culture-impact problem is one not merely of discovering in what way and to what degree the culture imposes restrictions upon the developing child, but also of determining in how far the culture is built up in response to the inner needs of the group.

Structure of Children's Groups.—Even very young children tend to build up a social structure in which some become leaders, others followers, and still others social outcasts. The mapping of group structures and the measurement of the strength of bonds between one group member and another recently has been given the name of *sociometry;* but essentially the same methods and objectives were employed in earlier studies of children's friendships and social contacts.

Observational Methods in Social Studies.—Because social behavior loses much of its spontaneity or disappears altogether if it is brought into the laboratory for analysis, it has to be studied largely by observational methods. Human observation is notoriously fallible; so students of social behavior have spent much time and thought on the perfection of observational methods. About ten years ago a great deal of hope was held for the *time-sample* technique for measuring children's spontaneous behavior. The observer selected a particular type of response to be observed—the child's physical contacts with others, let us say—and he made out in advance a list of specific types of contact that were likely to occur, such as hitting, pushing, leading, patting. The observer then moved about from child to child observing each for a short time interval of one, five, or at most ten minutes, checking the items that occurred. Similar short time-sample observations were made on each child every day until a long series was obtained. The frequency of each behavior item for each child was then found by counting the number of occurrences, and the scores yielded a rough measure of the child's proclivity for each type of contact. Sixty single minutes of observation made over a period of two or three months yielded a better measure than a whole hour of continuous observation for chance factors, ill health, or temporary upsets, tended to be equalized for all children over the longer period.

Although these techniques proved to be very reliable, they are less useful than they promised to be. The setting for the child's behavior and the consequences of it are not observable in so short a time span. One needs rather a large chunk of the child's behavior all in one piece in order to see what it is all about. Hence the present trend is away from the more formal, prearranged short-sample observations toward longer observations, more impressionistic recording, and more theoretical analysis.

Factors Influencing Group Formation.—Although the most fruitful period of this field probably lies in the future, a number of products have already been gathered. At preschool ages boys form the closest attachments to other boys about their own age; girls likewise show a preference for the companionship of girls, but they are more likely to attach themselves to a younger boy or girl and to stand in a fostering or protective role to it than are boys. Both the size of groups and the degree of structuralization within them increase with age. In the late preschool period children indicate by their behavior not only that they know their own status in the group structure, but also that they recognize the status of the other members in it.

Leadership is not always to the strong even in nursery school. One child dominates by brute force; another by strategy and guile.

A child's position in the social structure is subject to change with growth to some extent; at least it is influenced by the departure of older children and more dynamic leaders from the group, so that a younger and relatively non-aggressive child may develop leadership the next year when his elder competitors have graduated to kinder-garten. Specific training in tasks that develop self-confidence has been found to help a non-ascendant child toward a more ascendant position in the group.

THE CHILD AS AN INDIVIDUAL

(*Nurture-Individual Quadrant*)

Now we have straddled the generic child-individual child fence and are ready to explore the east half of the field where child psy-chologists grow facts about the particular Johns and Marys. We come first to the plot of topology where the child presumably moves about in a field of forces among objects that shed positive and negative valences upon him.

The Child's Life Space.—Every child's life is circumscribed by a boundary that is set by the limits of his experiences and his abili-ties. The infant's life space is very small; there are few things that he has seen and known, and few that he can do. But his universe ex-pands with his increasing motor skill and intellectual grasp until as a run-about child he has quite a *space for free movement*. If he could always approach the positively valent objects in his life space and retreat from those of negative valence all would be well; but bar-riers often obstruct his *path to the goal*. As the child reaches the meddlesome age many of the attractive objects and delightful pursuits that have plus valences for him acquire an induced negative charge because of his parents' prohibitions. A succinct description of this type of restriction of the child's life space was given by a well-disci-plined two-year-old who, when calling with his mother, looked wist-fully around the strange room at all the enticing bric-a-brac and exclaimed, "Mamma, see! All the pretty no-no's!"

Lewin [2] has drawn a useful diagram which shows a child's life space so cluttered up with things he is forbidden to do and things he is incompetent to do that no free space is left for him in which to move. In such a cramped life space a child *encysts*, draws into himself, becomes negativistic and stubborn. There really is nothing else he can do unless someone clears out some of the prohibitions and gives him some freedom for movement.

Frustration.—Recently topological psychologists [3] have performed experiments to discover how children react to a frustrating situation. A child is brought into an experimental room and allowed to play for half an hour with some simple toys—blocks, boats, a doll, a truck, a duck. The experimenter carefully watches the child's play and notes its *level of constructiveness*. Merely pushing the truck back and forth represents a low level of constructiveness; loading it with blocks and hauling them across the room is a higher level of constructive play; and using the truck, the blocks, and the boats all three in constructing a wharf for shipping is even more constructive. Thus constructiveness ratings can be worked out for every activity in which the child engages during the period and his total play can be given a score on this basis.

At the next session the child enters an altered playroom. The old toys are there, but they are placed in a setting of fine new ones. The doll now resides in a house with furniture, tea set, and an interesting wardrobe; the boat and ducks float on a pond of real water; the blocks are built into a garage for the truck; in short everything is arranged so that the child's play can be more complete and more satisfying. But after a few moments in this more delightful setting the experimenter gathers up the old toys, and, leading the child to the other end of the room, locks him out of paradise by lowering a firm wire partition. Since the child still has access to the original toys the play situation is, objectively considered, the same as it was the first time. But psychologically it is very different. Although the child is effectively barred from the coveted playthings, he can still see them through the wire netting; and because of their greater attractiveness the old toys have now depreciated in value or "valence" for him. In this situation 23 of 30 preschool children regressed to a lower or younger level of activity. Some spent most of the time at the screen, longingly looking at the forbidden fruit; some begged or demanded that the experimenter remove the barrier; some cried. Their play with the old toys was less constructive than during the first period; a former hauler and builder, for example, reverted to a mere truck pusher. The average loss in constructiveness of the 30 children was equivalent to a regression of 18 months in mental age; during this frustrating half-hour the children behaved as if they were a year and a half younger!

Nevertheless one child showed no loss whatever in constructive activity, and six actually gained in constructiveness score under the thwarting situation. Even to the young child frustration may present a challenge that leads him to higher accomplishment, but regression to more infantile behavior is the more common response.

By experiments such as this it is possible to study the dynamics of the child's behavior at a given moment or in a given situation, but let the child's *inner tensions* change, his physiological state of hunger or fatigue, his excitement over the coming circus, his bewilderment at the arrival of a baby brother, or even his desire to join other children outdoors on a fine spring day—and the dynamics so carefully worked out for the original situation no longer hold. Challenging and fruitful as these topological analyses are, they have an almost momentary application, and a new set of dynamics must be worked out almost hourly if one is to keep an accurate map of the child's expanding and contracting, thwarting and encouraging life space.

The Dynamics of Needs and Presses.—Analytical psychologists take a longer view of the child's dynamics. Their technique is the analysis of case history extending back to infancy and if possible to prenatal life. From it they are able to see the operation of certain needs, pressures, and lacks over a long period of the child's life. Different workers have made up different lists of needs in accordance with their own points of view. A sociologist, for example, lists four fundamental wishes or needs—for security, for recognition, for response, and for adventure, all of which are primarily social needs. A psychoanalyst would list more personal needs such as a need for love from the mother, a need for oral stimulation and gratification during infancy.

Perhaps the most comprehensive list of *needs* is that recently published by Murray.[4] Among his list of more than twenty-five are such antithetical social needs as nurturance and succorance; dominance and abasement; affiliation and seclusion; and more personal needs such as sentience, the need for sensory experience; cognizance, the need to acquire knowledge; and needs to avoid harm and blame. The individual is also subject to a number of *presses* from the environment—to the press of family insupport, perhaps, or of danger or misfortune, domination, rivalry, or aggression. A child does not possess all these needs and presses in equal amounts; instead there is a different constellation or *thema* of needs and presses for each. In one child the nurturant need is particularly strong and she tends to mother other children; in another the chief need is for exhibition, and she constantly seeks an audience for her tap dancing and singing.

Fantasy and the Projective Method.—One of the important findings of psychoanalysis is that individuals who are blocked in their direct approach to their goals take refuge in the indirect attainment of their desires through dreams or fantasy. Child life is particularly rich in fantasy; make-believe characterizes the play of children in the late preschool years, and much of the small fry's swaggering joy in playing policeman or fireman is attributable to the compensatory function such play serves in the life of a person who is neither very big nor very brave.

Lonely children sometimes invent imaginary playmates as their companions. One little girl of three was constantly accompanied by an imaginary character whom she designated as "My Nephew." "My Nephew" was sometimes a girl and sometimes a boy, sometimes a grown-up and sometimes a child; but always he was a person of superior accomplishments and broader liberties than little Jane herself. Jane was not allowed to cross the street except when she held tightly to her mother's hand; but Jane sent "My Nephew" bounding across in reckless defiance of traffic; Jane's mother might deny her an ice cream cone, but "My Nephew's" mother always indulged him in cones and candy. Through the fuller life of her imaginary playmate Jane was able to obtain a substitute gratification of some of her own thwarted desires.

Since fantasy is a mechanism whereby the individual seeks to fulfill or to compensate for his deep inner needs, it is possible through careful observation and analysis of fantasy to determine what needs are most important to the individual. The technique of getting the child to reveal his inner needs through fantasy is called the *projective method*. Murray has developed a series of pictures which he shows to the child one by one with the request that the child tell a story about each. Upon analysis of the child's several stories according to the conceptual framework of needs and presses, the same thema of group of needs and presses appears again and again. Very different themata are found in the stories of different children.

A simpler technique for use with younger children is to show the child a series of pictures,[5] each one of which represents a different need, and allow him to look as long as he likes at each one; at the end of the series he may be asked which one he liked best. If after several series of pictures a child has shown rather consistently by his time choices and his stated preferences that he prefers pictures representing companionship—children swinging, boys coasting, children playing tag—he is thought to have a strong need for affiliation; if he prefers such pictures as a child eating his dinner, a boy sucking a stick of candy, a baby taking its bottle, his oral need would seem strong; and if he enjoys most pictures of a mother tucking a child in bed, a nurse binding up a boy's hand, a father carrying his son, the child is considered to have a need for succorance.

Another device for releasing fantasy is the Rorschach ink-blot test. In describing and explaining what "pictures" he sees in each meaningless blot the child often reveals his own wishes, fears, and imaginings. By methods such as these the relative strength of different needs for the individual can be obtained. Thus the child *projects* his inner dynamic mechanisms onto the materials which he is given so that the trained observer can see them.

Play Techniques and Play Therapy.—Another approach to the child's dynamics utilizes play materials to stimulate his fantasy. Finger painting and clay modeling are good materials for releasing fantasies, for the child readily becomes engrossed and accompanies his ever-changing picture or model with a running commentary. One investigator [6] uses a group of small dolls, a doll house, and furniture, a few automobiles and trucks, and some animals, and asks the child to create a dramatic scene. Although this method cannot be used with very young children, they can be given a series of dolls and encouraged to name them. From the child's treatment of the mamma doll, the papa doll, the child doll, and the baby doll, the trained person gains considerable insight into the child's own home life. If a child is emotionally ill with apprehension or jealousy it is sometimes possible to treat him successfully by means of *play therapy;* with guidance and encouragement he can be induced to work off his aggression and jealousy in fantasy on the baby doll and thus spare baby brother.

Play therapy in the hands of a skilled person may be very beneficial, but in the hands of a mere enthusiast it may be useless or even harmful. The logic behind some of it is rather difficult to comprehend. First the therapist furnishes the playroom with toys, to each of which he gives a symbolic meaning. Often the materials can be manipulated in only one way. At a certain age, for example, a child can do nothing with clay but roll it into "snakes" or balls. The child must play with one or another of these toys or materials; there are no others. And whatever he chooses, his play will be saddled with the symbolic interpretation with which that toy has already been endowed. Although some conceptual framework is necessary before any interpretations can be made, nevertheless a too rigid conceptual framework accompanied by too scant a knowledge of the child's level of motor and intellectual maturation inevitably leads to errors in interpretations. Yet play analysis offers one of our most promising techniques not only for diagnosis and therapy of problem children, but also for research upon the dynamics of child behavior.

Family Constellation and Child Dynamics.—Clinical psychologists are agreed that a child's status in the family group has a great deal to do with the dynamics of his behavior. Birth order alone has not proved to be particularly important, although among child guidance clinic patients the percentage of children who are firstborn is somewhat higher than the per cent of firstborn in the child population. It is the child's psychological position among his parents and siblings, his acceptance or rejection as a person in his own right, that influences his behavior so markedly. Acceptance and rejection of the child often occur long before birth, and sometimes extend far beyond the limits of the immediate family. In monarchies a whole nation awaits almost breathlessly the birth of an heir and sighs with disappointment if the infant is a girl. Parents often have their desires so fixed as to the sex and the physical and emotional characteristics of their unborn child that the cards are stacked against a baby that does not meet their prenatal specifications.

Children have an uncanny way of detecting their parents', particularly their mother's, true attitude toward them and of acting in accordance with it. A very young baby picks up the emotional tone of the home as accurately as the radio picks up sound waves from the ether; and he broadcasts it just as loudly. The sensory mechanism by which he does it has not been discovered; most probably the mother reveals her attitudes through tensions and slight withdrawals from the baby as she nurses and cares for him. She herself may be wholly unaware of them, but the newborn, who has so recently left a snug nest, well-insulated from shocks and jars, and who because of his helplessness must be almost completely enfolded in his mother's arms, is probably highly sensitive to jitteriness and tension in her handling.

So important is that warmth and nurturing care called *mother love* that an infant who is deprived of it may be badly warped throughout life. One psychiatrist [7] designates the complete lack of maternal love as *primary affect hunger* and likens it to a vitamin deficiency. According to his observations the child who suffers from affect hunger sometimes becomes unable to form warm emotional attachments to anyone and he grows up into a cold and perhaps a sadistic adult. Or he may demand an excess of affection and fondling from everyone and remain childishly helpless and appealing even after he is grown. The number of children suffering such marked maternal rejection fortunately is not large, but several cases annually find their way into child guidance clinics, where they manifest a variety of problems. Such children are almost impossible to treat successfully unless the mother's attitude can be changed so that she offers the child more affection, or unless some other person in the child's environment, the father, a relative, or sometimes a teacher, can furnish the love and fostering care he so sorely lacks.[8]

The child that is smothered by *overprotective love* is almost as badly off. Overprotection sometimes represents genuine love of the child; but sometimes it is a device whereby the mother conceals from herself and from others her real rejection of the child and thus absolves herself from a sense of guilt. Regardless of whether it is based on genuine or sham devotion, overprotection cramps the child's development of independence and initiative and gives him poor preparation for meeting a world in which he must stand on his own feet. An attitude of *ambivalence* toward the child is perhaps more common than either overprotection or rejection. The child is now a treasure, now a nuisance to his parents; one moment they overwhelm him with affection and attention, and the next they turn him over to a nurse or pack him off to a summer camp so that they can live their own lives as if he did not exist. Such shifts in the parents' attitudes are extremely bewildering to the child and encourage his developing attention-getting behavior in his effort to stabilize the family attitude at what, to him, is the desirable end of the scale.

Contributions of Clinical Methods to Child Psychology.—Child therapy is in the hands of psychiatrists and trained clinicians, but the clinical method makes its contribution to theoretical as well as to practical child psychology. Perhaps one of the most important is the clinical system of two-way interpretations. Clinicians recognize that too much of a good thing is as bad as too little; they see the one-man's-meat principle at work every day. Identical behavior may spring from opposite motives; and similar environmental pressures may lead to very different behavior in different children. This elasticity in the clinicians' interpretations of child behavior is attributable partly to the fact that they deal more with the deviates than with the norms in behavior; with the cases in the opposite tail ends of the distribution curve rather than with those in its mountainous middle. These paradoxical interpretations of clinicians and particularly of psychoanalysts are very confusing to statistically-minded psychologists who have looked too exclusively for direct, straight-line relationships in human dynamics. As the Murphys [9] recently have pointed out, there is just as good evidence, by analogy with physics and chemistry, for the existence of u-type curves as for straight-line relationships among human traits.

Organizing and integrating facts with the individual child rather than the trait as a center of reference is another real contribution of the clinical method. Individual case study involves not only a comprehensive examination of the child's present status in physical development, health, mental development, emotionality, personality, and family relationships, and as complete and accurate history of all these aspects from birth as it is possible to get; but also it demands the weighing, judging, evaluating, and interpreting of these facts. To the clinician intensity of response is more important than mere frequency; and his ability to high-light one bit of the child's behavior as significant and shadow another as irrelevant makes the clinical study of child dynamics an art instead of a purely scientific procedure.

Clinicians deal with one child at a time, but their interpretations and the conceptual framework within which these are made are based on a broad knowledge of many individual children. Because of their cleverness in dealing with all or nearly all aspects of one child at a time, clinicians have developed and demonstrated the soundness of many hypotheses concerning child dynamics that have eluded those psychologists who deal with only a few aspects of many children all at once.

NATURAL INDIVIDUALITY

(Nature-Individual Quadrant)

Once more we scramble over the nurture-nature wall and find ourselves in the chip-off-the-old-block or the blood-will-tell section of child psychology. Here the students of child personality are trying to discover how early a child manifests a distinctive *life style,* and to what it may be attributed. The characteristics of personality, as one child psychologist [10] has described them, are *all-pervasiveness, persistence, pattern,* and possibility of development in a *consistent direction.* If these qualities of personality are true, then no matter what bit of the child's behavior we chance to observe or when we chance to observe it, the pervasive, persistent pattern of personality should manifest itself. Such omnipresence ought to make child personality very easy to study; but to the contrary it makes it more difficult. For attributes that are always in view soon pass unnoticed and discrepancies or exceptions attract more attention. Furthermore the same persistent trait manifests itself in different behavior at different ages and in different situations. Shyness is heard in the cry of infants, is seen in head ducking at six months, and is indicated by silence and toe-twisting fidgetiness at three years.

Tools for Studying Child Personality.—Adult personality usually is studied by paper-and-pencil tests or ratings that are filled out by the individual himself and by his associates. The personality variable extroversion-introversion is one commonly studied by this method. Many years ago, as time is reckoned in child psychology, an extrovert-introvert *rating scale* was worked out for nursery school children, validated by some observations on the child in controlled experiments and by records of his meanderings during a trip to a museum. Many other traits of the child's personality have been studied by rating-scale and *ranking* techniques. The ratings usually are made by nursery school teachers who know the child only in the school situation and who, in making their judgments, compare the child to other children in the group. Although the child's home behavior is not included in these ratings, the teacher's judgment is based on her knowledge of a large number of children, and probably it is less biased than a mother's rating. At best the rating technique is imperfect and has many undesirable features.

Personality pattern or configuration is usually studied by the technique of *profile graphing*. The child's scores or ratings in a number of traits are converted into *percentile* or *sigma* units, which make the child's standing relative to the distribution of the group. Then the new scores are plotted in a zig-zag row down the page and this graph is called the personality profile. It takes a very skillful person to identify a given child from such a bolt-lightning-like picture of his personality. Since statisticians as yet have given us nothing better than these procedures for integrating facts about the individual, much of the personality work on young children is still on the descriptive level.

Personality of the young child is studied perhaps more success-fully by repeated observations in a variety of situations. Later the personality picture must be extracted from these observations by skillful analysis and judgment. Lois Murphy [11] gives an example of four types of observation on a seven-year-old girl, a Rorschach test, a meal with other children, a period of housekeeping play, and an interview. From each the same consistent personality picture can be extracted. To the Rorschach ink-blots the child responded re-luctantly and tentatively, calling most of the blots "just a blotch." At the meal she ate daintily and smiled indulgently at the other chil-dren who were voting by an enthusiastic show of hands about their food likes and dislikes. In housekeeping play she deferred to the observer with many "Now what shall I's" and "Isn't it's"; and she put each member of the large doll family, including the dog, through a cleanliness ritual—wash before dressing, wash before eating, wash before going to bed. At the interview she stated her preference for quiet games, but added that she really enjoyed rowdy, noisy games if a teacher initiated them. In the four situations the girl indicates by her deference to the adult observer, her suppression of childish spontaneity and her overmature, meticulous, lady-like behavior a desire to be like grown-ups and to be accepted by them as equals. These four observations give one more *insight* into the child's life style than a dozen percentile scores drawn into a profile.

Personality Manifestations in Babyhood.—To attribute person-ality to a newborn infant seems absurd, yet in the hospital nursery babies begin to display their temperamental differences. One is easily irritated, another is placid; one looks neat and tidy, another frowzy and unkempt; one cries plaintively, another yells lustily; one the nurses pronounce "adorable," another they call "a brat." The definite impressions that newborns make on the nurses that care for them is some evidence that they are born with at least a nucleus of tempera-ment traits that will eventually become the core of their personali-ties. It is also evidence that from the moment of birth babies are subjected to a differential care that tends to accentuate their native differences.

Allport [12] reports the observations of a psychologist-father who was able to detect nothing that he considered personality in his son until the baby was four months old. At that time the father wrote a personality sketch of the baby and kept it for future reference. At yearly intervals thereafter both the parents and later the teachers described the boy's personality; even at nine years the boy continued to manifest the many interests and the sense of humor that had been forecast from his inquiring, smiling manner at four months.

Another worker [13] observed several babies during their hospital periods, saw them at weekly intervals in their homes the first year, biweekly the second, and twice a year until they were four and a half; at ten years she again saw them briefly. In most of them the personality characteristics that had been prominent in babyhood were still noticeable at ten years. The child that had cried timorously in the newborn nursery, and that became the shyest baby of the group was, at ten, a *painfully shy* boy that grimaced, twisted his legs around his chair, and went through bodily contortions in the visitor's presence. The girl that, as a newborn, had achieved a bandbox neatness clad only in a hospital diaper, and that as a girl of three or four had displayed an orderly clothes closet and a perfectly arranged doll house, at ten showed the visitor her even-stitched embroidery and crocheting. The boy who in babyhood was a fun-loving clown, and who early used a pencil with skill and interest, at ten brought four drawings to show the visitor; each was obviously a cartoon. Not only had his fun-loving and his drawing interest both been preserved; they had become integrated!

Such observational and interpretive studies of personality leave much to be desired but they do suggest that babies are something more than plastic lumps of clay to be molded entirely by cultural and familial impact. They suggest that impact is not a one-way proposition, but that at every punch the child hits back, feebly perhaps, but nevertheless he hits. Though the cultural and familial impact certainly warps the child, the child makes his small dent in the culture, and particularly in his family.

Self-Direction.—At one stage of progressive education when the single goal of formal education had been given up for individualistic goals, the child was looked upon as one endowed with potentialities to last a lifetime. Educators were supposed to surround the child with a rich environment that would offer him materials for developing any and all of his potentialities, and then to leave him alone. The child's inborn and eager-to-grow talents were supposed to guide him unerringly toward what, for him, was the good, the beautiful, and the true. Self-direction, with a very minimum of guidance, was the newest educational pattern. Already there is a backward swing from this rather extreme view. It is now recognized that the burden of self-direction is too great for young shoulders to bear, and that children should be required to make and be held responsible for only a limited number of decisions that are within the scope of their foresight and understanding. Supervision and guidance again have their place in the educational program.

A Brief Review

For a quick review tour of the field let us take with us a stubborn little two-year-old boy, the eldest son of our surly janitor; we shall see what explanations of his negativism grow in each plot, beginning again in the lower left quadrant.

Nature-Generic Quadrant:

Natural Unfolding Plot.—Negativism is a common trait in children that develops about 18 months, reaches a peak around two or two-and-a-half years and declines thereafter. The janitor's boy is following the usual pattern.

Native Differences Plot.—Negativism is more pronounced in boys than in girls; and it is more common in children of the lower socio-economic levels. Since this child fits both these categories it is to be expected that he show negativism.

Nurture-Generic Quadrant:

Culture-Impact Plot.—Negativism is one way in which a child reacts when cultural restrictions are imposed upon him too suddenly and too severely. The janitor and his wife are strict with their little boy, desiring him to grow into a polite, desirable person who will get ahead in the world. Ergo—

Social-Atom Plot.—Negativism is one way by which a child struggles to achieve status among his associates. Other tenants do not let their children play with the janitor's boy; hence he feels insecure socially.

Nurture-Individual Quadrant:

Topological Plot.—Negativism results from too great restriction of the child's life space, and from cluttering it with barriers and prohibitions. The janitor's boy must not meddle, must not disturb, must not destroy the peace or property of other tenants.

Clinical Plot.—Negativism is often a device whereby children strive for attention from their parents. They prefer to be punished rather than to be ignored. Mrs. Janitor just now is very busy with the new baby boy; and the janitor himself is always in demand by the tenants, so Jan, Jr., gets little attention.

Nature-Individual Quadrant:

Persistent Personality Plot.—Negativism, like other personality traits, runs in families. The janitor himself is often grudgingly compliant with tenants' requests and Mrs. Janitor seldom is obliging. Like father, like son!

The contribution of every plot is needed to explain adequately the stubbornness of our little friend. So it is with every other feature of the child's behavior. No patch can be plowed under or allowed to lie fallow. In some fields the crop is larger and more nearly mature. But if the eager consumers of child psychology try to subsist on the products of any one plot their diet will be sadly deficient in other essentials. Although each field must keep up its own production, there well might be a cooperative market where producers could mill and box their produce into balanced packages, and where they might buy tested tools and fertilizer, and might exchange ideas about what crops were most worth cultivating in their individual patches.

REFERENCES

Nature-Generic Quadrant:

   Bühler, C. The social behavior of children, in Murchison's *Handbook of Child Psychology*. Worcester: Clark University Press, 1933, 374-416.

   Gesell, A. Maturation and the patterning of behavior, in *Ibid.*, 209-235.

   McGraw, M. B. *Growth: A Study of Johnny and Jimmy.* New York: D. Appleton-Century Company, Inc., 1935.

Shirley, M. M.   Locomotor and visual-manual functions in the first two years, in Murchison's *Handbook of Child Psychology. Op. cit.* 236-270.

Nurture-Generic Quadrant:

Frank, L. K.   The fundamental needs of the child, *Mental Hygiene,* 1938, 22, 353-379.

Mead, M.   The primitive child, in Murchison's *Handbook of Child Psychology. Op. cit.* 909-926.

Nurture-Individual Quadrant:

Isaacs, S.   *Social Development in Young Children.*   New York: Harcourt, Brace and Company, 1933.

Lewin, K.   Environmental forces, in Murchison's *Handbook of Child Psychology. Op. cit.* 590-625.

Macfarlane, J. W.   Family influences on children's personality development, *Childhood Education,* 1938, 55-59.

Nature-Individual Quadrant:

Chave, E. J.   *Personality Development in Children.*   Chicago: University of Chicago Press, 1937.

CHAPTER VI

THE CONCEPTS AND METHODS OF SOCIAL PSYCHOLOGY

By DANIEL KATZ, *Princeton University*

Social psychology is a relatively late chapter in the story of psychology. At first psychologists were content to investigate man as a biological organism responding to changes of energy in the physical world called stimuli. Today an increasing emphasis is being placed upon man in relation to his fellows. Social psychology is that field of psychology which deals with living creatures as they affect and are affected by their fellows.*

Social psychology thus treats many of the problems of the economist, the political scientist, the anthropologist, and the sociologist. But while these specialists are concerned either with the end result of social interaction or with generalizations about social events which are independent of individual human beings, the social psychologist concentrates upon the principles of human behavior involved in wars, depressions, strikes, elections, and other social happenings. The economist describes the business cycle in terms of commodity prices, car loadings, market fluctuations, and other indices of economic activity. The psychologist turns instead to the buying and selling habits of human beings and to their motives in buying and selling.

THE NATURE OF HUMAN GROUPINGS

In dealing with men in relation to their fellows our first inquiry may well concern the nature and type of human associations. There are many different kinds of groups. An individual belongs to a fraternity, he associates with a certain clique, he comes from the right side of the railroad tracks, he is a member of a certain church, etc.

---

* The writer wishes to express his indebtedness to Richard L. Schanck with whom he has collaborated so often in the past. Many of the ideas which appear in the following three chapters have come from this close association.

It is essential to analyze the nature of various groupings so that we do not confuse different facts of social relationship by calling them all groups or associations. To help in this analysis the following four criteria may be usefully employed.

Primary and Secondary Groups.—In the first place, we need to know whether a group is *primary* or *secondary*. The sociologist, Cooley, emphasized the difference between a group in which all the members were physically present, and hence could directly stimulate and respond to one another, and a group the members of which were not physically present.[1] The family belongs in the former category whereas the followers of the actress, Carole Lombard, comprise a secondary group. The importance of this distinction is that people organized in secondary groups tend to show less personal responsibility for their actions than people associated in primary groups.

Partially and Totally Inclusive Associations.—A second criterion for analyzing groups is furnished by Allport's distinction between *partially inclusive* and *totally inclusive* associations.[2] Some groups include practically all of the individual's personality. Other groups may include only a segment, or fragment, of the individual. For example, a professional ball player may live his life in terms of his ball club. He eats, drinks, and sleeps baseball. The baseball league, to which he belongs, is for him a totally inclusive grouping. He has relatively few interests outside of it and these are of minor importance. If we know him as a baseball player, we have an adequate description of his personality. On the other hand, the professional joiner may belong to a score of organizations. A small fraction of his interests is given to his golf club, another small fraction to his political party, and still another fraction to his church. Each of these groups, however, includes only a small part of the man. If we saw him in any one of his group roles we would know very little about his personality.

Perhaps it is wiser not to distinguish sharply between a wholly inclusive as against a partially inclusive grouping. Instead we should use this criterion as a scale of more or less inclusion. Thus the baseball league may include ninety per cent of the ball player's activities and interests. The professional joiner may give ten per cent of his time to his golf club, two per cent to his church, and one per cent to his political party.

It is also important to include a qualitative consideration when we use this criterion of how much of the individual's personality is included in a given association. An individual may give relatively little time to a group and take part in few of its activities and yet his ego may be deeply involved in it. Practical considerations of making a living prevent him from playing the role he otherwise would. In addition, therefore, to describing the time and activities as a measure of inclusion we need to know the intensity of the attachment to the group.

Group Relationships.—A third criterion is the nature of the relationship within the group and the relationships toward other groups. These relationships are defined by the objective reference of the actions of the group. In other words, how do the people in the group behave toward one another and how do all of them behave toward non-members? Many types of relationship are possible. A very common relation in human associations is the *in-group* and *out-group* difference in attitudes. Hostility is maintained toward anyone not a member of the group, whereas among those who belong to the in-group a relation of friendship and cooperation prevails. The technique is often employed, therefore, of discrediting someone we do not like by labelling him with some characteristic of the out-group. He may be typically American but if we call him a Communist this often has the effect of placing him outside the group. Other relations in the group include a polarization of attitudes toward a common stimulus-source, perhaps an official or leader, a reciprocal set of cooperative habits, and a master-slave relation of dominance and submission.

Permanence of a Group.—A fourth criterion is that of *permanence*. How long do the relationships between people last? A crowd is a temporary group. People stay together in a crowd for a few hours and then may never see one another again. The nation as a secondary grouping is relatively permanent. Obviously some degree of permanence is necessary, if we are going to speak of groups at all. The more stable and the more permanent the group, the more we are justified in using it as a concept in social psychology. Older writers were so impressed with the permanence of the human relationships which constitute the group that they regarded the group as of the same type of stable unity as a biological organism. The state for them was an entity with the same reality as the human being. Its parts were individuals just as the cells of the body are parts of the individual. As a matter of fact, however, groups lack the permanence of individuals and so cannot be considered entities. After all, individuals can leave one group and join another but cells do not wander away from the human being and become part of another person. Therefore, even though we do get in the habit of speaking of a group as an entity, we must always be alert to watch its stability. Otherwise we may wake up to find the group has vanished over night as did the German labor unions after the advent of the Nazis to power.

THREE SOCIAL GROUPINGS

With the aid of these four criteria we can now turn to consider three very important groupings in our society: *The community, the public,* and *social classes.*

The Community.—In popular usage the term community is indiscriminately applied to any group with certain common interests. In social science, however, community refers to a definite type of human association. It refers to a number of people living together within a short radius whose psychological needs are for the most part satisfied within the group itself. The rural village sixty years ago was a good example of a community. The radio, the automobile, and the chain store have broken down the old village barriers so that it is hard to find a pure community today. Neighborhood sections in large cities, the faculties of some colleges, and the officials of some business organizations sometimes approximate the community type of grouping.

The community is essentially a *primary* grouping. Not all of its members are in face-to-face contact with one another all the time, but the possibility of face-to-face contact is great and all members are known personally to one another. The community is also a *totally inclusive* group. Within its boundaries the members express their personalities and satisfy their needs. People do play roles in the social life of the community which are not without their standardized aspects—instance the village philanthropist, the village fool, the village gossip. Nonetheless, people tend to find the role which suits their personality within the community. The village busybody creates her own part and so, too, do the other community characters.

The relations within the community, therefore, are many and varied. They vary according to the personalities of the individuals and according to the patterns of association. Friendship, enmity, tolerance, derision, cooperation, and non-interference appear between different people and at times between the same people. Toward the outsider, however, is a universal feeling of mistrust and mild hostility. This general attitude does not govern every action, for if a person appears as a visitor he will be treated hospitably. If he comes in any other capacity, however, he finds the community solidified as an in-group against him. The community is a relatively permanent grouping. Since it is based upon personal contacts between its members, there is a strong tendency for it to survive as long as these individuals live.

At present the community grouping is found less frequently than in the early days of our culture. We were once a nation of communities. Today we are a nation of publics. Members of the older generation are apt to bewail the good old days of the community. This is largely because they spent their childhood in this personal type of living. As adults they find it hard to adjust to a less personalized social life and they look back with a nostalgic longing to a golden age.

Publics.—At the opposite pole from the community stands the public. A public is a group of individuals who hold in common some interest or some attitude or some emotion. Practically the number of publics seems unlimited. There are as many possible publics as there are human interests and attitudes. In our culture the supporters of Townsend's Old Age Pension Plan constitute one public, the radio audience of Charlie McCarthy another, the readers of *Life* still another, the members of the Democratic Party a fourth, the buyers of Ford cars a fifth, and so on.

The public is generally, though not invariably, a *secondary* group. Its membership transcends the spatial limitations of direct physical stimulation. A coal miner in Illinois and a store owner in Jersey may both belong to the same political public. More important than the criterion of the primary or secondary nature of association in describing the public is the criterion of the degree of inclusion of the individual's personality. The public is almost always a *partially inclusive* group. A person enters into a public with but a segment of his personality. Hence he can belong to many publics but to only one community. The number and variety of publics to which a man belongs is an index of the extent and variety of his interests and sometimes of the integration or lack of integration of his personality.

The relationship which characterizes a public is the polarized attitude of acceptance or submission to a common stimulus source, found in almost all audiences. The common stimulus-source may be a leader, such as Townsend, a radio program, or the object of people's material desires. There is little reciprocal interaction between members of the public. They intensify one another's allegiance to the group through the facilitating effect of numbers, but extended give-and-take between members or between leaders and followers is lacking.

The public is a relatively impermanent group. Since it competes with many other similar publics for the time and support of the same people, any one public may disappear with startling quickness. Some publics do endure but the average public does not have a long life.

In general it is useful to distinguish between two types of publics: The *interest public* and the *identification public*. The interest public is a group of people with a common economic motive. The retailers' association is an interest public; so, too, is the National Manufacturers' Association or the consumers' union. An identification public, on the other hand, is a group of individuals who ally themselves with a leader or symbol to enjoy vicariously a success not easily available to them in their own lives. The sporting public, who follow the fortunes of a particular prize fighter or a particular baseball team, identify themselves with their heroes and so participate in the victories of their champions. Identification publics thus can flourish only in an age when many people are thwarted in living the type of life they would like to live. Vicarious enjoyment through identification takes the place of direct satisfaction with life itself.[3]

The proper analysis of publics enables us to predict the outcome of social trends. The mistake is frequently made of regarding publics as vague forces or as entities in and of themselves. Before an election it will be assumed that Candidate A will be elected because he has the support of the Ku Klux Klan, the American Federation of Labor, the Republican Party, and the advocates of a new prohibition law. This assumption obviously overstates the strength of Candidate A because these groups are overlapping. Moreover in each of these publics are individuals who belong to other publics which may oppose Candidate A. For example, though the American Federation of Labor may officially bless the candidate in question, many of its individual members may belong to the Union for Social Justice. On election day the allegiance to this union may prove more important than loyalty to the Republican Party and the American Federation of Labor. To predict accurately we must regard publics as segments of human beings and not as entities in themselves. Moreover, it is necessary to measure in advance the relative strength of the allegiance to different publics of the same individuals. Will John Jones, a lifelong member of the Democratic Party and also an ardent labor man, vote for a Democrat who is non-labor in preference to a pro-labor Republican?

Social Class.—Somewhere between the community and the public should be placed the grouping called social class. In the United States it has never been considered nice to talk about classes because we are a democracy with all citizens equal before the law. Nevertheless, classes seem to exist in almost all societies and they are a useful concept for the social scientist. By class is meant the role people play in the process of creating and distributing wealth.

After all, the bulk of the average individual's waking hours is given to his vocation. People, therefore, who pursue fundamentally the same way of life in earning a living tend to have the same attitudes, the same habits, and the same interests. Moreover, a man's way of earning his living determines his outlook on life because it sets limits on his actual and potential share in the nation's income. In improving their lot in life men band together according to class because of similar interests. Manufacturers organize to secure tariff laws which benefit them; farmers get together to preserve their A.A.A. subsidy; factory workers strike to raise their wages.

Social class is both a primary and secondary group. Farmers as a social class include both the local group of intimate associates and fellow farmers distributed over the whole country. The primary aspect of this grouping brings home to each individual the similarity of interest and the identity of attitude through a common way of life. This *consciousness of kind* is then extended beyond immediate associates to include colleagues never even seen.

Social class is closer to the community than to the public with respect to the criterion of inclusiveness of personality. In modern society members of a social class belong to other groupings as well. Hence social class is not totally inclusive. Nevertheless, in terms of the intensity of the involvement of the individual's personality social class is not to be compared with the public. The test of a social class is whether it involves the central basic attitudes of personality. Other group memberships are generally abandoned when they clash with membership in the social class. One reason for holding that social class in this country is relatively unimportant as compared with Europe is that members of the alleged social classes in the United States follow other than class allegiance in general behavior and attitude.

The relations within a social class are those of equality as Ginsberg points out.[4] Toward other classes the relation is one of inferiority or superiority. The upper classes expect and receive deference from the lower classes. Within a class, attitudes of superiority shown by one man toward his fellows are regarded as bad manners or an attempt to renounce his class.

Social classes are among the most permanent of groupings because they are rooted in the methods of earning and distributing

wealth basic to a given culture. Until a people changes its fundamental economic habits, classes will tend to be stable. Social classes
thus follow the objective relationships in society, and change when
those objective relationships change. Often, however, there is a lag
between the objective picture and the psychological groups which
emerge. In the United States we are approaching a period in which
economic opportunities are no longer as plentiful as they were when
our natural resources were still unexploited. Hence we may expect
to see social classes become more clearly defined in this country within the next generation.

A social class is popularly differentiated on the basis of amount
of income. A better criterion is the source of income. Does a man's
income come from wages, or from investments, or from his own
business? The reason for following source of income rather than
amount is psychological. A man who has his own small business
may make no more than a skilled mechanic. Nevertheless he belongs
to a different social class. For one thing he has the possibility of doubling or tripling his income if business conditions are good. All the
skilled worker can hope for is a slightly higher wage scale. Hence the
small business man has the psychology of the big business man, though
his income is close to that of the skilled worker. For another thing,
whereas the worker earns his living through manipulating objects
the business man manipulates people. There is a different psychology
associated with these two kinds of activity which further differenti-
ates the worker and business man.

Social classes have not been clear-cut in this country because of
the many psychological devices for eliminating differences between
economic groups. For example, a large oil concern will not bother
to own all of its gas stations. It will sell gas to the small station
cperator who might just as well be an employee of the company. As
an owner, however, he is under the delusion that he may some day
make his fortune. But since the price of the oil he buys is beyond
his control he can do little to regulate his degree of profit. And
since he is also limited in the number of gallons he can pump a week,
he might just as well be working for wages and enjoy shorter hours.
Similarly many farmers work their farms for the banks which hold

the mortgages. Yet these farmers feel themselves independent business men and their psychology is that of an owning class.

An interesting description of social classes in modern industrial society is furnished by Bukharin who calls attention to five kinds of groupings.[5]

(1) The *basic classes* of a given social order are the owning or upper class and the non-owning lower class. The lower class does not possess factories, land, or tools, and hence must work according to the conditions laid down for them by the owning class. These major divisions may be broken down further into smaller units. The commanding class can be subdivided into bankers, manufacturers, and large-scale merchants. The lower class may be divided into skilled and unskilled workers.

(2) Frequently groups can be found which are a survival from a previous social order and which are in the process of deterioration. As these *transition classes* gradually go to pieces their members become absorbed into the basic classes. After the Civil War the old slave-owning aristocracy gradually lost its distinctive characteristics in the new economic system. Similarly, the artisans and peasants of the feudal order are in the process of transition to the more basic classes of modern industrialism. In fact the artisans have almost all become merchants and wageworkers, but the small farmers are still an important group.

(3) The *intermediate classes* comprise the groups who belong somewhere between the commanding and the lower classes. They are not a remnant of a previous social order, but are an organic part of the present society. Doctors, college professors, engineers, and trained technical workers belong in this category. Radicals are inclined to underestimate the importance of the intermediate classes and to overestimate the importance of the basic socio-economic groups.

(4) It is also possible to find *mixed class types,* comprising individuals who have membership in more than one class. For example, a skilled mechanic may own a farm, for the operation of which he may hire a farmer. The mechanic is thus both an owner and employer and a wageworker. Unlike the public, however, the class

grouping does not as a rule permit the individual to belong to more than one class. But so long as people have a scrap of objective evidence for regarding themselves as members of a higher socio-economic group than they are, they proceed to comport themselves in a fashion befitting the higher status. The man who works in a factory may own a few shares of stock from which he may derive two per cent of his income. Yet his psychological identification is with the class of investors rather than with his fellows in the shop. Studies of the voters in the 1936 campaign by the American Institute of Public Opinion confirm this observation. Members of the low income groups who had investments, no matter how slight, were more conservative than people in the same income bracket who had no investments.

(5) Finally may be mentioned the *declasse groups,* the men who don't fit in. Beggars, vagrants, psychopaths, and non-racketeering criminals would belong in this category.

The Groupings Are Intermingled.—The structure of society is the patterning of communities, publics, and classes within it. To understand how social life operates in any culture it is necessary to break down the complex pattern and see how it is put together. At different periods in history different types of groups predominate. The America of a century ago was a society of communities. Today we are a nation of publics. Many European countries are built about social classes. The social processes in these different set-ups are accordingly different. In the community era people are controlled and control others through personal opinion, personal merit, and recourse to a common set of beliefs and attitudes based upon a common way of life.

In the period of publics we find the agencies of mass impression like the radio and the newspaper more important. A common set of beliefs grows out of the coordination of information and propaganda supplied from above. Individuals no longer count and the dominant criterion becomes the quantitative yardstick according to which it is possible to say that this bridge is the biggest in the world, this highly advertised product is used by ten million Americans, this university has the largest enrollment in the world. No one really knows anyone else though he may be acquainted with the recreation habits, the business activities, and the political attitudes of many actors in the social drama. In this age of the lost individual, public opinion assumes huge proportions as a means of social control, but exactly what this public opinion represents no one precisely knows.

In a society of social classes, on the other hand, individuals are less confused but the social order is more chaotic. The various classes represent opposed interest groups at war or potentially at war with one another. The tug of war between them produces not equilibrium but a see-saw of tensions. Within a given class, however, individuals feel at home as they did back in the days of the community. Again there is a common way of life and a common psychology growing out of it.[6]

Rarely, however, do we find a people organized exclusively into any one of these types of groupings. All three groups may be well represented at certain periods in history. Publics, for example, may cut across a community set-up and unite like-minded individuals at least with respect to some of their interests. But often a given type of group will prevail and will determine the social processes operative within its boundaries.

SOCIAL INTERACTION

In starting our description with the nature of groups we have done violence to the facts in a certain sense. Historically we should start with men as self-interested creatures struggling to make a living against one another and against the natural environment. Out of this struggle develop the stratified adjustments known as group organizations. Once a grouping has been achieved it exerts a directive influence upon subsequent strivings of men after various biological and social goals. It exerts an influence not as an impersonal force but because it is embodied in the habits of people and taken over by their progeny through a process of social learning.

The dynamics which produce group organization are usually described under the heading of processes of social interaction. Men in their struggles to attain their goals do not wage solitary battles against a non-human world. They fight together and against one another. Their struggles at adjustment are generally collective in some measure. They may get together to rob a foe or protect themselves against an avaricious enemy. Even an individualistic people carry on a number of activities in cooperative groups.

Processes of Social Interaction.—Four processes of social interaction are generally distinguished: *Conflict, cooperation, competition,* and *accommodation. Conflict* is distinguished from competition in that in conflict the individuals direct their energies at the destruction or injury of their opponents. In *competition* they often pursue parallel courses of action directed at the same common goal. Their attention is upon getting there first or getting more of the objective. For true competition both parties must agree implicitly upon the rules of the race. *Cooperation* does not imply an altruistic set of motives. It merely describes a joint coordinated effort by two or more individuals. *Accommodation* refers to the settlement of conflict either through the subjugation of one party by the other and a consequent imposition of a master-slave relationship or through a process of compromise.

Societies are sometimes characterized as competitive, cooperative, or individualistic. As a matter of fact all four processes of social interaction (conflict, cooperation, competition, and accommodation) occur in every society, though the emphasis upon the several processes may vary. As a general rule even these dynamic processes become channelized in standard patterns. The aggressive impulses which among children are discharged directly in fights with one another are inhibited in adulthood and directed against the enemies of the group—real or imaginary. These aggressive impulses are not the result of an instinct of pugnacity. They are the direct overflow into action of emotions produced through a blocking or thwarting of some desire of the child. In the interests of social living, aggression is limited to certain types of expression, often expression which is relatively harmless or expression against outsiders which solidifies the in-group.[7]

The particular conditions which favor competition over cooperation or individualistic conflict over compromise are very complex. Anthropologists have sought an answer in their studies of primitive societies. They find that the frequency of cooperation in relation to competition is not a function of the cultural complexity of the group nor of the type of natural environment in which the group lives.[8] It is related to the total complex of natural and social factors found in a given society. Thus men may hit upon cooperative devices as the most profitable means of hunting. The large game they hunt and their limited technical equipment may make hunting under simple competitive procedures almost impossible. Once having developed cooperative hunting habits, however, they are likely to preserve them even after the discovery of weapons which would make individualistic hunting practical. The cooperative practice may remain because even under the new set of conditions it is still a good adjustment. This practice has come to be highly valued and as long as it brings results it is going to be difficult to change men's habits.

Similarly, competition arises out of environmental circumstances which make cooperation difficult. Hunting small game, for example, may be done more effectively by the lone hunter than by a group of clan-mates. Again, once the practice becomes established in the habits of men they rationalize its objective basis and teach their children competitive values. In other words, the dominant activities of a society cannot always be inferred directly from its natural environment because men need not make the best possible adjustment to a set of conditions in order to survive. Alternative adjustments exist. The particular adjustment which becomes standardized as the institution of the group may survive for a long time, even though better ways of social living are possible.

Sometimes people are so impressed by the way old customs endure that they hold that the only reason for different customs in different groups is the historical accident which originated the custom. This belief overlooks the important fact that customs remain because they do have some psychological utility. When the psychological utility vanishes the custom changes. Men do cling to old customs but let those customs cease to provide satisfaction of needs and men will find new ways to meet their problems.

Mechanisms in Social Interaction.—The processes of social interaction just described are fairly complex relationships between people. To describe cooperation or competition adequately, reference must be made both to the interacting individuals and their objectives. Social psychologists have also been interested in describing the more elementary mechanisms at work in social interaction. Five such mechanisms are *social facilitation, social inhibition, imitation, suggestion,* and *identification.*

Social Facilitation.—Social facilitation refers to the increase in speed and amount of activity due to the sight and sound of one's fellows engaged in similar activities. This increase, moreover, is not solely a matter of rivalry. When we are in the presence of coworkers we are actually receiving more stimulation than when we are alone. We eat more in company than in solitude and we tend to speed up our actions generally when in the presence of similarly-acting individuals. Experiments have demonstrated that people will turn out more work in a room with others busy at the same type of task than they will when alone.[9] There is even some evidence to show that the best seats for students in lecture courses are not those on the front row but those in the center of the group where the amount of social stimulation is greatest. Certainly in a crowd the people at the fringes do not feel the impulsion to follow their fellows as violently as do those in the center. Every track man knows he can make better time running against competitors than when running by himself against time, even if his time record will be used to qualify or disqualify him for a team.

Although social facilitation means an increase in speed and amount of activity, it does not imply an increase in quality of performance. In fact, experiments show that individuals are more accurate when working alone than when working together. Moreover, research proves that in tasks calling for thought, the solitary performance of an individual is better than his performance in a group. The most desirable conditions for taking an examination would include a room in which the candidate is left to himself.

Social Inhibition.—The poorer quality of performance in a group shows that we have an opposed process to facilitation, namely social inhibition. Facilitation applies to the gross patterns of response of the individual. Inhibition is more likely to affect the subtle patterns involved in thought.

Social stimuli, like other stimuli, release energy in the nervous system in the form of nerve impulses. A gross pattern of response like that of running, which involves many muscle fibers, is strengthened by the additional energy which derives from additional stimulation. A highly discriminating adjustment on the other hand involves the selection out of a few muscle fibers. This type of neuromuscular adjustment is easily disrupted by an increase in energy. The overexcitement in group situations thus tends to destroy sustained patterns of thought and other delicate adjustments such as skilled coordination. For example, very few people can think well on their feet when addressing a group. The golfer is easily disturbed on the green by a noisy gallery and his putt may go astray. The basketball player can sink more goals in practice than in a game with a large audience watching him.

The additional stimulation which floods the nervous system in social situations comes only partly from the sight and sound of the people about one. A great deal of it is supplied by the functioning of the autonomic system which has been aroused by the original social stimulation. It often happens, therefore, that the individual who is emotionally insensitive will not be socially inhibited. People vary with respect to their susceptibility to social stimulation, but most individuals find their skilled coordinations and their thinking adversely affected by the group. Stage fright is an extreme instance of this phenomenon and its cure lies in giving the individual a simple part with considerable action but with few lines. As he becomes habituated to appearing before an audience, he can be entrusted with more difficult roles and longer speeches.

Imitation.—Early writers on social psychology like Tarde and Ross were very much impressed by the eagerness with which people follow fashions in clothes, personal habits, and ideas.[10] They explained group conformity and crowd contagion by postulating an instinct of *imitation*. Today we still accept the importance of imitation as a process of social interaction but we question its instinctive basis. Imitation can be defined from an objective point of view as a close similarity between stimulus and response. Two forms of imitation can be distinguished: *Elementary imitation* and *complex imitation*.

(1) *Elementary Imitation.*—*Elementary imitation* refers to the setting off of a circular response by a stimulus similar to the response itself. For example, an infant a year old will respond to a laugh with a laugh or will repeat a stimulus-syllable, if that syllable is already part of its repertoire of babbling sounds. The mechanism at work is the conditioned response. The infant in its random articulation has stimulated its own ear with various sounds. The sound of a particular syllable thus becomes tied to the motor pathway for producing that very sound. Hence, upon hearing that sound, whether spoken by himself or some one else, the infant is conditioned to respond with a repetition of the syllable.

Elementary imitation really includes only those cases where the simulation of another's speech or actions calls for no new responses. The person who imitates is neither socially nor individually original, for he is merely showing some previously acquired mode of response. We follow suit in the group by smiling, laughing, or yawning primarily because those reactions are part of an old repertory which has been conditioned to the sight and sound of others similarly behaving.

(2) *Complex or Generalized Imitation.*—All imitation, however, is not at as simple a level. Everyday observation reveals many cases of a generalized tendency to imitate which is more complex than the eliciting of actions previously acquired. We deliberately try to emulate the people we admire. During the freshman year the student sheds many of his high school values and habits and models himself after the campus leaders. Nor is the college world unique in its imitative tendencies. In all walks of life people aspire to be copies of the correct ways of thinking and acting as exemplified by a few leaders. But successful imitation of this description comes only after a period of trial-and-error learning.

Generalized imitation refers both to *mechanism* and to *motive*. The *mechanism* is to be found in the nature of human behavior. Behavior is a function of the stimulating world in the sense that it is directed specifically by the nature of the stimulus-pattern. To respond differentially to the objective features of the environment the organism must approach some point-to-point correlation between its actions and the details of the stimulating situation.

The child explores his world by following the contours and qualities of objects with his eyes and hands. A square means describing four motions at right angles to one another, either with the hands or the eyes. Response thus implies motor re-creation or imitation. Later these detailed movements of imitating, or following, become so abridged that they are no longer good reproductions of the outside world. Nonetheless this internal mimicry is the basis of perception. It is explained by the principle of *adience* or the tendency of an organism to get more of the stimulus.[11] As the child explores a toy the movements he makes are further energized by stimuli arising from the process of exploration. The visual stimulation provided by the bright colors, the tactual stimulation from contact with the toy, and the proprioceptive stimulation from the movements of his arms all feed the activity in process, since the nerve impulses aroused are discharged over the most open pathways. And the most open motor pathways are those in use at the present moment, namely those which are responsible for the exploratory behavior. So the child continues to explore and in his exploring reproduces in his own movements the pattern of the objects examined. Similarly, in adult behavior when people seek to discover the exact nature of a situation, they re-create in their behavior its objective features.

To understand generalized imitation, however, it is necessary to know more than its mechanism. The mechanism tells us how the process goes on but it does not tell us why people tend to imitate certain actions rather than others. Hence a consideration of *motive* is indispensable to a thorough understanding of man's imitative behavior. The most general motive behind imitation is the wish to be like the person one imitates. By imitating some model the individual in his own eyes becomes the model.

For example, the child who plays soldier feels himself a military hero in the process. Likewise the stenographer who buys copies of Parisian frocks elevates her status to that of the society girl who wears the originals. Many devotees of swing music are proving their social alertness and sophistication in following this musical fad. Advertisers and propagandists have long understood the motivating force back of imitation and have accordingly tried to present their wares as the accepted products of prestiged individuals. Once the upper class takes up a custom its spread throughout society is generally guaranteed. Not so many years ago only women of doubtful reputation smoked in public. But after the practice was adopted by upper-class women it did not take long for smoking to become widespread.

Other motives underlie imitation though they are not as potent as the wish to enhance status or to take on the desirable attributes of the model. People follow leaders and ape one another because it is easier to imitate than to be original. Then, too, once an idea or action has the sanction of majority opinion, people accept it rather than take the chance of finding themselves in the out-group. In our culture there is also a premium placed upon imitation in the training of the child. At home the youngster who patterns himself after his elders is praised; at school the pupil who can echo the teacher's words or the lessons in the school book is rewarded.

Similarity in group behavior is not always the result of imitation. Human beings are sufficiently alike in their biological equipment and in their training so that they may all hit upon the same solution to the same problem. When grain is thrown to a group of hungry chickens they will all start pecking, not in imitation of one another, but because they are all hungry. In human behavior many instances of crowd contagion show a complex mixture of imitation and independence of motive. People bid at an auction, for example, partly because they are imitating one another and partly because they are moved by their cupidity to get their share of the bargains.

Suggestion.—The most important of all the mechanisms of social interaction, however, is suggestion. Suggestion is a process so difficult of measurement, yet so potent in its results, that its early psychological use was regarded as sheer magic. Mesmerism, a supposedly magical form of healing, was merely a special case of the working of suggestion. Suggestion is the uncritical acceptance of an idea or the uncritical following of an action. Suggestion is of two types; it is either *direct* or *indirect*.

(1) *Direct suggestion* refers to the acceptance of the stimulus-pattern because the individual's critical thought processes are temporarily inhibited. In subjective terms there is a narrowing of the field of consciousness. In moments of excitement, for example, the person cannot think because emotional energy blocks out his sustained ideational patterns. Hence he is a prey to any passing suggestion. The same thing is true in moments of fatigue. The individual is too tired to think and so accepts some one else's idea.

(2) *Indirect suggestion* is likewise an uncritical acceptance, but it is uncritical because the thought processes are occupied with another problem. The constant repetition of advertising slogans is often effective because people unwittingly absorb them while they are attending to more important matters. The clever political speaker suggests ideas by implication, while ostensibly discussing an issue unrelated to the suggestion. An oversimplified example of indirect suggestion is furnished by the old question: Have you stopped beating your wife? Attention is centered upon whether or not the individual is still abusing his spouse with the implication suggested that he is a wife-beater. In indirect suggestion the technique is to direct the attention of the victim to an irrelevant problem and then to slip by his critical judgment the desired innuendo. The difference between direct and indirect suggestion is essentially a matter of whether the individual's ideational processes are inhibited or whether they are dissociated from his other behavior.

From our knowledge of the nature of suggestion it follows that any factor which makes for inhibition or for distraction of the thought process is conducive to suggestion. It is also true that the less intelligent the individual and the less experienced the person, the fewer sustained responses will be maintained toward the many objects and relationships in his environment. The unintelligent and the inexperienced individuals are suggestible because in their case, there is less critical intelligence to inhibit or to distract. Experimental studies of children show that they are more suggestible than adults.

Moreover, the curve of suggestibility gradually declines with age from the age of six to the age of sixteen.[12]

The conditions which lead the individual to accept suggestion have been the subject of considerable investigation. Their importance is obvious, for a thorough acquaintance with these predisposing factors is becoming the stock in trade of the advertiser, the propagandist, and the educator. Predisposing conditions can be described in fairly objective terms, but the actual operation of suggestion always is a relational matter between the objective situation and the individual. For example, the prestige of the source of the suggestion makes for blind acceptance, but what one individual regards as a prestiged source another individual holds in contempt. Three important factors which load a situation with suggestive possibilities are: (1) Numbers and quantity, (2) the prestige of authority or of status, and (3) the mere fact of existence.

Sheer size and sheer numbers not only compel respect, they also make most people very suggestible. Quantity as the most obvious aspect of things is often taken as a comparative measure of merit. Bigger becomes synonymous with *better*. The advertiser assures the public that his product is the best because it has the largest sale; the politician urges voters to get on the band wagon and not to throw away their votes on a minority candidate; some college presidents even use the yardstick of quantity or number of publications to measure the excellence of their scholars.

The deference to numbers and quantity is deeply rooted in the personality. As children we were unable to cope with objects and animate beings larger than ourselves. The approval of numbers in our immediate social group was equivalent to the satisfaction of our basic needs. Their approval meant security. Moreover, in our culture of large scale production and a mechanized way of life, not only is size important but everything seems capable of being reduced to numbers. Small wonder that the child grows up sensitive to what everybody else is doing and saying.

Experiments have confirmed the importance of numbers in determining the beliefs of the individual. Moore asked students to indicate their preferences for various ethical concepts, for linguistic expressions, and for musical expressions.[13] Later the same type of judgment was obtained, but this time the students were told the majority verdicts on these matters. Many of the students who had been in the minority reversed their opinions to accord with the majority. The suggestive effect of majority opinion was greatest in the field of ethical judgment.

An interesting study of the individual's psychogalvanic response when he knows he is expressing a minority opinion has been made by Smith.[14] The psychogalvanic skin response can be obtained by placing electrodes on the fingers and measuring the resistance of the skin to electric current. This measure is an index of emotion. Before recording the psychogalvanic response the subjects had been asked to indicate their agreement or disagreement with a number of statements. Four weeks later they were brought into the laboratory and again asked to indicate agreement or disagreement. This time their psychogalvanic responses were recorded. The psychogalvanic responses were considerably greater when the subjects differed with group opinion than when they agreed with group opinion. To go against the group produced conflict and emotional tension.

The belief that one's fellows are acting or thinking in the same manner has been termed by Allport *the impression of universality*.[15] This impression of universality rather than the real degree of agreement with the group is the important factor in suggestion. In political psychology much has been made of the *band-wagon effect*— namely the tendency of people to follow the majority. Yet in the 1936 election the *Literary Digest* poll which announced a decisive majority for the Republican candidate was widely publicized and dramatically broadcast over the air. No apparent band-wagon effect could be discovered on election day when the voters proceeded to contradict the *Digest* poll.

Some observers have interpreted this event as decisive proof that there is no band-wagon effect and that people are not susceptible to the suggestion of majority opinion. This interpretation overlooks the subjective character of the impression of universality. The important consideration for the individual is not the total universe but the universe with which he identifies himself. In national elections the voter is concerned not with sheer numbers but with the way in which his group is voting. The people outside the group or groups which he considers important *do not count*. The effect of numbers as such has to be qualified to include the numbers which the individual is willing to count. The middle classes do not care to model themselves after the lower classes even though the lower classes may outnumber them.

To qualify the effect of numbers by a consideration of the class-membership character of those numbers is to introduce another factor as a determinant of the suggestion process—namely the factor of the prestige of authority or of social position. In the minds of many individuals there is no conflict between what is commonly done and what the best people do. Those who do not follow the example of the best people are not included in the psychological universe of the individual. Thus one believes he is on the side of the best minds and that the majority of right-minded people are with him. It is the exception rather than the rule to find a person who deliberately opposes in his mind the opinion of the expert and the opinion of the majority.

In a sense it is circular to speak of the prestige of the source of suggestion. A position, an individual, or a symbol has prestige only for those who accept their suggestions. In the final analysis prestige is less a matter of the objective nature of the stimulus-pattern and more a matter of attitudes of deference. In other words prestige is another term for the phenomenon of suggestion. Its use is justified, nonetheless, by the fact that it enables us to relate suggestion to many already familiar facts of social life. For example, we know that for most people prestige attaches to positions of authority in large organizations, to specialists or experts in a given field of endeavor, to upper class membership, and to certain values in a particular culture.

Just why people should accept without critical evaluation the ideas of prestiged persons is a complex problem. One reason is the individual's inadequacy to cope with more than a very limited area of life. He lacks the knowledge and the training to oppose the views of experts. The prestiged person, moreover, has achieved some success denied to the average man. The average man is not analytical about this success and assumes that if Thomas Edison was great enough to give the world practical inventions, he was also great enough to give the world sound political advice. Again we find the mechanism of the conditioned response at work. The deference to Thomas Edison as an inventor is carried over to everything that Thomas Edison says or does. Then, too, the prestige of authority is related to childhood acceptance of the authority of parents and elders. The individual learns through experience to bow to superior force and this becomes an unquestioning obedience to symbols of authority. Distinctive symbols have been set aside to represent the authority of the state such as the uniform of the police, the robes of judges, the seal for official documents, and the titles of officials.

Numerous studies have demonstrated the prestige value of the names of experts in inducing acceptance of ideas. The testimonial of the advertisement is supposed to be effective only for the unsophisticated, yet college students will judge literary passages, musical compositions, paintings, and political utterances according to the names attached to them. For example, a passage accredited to Edgar Guest (but really written by Shakespeare) will be regarded as very poor, whereas the same passage attributed to Browning is judged as an excellent bit of writing.[16] Similarly, political ideas presented as the statements of Karl Marx are rejected as false, but if presented as the statements of Calvin Coolidge they are accepted as true.

Reference has already been made to the way in which success in one field is sufficient evidence for people to accept the successful individual as an authority in all fields. In an experimental verification of this fact Bowden, Caldwell, and West asked students to rate the following seven men on the basis of their authoritative command of fifteen fields of knowledge: Herbert Hoover, Charles Lindbergh, Albert Einstein, John Pershing, Thomas Edison, Theodore Roosevelt and John P. Morgan.[17] All of these men were ranked as authorities in most of the fields of knowledge listed. Thus Pershing was regarded as an outstanding authority not only in military affairs, but also in mathematics, engineering, and government. Theodore Roosevelt was considered an outstanding authority in government, military affairs, economics, education, and law. In general military prestige seems to overshadow other forms of prestige, for Pershing was only slightly below Einstein as a mathematician and decidedly above Hoover in this respect.

The third predisposing factor in the suggestion process is the readiness to accept the established fact. One of the techniques of politics is to confront people with the *fait accompli*. Whatever is, tends to be accepted as right and proper by virtue of the fact that it exists. The basis of this acceptance of the status quo stems from a wholesome acceptance of reality. As children we learn we cannot wish away facts.

The acceptance of the accomplished fact, however, ceases to be the same type of wholesome adjustment in the social world that it is in the natural world. We cannot change the climate though we can protect ourselves from it. In the social world, on the other hand, the social realities are often amenable to change because we ourselves are the social realities. Thus if a dictator were to seize office in this country, we would be confronted by an accomplished fact. If our critical processes of thought were not overwhelmed by this fact, we might find that he could be overthrown without too much difficulty if most of us did not want him. In other words, the accomplished fact in the social world remains the accomplished fact largely because people accept it. It is like the circular argument of the prohibitionists in the days of the Volstead Act. They maintained that prohibition would work if people only observed the law. But people did not accept the accomplished fact that a prohibition law was on the statute books. This law failed to be accepted as a suggestion, because it ran counter to too many fundamental wishes of the American people.

In general, however, people will bow before the statement that a certain condition exists as a fact and not a theory. The mere existence of a state of affairs is taken as presumptive evidence of its necessity and even of its righteousness. Katz and Cantril asked students about their attitudes toward Communism and Fascism.[18] Though the overwhelming majority were opposed to both Fascism and Communism, a majority thought that Fascism was a good thing for Italy and Germany and that Communism was a good thing for Russia. Whatever system prevailed in a given country was regarded as the desirable state for that country, no matter how contradictory the systems were.

In addition to the predisposing conditions just described it should be added that suggestibility is a function of the individual personality. People differ with respect to their readiness to accept suggestions in general. On the whole the well-integrated personality is less suggestible than the poorly integrated personality. The person, whose personality comprises many unrelated segments, cannot bring to bear upon a problem the many experiences which might aid in its solution. He is dissociated and meets the situation with only part of himself. The well-integrated individual, however, has a unified point of view which is the result of the fusion of many experiences. Hence he can meet a situation and examine all of its implications. Thus he can resist suggestion more effectively than the poorly integrated person.

Unfortunately our complex culture makes integration a difficult process. The child grows up in an institutionalized world with the school, the home, the play group, the Boy Scouts, and the Sunday School making demands upon his time and allegiance. Often these demands are unrelated and even conflicting. No central coordinating thread runs through the many activities in which the child finds himself. Hence many youngsters grow up with no unified interests in life. Even when they enter college they do not know what vocation they want to follow. As adults they have no central philosophy of life and blindly accept the "easy solutions" suggested by the propagandist.

Identification.—Human beings prefer a group way of life to a hermit-like individualism because they are neither economically nor psychologically self-sufficient. The mechanism which compensates for their psychological insufficiency is known as *identification*. Through identification the individual enters into the lives of his fellows and thus enjoys a fuller and richer experience than his own activities would permit him. Identification enables him to be an active member of the group, for his ego becomes involved in its symbols. Identification also makes possible the vicarious enjoyment of adventure and of a life of glamour offered by the movies, the radio, and literature.

Identification may be defined as the process in which the individual extends the boundaries of his ego to include more than his physical self. People, objects, and symbols are psychologically regarded as part of one's self. Freud has described identification as the earliest expression of an emotional tie with another person.[19] The little boy takes his father as his ideal and patterns his behavior after that of his father. Early identification also extends to favorite toys. The child will be so attached to a toy that he will carry it about with him and take it to bed at night. The cherished toy is almost part of his personality.

Patterns of similarity between the person who does the identifying and the people or things he identifies himself with facilitate the process. The girl finds it easier to identify herself with other girls than with boys. Horowitz has shown that white children identify themselves more with other white children than with Negro children and similarly Negro children identify themselves more frequently with other Negro children than with white children.[20] In fact the Negro children showed less tendency to identify themselves with white children than the white children did to identify themselves with Negro children. Probably social influences had taught the Negro children to be conscious of themselves as a distinctive group.

The leader or official of the group often has the function of being the symbol with which the followers can identify themselves. Impersonal symbols like flags or slogans are not as effective devices for securing group identification as a human being. The personality of an individual can sum up the aspirations and characteristics of the group. Hitler's hold upon the German people is due in part to their ability to identify themselves with him. They suffered crushing defeat in the World War; Hitler was a corporal in the defeated army. They suffered from a ruinous inflation; Hitler was one of the underprivileged masses. They longed for the time when Germany would avenge the ignominious peace terms of 1918; Hitler voiced their wishes and embarked upon a policy of rebuilding the empire. They wanted employment and security; Hitler expressed this wish in aggressive and decisive terms.

The advantages of a human symbol in intensifying the process of identification explains why a political democracy like England has kept its king. Hitler is both an active leader and a symbol, but the King of England is pure symbol. Englishmen all over the world find in their king a symbol of the unity of the British empire. They feel their membership as Englishmen in this empire all the more keenly because they can identify themselves with the typical English character which the king represents. Our presidents do not serve quite this function because as active participants in political affairs, they are too much like other ordinary men. Their partisans identify themselves with these leaders, but the members of the opposition party will have none of them.

The mechanisms of facilitation, inhibition, imitation, suggestion, and identification are the explanations of why people behave differently when together than when isolated. All these mechanisms make for similarity of conduct and belief. Group living can be carried on only under conditions of uniformity and orderliness in human behavior. Human groupings are the stratified results of the dynamic processes of interaction. These processes socialize the egoistic and atypical wishes of the individual.

The Methods of Social Psychology

Most of us are more interested in answers than in the process by which answers are derived. Like the layman we accept the findings of scientific investigation in the same manner in which we receive any suggestion from a source of great prestige. Unlike the layman, however, it is possible for us to acquire some appreciation of the relevant methodology in the various provinces of psychology. On the basis of this knowledge we can form our own opinion about the answers of the specialists. In our present exploration into the field of social psychology we have gone far enough to have some idea of the nature of the discipline. Before we attempt a more thorough penetration into its answers we need to know the processes by which these answers have been formulated. Four main methods can be distinguished: The *laboratory approach,* the *cross-sectional field study,* the *longitudinal or developmental approach,* and the *actuarial method.*

The Laboratory Approach.—The laboratory approach is the basic method of all psychology. As such it is already familiar to the student and needs no detailed exposition here save as it raises particular problems for social psychology. The great advantages of the experiment carried out within the laboratory are the control, isolation, and measurement of the many factors related to the process under investigation. Everyday observation may tell us that there is an increase in activity in the group situation as compared with solitary performance. The significant factors associated with this increased activity can be isolated in the laboratory and their relative importance determined.

Experiments with Human Subjects.—For example, is the increased performance in the group due to the mere presence of others, to the fact that they are working at the same tasks, to the emotional rivalry engendered by a competitive situation, or to the mere knowledge that others are working on the same problems? In an attempt to measure the importance of all these factors, Dashiell has carried out experiments (1) in which the performance of people working alone with knowledge of fellow workers in other rooms was compared with performance of individuals working alone without knowledge of coworkers, (2) in which the performance in presence of spectators was compared with the performance in presence of coworkers, (3) in which the performance of individuals in a group motivated to compete was compared with performance of individuals working alone but also motivated to outstrip their fellows, and (4) in which an attempt was made to remove conditions of competition and rivalry for both group and solitary performance.[21] By this type of controlled experimentation it can be demonstrated that competition is the most effective factor in increasing group performance, but that the mere presence of fellow workers also increases the amount of work done.

Laboratory experimentation in social psychology has obvious limitations. Human beings are poor guinea pigs. We cannot keep them in the laboratory and control their experience and their motives as we can in the case of lower animals. For example, even in Dashiell's careful study the effect of rivalry could not be completely eliminated in individuals who were not encouraged to compete. Their many previous habits of competition in group situations may have affected their performance. To overcome this directly, it would be necessary to rear a number of human beings under laboratory supervision. Unfortunately the limitation of the uncontrollability of the experience and motives of the human subject is greatest in relation to some of the most significant problems in social psychology. Crowd behavior, strikes, social movements, wars, elections, nationalism, and institutional change, to cite only a few instances, cannot be brought into the laboratory.

Experiments with Animal Subjects.—To overcome the uncontrollability of human subjects, animals are being used more and more in social experimentation. One experimenter established a taboo in a group of monkeys in the following manner.[22] A banana was suspended from a pole out of reach of a group of monkeys in a cage. When one of the monkeys climbed the pole and grabbed the banana, hot water was released into the floor of the cage to the discomfort of all the monkeys save the one who was on the pole eating the prize he had secured. It did not take the group long to learn the cause of the flooding of the cage and soon any enterprising monkey who started after the banana was punished. The coveted fruit was admired from a distance and became taboo for all the monkeys in the cage. This situation illustrates the nature of many of our social taboos and shows how even complex situations can be set up experimentally and studied.

Animal experimentation on social problems has an advantage which is for other purposes a disadvantage. Animals lack the many social traditions which color and determine human behavior. Hence by studying the social psychology of animals we can discover what is fundamental to processes of social interaction and what is due to the particular cultural complex of the group. On the other hand, these cultural or traditional factors are frequently of great importance in a study of social problems. Hence animal experimentation can shed little light on many of the social processes about which we are most concerned.

In general, we may conclude that laboratory experiment is the most valid method but that it is not adequate for the study of all social phenomena. It is valid in the accuracy of its findings, but its answers are limited to a narrow range of situations. The mistake is sometimes made of overgeneralizing from a simple laboratory experiment to a complex life situation. Experimental findings are valid, of course, only for the type of process which is controlled within the laboratory setting. On the other hand, the student should realize that the laboratory method is in its infancy with respect to social experimentation. Though there are limits to its use, we are very far from reaching those limits. Moreover, some problems which seem at first glance to lie outside the laboratory can be neatly fitted into controlled experiments by the ingenious investigator.

The Cross-Sectional Field Study.—To obtain a more comprehensive picture of the social scene the psychologist may abandon his laboratory and observe and record the sayings and doings of people in their everyday adjustments. The field study is crosssectional when it is limited to a brief period of time. It is a slice taken through the lives of a large number of individuals. Most of our observations when we travel to other countries are cross sectional in nature. We see customs, witness events, hear new songs, and come away with an impression of the foreign culture but with little knowledge of the personalities of the people in it.

Statistical Studies.—The cross-sectional study tends to be either *statistical* or *topological*. The most common form of the crosssectional method is the statistical. The social psychologist, like the enquiring reporter, posts himself at an advantageous position and either records on a quantitative scale the behavior he observes or asks questions of people, the answers to which can be quantified. One example is afforded by Allport and his students who have studied institutional behavior.[23] Their procedure was to note the degree of conformity evoked by such institutional symbols as the traffic policeman, the traffic sign, the factory whistle, the religious requirements of certain churches. The results of these studies illustrate how the normal tendency for people to scatter about a central tendency is regimented into rigid conformity with only one type of deviation.

Another example is furnished by large scale attitude studies which tell us about the social, political, religious, and economic beliefs of a given population. At Syracuse University over four thousand students reported to their regular classes one morning and spent two hours in answering a detailed series of questions pertaining to all aspects of student life. In recent years a commercial organization, the American Institute of Public Opinion, has found it profitable to sample people's opinions on various issues.

The statistical cross section can be broken down to make possible an analysis of the attitudes and behavior sampled. The American Institute not only can announce how many people are in favor of our armament program but it can also tell us how many of those in favor are Republicans, how many come from lower income groups, and how many live in the city. Thus significant and reliable groupings of factors can be determined by the cross-sectional approach. For example, upper income groups of Republican sympathies show one constellation of attitudes and low income groups of Democratic sympathies show another constellation of attitudes. It is difficult, however, to detect causal relationships by means of cross-sectional study.

The statistical cross section is really the research method of social science and it has to be used very cleverly to elicit information of a genuinely psychological character. This is because the breakdown of its data tends to follow standard economic and social categories which are fairly easy to include in the schedule or questionnaire form. Such categories as party affiliation, urban or rural residence, amount of income may be important but they tell us little about the psychology of the individuals so classified. It is difficult to evaluate questions of a more psychological nature for a number of reasons. Individuals vary in the amount of cooperation they give the questioner. They vary in the insight they have into their own motives. If radicals have more insight into their personalities than conservatives, they may make a higher neurotic score on a personality inventory than conservatives even though there may be no real personal difference between the two groups.

Another important pitfall in psychological questioning for a statistical cross section is the halo error. If an individual is feeling depressed at the time he is questioned, his answers to all questions may reflect a pessimistic point of view. Terman in a recent study of marital compatibility concluded that childhood happiness and the happiness of the parents were significant correlates of marital happiness.[24] Yet, as Hollingworth points out, this correlation could be due to a halo effect.[25] If the person were in a depressed emotional mood when he answered the questionnaire he may have checked all items pertaining to his present happiness and his past happiness unfavorably. The correlation Terman reports, therefore, may possibly reflect the consistency of present emotional mood without telling us anything about its causes.

Topology, or Field Theory.—The second cross-sectional method is that of field theory. Instead of counting noses and classifying frequency of responses according to definite categories, topology or field theory regards the relationships existing within the field studied as a function of the total field. This is essentially an application of Gestalt psychology to social psychology.

The statistical approach would give us a picture of a nation at war in terms of the number of combatants on the front line, the number of casualties, the number of aliens arrested, the number of subscriptions to war loans, the number of dollars being made by war profiteers, etc. Field theory would regard everything that happened as a function of relationships within the total field. It would point to the demolition of barriers between classes, to the breakdown of barriers between the sexes as groups with distinctive economic roles, in short to the weakening of all local divisions in the interests of national unity against a common enemy. The nation is at war and everything else is to be viewed as a function of this organization of the social field. Having ascertained the nature of the total situation the field theorist can predict without counting that huge profits will be made due to the increased demand and the limited supply of commodities. He can predict without statistics that more women will be found in industry, that officers from upper class families will marry nurses from lower class families. The nation is at war and this fundamental relation is the determining factor.[26]

Another way of saying this is to point out that field theory is bitterly opposed to *local determination*. Local determination means

that units in the social field are determined by their nature as units
and by the influence of surrounding units. Field theory affirms that
these units to the extent that they exist are determined by the total
relations obtaining at the moment in the whole situation. The lynching of an alien, for example, during a war is not determined by the
sadistic nature of a few bullies who happen to be in the crowd. The
lynching is a function of the total war situation in which people's
emotions are aroused and find expression against almost any alien
object.

Field theory thus is a wholesome influence in correcting the
tendency to neglect the woods for the trees. Too often, conclusions
are drawn on the basis of detailed statistical analyses which miss
important determinants in the total situation. Like other cross-
sectional approaches, however, field theory is weak in portraying
basic motives or in formulating predictions for future events. The
field theorist is committed to the doctrine that explanation is to be
found only in the present situation. Motives, he contends, are not
past forms of energy but are dynamic processes effective only if
they are contemporaneous. Logically this answer is correct but we
are limited, indeed, if we must investigate each situation anew to
know anything about it. It is only when we can relate the present
to the past that we can make realistic predictions. Men's actions
tomorrow are the logical extension of their behavior yesterday. Even
a new total relationship such as the nation at war does not affect
everyone alike.

The Longitudinal or Developmental Approach.—Cross sections through experience are valuable in analyzing the relationships
which hold true for a limited period of time. Life, however, is a
dynamic process in which relationships are often in flux. To understand human beings fully, we must follow them over a period of
time. Their transformations from situation to situation assume a
constant pattern after we have studied them developmentally. The
individual who does not understand children does not truly understand adults, any more than the person who drops in for the last
act of the play appreciates the dramatic resolution of forces.

Studies of Personality.—The usual psychological study of development is the investigation of personality. The most revealing data on the underlying motives of a particular individual come not from tests but from continuing observation of his behavior in many situations. If it were possible to follow a number of German citizens through all their activities for just one week we would know a great deal about the stability of the Nazi regime. At work we might see only a complete adherence to the official code, but at home we might see indications of suppressed hostility or we might find evidence of a psychological feeling of economic security. The meaning of a bit of behavior in the life of an individual is revealed by its relation to the rest of the temporal pattern. The politician who appears in the afternoon to praise the work of the Ladies' Aid Society may be found in the evening at the corner saloon buying the boys a round of drinks. Thus we can discover the constant reference of a person's actions by continued observations.

The obvious difficulty with the developmental study of personality is its impracticability. We cannot follow the technique of the detective novel in which suspects are shadowed by trained human watchdogs. Public characters, however, are an exception in that they leave a record of many of their sayings and actions for the perusal of the curious. The practical way out of the difficulty is the use of the case study method. In this procedure, the individual's life history is reconstructed from his own story, from the accounts of friends and associates, and from existing objective records. This method has been applied by Opler [27] to the study of primitive peoples with results much more revealing than the usual descriptions of primitive customs and rituals.

Studies of Situations.—A second type of developmental study applies to situations rathers than to individuals. We may choose to study that multi-individual institution known as Harvard University. Our interest is not so much in specific people because various individuals come and go. Contrary to student belief, even the faculty does not go on forever. A newcomer tends to play a very similar role to his predecessor and for that reason we do not stress the personalities involved. This has led some social scientists to regard the study of institutions as the study of superorganic entities rather than as the study of human behavior. We are still studying human nature, however, but we are emphasizing the standardized roles of people rather than their distinctive traits as personalities.

A longitudinal study of a situation tells us what the basic human reactions are in a given setting. It gives considerable information, moreover, about the shifting group pattern over a period of years. It is weak in a complete evaluation of motives though it does show something of the immediate motivation in a given type of situation.

The Actuarial Method.—The actuarial method is a compromise between the cross-sectional and the longitudinal approaches. It consists in taking a series of cross sections through the lives of people. Comparisons are then possible between past and future events. It lacks the continuity of the longitudinal method. The time gaps between observations are filled in by guesses which can be checked statistically. This is the method of the insurance actuary who takes repeated samples of the mortality rates and then predicts group trends. He can tell how many people over seventy will die in the next year but he cannot tell who these specific individuals will be.

The actuarial is the most commonly used method in the social field and the most practical. It overcomes some of the failings of the single cross section and it avoids the cumbersome problems of the developmental study. It has two limitations. First it tells us only about general trends and not about specific individuals, and second it predicts recurrence and not novelty. So long as the same series of factors continue to operate, it can predict the repetition of events.[28] But if a new condition arises actuarial prediction easily goes astray. A new disease, for example, may throw off the mortality table of the insurance actuary. As a rule insurance companies can allow themselves sufficient margin of error to survive one or two mistaken predictions.

One practical difficulty with the actuarial method is the proper equating of successive samples. The many cross sections are related together as if they sampled the same basic type of situation. Sometimes this may not be true. Since it is impractical to include all of the population in successive cross-sectional studies the investigator is satisfied with a relatively small sample of the total group. Now if successive samples are not taken in the same way a comparison of their findings is not a reliable index of trend. Suppose we ascertain the attitudes of all entering freshmen in a state university next fall toward socialism. Two years later we repeat our attitude test and find that the incidence of favorable attitudes has increased and two years from that time we again find an increase of favorable attitudes.

It still may not be true that there is a trend toward socialism among American college students. The increase in favorable attitudes in successive samples may be due to the fact that there has been a shift in the type of students who are now coming to the state university. If economic conditions have improved during the period when the samples were taken, the well-to-do families who sent their children to the state university during depression years may now be able to send them to private institutions. Hence the shift in attitudes reflects a different composition of the population of the state university rather than a trend away from conservative values among American college students. In relating cross-sectional samples together to predict trends it is necessary to equate the samples in the first place. The American Institute of Public Opinion does this by always selecting its sample according to the same criteria of income, party affiliation, rural or urban residence, and age. Even with these precautions it is possible that some other variable than income, party affiliation, residence, and age may be present in unequal proportions in the different samples and so destroy the accuracy of the prediction.

On the whole it is an advantage rather than a disadvantage to have these many methods of studying social behavior. The great difficulty lies in attempting to integrate the findings which diverse methods give us. We tend to overlook the limitations of a given set of data which necessarily result from the way in which they have been discovered. Cross-sectional studies tell us very little about the deep-lying motives of individual personalities. Yet we assume in everyday life that a legal classification of people into criminal and non-criminals is a good index of personality types. This classification, however, is cross-sectional rather than the outcome of a longitudinal study of individuals. A man is convicted or acquitted of the crime charged on the basis of whether or not the evidence indicates he committed the crime. His motive is often irrelevant so long as some motive is established. Thus a man may be in prison because he is truly vicious and antisocial or he may be there because he lost his head in an emotional situation, or because he was trying to provide for his family, or for any one of a number of reasons. A criminal type of personality cannot be established, therefore, on the basis of legal statistical classification.

If we know the process by which answers have been formulated, we know how well these answers hold for the phenomena to which they refer in varied situations. We know, moreover, that we cannot fuse answers obtained with different methods unless we make some correction for the method used. The failure to take methods into account is one reason for the blurred and confused image many people have of the social world. It is as if they looked at the world with different colored glasses with lenses of different degrees of distortion, changing rapidly from one pair of spectacles to another. No wonder their impression of social events is much like a surrealist painting.

REFERENCES

Allport, F. H. *Institutional Behavior.* Chapel Hill: University of North Carolina Press, 1933.

Allport, F. H. *Social Psychology.* Cambridge: Houghton Mifflin Company, 1924.

Brown, J. F. *Psychology and the Social Order.* New York: McGraw-Hill Book Company, Inc., 1936.

Cooley, C. H. *Social Organization.* New York: Charles Scribner's Sons, 1909.

Dollard, J., et al. *Frustration and Aggression.* New Haven: Yale University Press, 1939.

Holt, E. B. *Animal Drive and the Learning Process.* New York: Henry Holt and Company, 1931.

Katz, D., and Schanck, R. L. *Social Psychology.* New York: John Wiley and Sons, Inc., 1938.

Mead, M. *Cooperation and Competition Among Primitive Peoples.* New York: McGraw-Hill Book Company, Inc., 1937.

Terman, L. M., et al. *Psychological Factors in Marital Happiness.* New York: McGraw-Hill Book Company, Inc., 1938.

CHAPTER VII

THE PSYCHOLOGY OF THE CROWD

By Daniel Katz, *Princeton University*

The psychology of the crowd, is the best chapter in descriptive social psychology. Le Bon's classical contribution set forth the problem in brilliant fashion. He described the emotional nature of the crowd man and suggested the importance of unconscious motivation in crowd behavior.[1] His account, however, was biased by his conservatism and weakened by the lack of analytical tools. Martin and Allport have improved the description from the analytical side.[2] Both have been very much influenced by Freud and both have succeeded in reducing the problem of crowd psychology to the problem of individual behavior under special types of motivation. The mechanisms described by Allport are difficult to improve upon and his chapter on Crowd Psychology is perhaps the most excellent chapter in his text on social psychology.

THREE TYPES OF CROWDS

Because these authors ignore the problem of social contexts, however, they tend to make all crowds essentially alike. Impressed certainly with the common mechanisms which occur in crowds— such as high suggestibility, intolerance, and strong emotion—they fail to see three very different types of crowds, which though dependent upon similar mechanisms, operate toward very different end results. These crowds may be called the *community crowd*, the *fanatic public*, and the *class crowd*.

The Community Crowd.—In early American history and to-day in undeveloped rural sections of the country we find the *community crowd* which takes the direction of *lynch law*. Cattle rustlers, horse thieves, bank robbers, and claim jumpers have all been subjected to the justice of crowd rule. Thus gamblers, drunkards, and other individuals of loose morals, have been treated to tar and feathers or ridden out of town upon a rail. In these cases we see the community joined to enforce an ethic which they feel together, rather than to overthrow such an ethic. The community crowd functions to protect existing social norms.

The Fanatic Public.—The *fanatic public*, which appears in the more developed state of an economy, is different from the lynching crowd. Most individuals in the fanatic public are seeking some sort of self-expression which may be quite independent of any community feeling. The Valentino public showed all the signs of crowd behavior, but the emotion was in no sense directed toward elements which jeopardize community life.

The Class Crowd.—The *class crowd*, on the other hand, is a struggle group, which is not inclined toward protection of community ethics. Its members are bent upon discovering rationalizations and other incentives by which they may abandon traditional institutional attitudes for more fundamental beliefs which have long been repressed. The class crowd is on the objective side a threat to the state, and to principles of law and order which benefit other groups.

Crowd Mechanisms.—Yet the same crowd mechanisms operate to produce these three different results. This fact most authors have failed to see. As a consequence, the French Revolution which is an affair of classes, and includes the overthrowing of the feudal state, is treated as if it were identical with a religious revival or with frontier mob rule. Each type of crowd involves, however, different elements. The problem of the community crowd is the problem of individuals with a set pattern of behavior of a very fundamental sort which is jeopardized by the behavior of other people. The sex crime seems a threat to every law-abiding citizen in his own pattern of life. The cattle rustler who steals some other person's cattle may eventually turn toward your own.

The problem of the fanatic public, however, is one of finding new and common modes of expression for all sorts of repressed wishes. The new modes of expression serve as a safety valve for the release of repressions. In obtaining this release the members of the fanatic public are not waging a war either against the community or against the enemies of the community. They are merely seeking relief from the many institutional attitudes of their culture. They do not want to discard these attitudes completely, but they want to forget for a moment that such values exist. Hence fanatic crowds are silly, exuberant, intoxicated, enthusiastic, and vain, but not revolutionary.

The class crowd creates situations which are revolutionary in their implications. The phenomena which appear in the class crowd like the phenomena of the fanatic crowd are based upon thwarted wishes. The chief repressive agent in the case of the fanatic public is the institutional pattern of behavior located in the members of the fanatic public themselves. On the other hand, the chief repressive agent in the case of the class crowd is the organized police power of the state. In the fanatic public the individuals are rebelling against themselves; in the class crowd the individuals are rebelling against their external enemies.

The Formation of a Crowd

Because the fanatic public is slower in formation than a community crowd or a class crowd, it affords a better opportunity for the study of early crowd mechanisms. Mob action and class crowds are generally precipitated by some striking event such as the rape of a white woman or 'scabs' entering a factory on strike. The impact of the exciting condition produces sudden and drastic changes in the individuals who become the crowd and the psychological development of the crowd process is difficult to trace. The formation of a fanatic public can be observed, however, in which a great orator can start with individuals in their everyday attitudes and by the end of his speech have his auditors whipped up to a frenzy of crowd emotion. This audience situation provides an opportunity to observe each stage of crowd development in detail.

Polarization.—Crowd action is predicated upon the ability to secure what Woolbert has called a *polarized audience*.[3] *Polarization* represents a condition in which the audience members are under the complete control of the speaker's words and gestures, in which attention is riveted upon the speaker. In the case of mobs and class crowds, polarization is a fairly easy task for any speaker who represents the cause of the crowd members, because the community and class crowds are selected groups. They comprise only those individuals who are fundamentally prepared in advance for unusual action. In the development of an audience into a fanatic public, however, the speaker must secure polarization by the careful use of the following techniques.

(1) *The speaker attempts to remove all counterattractions.* It is obvious that all stimuli are not completely under a speaker's control, but many of them are. He cannot prevent individuals from eating too heavy dinners, but he can control the heat, light, and comfort within the auditorium. He can see to it that nothing about his own appearance (watch charms which twinkle, gestures which distract, nervous walking which annoys) leads away from his message. He can ask other people to stay off the platform (a noisy choir adds nothing to a sermon). Those factors which he cannot control he must eliminate by suggestion, especially if they are genuine counterattractions. The engine that whistles on the siding, the fire truck going down the street, or other such uncontrollable stimuli obviously cannot be eliminated. But the experienced crowd orator weaves these stimuli into his speech. They become a part of the stimulus pattern and not a counterattraction. (Thus the experienced speaker interrupted by the class bell, stopped and said, "I have been warned about that bell. A good speaker like a railroad should have good terminal facilities. I therefore come to the last point in my speech." He then continued to speak for twenty minutes uninterrupted, whereas if he had not included this reference, many of his audience would have become restless).

(2) *The speaker uses attention-getting devices of high value.* The crowd orator also must know devices of high attention value. Conflict, suspense, human interest, action, humor, and novelty are introduced into his speech. He knows the rules of vividness: That recent events are more vivid than far away occurrences, that often repeated behavior strikes deeper than occasional happenings, and that emotional experiences are more effective than nonemotional experiences. He recognizes the value of the concrete over the abstract, the

specific over the general, the pictorial over the nonpictorial, and the principle that an appeal to many senses is more effective than an appeal to just one.

If he is able at these tasks, he soon has the attention of his audience. Woolbert has suggested the process of development of polarization by stages in the following diagram.

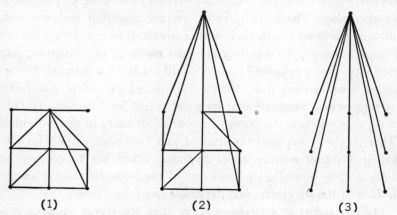

(1)   (2)   (3)

FIG. 12.—ILLUSTRATING THREE LEVELS OF ORGANIZATION OF AN AUDIENCE.

In (1) we have a nonpolarized audience, in which attentions of the members are variously distributed, the leader having not yet appeared. In (2) we have a partially polarized audience, most of the members being partly conscious of their neighbors, although their attention is directed toward the leader. In (3) we have complete polarization, where each member is concentrated upon the leader and is vaguely or not at all conscious of his neighbors. Such a level is usually of short duration. (Adapted from C. H. Woolbert, "The Audience," Psychology Monograph, 1916, Vol. 21.)

In addition to the ability of the speaker, Gurnee has suggested that certain characteristics of the audience contribute to this process: (a) *General receptivity.* Most audiences come predisposed in attitude to hear the speaker. Some audiences may be hostile or disinterested. In this instance, the speaker has a harder task before him and must present material which gains their interest. (b) *Mental homogeneity.* Gurnee points out that individuals of different age, interests, prejudices, etc., make a difficult audience.[4] A homogeneous audience is obviously easier to unify. (c) *Audience training.* Moreover, audiences with experience are most easily dealt with, for they have already established appropriate responses which aid the speaker.

(3) *Polarization is socially facilitated.* A polarized audience is, however, not a crowd. A crowd does not exist until emotion runs high in an audience and until the speaker's words are reinforced by contributory stimuli from the crowd members. It is granted that an audience, rapt in attention, is more suggestible than a less attentive audience. It will be recalled from the description of suggestion in the previous chapter that suggestion involves a narrowing of the field of consciousness. The techniques of getting attention and removing counterattractions are, by their nature, methods of restricting the field of consciousness. Hence they are also methods of enhancing suggestibility. But a polarized audience will not lynch a man nor tar and feather a woman any more than a hypnotized individual will follow any suggestion. Suggestion at its most potent level cannot overcome strong inhibitions in the form of dynamic attitudes in the individual. (There is the example of the student in a European clinic who after putting a young woman under hypnosis asked her to remove her clothing. She immediately came out of the hypnotic trance, slapped the face of the suggester, and departed from the clinic.)

Allport points to a stronger force than the direct suggestion of the speaker. That is the force of social facilitation. The crowd speaker uses special methods for eliciting emotional demonstrations in his audience such as applause, laughter, weeping, shouting, or stamping. Allport writes:

> "In our study of group influence we found that the social increment was in direct proportion to the overt evidence of the coworking of others. The same rule applies to crowd excitement and is practiced by those skilled in the art of public control. Speakers who wish to stir their audiences use special methods for eliciting responses *of a demonstrative sort,* so that an abundance of contributory social stimuli may be in evidence. . . . Appeals are made to emotional rather than to thought responses; for emotional expression is the very material of which crowd facilitation is made. A crowd cannot be made of reasoning individuals, because reasoning involves few outward responses through which individuals stimulate one another. Sentiments common to all are touched upon, since these involve postures of stimulating value." [5]

Socially facilitated polarization is then a condition of intense attention of audience members to a speaker in which the suggestibility of members is farther enhanced by the contributory stimulation of other audience members. It is as if the members of the audience had become part of the same stimulus field in which the speaker is the dominant object. The contributory stimuli are the background.

(4) *Other techniques for enhancing suggestibility of audience members.* There are other conditions which aid in increasing the suggestibility of audience members. The crowd speaker must be fluent. His English may be broken, his pronunciation incorrect, his sentence structure faulty, but his words must flow like a cascade. This gives a rhythm to the speech which has a special effect. Repetition is also effective in increasing suggestibility. "For Brutus is an honorable man" is repeated over and over, each time with increased effect. The progress of enhanced suggestibility should look like a bull stock market chart. The speaker takes the audience a limited distance and allows it to rest a moment and to recede in emotion. But from each valley he takes it to higher peaks. It is very difficult to take an audience from everyday passivity to a high state of emotion without stages of rest.

THE OPERATION OF MECHANISMS IN CROWDS

It is now possible to superimpose this crowd description upon different types of crowds. The lynching mob passes through certain of these stages in short order. No crowd speaker needs to use special devices to get the attention of such a group if he confines himself to the subject at hand. In a process called milling, group members have already worked themselves up to a fairly high degree of suggestibility. Milling is a form of interstimulation of a direct face-to-face sort. The word has gone round that a sex offense has been committed against a child. The community gathers at the post office to talk the matter over. Everyone is excited. Each intensifies the emotion of the other, but as yet no crowd exists. In the same fashion a class crowd, for example, a labor union on strike, has gone through a preliminary period of preparation. The crowd orator in these situations is handed an audience in a state of high suggestibility which polarizes immediately.

Nor is there any difficulty in producing expressive behavior. Any statement which accords with the prevailing temper is greeted with cheers, any mention of the enemy with boos. The art of crowd making in all three situations is essentially the same in its psychology, but not in the ease with which it is accomplished. The building of an audience from a passive group into a crowd is an art. The polarization of a milling group is merely the acceptance of an invitation. If one individual does not do it another will. A community or a class crowd finds leaders.

Social Projection and the Feeling of Universality. —The chief differences between the community crowd, the fanatic public, and the class crowd arise, however, at another point. Allport has demonstrated the existence of two other mechanisms in the crowd situation which have a great deal of importance for our theory. The situation is more than one of a small audience of individuals within sight and sound of each other. In addition to the social facilitation of his fellows, each individual possesses some notion of the greater numbers who are beyond range of immediate stimulation. Allport states:

> "In terms of behavior we may say that the individual reacts to stimuli which he actually receives *as if* they were coming from an enormously greater number of individuals. In terms of consciousness he imagines that the entire vast assembly is stimulating him in this fashion. He has mental imagery—visual, auditory, and kinaesthetic—of a great throng of people whom he knows are there, although he does not see them. These people moreover are imagined as reacting to the common crowd object. There is vivid visual and motor imagery of their postures, expressions and settings for action." [6]

An audience has been polarized by attention-getting mechanisms, and by reducing counterattractions; this attention has been augmented by social facilitation so that an enhanced state of suggestibility exists. Now the impression of universality enters to add further prestige to the words of the speaker, the prestige of numbers.

Crowd behavior is dependent upon emotion and crowds are seldom characterized by logical thinking. One requirement for a crowd is expressive behavior, because of the necessity of enhancing the speaker's words with the social facilitation of audience responses. And expressive behavior tends to be emotional behavior. But there is also another implication to emotional behavior.

The Mechanism of Projection.—We interpret the expressive emotions of others in terms of our own wishes. We read into them our own mental content. This mechanism is called *projection*. When we are melancholy we find the world a sad place; when we are joyous the world takes on a cheerful hue. The world has not changed; we have merely projected into it our changing emotional mood. In the crowd situation the individual who is moved by the speaker projects his own acceptance of the speaker's ideas into the other members. Thus he finds support for his belief in the numbers about him whom he assumes are feeling as he is feeling. In this manner projection and the impression of universality work together in circular fashion to intensify the attitudes of the individual. The circular effect, moreover, extends beyond the individual, because the more expressive a man becomes as he feels the group is with him, the more he stimulates his fellows to emotional behavior which in turn reinforces his emotion still further.

The Impression of Universality.—The mechanisms of projection and of the impression of universality are two important features of crowd behavior. In as much as emotion dies off slowly, expressive behavior often lasts long after the instigating stimulus has passed. A speaker who is quick finds it possible to exploit this psychological moment. While the audience is still applauding some statement which the speaker has made, he presents another idea which would not be usually accepted. Owing to the lag of the expressive behavior, the individual as he looks around sees acquiescence upon every hand. The audience has been previously agreeing with the speaker; they still seem to be agreeing with him. Add this condition to the already heightened state of suggestibility and we have the basis for the acceptance of some proposition which under other circumstances would be turned down. When this accepted idea is further projected into the multitude and blessed with their apparent approval, it becomes a proposition which the individual cannot be expected to refuse.

The Class Crowd.—It is interesting to compare this generalized picture of crowd behavior with a more specific type of crowd such as the class crowd. In this case we have a long history of preparation. Those who are members of labor unions have had experience with past strikes. Many may have been in demonstrations in which either they or some friend were injured. Some of them have been jailed for picketing. Conflict and repression have provided a reservoir of emotion. To go on strike means to go without wages. This means privation and suffering. More than any other thing a 'scab,' a non-union man who will go to work during the strike, is to be hated. Thus there is built up in the worker a background of hostility and hatred.

"The menacing of the drives of a large number of individuals simultaneously both draws them together and incites them to common action," to use the words of Allport. He continues, "It is often said that crowds are creatures of hate and invariably demand their victims. There is, however, sufficient psychological reason for this: The formation of the crowd springs from the collective struggle responses of individuals. The mob members do not demand a victim merely in order to shed blood, but to restore their thwarted responses to their normal operation." [7] The picture seems to be reasonably clear, but Allport forgets that in many instances it is difficult for workers to restore their thwarted responses to their normal operation. They may be fortunate during certain periods if they can even secure a subsistence standard of living, let alone normal desires.

Moreover, it is not enough to point out the fact that the crowd members in this instance have a background of repression and regimentation. It is also important to see how they localize the causes of the repression. Their emotion runs highest against scabs and against the company, but it also may be oriented against the State. If the workers go on strike, the police prevent their picketing a factory. If the workers attempt to keep scabs out by force, the militia is called out to protect lives and property. Increasingly labor may find the forces of the state lined up on the other side. Thus the apparatus of the State interferes with the accomplishment of labor's objective. On the other hand, the education of the individual member has taught him that he should respect private property and lives, that justice is given through the courts, and that as an individual he must abide by these legal attitudes.

The crowd process in this situation becomes a device by which the individual overcomes his scruples about obedience to law, his attitudes about human life, and his fear of the police or the militia. In general, the class crowd is a revolutionary thrust at the state. Through polarization and social facilitation the crowd is raised to a high state of suggestibility. Thus Allport describes a group of strikers who seized a certain number of scabs and paraded them through the city. As the line of march proceeded, feelings ran higher and higher. Finally, the leaders became afraid of the situation and advised the scabs to run for it. The tail of the crowd started in pursuit and as it passed the leaders they, too, turned and pursued the scabs, who were then beaten up.

Crowd Psychology as a Technique for Displacing Institutional Regimentations.—Allport points out that in a crowd an individual often does what he has wanted to do all along, but now more so. In a highly developed crowd situation some one starts some form of action. Allport suggests that the first individual to act may be a person of high suggestibility.

Unless the crowd is very unusual the members have already been given various high-sounding rationalizations to prove the justice of their cause. Personal rights are represented as higher than property rights; every man has a right to live; the other side has proved its perfidy by hiring scabs, labor spies, and brutal company police; the Constitution gives the right to free speech and assembly.

A sense of anonymity is already created. Allport shows these steps as operating in this respect. The individual argues with himself "(1) I could do this thing which I want to do as a member of a crowd because no one would observe me, and I would therefore escape punishment. (2) Even if I should be detected, no one could punish me without punishing all the others. But to punish all would be a physical impossibility. And (3) more than that, it doesn't seem possible to punish a crowd, because that would be making a large number of people suffer. And that is unjust; it is the interest of the many which must always be safeguarded. Hence (4) since the whole crowd show by their acts they wish the deed to be done, it must be right after all. So large a number of people could not be in the wrong. And finally (5) since so many people will benefit by this act, to perform it is a public duty and a righteous deed." [8]

With this background the first overt act is taken not as a single act but as a genuine signal that everybody intends to participate in the action. The individual is in no position to refuse participation. Whereas the impression of universality in the past has always been connected with institutional attitudes such as property security and human security, now the impression of universality is apparently on the side of his repressed attitudes. The crowd becomes *a technique for transferring this impression from the conformity side of a set of regimented attitudes to the private attitude side.* It is the last needed increment to make crowd behavior appear completely reasonable.

The Crowd as a Fanatic Public.—Crowd psychology in a fanatic public may show a similar mechanism to that of a class crowd, but it also has points of difference. Generally no history of repression from a common agency exists. A common emotion and a common orientation have to be rather artificially generated from general attitudes arising out of the experiences of life. The "get rich quick" attitudes which characterize such manias as the "Mississippi Bubble," "Tulipmania," "The Florida Land Boom," Auctions, and "Chain Letters," are not felt by the average individual to be attitudes repressed by "the State," or by any other specific agency. They are prepotent attitudes of high emotional value which have not been fully expressed because the average individual has little opportunity to get rich quick. Crowd psychology is used upon these people not to overcome institutional repressions, but to overcome the individual's fund of common sense and to make him accept as a good proposition one which is obviously logically false.

In the same fashion a religious revival is successful because it can exploit a certain reservoir of strong emotional attitudes and find a common orientation for them. The success of religious revivals cannot be traced to frustration which people attribute to a specific institution. Rather it can be traced to frustration by life itself. Tired, discouraged, and unsuccessful individuals present a psychology open to exploitation. The basis of the exploitation is not the overcoming of some institutional attitude, as much as it is a victory over human intelligence. The drunk believes that if he accepts the Christian life he will be saved. The tired and discouraged accept the notion that by humility and service, they can secure peace in an after world.

In as much as these types of crowds start from a different and less emotional background, it takes much more effort to bring them to the state of suggestibility necessary for the end sought. The evangelist is trained in the methods of polarization, and of polarizing social facilitation. He often has trained assistants to start the crowd into action.

Crowd Psychology as a Technique for Integration.—In the fanatic public the impression of universality and the processes of social projection are utilized for a different purpose than in a class crowd. In the class crowd these mechanisms of crowd psychology are utilized to allow the individual to rationalize conditions under which he can do what he has been wanting to do all along. In the fanatic public, the techniques are utilized to create a new want in the individual. Moreover the want may be very unusual and the means of satisfying it a bizarre method. Under any other conditions than crowd psychology the new means would be completely repudiated by the common sense of the individual.

The evangelist develops old attitudes regarding childhood life, mother, home, and family. He develops the desire for contentment, rest, and security. He suggests the punishments that flow from sin, and dissipation. He concludes with the rewards and satisfactions that arise from genuine repentance. All of these attitudes have a strong emotional value in their own right. Under the influence of crowd psychology, however, they take on an intensity not hitherto recognized. The drunkard signs the pledge and it seems a perfectly reasonable thing to do. Moreover, if he really changes his environment it may represent a genuine conversion. But in most cases the individual returns to his old environment. The stimulating factors of crowd psychology are gone and soon the individual returns to his old ways.

Similarly, the progress of a real estate boom sets off a series of strong positive values. Florida is the land of plenty. It represents a climate where ease and relaxation are possible. There is no heating problem, no winter, no need for winter clothing. It seems reasonable that everybody should be interested in owning land in this climate. Real estate salesmen succeed in starting a movement to Florida. Soon lots are being laid out in every direction. Everybody seems to be on the road to Florida. There are great sums to be made in Florida land. The get-rich-psychology gets stronger and stronger. Many begin to believe it will last forever.

The Crowd as an Indignant Community.—The community crowd presents points of similarity with both class and fanatic crowds. As in the case of the public there is generally no history of systematic repression by some single agent. Such instances as border warfare in which the community takes common action against marauding Indians are generally not considered as cases of crowd psychology, though they have many common elements. The union of the community in violent counteraction is generally considered as war psychology rather than crowd psychology. Crowd psychology seems more often, in the case of the community, to be used against the violation of the community mores by a single person or a very few individuals. The rustler who steals cattle, the Negro who commits a murder, the individual who kidnaps a child are more often the victims of community crowd psychology.

It should be observed that the mores themselves represent emotional taboos. Although very few individuals in the community may suffer from a particular violation of the code (for it is not their child who has been stolen, their sheep which are being killed, or their relative who has been murdered), still the deed stands as a very "wrong" sort of behavior. Because this fact has been long recognized, there generally exist legally constituted agencies for carrying out the punishment of the offender.

Crowd psychology in this community situation operates not to overcome the state, or to suggest some new unthinkable form of behavior, but to allow individuals to anticipate the usual governmental processes. This they know they are not ordinarily allowed to do.

because due process of law is worked out to protect the innocent from being misjudged. As in the class crowd, under the mechanism of crowd behavior the individual finds anonymity. Whereas most often the feeling of universality is on the side of the due process of law, it is now on the side of the proposed crowd behavior. In England where law is carried to swift execution, crowds of this kind are much less frequent. The rationalizations which justify the community crowd are that the courts are slow, the politicians corrupt, and the officials inefficient.

Crowd Psychology as a Failure of the Division of Labor. —In the community situation the crowd represents a distinct failure of the division of labor. Unlike the class crowd oriented against the state, there is no feeling that the governmental agencies are in the hands of another class. It is rather a feeling that governmental agencies are unable to carry out community will and, therefore, community members take the decision into their own hands.

In some cases, no special agency exists to cope with the infraction of the community code. Many of the early lynchings were really a primitive attempt to set up a method for dealing with violations of the community mores.

The Problem of Mistaken Identity. —Sometimes crowds which appear as community crowds are really class crowds. Thus, though many writers attempt to make certain Negro lynchings an instance of community justice, a thorough examination will show the affair to be a class crowd of poor whites who are in economic competition with the Negro. The whites have localized the Negro as the cause of their own frustration instead of localizing the State as the chief agent in the way of a good life. It must also be recognized that it is possible for a crowd to represent an instance of enforcement of community mores to some members, a means for achieving a new integration for others, and a technique for finding release for repressed private attitudes from their institutional limitations for still others.

Crowd Psychology in General. —Upon the basis of the previous analysis it is possible to comment upon the general theories of crowd psychology in the literature. Thus Martin is very much interested in the logic and violence of the crowd, but is unable to understand the nature of either.[9] He feels all crowds to be paranoic in the sense that to him they seem to reflect logic-tight delusions of grandeur and persecution.

The Logic of Crowds.—There is no difference between the logic of men in crowds and their logic elsewhere. This fact seems so potent in the light of modern psychological knowledge and has been so often demonstrated by Pareto, Freud, and others that it hardly bears comment. Men think scientifically only in restricted fields, and then only when their goals are fairly rigidly defined. Nor is the logic of the men in the crowd more of a systematized delusion than is the economic philosophy of the member of parliament. The logical doctrines of any group are principally systematized rationalization of the wants, desires, and motives of the group members. Seldom is group ideology formulated in an objective impersonal manner. It has the emotional and absolutistic characteristics which Martin finds in crowd thinking.

The Violence of Crowds.—There is a difference in crowds in regard to violence. Here again Martin fails in his analysis. The amount of violence is in good part a function of repression. The reason that the member of parliament speaks his economic theories in good temper is because he is not repressed in his expression. As parliaments have had to debate subjects on which there was a distinct and real difference between members on fundamental presuppositions, they have become increasingly violent in their expressions. The member of the labor class who has long been regimented by another class in his expressions so that he hardly dares to express his ideas develops a fund of emotion behind his attitudes. This frustration leads to violence in behavior once the proper rationalizations are developed to allow him to give manifestation to his desires. In the same fashion the poor white, who has long been frustrated in his economic endeavors by the cheap labor of the Negro, develops attitudes which cannot be socially expressed without running into difficulty. In the mob situation he finds the opportunity to express long pent-up feelings. The Fascist developments of modern times have indicated that many of the members of the class of good temper can develop violent feelings once their property rights are frustrated by the development of the labor movement.

Delusions in Crowd Psychology.—Two characteristics of paranoia are the delusion of persecution and the delusion of grandeur. Two very similar mechanisms are found in crowd psychology. The delusion of the paranoiac is founded upon false reference. He misinterprets the actions of people as directed against himself. His own failure is blamed upon some agent whose reference to himself can be shown to have nothing to do with the matter.

Delusion of Persecution.—Martin seems to believe that the crowd never has grounds for belief in persecution and this belief must always be a delusion, or a false judgment. Because some crowds are led to believe that the devil is their enemy and the cause of their misfortune, others that witches are spoiling their crops, and still others that the Jews are the cause of their economic misfortune, Martin would seem to believe that the early settlers were deluded in blaming the Indians for the burning of their frontier villages, the feudal serfs and rising bourgeoisie were deluded in blaming the nobility for the restrictions on their economic activities, and the modern labor movement in blaming its subsistence level upon modern production relationships. Because some crowds have no ability to localize correctly the real cause of their misfortunes, he assumes that all crowds lack this ability.

There is, of course, some justice in his claim. The cartoonist who blames the present amount of economic disorder upon conspiring capitalists is distorting the picture. Few of us know of instances in which industrial barons sit up nights attempting to starve laborers. Many individuals, however, are convinced that modern production relations, defended by unconscious motives of the property owning classes, do result in the persecution of the laboring class. And the persecution may be as relentless as if it were conscious. Nor is it denied that the laboring class in seeking to localize the agent responsible for its condition often blames the wrong individuals, "the politicians," "the wall street banker," or "foreigners and Jews," before it arrives at the correct answer to its problem. This is a complex social world in which we live and few individuals are trained to see it in its entirety and in correct perspective.

Delusion of Grandeur.—The delusion of grandeur, on the other hand, arises from other sources. It is undoubtedly connected with the type of crowd psychology we have already described. Social facilitation, the impression of universality, and social projection do make it seem possible that the crowd members can accomplish anything that they have a mind to accomplish. There is still, of course, one caution that should be sounded. Upon occasion it is probably true that a crowd of sufficient members can accomplish what the group members desire. Such a crowd represents revolution. And if enough people in any culture have come to the conclusion, under crowd psychology or any other psychology, that they intend to change the prevailing order, there is little that can be done to prevent it.

Whereas the delusion of grandeur is assumed in paranoia to compensate for feelings of inferiority, a real feeling of immense collective power is a very different thing.. The surge of creative enterprise which followed the French Revolution was based upon real fact. The middle classes who found power in that epoch virtually remodeled the world. The path between illusion and fact, between delusion and reality, is often hard to detect.

REFERENCES

Allport, F. H. *Social Psychology*. Cambridge: Houghton Mifflin Company, 1924.
Gurnee, H. *Elements of Social Psychology*. New York: Farrar and Rinehart, Inc., 1936.
Hollingworth, H. L. *The Psychology of the Audience*. New York: American Book Company, 1935.
Le Bon, G. *The Crowd*. London: T. F. Unwin, 1917.
Martin, E. D. *The Behavior of Crowds*. New York: Harper and Brothers, 1920.
Woolbert, C. H. The audience, *Psychol. Monog.*, 1916, 21, No. 92.

CHAPTER VIII

THE PSYCHOLOGY OF NATIONALISM

By Daniel Katz, *Princeton University*

Nationalism has been widely acclaimed the most important and the most striking phenomenon of the past two hundred years. "The most significant emotional factor in public life today," writes Hayes, "is nationalism. Of the current age it is the mark at once intense and universal." [1]

A scrutiny of the world scene seems to confirm Hayes' observation. The fury of an aroused nationalism in Japan is driving the Japanese people to the most ambitious conquest of modern times. In Germany nationalism is holding together a disgruntled people, many of whom would otherwise be at swords' points. Aided by nationalistic spirit, the German rulers are absorbing central and southeastern Europe. Italian nationalism bids fair to make the Italians masters of the Mediterranean. In Russia nationalism is diverting an experiment in economic reconstruction into a national movement.

Likewise, from a historical point of view nationalism looms as a central fact of the past two centuries. During this period strong national states emerged in the Western world. They proceeded to subjugate the people of other lands. Britain established an empire upon which the sun never sets. France became a colonial power. Italy and Germany achieved unification relatively late and had to be content with the less attractive parts of the globe. Even conquered peoples retained their nationalistic spirit. The Czechs, for centuries a part of the Austrian empire, had had their leaders executed and their language replaced by German as the official language of their land. Yet in the World War Czech nationalism burst into flames and Czech troops in the Austrian army deserted to the Allied cause.

How then are we to account for this potent consciousness of kind known as nationalism? Is it primarily a matter of physical proximity, of men living together in the same part of the world?

Geographical residence hardly seems an adequate explanation, or the Czechs would have been Germans long ago. National boundary lines tend to be arbitrary. They do not necessarily follow natural barriers.

Does nationalism derive from race as the German ideologists would have us believe? Almost every national group has a set of beliefs that its members are biologically superior to other national groups. Yet no myth has been·more frequently exploded by social scientists than the myth of racial superiority. The latest version of the Aryan doctrine which emphasizes the superior genes of the Nordics has met the same fate as its predecessors.[2] To find consistent ethnic differences in Europe it is necessary to go to its geographical extremes, to compare, for example, the Scandinavians and the southern Italians. Wars, migrations, and conquests have scrambled European peoples racially.

Is nationalism a function of a common language? A common language makes possible common traditions and thus is productive of consciousness of kind. But England and the United States in spite of a common language have preserved an English nationalism and an American nationalism. Why is it, then, that people should identify themselves with the concept of the nation? "Why" asks the Martian observer—and his question is a fair one—"Why do not people identify themselves according to the color of their hair?" [3] Why not a red-haired league opposed to a group of brunets? Why not all the introverts against all the extroverts?

To find an answer to the problem posed by nationalism we may well start with a general characterization. In this way we can link up the problem of nationalism to psychological knowledge with which we are already familiar. Then we can narrow down the description to apply it more specifically to nationalism. *Nationalism may be defined as the religion of the state.* It is the emotional identification of the personality with the symbols of the state. The general formula for nationalism thus reduces to the well-known phenomenon of individuals identifying themselves with symbols which stand for the group. Since a person's verbal and imaginal processes are not checked at all points directly by physical realities, he can transcend the boundaries of his self in imagination. He becomes part of a greater world in his own mind. This expansion of the ego in nationalism can be studied profitably with respect to (1) the motivation of identification and (2) the mechanism of identification.

IDENTIFICATION AND NATIONALISM

The Motivation of Identification.—The motivating force behind identification can be traced to three sources: (1) It makes possible a greater satisfaction of men's material needs. (2) It makes possible an enhanced psychic income. (3) It supplements the projection of hatred and hostility upon the out-group.

(1) *Greater Material Returns.*—In the first place, the concerted effort of many individuals through their attachment to group symbols provides a greater material return to group members. In the old agrarian family the identification between members resulted in coordinated labor which was to the advantage of all. In the nation there is always an *interest public,* the members of which stand to gain by identifying their material interests with those of the group.

At various times in American history certain individuals who owned oil wells in Mexico were eager to have the United States take over Mexico to protect their oil interests. Nor were these people always deliberately conscious of the basis of their imperialistic wishes. They had sufficiently identified themselves with the American flag and other American symbols so that they regarded their interests in Mexico as the interests of the American nation. So, too, in the World War bankers who had loaned money to the Allies felt in 1916 that *American* investments were at stake. Since the symbols of the state can be used to protect and foster the interests of any one of its members, there is an objective basis for a materialistic identification with the state. The objective basis is greater perhaps for the privileged minority groups than for the masses.

(2) *Enhanced Psychic Income.*—In the second place, psychic income is raised immeasurably by the identification with group symbols. The larger a group to which an individual belongs, the greater its organized strength, the greater the personal satisfaction accruing

to the individual in being a part of it. People are inordinately proud of their families, students are excessively exhilarated by the victories of their football team, and citizens are fiercely proud of their nation's record in war and peace. Identification provides a wonderful means for the individual to increase his stature through attachment to his group.

Perhaps the ego-enhancement in group identification has always existed but the phenomenon varies considerably in certain respects from culture to culture. At times the need for this type of personality satisfaction is greater than at other periods in history. Basically, the ego-enhancement through group identification is compensatory in nature. If people could live full and rich lives as individuals, they would have less need for the vicarious experiencing of the group's greatness. It is precisely in those countries where people's lives have been the most hopeless and the most thwarted that we find the fiercest type of nationalism. Observers agree that the German people would not have accepted Hitler, had it not been for the frustrations of the post-war years.[4]

The real world is frequently too much for the individual. Its limitations restrict and cramp him at every turn. Very few of us can mold it to our desires. Yet to seek release in sheer escape in the fictional world of the "pulps" is not thoroughly satisfactory for most of us. The unrealistic nature of this dreamworld is too apparent. Group symbols, however, have an objective existence. The activity of the group is real. Hence by attaching ourselves to these symbols and engaging in group activities we derive an ego-enhancement, the escapist function of which we do not realize.

Moreover, we enjoy the advantage in group identification of transcending our own limitations and of apparently not being restricted by the limitations of the group symbols. To the student his fraternity is very much a part of himself. The successes of its members are his. Yet he can often rationalize himself out of individual responsibility for the failures of the fraternity or for the reprehensible actions of its members. Such actions were the work of individuals and had nothing to do with the real merit of his fraternity. The stock rationalization for every abuse which is found within our institution is that the abuse represents only the behavior of individuals.

In the long run, however, the individual pays dearly for his un-analytical acceptance of group symbols. The advantage of immediate psychic income is frequently outweighed by the consequences of group identification. The individual can be manipulated through the use of group symbols into actions which are contrary to his own interests. The great majority of people in most nations do not want war. But their blind identification with group symbols permits them to be propagandized into conflict.

In fine, the psychic income in group identification flows from the expression in group symbols of the thwarted and repressed wishes of the individual. Frustrated *personally*, we achieve success *collectively* through our subjective participation in the attainments attributed to the group. In Freudian terms the libidinal wishes of the personality become displaced upon group symbols.

(3) *An Outlet for Hostilities.*—In the third place, identification possesses motivating power because it helps to release the inhibited aggression of people. The strongest identification with the group occurs when the *in-group*, or *we-group*, can be sharply differentiated from the *out-group,* that is, when the in-group stands out as a *figure* against the out-group *ground*. Against the out-group can be directed the hatred stored up by the individual as a result of his frustrations in life.

The essential condition for struggle and anger is interference with the individual's wishes. If the movements of the child are restrained, he will show unmistakable evidence of rage. In adult life we recognize that even a mild-tempered person is goaded to aggression when he is crossed, that is, when his basic wishes suffer interference. Now it frequently happens that the individual must inhibit overt manifestations of his hostility toward the world which thwarts him. This inhibited hostility does not always evaporate with the passing of the immediate situation. It may remain with the individual and form a reservoir of resentment and hatred. It is sustained or at least reinstated from time to time by similar thwarting situations or some reminder of them. The reminder may be a more successful person, a chance derogatory remark, or the expectations of a friend or relative.

Moreover, repressed hostility seeks expression. Laws, taboos, and customs localized within the individual himself and reinforced by the conduct of his fellows prevent direct expression of this hatred. People, however, who lie outside of the group are an admirable object for the suppressed aggression of group members. Since members of the group have identified themselves with group symbols they feel that their aggression is in the interests of the group and is not antisocial activity. The process here is very similar to that described in crowd behavior by which the individual can indulge his antisocial desires because his fellows (who represent the social) are with him.

People join up with the group, or at least intensify their allegiance to it, in part because group membership gives them an approved outlet for their feelings of resentment and hostility. Just as they derive ego-enhancement through participation in group activity so they experience pleasure in chastising the group enemies in word or deed. Group leaders consciously and unconsciously capitalize upon this psychology by furnishing a common scapegoat for the group. Many organizations have flourished with a *vague positive* program because of a *definite negative* program. They have been more specific in persecuting their alleged enemies than in positive proposals for reform. Fairly extreme instances of this sort can be found in the Know Nothing Party, the Black Legion and the Ku Klux Klan. Present-day German nationalism shows the operation of the same principle in a large-scale plan. The Jews, the bankers, and the Marxists betrayed Germany in the World War, brought about a devastating inflation, and monopolized the good jobs, according to Nazi propaganda. Hence they have been made the victims of organized pogroms.

The Mechanism of Identification with Group Symbols.— It is not enough to understand motives; we need to know also *how* identification operates. The mechanism of identification can be described with reference to (1) the nature of personal identification, (2) emotional conditioning, (3) projection, and (4) the confirmation of the belief in the reality of the projected idea.

(1) How do people come to feel that the American flag, the American eagle, the Constitution, and other national symbols are part of their personalities? The explanation lies in good part in that these abstract group symbols have taken on meaning through association with human symbols. The child cannot readily identify himself with an abstract symbol which stands for the group. He can, however, identify himself with people who are very like himself. Other humans not only resemble the child, they also carry out his wishes and so form an extension of his personality. From his identification with his parents, his teachers, and his friends, the child finds it easy to attach himself to other people who stand in a pleasantly-toned relation to him.

The *personal* symbols of the state thus are the first symbols to draw the allegiance of the child. The childhood of national heroes is described to the youngster and he is encouraged to be as truthful as George Washington, as honest as Abraham Lincoln, as courageous as John Paul Jones. Other personal symbols include marching soldiers and public officials. Without the mediation of these human symbols the child would find difficulty in identifying himself with the state. Even at the adult level we know that college students can experience a more intense identification with their group when they know personally the star halfback on the football team.

(2) The process of group identification is aided by direct emotional conditioning. The symbols of the state are marshalled before people on gala occasions. For the child the vivid pleasure of the parade with its bands and colors becomes associated with the American flag and the American uniforms which are conspicuous features of the parade. Most American children raised in small towns look forward to the Fourth of July celebration with its town parade, its games, its free ice cream, and its fireworks. National symbols, moreover, are dramatized in many ways to bring about a lasting association with favorable emotional states.

(3) The abstract symbol permits of identification because we project our mental state into it. Then we accept the projected idea as external reality.[5] We recoil in horror at the thought of anyone desecrating the American flag. Our recoil is not based solely upon

the symbolic significance of his action, that is, upon anger toward a person thus proclaiming himself our enemy. We feel that the flag has been sullied, that actual harm has been done to our nation and to ourselves. We have subjectively added to the physical properties of the American flag our emotional meaning which we regard as existing in the flag itself.

The New York *Times* of October 20, 1938, carried this news item:

> "Deferring to the protests of patriotic organizations, the Treasury department completed today the removal of two aluminum reproductions of the Great Seal of the United States from the floor of the principal entrances of the Newark Federal Building. The seals will be replaced with the inlays.
>
> "For the last six months, Stephen F. Walker, Scoutmaster of Boy Scout Troop 77, and other persons have protested that it was desecration to permit persons to walk on the seals. Mr. Walker wrote to President Roosevelt and other Federal officials in his efforts to stop it and threatened to march his troop into the building and encircle the emblems with Scouts to protect the seals from pedestrians."

The patriotic individuals who were upset by people walking on our national symbols had projected their emotional feelings into the seals themselves. For these patriots it was *as if* the pedestrians were stepping upon the American people. Although the seals were not being harmed in actuality, the subjective *it is as if* becomes for the individual identical with *it is*. Though many Americans might not be upset by this incident of the United States seal, they would probably react as did the Boy Scout leader if some symbol particularly sacred to them had been similarly desecrated. Sophisticated people who do not confuse their emotions with impersonal symbols are often aroused when national heroes like Abraham Lincoln or Thomas Jefferson are treated realistically by historians. This is one reason why many people do not like to see historical plays. They have built up so much subjective addition of their own about historical characters that the dramatist's picture does not accord with their preconceptions.

(4) Identification with the group becomes firmly established, finally, because people find evidence to confirm their belief in the

reality of their projected emotions with respect to group symbols. The evidence they encounter is fourfold:

(a) Other people behave as if the group symbols were real. The flag goes by and all men remove their hats. The President proposes a reform of the Supreme Court and the defenders of the Court are legion. Thus the individual is strengthened in his own belief in the reality of the nation by large numbers of his fellows who act as if it were real.

(b) Noble edifices have been erected to house the officials of the nation. These great buildings are older in many cases than anyone now living. Since they cannot be the work of a single individual they must embody the spirit of the nation. The physical plant of the institution is taken as the objective proof of the greater reality with which the individual identifies himself.

(c) The leaders constantly keep the ideology of the group before the group members. The might and righteousness of the state is the constant story told by the journalist, the artist, the propagandist, and the educator. The symbols of the group become more than symbols because they are backed by the prestige of the printed and spoken word.

(d) Then, too, there must be something to our national character as represented in our flag, our Constitution, and our institutions, reasons the individual, because we are different from other people. Foreigners have queer ways. The author of *With Malice Toward Some* found that even the English were a bizarre people. What greater proof could be needed for the average citizen to convince him of the reality behind the symbols to which he attaches himself than the distinctive nature of his own culture?

No wonder, then, that the nation seems more real to people than any objective fact. It takes an unusual set of experiences to make the average man gain insight into his identification with the ideas and emotions he has projected into the world. Only after the layman has fought in the trenches for several months does he begin to wonder whether or not it would be more sensible to be identified with a League of Extroverts or with the national state.

Totemism as an Ancient Example of the General Formula.—We have been describing the nature and mechanism of group identification. With minor exceptions this general formula holds not only for nationalism but for group solidarity of all kinds. Nationalism as far as some of its basic aspects are concerned, is not quite the unique and startling phenomenon which historians tend to make it. Group identification is an old story and group solidarity can be found in almost all societies.

Consider that common system found in primitive cultures—*totemism.*[6] Primitive peoples are divided into clans or groups of blood-relatives (or individuals considered blood-relatives). Each clan has its totem animal which is the symbol of the clan. Clan members all claim descent from the totem animal. It is taboo to them and they may not hunt it. It stands for and psychologically is the group. All clan members identify themselves with one another through the symbol of the totem animal. If it should be an elk, they are all brother elks. And all good brother elks stand together against the beaver clan. Moreover, since all the men and women in the clan feel this close bond of unity with the group and with one another, they must marry outside the clan group. For a man of the beaver clan to cohabit with a woman of the beaver clan would be incest.

Totemism is similar to nationalism in the psychological mechanisms involved. It is group identification at a much simpler level. Primitive peoples have not developed very abstract symbols. Yet men like themselves are not sufficiently mysterious to make into symbols. But, their companions, the animals fascinate the native peoples. Animals present just the right mixture of familiarity and mystery to be used as symbols. The primitives were impressed with some trait of an animal species which they admired—some trait which they wanted to possess in greater measure themselves.

SPECIAL FEATURES OF NATIONALISM

Nationalism differs from previous forms of group solidarity less in terms of its unique features and more in terms of the particular patterning of characteristics. Moreover, early nationalism reveals a different patterning of psychological features than the nationalism of the present period.

Nationalism differs from totemism and feudal loyalty to the lord in its *extensity*. It applies not to a community type of face-to-face grouping but to the organization of great numbers of individuals into an institution—or a permanent public.

Nationalism differs from the emotional attachment of people to their many publics in that its symbols are *master symbols*. National symbols comprise a master pattern under which many minor patterns are subsumed. The minor groupings exist only in so far as they can be integrated into the national structure. Thus wageworkers may be organized into a federation of labor but it is the *American* Federation of Labor; manufacturers may be organized into an association but it is the *National* Manufacturers Association. No explicit conflict in allegiance between the nation and other groups is permitted.

During the middle ages the allegiance to the Church was similar to the nationalism in the features mentioned above. The Church like the state extended over many communities and many groups. Moreover, its symbols at the time were the master symbols of the period. Loyalty to the Church came first and feudal lords and kings alike dared not oppose their symbols of power to those of the Church. In effect the Church during this period was a political empire as well as a religious institution. The national state differs from the Church, however, in that its symbols are related more to this world, religious symbols more to another world.

Symbols, Martin reminds us, can be of two kinds.[7] They can be *maps* or *flags*. The map symbol has objective reference. It conceptualizes objective relationships. The flag symbol has subjective reference. It stands for emotional projection and does not describe features of the external world. Though both Church and state abound in flag symbols the Church deals more completely in this commodity than does the state. The concepts of the Church transcend the natural world. They refer to a future life, to divinity, to forces over and above this earth of flesh and material. The symbols of the state are not so exclusively lacking in objective reference. They do refer to specific people of common customs and a common language living within a certain territory and to the particular individuals who are their leaders.

Differences between Early Nationalism and Present-Day Nationalism.—The group solidarity of early nationalism was similar in mechanism but different in motivation from present-day nationalism. When England was on her way to becoming an empire, when France was expanding after the Revolution of 1789, when the United States was pushing its frontiers across the American continent, nationalism was a psychological state of hope and optimism. The extension of the master national symbols over the minor group symbols of the period meant the removal of the restrictions which fettered economic life. The growth of a nation or the building of an empire meant that men could expand their activities on an unprecedented scale. The local storekeeper had the chance to become a national merchant. The small manufacturer had the opportunity to supply the people of the nation and become wealthy. The small town politician could become a national statesman.

During the period of early nationalism it is important to recognize that the new opportunities existed in fact as well as in men's minds. The period following the French Revolution was a period of rising standards of living. Material well-being was improved even for the masses.

Of course the upper middle classes took up the doctrine of nationalism first and were its most vigorous supporters. They had the most to gain from this new religion. Though material gain was not the only motive it played its part. To quote Hayes:

> "The middle class . . . proceeded to think of the state, of the national state, as peculiarly their own and to love the nation as it had never been loved before. . . . Nor was it long before the liberal and democratic middle class discovered that the rewards of love were not merely love. . . . By preaching nationalism to the masses they acquired in marked degree that respect and veneration which worthy disciples are wont to pay spiritual leaders. By securing the trust and confidence of the masses they were better enabled to identify national aspirations with their own interests." [8]

Nonetheless in many countries the masses shared to some extent in the new prosperity. The new prosperity grew out of mechanization and the increase in the size of productive units made possible by a large national state. To apply machine methods on a large scale involved a large-scale political state which could maintain the same legal standards over a large territory. The forward progress in standards of living under the national state was not uniform, but there were enough people in the lower classes who improved their lot for most men to feel that they had a real chance in this world.

Psychologically, early nationalism owed its tremendous motivating force to the fact that it represented an integration between man's *bread-and-butter drives* and his *egoistic* wishes. The individual prospered as his country grew in size and importance. His psychic income and his material income were derived from the same source. For example, the early industrialization of England gave the English people a higher standard of living—some of it at the expense of the rest of the world. English imperialism thus inflated the ego of the English citizen as the British empire was extended beyond the seas and it also gave him a better material way of life.

The nationalism which rages today in Germany and Italy, however, has a different motivation. It no longer represents a fusion of psychic and material satisfaction. Instead it furnishes a compensatory psychic income for individuals whose material income has been reduced. European peoples today accept nationalism because they find solace in group-identification for their frustration in everyday life.

It will be remembered that the German people following the war went through a series of thwarting experiences. Defeat in the war, demotion to the status of a second-rate power; a ruinous inflation, widespread unemployment, and restriction of economic opportunity demoralized the people. The Nazi movement with its glorification of the German people was salve to their wounds. Moreover, it furnished a scapegoat upon whom the people could turn their stored up hatred and hostility. In identifying themselves with the new German Reich, the German people could find temporary relief from the miseries of their daily existence.

It is important to recognize the differences in motivation between early and late nationalism. Whereas early nationalism could be maintained at a high pitch over a period of time, present-day nationalism has less enduring qualities. Early nationalism represented men's open road in their struggles both to make a living and to expand their personalities. In some quarters the nationalism of our time is more like a week-end drinking debauch in which people forget their troubles and take out their repressions upon any convenient object. The result may be a Monday morning headache and a feeling of despondency at the week of effort before the next Saturday night release.

Functions of the National State.—Universal agreement does not exist among students of social science concerning the function of the national state. Three main views have been vigorously championed.

(1) The state is often regarded as a cooperative organization of people for the purpose of solving the problems of social living. To live together in any satisfactory fashion people have to agree on traffic regulations for social life if they are not to exterminate one another. They delegate to a few of their number the authority to enforce regulations for social living and these special agents are the officials of the state. Thus the state not only protects the citizen from marauding criminals, it also preserves public health and public safety through such regulations as sanitation laws and quarantine rules. In this capacity the state is regarded as the agent of all the people and its officers are public servants.

This conception of the state was developed in complete form by Rousseau in his social compact theory. According to the theory of social compact the state emerged when men gave up their individual freedom and delegated authority to a few of their number who were to act for them.

(2) The state has also been regarded as the coercive agent of special interest groups. In their hands it is an instrument to preserve their privileges against less privileged groups. This function of the state has been emphasized by writers who trace the origin of the state to conquest and confiscation.

Thus Herbert Spencer believed that the state was the military organization which survived from wars of a predatory nature. Oppenheimer has elaborated this theory very fully.[9] History is the story of a war-like people moving in upon another group, conquering them, and imposing their rule upon them. The state is the organization by which the conquest is achieved and through which the conquered group are kept in permanent subjection. "Everywhere we see," writes Oppenheimer, "a militant group of fierce men forcing the frontier of some more peaceable people, settling down upon them and establishing the State with themselves as the aristocracy." [10]

In time the aristocracy gives way before the onslaught of some new foreign aggressor. In Britain the Saxons conquered the Gallic population and established themselves as rulers but centuries later the Saxons were enslaved by the Normans. In Italy the Romans gave way to the Ostrogoths, then came the Lombards and the Franks. In France the original Gauls were conquered by the Romans; the Roman rule was overthrown by the Franks and still later came the Norman invasion. In every case the invaders set themselves up as rulers and the agencies and devices by which they maintained their rule comprised the state.

The first stage in the development of the state consisted of the conquest of one tribe or one race by another tribe or race. In time, however, the cultural differences between the invaders and their victims ceased to be the dividing line between ruled and rulers. In England the culture of the conquering Normans became fused with the culture of the defeated Saxons. Although this national or cultural differential disappeared the state remained as the means for preserving the privileges of the upper class. The coercive methods and the centralized authority which arose from the imposition of the rule of one tribe upon another did not vanish because the two tribes intermarried and acquired a common culture. They were still employed by the dominant group to protect their favored position.

A modern illustration of this conception of the state can be found in the criticism of the government made by the party out of power. When the Democrats were out of power before the New Deal they charged that the Republicans ran the government in the interests of the bankers and manufacturers, that the tariff laws benefited Eastern industrialists and that Hoover depression measures aided the bankers. On the other hand, the Republicans assailed the

Democratic administration which succeeded Hoover as utilizing the powers of government to redistribute the wealth of the nation by overtaxing the upper and middle classes for relief purposes.

(3) Finally the state has been conceived of as an exploitative institution in its own right. There are those who assert that the state functions neither in the interests of all the people, nor in the interests of the privileged classes but that it functions in the interests of the official bureaucracy.[11] State officials, it is pointed out, generally exempt themselves from taxation. Politicians and bureaucrats are supposedly self-interested individuals who run the machinery of the state for material gain and for power.

The traditional American view of government has been colored by this conception. That government is best which governs least is an applauded sentiment. We have been loathe to entrust great power to public officials. The Child Labor Amendment was defeated because people were made to believe that the government could invade the home and dictate to parents about their children. Our federal structure is a system of checks and balances to prevent any single branch of government from becoming too powerful. The first Reorganization Bill was defeated because people did not wish the President to increase the scope of his authority.

These three conceptions of the state present opposed points of view. Does the state function as a cooperative agency in the interests of all the people? Is it the instrument of an entrenched minority group for maintaining their vested interests? Or is it the creature of politicians and bureaucrats who use it to enrich themselves at the expense of the people?

Our study of the differences between early and late nationalism should suggest the difficulty of generalizing about the functions of the state throughout history. The proponents of the three conceptions of the state can all find evidence to support their contentions because history has seen not one but many types of states. Moreover, in any one period of history the state may exhibit in different areas of life all three of the functions—incompatible though they seem. Politicians operate in their own interest to be sure, but in order to stay in office they must satisfy the wealthy groups who contribute to their campaign coffers and they must also render some measure of service to all the people to secure reëlection. In other words government is an arena in which public interest, private interest, and personal gain all compete.

Undoubtedly the centralized coercive authority of the state arose originally in conquest and confiscation as Oppenheimer contends. But in time public service functions were grafted on to the state apparatus especially in democratic states. The achievement of popular suffrage gave the people a real check upon the use of governmental power for personal and private ends. Though the people do not always use this check wisely or thoroughly, they can prevent the state from becoming a purely repressive agent.

The Democratic versus the Fascist State.—The Fascist state is a reversion to the police state described by Oppenheimer in his theory of conquest and confiscation. Under Fascism all the organizations of the people from labor unions to bowling clubs are smashed lest they become the focus for an opposition movement to the government. The industrialists and financiers in other words are protecting their favored positions by using the state to crush their opponents in the lower classes. To this end they finance the Fascist movement.

Fascism makes little pretense at democracy and at giving each citizen a share in political decisions. Its pretense lies in the national glory it makes available for the most lowly citizen. This glorification of the nation has as its purpose the unification of the people through submerging their many group and class differences. The farmer, the worker, the shopkeeper, and the industrialist are to forget any differences in income, opportunity, interest, and values in their identification with the national state.

Quantitative evidence of differences between the way of life in a Fascist state and in a democracy are lacking. An interesting comparison could be made between the two states, if we could follow typical citizens through a week or more of their daily lives and see how many decisions during the course of the day were made by the citizen himself and how many were made for him by state officials. This would give a measure of the freedom enjoyed in the two states.

Competent observers have pointed out that the life of the Fascist citizen is much more regimented by external coercion than is the life of the citizen in the democratic state. Brown has differentiated four types of freedom: (1) Economic freedom includes the freedom to work, to select a vocation, to satisfy basic needs and derived drives. (2) Personal-social freedom includes the liberty to choose one's friends and to live a congenial social life of one's own choosing. (3) Intellectual-action freedom refers to the right to think and say what one pleases. (4) Political freedom refers to self-government, to suffrage, to the participation in governmental action.[12]

Under Fascism all four types of freedom are greatly restricted by the state. Compulsory labor service, the regimentation of industry, and the outlawing of unions have destroyed freedom in the economic sphere. Intellectual-action freedom is limited to echoing the ideas of the official propagandists. Personal-social freedom is hampered by the fear of spies. Congenial social groups are reduced to a few close intimates lest one's remarks be reported to the secret police. Political freedom is limited to a small minority within the ranks of the Fascist party.

In a democratic state citizens enjoy a considerable measure of personal-social, political, and intellectual-action freedom. Economic freedom, perhaps the most basic, is however not guaranteed to all citizens in equal measure. During depression years when unemployment is widespread the lack of economic freedom is most striking.

An interesting psychological problem presents itself in relation to Fascism and democracy. What is the effect upon the personality of the individual of the democratic way of life compared to the Fascist way of life? The complete answer to this question is not yet available but two stimulating experiments (those of Mowrer, and of Lewin, Lippitt and White) have produced suggestive findings. In Mowrer's experiment a group of children, living in a cottage at the New Haven Community Center, were reared under conditions of modified self-government.[13] With adult supervision they were allowed to make their own rules and to discipline transgressors against the rules. Adult intervention was not carried out autocratically but was explained in terms of the values of the children's group. Prior to this regime of democratic self-government the children had been under the usual institutional pattern of authoritarian adult rule. The effects of the democratic system were marked. There was a decrease in fighting and a decrease in the number of infractions of rules and an increase in cooperativeness. Evidently under the older regime the arbitrarily imposed standards produced frustration with a resulting intragroup hostility.

Similar results have been reported by Lewin, Lippitt, and White who equated two groups of nursery school children for sex, age and intelligence.[14] One group was reared democratically with participation in group decisions, the other autocratically with no participation in group decisions. In the autocratic group about thirty times as much hostility was expressed as in the democratic group. On occasions the children under the autocratic regime combined against one of their number to make him the scapegoat. Under the democratic regime the group structure was more stable and the feeling for group goals better developed.

REFERENCES

Allport, F. H. *Institutional Behavior.* Chapel Hill: University of North Carolina Press, 1933.
Brown, J. F. *Psychology and the Social Order.* New York: McGraw-Hill Book Company, Inc., 1936.
Dollard, J., Doob, L. W., Miller, N. E., Mowrer, O. H., et al. *Frustration and Aggression.* New Haven: Yale University Press, 1939.
Goldenweiser, A. A. *Early Civilization.* New York: Alfred A. Knopf, Inc., 1922.
Hayes, C. J. H. *Essays on Nationalism.* New York: The Macmillan Company, 1926.
Lasswell, H. D. *World Politics and Personal Insecurity.* New York: McGraw-Hill Book Company, Inc., 1935.
Martin, E. D. *The Mystery of Religion.* New York: Harper and Brothers, 1924.
Oppenheimer, F. *The State.* Indianapolis: Bobbs-Merrill, 1914.
Radin, P. *The Racial Myth.* New York: McGraw-Hill Book Company, Inc., 1934.
Rumney, J. *The Science of Society.* London: Duckworth, 1938.

CHAPTER IX

ABNORMAL PSYCHOLOGY

THE SIGNIFICANCE AND CAUSES OF ABNORMAL BEHAVIOR

By Laurance F. Shaffer, *Carnegie Institute of Technology*

Unusual or abnormal human behavior invariably arouses popular interest. When a newcomer moves into a community he is soon evaluated by his neighbors. If he converses about the weather or about his garden, he is a commonplace fellow and interest in him develops slowly. But let him paint his garage a bright pink with blue trimmings, and the response will be quite different. Or, suppose that the newcomer tells about a nation-wide plot against himself, that he is the victim of a sinister and far-reaching conspiracy all of whose members are seeking to injure him personally. Immediately gossip is rife, and the man receives more than his share of attention. Thus the touch of abnormality arouses widespread concern and curiosity. Abnormal psychology shares this appeal, for it endeavors to explain human conduct and thought that cannot be understood in terms of ordinary common sense.

What Is Abnormal Psychology?

Pictures of Abnormalities.—The subject matter of abnormal psychology is encountered in everyday life, but usually is poorly observed and incorrectly understood. Therefore it is necessary to picture some of its problems before attempting to define the field precisely, since the conditions may be unfamiliar to students. The following illustrations describe only the "present condition" of the individuals; any attempt to trace their histories or to ascertain the causes of their disabilities must be deferred until later. The first four cases are patients in mental hospitals.

Withdrawing.—(Case 1). The patient is a young woman about 24 years of age. She walks stiffly across the room when propelled by a nurse, but does not sit down when a chair is offered her. Pushed into the chair, she sits in an uncomfortable position which she makes no move to remedy. In fact, she remains motionless for five minutes, and does not respond to questions. When her arm is lifted to an awkward horizontal position she allows it to remain there, holding the arm rigid for a longer time than a normal person could. She has not spoken a word since her admission five months ago, and ignores the relatives who visit her. She will not feed herself, but swallows food that is placed in her mouth. This patient shows a very complete *withdrawal* from the usual activities of living.

Deterioration.—(Case 2). A mature man walks with a dragging, slovenly gait, has tremors of the hands, and shakes almost constantly. The most striking symptoms are revealed by his answers to questions of common information. Asked his age, he at first says that he doesn't know; he would have to look at a calendar. Later he says that he is 29. (His real age is 36.) He knows the name of the present President of the United States, but not that of the preceding president. He can give his name, but looks puzzled when asked where he is. Simple arithmetic problems are answered incorrectly: Four times two is forty, five plus ten is one hundred. He does not know the date. This man shows marked *deterioration of intellectual functions* that he once could perform. He is also said to be *disoriented* as to time and place.

Distorted Thinking.—(Case 3). This young man hears voices that speak to him constantly, sometimes scolding him and sometimes giving him instructions (*hallucinations*). He talks freely, however, and is eager to give an account of his experiences. He says that he received a course in X-ray work by radio. As a result of this instruction, he can throw X-rays from his eyes and can look through solid substances. He can see into the ground and has discovered treasures of gold, silver, and jewelry. People are jealous of this great power, he says, and his wife tried to poison him. He recovered some of the treasures from the ground, but "three gentlemen, one of them Herbert Hoover," stole his power. He steadfastly holds to these *delusions,* or distorted beliefs, and cannot be persuaded of their falsity.

Excessive Variations in Activity.—(Case 4). A woman about 50 years old talks in a low and moaning voice. She answers questions very slowly, but the replies are relevant and correct. She knows her name, her age, the date, and where she is. She says that she does not feel well, that "her head isn't right." She is worried constantly. When asked what she worries about she replies, "Everything." This woman weeps frequently, and seems overwhelmed with disaster. She is *depressed*, and also retarded in her speech and movements.

A year later, this same woman presents a striking contrast. She is now laughing and active, and talks so rapidly that one can hardly understand what she says. She runs up and down the corridor, and shows a great amount of muscular activity. Sleeping very little, she keeps up a prattle of talk, song, and laughter all day and most of the night. She is still capable intellectually and answers questions correctly when her attention can be secured, although she tends to give joking replies. At times she tears off her clothing, not viciously but gaily. She is *agitated, accelerated,* and is said to show *manic* symptoms.

In addition to the serious conditions that usually require hospitalization, abnormal psychology also studies the minor deviations of behavior that are found among persons in ordinary walks of life. There are many forms of these less severe disorders of behavior of which only one will be illustrated now.

Fearful Behavior.—(Case 5). A college sophomore was questioned by the head of his department after he had persistently refused to recite in class. The young man confessed that he is unable to speak in public because of an uncontrollable fear that seizes him whenever such a demand is made. If compelled to recite he becomes very red in the face, his heart pounds wildly, and at times his throat seems to become paralyzed so that he cannot talk. He is a fairly capable student, and has been able to pass his courses because he suffers no difficulty in expressing himself on written examinations, or in performing laboratory work. He believes that these symptoms are caused by a defective heart, but a careful examination by a physician reveals no organic heart disease. The heart symptoms probably arise from the physiological effects of emotion. The fundamental problem is his abnormally fearful reaction to public speaking.

The Definition of Abnormal Behavior.—Abnormal psychology is the application of scientific psychology to the study of abnormal behavior. Having illustrated some typical abnormalities of behavior, the next task is to make a more precise definition of "abnormal."

Abnormal Behavior as Different Behavior.—Fundamentally, "abnormal" means *deviating from some average or standard.* By derivation, the word signifies *ab,* "away from," a *norm* or average. Abnormal behavior is therefore different behavior, conduct that is not like that of most of mankind. All important human characteristics exist in various degrees. People differ in height, in visual acuity, in health, and in numerous other physical, psychological, and social characteristics. They also differ in excitement or apathy, exaltation or depression, flighty fancy or stubborn tenacity. To be sufficiently different in some of these respects is to be abnormal.

The conception of abnormality as different behavior leads to one especially important conclusion. Abnormality exists in various *degrees.* Everyone knows that all people cannot be classed as short or tall. Instead, there are all quantities of height between the extreme cases. Similarly, all forms of behavior cannot be classed as normal or abnormal. For example, the characteristic of elation-depression exists in many gradations. The person who is extremely elated, constantly shouting, laughing, and singing, is clearly abnormal in this respect. So is an individual who is very depressed and who moans continually about his misery. But there are also persons who are a little overactive, or quite neutral, or a little depressed. Traits are not divisible into two classifications, or into three, but show many small variations in quantity. Variations in degree extend continuously from the average to both extremes. Therefore, all persons cannot be classified precisely as "sane" or "insane," but only as possessing a greater or less degree of some characteristic.

Abnormal Behavior as Inadequate Adjustment.—The concept of abnormal behavior as different behavior needs to be supplemented by another criterion. There still remain the questions of the *direction* of deviation, and of the *amount* of difference that must exist in order for behavior to be called abnormal.

In the sense of the first definition of abnormality, any great deviation from average is abnormal. In practice, however, good variations are distinguished from unfortunate ones. Persons who display broad social participation and leadership, a superior capacity for rational thinking, or a high intelligence are not considered abnormal, while the opposite extremes of withdrawal, delusion, and deterioration are so regarded. In some traits, such as elation-depression, both extremes are abnormal. This is because both great joy and great grief hinder effective social adjustment and prevent the achievement of life purposes. The "good" extremes, in general, facilitate the accomplishment of social and individual adjustment. Of course, what is a good adjustment depends considerably upon social opinion. A deluded individual might become the "medicine man" of a primitive tribe, or even the leader of some religious or political sect in a civilized group.

The definition of how much an individual must vary to be abnormal is also a matter of social opinion. In a complex city environment a man who mutters constantly to himself might be judged abnormal, whereas he might adjust well enough on a lonely farm or as a solitary trapper. Both the direction and the degree of deviation that will be considered abnormal depend on their effect upon the total adjustments of the individual.

"Mental" Disorders.—Another way that abnormal psychology is often defined is to say that it deals with "mental" disorders. This is a convenient term, since it distinguishes the subject matter of abnormal psychology from other abnormalities, such as physical, physiological, economic, or social ones. The term "mental" is troublesome, however, for it seems to ascribe the conditions to some realm of "mind" that was once believed to be quite separate from the physical body. Today, the word "mental" means no more than *psychological*. Psychology is the study of man as a whole individual as he adjusts to his environment. Psychological disorders, or mental disorders, are therefore abnormalities of whole conduct, of perceiving, of thinking, and of adjusting. Calling these abnormalities

"mental" merely distinguishes them from other disorders, but does not explain them.

Psychology and Psychiatry.—Two professions are concerned with abnormal behavior, each of which has a distinct field of activity in spite of the overlapping of their subject matters. *Psychiatry* is a medical specialty that deals with the diagnosis, care, and treatment of abnormalities of the kind considered here. A *psychiatrist* is a medical doctor who has the requisite knowledge and skill to perform the practical tasks demanded by the problem of mental disorder. It is proper for a physician to do this work, since many of the concepts and techniques that he uses are common to general medicine. Psychiatrists tend to be empirical and practical, more concerned with predictions and results than with refinements of theory.

Abnormal psychology differs from psychiatry in that its aim is to understand the origins of abnormal behavior, rather than to classify it or to cure it. The psychologist is the scientist rather than the practitioner. Psychology contributes basic concepts to psychiatry, just as the chemist does to the chemical engineer, and the anatomist to the surgeon. Lacking the related medical knowledge and the practical experience, psychologists usually do not assume responsibility for the treatment of serious abnormalities of behavior.

THE SIGNIFICANCE OF ABNORMAL BEHAVIOR

The extent, cost, and significance of mental disorders are unappreciated by those who do not have professional contact with them.

The Major Abnormalities.—The greatest loss, both in money and in human values, arises from the serious disorders that ordinarily require hospitalization. These most severe conditions are termed *psychoses*, and the patients are referred to as *psychotic*.

Extent.—At any one time there are about 450,000 psychotic patients in mental hospitals in the United States. In the course of a year, approximately 140,000 new patients are admitted, while almost the same number die or are discharged as recovered or improved. There is thus a large turnover in the population of mental hospitals, so that many more persons are psychotic at some time in their lives than are affected at any one date. Also, there are large numbers of mentally disordered who are not in mental hospitals, but who are cared for at home or in institutions for the aged or indigent. Summarized in terms of the general population, the figures concerning the frequency of mental disorders are:

(1) From 8 to 10 out of every thousand persons are in a mental hospital at some time during each year.

(2) About 15 persons out of every thousand are psychotic, whether hospitalized or not.

(3) Of every thousand persons born, about 50 will be in a mental hospital at some time during their lives.

Cost.—The annual cost of maintaining mental hospitals in the United States is about one hundred million dollars, and about five hundred millions are invested in buildings and equipment. This cost is large even when compared with the cost of all sickness, since about half of the hospital beds in the United States are in psychiatric hospitals.

Not all of the cost of abnormal behavior is represented by the hospital expense. Approximately 200,000 of the patients are men between the ages of 20 and 60. If these men could be gainfully employed at an average value of only five hundred dollars per year each, the total loss of wages would be an additional one hundred million dollars annually. Serious mental disorders therefore represent an economic problem of great proportions.

The Minor Abnormalities.—The minor deviations from healthful adjustive behavior are less severe than the psychoses, but they are much more numerous. Most of these less serious disorders fall into the class of the *psychoneuroses*, and include abnormal fears, anxiety, and a number of other conditions that are described in the next chapter.

Extent.—It is difficult to estimate the extent of the psychoneuroses, since cases seldom are hospitalized and often do not even consult a physician. The proportion of psychoneuroses in the general population must be very large, however, if some estimates and judgments can be trusted. Many physicians have estimated that at least half of all medical patients suffer from psychological disorders rather than solely from physical disease. This includes the vast number of "nervous" persons, some persons who go to physicians because they mistake the accelerated heartbeat of emotion for an organic heart condition (as in Case 5, previously described), and many others. Some authorities have estimated that almost every person is at least a little psychoneurotic at some time in his life, and that about ten per cent of the population is affected all of the time. Several surveys of the mental health of industrial employees have shown that psychoneuroses are a significant problem in business. From 12 to 20 per cent of the employees of department stores have been found to be handicapped by "nervousness" or other psychoneuroses. In a careful study of a large number of industrial and clerical employees in Great Britain, 30.6 per cent were found to display noticeable psychoneurotic symptoms.

Social Significance.—The social significance of abnormal behavior goes far beyond the statistical and economic facts. A very large proportion of human misery is associated with psychological ills. Persons who cannot get along with their fellow men, who are quarrelsome and uncooperative or else timid and fearful, suffer from psychological maladjustments. Other maladjusted persons include those who cannot retain employment because of peculiar personal traits, those who cannot live at peace with their parents, husbands, wives, or children, and those who are always "just miserable." Abnormal psychology presents a way of understanding these forms of behavior, and, in some instances, points toward their control and cure.

The study of abnormal psychology has another broader social significance. Literature, drama, and history are full of characters who can be understood only in terms of abnormalities of behavior. Some of these personages show major mental disorders, and many more of them display the lesser deviations of behavior. Individuals who are queer or unusual are more interesting than ordinary people; hence they are frequently found in literature, and also in history. Not only do Hamlet and Macbeth become more understandable through the study of abnormal psychology, but also Caesar and Napoleon.

Two Interpretations of Abnormality

There are two chief interpretations of mental abnormalities, both of which must be examined if a thorough understanding is to be achieved. These points of view may be illustrated by a simple example. Suppose that we say to each of two persons, "Lift up your hand!" Neither one of them complies. The causes of these failures to follow our directions may now be investigated. One individual, we will discover, is totally deaf. Some years ago he suffered an infectious disease that attacked the inner ear and permanently damaged its mechanism. The other person, however, is not deaf, nor does he show any other organic disability. But he is a native Frenchman, has never learned English, and hence cannot understand what we say to him. Thus behavior may be affected by a deficiency of *structure*, or by a deficient *functioning* of a normal structure. Broadly speaking, the functional variations are caused by what a person has *learned* or by what he has *not learned*.

The Neurophysiological Interpretation.—Neurology and physiology view the individual as a complex machine. Any failure of this machine to function satisfactorily, then, must be explained as a defect in the mechanism, some part being out of order. The maloperation may be caused by the destruction of some part of the nervous system by an accidental injury or by a disease process. This falls within the province of the *neurologist*, whose specialty is a detailed knowledge of the structure of the neural pathways. Or, the nervous system may be prevented from operating properly by an externally acquired poison such as alcohol, or by some internally secreted toxic substance. A part of the field of physiology is concerned with these conditions.

In recent years the neurological and physiological approach has received increasing emphasis because of new findings concerning the cure of certain psychoses. These discoveries suggest that several disorders that were formerly explained in psychological terms are greatly influenced by subtle physiological conditions, such as the metabolism and nutrition of the brain cells. A more detailed account of this point of view will be given in the second chapter following.

The psychologist cannot ignore the neurophysiological interpretation if he is to achieve a comprehensive understanding of mental disorders. Although the *causes* implied by these interpretations are not within the field of psychology, their *results* are unmistakably psychological. If, as a result of neurophysiological disorders, the individual shows disturbances of behavior, cannot remember, or does not reason or judge adequately, then psychologists must be interested in these causes and must include them in any study of abnormal psychology.

The Psychological Interpretation.—Psychology sees the individual as a reacting, working, adjusting, conscious organism. Its chief concepts are therefore the individual's motives, adjustments, habits, and memories, rather than his neurones or his chemical composition. The fundamental principles of abnormal psychology come from normal experimental psychology. The ways in which individuals adjust and learn are basically the same, whether the end-result is normal behavior or abnormal behavior. Wrong answers or right answers, whether to school questions or to life problems, are learned by essentially the same processes.

The psychological point of view holds that abnormal behavior is an inadequate adjustment to the demands of the environment, the result of an unfortunate learning process. An illustration will serve to make this clear. A young child cries out in the night. This may be due to a stomach ache or to some other illness, in which case the physiological hypothesis will hold. But the child may cry when he has no pain or other ailment. Upon investigation, we find that his parents have come into his room whenever he has cried, and have petted him and played with him until he was sleepy again. From the child's point of view this is a satisfactory end result. He therefore *has learned* to cry when awake and alone, and the parents unwittingly have taught him to do so by rewarding his cries with fondling and attention. The principal concepts of the psychological approach may be drawn from this example. The child has certain needs for attention, companionship, and play, which are normal and worthwhile motives. He learns that his wails will bring about a satisfaction of these motives, a result that is individually and personally adjustive for him. But this solution of his needs is antisocial since it inconveniences others, and is generally undesirable because it hinders the development of independent adjustive behavior. This illustration is very simple, but the same processes occur in more serious instances. Adults learn to fear, to withdraw, to hold false beliefs, or to show other abnormalities, as a result of inadequate processes of adjustment.

The psychological approach is not antagonistic to the physiological type of explanation. Physiological changes occur in the nervous system whenever a person adjusts or learns. The psychological hypothesis explains mental disorder in terms of the socially unfortunate operation of an *intact* nervous system, rather than in terms of diseases or injuries of the nervous system.

From the descriptions of the two hypotheses, the student must not conclude that some mental disorders are entirely physiological, while others have only a psychological basis. Instead, all mental disorders are probably due to some combination of *both* kinds of causes. There are differences among mental disorders, however, in the degree to which neurophysiological or psychological approaches are applicable. Some disorders are more physiological, some more psychological, but both factors enter all cases in some measure.

Structural Defects and Abnormal Behavior

The neurophysiological point of view has been strikingly successful in explaining some forms of mental abnormality. This approach is very complex, since the anatomy of the nervous system is exceedingly intricate, and the injuries and disorders that may affect it are even more so. It is impossible to describe many details of the neurophysiological approach in a book of this scope, but a few samples may be cited with some simplification to show how the neurophysiologist goes about his work. A spinal disorder, one involving a limited part of the brain, and one that affects the brain generally, will be used as examples.

An Ataxia.—(Case 6). A not infrequent sight on the street is a man who walks with a peculiar gait, assisting himself with a cane. His legs are thrust far apart, are thrown forward irregularly, and are brought to the ground with a sharp stamp, the knee being held stiffly. Both legs are affected. This is the picture of *tabes dorsalis* or "locomotor ataxia," a condition that can be explained quite satisfactorily from the neurophysiological point of view. The disorder as a whole has other symptoms, including severe pains in the legs, gastric crises, and impairment of the skin senses. We will consider here only the *ataxia* or motor incoordination of the legs.

A clinical examination of a case of tabes dorsalis reveals certain features of the disorder in more detail. The patient can stand erect with his eyes open so that he can watch his surroundings, but sways and falls when his eyes are closed. The knee-jerk reflex is likely to be diminished or absent. The pupillary reflex of the eye is peculiar, for the pupil contracts normally when accommodating to distant vision, but does not contract when a light is made to shine in the eye. If the patient is asked to put his finger on his nose with his eyes closed, his aim is found to be very poor. Various other tests show that the man has lost the kinaesthetic or muscle sense of the movement and position of parts of his body. He does not "know where his feet are" unless he watches them. This is a kind of sensory impairment, therefore, and the man walks poorly because he lacks the normal "feel" of movement.

The disorder can be located even more specifically by the neurologist. It is due to a degeneration of the posterior columns of the spinal cord (see Fig. 13). Through these columns of neurones pass the kinaesthetic impulses from the peripheral nerves to the brain. The damage causes the effect that has been noted, the loss of kinaesthesis. Moreover, this condition is due, in an overwhelming majority of cases, to a syphilitic infection of the cord that particularly affects these posterior columns. The neurologist can thus give a complete picture of this disorder in terms of neural mechanisms.

An Aphasia.—(Case 7). An accumulation of gas in a business building exploded with great violence just as a street car was passing. Many passengers in the car were injured, including one young man who suffered a severe skull fracture when a piece of steel penetrated his brain from the left side just above the ear. He survived this injury rather remarkably, but when the first shock was over it was discovered that he could not talk. He understood language fairly well, and was able to communicate by means of signs and gestures, but when he tried to speak only a meaningless jargon passed his lips. This case belongs in the broad class of *aphasia*, a disorder involving the ability to communicate by means of words.

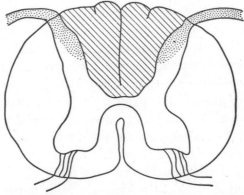

Fig. 13.—Typical Spinal Cord Degeneration in *Tabes Dorsalis*.

The shaded area represents the damage to the posterior columns which carry the impulses for the sensations of movement, balance, and equilibrium to higher centers. The sensory nerve roots are also affected as shown by the dotted areas.

Aphasia, of the structural sort here considered, is caused by an injury to the brain areas that control the language functions (Fig. 14). These are located at the side of each half of the cerebrum, the left hemisphere being more important in right-handed persons. Parts of each of the four lobes of the brain are involved, each correlated to some extent with distinct functions. According to the classical view of aphasia which is somewhat disputed by some authorities, there are two main sorts of this disorder, *motor aphasia* and *sensory aphasia*. The case described here is principally of the motor variety. The young man's ability to understand language is little affected, but he cannot make the complex coordinations necessary for speech. This function is ascribed to a part of the frontal lobe. Among the sensory aphasias are distinguished *auditory aphasia*, the inability to understand spoken language, and *visual aphasia,* the loss of ability to read. Most actual cases of aphasia cannot be classified into these categories sharply, both because the brain functions are not so clearly differentiated as the classical theory would imply, and because injuries usually affect more than one limited area.

Many cases of aphasia recover gradually. The young man described was wordless for ten days, then nurses succeeded in teaching him to say a few simple words, such as "drink," "orange," and "milk." After three months he had relearned his vocabulary fairly

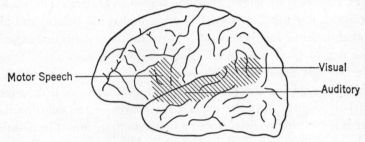

Fig. 14.—Brain Areas Most Often Damaged in Cases of Aphasia.

The left hemisphere of the cerebrum is represented. The shaded area in the frontal lobe is affected in *motor aphasia,* that in the temporal lobe in *auditory aphasia,* and that in the parieto-occipital lobe in *visual aphasia.*

well and would pass for a normal person. Examinations of the brains of aphasic persons, and analogous experiments with lower animals, show that the damaged brain area does not recover its former functions. Instead these processes are taken over by adjacent undamaged areas as reëducation goes on. If too wide a damage has occurred the possibility of retraining may be very limited.

A General Neural Infection.—(Case 8.) A man in a mental hospital shows a variety of symptoms, three of which will receive particular attention. First, he displays a notable *ataxia,* somewhat like that of Case 6. He has a shuffling gait, a general incoordination of movement, and shows the same clinical reflex signs as did the case of ataxia. Second, he shows rather pronounced *mental deterioration,* like that of Case 2, described on page 183. He does not know the date, where he is, or who his associates are. His information is scanty, and he cannot perform arithmetical tasks. The neurophysiologist, from these symptoms and others, recognizes this as a case of *paresis,* a general syphilitic infection of the nervous system. Asked to explain the intellectual deterioration, the neurologist will say that the entire brain is affected, and this observation has been widely confirmed. Moreover, the cause of the infection is known to be syphilitic, a very valuable fact.

But the patient shows a third kind of symptom of even greater psychological interest. He has "expansive" *delusions* of a very intense nature. When questioned, he says that he has millions of dollars, hundreds of wives, and thousands of children. He is a king, a president, a general, or God. The hospital is his palace, and all of the other patients are his servants. How are these delusions explained by the neurological approach? The neurologist says again that the whole brain is affected, which is true enough, but not sufficiently specific. It explains the poor judgment that permits a delusion to be harbored, but it does not explain the source of the delusion itself. There is something positive about a delusion that cannot be dismissed merely as a "weakness of judgment." Moreover, not all paretics show expansive delusions. Some simply deteriorate, some are depressed, while others are agitated. There are no known differences in brain degeneration that distinguish these types. Psychiatrists usually point to the patient's past history, to his *habits,* as the factor that leads to one type or another of paretic behavior. Thus the psychological theory is brought to bear where the neurological theory leaves off.

Merits and Shortcomings of the Neurophysiological Approach.—The neurological and physiological explanations of mental disorders have the advantages of being definite and practical. They are satisfying because they point to the identifiable defects in the present structure of the man that make him act as he does. This approach is practical because it suggests definite methods of treatment and prevention. Many neurological defects due to diseases or tumors can be cured by medicine or surgery. Paresis can be prevented by the eradication of the syphilis from which it develops.

The neurophysiological interpretation is at its best when it deals with relatively simple and limited disorders such as paralyses, ataxias and aphasias. It provides an invaluable background for many of the more complex disorders, but it cannot cope with problems involving the individual's whole behavior and thought. For these conditions the psychological approach is also necessary, since the basic explanations arise from the individual's habits of adjustment.

ADAPTIVE FAILURES AND ABNORMAL BEHAVIOR

The psychological interpretation of abnormal behavior is an application of the objective, experimentally established principles of normal psychology. Not all of general psychology can be applied to the problems of mental disorder, but the studies of how an individual adjusts to his environment, of how he learns and forms habits, and of how his personality traits develop, are very pertinent. Some of these fundamentals are reviewed here, and are illustrated copiously in the two following chapters.

The Adjustment Process.—The course of a normal life may be regarded as a series of adjustments, in which each individual modifies his behavior in response to the combined situation created by his *needs* and by the opportunities of his *environment*. In order to be normal, an individual must be able to adjust flexibly. He must show varied responses that are appropriate to each situation encountered, and that are successful in fulfilling his motives.

The nature of adjustment has been investigated by many animal and human experiments, as well as by observations from everyday life. The familiar puzzle-box and maze experiments illustrate this process clearly. At the outset, the animal is motivated by some physiological need; he is hungry or thirsty, or confined. The fulfillment of this need is prevented by the conditions of the environment, that is by the puzzle box or maze. Next, the animal engages in varied activity typically of the trial-and-error sort, until finally he stumbles upon a solution that leads to the reward and reduces the drive. The total adjustment process can then be outlined in four terms: (1) *Motive*, (2) *thwarting*, (3) *varied response*, (4) *solution*.

The same sequence may be observed in the complex social adjustments of human beings. If a man loses his employment, an adjustment is demanded, since this situation thwarts not only his economic drives but important social motives as well. The man may look and make inquiries (varied responses) until he secures another position, thus solving his adjustment. The notable thing about human social adjustments is the tendency to make *inadequate substitute solutions*. Instead of looking for another job, the man may sit at home and nourish grievances against the economic system. Or, he may blame others for his lack of employment, claim that he is persecuted, or demand that others support him. These inadequate substitute adjustments are of the greatest interest to abnormal psychology.

Certain features of each of the four steps of the adjustment process demand separate consideration.

Motives.—Adjustive behavior may be evoked by any motives whatsoever, but in civilized communities the social motives are probably most significant. Human social motives are very complex, and cannot be reduced satisfactorily to a list of names. They are acquired through life experiences, chiefly as modifications of emotional reactions. Among the important human social motives are the needs for *preëminence, mastery, excelling rivals,* and *overcoming obstructions,* which are related to the emotional pattern of anger or rage. Derived from positive social experiences are the strong motives for *recognition, social approval, praise rather than scorn, attention,* and *gregariousness.* Other significant social motives are the needs for *conformity* with the group, *security,* and *sex.* There is reason to believe that the frustration of these motives leads to inadequate adjustments more frequently than any others.

Thwarting.—A thwarting or frustration is a situation that prevents the fulfillment of a motive. When a motive is aroused under circumstances that prevent its prompt satisfaction, it continues to operate, and stimulates the individual to activity. Three classes of thwarting have been distinguished. Thwarting by *environmental obstacles* usually leads only to constructive activity, since the individual ascribes his difficulties to impersonal and external circumstances. This type blends into a second class, thwarting because of *personal defects* of the indivdual. Persons often lack physical, mental, social, and other qualities to such an extent that they are hampered in the attainment of their motives. Personal defects arouse strong secondary motivation and are more likely to lead to inadequate adjustments. Frustration also may occur because of a *conflict of motives*. If a situation impels an individual to two antagonistic courses of action, he must choose one of them, compromise, or else remain futilely stirred up. Since many conflicts cannot be compromised except with inadequate substitutes, this is a very common cause of maladjustment.

Varied Responses.—Impelled by unsatisfied motives, an individual who is making an adjustment tries one course of action after another, until he hits upon a response that is satisfactory in some degree. Healthful adjustment depends very considerably upon the maintenance of varied behavior until a good enough solution has been discovered. The individual who has a limited repertory of adjustive responses, or who is too easily satisfied with the first partially adjustive response that he makes, is likely to show maladjustment. Flexibility of behavior and the possession of many socially adaptive habits make for good adjustments.

In some instances, a person displays strong emotion when he is frustrated, which hinders constructively varied activity. A fearful or enraged person is likely to perform the same reaction over and over again, trying some partial solution repeatedly instead of varying his behavior. Such a response is known as a *persistent nonadjustive reaction* and is especially significant in abnormal behavior. Excessive emotional states are the chief causes of persistent nonadjustive reactions.

Solution.—A solution of an adjustment problem, from the psychological point of view, is any act that reduces or satisfies the motivation that initiated the adjustive sequence. Thus, if an adjustment is demanded by a need for preëminence or mastery, anything that will cause the individual to think better of himself and to feel successful will constitute an adjustive solution. Adjustments, of course, vary greatly in quality. A man may secure a satisfaction of his mastery drives by actual achievement, by substitute achievement in a hobby or a sport, or by joining some group or movement that makes him feel more important. These are not undesirable solutions. But he can also receive motive-satisfaction by finding excuses for lack of achievement, by exaggerating his disabilities, by daydreaming of accomplishments, or by developing delusions of grandeur. Here lies the key to the psychological interpretation of mental disorders. *The abnormal behavior is satisfying to the motives of the individual.* The understanding of any psychological symptom, therefore, is clarified by asking these questions. "What adjustive need does the symptom fulfill?" "What shortcoming is the symptom designed to conceal?" "What is the individual gaining from his abnormality?" When these questions can be answered, the causes of the disturbance can be discovered.

Adjustive Learning.—When an individual has secured satisfaction from a certain solution of an adjustment problem he tends to repeat that solution when the same problem arises again. Persons thus *learn* their typical habits of adjustment, whether adequate or inadequate.

Trial-and-Error Learning.—Most instances of adjustive learning follow the pattern well known to general psychology as trial-and-error learning. When a rat is placed repeatedly in the same maze and is given food at its end, he comes to run the maze more quickly and to take the most direct course to the reward, omitting the unrewarded varied responses ("errors") that he made in the earlier trials. Similarly, human beings tend to repeat and to learn the responses that lead to the completion or satisfaction of motivated activity.

There is considerable variation in the degree of *insight* shown in human learning. At times a person will plan his action to achieve the end in view, and will consciously and deliberately work toward a goal. This rational or insightful behavior usually leads to good adjustments. In other instances persons "stumble upon" their adjustive solutions, retain them because they are satisfying, and yet are not clearly aware of why they act as they do. This has been termed *blind trial and error.* The same effect can be seen in the laboratory. A blindfolded subject can learn to trace a finger maze without error, and yet he may be entirely at a loss when called upon to describe or to explain in words the path that he took. Thus many traits of personality and character are learned only because they satisfy motives, not because they are rationally and consciously selected. No person "chooses" to become deluded, but the individual with delusions gradually learns his distorted ways of thinking because they are so satisfying to some of his personal drives. This fact has led to the theory of "the unconscious," a hypothesis that is unnecessary in the light of the experimental findings that learning and understanding do not always occur together.

The Conditioned Reaction in Abnormal Psychology.—Another approach to the process of learning that has many useful applications in abnormal psychology is the conditioned reaction. Conditioning, or associative learning, takes place when two responses are elicited from an individual simultaneously or almost simultaneously. To cite a well-known example, Pavlov's dog learned to salivate when a bell was rung because the bell had accompanied the presentation of food for a number of times. Further experiments in conditioning define the circumstances under which animals and humans can learn to discriminate between stimuli, and to inhibit responses to stimuli. All of these are as applicable to abnormal as to normal behavior.

It may be noticed at once that for a dog to salivate when a bell is rung is "abnormal" in itself. The bell has no rational connection with the food, and salivating-for-bells is not a part of the normal and usual behavior of a dog in his everyday adjustments. The force of conditioning, of the simultaneous association of responses, is stronger than logic in determining the behavior of organisms. Many abnormal fears and elements of compulsive and stereotyped behavior found among the mentally disordered can be understood only in terms of the conditioned response. In this form of learning, as in trial and error, "unconscious" learning is significant. Experiments have shown that persons can become conditioned to incidental, almost unnoticed stimuli, and that unconscious responses such as the pupillary reflex can be attached to substitute signals. It is very common for a person to display a habit acquired by conditioning even after he has forgotten the experience by which this habit was learned. Thus bizarre, useless, and maladjusting behavior can be acquired through conditioning, as will be illustrated later.

Personality.—Maladjustments and mental disorders rarely make a sudden appearance; instead, they develop gradually over long periods of time. An investigation of the past history of a maladjusted person will reveal that he has shown for a long time traits of personality that lead to his final state. A person who withdraws acutely is found to have had a shy, retiring, excessively quiet disposition in the past. The deluded person is likely to be described as "always suspicious of others and conceited about his own abilities." From these facts, the theory has evolved that the *personality* of the individual is the basic or predisposing cause of abnormality. This is a valuable theory but is susceptible to a serious misinterpretation.

The individual does not act as he does "because" he belongs to a certain personality type. Instead, what is called his personality type is merely evidence of the habits of adjustment that he already has acquired. A theory of inherent personality types therefore puts the cart before the horse. It is incorrect to say that a person withdraws because he has a withdrawing or "introvertive" personality. The withdrawing behavior shows that the individual's experiences and training have taught him to use this form of adjustive reaction, rather than others. Fearful, self-centered, excuse-making, withdrawing, or complaining personalities are the *end results* of processes of adjustive learning, rather than the sources of these adjustments. In keeping with this interpretation, an individual's personality may be defined as his *persistent habits of making certain kinds or qualities of adjustment*. This is the most useful conception for a psychological theory of abnormal behavior.

REFERENCES

See Chapter XI, page 250, for references on abnormal psychology.

CHAPTER X

ABNORMAL PSYCHOLOGY

THE MINOR ABNORMALITIES

By LAURANCE F. SHAFFER, *Carnegie Institute of Technology*

MALADJUSTMENTS IN EVERYDAY LIFE

The concepts of abnormal psychology apply not only to persons who are seriously disordered, but also to many characteristics of normal people. Most individuals are normal in the sense that their reactions are common, usual, and not too much out of keeping with their life aims. But no one is perfect, and every person shows at least some small signs of inadequate adjustment. "The abnormal psychology of normal people" is a significant field of study, for it contributes to an understanding of one's own behavior more directly than does any other branch of psychology. It is also a necessary preparation for the study of the more serious disorders. No one can understand the nature of "delusions" unless the concepts of "compensation" and "rationalization" first are understood. This chapter describes some of the applications of abnormal psychology to normal behavior, and to a number of the less seriously disabling abnormalities.

Adjustment Mechanisms.—The habits by which persons satisfy their motives are known as *mechanisms*. If, for example, an individual adjusts to a need for recognition by showing-off, exhibiting loud and boisterous behavior, and interrupting others, these responses constitute his mechanisms of adjustment. It is convenient to give names to related groups of adjustive responses. Those in the example just cited are known as "attention-getting mechanisms," a term that describes their nature and utility. Every person shows many mechanisms of adjustment, and all mechanisms are therefore normal in the statistical sense. Mechanisms vary greatly in adjustive merit, however, and in the intensity and frequency with which they are used. An individual who is comparatively well adjusted, or one who is in the early exploratory stages of a difficult adjustment, tends to use many different mechanisms in his trial and error. This is desirable, for by trying many adjustive responses he is likely to hit upon a satisfactory one. In the later stages of maladjustment a person may limit his adjustive behavior to one mechanism that becomes the dominant factor in his personality. This is characteristic of the more serious disorders.

Defense Mechanisms.—The *defense mechanisms* constitute one very important and inclusive class of adjustive habits. Defensive behavior consists of responses that tend to make up for, conceal, or disguise a personal defect or conflict. Defense mechanisms are employed to adjust to a thwarting caused by a subjective inferiority. If a person believes that his inability to satisfy his motives arises from inferior strength, skill, appearance, intelligence, or social status, he is likely to behave defensively. The subjectively sensed inferiority has little relationship to real ability. Some able people believe themselves inferior, while many incompetent persons are never troubled with such thoughts. Defense mechanisms, then, do not arise from genuine inability, but from subjective factors in the individual's personality. A long period of habit formation, usually beginning in childhood, establishes a fearful reaction to personal criticism. This may be caused by experiences such as excessive scolding and punishment at home, ridicule or physical torments from playmates, or persistent failures in school. An individual who has learned this fearful attitude is always ready to believe his own inability and hence to act defensively. Defensive habits set up in childhood are often carried into later life, long after their original causes have disappeared. Since all persons experience some situations in childhood that are productive of an attitude of inferiority, all show defense mechanisms in some degree. Only the more severe and prolonged defenses are mental abnormalities.

Aggressive Defenses.—Defense mechanisms are divided into two convenient, if somewhat arbitrary, groups. First, there are the defenses that are relatively aggressive in nature usually involving social participation. A second class consists of the withdrawing defenses, characterized by retreat from social situations.

Compensation.—A compensation is a pseudo-achievement, developed as a defense against the imputation of failure in real achievements. Compensations have two adjustive values. They are substitutes for genuine achievement, and therefore indirectly fulfill the motives that have been frustrated. Also, they distract the individual from thinking about his shortcomings, and direct the attention of others to his substitute accomplishments.

Compensations are easily detected in many behavior problems of children. One boy was referred to a clinic because of persistent troublemaking in school and bullying on the playgrounds. He also stole small articles from stores in the neighborhood. Investigation showed that beneath this aggressive exterior, the boy had a severe attitude of inferiority toward his physical abilities. He had suffered an unusual number of injuries during the few years before, breaking bones three times while engaged in active play. Consequently he shunned contacts with other youngsters of his age. His motives for physical mastery and for recognition found compensatory outlets in classroom disorder and in bullying younger children. He stole to appear a "tough guy" before his companions. Thus he strove to conceal his fear of being puny by compensatory aggressiveness.

Compensation appears in many other forms. Lack of social recognition may give rise to attention-getting mechanisms, especially in young or naïve persons. Intellectual shortcomings have their typical compensations. For example, a mechanic employed by a college, who was constantly thrown into the company of more educated persons, became addicted to the use (and misuse!) of very long words, thus endeavoring to disguise his lack of formal schooling. Parents often endeavor to secure compensation through the accomplishments of their children, and therefore urge the youngsters into careers that they themselves would have liked to pursue. Many hypermoral attitudes are compensatory in character, for often an individual tries to overcome his own temptations by loudly preaching the opposite virtue. The reformed drunkard is proverbially the best temperance lecturer.

The results of compensation are not always unfortunate. If an individual is prevented from real achievement by unavoidable circumstances, compensations in the forms of hobbies, collections, and other avocational interests may represent the best way of securing a passable adjustment. On the other hand, evidences of compensation can be found in some of the behavior of the seriously mentally disordered.

Identification.—Another common defense mechanism is identification, in which the individual secures motive-satisfactions by participating in the achievements of other persons or groups. A person "identifies himself" with another individual or with an organization. Identifications occur at all ages, ranging from the child's pride in his father's position, through the collegian's adulation of the football captain, to the adult's participation in lodges, societies, and political parties. Identification is a normal source of adjustive satisfaction, but is also seen in extreme abnormalities. It is basic, for example, to delusions of identity, in which patients believe that they *are* a god, a king, or a Napoleon.

Projection.—As a means of defense against tendencies that he will not admit in himself, an individual will sometimes ascribe these same desires to other people. A student with a strong temptation to cheat will see evidence that everyone around him is cribbing. A prudish person is sometimes one who is struggling with sexual drives that he regards as unworthy, hence he sees obscenity in every book and theatrical performance. The tendency to be oversensitive about one's own weaknesses, and to detect them more readily in others, is a common human adjustive trait. It is also characteristic of some delusions, such as those of persecution. If a mentally disordered person is suppressing a tendency to do away with his family, he may easily shift to a belief that they are trying to poison him.

Rationalization.—As compensation is to conduct, so rationalization is to thinking. The person who rationalizes gives "good" reasons to justify courses of action that he believes to be inferior, or else to excuse away his shortcomings. Normal rationalizations are illustrated by the excuse-making that follows having failed an examination, having been reprimanded by one's employer, or having lost a set of tennis. In these situations it is very consoling to believe, respectively, that the instructor was unfair, that the mistake was made by someone else, or that one's racket must be restrung.

The habit of "passing the buck," verbally and in thought, to explain every failure is closely related to the structure of many delusions. The patient who believes that he has been imprisoned in order that others may get his money is spared the embarrassment of recognizing his mental breakdown.

Withdrawing Defenses.—A rather different type of defensive behavior is illustrated by simple withdrawing or *seclusiveness*. An individual who is frustrated in his social adjustments may give up the attempt to adjust socially, and may withdraw from the stimuli that cause his difficulties. Seclusive persons shun the company of people, prefer solitary amusements to competitive ones, and would rather watch other individuals than participate in their activities. This reaction is adjustive, for a person who will not try to make social adjustments cannot experience painful failures. The withdrawing adjustment is tried by almost all persons who encounter social thwarting, and frequently alternates with the more aggressive adjustments. A socially maladjusted individual is typically shy and retiring at one time, and aggressively compensatory at another, with seeming inconsistency.

Excessive seclusiveness is usually caused by a strong conditioned fear of social situations, or else by the persistent frustration of more active attempts to adjust to them. Many timid children have histories of harsh treatment from parents, or of demands made upon them that were far beyond their capacity to fulfill. If compensatory adjustments are suppressed by severe discipline, the child has no alternative except to withdraw. This is one of the dangers of a repressive type of discipline that stamps out undesirable adjustments without providing other constructive means for the satisfaction of motives.

The withdrawing defenses are usually regarded as more perilous than the aggressive sorts. They are less likely to be detected and to receive constructive attention, since they represent quiet and orderly behavior that is not a nuisance to parents and teachers. They are also harder to modify, since the individual is less actively seeking an adjustment. The most common serious mental disorder, dementia praecox, is also characterized by extreme withdrawing. While this may be due in some degree to physiological factors, patients suffering from dementia praecox often have a long history of prior seclusiveness.

Negativism.—Withdrawing that is very vigorous and strongly emotionally toned is called *negativism*. It is shown by stubbornness, rebellion, refusal, and a negative kind of response to any social suggestion. The concept of negativism has three applications. It is an almost normal form of behavior in young children, an inadequate adjustment in older children and adults, and a symptom found in some psychotic states. Very young children, especially from about two to three years of age, show spells of negativism rather frequently. Children of this age have limited means for asserting themselves, but can gain their point and attract attention by unreasonable refusals. Negativism is related to temper tantrums and is a rage-like form of behavior. Under desirable conditions of habit formation this phase passes. If training circumstances are unfortunate, a negative attitude may persist into the adolescent or adult periods as an inadequate response to social frustration.

Some persons with serious mental disorders also show negativism, refusing to comply with routine, refusing to eat, or doing the opposite of whatever they are commanded to do. This has the same significance as childhood negativism, for it is a means of personal expression under conditions that limit the range of other assertive behavior.

Phantasy.—Phantasy, or daydreaming, is an adjustive mechanism that almost everyone uses to some extent. To imagine the attainment of satisfactions that are not obtained in real life is an easy and available form of adjustment. Since such a large proportion of people daydream, this outlet must be considered normal. In one questionnaire study of college students, 98 per cent admitted that they had daydreamed recently. The most common types of normal phantasy represent the most frequently thwarted of common ambitions. Daydreams of possessing physical strength or attractiveness, of having money and possessions, of being successful vocationally, and of securing a desired partner of the opposite sex, are among the most common phantasies of young people.

An individual who is withdrawn and seclusive usually daydreams immoderately, since this is the one positive means of substitute adjustment that requires no social participation. Excessive daydreaming is not conducive to good adjustment, since a person will not try to make overt adjustments when his needs are satisfied imaginatively. Many fanciful delusions of the mentally disordered are very similar to normal daydreams, being in no way more unreal or wishful. An important difference is that the normal person recognizes his daydreams as not real, while the phantasies of the abnormal person may be accepted as facts.

HYSTERIA

Conversion Hysteria.—Among the psychoneuroses, one of the most common and yet one of the most severe disorders is hysteria. Hysteria is not a clearly defined single maladjustment, but rather is a name traditionally applied to a large group of conditions. These are related by one common characteristic found in the personalities of individuals who show hysterical symptoms. The hysteric is said to be *dissociated*, unintegrated, or lacking in unity of behavior. This is a difficult concept which will be made more clear by subsequent illustrations.

The most frequent form of hysteria is called *conversion hysteria*, the name having arisen from a now discarded theory that the individual "converted" his mental conflict into a physical symptom. This type of disorder simulates various evidences of physiological illness, such as paralyses, pains, or anaesthesias (loss of sensation). Untrained observers, and most of all the patient himself, believe that these symptoms are physiological, but there is conclusive evidence of their psychological origin. The symptoms are usually local ones and involve a limited part of the body such as a paralyzed leg, a sore throat, or numbness of the hand. They conform to the conception of hysteria as a disorder of dissociation. A man with a hysterically paralyzed arm, for example, quite literally "does not let his left hand know what his right hand is doing." The paralyzed member is shut off or dissociated from his total adjustive reaction. In more severe classes of hysteria such as *somnambulisms, fugues,* and *multiple personality,* whole segments of experience are dissociated from the rest of the individual's thought and behavior.

A Case of Hysterical Paralysis.—(Case 9.)[1] Kate F., a very attractive young girl thirteen years of age, was admitted to a hospital suffering from a partial paralysis of the left leg, extreme nervousness, and marked loss of appetite. Several months before, while she was in school, her left leg suddenly "gave way," felt numb, and had a tingling sensation of "pins and needles." She was confined to bed at first, then used crutches for a time, but made a partial recovery during the summer months. Upon starting school again in the fall, the symptoms recurred and she was brought to the hospital. Careful medical examinations indicated that there was no disease or organic disorder of the nervous system to account for her condition.

In a series of interviews with a psychologist the history leading to her attack was brought to light. After much hesitation, she tearfully related the story of a triangle situation involving her parents. Three years previous, her mother and a roomer in the home fell in love and eloped. The father and sisters found her mother, and brought her back home. Then for many nights there were violent and abusive scenes, as the father upbraided the mother, and she in turn also accused him of infidelity. Kate reacted to these scenes with crying and praying, and felt that she had lost all faith in her beloved parents. Other quarrels followed for some time, but at last the parents assumed an outward calm for the sake of the children. Kate continued to brood over the situation, however, and began to avoid the company of other children. She often stayed in during recess at school rather than face the other girls. It is notable that the leg paralysis appeared just before a recess period. In a long series of talks over many months, the psychologist made the girl tell the story of her parents' conflict over and over again. Gradually, Kate came to accept it as a misfortune that was entirely in the past and no longer a source of fear. With the assimilation of the experience, her symptoms disappeared.

The Interpretation of Hysteria.—There are two things to explain in a case of "conversion hysteria." One is the source of the disturbance or dissociation of personality, and the other is the origin of the particular symptoms shown. One common source of dissociation is the development of *inharmonious and conflicting reactions toward some situation.* This is illustrated clearly by the case of Kate F. In earlier life she had learned to love and idealize her parents; now she finds them unworthy. She continues to live with them and outwardly to respect them, but in an unanalyzed and deeply emotional manner she is disgusted, repulsed, and disillusioned. Thus she learns to divorce her overt behavior from her emotional attitudes, to think one thing and do another. This is the essence of dissociation, the development of an inconsistent and fragmentary response to a situation.

The particular symptoms of hysteria have value as defense mechanisms, and are developed as partial, though inadequate, adjustments. For example, Kate wished to avoid social contacts with her schoolmates during the recess period, and had already resorted to many excuses. The paralyzed leg provided a perfect reason for withdrawing from company, and so was adopted or "learned," the dissociated personality permitting this irrational solution. The physical disability in most cases of hysteria is *suggested* by some real but temporary physical disorder. It is probable that in Kate's case her leg "went asleep," a common phenomenon due to pressure that almost everyone experiences from time to time. Most persons take the leg "asleep" calmly, and stamp or move it until it is restored. The hysteric, however, both fears the worst and is ready to believe that the leg is really paralyzed. Also, the paralysis serves an adjustive end, so it is exaggerated and used as a defense mechanism.

The hysterical individual is entirely sincere in believing in his ailment. It is not a "pretended" or "imaginary" disability but a very real one, even though it arises from psychological causes. The individual is entirely unconscious of the source, nature, and utility of his symptom. He has hit upon it by blind trial and error, without realizing its significance. When the patient gains insight into the origin of the symptom and becomes reconciled or adjusted to the conflict that caused it, the disability usually disappears.

Other Cases of Hysteria.—Hysteria is a very common maladjustment, if the less striking cases are considered. Many a neglected housewife develops hysterical "sick headaches" that excuse her from irksome duties and elicit the sympathy of her husband and family. Hysterical vomiting is not infrequent in young children who can gain their ends by being ill. Vomiting seems very physiological, but it is only a reflex and can be conditioned to substitute stimuli. One of the commonest hysterical adjustments is the "nine o'clock headache" whereby a child may escape being sent to school, only to be quite well again when it is too late to go.

A number of cases of hysteria were precipitated by the war of 1914-1918. Facing a severe conflict between fear and "patriotism," many dissociated young men solved it by developing hysterical paralyses or blindness that excused them from active service. Disabilities that arise from industrial accidents or from automobile collisions are occasionally of hysterical nature, originating from the fear produced by the situation rather than primarily from physical injury. Since hysterical ailments can simulate almost all real illnesses, laymen cannot distinguish them reliably, and even general practicing physicians are often deceived. Experienced psychiatrists can detect most cases, either from the nature of the symptoms, the course of development, or the success of psychological treatment.

Somnambulisms and Fugues.—A more pronounced degree of dissociation than that of conversion hysteria is found in somnambulisms and fugues, which are more severe and less frequent forms of hysteria.

Somnambulism.—In somnambulism, which literally means "sleepwalking," the individual goes into a trance-like state in which he reënacts some scene that had occurred in an emotional crisis. A classic example of somnambulism is Janet's case of Irene, a twenty-year-old French girl.[2] (Case 10.) Irene's mother had died under most harrowing circumstances. For some time afterward, Irene would occasionally go into a trance-like condition in which she would reënact with great manifestations of grief the scene at her mother's death, and her own subsequent attempted suicide that she had planned but had not carried out. During the somnambulism she was entirely oblivious of her surroundings, talking with her mother as if she were present, and ignoring anyone else. Between attacks, on the other hand, she showed no grief about her mother and went about her ordinary business normally. She had entirely dissociated her mother's death from the rest of her experience, reserving it for the hysterical episodes.

Fugue.—A *fugue* is a prolonged somnambulism during which a person forgets his identity, and often travels to a different place. After some time the individual usually "comes to himself," does not know where he is, and remembers his past life but not the period of the fugue. The fugue, therefore, is a temporal segment of his experience that is almost entirely dissociated from the rest of his life. The chief symptom of a fugue is termed *amnesia,* which means a loss of memory. This disorder is not especially rare, and cases of it are reported in the newspapers from time to time. The "amnesia victim" is found wandering in the streets, and regains his former character gradually after he has been identified and restored to his family. A fugue is usually precipitated by an intense emotional crisis, toward which it has two adjustive functions. First, the individual spares himself from harrowing thoughts by forgetting all of his past, and second, his flight is a withdrawal from the stimuli that stir up his emotion.

Multiple Personality.—The most extreme form of hysterical dissociation is found in *multiple personality,* a disorder that is an exaggerated, alternating, and long-continued fugue. One case citation will make this condition more clear than many paragraphs of description.

A Case of Multiple Personality.—(Case 11.)[3] Mrs. X had shown severe hysterical symptoms throughout childhood. She had fainting spells, somnambulistic episodes, and hysterical pains and paralyses. At times her arm would hurt, again she had a stiff leg, and on one occasion she could not walk for two months. She was in constant conflict with her father, who punished her severely. Largely to escape an unhappy home she married a young man who was disapproved by her parents. Her husband was exacting, however, and she soon was weighted down with the domestic responsibilities of a baby. It was to escape these burdens that the first secondary personality appeared.

The secondary personality, which the psychiatrist named "Susie," was a mischievous and irresponsible childlike character. At times Mrs. X was a normal mother, at other times for hours or days she was "Susie," neglecting her housework for play or for wandering about the streets. Her infant died of neglect during one of these periods. "Susie" was unknown to the normal Mrs. X (amnesia), but "Susie" wrote notes in which Mrs. X was referred to as "she." "Susie" never spoke and was almost entirely insensitive to pain. Later, this patient developed two other secondary personalities. One, called "Jack" was a masculine character into which she would pass occasionally. At one time she was "the Baby," acting for several weeks as if she were an infant about one year of age. It is interesting to note that this patient became quite normal several years later, partly through psychiatric treatment, and partly because of her removal to a remote mining town where her responsibilities and conflicts were minimized.

PHOBIAS AND COMPULSIONS

Phobias.—A phobia is an irrational and unaccountable fear of some definite situation. The stimuli that may evoke phobias in various persons are almost unlimited. One person fears the dark, another is thrown into a panic by crowds, while others fear animals, high places, small enclosed places, running water, eyes, and a host of other things. Phobias vary greatly in intensity, ranging from a mild uneasiness in the presence of the stimulus, to a severe and continued panic that disorganizes the individual's entire adjustive conduct. The milder cases are very common, and instances of them can be found in almost every classroom group. Phobias, along with compulsions, obsessions, feelings of doubt and unreality, and some similar symptoms, are classified traditionally as *psychasthenia*, in the general group of the psychoneuroses.

A Case of Phobia.—(Case 12.) One of the classical cases of phobia was reported by Dr. W. H. R. Rivers, a British psychiatrist.[4] The patient was a young physician who had suffered throughout his life from an intense fear of enclosed places (a "claustrophobia"). He was in anguish when in a small room with the door closed, and was unable to attend the theatre, since the exits seemed to be blocked by crowds of people. During the war he displayed a fear of dugouts, and preferred to be in an open trench under fire. Only then did he realize that his fear was abnormal. It was unaccountable to him, and he could remember no experience that might have caused it.

Dr. Rivers instructed the young man in how to recall memories of his earlier life that might be related to the phobia. After a number of attempts he recalled a significant incident that had occurred when he was four years old. He had found a piece of junk and had taken it to a junk merchant. After finishing this transaction, he returned through a dark narrow passage only to find the door to the street shut. A dog in the passageway began to growl, and the child became terror stricken and frantic in his attempts to get out. He had not recalled the incident during the interval, but the phobia had resulted, and he had terror dreams of being confined. After the memory of the experience was restored and assimilated, the phobia and dreams disappeared.

The Origins of Phobias.—Some of the principal characteristics of phobias can be enumerated. First, phobias often originate in an intensely fearful experience in childhood. Many cases have been traced to such a source, while in other instances this origin may be suspected even when it cannot be proved definitely. Second, the critical experience is peculiarly forgotten in spite of its great influence on behavior. The memory for the incident is said to be "repressed." Third, when the incident has been recalled by the aid of the psychologist's techniques, and when the individual has adjusted to it, the phobia disappears. Fourth, most sufferers from severe phobias show other maladjustments, frequently being subject to "nervousness," anxiety, stammering, bad dreams, and other symptoms. This was true of Rivers' case, although it was not cited in the brief description above.

The easiest thing to explain about a phobia is the source of the particular fear for a certain stimulus. It is a conditioned fear reaction, learned by association. If an individual fears dogs, or high places, or the dark, it is because a strong fear was provoked at the same time that the substitute stimulus occurred. This is true in most cases of simple phobia. In a few cases, however, a double learning process occurs so that the feared thing is a secondary rather than a primary conditioned stimulus. For example, a person may be conditioned to fear death, and may transfer this to an apparent fear of the dark, because "death" and "darkness" have become associated in his thinking.

The most significant elements in a phobia, however, are not the conditioning experiences, but the underlying personality traits, and the fact of "repression." If a fear experience is remembered clearly, it is usually overcome in time. On the other hand, rather trivial conditionings have resulted in phobias if the original experience cannot be recalled. This significant phenomenon will be investigated later. Also, a person who is generally well adjusted rarely develops a serious phobia. Apparently, the same factors in the formation of habits of personality that cause repression and phobia are also responsible for other evidences of inadequate adjustment.

Compulsions and Obsessions.—A *compulsion* is a strong impulse to perform some irrational act, often repeatedly. Persons who suffer from compulsions realize that their behavior is absurd, yet they cannot curb the impulse. Compulsions often accompany phobias, and have a similar psychological significance. A young woman who had a fear that something was behind her, also displayed a compulsion to make a thorough inspection of the room from time to time, although she realized that there was no one present.[5] The compulsion thus had an adjustive effect; it reduced the fear reaction of the phobia. Other compulsions usually are either reductive of phobias, or else the substitute for a phobia. They resemble phobias in their histories and in the means by which they may be cured.

An *obsession* is a recurring thought that the individual cannot prevent, even though he knows it to be silly, meaningless, or useless. For example, one girl who had a phobia for eyes also was obsessed with the phrase "fear looking out of her eyes," which kept running through her thoughts. A man was obsessed with the number 13. He was always looking for this number, and even counted the letters in words and phrases to see if there were thirteen of them.[6] This obsession was traced to a sexual conflict. In earlier life he had an affair with a superstitious young woman who was afraid of the number thirteen. He was very ashamed of this episode and had repressed a direct memory of it, but the obsession with "thirteen" acted as a substitute for his preoccupation, and as a distraction that kept him from recognizing the real source of his anxiety. Obsession has its counterpart in normal life, as do almost all abnormal symptoms. "A tune running in one's head," is a familiar obsession that happens to almost everyone.

Repression and Adjustment.—Repression is the most generally interesting psychological phenomenon found in phobias, compulsions and obsessions. To ordinary common sense it is inconceivable that an experience that exerts so profound an influence on an individual's life could be "forgotten." There is ample evidence, however, that repression does occur. The case histories of persons who suffer from phobias offer clear indications of its presence. More fundamentally, a large number of experiments with normal people show that there is a general tendency to forget experiences that are fearful or shameful. If this occurs in the ordinary unpleasantnesses of normal life, it is even more likely to happen in the intense cases that result in abnormalities of behavior.

Repression is interpreted most satisfactorily as a form of *inhibitory adjustment*. There are many other examples of how people may adjust by *not doing* (inhibiting) some act that would have unpleasant results. A person may adjust to a social rebuff by withdrawing from company, that is, by inhibiting his normal tendency to seek companionship. People tend to avoid the places or situations in which shameful experiences have occurred. Similarly, an individual may adjust to a painful event in his past by inhibiting any recall of the affair. Recall is an act, a response to a stimulus, and is just as susceptible to inhibition as any muscular activity. There is evidence that repression is usually incomplete at first. Soon after a fearful or shameful act has happened, it can be recalled without great difficulty. With practice the individual becomes more adept at the task of "not remembering," and so finally can recall the experience only with the greatest difficulty. Repression is thus an inadequate or partial adjustment, achieved by inhibiting the recall of painful circumstances.

It is not hard to explain how a "forgotten" experience can continue to cause a phobia. It is the general rule in habit formation that a reaction may be retained long after an individual has forgotten the situation in which it was learned. We all know "$2 \times 2 = 4$," but how many can remember the occasion on which it was learned? This phenomenon is even more likely to occur in the case of phobias, since fear reactions are largely autonomic and are not easily controlled or inhibited, while the more cortical memory reactions are subject to inhibition more readily.

Repression causes a phobia to persist because it prevents the most available method of reëducation from being used. To cure a child's fear of a dog he should become accustomed to that dog by repeated friendly and fearless contacts. But if he fears a dog long dead and buried, reëducation can only be achieved verbally, through talking about the former fear experience and making a new adjustment to it. For the individual to be educated to make a new adjustment to any stimulus, which is the essence of the cure of maladjustments, that stimulus must be present, either actually or in the substitute form of words and ideas. When the words or ideas are repressed reëducation is rendered more difficult or even impossible. The reinstatement of the memory permits the individual to learn a new and more adjustive response to the source of his fear. This is why the recall of the causal experience of a phobia usually results in a cure.

A tendency to repress the recall of unpleasant experiences is a general characteristic of maladjusted persons. This unfortunate habit of personality is acquired in childhood through unsympathetic treatment received from parents or other advisers. Children usually like to confess their fears and troubles. If they are often rebuffed, or if they have no one in whom to confide, some other adjustment has to be made. The habit of repressing is hit upon by some children, just as others learn to daydream, compensate, or rationalize. Since phobias occur chiefly in persons who have a habit of repression, these individuals often show other maladjustments. Intense phobias therefore are found most often in persons who are "a bit queer" in other ways as well.

Νeurasthenia, Νervousness, and Anxiety

Nonadjustive Emotional Reactions.—An individual who is unable to achieve an adjustment, either by direct means or by one of the typical substitute mechanisms, is likely to remain in a strong emotional state. Since the presence of emotion inhibits constructive and thoughtful adjusive behavior, the individual may then show *persistent nonadjustive reactions.* He repeatedly performs acts that have little or no adjustive value, stimulated by his need to make some attempt to adjustment, and by the visceral effects of his persistent emotional state. Common evidences of this condition are found in worry and nervousness, which almost all people experience from time to time.

Persistent nonadjustive emotional reactions to baffling difficulties usually result in three kinds of symptoms. First, the individual may show evidence of the *visceral* condition that accompanies all strong emotional reactions. At first this may include a quickened pulse, increased blood pressure, and other signs of the emergency state of emotion. But this heightened tonus is exhausting, and may result later in lowered blood pressure, fatigue, impaired digestion, and similar indications of depletion. Second, nonadjustive emotional states are usually accompanied by *motor* signs, including "jumpiness," irritability, and a tendency toward useless and repeated muscular movements. Third, worry or anxiety may be present, as a *verbal* reaction to the frustration. All three of these kinds of symptoms, visceral, motor, and verbal, are usually present together, but one or another of them may be unusually prominent in any particular instance.

More serious cases of persistent nonadjustive reactions are usually classified among the psychoneuroses. Three categories have been named, corresponding to the three classes of symptoms just described. *Neurasthenia* or "nervous exhaustion" is a psychoneurosis in which the visceral effects of emotion are most prominent, especially in their secondary form of depletion after chronic emotional excitation. *Nervousness* is often used to designate the predominance of diffused and useless motor behavior in a nonadjustive reaction. The verbal responses to emotion constitute worry, or in a more severe form, *anxiety neurosis.* It is not altogether satisfactory, however, to inter-

pret these psychoneuroses from an entirely psychological point of
view. Toxins, exhaustion following illnesses, glandular disturbances,
and other physiological conditions may contribute to nonadjustive
behavior. These disorders must then be examined from both the
psychological and the physiological aspects. Some cases show a preponderance of organic causes, some are almost entirely psychological,
while still others are due to a combination of the two causes in
varying degrees. Psychiatrists often have difficulty in separating the
psychological and physiological factors, and laymen should not attempt to do so.

Neurasthenia.—(Case 13.) Nancy N., a twenty-five-year-old
college graduate, showed a varied assortment of symptoms that
seemed to be chiefly of a "physical" nature. At the end of a day's
work she was utterly fatigued, and complained of vague aches and
pains. In the evening she moped in her room, lacking the energy to
do housework and the interest to read or to engage in other amusements. She had no appetite and her digestion was poor. Nancy was
"absent-minded," could not concentrate, and made an unusual number of errors in her work. Recently she had refused to consider a
more attractive position because she felt that she could not assume
the responsibility. Her physician could find no definite illness, and
said only that she was "run down."

Nancy's symptoms can be interpreted as a neurasthenic reaction.
She lives with her invalid mother who depends solely upon her for
support and care. Nancy feels hopelessly restrained by this situation.
Many of her friends are marrying, and she feels that she may never
be able to do so. An intelligent young woman of high ideals, she
refuses to shirk her responsibilities consciously, or to employ the
cruder kinds of defense mechanisms against them. She thus cannot
escape the conflict, but remains emotionally stirred up by it. The
disruptive influences of emotion on visceral processes cause her indigestion, restlessness and, indirectly, her fatigue and inertia. Although no direct solution was possible, a series of talks with a psychologist helped her to assimilate and accept her difficulties, and the
symptoms then diminished.

Neurasthenia offers an excellent example of the interrelationship between physiological and psychological factors in adjustment. In some cases a person may be at low ebb physically, and his lack of energy and stamina predisposes him to weak psychological adjustments. On the other hand, the physiological symptoms of neurasthenia may arise from entirely psychological causes. Long continued emotion is exhausting, because it is an emergency state not intended to be maintained over a period of time. If a person is fearful for a prolonged interval, he burns up his surplus nutritional energy because of his heightened metabolism. The after-effects are fatigue and weakness. In many cases these symptoms are treated most effectively by rest and medical care, even though they arose from psychological causes originally.

In some cases, neurasthenia has a slight adjustive value of a low quality. If the individual persuades himself that he is really ill, he can explain his failures on this basis and get out of irksome duties. The symptoms also gain him the sympathy, recognition and consideration that are ordinarily given to a sick person. A neurasthenic ailment thus has an adjustive function similar to that of a hysterical one.

Nervousness.—Ordinary nervousness is a very common form of maladjustment, but usually is poorly understood. The best interpretation of nervousness is to regard it as a persistent, nonadjustive emotional state, with the motor reaction symptoms predominating. The nervous person cannot relax; he constantly engages in minor meaningless movements. He squirms in his chair, fusses, fidgets, and constantly moves about. He is irritable, complaining, and likely to be quarrelsome. Small distractions, such as persistent noises, annoy him excessively, and he is too much disturbed by sudden shocks. Along with these motor symptoms a nervous person usually shows some visceral ones such as "nervous indigestion," and some verbal signs in the form of worry and indecision.

Organic factors may contribute to nervousness, but not in the way that is believed popularly. Nervousness is not due to "weak nerves," a common conception that has no scientific foundation. It is true, however, that the symptoms of nervousness can be caused by toxic conditions, such as a chronic infection of the tonsils or the appendix, or by glandular disturbances, especially by an excessive secretion of the thyroid gland. In many instances, disease is an *indirect* cause of nervousness. If a person has a painful disease, or if he fears that he may not recover, nervousness may arise as an emotional reaction to his hopeless difficulties. In such cases the organic disease is the thing that is feared, but the nervousness itself is primarily psychological.

Much nervousness has no organic basis, but represents a persistent nonadjustive reaction to unadjustable frustration. A person who is responding to a problem to which he cannot adjust has an excessive tendency to react. He is "all keyed up" to make a response, but is inhibited because he cannot discover any adequately adjustive behavior. An inhibited strong impulse tends to raise the general level of readiness to respond to other stimuli. The individual therefore "releases" his readiness, so to speak, by means of the nervous symptoms. The motor agitation of the nervous person is the most direct evidence of this. The irritable behavior shows that the person is easily aroused to fear, anger, or complaint by petty stimuli to which he would not react emotionally except for this exaggerated responsiveness. The tendency of a nervous person to jump when there is a noise and to be bothered by small distractions are further indications of this same condition.

Examples of nervousness vary greatly in intensity. Temporary nervousness in embarrassing situations is common and is soon overcome when an adjustment has been made. Persistent nervousness, however, is a habit of personality. A chronically nervous person often carries the stimuli for his maladjustment around with him as a feeling of incompetence or inferiority. Other persons have developed intense habits of wanting to carry out every act or idea immediately, and consequently are irritable and nervous when they meet the slightest obstacle. Such cases are hard to cure since they represent the end result of a lifetime of habit formation.

Worry and Anxiety.—Little need be said about the origin of worry and anxiety, except that they are the verbal equivalents of "nervousness." Just as the individual who cannot adjust to a difficulty is impelled to engage in useless motor activities, so also he is stimulated to think and talk about the frustrating situation. Worry is persistent nonadjustive *thinking,* in which the worrier goes over his troubles again and again, unable to arrive at a constructive solution. Anxiety differs from worry in being more intense and in having a more general effect on the individual's whole adjustment. A simple worry usually concerns a limited and fairly specific problem, while a person with anxiety neurosis may appear anxious in all situations.

Repression is often an accompaniment of anxiety. If a person refuses to admit to himself the real cause of his fear, he may transfer the emotional reaction to all sorts of other situations. For example, a young man was prevented from adjusting to his problems by his father, who dominated him and made all decisions for him. Inhibiting a recognition of the real cause of his fear, the boy showed a widely generalized anxiety about his health, his studies, and his social relationships. Anxiety, like many other characteristics of personality, may become habitual. A habit of worrying is formed by the repeated occurrence of this reaction in situations involving frustration, and then is more likely to appear again when another thwarting is encountered.

To relieve a state of worry, an individual should talk about his problems freely with a person in whom he has confidence. The persistent nonadjustive response may be overcome by seeking advice and assistance. Any active and constructive attempt to adjust will reduce worry, even though it is not entirely successful, because it gives the worrier a sense of having done something about his difficulties. The basic cure of worry and anxiety, of course, is the full readjustment of the individual to the situations that have baffled him.

Mental Hygiene

The aim of mental hygiene is to prevent maladjustments and mental disorders. This aim is accomplished in two general ways, by treating minor disorders before they grow more serious, and by arranging the influences acting upon individuals so that they are made capable of solving their adjustive problems adequately. The treatment of incipient maladjustments and psychoneuroses is carried out chiefly by psychiatrists or psychologists, or by clinics in which these professions work together. This practice is a part of *clinical psychology*, and is described in Chapter XV. On the other hand, the primary responsibility for preventive and positive mental hygiene lies with parents, teachers, employers, and people in general. Whenever one person has a contact with another, he may be a desirable or an unfortunate influence from the standpoint of mental hygiene.

Principles of Mental Hygiene.—The principles of mental hygiene arise from a knowledge of the nature and causes of maladjustments. The chief thesis of the psychological approach is that abnormal behavior originates from inadequate adjustments to the thwarting of a person's motives. Since everyone meets with some frustrations, the person with better mental health is the one who can make good adjustments when difficulties occur. The ability to make good adjustments comes from the habits of adjustment that the individual has acquired through his past experiences. In a limited space, it is possible to state only what some of these desirable habits are. The methods by which such habits may be trained would require several volumes, and touch the fields of child psychology, educational psychology, and psychiatry. A few of the most essential characteristics of mental health will be described.

Individual Factors in Mental Health.—The mentally healthful person has an *objective attitude* toward himself. He sees his problems rationally, and is guided by facts and circumstances rather than by wishes and desires. Because of this objectivity, the ability to "sit back and take a look at himself," he can detect defensive behavior when it is incipient. The well-adjusted individual has *insight* into his own conduct. He has learned his typical ways of behaving not by "blind trial and error," but with some perception of the relationships between ends and means. Since he "knows himself," he can assimilate his shortcomings without having to compensate or rationalize. Another important characteristic of the well-adjusted person is that he has acquired *consistent reactions* toward his problems. He does not wish and fear the same thing, but has learned harmonious and unconflicting responses to the major factors in his life. A lack of consistency in reactions leads to dissociation, one of the basic factors in maladjustment.

Social Factors in Mental Health.—Many of the most significant criteria of good adjustment pertain to the individual's social relationships. First, the well-adjusted person engages in adequate and varied *social activities*. He does not keep too much to himself, or shun the ordinary amusements that are enjoyed by his group. Maladjustments thrive on solitude, and are less often found in genuinely sociable persons. Moreover, good adjustment demands *social objectivity*, or "fair-mindedness," the ability to see the other person's reasons, to understand his conduct, and hence to compromise more effectively. It is very important for every individual to have someone in whom to *confide*. Many maladjustments are made worse because an individual has no one with whom he can discuss matters that seem shameful or fearful. Consequently he worries alone, or else succeeds in repressing the unpleasant thoughts. A thorough talk about one's troubles, with a person in whom one has great confidence, will do much to relieve worry and to prevent repression.

Any individual who is able to guide his life by these principles of mental hygiene can scarcely develop maladjustments or psychoneuroses, and will achieve good mental health.

REFERENCES

See Chapter XI, page 250, for references on abnormal psychology.

ABNORMAL PSYCHOLOGY
THE MAJOR ABNORMALITIES

By LAURANCE F. SHAFFER, *Carnegie Institute of Technology*

CHARACTERISTICS OF THE MAJOR ABNORMALITIES

The most serious mental disorders are the *psychoses,* which are so severe and so inclusive in their effects that the individual is unable to make the simplest adjustments demanded in everyday life. The psychoses are approximately equivalent to "insanity," but the latter term is a legal one and has no precise psychological definition. Most psychotic patients should be cared for in mental hospitals, although numerous cases are not in institutions.

Certain characteristic symptoms are common to the psychoses, and are found in disorders that arise from very different basic causes. These psychotic symptoms are not entirely unlike certain aspects of the behavior of normal people, but they differ strikingly in the degree of intensity with which they occur. For purposes of description, psychotic symptoms may be divided into two general classes. The first group includes the *inhibition of normal systems of behavior,* the things that the psychotic patient *does not do* that would be expected of normal people. The second group comprises the more positively *abnormal systems of behavior.* Not all of the symptoms described occur in all psychoses. Indeed, one psychosis is distinguished from another chiefly by the typical pattern of symptoms that each presents.

The Inhibition of Normal Systems of Behavior.—Many symptoms of the psychoses consist of the suspension of activities that are typical of normal persons. These are among the less spectacular characteristics, but are very important in identifying and understanding the grave mental disorders.

Disintegration.—A significant symptom common to many types of psychotic conditions may be termed *disintegration.* The disintegrated patient cannot relate his various experiences and thoughts, and cannot combine them into a consistent whole. Figuratively speaking, the reactions of such an individual have "fallen apart." He has lost the ability to perceive the connection between the real world of experience and his own desires, thoughts, and fancies. He does not discriminate, judge, or reason clearly. Especially significant is the failure of the function of self-criticism. The patient readily and uncritically accepts ideas that are out of keeping with circumstances and ordinary observation, and hence is susceptible to the development of delusions. He is prone to display emotion that is inappropriate to the present conditions, and to harbor beliefs that common sense would reject immediately.

A very pronounced degree of disintegration is *confusion*. In this state, the individual is bewildered, perplexed, and unable to perceive anything clearly. The introspective side of this condition is sometimes called *clouding of consciousness*, which means that the person has only a vague and chaotic awareness of external events.

Apathy and Withdrawal.—Another striking symptom is the tendency of many psychotic persons to withdraw from social contacts. This seems to be caused by a great *apathy*, an utter indifference, to persons and events in the environment. When such a patient is asked how he feels, the typical reply is "all right," and when asked how he likes the hospital, "it's all right." These answers are spoken with little trace of feeling, and it is evident that the patient does not care what happens to him, to others, or to the world in general.

Very apathetic patients are *inaccessible* in various degrees, that is, they cannot hold dependable communication with other persons. Sometimes psychotics appear to shut out the impressions from the environment. They do not know what is said to them because they are paying no attention. In other cases, evidence indicates that the individual can understand, but that he is inhibited from answering. An apparently inaccessible patient of this type, in a clearer moment at a later time, may give a correct account of all that has happened in his presence.

A related symptom is *retardation*, or the slowing down of all responses. The individual moves slowly, talks slowly, and may remain silent for a long time before answering a simple question. With-drawn patients also often show *stereotypy* of speech or of manner-isms. One mutters "never die, never die, never die" in a scarcely audible undertone from morning to night; another constantly paces in his room, three steps forward and three steps backward.

The extreme of withdrawing is found in the symptom of *catalepsy* or *catatonic stupor*. Patients showing this symptom are often bed-ridden and completely helpless. They hold themselves in one posture for long periods of time, are mute, and sometimes do not even make the effort to eat. In less pronounced cases, the catatonic symptoms are displayed by great retardation, absence of voluntary activity, and a tendency to retain any posture in which the individual is placed. (See Case 1, on page 182 f.)

Dementia.—When used alone, the term *dementia* does not imply a type of disorder, but refers to a symptom found in many psychoses. Dementia means the deterioration of the intellectual behavior of the individual. As a psychosis progresses, many patients become pro-gressively less competent mentally. Dementia is shown in two prin-cipal ways. First, the patient has difficulty in *remembering;* he forgets common information that he had learned in school or at his work. At the extreme he may not remember his name, the names of his parents or his children, and other things that are equally easy for normal persons to recall. Second, the demented person is usually incompetent in *learning* and in solving new problems. Even if his cooperation can be enlisted, he cannot learn skills that formerly he could have acquired with ease. Dementia seems to be permanent in many cases, that is, the lost mental competence is not regained even when other symptoms of mental disorder may have disappeared.

Disorientation.—Many psychotic individuals are disoriented, which means that they do not know time, place, or person. An in-dividual is said to be disoriented in time if he does not know the approximate date, and disoriented as to place if he does not know where he is. He is personally disoriented if he does not know who he is. In some cases disorientation is evidence of disintegration or confusion, while in other instances it may be caused by dementia.

Abnormal Systems of Behavior.—The most interesting symptoms of the psychoses are the definitely abnormal systems of behavior that are shown by psychotic patients, but not by normal people. These include hallucinations, delusions, and excessive variations in emotional tone.

Hallucinations.—A hallucination is a sensory perception in the absence of an appropriate external stimulus. A hallucinated individual reports that he sees things and persons, hears voices, or smells odors that are not actually present. Hallucinations may occur in all types of sensations. The simplest visual hallucinations consist of flashes of light or color. A little more complex are hallucinations of vague visual shapes that the patient interprets as snakes, ghosts, or unnamed beasts. Most visual hallucinations, however, concern actual objects and persons. One patient describes the pictures that he sees on the walls, where there really are none. Another sees a man and a woman following him around the hospital, and reports their appearance in considerable detail. Auditory hallucinations are probably the most common type. They range in complexity from a buzzing in the ears, through hearing a sound such as the constant ringing of church bells, to hearing human voices that scold, accuse, or curse the patient. Some patients carry on long conversations with the voices that they claim to hear. Hallucinations of touch are sometimes reported, as when a patient feels worms crawling on his skin. Another psychotic person reports that he constantly smells the odor of a skunk, which he believes to emanate from his own body. Hallucinations of sweet or bitter tastes also occur. Hallucinations are often related to the patient's delusions. An individual with delusions of persecution often reports that he sees his tormentors, and even more frequently that he hears their accusing voices.

Somewhat similar to hallucinations are the *illusions* sometimes seen by psychotics. These differ from hallucinations in having some external stimulus, which is misinterpreted. Thus a patient calls a strange physician by the name of an old friend and seems to recognize him as such. Or, an affected individual may hear voices in the sound of running water, which cease when the water is turned off.

Normal persons experience illusions too, but the illusions of the insane, like their hallucinations, are accepted as being real.

Delusions.—Delusions are abnormal, false beliefs that are cherished in spite of their manifest absurdity and in the face of contrary evidence. Delusions shade gradually into the "crank" opinions held by some apparently normal people. It is difficult to draw an exact line between the tenets of the parlor statesman who knows just how to save the country, and the overt delusions of the mentally disordered. The delusions of the psychotic vary greatly in consistency and elaboration. *Systematic delusions* may be detailed and apparently plausible, requiring careful checking to discover their falsity. At the opposite extreme, some delusions are very *unsystematized,* being transparently false, internally incoherent, and variable from time to time. Psychotic delusions may show any degree of systematization, from great to small.

(1) *Melancholy Delusions.*—Three chief kinds of delusions are usually distinguished, in terms of the general attitude accompanying the false belief. An individual with *melancholy delusions* believes that he is sinful, guilty, and cast out by the world, or that he suffers from some impossible organic loss. In this group, delusions of sin or of self-accusation are most common. The patient acknowledges that he has committed the "unpardonable sin," or that he is responsible for all the misfortunes in the world. This delusion is accepted with humility, and the individual believes that he deserves any punishment that might be inflicted upon him. In other cases of melancholy delusions the individual asserts that he has no stomach, or that his legs are rotting away.

(2) *Delusions of Persecution.*—A second general type of false belief is the *delusion of persecution*, which has some similarity to the melancholy delusions, except that the individual blames his state on the conspiracy of other persons. The patient often gives an elaborate account of a great plot to poison him, to keep him in confinement, or to kill him. Prominent public figures or well-known societies frequently are accused of directing the persecution, and patients sometimes have detailed plans to defend themselves from

the oppression. In recent times, many patients have harbored delusions that electric power companies or radio stations are maliciously sending shocks through their bodies. Many years ago the devil was most often accused of torturing the deluded; now it is the radio. Thus delusions keep pace with scientific progress.

(3) *Delusions of Grandeur.*—The third general class consists of *delusions of grandeur.* The patient in this condition believes that he has great wealth or power, or that he is some great person. Most grandiose delusions are less well systematized and less plausible than are typical persecutory delusions. An occasional patient consistently will act out the part that he is a king in exile, or a great inventor who has been robbed, but most delusions of grandeur are shallow, changeable, and not well integrated. They are more likely to occur in the later stages of a disorder after some dementia has set in.

There is some relationship between the three chief classes of delusions, and a succession of delusions is often found in the same patient, first melancholy, then persecutory, and finally grandiose. This sequence has a psychological significance. First, the patient feels very distressed, and develops melancholy beliefs. Then to explain why he is so miserable, he blames his apparent misfortune on others, developing delusions of persecution. This is very similar to the "rationalization" process found in normal people. Finally, to explain why he should be singled out for persecution, the delusions of grandeur appear.

Excessive Emotional Changes.—One large class of psychosis is characterized by extreme emotional reactions which may be either positive or negative. Severe *depression* is a term that explains itself. The individual seems to suffer greatly, his outlook is very pessimistic, and he is in the depths of despair. This condition is usually accompanied by a slowing down of all reactions. Often the depressed patient attempts suicide, since life holds nothing for him. Morbid depression differs from the despondency that might be shown by a normal person in having no logical cause sufficient for the response shown. As in the case of all other symptoms, depression may exist in various degrees, from small to great.

The opposite of depression is called *euphoria* ("good-feeling") or elation. The patient in this state is excessively happy without knowing why. He is optimistic and jocular, and nothing bothers or worries him. Laughing, loud talking, and heightened motor activity frequently accompany euphoria. Thinking is likely to be very quick but superficial, resulting in *flight of ideas*. A state of euphoria and overactivity together is called an excited or *manic* condition, which may exist in any degree.

Another emotional excess found occasionally in psychotic persons is *morbid anger* or irritability. A patient may be quarrelsome or irascible persistently, or he may show great outbursts of furor for short periods of time, often unprovoked by any sufficient external circumstance. These are accompanied with a great show of muscular activity and strength. Patients in extreme manic excitement or morbid anger satisfy the popular conception of a "madman." It should be noted that few psychotics have these spectacular outbursts. The great majority of patients are quite tractable, and offer few difficulties of control.

THE CLASSIFICATION OF THE PSYCHOSES

For a number of years it has been customary to classify severe mental disorders into two large groups, the *organic psychoses* and the *functional psychoses*. The organic disorders have fairly well-known physiological causes, including conditions due to old age, hardening of the arteries of the brain, syphilis of the nervous system, alcoholism, brain injury, epilepsy, and a large number of other organic factors each of which contributes relatively few cases. The so-called functional psychoses were believed at one time to be entirely psychological in origin. Although this conception is being broken down, the group still presents a useful classification for descriptive purposes. It consists of schizophrenia (dementia praecox), manic-depressive psychosis, and paranoia. In spite of the classification of the two groups, it is incorrect to suppose that the neurophysiological approach is applicable only to the organic psychoses, and the psychological point of view pertinent solely to the functional disorders. There are organic factors in both classes, but these are more definitely known for the "organic" group. Psychological causes also play a part in determining the symptoms of both categories.

The various psychoses are not equally common, for more cases exist of some than of others. An approximate tabulation of the "first admissions" to mental hospitals during 1934 may be of some service in giving the picture of the relative frequency of the disorders.

Organic group (total)		40%
Senile and arteriosclerotic	18%	
Paresis	8%	
Alcoholic	5%	
Other organic conditions	9%	
Functional group (total)		45%
Schizophrenia (dementia praecox)	19%	
Manic-depressive	15%	
Paranoia	2%	
Other functional conditions	9%	
Without psychosis		15%
Total		100%

The "other functional conditions" of the table refer chiefly to severe psychoneuroses of the kinds described in the preceding chapter. Of the mental hospital patients "without psychosis," the largest single group are alcohol and drug addicts who, while not yet mentally disordered, are receiving treatment in such an institution.

ORGANIC PSYCHOSES

Senile and Arteriosclerotic Psychoses.—In old age, malnutrition of the brain frequently causes changes in conduct, and especially an impairment of the intellectual functions. In many cases this is complicated by arteriosclerosis (artery-hardening) of the brain.

Senile Dementia.—Unmixed senile dementia presents a simple picture that is just what the name implies, a deterioration of intellect in old age. In a number of very elderly persons the sense organs, skin, glands, and hair show the changes characteristic of senility. The brain undergoes the same type of degeneration also. It loses weight, the convolutions become shrunken, and many nerve cells degenerate. The mental symptoms develop gradually. The usual first signs are failures of immediate memory. The senile individual cannot remember persons recently met, although he may still recall childhood events in great detail. In a further stage of dementia, even long-learned things may be lost, and the individual is unable to tell his name, his age, or his former occupation. The deterioration of memory may be irregular in some instances. For example, one old patient was not sure of his own name, but could remember the names of two teachers with whom he studied as a child. Senile dements often die of concurrent diseases such as pneumonia, or else lapse into unconsciousness and succumb quietly to sheer old age. None recover.

While many senile dements are contented and cheerful, others show behavior that makes them hard to live with. Some become irritable, selfish, and quarrelsome, which probably are reactions to their inability to do things for themselves. Occasional delusions occur, in which the patient may believe that his family is trying to poison him or to defraud him. These delusions usually develop in persons who have been suspicious and distrustful in earlier years. The disintegration of senility releases and intensifies the habits of distorted thinking that have been formed during an entire lifetime.

Senile dementia rarely is found in persons younger than sixty years. One study found the average age of onset to be 74. Some persons are senile at sixty while others live quite unaffected into the nineties. This variation is due to the same factors that determine physical old age, such as constitution, diseases, nutrition, and the nature of the individual's life work. There is some evidence that alcoholism and certain infectious diseases hasten senility.

Cerebral Arteriosclerosis.—The hardening of the arteries of the brain progresses with the hardening of other arteries, and is often found in old age. This seriously affects the nutrition of the brain and results in an intensification of the symptoms of senile dementia. High blood pressure together with hardened arteries may result in the bursting of cerebral blood vessels, which causes local damage to the brain. A sudden rupture of a cerebral blood vessel is *apoplexy,* commonly called "a stroke." The individual is unconscious for a time, and subsequently has a motor impairment such as a paralysis of one side of the body. Apoplexy is frequently associated with senile dementia.

Alcoholic Psychoses.—Excessive indulgence in alcohol causes several types of mental disorder.

Intoxication.—Common drunkenness is itself a psychosis although fortunately a temporary one. The mildly intoxicated person becomes genial and happy (euphoria), and shows some excitement and flight of ideas. With more alcohol he may display an irrational exaggeration of his normal personality trends, becoming loud, aggressive, suspicious, boastful, or sad. Normal inhibitions of conduct are weakened, the individual remembers poorly, and finally lapses into a stupor. This condition would be regarded as a serious mental disorder except for the speed with which persons recover from it.

Intoxication often functions as a defense mechanism against an individual's maladjustments. When under the influence of alcohol, a person forgets his troubles, and escapes from an awareness of his conflicts and frustrations. This explains many persistent tendencies toward alcoholism. A permanent cure of alcoholic excesses seldom is achieved by physiological measures alone. It is necessary also to treat the psychological maladjustments that made the man take to drink.

Drunkenness is a not infrequent expression of an already existing mental disorder of some other type. If a mental patient has been drinking when his symptoms develop, it does not always mean that his psychosis is of alcoholic origin. Instead, the alcohol may be only an incidental or contributing factor.

Chronic Alcoholism.—Continued alcoholism causes changes in the nervous system as well as in other organs of the body. The behavior symptoms include tremors, loss of memory, and some degree of dementia. The chronic alcoholic has a poverty of ideas, his judgment is poor, and he does not reason clearly. Emotionally, he is likely to be indifferent to the opinions and feelings of others, but irritable and impulsive when his own acts meet with interference.

Delusions sometimes develop in deteriorated chronic alcoholics, just as they do in other persons whose rational appreciation of reality has been impaired from any cause. Delusions of self-accusation and of unworthiness are common, the origin of which is apparent. Other frequent delusions are that the patient's wife is unfaithful to him, or that his family are persecuting him. These seem to arise from "projection." Feeling that he is unfaithful to his family, the alcoholic defends himself by believing instead that they are unfaithful to him.

Since alcoholic dementia is due to an organic deterioration of the brain cells, the outcome is unfavorable. Treatment can check the disorder from developing further, but cannot restore what has been lost.

Acute Alcoholic Psychoses.—A chronic alcoholic may have acute psychotic episodes, precipitated either by an intense or prolonged spree or by some accident or illness that lowers his vitality. There are several varieties of these outbursts. One of the best known is *delirium tremens,* a very acute condition of short duration. The most prominent mental symptoms are an extremely fearful and agitated emotional tone, and visual hallucinations of a terrifying nature. Fantastic animals such as snakes, rats, and lions are often seen, or else hideous leering faces. These hallucinations are sometimes accompanied by delusions of persecution. The patient trembles, is restless and excited, and cannot sleep. After a course of three to ten days, the outcome of delirium tremens is either recovery or death.

A slightly different acute condition is *alcoholic hallucinosis.* The hallucinations are characteristically auditory and consist of accusing, threatening, or insulting voices. There is less clouding of consciousness than in delirium tremens, but the duration of the disorder is longer. It occurs only in chronic alcoholics. A particularly interesting disorder, *Korsakow's psychosis,* is usually associated with alcoholism, although it arises fundamentally from another cause. Recent studies indicate that it is due to a deficiency of vitamin B, which chronic alcoholics often have because they neglect their normal diets. In addition to agitation and anxiety, the patient has a striking loss of memory. To fill the gaps that he cannot remember, he "romances" about supposed experiences. A patient who has been in a hospital for days, for example, will give an account of a play that he saw on the preceding evening, or of a conversation that he had with friends.

Other Drug Psychoses.—Prolonged addiction to morphine, heroin, hashish and other habit-forming drugs results in mental deterioration that may amount to a psychosis. The withdrawal of the drug produces acute symptoms of anxiety, agitation, prostration, and sometimes delusions and hallucinations.

Paresis.—Paresis, which is also known by the names of "general paralysis of the insane" and "dementia paralytica," is the principal psychosis caused by syphilis. Its diagnosis depends upon physiological evidence as well as on the development of the characteristic symptoms. A Wassermann test is made of the spinal fluid of the suspected patient which, if positive, indicates a syphilitic infection of the nervous system. Although all paresis is caused by syphilis, only about three per cent of syphilitic individuals develop this psychosis. To explain this fact theories have been advanced that paresis develops from a special strain of the syphilis germ, that it is precipitated by accidents, alcoholism, etc., or that persons vary in their susceptibility. The last theory has the most to commend it. For example, no case of paresis ever has been reported among the American Indians, although many of them have syphilis. A case of paresis has been cited (Case 8 on page 195 f.).

The Development of Paresis.—Paresis typically begins in middle life, ten to twenty years after the initial infection with syphilis, and has a long course of development. In the first or *preliminary* period the first changes noted are in mood, judgment, and character. Because of failing memory and judgment the individual may make blunders in business, sometimes losing much money. His moods are irregular, and he may be foolishly optimistic at one time and deeply depressed at another. Paretics in the early stage frequently show a loss of inhibitions, and engage in alcoholic and sexual excesses. Often these are regarded as character faults, and the nature of the disorder is not recognized. Disturbances of reflexes also occur at this time, but these are not detected unless the person is examined by a physician.

The second or *fully developed* phase of paresis develops gradually from the first stage. The symptoms are now unmistakably abnormal. The patient usually develops a stumbling, incoordinated manner of walking. His voice is thick because of an inability to control the muscles used in speech. Seizures or "fits" sometimes occur. Mentally, he shows an increasing dementia and often is disoriented. At this stage several types of paresis may be classified. The simple demented type merely deteriorates. The "expansive" type develops unsystematized delusions of grandeur. Such a patient is happy, talkative, and tells silly stories of his great power, wealth, or virility. The "depressed" type has melancholy delusions, believing that his inner organs are wasting away, or that he is being punished for sin. The expansive or grandiose delusions seem to be most frequent.

In the third or *terminal* stage of paresis, if effective treatment has not arrested the disorder, the patient is in constant tremor, emaciated, helpless, and paralyzed. His delusions disappear in utter dementia, and the termination is fatal.

The Treatment of Paresis.—The ordinary remedies for primary syphilis are ineffective for paresis, but in 1917 it was discovered that a prolonged fever would often leave a paretic patient in an improved state. The fever treatment, which is now standard, is administered in two ways. The patient may be innoculated with malaria, a disease that produces fever and can be controlled. High-frequency electrical devices also may be used to raise the body temperature. With these treatments the disorder often can be arrested in the earlier stages and the symptoms lessened in severity. Many patients are improved enough to be discharged from hospitals, although complete cures are not common.

Juvenile Paresis.—Juvenile paresis develops in some children who have congenital syphilis. Its symptoms are motor incoordination, intellectual deterioration, and sometimes queer, impulsive behavior. It is not treated as successfully as adult paresis and is almost invariably fatal.

Epilepsy.—Epilepsy is not precisely a psychosis but is a serious disorder that probably has an organic basis. The typical sign of epilepsy is the fit or *seizure,* which is an episode having considerable uniformity from case to case. Before a seizure the epileptic has preliminary signs, which consist of flashes of light, subjective sounds, or moments of nausea. The seizure proper begins when the patient becomes rigid, falls, and loses consciousness. After some seconds, convulsions begin as rhythmic contractions and relaxations of the muscles. Saliva foam is whipped up by the movements of the mouth, and the tongue may be bitten during the convulsive jaw movements. A typical seizure lasts a few minutes, after which the patient remains unconscious for a time, although relaxed. Following a seizure, the individual is usually fatigued and depressed.

Epileptic seizures have a great range of intensity and frequency. In mild forms the seizure may appear only as a shudder and a momentary lapse of consciousness. The number of seizures may vary from a few in a lifetime to several in a day. Extreme conditions of "epileptic insanity" show delirium, confusion, and great excitement. This state develops in some epileptics, who may then become patients in mental hospitals.

The causes of epilepsy are probably organic, but they are not known with certainty. Studies of particular groups of epileptics have suggested that brain injuries at birth, intracranial pressure, deficiency of the parathyroid glands, and faulty nutrition of the brain are causes. Probably epilepsy has no one cause, but several that lead to approximately the same end result. It cannot be cured dependably, but can often be aided by medication, diet, and the avoidance of undue emotional excitement.

THE "FUNCTIONAL" PSYCHOSES

Manic-Depressive Psychosis.—Manic-depressive psychosis has been called the disorder of emotional extremes. The affected person is either in the *manic* or excited condition or else is *depressed* and retarded. Up to about fifty years ago these states were classed as two separate psychoses, but they have much in common. The first point of similarity is that both mania and depression affect the emotional tone and the activity level of the individual, although in opposite directions. Intellectual functions are not disturbed seriously in either condition, and little or no permanent dementia results. The second reason for grouping the two together is that they often occur in the same person. An individual may show a deep depression at one time, and then, perhaps a year or two later, have an attack of a maniacal type. This characteristic alternation may take a number of forms. Several attacks of mania or of depression may be separated by intervals of normality. Or, a patient may change from a depressed to a manic condition or vice versa without any appreciable period of normality between. Many individuals, however, have only one attack of one form, without subsequent recurrences. Manic-depressive psychosis is typical of middle life, the greatest number of first admissions to hospitals from this cause being in the decade from forty to fifty years. Recovery from a single attack is comparatively rapid, and about 65 per cent of cases recover within one year of the onset of the trouble. A case of manic-depressive psychosis has been described. (Case 4 on page 183 f.)

Manic State.—No one else in the world seems as happy as a mild case of mania. The individual is joyous, optimistic, and smiling. He is also accelerated in all activities, moves quickly, talks rapidly, and even thinks with more than ordinary speed. Irritability and anger are shown only if he is prevented from carrying out his wishes. The individual's attention is flighty, however, and he talks and acts at random, thereby easily betraying his abnormality. In "acute mania" these symptoms are exaggerated. A patient in this condition moves constantly, shouts, sings, and may be very destructive of clothing and furniture. Since he sleeps little, an acute case of mania may wear himself out physically from the continued exertion. The patient may be disoriented and confused temporarily, but often shows a surprising degree of insight into his condition. Delusions of persecution or grandeur of a fleeting sort are sometimes seen, but they are not common among patients of this class.

Depressed State.—The depressive psychosis is the opposite of the manic condition in all essentials. The individual is grief-stricken, sad, and depressed. Retardation of speech and movement is also typical. The patient talks in a low, plaintive voice, and very slowly. Often some time will elapse before a question will be answered. Most mildly depressed patients are oriented and understand that they are not normal. The greatest danger to depressed persons is that of suicide. Many are committed to hospitals after having threatened or attempted to kill themselves, and it is suspected that a large number of actual suicides are motivated by this condition. Some depressed patients have delusions of sin and unworthiness or of incurable disease, but the majority are not deluded.

Theories of Manic-Depressive Psychosis.—The causes of manic-depressive psychosis are not well agreed upon. Both physiological and psychological theories have been advanced to account for it. Some cases may be due to *glandular disorders,* especially those of the thyroid gland which regulates metabolism and hence determines the level of activity. Selected cases of depression have been treated successfully with glandular preparations, yet this method has proved not to be a cure-all. *Focal infections* such as those in teeth or tonsils possibly account for a number of cases. In a greater number of instances than chance would allow, a manic-depressive patient has suffered recently from typhoid fever, scarlet fever, or fevers following childbirth. These *infectious diseases* may be a predisposing factor, but the evidence is inconclusive as yet. *Heredity* is often mentioned as a cause of insanity, and especially of the manic-depressive psychosis. This is not proved, however, since the statistics used are known to be faulty in many respects.

The psychological theories rest upon the observation that manic-depressive patients usually show a certain "type" of personality before the critical attack, and that normal persons also vary with respect to this trait. The *cyclothymic* personality is subject to ups and downs of mood, is unstable in emotional reactions, and tends to be too elated by success and too depressed by difficulties. A "cyclothymic" person has not learned how to compromise, but sees all situations either as entirely good or entirely bad. This trait may be the result of certain processes of habit formation in infancy and childhood, which later serve as a predisposition toward the psychosis.

Neither the physiological nor the psychological theories of manic-depressive psychosis are very satisfactory, and it is hoped that future research will reveal a more adequate explanation.

Involution Melancholia.—One variety of depressive psychosis that is sometimes classified apart from the manic-depressive group is *involution melancholia.* It occurs at the involution period or climacteric, the time of life at which the sex glands cease to function in persons of either sex. The symptoms include irritability, depression, anxiety, delusions of sin or of persecution, and frequent attempts to commit suicide. The patient is more agitated than in simple depression.

This disorder illustrates clearly the interlocking of physiological and psychological factors. The glandular causes are apparent, and cases treated with gland extracts usually improve. But psychological factors contribute also. A woman in middle life sees that her children are grown and no longer require her care; a man sees the time ahead when he can no longer pursue his work. These are depressing situations, as is felt by almost all normal people who pass through them. It is not surprising, therefore, that the combined glandular and adjustive causes should coincide in some instances with enough severity to produce a psychosis.

Paranoid Conditions.—The nature of delusions, which are an important factor in many mental disorders, may be investigated most successfully in connection with the psychoses in which they are the chief symptom. Some years ago the term *paranoia* was applied to all disorders characterized by systematized delusions, but this diagnosis now is limited to the infrequent cases in which the delusions are the *only* consequential symptom. Pure cases of paranoia have systematic delusions, but show no dementia, disorientation, confusion, or excessive emotion. It is probable that most paranoics are not in mental hospitals, for the very reason that they are normal in everything except the delusion. Several varieties have been designated by special names. *Religious paranoia* consists of a belief that the individual is divinely inspired to found a new religious practice. Many religious paranoics attract followers and establish cults of more or less consequence. *Inventive paranoics* believe that they have made great discoveries, and *litigious paranoics* engage in endless lawsuits. Underlying these conditions in varying degrees are the fundamental delusions of persecution or of grandeur.

"True" paranoia is not as common as some similar psychotic states that are called *paranoid* (paranoia-like) conditions. Paranoid schizophrenia, the other symptoms of which are described in the next section, is quite prevalent. A case of this sort will be cited.

A Paranoid Case.—(Case 14.) Gregory E. was a college senior when he developed his delusions. He had always been a quiet, studious boy, although not of the highest intelligence. In spite of the fact that he was a good athlete, he had few friends, kept to himself, and was inclined to be suspicious of others. He was excelled both in studies and athletics by his brother, to such an extent that his college career had been disappointing. Although previously in good health, he began to complain of feeling ill. Eventually he disclosed a belief that his illness was caused by poisoning. He thought that the men of the fraternities, of which he had not become a member, were poisoning his meals. They stood behind him in restaurants, he said, and made secret signs to the waiters to put poison in his food. To escape his tormentors he fled to a distant city, where his queer behavior attracted attention, resulting in his commitment. Later, in the mental hospital, he developed delusions of grandeur. He claimed that he was the greatest athlete of all time, and was imprisoned and poisoned because the fraternities would not permit such eminence to a non-fraternity man.

The Development of Delusions.—The development of Gregory's delusions offers an excellent opportunity to investigate the process psychologically. First, there is a long-standing *habit of distorted thinking* by which he is suspicious of other people, and blames them for his own shortcomings. This is an adjustment mechanism, hit upon by trial and error, and retained because it is satisfying. Thus he has been *learning to be a paranoid* for a long period of time. Second, the precipitating factor appears. He feels *ill*, just generally physically ill and miserable, and also somewhat *confused* in his thinking. There is reason to believe that this factor may be physiological. But why should he, who has been in robust health, feel ill? In keeping with his long-established habit of blaming others, the thought of poison occurs to him. Perhaps this idea is rejected at first, but it is such a satisfying explanation that he finally accepts it. This is aided by the growing state of confusion. The delusion of *persecution* is now formed. He retains enough rationality, however, to ponder on *why* he was persecuted. This is solved by the thought that *great people are always persecuted. If* he were the greatest athlete of all time, people naturally would be jealous of him. This idea is pondered for weeks until the "if" becomes accepted as a fact, and the ideas of *grandeur* complete the delusional system.

Delusions, therefore, occur because they are adjustments. They permit the individual to reach an understanding that is personally satisfying to him. The same process operates in the formation of the unproved beliefs of normal people. The paranoid state is an exaggeration of the normal process, under conditions of disintegration.

Schizophrenia (Dementia Praecox).—The most prevalent of all psychoses is known by the alternative names of *schizophrenia* and *dementia praecox,* the former being preferred. These names refer to two important symptoms of the psychosis. Schizophrenia literally means "split-mind," a separation or disharmony among the various aspects of personality. Dementia praecox, "precocious deterioration," signifies the intellectual retardation that appears in many cases, though not in all. This dementia is "precocious" in that it occurs earlier in life, as distinguished from senile dementia. In fact, dementia praecox is a psychosis of youth. Although some cases occur at all ages from five to seventy, the greatest number have their onset in the decade from twenty to thirty.

Cases of schizophrenia have a number of common characteristics. The outstanding symptom is emotional *apathy*. The schizophrenic is indifferent to events that stir feeling in a normal person. He does not care about his friends, family, or business. He also neglects his person, and is slovenly and dirty. Schizophrenics show the symptom of *disintegration* in striking degree. They laugh when there is no cause, but may show no emotion when there is a sufficient reason for it. Their reactions are quite divorced from the real world of experiences. *Delusions* and *hallucinations* occur in most instances. More than half of the patients in this class show *dementia*, the symptom that gave the disorder its earlier name.

Within the general frame of schizophrenia four special types are usually described. These have the common symptoms in varying degrees, and also other particular symptoms. Not all schizophrenic patients can be classified definitely in one of the four types, since there are intermediate and mixed cases.

Simple Schizophrenia.—A few cases of dementia praecox show apathy, indifference, deterioration, and no other striking symptoms. These constitute the "simple" form of the disorder. The onset is usually gradual, and the changes may not be noticed until they have progressed far. Typically, an adolescent or young adult becomes indifferent, listless, and devoid of any ambition. He may do more and more poorly at school or work until finally he does not bother to try at all. He sits at home and shuns the company of other persons. There is some indication that the idle time is filled with pleasant daydreams. Emotional delapidation and intellectual dementia may appear later. Only a few of the hospitalized cases are classed as "simple" schizophrenia, but these statistics are unreliable, as many such persons may be cared for at home, while others may become tramps and vagrants.

Hebephrenic Schizophrenia.—The word *hebephrenic* means "child-minded," but this term does not give an accurate description of the type that it names. The hebephrenic classification is the broadest among the types of schizophrenia and a considerable variety of patients are so designated. The classical hebephrenic type is distinguished by a more *sudden onset* than the others, and by *greater disintegration.* The chief characteristics are *silliness* of attitude, and *incoherence* of speech and behavior. *Hallucinations* are common, but delusions are shallow and changeable. A case of this type will be cited.

(Case 15.) Helene W., nineteen years old, finished the ninth grade two years ago after an undistinguished school career, and henceforth remained at home. The first symptoms were noticed about six months ago. She would quarrel with her mother, and then go to stay with a married sister. After a few days she would become angry with the sister and return home again. Gradually her family noticed a foolish trend in her conversation. On several occasions she screamed in the night, saying that a man was under her bed. At other times she acted as though she were being chased by someone, which may be evidence of hallucinations. Finally she took to crying and jabbering constantly, and threatened to kill her father and herself. She was then committed to a mental hospital. Examination at the hospital showed that she was completely disoriented. She gave irrelevant answers to questions about school subjects and common information. She has a few scattered delusions of being chased by men, and calls the physicians by the names of former acquaintances. She is overactive and very destructive, tearing her clothing and dishevelling the furniture in her room. She lies on the floor and rolls over and over, striking herself lightly with her hand while doing so. Frequently she laughs for minutes, but at other times she screams or cries. She makes foolish grimaces and mannerisms, and it is impossible to carry on a connected conversation with her. This girl shows many of the typical symptoms of a newly developed case of "hebephrenic" dementia praecox.

Catatonic Schizophrenia.—The *catatonic* type has two varieties, catatonic stupor and the rather misnamed catatonic "excitement." The distinguishing feature is *stereotypy,* that is, the persistence either of a posture or of a type of movement. The onset is like other classes of dementia praecox but is often more gradual, requiring several years to develop fully. A rather typical case of catatonic stupor follows. Another case has been described before. (Case 1 on page 182 f.)

(Case 16.) Daniel E., a well-educated young man, developed a psychosis at the age of thirty-one. For ten years before this time he had been increasingly "nervous" and "absent-minded." He would start for a visit, and then forget his destination. At times he mistook strangers for acquaintances, and often seemed unable to understand what was said to him. A few weeks before commitment he left his job, became despondent, and showed an almost complete lapse of memory. He had no sense of responsibility but depended entirely on his wife and others to tell him every little act that he should perform. He bought poison, but never actually attempted suicide. He had no delusions, although he once said without any evidence of emotion that his mother-in-law was poisoning him. In the hospital he took no interest in his surroundings, stayed in bed most of the time, did not attend to his personal needs, and had to be aroused for his meals. He varied greatly from day to day, however, and on one occasion talked enough to demonstrate a good memory for past and recent events. Gradually he became worse. He did not speak for several months, but sat bent over in a chair looking at the floor for hours at a time. He showed "waxy flexibility," retaining for a long period any posture in which he was placed. About one year after admission he was given the metrazol treatment, which is described in the next section. He grew more lucid, answered questions, said that he felt better, and appeared almost normal at times. His behavior, however, was still apathetic and lacking in interest. Characteristically, he remembered many things that had happened while he was mute and apparently inaccessible.

So-called catatonic "excitement" sometimes alternates with the stuporous form. It is active in motor behavior, but devoid of emotion or feeling. A catatonic patient will sometimes throw articles of furniture about, attack other persons, or cry out loudly. More common than these extreme outbreaks are stereotyped movements. The individual will pace up and down for hours, or will execute repeatedly a fantastic series of gestures. Although active instead of stuporous, such patients are very withdrawn. Their behavior is automatic and not responsive to the environment, hence it is appropriate to include them in the catatonic group.

Paranoid Schizophrenia.—The delusional form of schizophrenia is the most common, and the least likely to recover under ordinary conditions of hospitalization. The symptoms include disintegration, apathy, withdrawing, and often dementia, as well as the characteristic delusions. This condition has been described in the preceding section, with illustrative cases. (Case 14 on page 243, and Case 3 on page 183.)

Interpretations of the "Functional" Psychoses.—For many years the functional psychoses have been difficult to understand, and the various explanations commonly offered have been unsatisfactory to critical thinkers. Very recently, however, a number of discoveries concerning the treatment of the functional psychoses have led to a new approach that promises to provide a reasonably satisfactory interpretation.

Physiological Evidence.—Since 1937, a number of new physiological treatments for the functional psychoses have yielded promising results. Although a diversity of methods have been used, it is significant that they all act upon the same fundamental characteristic, the *metabolism of the brain.* The earliest of these treatments is that given by means of *narcotics.* A sleep-producing drug, such as sodium amytal, is administered to put the patient into a deep state of unconsciousness, which is continued for hours and repeated at frequent intervals. After coming out of the influence of the drug, the patient is often improved mentally. From 22 to 60 per cent of cures of various functional psychoses have been reported by experimenters who used this method. The sodium amytal is known to dilate the cerebral blood vessels and to decrease the oxygen and sugar "uptake" of the brain tissues. Another treatment has made use of *oxygen deprivation.* The patient is made to breathe a mixture of oxygen and carbon dioxide, or of oxygen and nitrogen. The oxygen content is gradually decreased until the patient becomes unconscious; then he is revived by increased oxygen. Marked improvement has followed this treatment, especially in cases of catatonic schizophrenia, but the gain has proved to be temporary in most instances.

Another treatment that has received wide trial uses is *insulin,* the hormone that regulates the concentration of blood sugar. The patient is given large doses of insulin, which reduce the sugar content of the blood until he becomes unconscious. This treatment is repeated at intervals, and has resulted in a large proportion of cures in some selected groups. More recently *metrazol,* a drug related to camphor, has been used similarly. The injection of metrazol produces almost immediate unconsciousness, and brings about convulsions like those of an epileptic seizure which last for several minutes. Ten to twenty such treatments are given at the rate of two or three per week, after which psychotic patients often show marked improvement in rationality and accessibility. Case 16, described on page 246, was so treated. Both insulin and metrazol treatments affect brain metabolism. Insulin starves it for sugar, and metrazol decreases its assimilation of oxygen. After this temporary deprivation, a "rebound" seems to occur, resulting in an increased metabolic rate with consequent improvement. As yet, no way has been devised to stimulate the metabolism of the brain directly without first starving it. Such a method, if discovered, would be very promising.

It is significant that cases both of schizophrenia and of manic-depressive psychosis have been benefited by these treatments. This confirms the long-standing suspicion that there is no hard and fast boundary between these two psychoses. In general, the largest number of cures have been secured with early cases. Thus one experimenter who used metrazol reported 85 per cent cures of schizophrenics who had been ill less than six months, but no cures in cases of over three-years standing. It is probable that the permanent damage to the brain shown by the dementia of the older cases prevents a satisfactory cure.

Psychological Evidence.—The physiological evidence just cited does not exclude the importance of psychological factors in the functional psychoses. In many cases that have been studied in sufficient detail, the origins of personality trends and of delusions have been found in the life histories of the patients. The particular conflicts and frustrations that the individual encounters determine the nature of his inadequate adjustments. Delusions are false thinking, an exaggeration of the normal tendency to rationalize and to excuse one's self. Therefore they can be explained only in terms of thinking mechanisms, that is, psychologically.

Many of the research workers who have investigated the physiological treatments also have emphasized the importance of concurrent psychological treatment. The treatments by insulin, metrazol, and other drugs render the patient lucid, accessible, and able to talk sensibly about his troubles. The other essential part of the treatment utilizes this increased clarity to help the patient understand the sources of his abnormal reactions, and try to make more effective adjustments.

Psychological treatment or *psychotherapy* is carried out by means of interviews. The patient talks about his life history, his attitudes and his frustrations, under the guidance of the psychiatrist. Gradually he develops insight into the psychological causes of his abnormality, is no longer so sensitive to his frustrations, and so is prepared to attempt new means of adjustment. Evidence shows that the new physiological treatments give rise to many more cures when they are accompanied by psychotherapy than when they are given alone.

Concluding Orientation.—By combining the physiological and psychological evidences, a fairly satisfactory tentative hypothesis concerning the functional psychoses may be suggested. The "inhibition symptoms" such as disintegration, apathy, disorientation and dementia probably are due to physiological causes, such as inadequate nutrition of the neurones of the cerebral cortex. On the other hand, the more positive indications of abnormality, including hallucinations, delusions, and excessive variations in emotional tone, seem to arise from the individual's experiences, habits, and frustrations. It might be said that *who* will become psychotic depends chiefly on physiological conditions, whereas *when* the individual will break down and *what* symptoms he will show are psychological matters. These two factors, however, are interrelated. A person with relatively little physiological disturbance would develop a psychosis only if he experienced a very great psychological conflict, while one who was badly predisposed physiologically would become upset by a relatively milder adjustive frustration. In all cases, both physiological and psychological approaches are essential to an understanding of the functional psychoses.

REFERENCES

Bagby, E. *The Psychology of Personality*. New York: Henry Holt and Company, 1928.

Bentley, M., and Cowdry, E. V. *The Problem of Mental Disorder*. New York: McGraw-Hill Book Company, Inc., 1934.

Conklin, E. S. *Principles of Abnormal Psychology*, Revised Edition. New York: Henry Holt and Company, 1935.

Dorcus, R. M., and Shaffer, G. W. *Textbook of Abnormal Psychology*. Baltimore: Williams and Wilkins Company, 1934.

Fisher, V. E. *An Introduction to Abnormal Psychology*, Revised Edition. New York: The Macmillan Company, 1937.

Landis, C., and Page, J. D. *Modern Society and Mental Disease*. New York: Farrar and Rinehart, Inc., 1938.

Morgan, J. J. B. *The Psychology of Abnormal People*, Revised Edition. New York: Longmans, Green and Company, 1936.

Moss, F. A., and Hunt, T. *Foundations of Abnormal Psychology*. New York: Prentice-Hall, Inc., 1932.

Rosanoff, A. J. *Manual of Psychiatry and Mental Hygiene*, Seventh Edition. New York: John Wiley and Sons, Inc., 1938.

Shaffer, L. F. *The Psychology of Adjustment*. Boston: Houghton Mifflin Company, 1936.

CHAPTER XII

THE NATURE OF INDIVIDUAL DIFFERENCES

By ANNE ANASTASI, *Queens College, New York*

Differential psychology in its broadest sense is concerned with all of the differences in behavior among individuals and among groups. Its fundamental aim is similar to that of all psychology, namely, the understanding of behavior. Differential psychology approaches this problem through a comparative analysis of behavior under varying environmental and biological conditions. By relating the observed differences in behavior to other known concomitant phenomena, it may be possible to tease out the relative contributions of different factors to behavioral development. If we can determine why one person acts differently from another, we shall know what makes people react as they do.

SCOPE OF DIFFERENTIAL PSYCHOLOGY

Individual variation is a universal phenomenon throughout the organic scale. Superficial and inadequate observation often creates an impression of similarity and even identity among the members of a group while the differences pass unnoticed. "All cats look gray at night" but upon closer inspection each becomes an individual in his own right. Every psychological investigation in which more than one subject was employed has revealed wide individual differences.

From the lowest form of life to man, no two individuals react alike when presented with the same objective situation. Thus in experiments on conditioning,[1] the number of trials required to establish the conditioned reaction ranged from 79 to 284 in a group of 82 protozoa; from 34 to 1112 in a group of 14 crustacea; from 3 to 35 in a group of 59 fish; from 30 to 40 in a group of 13 pigeons; and from 3 to 17 in a group of 11 sheep. Equally wide differences were observed in a series of learning projects[2] in which small samplings of guinea pigs, albino rats, common short-haired cats, and monkeys of two species were tested with the same type of problem

box containing a series of steps of increasing difficulty. The range
of trials required by each group to learn step I was as follows: 16
guinea pigs, 53 to 407; 24 albino rats, 30 to 453; 62 cats, 9 to 136; 17
rhesus monkeys, 19 to 310; 6 cebus monkeys, 42 to 327.

Within the human species, individual differences have long been
recognized. Many of our basic social institutions, and in fact the
patterns of societies themselves, are largely colored by the fact that
individuals differ from each other. In our everyday activities, we
are constantly adjusting ourselves to individual differences among
our associates. Certain broad biological or cultural groupings, such
as age, sex, racial, or national groupings, also play an important part
in social interaction. Such group distinctions have frequently been
made the basis of social institutions and attitudes, to the almost complete exclusion of any consideration of individuals. It is a further
aim of differential psychology to inquire into the nature and origin
of any behavioral differences which may exist among these major
groups.

Heredity and Environment

Basic Mechanisms.—The causes of individual variation are to
be sought in the individual's heredity and in the environmental conditions to which he has been exposed. Every trait or reaction of the
individual depends both on his heredity and on his environment.
Traits and activities cannot be classified into those which are inherited and those which are acquired. The problem resolves itself
into a determination of the relative contribution of hereditary and
environmental factors in the development of the individual. To what
extent can the development of any given characteristic be altered by
the control of environmental influences, and to what extent is such
modification limited by hereditary conditions? Individual variations
found under similar hereditary conditions may be attributed to the
operation of different environmental factors. Similarly, when the
environments are sufficiently alike, any dissimilarity in behavior may
be attributed to differing heredity.

The understanding of the mechanism of heredity has been greatly
furthered by the concept of the *gene*. The individual begins life at
conception with the union of one germ cell from each parent, the

ovum of the female and the spermatozoön of the male. Each of these cells contains hundreds of thousands of very minute particles, called genes. A gene is the carrier of a "unit character," that is, a hereditary factor or influence which always operates as a unit or in an all-or-none fashion. These unit characters of the geneticists are not to be confused with psychological traits, but are of a much more elementary nature. Thus even such a relatively simple characteristic as eye color depends upon the combined influence of a very large number of separate genes. Such complex hereditary determination would of course produce varying degrees of a trait, even though the individual genes may be characterized only by presence or absence. It is obvious that any attempt to identify psychological characteristics, and especially such a manifold and ill-defined phenomenon as "intelligence," with unit characters is entirely inconsistent with the concepts and data of genetics.

The hereditary basis of *individual differences* is to be found in the almost unlimited variety of possible gene combinations, especially in the case of such a complex organism as man. It is not surprising that duplicate individuals are not produced by chance, when we consider, first, the extremely large number of genes; secondly, the variation in gene pattern among the individual germ cells of a single parent; and thirdly, the union of germ cells from two parents in the production of any one individual. The only exception to this individual diversity of gene constitution is that of *identical twins,* who develop from the union of a single ovum and spermatozoön. Such twins are always of the same sex and identical in appearance. *Fraternal twins,* on the other hand, do not reveal such close resemblance and may be either of the same or opposite sex. The hereditary similarity of fraternal twins is no greater than that of ordinary siblings,* since they result from the simultaneous development of two fertilized ova.

There is a popular belief that inheritance is indicated only by resemblance to parents or immediate ancestors. This is shown to be false by a consideration of the mechanism of inheritance. The germ plasm is not produced by the individual parents, but is transmitted

---

* "Siblings" is a general term employed to cover both brothers and sisters.

by them to their offspring. Hence the individual inherits from all of his direct ancestors, and not from his parents only. Some characteristics which may have been latent for many generations may become dominant because of a particular combination of genes, and the result will be an individual very unlike his parents in some one respect. Instances of this sort are not uncommon in family histories.

Another popular misconception is that the influence of heredity ceases at birth and that of environment does not begin until after birth. Both parts of this statement are false. Hereditary factors may influence the development of the individual throughout the life span and their manifestation may be delayed until a relatively late age. Similarly, environmental influences operate from the moment of conception and are not limited to any phase of the life cycle. Thus the importance of temperature, chemical, and other types of stimulation in the prenatal surroundings of the developing embryo is rapidly coming to be recognized.

A further source of confusion is to be found in the common habit of speaking about functions and activities as being inherited. Heredity can exert a direct control only over the development of *structures*. In so far as a given activity involves the presence of certain structures, such as vocal organs, hands, glands, nervous system, the hereditary factors underlying the development of these structures will influence activity. Likewise, the nature and degree of development of organs will affect their functions. But this is only a *limiting condition* imposed upon the development of a given type of behavior. Hereditary factors may prevent the appearance of a function through the absence of the necessary structures, but the converse does not hold. Within the limits set by the individual's structural characteristics, there are almost infinite possibilities for varied behavioral development.

The concept of *environment* itself requires some clarification. The popular definition of environment is a geographical or residential one. A child is said to have a "poor environment," for example, because he lives in the slums. Or his "environment" may be described as a French village, an American small town, or a British mining community. To the psychologist, this is a very inadequate designation of environment. Psychologically, environment is to be regarded as the sum total of the *stimulation* which the individual receives from conception until death. It will be noted that this is an active concept of environment. The mere physical presence of objects does not constitute environment unless the objects serve as stimuli in the experience of the individual. The definition is also a more inclusive one, covering all forms of stimulation and extending over the entire life cycle.

Experimentally Produced Variations.—In general, it may be said that the earlier an environmental condition operates in the life of the individual, the more pronounced will be its effect. After an advanced stage of growth has been attained, the organism is much less modifiable. For this reason, the stimuli to which the organism is exposed during the embryonic period exert a pronounced and lasting influence upon its future development. Variations in diet and nutrition, glandular secretion, and other conditions of the mother which affect the chemical constitution of the blood have a marked effect upon the characteristics of the embryo. The structural development of the individual is definitely influenced by such environmental factors. It is also possible that a certain amount of rudimentary learning may occur during prenatal life. The presence of certain reflexes and other simple movements in young embryos has been definitely established. Such responses may early become conditioned in various ways to changes of temperature, pressure, and other stimuli furnished by the intrauterine environment. The study of prenatal behavior opens interesting possibilities, although so far it offers only very meager information.

In the field of *structural development*, however, specific data on prenatal influences are more plentiful. In the fruit fly, for example, a defective gene causes the animal to produce "reduplicated legs," that is, certain joints of the legs, or entire legs, may be doubled. Although the inheritance of this defective gene has been definitely traced, this characteristic will not appear under certain environmental conditions.[3] If animals known to have the defective gene are kept at a sufficiently warm temperature, the additional leg or joint will not develop. Successive generations bred under these conditions will have a normal appearance. If, however, any of the offspring are allowed to develop in colder temperatures, the defect will reappear. This furnishes a definite illustration of the fact that even a clearly demonstrable "inherited defect" is actually only a tendency to develop in a given way under certain environmental conditions.

Experimentally produced "monsters" furnish very striking examples of the influence of prenatal environment.[4] In experiments on fish eggs, "Siamese twin" fish have been artificially produced by inhibiting or retarding the rate of development at an early age through cold, insufficient oxygen, or by the application of ultra-violet rays. In some cases, one twin is much smaller than the other and is deformed, the larger twin being perfectly normal. Two-headed monsters have been produced among tadpoles and several species of fish by the application of various chemical or mechanical stimuli. Striking variations in the number and position of the eyes of minnows have likewise been induced. If the eggs of the minnow are allowed to develop in sea water to which has been added an excess of magnesium chloride, peculiar eye conditions will appear in a large majority of the embryos. Instead of the usual two eyes, many will develop a centrally placed "Cyclopean" eye; others may develop a single lateral eye to the right or left of the head, or two eyes which are abnormally close together. In the human, the influence of environmental factors upon the development of stature and weight of the body has been attested by a considerable body of data.[5]

Numerous experiments have demonstrated the possibility of pronounced alteration in *behavior* through postnatal environmental variation. Animals reared in isolation from other members of the species or from individuals of the opposite sex, or in close association with a human child, have developed curious modifications of behavior. Activities which are commonly assumed to be "unlearned" or "instinctive" have proved to be susceptible to marked changes. Thus experiments in which birds were reared in isolation or in exclusive association with birds of other species have demonstrated that, although the birds will develop some sort of song when they reach a certain stage of structural development, the specific nature of the song depends upon stimulational factors.[6] Sexual behavior has also proved to be dependent upon learning in its specific manifestations. Some form of sexual activity will occur at a definite developmental stage because of the presence of glandular secretions in the blood and other physiological factors, but the particular way in which such activity is expressed and the object towards which it is directed will vary according to environmental circumstances.[7]

A recent investigation in which a young chimpanzee was reared for a short period in a typically human environment throws further light upon the factors affecting behavioral development. The animal showed remarkable ability to develop typically human behavior in its feeding and sleeping habits, play and social behavior, response to language, reaction to clothing, and similar activities. The degree to which it proved possible to "humanize" the behavior of this ape is indeed suggestive, especially in view of the fact that the period of residence in the human environment was only 10 months, and did not begin at birth, but when the animal was $7\frac{1}{2}$ months old.[8]

Children Reared in Isolation.—Several cases are on record of human children who were brought up either in isolation or in exclusive association with lower animals. The most famous case is probably that of the "Wild Boy of Aveyron." In September, 1799, three hunters came upon a boy of 11 or 12 in a French forest. The boy was completely naked, unkempt, scarred, unable to talk, and seemed to have been leading a wild, animal-like existence. He finally came under the observation of the French physician, Itard, who subsequently published a detailed account of the case.[9] When found, the boy seems to have been markedly deficient in all forms of behavioral development, including the sensory, motor, intellectual, and emotional.

After five years of ingenious, painstaking, and methodical training, Itard abandoned the task, having failed to bring the boy up to normal. This has led many to conclude that the Wild Boy of Aveyron must have been an imbecile from birth, who had been abandoned by his parents because of his mental deficiency. Such a conclusion, however, overlooks several important points. In the first place, marked improvements were effected by the training, even though a normal level was not attained. For example, although the boy could not learn to articulate sounds, he succeeded in learning simple written language, being able to reproduce written words from memory and to use them to express his wants, as well as to understand their use by others.   Secondly, had the boy been feebleminded because of a basic structurally imposed deficiency, he should probably have been unable to survive in the very trying circumstances of his primitive environment. Finally, the fact that the training was begun so late in life may furnish an adequate explanation of its lack of success. Subsequent educational efforts are inadequate to undo the effects of prolonged earlier nurture.

The more recently discovered "wolf children" of India represent a similar case. These were two girls, aged about two to four and eight to nine, respectively, who were found living in a cave with wolves in a sparsely settled region in India and were subsequently adopted by a local missionary who attempted to train them.[10] Mention should also be made of the celebrated case of Kaspar Hauser about whom so much has been written. Some accounts suggest that this boy was an heir to some princely house and was put out of the way by political enemies. He was apparently confined from early childhood in a dark cell not large enough for him to stand upright. When he awoke he was accustomed to find bread and water, but he never saw the person who brought them and had no knowledge of the existence of other human beings. He lived under these conditions up to the age of about 17, when he was released.[11]

In all of these cases, the child's behavior when first brought into a civilized human community was very unlike that of "normal" children. Sensory acuity, posture, locomotion, language, emotional expression, reactions to other human beings, and other forms of behavior which are generally regarded as more or less "fixed" by the individual's constitution were found to be markedly altered in these children. The implications of these observations have been very aptly summarized by Stratton [12] as follows:

> "Lack of association with adults during a certain critical period of early childhood, it seems likely, produces in some or all normal children marks like those of congenital defect. The evidence seems against the romantic view that a civilized community is a chief

obstacle to the development of personality. On the contrary, the higher forms of personality become possible only in and through such a community. By our biological endowment alone, or by this as developed by maturing and learning in an infrahuman environment, we remain man-beasts. We become human only by active intercourse in a society of those who already have become human."

Isolated Communities.—The study of children reared in relatively isolated communities, in which educational and cultural facilities are very limited, presents in a milder form the same situation encountered in the cases of the "wild children" described above. These investigations have ordinarily dealt with fairly large groups and have employed standardized tests and better controlled observations than the case studies reported in the preceding section. In one investigation conducted in England, the Stanford-Binet Intelligence Examination was administered to 76 canal-boat children and 82 gypsy children.[13] Both groups had very limited schooling, the canal-boat children attending school on only about 5 per cent of the total number of school days, and the gypsy children on about 35 per cent. The home surroundings were also intellectually very inferior, the canalboat children leading a more isolated existence, with fewer social contacts than the gypsy children.

In both groups, the results indicate very vividly the influence of schooling and home environment upon intelligence as measured by current tests. The average IQ of the canal-boat children was 69.6, that of the gypsy children 74.5. This difference is in keeping with the better school attendance and greater opportunity for social contacts of the gypsy children. It will be noted that both group averages are well below the "normal" IQ of 100. Taken at face value, these averages would suggest at best a borderline group, with a few distinctly feebleminded individuals. Further analysis, however, brings out the influence of the restricted educational facilities. Thus a marked tendency was found for the older children to obtain lower IQ's than the younger. The correlation between age and IQ was —.755 among the canal-boat children and —.430 among the gypsy children.

Such a finding is quite contrary to the data on growth of intelligence under ordinary conditions, which show that the IQ tends to remain quite constant throughout life. The discrepancy can only be explained in terms of specific environmental influence. The intellectual environment of the younger canal-boat or gypsy children is not so far below normal as that of their older brothers and sisters. The younger child in any home is exposed to relatively simple intellectual stimulation; as he grows older, differences in schooling and in the cultural level of the home become more apparent. The above explanation is corroborated by a comparison of siblings *within the same family* in both the canal-boat and gypsy groups. Such a comparison revealed a fairly consistent drop in IQ from the youngest to the oldest children within each family, the IQ's of the youngest children falling within the normal range.

Similar results have been obtained in a number of studies on children living in isolated, backward mountain communities and rural districts in the United States.[14] In such studies, scores on performance tests, which are less dependent upon schooling, tend to be higher than scores on the more highly verbal type of tests. All tests, however, show a marked and consistent age decrement. Thus in one investigation, the average IQ on the Pintner-Paterson Performance Scale dropped from 91 at ages 6-8 to 75 at ages 14-16; in the Goodenough test of Drawing a Man, it dropped from 80 to 49. In another study, the median IQ on the Myers Mental Measure, dropped from 83.5 at age 7 to 60.6 at age 15. Commenting upon this age decrement which is commonly found in such communities, the authors of one of these studies write:[15]

> "An estimate of intelligence is based on the information the child has been able to obtain. In the mountain environment increments of information become less large with increases in age, and the seven-year-old has relatively more chance to gather information than the 12-year-old in the same environment."

Family Resemblances.—It is a common belief that family resemblances in psychological traits are entirely attributable to heredity. The study of family likeness has traditionally been the hereditarian's favorite source of data. It is not uncommon to hear a child described as having his father's business acumen, his aunt's musical talent.

"taking after" his grandfather in obstinacy, and perhaps inheriting a keen sense of humor from an Irish grandmother on his father's side! The successful son of an eminent family attributes his accomplishments to the fact that he is "well-born." A lecturer's vigor and zeal are explained by his coming from "pioneer stock." A boy's ingenuity with mechanical toys is regarded as being "only natural" when one finds that he is descended from a "long line" of boat builders and inventors.

Nor is this type of interpretation limited to popular and everyday discussions. Many otherwise accurate and well-conducted scientific investigations on family resemblances contain the same logical fallacy, that is, they ignore the fact that close relatives generally *live together*. The environment of individuals within a single home is certainly more similar than that of persons picked at random. The closer the hereditary relationship, furthermore, the greater the environmental proximity. Thus parents and children, and brothers and sisters usually live in the same home, whereas more distant relatives, such as uncles and nephews, or cousins, come into less frequent contact. Related individuals also constitute in part each other's environment and may be rendered more alike by this mutual interaction. Thus it appears that a hierarchy of family resemblances could be produced by environment alone, which would coincide with that actually observed.

The two major methods employed in the study of family resemblances and differences are *family history* and *correlation*. The former has been applied chiefly by eugenists. Genealogies are traced and elaborate pedigree charts drawn up for families which are outstanding either for their talents or their deficiencies. This method was launched by Sir Francis Galton in his book on *Hereditary Genius*,[16] in which he reported data on 997 eminent men in a total of 300 families. Similar studies subsequently conducted in different countries have all yielded essentially the same results.[17] All show that eminence tends to run in families. Similarly, the investigations on degenerate and feebleminded families, the best known of which are probably the Jukes[18] and the Kallikaks,[19] show that such characteristics as mental deficiency, crime, and pauperism tend also to run in families. To argue from such results to heredity, however, is quite unjustifiable. The operation of environmental influences in each case is too obvious to overlook.

Investigations by the correlation method have revealed a hierarchy of family resemblances in mental-test performance.[20] Identical twins show the closest resemblance, the correlations between their scores often being in the neighborhood of .90. The next highest correlations are found between fraternal twins. Sibling correlations are lower, and parent-child correlations the lowest of the family relationships which have been investigated. The correlations vary somewhat with the nature of the test and the age of the subjects. It is interesting to note that the correlation between fraternal twins is quite generally higher than that between siblings, although the hereditary similarity is no closer in the latter than in the former.

Special Family Relationships.—Investigations on foster children and on identical twins reared apart suggest the degree to which ordinary family resemblances may have resulted from environmental similarity. *Foster children* show a rise in IQ after adoption into a foster home, this rise being greater the younger the child and the higher the socio-economic level of the home. The resemblance between siblings living in different foster homes, furthermore, is much less than that ordinarily found between siblings in the same home. Thus in one group of 125 pairs of siblings, each adopted into a different foster home and separated for a period of 4 to 13 years, the sibling correlation in Stanford-Binet IQ was only .25, in contrast to the correlation of about .50 usually found between siblings living in the same home.[21]

The study of *identical twins* who have been separated in infancy and reared apart in different foster homes yields data which are particularly crucial for the problem of heredity and environment. In a recently published investigation,[22] 19 pairs of such twins were tested and observed. The findings varied from one pair to another, but when the environments were sufficiently unlike, the twins revealed marked discrepancies in all traits, including intellectual, emotional, and even such physical characteristics as general health and bodily vigor. Naturally, when the twins were adopted into homes which offered very similar intellectual and emotional stimulation, their behavioral development was also quite similar. Mere geographical disparity does not constitute a difference in psychological environment. As an illustration of the results obtained when the environmental difference was sufficiently large to yield clear-cut results, the following case study is reported:

> Case IV: Female twins, separated at the age of 5 months and reared by relatives; 29 years old when examined. Mabel had led the life of an active farm woman on a prosperous farm. Mary had lived largely a sedentary life in a small town, clerking in a store during the day and teaching music at night. Mabel had only an elementary school education, while Mary had had a complete high school course in an excellent city school. At the time of examination, a vast difference was noted between the twins in intellectual, emotional, and physical traits. Physically, Mabel is described as robust, muscular, and in perfect health, while Mary was underweight, soft-muscled, and in poor general condition. Mabel weighed 138½ lbs., Mary only 110¾ lbs. Intellectually, an equally striking difference was found, but in favor of Mary, whose Stanford-Binet IQ was 106 as compared with Mabel's IQ of 89. Even larger differences were found on some of the other tests. Temperamentally, these twins are described as no more alike than two persons chosen at random.

TRAINING AND GROWTH

The Concept of "Mental Growth."—When the psychologist studies "mental growth," he compares the individual's performance at successive ages or, more often, he compares the performance of different individuals from each age level. The differences found in such an investigation may be properly designated age changes in mental traits. To call them "growth," however, is to make assumptions which extend far beyond the scope of the data. Attempts have been made, for example, to plot "growth curves" of mental traits, by analogy with the growth curves found in height, weight, bodily proportions as indicated by various indices, and the like. Such mental-growth curves show merely the performance of individuals at successive ages in some standard test situation.

Such a curve does not differ in any essential respect from a learning curve. In both cases the subject is tested under similar conditions at successive intervals and his progress is charted on the curve. Learning curves usually cover a shorter period of time than growth curves, although a learning experiment could conceivably extend over several years. The major difference between learning curves and growth curves, however, seems to be that in the former the subject is given special training under rigidly controlled experimental conditions, while in the latter he is left to his own resources. Thus it would seem that a mental-growth curve is at best a practice curve obtained in the absence of controlled conditions. It reflects the cumulative effects of the random training and experience of everyday life, without adding anything essentially new to the picture. It also follows from this analysis that growth curves are specific to the cultural milieu in which they are obtained. If the learning conditions differ from one group to another, the curves of "mental growth" should likewise be expected to differ.

Age Changes in Mental Traits.—If we reformulate the question of mental growth in terms of operationally defined concepts, many of the scattered findings on this problem will become more meaningful. Rather than discuss the growth of some vague, hypostatized mental function which exists over and above concrete behavior, we shall inquire into the specific age changes in behavior which occur within a given cultural milieu.

Performance on most of the common intelligence tests tends to improve until the late teens or early twenties.[23] This improvement, furthermore, continues longer among subjects in the higher educational levels. Thus high school students, for example, show a continued improvement beyond the age when such improvement ceases in individuals with only an elementary school education. Such results suggest the dependence of mental development upon schooling, as well as upon other experiential factors.

It has been frequently suggested that the curve of mental development is negatively accelerated, that is, progress is most rapid at the outset, the successive yearly increments becoming progressively smaller as the individual approaches maturity. This, however, is a difficult point to determine. In place of the more familiar negatively accelerated curve, a straight line or a positively accelerated curve may be obtained, depending upon such factors as the units in which the test scores are expressed, the difficulty of the test, and the age range and intellectual and educational level of the subjects. The question of the *form* of the mental-development curve is submerged in a tangle of technical controversy from which it is not yet possible to glean a single clearly established fact.

A question of considerable practical interest concerns *adult intelligence* and the decline of mental ability.[24] On such tests as the Army Alpha and the Otis Self-Administering Intelligence Scale, the average scores exhibit relatively minor changes in the twenties and thirties; between 30 and 50 years there are small but consistent decreases; beyond 50 the decline is more rapid and continues up to the oldest age groups tested. Several factors must be taken into account in interpreting these age changes. In the first place, the age decrement is not found uniformly in all types of tests. Thus in such tests as arithmetical reasoning, naming the opposites of words, and general information, all of which are part of intelligence scales, no decline with age was found. It should be noted, in the second place, that individual differences are large at all ages and that overlapping of different age groups is very marked, the range of scores within any one age group being much greater than the largest average difference in score between groups. In spite of the drop in average score, individual differences show no consistent tendency to decrease with advancing age.

A further point to consider is the relation of age changes to the educational level of the subject. In one investigation,[25] the subjects were classified into four groups with reference to the amount of education which they had received, as follows: (A) four years of college plus graduate or professional training; (B) one year of college or more, including the subjects in group A; (C) one to four years of high school; (D) eight grades of elementary school or less. Although all groups showed a decline in average intelligence-test score from the younger to the older age levels, this decline was smaller for the higher educational groups. These results are shown graphically in Fig. 15. It is also interesting to note that the lowest point on curve A, reached by the 70-year group, is still higher than the highest points on curves C and D. Thus a 70-year-old person who had

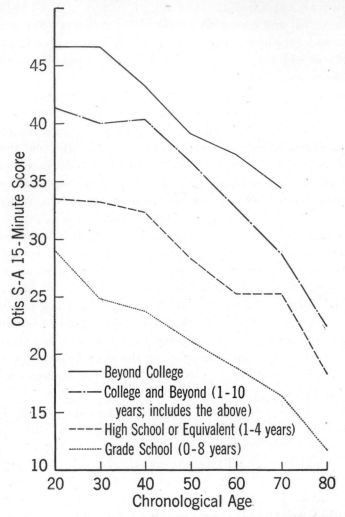

Fig. 15.—Age Changes in Intelligence Test Score at Different Educational Levels.

(From C. C. Miles and W. R. Miles, in "The Correlation of Intelligence Scores and Chronological Age from Early to Late Maturity," Amer. J. Psychol., 1932, 44, 70, by permission of W. R. Miles and Amer. J. Psychol.)

pursued at least one year of graduate work would be expected to score higher than a 20-year-old elementary or high school graduate. In extreme old age, of course, the influence of increasing structural deficiencies must also be considered.

One often hears that adults cannot *learn* as readily as young people. Learning tests administered to persons of different age levels have shown, however, that the age decrement in learning ability is very slight, one investigator [26] estimating the loss to be less than one per cent a year between the ages of 22 and 42. Studies of still older groups reveal somewhat larger drops,[27] but in every case the drop was greater in the rote learning of meaningless material than in the more meaningful and practically useful tasks. The loss was still greater in tasks which involved the breaking down of old associations. When learning material which is meaningful, useful, and interesting, the older adult can usually compensate for any slight handicap he may have by additional effort, information, and skills, and may actually surpass the younger subjects. It is also interesting to note that individual differences in learning ability tend to increase with age, in spite of the drop in average scores.

The Effect of Special Training.—It appears from various types of data which have been collected on age changes in mental traits that such changes can best be understood in terms of *training* and the subject's experimental biography. The so-called growth curve of mental development can be considered to be an extended learning curve. Similarly, the slight decrement observed in older adults may be regarded as forgetting through interference from other activities, except when complicated by the structural changes of extreme old age. Most psychological tests consist of tasks which are very similar to school work. The longer the individual has been out of school, therefore, the more chance he will have had to lose the facility in performing such tasks, which he had acquired during his period of schooling. The effect of length of schooling and occupational level upon age decrement becomes intelligible in these terms. The adult who has for many years been engaged in other activities will be less proficient in the sort of task which he himself had at one time performed in school. Those adults whose work involves material of the same sort as that found in the intelligence tests, however, may show a continuous increment with age.

Investigations on the effect of special training upon mental-test performance throw some light upon the nature of the training process itself. Contrary to popular belief, training does not consist in the improvement of any alleged underlying "capacity," but furnishes him with specific skills and techniques which will be useful to him in the performance of certain tasks. The concept of training has been unduly colored by the analogy with the strengthening of a muscle through exercise. Training in psychological functions cannot be considered in these terms.

Although most psychologists are agreed concerning the highly specific function of training, the failure to consider certain of the implications of this fact has led some to conclude that the type of behavior measured by intelligence tests is not susceptible to training. This conclusion is based upon a number of studies on the effect of specific training or coaching upon Stanford-Binet IQ, memory span, and other similar tests. The results of these studies indicate that the individual's score on such tests may be raised markedly by even a brief period of training, but the effect seems not to be permanent. In an investigation [28] with the Stanford-Binet, for example, in which a single coaching period of approximately two hours was employed, the average IQ's of coached and control groups were 100.18 and 133.09, respectively, three weeks after the coaching; but after three years, the averages of the same two groups were 96.18 and 102.82. Other training experiments which employed a similar set-up have yielded the same general results. The eventual reduction and almost complete disappearance of the effects of such training has commonly been taken to indicate that the "underlying mental capacities" measured by the tests were not affected by the training.

If we restrict ourselves to the objective facts, however, a much simpler explanation can be found for the gradual decline in the effects of such training. When the training is of brief duration and is *discontinued,* as was done in all of these experiments, we should naturally expect the improvement to fall off through forgetting. If, furthermore, children are tested in different functions at successive ages, as is done largely in the Stanford-Binet, the effects of training will not be manifested over a long period. It is futile to expect that a brief period of highly specific instruction or practice should raise the "general mental level" of a child, especially since such a mental level is itself a manifold of widely diverse and loosely interrelated functions. Training does have a very real effect, however, upon the individual's performance on specific mental tests. And this is of prime importance, since all our observations regarding the subject's psychological make-up are ultimately based upon such concrete be-havior.

The Problem of Training and Variability.—Since it has been demonstrated that training can bring about a pronounced change in mental-test performance, a further question may be raised re-garding the differential effects of such training upon individual subjects. Will such training reduce *variability,* or the extent of in-dividual differences in the group? Will the initially better individuals benefit more than the initially poorer? Will subjects tend to maintain the same relative standing in the course of training? If some of these questions are still unanswered, it is not for dearth of data, for they have been repeatedly investigated with a wide variety of ma-terials, methods, and subjects. The entire problem is so beset with technical difficulties, however, as to have been declared insoluble by some. The crux of the matter is that entirely opposite conclusions can be drawn if the results are expressed in different forms, a fact which has cast an aura of artificiality over all the data.

One of the chief controversies in this problem centers about the concept of *equal practice*. Does equal practice mean equal amount of *time* spent in training or does it mean equal amount of *work* done? With the time-limit method, the slower worker receives practice on less material than the fast worker during the training period. On the other hand, if amount of work done is held constant, then the fast worker will receive practice for a shorter period of time. In either case there is an inequality of conditions. From a practical standpoint, however, the definition in terms of equal time will prob-ably prove more serviceable, since it fits more of the situations en-countered in everyday life. When, for example, a person takes a course in music, or golf, or French conversation, he is given a specified number of lessons, each of the same duration. No adjustment is made for the fact that during that period the number of times a piano key is touched or a golf ball hit, or the number of words spoken differed widely from one individual to another. Among the other questions which have to be considered in defining the problem of practice and variability are the units in which achievement is measured—whether in terms of time required for each task or amount of work per unit of time—and the method of expressing improvement, whether in absolute gains or relative to the individual's original standing.

If, now, we redefine the problem in specific operational terms and inquire whether the absolute extent of individual differences in amount of work successfully completed during a constant time will increase or decrease after all the individuals have spent an equal amount of time in practice, a definite answer can be found in the experimental literature.[29] Investigators who have defined the problem in these specific terms have consistently found an *increase in individual differences* with continued practice. Individuals tend to maintain the same relative standing in the group in the course of practice, the initially better individuals maintaining their superiority in the group and the differences among them being even greater after the period of equal training than they were at the outset. Thus it appears that the individual's reaction to training, his ability to profit from training, is itself contingent upon the training he has received in the past and his general experiential background. The more the individual has learned in the past, the more he will be able to learn in the present. To use a rather crude analogy, we might say that practice does not add to the individual's ability but multiplies it. If one individual's past experience has made him more proficient than another in a given type of activity, he will be better fitted to profit from further instruction for that very reason.

THE PROBLEM OF CONSTITUTIONAL TYPES

Type Theories.—In the effort to simplify the problem of individual variations, a number of type classifications have been proposed from time to time. The entire range of human variation would thus be reduced to a small number of basic types, and each individual would be described as a more or less close approximation to one of these types. Such type theories date back at least to the fifth century B.C. when Hippocrates first formulated his twofold classification of mankind on the basis of physical constitution into *habitus apoplecticus* and *habitus phthisicus*. Many similar theories have been proposed since that time, and even now exponents of type psychology can be found. The terminology of type theories has become such an integral part of our everyday language that it is almost impossible for us to speak about people without reference to some such hypothetical categories.

Kretschmer's Theory.—In recent years, the type theory proposed by Kretschmer [30] has probably been the most influential in stimulating psychological research. Physically, Kretschmer classifies individuals into four groups, the pyknic, athletic, leptosome, and dysplastic. The *pyknic* type of body build is short and thick-set, with relatively large trunk and short legs, round chest, rounded shoulders, and small hands and feet. The *athletic* has a more proportionate development of trunk and limbs, well-developed bones and muscles, wide shoulders, and large hands and feet. The *leptosome* is generally characterized by small body volume in relation to height. He is tall and slender, with relatively narrow chest, long legs, elongated face, and long, narrow hands and feet. The *dysplastic* is a relatively small category in which are placed all individuals manifesting some marked abnormality of development, disproportion, glandular imbalance, or other defect.

The basic contention of Kretschmer's theory is that there exists a relationship between the body types which he describes and two fundamentally opposed "temperaments," the cycloid and the schizoid. The cycloid individual manifests personality traits which in extreme cases would be classified under the circular or manic-depressive form of insanity; the schizoid tends toward schizophrenia (dementia praecox). Kretschmer maintains that the cycloid is usually pyknic, whereas the schizoid is leptosome or, less frequently, athletic. This theory has subsequently been extended to apply to normal individuals who exhibit no personality disorder. The terms cyclothyme and schizothyme have been employed to denote these two normal types.

The former is described as social, friendly, lively, practical, and realistic; the latter is quiet and reserved, more solitary, timid, and shut-in. It will be noted that these descriptions correspond closely to the familiar classification into introvert and extrovert, first proposed by Jung.[31]

The Distribution of Psychological Traits.—Type theories have been most frequently criticized because of their attempt to classify individuals into sharply divided categories. Such a classification implies a *multi-modal distribution* of traits, that is, a distribution curve with more than one peak or mode. Thus the introverts, for example, would be expected to cluster at one end of the scale, the extroverts at the other end, and the point of demarcation between them should be clearly apparent. Actual attempts to apply such a classification, however, prove that it is very difficult to place a given individual definitely into any one category. When confronted with this difficulty, the typologists have often proposed intermediate or "mixed" types to bridge the gap between the extremes. Thus Jung suggested an ambivert type which manifests neither introvert nor extrovert tendencies to a predominant degree. Objective surveys with standardized tests, however, have shown that the ambivert category is the largest, and that the decided introverts and extroverts are relatively rare.

The same type of distribution curve has been found for any trait in which individual differences have been measured. The majority of individuals cluster in the center of the range and, as the extremes are approached, there is a gradual and continuous tapering off. The curve shows no gaps or breaks; no clearly separated classes can be discerned. The curve is also bilaterally symmetrical, that is, if it should be divided by a vertical line through the center, the two halves so obtained would be nearly identical.

In general, the larger and more representative the sampling of individuals tested, the more nearly does the distribution approach this typical, bell-shaped *"normal distribution curve."* This is illustrated in Fig. 16, which shows a composite curve for college freshmen, obtained by combining the results of 11 different intelligence examinations administered to groups of 623 to 5495 freshmen in various American colleges.[32] The theoretical normal curve is shown in broken line on the same graph. Similarly, in Fig. 17 will be found the distribution of total introversion-extroversion scores obtained with a self-rating questionnaire administered to 200 college students.[33] Similar curves have been obtained for any psychological trait which has been adequately measured in a sufficiently large and representative sampling of the population.

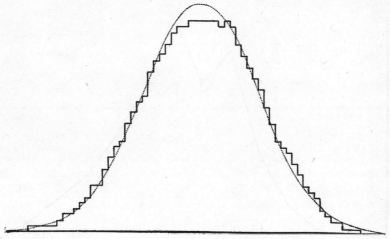

FIG. 16.—COMPOSITE CURVE FOR COLLEGE FRESHMEN, DERIVED FROM ELEVEN INTELLIGENCE-TEST SCORES.

The broken line indicates the theoretical normal curve. (From Thorndike, *et al.*, "The Measurement of Intelligence," by permission of Teachers College, Columbia University Bureau of Publications.)

The Relationship Between Mental and Physical Traits.— A further implication which underlies type theories is some form of interrelation between the individual's behavior tendencies and his physical, or structural, characteristics. Certain psychologists, realizing that any classification of individuals into clear-cut categories is untenable, have pointed out that type theories may be formulated so as to refer only to types or breeds of man which were at one time pure "biotypes." Through successive generations of interbreeding, mixed types could have been produced which now outnumber the remaining specimens of pure types. It is well known that through the mechanism of heredity, interbreeding will in the long run produce a larger number of mixed than pure individuals. This situation would thus present a normal distribution of traits, with the largest number of individuals in the center of the distribution, corresponding to the numerically largest mixed group.

When so conceived, the problem of types is reducible to a consideration of the relationship between structural and behavioral qualities. Apart from its bearing upon type theories, the study of this

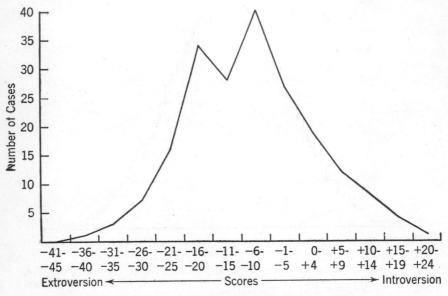

Fig. 17.—Distribution of Introversion-Extroversion Scores of 200 College Students.

(Data from Heidbreder, in "Measuring Introversion and Extroversion," by permission of Journal of Abnormal and Social Psychology, and adapted from Anastasi "Differential Psychology" by permission of the Macmillan Co.)

relationship has stimulated interest from many points of view. Among the other problems which touch upon it, may be cited the various attempts to discover physical "signs" of aptitudes, the role of the endocrine glands in behavior, the effect of sensory handicaps upon the development of mental traits, and the "explanations" of behavior in terms of the nervous system which have been essayed from time to time, not to mention the traditional mind-body problem of the philosophers.

In any discussion of the relationship between mental and physical traits, we must recognize at the outset the existence of certain abnormal conditions of the organism which have characteristic physical as well as behavioral symptoms. The cretin, the microcephalic idiot, and the paretic are good examples of this. It is unwarranted, however, to generalize from the association found in such pathological cases to a possible connection among individuals in general. To take an obvious and extreme illustration, an individual whose legs have been amputated to the knee is unable to dance; but we cannot conclude from this that length of leg is correlated with dancing ability and that those persons with longer legs will be the better dancers within a group.

If we turn to the specific investigations on the relationships between mental and physical traits within normal groups,[34] we find a variety of uncontrolled conditions which make interpretation difficult. Slight general trends in groups have often been unduly emphasized and the extensive *overlapping* of groups has been ignored. *Age* differences were sometimes present among the groups to be compared, thus producing a spurious connection between certain physical characteristics and mental level. Similarly, the factor of *social status,* which is of the utmost importance in any investigation of the relationship between mental and physical condition, has often been overlooked. The individual reared in a superior home will have richer opportunities for intellectual development and at the same time receive better physical care. He will be brought up under more sanitary conditions, will receive better medical attention, and will thus run less risk of contracting disease than the child in a city slum or remote rural district. This factor is probably responsible for what little correlation has been found between many physical conditions and mental development.

The *direct behavioral handicap* resulting from certain physical deficiencies must also be taken into account. Visual and auditory defects are among the most serious handicaps for man, in this connection. Since our culture is built to such an enormous extent upon a foundation of language, and the latter is acquired chiefly through the eye and the ear, the significance of deficiencies in these fields is apparent. Environmental stimulation is cut off by blindness or deafness. The individual who is so afflicted is psychologically "isolated" from cultural contacts in the same sense as the Wild Boy of Aveyron, the wolf children of India, or Kaspar Hauser, discussed in a preceding section. It is not surprising, therefore, to find that the average IQ of the blind is closer to 90 than to 100, and that of the deaf in the neighborhood of 80, even when they are examined with specially adapted intelligence scales.[35]

When we inquire into the relationship between hair and eye coloring, facial characteristics, head dimensions, and various cranial indices * on the one hand and intellectual and emotional traits on the other, we find consistently negative results. All investigations by psychologists in which objectively observed or tested behavioral traits have been compared with accurately measured physical characteristics yield consistently low and insignificant correlations.[36] Of special interest in connection with type theories are the various indices of *body build* which have been proposed from time to time. Among the most widely used of these are the height-weight ratio and the morphologic index. The latter is based upon an elaborate series of measurements and is computed by adding the length of one arm to the length of one leg, and dividing this sum by the trunk volume. Individuals with a high morphologic index are generally tall and slender, with relatively long limbs; those with a low morphologic index are stocky, with a relatively large trunk.

Such indices have also been found to have no significant correlation with behavioral traits. Thus in one investigation on 500 college freshmen of each sex, the correlation between height-weight ratio and intelligence-test score proved to be only .03 for the men and .04 for the women.[37] In another study, the correlation between morphologic index and intelligence-test score in a group of 434 male freshmen was .14.[38] Accurate consensus ratings of five personality traits by five judges likewise yielded either zero or low and insignificant correlations with morphologic index.[39] It appears, therefore, that the study of the relationship between mental and physical traits

---

* The best known of which is probably the cephalic index.

also yields no evidence in support of type theories. One more approach remains to be examined.

Direct Investigation of "Types."—A number of investigations have been conducted as a direct test of some specific type theory. Most of these studies have been concerned with Kretschmer's theory. This theory was originally formulated by Kretschmer on the basis of his observations on psychotic patients. In comparing the body build of schizophrenics and manic-depressives, he had consistently found a greater proportion of leptosomes among the former and pyknics among the latter. The chief difficulty in the interpretation of such results on psychotic cases is inadequate control of the age factor. Schizophrenia is more common among younger subjects, whereas older people are more susceptible to manic-depressive psychoses. It is also a well-established fact, which Kretschmer himself recognizes, that older subjects tend more toward the pyknic body build, younger subjects toward the leptosome. For this reason, it is essential that age differences be ruled out in any comparison of the body type of different psychotic groups.

In a recent investigation,[40] 130 manic-depressives and 130 schizophrenics were selected so that the two groups would be closely matched in age. In the effort to test Kretschmer's hypothesis, extensive physical measurements were taken and a number of ratios between horizontal and vertical bodily dimensions were computed. All showed an almost complete overlapping of the two psychotic groups. Not only were the averages closely similar, but the range and general form of the distribution were practically identical in the two groups.

Similar results have been obtained in investigations on normal subjects who were carefully chosen on the basis of physical measurements so as to be distinctly pyknics or leptosomes.[41] The groups thus selected have been tested with intelligence scales, personality tests, as well as a variety of more specific tests directly suggested by Kretschmer or his followers and including visual reaction time, speed of tapping and of writing, cancellation, substitution, color fusion, Rorschach ink blots, etc. In no case was the difference between the average test scores of pyknics and leptosomes significant, when other factors such as age and occupational level were held constant.

The Nature and Interrelationships of Mental Traits

Variation within the Individual.—The study of variations from trait to trait within the individual is of both practical importance and theoretical significance. When a child is classified as intellectually inferior on the basis, let us say, of Stanford-Binet IQ, there is still much that remains to be know about his mentality. Is he equally inferior in all respects or does he exhibit significant discrepancies in his mental development? Is he normal or even superior along some specific lines? Similarly, in the case of a child with a very high IQ, we may inquire in what ways he is superior. How uniformly does he excel the average child in intellectual performance? The intelligence test, furnishing a single summary figure to characterize the child's general mental level, often obscures important facts. Two individuals who obtain the same total score may present very different "mental pictures," or *psychographs,* when their performance along specific lines is analyzed.

If the individual's abilities were all more or less on a dead level, a single summary score would be quite informative. But if appreciable variation in the individual's standing in different traits is the rule, then such a score is crude at best and may at times be definitely misleading. It is therefore necessary to inquire into the extent of variation within the individual. The data on this question have been gathered from a variety of sources. Case studies are available of individuals who exhibit marked asymmetry of development along different lines. Such individuals can be found among the feebleminded and the intellectually superior, as well as among the normal. Quantitative measurements of the extent of variability from trait to trait in large random samplings have also been obtained. Finally, correlational analysis has further clarified and has introduced certain refinements into the problem of trait relationships and the identification of basic traits. Typical data obtained by these three approaches will be presented.

Case Studies of Asymmetrical Development.—Among the feebleminded, individuals are occasionally found who display an exceptional talent along some specific line. Such persons have been designated *"idiots-savants,"* a term which has been criticized for being somewhat misleading. The usual idiot-savant is neither particularly wise nor an idiot. He is not sufficiently deficient to be classified as an idiot, but frequently falls at the moron or borderline level. And he is "wise" only in a very limited field. In the practical management of his own life he is ordinarily a complete failure. He is sufficiently deficient in other respects as to be unable to capitalize his own special talent in making an adjustment to normal everyday life. Like all extreme deviations in the distribution of any trait, idiots-savants are relatively rare. Because of their unusual characteristics, however, they attract a good deal of attention and as a result, a number of fairly complete descriptive accounts are on record.

The special talent of the idiot-savant may be observed in almost every type of mental activity. Mechanical aptitude, ability in drawing and painting, a phenomenal memory, arithmetical proficiency, a special gift in music, all are represented. Two of the best known examples [42] are Gottfried Mind, known as "the cat's Raphael" because of his excellent drawings of cats, and J. H. Pullen, "the genius of Earlswood Asylum," who displayed extraordinary mechanical ingenuity coupled with talent in drawing and carving. Several cases of special musical talent have also been reported. The feats of memory and of arithmetical calculation performed by some feebleminded individuals have frequently attracted notice.

The one field from which idiots-savants seem to be conspicuously absent is that of linguistic or verbal aptitude. This fact throws some light upon our concept of general intelligence. It is gradually coming to be recognized that the latter is largely *identified* with verbal ability. Most intelligence tests consist, to a large extent, of verbal tasks. Success in the practical business of everyday life is also more closely linked to linguistic facility than to other traits. A serious deficiency in the power of verbal expression will thus brand an individual as incompetent from many points of view. Conversely, a person who is especially proficient in verbal traits may thereby compensate for deficiencies along other lines and will rarely, if ever, find his way into an institution for the feebleminded. No other single talent seems to be such a saving grace in our civilization.

Marked asymmetries of development may also be found among those classified as normal or superior on the basis of general intelligence tests. Case studies of such individuals reveal the same traits that are found in a survey of idiots-savants. Thus special aptitude in music, drawing, and mechanics may be found in persons of normal intelligence. Or conversely, marked deficiencies in these traits may be combined with superior intelligence. Numerous cases of mathematical prodigies and so-called "lightning calculators" have been investigated by psychologists. Such case studies suggest that numerical aptitude also may occur as an independent trait. Verbal ability alone cannot be differentiated from the individual's alleged "general mental level."

The Measurement of Trait Variability.—In a few investigations, attempts have been made to obtain a measure of the extent of *trait variability,* that is, the variability from trait to trait within the individual. In such studies, standardized tests were given to large groups of subjects who were not specially selected because of asymmetrical development. The same statistical techniques commonly employed to measure individual differences can also be applied to the measurement of trait differences, provided the scores on the different tests are reduced to the same units.

In one investigation, the scores obtained by 107 high school freshmen on 35 tests were analyzed from the standpoint of both trait and individual variability.[43] The tests included several subtests from intelligence scales, as well as tests of motor characteristics, perception, attention, and personality traits. After all of the scores had been converted into comparable units, the standard deviation of each individual's scores on the 35 tests was computed as a measure of trait variability, and the standard deviation of the 107 individuals in each test was computed as a measure of individual variability. From these measures it was found that the trait variability was approximately 80 per cent as large as individual variability. Although the exact figure would differ with the nature of the group employed, it is apparent that a large amount of trait variability will be found within a random, normal sampling of individuals. No tendency was found for the brighter individuals to be either more or less variable than the duller. Thus the correlation between each individual's average score on all the tests and his trait variability was only .03.

Similar results were obtained in an investigation on gifted children.[44] A group of 100 children whose IQ's ranged from 136 to 180 and averaged 149.4 were compared with a control group of 96 unselected eighth grade school children of approximately the same mental ages as the superior group. Both groups were given the Stanford Achievement Test, as well as information tests in special fields. An examination of the inter-test variations within each subject's scores revealed many differences which were large enough to be significant. By means of a specially devised statistical formula, it was possible to determine the percentage of trait differences which exceeded chance. When every possible pair of tests was compared, the percentages of such significant trait differences ranged from 13 to 37 in the gifted group, and from 13 to 40 in the control group. The average percentages are 28.89 and 27.82 for gifted and control groups, respectively.

Evidence from Correlation.—The examination of extreme examples of asymmetrical development, as well as the measurement of trait variability in random samplings, suggests that superior talents in one line may be associated with inferior abilities along other lines. It is not to be concluded, however, that compensation is the rule. Superior standing in one trait does not imply inferiority in another. We have cited only examples in which individuals with a high standing in a certain trait A make a poor showing in a second trait B. We could with equal facility find cases of individuals superior in A as well as B, or superior in A and average in B. This is just the situation indicated by a zero correlation. If various abilities are specific and mutually independent, so that an individual's standing in one tells us nothing about his relative standing in another, the correlations among them will be either zero or very low.

The evidence from correlational analysis corroborates that from case studies. Little or no correlation is found among such traits as musical, artistic, mechanical, numerical, and verbal aptitude. The correlations between tests falling within any one of these groups tend to be high; when tests from different groups are compared, however, the correlations are low and generally insignificant. Similarly, tests of all of these traits, with the exception of verbal aptitude, correlate low with most intelligence scales.

The Quest for Differentiable Mental Traits.—The lack of correlation found between intelligence-test score and a number of abilities raises the question as to what constitutes "intelligence." The original purpose of intelligence tests was to sample a large number of different abilities in order to arrive at an estimate of the subject's general level of performance. In so far as the individual's standing in specific functions varies, such a general estimate is inadequate. It is apparent, moreover, that current intelligence tests do not furnish even a satisfactory estimate of the individual's average ability, since they are overweighted with certain functions and omit others. Thus in the nonlanguage and performance tests of intelligence, spatial aptitude plays the chief part. Most paper-and-pencil tests, on the other hand, measure primarily verbal aptitude, and to a lesser degree, numerical ability.

Since the latter type of test is by far the most frequently employed, the term "intelligence" has come to be used almost synonymously with verbal ability. Mental age on the Stanford-Binet, for example, has been found to correlate as highly as .91 with performance on the vocabulary test of the scale. This finding led Terman to suggest that "a mental age based on the vocabulary scale alone would not be far wrong in a large percentage of the cases." [45]

Thus the inquiry into the relationships among mental traits discloses an even more basic problem. The question may now be reformulated to refer to the identification and nature of the traits themselves. Various theories of *"mental organization"* have been proposed, ranging all the way from a strict specificity of all mental activities, implying almost complete absence of correlation, to the presence of a single general factor underlying all mental functions. The bulk of the available evidence at present points to an intermediate view in terms of a relatively small number of *group factors*. According to such group-factor theories, there are common elements only through certain limited groups of activities, such as those included under the caption of verbal, numerical, or spatial aptitude. The correlations among tests in any one of these groups would thus be expected to be high, while those between groups of tests would be low and unreliable.

The identification of mental traits which can be differentiated from each other and which vary independently is not based solely upon correlation coefficients. More refined statistical procedures have recently been developed for the analysis of relationship within a set of test scores. These methods have become known under the name of *factor analysis*. It is possible by such techniques, not only to determine the number and location of independent factors necessary to account for the obtained relationships, but also to estimate the weight or "loading" of each factor in each of the tests.[46] All of these methods, however, are ultimately based upon relationships among correlation coefficients. They are essentially descriptive techniques, however refined, and cannot get beyond the immediately observed response to the test situation.

Recent investigations by both genetic and experimental approaches suggest that the "mental traits" or factors revealed by factor analysis cannot be regarded as fixed and immutable. Apparently such factors do not correspond to underlying psychological entities, like the "faculties" of the Scholastic philosophers. Not only do factor patterns change with age,[47] but the location and weight of the differentiable factors can be experimentally altered by the introduction of relevant experiences.[48] The data suggest that the mental activities of the individual, although tending at any one time to be organized into certain major clusters or "traits," are susceptible to considerable reorganization as the individual undergoes new experiences. Thus the role of environment is again forcefully demonstrated. The existence of innately fixed patterns of trait relationship could scarcely be expected when the individual's behavior has been found to be so profoundly influenced by experiential conditions.

REFERENCES

Anastasi, A. *Differential Psychology*. New York: The Macmillan Company, 1937.

Freeman, F. S. *Individual Differences*. New York: Henry Holt and Company, 1934.

Garrett, H. E. *Statistics in Psychology and Education*. New York: Longmans, Green and Company, 1937.

Garrett, H. E., and Schneck, M. M. R. *Psychological Tests, Methods, and Results.* New York: Harper and Brothers, 1933.

Gilliland, A. R., and Clark, E. L. *Psychology of Individual Differences.* New York: Prentice-Hall, Inc., 1939.

Guilford, J. P. *Psychometric Methods.* New York: McGraw-Hill Book Company, Inc., 1936.

Jennings, H. S. *The Biological Basis of Human Nature.* New York: W. W. Norton and Company, Inc., 1930.

Kellogg, W. N., and Kellogg, L. A. *The Ape and the Child.* New York: McGraw-Hill Book Company, Inc., 1933.

Newman, H. H., Freeman, F. N., and Holzinger, K. J. *Twins: A Study of Heredity and Environment.* Chicago: University of Chicago Press, 1937.

Paterson, D. G. *Physique and Intellect.* New York: D. Appleton-Century Company, Inc., 1930.

Pintner, R. *Intelligence Testing.* New York: Henry Holt and Company, 1931.

CHAPTER XIII

MAJOR GROUP DIFFERENCES

By ANNE ANASTASI, *Queens College, New York*

In the preceding chapter, we surveyed some of the major problems and results on individual differences, and attempted to unravel the factors and conditions which produce variation from one person to another. With this background, we may now turn to an examination of certain *groups* into which individuals are commonly classified. Such groupings have been built up through social and cultural traditions, and illustrate the general tendency to employ rigid categories and sharp divisions. Thus individuals are popularly classed into the normal and the abnormal, the genius, the feebleminded, the insane, the neurotic, etc. Psychological differences are expected, or at least sought, between the sexes or among nations and "races." A large number of similar differentiations could be made, such as that between urban and rural populations, or among groups inhabiting geographically different regions, as mountainous or flat, inland or coastal, cold or warm.

From the standpoint of psychological traits, these various groupings are arbitrary and artificial, like all rigid classifications of individuals. The multiple and complex determination of the individual's behavioral development should in itself make us skeptical about any simple system of characterizing people. Yet it is an all-too-common practice to expect an individual to be dependable, or shiftless, or dull, or excitable, or poor in mechanics, or to ascribe to him dozens of similar characteristics, simply from a knowledge that such a person is a man or a woman, or that he belongs to a particular "race" or nation.

It is partly to clarify these muddled popular notions that the empirical study of group differences ought to be undertaken. To be sure, a careful examination of the principles underlying individual variation in general should suffice to show the fallacies inherent in many popular claims regarding group differences. But when beliefs are as deep-rooted and emotionally tinged as those regarding many group relations, they are not easily dislodged. Direct evidence on the nature of group differences is more convincing than deductions from generally established principles.

From a more theoretical point of view, the analysis of group differences is a valuable adjunct to the investigation of individual differences in general. The existence of culturally diverse groups may be regarded as furnishing a natural experiment in the production of human variability. If psychological differences among groups are investigated with reference to the factors which brought them about, the understanding of individual differences will have been considerably furthered.

It is not for lack of data that confusion prevails in regard to group differences in psychological traits. The field has attracted many investigators and there is now available a sizable collection of material on such differences. But these data are usually very difficult to interpret because of the multiplicity of uncontrolled factors operating to produce each observed difference. The same set of data has frequently led to opposite conclusions in the hands of different writers. It is therefore of basic importance to analyze the special difficulties encountered in making group comparisons. These difficulties can be resolved into two essential questions: *Who* shall be compared; and *how* is the comparison to be made. Each question will be examined in turn in the two sections which follow.

PROBLEMS OF SAMPLING

Sampling Error.—In any one investigation, only a sample of the entire population is employed. For example, if the population under consideration is defined as public school children in American cities, data may be gathered on some 5000 or 6000 children in a dozen schools. From these results the investigator generalizes to the entire population. If the sampling was carefully chosen to be representative of the given population, such conclusions will not be far in error. The figures thus obtained, however, will not be identical to those which would have been secured by testing the entire population of American city public school children. Nor will results from successive samplings of the same population coincide completely. Had a different sampling of 5000 city public school children been employed, slightly different results would have been obtained.

This variation in results from sample to sample within the same population is known as *sampling error*. Statistical measures of reliability furnish a theoretical estimate of the probable limits within which such errors will fall. Reliability means, in this case, the degree of consistency among the results obtained on different samples of the same population. Formulas are available for the computation of the sampling error of any statistical measure. The most common measures of reliability are the "probable error" (PE) and the "standard error" (SE or σ). The total estimated range within which a measure will fall in successive sampling is covered by ± 4 PE, and ± 3 SE.

A hypothetical example will serve to illustrate the application of such measures to group comparisons. Let us suppose that a group of sixth-grade public school boys and girls obtained the following average scores on an intelligence test: Girls, 90; boys, 80; the difference between the two averages being 10 points in favor of the girls. Let us assume further that the PE of this difference is 5. In different samples of sixth-grade public school children we should therefore expect the sex difference to vary from 30 points ($10 + [4 \times 5] = 30$) to -10 points ($10 - [4 \times 5] = -10$). In other words, the relative standing of the male and female groups would be reversed in certain samplings, and the boys' average might be as much as 10 points higher than that of the girls. This is what is meant by an *unreliable difference*. The same conclusion can be reached more directly by dividing the obtained difference by its PE. If the difference is 4 or more times as large as its PE, there will be no reversal of direction and the difference is said to be perfectly reliable. In the present example, it will be noted that the difference is only twice as large as its PE ($10 \div 5 = 2$). This value, called the *critical ratio*, is an index of the degree to which the obtained figures represent a reliable or consistent trend.

The probable error (and the standard error) of an obtained difference depends upon the *size* of the samplings employed as well as the amount of *variability* within the samplings. It is apparent that the larger the samplings, the more reliably will the results be established. If the samplings were infinitely large, the probable error would be zero, since the entire theoretical population would then have been included. In many of the investigations on group differences, the samples employed have been so small as to yield extremely large probable errors, had the latter been computed. The sex or race differences reported in such studies may have been due entirely to sampling error.

Similarly, wide variability within each group renders the differences between averages less reliable. If all men were of identical height, for example, and all women were likewise equal in height, then sex differences in height could be reliably established by comparing only one representative of each sex. All other samplings would yield the same difference, since variation within each sex would be zero. The greater the variability within either group, the larger will be the probable error of the obtained difference. In the computation of probable errors and standard errors, both the number of cases and the variability of each group are taken into account.

Selective Factors.—In any group comparison, selective factors may operate to vitiate the results. Whenever a group is not a random or representative sample of the population from which it is drawn, it is said to be a select group. It is impossible to generalize from the results obtained with such a sampling to the total population. An additional complication arises when two populations are compared, since selection may have operated differently in the two groups. Thus one group may represent a superior sampling of its population, while the other represents a mediocre or inferior sampling of the second population.

Immigrant groups furnish a good example of the differential operation of selective factors. Immigrants coming to the United States from different countries, for example, are usually neither fair samplings of their home populations, nor comparable among themselves. If it could be shown that immigrants from all nations were drawn consistently from, let us say, the lower socio-economic or intellectual levels, then such groups would at least be comparable with each other. But it is well known that, through purely historical reasons, the immigrants coming from certain nations at a given time may represent a relatively inferior sampling of their population, from others a more nearly random or average sampling, and from still others a relatively superior sampling.

It might seem that selective factors would not play such a large part in comparisons between the two sexes. Many investigations on sex differences have nevertheless proved inconclusive because of the operation of previously unsuspected selective factors. Thus in two investigations on sex differences, the Pressey Group Test of Intelligence was administered to 2544 elementary school children [1] between the ages of 8 and 16 and to 5929 high school seniors [2] ranging in age from 16 to 23. In the elementary school groups, the girls excelled at all ages, although among the 16-year-olds this difference was not reliable. Among the high school seniors, however, the relationship was reversed, the boys surpassing the girls.

This reversal becomes intelligible if we examine the relative number of pupils of each sex in the elementary grades and in the senior year of high school. Throughout the high school period, there is a much more rapid elimination of boys than girls. Boys whose academic work is unsatisfactory are more likely to leave school and go to work, whereas girls tend to be kept in school longer. Girls also seem to adjust better to the school routine in general. The less intelligent girls will exert more effort and manage to pass sufficient subjects to stay in school, while boys in the same situation are more likely to rebel against school work. This explanation was borne out by an examination of the scholastic history of those students who had dropped out in the course of their high school work.

Much of the evidence offered in support of the once popular doctrine of sex differences in *variability* is rendered invalid by selective factors. This doctrine proposed that although the average ability of men and women might be equal, the distribution of ability of men covered a wider range than that of women. Similarly, more men than women would be found at the extremes of the distribution, corresponding to feeblemindedness and genius. In support of this contention were cited the admission statistics of institutions for the feebleminded. Surveys conducted in several countries revealed a consistent excess of males among the inmates.

Subsequent investigations [3] revealed, however, that the discrepancy results from social and cultural factors which operate differently in the admission of men and women to institutions. Unless a woman exhibits a pronounced degree of mental defect, she tends to be kept at home, or she may earn her livelihood by turning to such activities as housework, prostitution, or marriage. The boy, on the other hand, is forced into industrial work at a relatively early age, and will soon reveal his mental deficiency in the severe competition which he encounters. Thus, although there is an excess of males in institutions for mental defectives, it seems that there are more feebleminded females outside of institutions. Direct investigation of several thousand cases in New York City showed that the women brought to a psychological clinic for examination were on the average older and more deficient than the men. The difference in IQ was even greater when the cases actually committed were compared.

Overlapping of Distributions.—Although one group may excel another in a given trait by a large amount, individuals can be found in the poorer group who will equal or surpass individuals in the better group. Owing to the wide range of individual differences within any one group as contrasted to the relatively small difference between groups, an individual's membership in a given group furnishes little or no information about his standing in any trait or behavioral characteristic. The poorer end of the superior group coincides with the better end of the inferior group, and this overlapping is very large even when the group averages differ markedly.

An example of overlapping will be found in Fig. 18. This shows the distribution curves of a group of 189 boys and 206 girls in the third and fourth elementary school grades on a test of arithmetical reasoning. The average score of the boys is 40.39 and that of the girls 35.81. The difference between these averages is nearly 8 times as large as its PE and can therefore be regarded as perfectly reliable. An examination of the distributions, however, reveals a large amount of overlapping between the two groups. Large proportions of the

boys' and girls' scores fall within the same limits. Further evidence
of overlapping is to be found in the fact that 38 per cent of the girls
obtained scores which were higher than the boys' average, and 24
per cent of the boys scored below the girls' average.

It is therefore apparent that because of overlapping of distributions, the relationships established for the averages of two groups

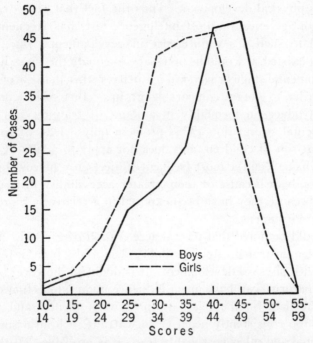

FIG. 18.—DISTRIBUTION OF BOYS AND GIRLS ON A TEST OF
ARITHMETICAL REASONING.

(Data from Schiller, in "Verbal, Numerical, and Spatial Abilities of Young
Children," by permission of Archives of Psychology, and adapted from Anastasi
"Differential Psychology" by permission of the Macmillan Co.)

may be entirely reversed when comparisons are made between individuals from the same two groups. This fact was very succinctly
put by Samuel Johnson who, when asked which was superior, man
or woman, is reported to have replied: *"Which man, which woman?".*
The individual, and not the group, should be the unit of observation.

Developmental Rate.—A further complication in the analysis of group differences arises from a possible difference in developmental rate. In connection with sex differences, for example, it has been clearly established that girls reach maturity earlier than boys. Moreover, at any one age during childhood, girls tend to be farther advanced than boys towards their eventual adult status.[4] A number of writers have proposed that girls might be accelerated in mental as well as physical development. Thus the fact that girls of elementary school age excel on most intelligence tests has frequently been attributed to such a sex difference in developmental rate. If this difference existed, it would be necessary to equate the sexes in regard to developmental stage or physical maturity, rather than chronological age, in order to obtain comparable groups. But such a procedure would introduce an inequality in amount of training and general environmental stimulation. This problem only arises, of course, in the comparison of children, and does not apply to adults. Children, however, have been the most frequent subjects for surveys on group differences, both because of their greater accessibility in large numbers and because they have been exposed to a relatively more homogeneous environment.

It should be noted that mental acceleration of girls has not been directly demonstrated. Its possibility has only been inferred by analogy with physical development. It is doubtful, however, whether physical maturity can have much influence upon intellectual development. The data on the relationship between mental and physical traits are too consistently negative to warrant such an assumption.[5] In emotional and other personality traits it is probable that the onset of puberty and the relative physiological maturity of the individual introduce a disturbing factor into sex comparisons at certain ages. In intellectual development, however, the environmental stimulation to which the individual has been exposed is far more significant than slight differences in physical condition.

In connection with race differences, the suggestion has been made by some writers that the more "primitive" races may mature earlier, mentally as well as physically. Superficially, the comparison of the performance of children at successive ages would seem to support this view. In an investigation on American Negro children, for example, the median Stanford-Binet IQ was found to decline from 100 in the 5-6 year group to 78.4 in the 10-15 year group.[6] According to the theory of the earlier maturity of "primitive" group, the "intellectual inferiority" of such groups tends to be obscured in early childhood by their more rapid development but becomes apparent as development slows down at the adolescent level. The age decline in IQ, however, admits of other more objective interpretations. The reader may recall in this connection the similar decline which was found in the case of canal-boat and gypsy children, as well as children living in isolated rural communities. It should also be noted that at the upper ages the Stanford-Binet becomes increasingly verbal. Performance at the upper age levels would thus be more directly influenced by the intellectual stimulation furnished by the environment. There is some evidence that when tests are employed which are more homogeneous throughout their range, this age decrement is not found.[7]

PROBLEMS OF MEASUREMENT

It should be apparent from the preceding section that the choice of subjects for the investigation of group differences presents many difficulties. If we now raise the further question as to *how* these differences are to be measured, we are faced with the task of evaluating current mental tests and other measuring devices. Individuals who differ in their "race" or their sex also differ in many other respects. It is very difficult to *isolate* the factor of race or sex so as to determine its direct influence upon the individual's behavioral development. It becomes necessary, therefore, to try to determine the degree to which these other concomitant variables influence mental-test performance.

General Cultural Background.—Such conditions as the customs, traditions, habitual activities, or attitudes among which the individual is reared affect his mental development, and more specifically his mental-test performance, in countless ways. A few examples of their operation will have to suffice. Although reared in the same home, for example, brothers and sisters cannot be assumed to have been exposed to identical psychological environments. Even in the most "enlightened" and "progressive" homes, *sex distinctions* are introduced which cannot fail to affect subsequent development. Boys and girls are usually given different toys and games, and different books to read. Girls are generally considered to be weaker and more frail than boys; they tend to be sheltered more, and are taught to be neater and quieter than their brothers. Even in those few cases in which the parents themselves may not foster these differentiations, the child is sure to come into contact with such attitudes among his playmates or other associates outside the home.

In the field of racial comparisons, the influence of cultural background upon mental-test performance is more clearly apparent. The test often demands specific information which the individual has had little or no opportunity to obtain in his own environment. Thus the use of such objects as bicycles, electric bulbs, postage stamps, and mirrors in picture tests may place individuals in certain cultures at a considerable disadvantage. Certain traditional *attitudes* may also interfere with the subject's test performance. Thus Porteus [8] reports that he found it difficult to convince Australian aborigines that they were to solve the test problems individually, without assistance from their tribal brothers, because of their custom to settle all important problems in tribal conferences. Klineberg [9] reports that among the Dakota Indians it is considered bad form to answer a question in the presence of someone who does not know the answer, or to give an answer of which one is not absolutely sure.

Another important point to consider in evaluating racial differences in mental-test performance is the significant part played by *speed* in such tests, and the varying emphasis placed upon speed in different cultures. This was vividly demonstrated in an investigation on white, Negro, and Indian boys with the Pintner-Paterson Performance Scale.[10] In accuracy of performance, as measured by the number of errors on each test, the Indians excelled the whites, and the Negroes were either equal to or slightly superior to the whites. All measures of speed, on the other hand, favored the whites. A comparison of groups belonging to the same race but living in a different cultural milieu suggested that these differences in speed were cultural rather than biological. Thus New York City Negroes clearly excelled

West Virginia rural Negroes in every comparison. Similarly, the Indians attending a school run by the government and conducted by white teachers were consistently faster than those tested on the reservation. The relatively insignificant part which speed plays in the life of the reservation Indian or the rural southern Negro may fully account for these results.

Finally, the relatively intangible but highly effective factor of *social expectancy* should be mentioned. This operates to perpetuate group differences, however they may have been established. What is expected of an individual is a powerful influence in the determination of what he will do. When such expectation has the force of social tradition behind it and is corroborated at every instant by family attitudes, everyday contacts in work and play, and nearly all other encounters with one's fellow-beings, it is very difficult not to succumb to it. As a result, the individual himself becomes convinced that he is "superior" or "inferior," or that he possesses this or that talent, interest, or attitude, according to the dictates of his particular culture.

Education.—That the *formal education* of different racial and national groups differs in amount and in kind is too obvious to require much elaboration. Adult immigrants in the United States, such as the foreign-born groups of the army draft tested during the World War, have usually received much less formal schooling than the average native-born American with whom they are compared. American Indians and American Negroes, although born in this country, receive as a group an education which is far inferior to that of the white population. Apart from poorer equipment, fewer and less adequately trained teachers, and more inaccessible schools, school attendance is much lower among such groups. This results partly from poorer roads and less adequate means of transportation, partly from the demands of a rural community where the official school term is sometimes only six months in duration, and partly from the attitude of parents in a group which is not in complete sympathy with American standards.

Educational opportunities have likewise been very dissimilar for the two sexes,[11] although at present the environments of men and women are probably more nearly equated in this respect than in any other. Although America was in advance of most other countries in the education of women, until nearly the middle of the nineteenth century there was no institution of collegiate rank in this country which admitted women. Professional and post-graduate training was not available until a much later date. Even in the elementary and secondary schools, the traditional curriculum for girls was different from that for boys, including much less science and more literature, art, and other "genteel" subjects.

The more general opportunities for intellectual development furnished by the home and general cultural level in which the individual is reared also exert a marked influence upon intelligence-test performance. It is apparent that the *socio-economic level* of the homes of such groups as immigrants, Negroes, or Indians is far below the general American average. In one investigation on Negro children and white children of American and Italian parentage, all within a single school district, it was found that over 90 per cent of the Negroes and Italians fell into the "inferior" and "very inferior" categories with reference to father's occupation, in contrast to only 22 per cent of the white children of American parentage.[12] Similarly, in a study on Indian children, the average socio-economic rating of the homes proved to be 13 points, as compared to the white norm of 56 points.[13] In a series of investigations, a close correspondence was found between the social status of various Indian groups, as evaluated in terms of white standards, and the average intelligence-test scores obtained by children from these groups.[14]

Language Handicap.—The effect of language handicap upon mental-test performance has proved to be most serious when this handicap is present in a *mild degree*. Individuals with very pronounced linguistic difficulty are usually tested with a nonlanguage or performance scale. If the individual has a moderate understanding of English, however, it is frequently deemed unnecessary to give him a nonverbal test. Although such an individual may know the language sufficiently well to make himself understood and to follow directions in a test, he may lack the facility in the use of English or the range of vocabulary required to compete fairly on a verbal test. This situation is often met in immigrants who have lived in America for many years, or in the children of immigrants. The latter are frequently *bilingual,* speaking their own language at home and English at school.

That such relatively mild language handicaps may have a pronounced effect upon intelligence-test scores has been repeatedly demonstrated. In one investigation [15] on children of immigrant groups in America, it was found that among those who spoke a foreign language at home, 75 per cent obtained higher mental ages on performance tests than on the Stanford-Binet. In the English-speaking group, on the other hand, only 52 per cent scored higher on the performance tests, that is, there was no tendency for this group as a whole to excel in either test. In another similar investigation,[16] the intelligence-test scores of 165 third- and fourth-grade school children of foreign parentage were compared with those of 121 children of American parentage. On the Pintner Non-Language Scale, 50 per cent of the "foreign" group reached or exceeded the median of the "American" group; on the National Intelligence Test, which is highly verbal, however, this percentage was only 37.

The data on language handicap are not limited to immigrant groups from European countries. In investigations on American Indians, the influence of language deficiency upon intelligence-test performance has been vividly demonstrated. In an investigation [17] on 717 pupils attending Indian schools in Ontario, Canada, the children were divided into the "monoglots" who spoke only English, and the "bilinguals" who spoke an Indian language at home either all or part of the time. On the Pintner-Paterson Performance Scale, the bilingual children obtained a higher median score than the monoglots, while the reverse was true on the National Intelligence Test, the Pintner Non-Language, and the Pintner-Cunningham. In the case of the Pintner Non-Language Test, it is possible that the use of paper-and-pencil materials gave a disadvantage to the children from the less highly assimilated homes. Those children who were relatively unfamiliar with such materials would also tend to come more often from the Indian-speaking homes.

Similar results were obtained in a study of 570 American-born Japanese children between the ages of 10 and 15.[18] On the Army

Beta, there was no significant difference between Japanese and white children at ages 10 and 11, and a difference in favor of the Japanese group beyond this. On the Stanford-Binet, however, the median IQ of the Japanese children was 89.5, as compared with 99.5 for white children of the same districts. Moreover, a correlation of .87 was found between the degree of Japanese inferiority on each of the tests in the Stanford-Binet scale and the "verbality" rating of the test based upon the consensus judgment of seven psychologists.

The Criterion of "Intellectual Superiority."—In all group comparisons there is a tendency to go beyond the observed differences in behavior and to evaluate the *relative status* of each group in terms of some presumably universal criterion. Linear comparisons are made in terms of better or worse. Thus we frequently find national or racial groups arranged in a rank-order for "intelligence." Such a point of view implies either that one group is consistently poorer than another in all mental traits, or that certain behavioral processes are universally more significant, more valuable, or even more "mental" than others.

In regard to the first of these assumptions, it can easily be shown that groups vary in the relative inferiority or superiority which they manifest in different traits. Comparison of scores on different types of intelligence scales, or on different tests within a single scale, has repeatedly demonstrated the specificity of such group differences. It has frequently been argued, however, that racial or national groups can be arranged in a consistent hierarchy if we consider only the "higher mental processes." Tests of abstract abilities, for example, are considered more diagnostic of "intelligence" than those dealing with the manipulation of concrete objects or with the perception of spatial relationships. The aptitude for dealing with symbolical materials, especially of a verbal or numerical nature, is regarded as the acme of intellectual attainment. The "primitive" man's skill in responding to very slight sensory cues, his talents in the construction of objects, or the powers of sustained attention and muscular control which he may display in his hunting behavior, are regarded as interesting anthropological curios which have, however, little or no intellectual worth. As a result, such activities have not usually been incorporated in intelligence scales, but have been relegated to a relatively minor position in mental testing.

Upon closer examination, it will become apparent that this conception of intelligence is itself culturally conditioned. By "higher mental processes" is usually meant those aspects or segments of behavior which are at a premium in our society. Intelligence tests would be very different if they had been constructed among American Indians or Australian aborigines rather than in American cities. There are a few instances on record of the application of a test constructed from the point of view of some other culture. Porteus,[19] for example, having been impressed with the remarkable tracking skill of the Australian aborigines, constructed a test with photographs of footprints, the task being to match the two prints made by the same foot. On this test, the Australians did practically as well as a group of 120 white high school students in Hawaii who were tested for comparison.

The criterion employed in validating intelligence tests has nearly always been success in our social system. Scores on the test are correlated with school achievement or perhaps with some more general measure of success in our society. If such correlations are high, it is concluded that the test is a good measure of "intelligence." The age criterion is based upon the same principle. If scores on a given test show a progressive increase with age, it may merely mean that the test is measuring those traits which our culture imparts to the individual. The older the subject, the more opportunity he will have had, in general, to acquire such aptitudes.

Thus it would seem that intelligence tests measure only the ability to succeed in our particular culture. Each culture, partly through the physical conditions of its environment and partly through social tradition, "selects" certain activities as the most significant. These it encourages and stimulates; others it neglects or definitely suppresses. The relative standing of different cultural groups in "intelligence" is a function of the traits included under the concept of intelligence or, to state the same point differently, it is a function of the particular culture in which the test was constructed.

SEX DIFFERENCES

In view of many of the problems which have been discussed in the preceding sections, it would seem very difficult to formulate any summary statements regarding sex differences from the data of a number of independent investigations. This is especially true since such investigations differ widely in number and kind of subjects, specific tests or materials employed, and other important conditions. Similarly, all but the most recent and best controlled studies fail to report reliabilities, degree of overlapping, and other essential facts, thus making it difficult to evaluate their findings. Under these conditions, the most common available criterion for the acceptance of a conclusion is the *consistency* of results of different investigators. It should also be remembered that such findings represent only sex differences under existing conditions *in our society*. Although of limited application, however, such data are not without practical value.

Intellectual Aptitudes.—In general, boys have been found to excel in spatial and numerical aptitudes, girls in memory and verbal aptitude. These results have been established by special investigations with tests particularly designed to measure such aptitudes, as well as by the analysis of performance on different types of intelligence scales or different parts of such scales. In investigations of *spatial* or *mechanical* aptitude, boys generally obtain higher average scores on such tests as puzzle boxes, form boards, slot mazes, paper-and-pencil mazes, construction tests, and most of the tests included in performance scales. In some investigations, the boys were found to excel in mechanical aptitude even though the girls equaled or surpassed them in average Binet IQ.[20]

In *numerical* aptitude, a tendency towards male superiority has likewise been found, although the data are not so consistent as in the case of mechanical aptitude. This might be expected from social tradition and environmental conditions, since the sex differentiation in regard to mathematical work is not so pronounced as it is for mechanical pursuits. Girls are afforded relatively more opportunity for the development of mathematical abilities than for the exercise of mechanical functions. In the elementary school, for example, girls are taught arithmetic in the same classes as boys, but the latter are still segregated for "shop courses."

An analysis of the data employed in the standardization of the Stanford-Binet showed that the average percentage of boys who succeeded on the numerical tests was greater than that of girls. The difference in favor of the boys was 33 per cent on the arithmetical reasoning test, 15 per cent on the test of making change, and 10 per cent on the "induction" test in which a generalized numerical rule must be discovered.[21] An examination of the scores obtained by 834 high school students on the Army Alpha showed male superiority only on the arithmetical reasoning, number-series completion, and information tests.[22] The differences on these three tests were sufficient, however, to pull up the total scores and produce a sex difference in the scale as a whole in favor of the boys. An analysis of the scores obtained in 1930 by 4394 boys and 3318 girls on the Scholastic Aptitude Tests administered to entering college freshmen revealed a large and significant difference in favor of the boys in the mathematical portions of this test.[23] The critical ratio of this difference was 11.59. In a variety of special investigations, boys have been found to excel both in the mechanics of computation and in mathematical reasoning.

In *verbal* or linguistic aptitude, there is a fairly consistent difference in favor of the female sex, which is manifested from an early age and persists in successive age levels. Observations on normal, as well as gifted and feebleminded children have shown that on the average girls begin to talk earlier than boys.[24] Similarly, girls of preschool ages have a larger vocabulary than boys. Female superiority has been found consistently in such tests as speed of reading, naming opposites, and in all verbal association tests. Girls excel in sentence completion and story completion. The difference in favor of girls found in many of the common paper-and-pencil intelligence tests may likewise be attributed to the large verbal content of such tests. The analysis of the 1930 data obtained with the Scholastic Aptitude Test cited above, revealed a marked female superiority on the verbal portions of the test, the critical ratio of this difference being 13.52. It is particularly significant that this reversal in the relative status of the two sexes was found within the same group of subjects, and cannot therefore be attributed to selective factors or other irrelevant influences.

On practically all tests of *memory*, a sex difference in favor of the female has likewise been found. As in the case of verbal ability, these differences have been found from preschool age, and persist throughout life. The female superiority in memory has been established with a wide range of materials and methods of testing retention, and for direct as well as incidental memory. In this connection may also be mentioned the fact that women tend to have more vivid mental imagery than men in every sense modality. This finding, first suggested by Galton on the basis of his famous "breakfast table" questionnaire, has been subsequently corroborated by a number of investigators.

It is interesting to note that in *scholastic achievement,* girls tend to surpass boys, even in those subjects which should favor the boys. Achievement-test scores show the boys to be somewhat superior in such fields as arithmetic, geometry, nature study, and history, the girls excelling in reading and language usage. In school grades, however, girls excel consistently in nearly all subjects. Girls are also promoted in larger numbers, and are more often accelerated and less often retarded than boys. Among the explanations for these discrepancies might be mentioned the important part which verbal ability plays in all school instruction and especially in examinations. A further explanation can probably be found in personality factors, such as the greater neatness and docility of the girls, and the fact that they are more susceptible to school discipline and less frequently constitute "behavior problems" than boys.

Personality Traits.—A number of investigations, most of which have been conducted on adults, report a sex difference in *emotional traits.* Typical of the results of such studies are those obtained with the Bernreuter Personality Inventory.[25] On this test, men were found to be reliably more stable, or less neurotic, more self-sufficient, less introverted, more dominant, and more self-confident than women. In a more intensive investigation of introversion among college students, no significant sex difference was found in the introversion-extroversion variable itself, but a difference was found in another trait which seemed to cut across introversion-extroversion.[26] This trait seemed to be concerned with social relations. The introvert characteristics most often found among men were those which would interfere with social adjustment, such as keeping in the background on social occasions, and being outspoken. Those most often found among women were such as to interfere with efficient work, such as shrinking when facing a crisis, or working by fits and starts.

Interesting comparative data on the emotional differences between boys and girls at successive ages have been obtained with the Wood-

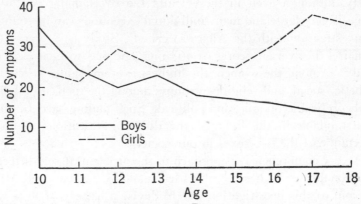

Fig. 19.—Median Number of Symptoms Reported by Boys and Girls on the Woodworth-Mathews Test of Emotional Instability.

(After Mathews, in "A Study of Emotional Stability in Children," Journal of Delinquency, and adapted from Anastasi "Differential Psychology" by permission of the Macmillan Co.)

worth-Mathews questionnaire, a measure of emotional instability and neurotic tendencies. This test was administered to 575 boys and 558 girls between the ages of 9 and 19. In the entire group, the median number of neurotic symptoms reported by the boys was 20, and by the girls 25.5. An analysis of the median scores of successive age groups, however, revealed certain rather suggestive facts, which are shown graphically in Fig. 19. It will be noted that at age 10, the boys reported *more* neurotic symptoms than the girls. At 11 there is no appreciable sex difference, and beyond this the girls show an *increase* in emotional instability and the boys a *decrease*. Such trends might well be expected from an analysis of the environments of the two sexes. The emotional problems and affective surroundings of boys and girls are quite similar in early childhood. Gradually, however, the environmental differentiation becomes more marked and this is reflected in the increasing divergence of the sexes in emotional stability with increasing age.

The administration of *character tests* to children of both sexes has revealed no difference in honesty, a slight tendency for girls to be more cooperative and more persistent, and a larger and statistically reliable difference in inhibition in favor of the girls.[27] In *interests* and *attitudes*, marked sex differences are found among adults in our society, although even in these traits the overlapping of the two groups is very large and many individual exceptions can be found. In an investigation with the Allport-Vernon "Study of Values" questionnaire, the average scores of 463 men and 313 women were compared.[28] Among the women, the highest average values fell into the aesthetic, social, and religious groups; among the men, they fell into the theoretical, economic, and political. Such findings are, of course, understandable in the light of the differing traditions and social expectancy of the two sexes in our society.

A very comprehensive approach to the problem of sex differences in personality traits has recently been made by Terman and Miles.[29] The aim of this investigation was to devise a battery of tests which would differentiate clearly between the characteristic male and female patterns of response and furnish an index of "masculinity-femininity." After an exhaustive survey of the literature and prolonged research, items were selected which revealed the most pronounced differences between representative samplings of the two sexes in our society. Data were collected on many hundreds of subjects, including elementary, high school, college, and graduate students, unselected adults, members of several occupations, and specially selected groups such as athletes, juvenile delinquents, and adult homosexuals. The scale as a whole proved very successful in differentiating between the responses of groups of men and women in our society, all average differences being statistically reliable. With regard to the origin of such differences, the authors offer only tentative hypotheses, and repeatedly point out the influence of cultural factors in producing many of the obtained differences.

Sex Differences and Culture.—The study of the typical behavior characteristics of the two sexes in different cultures offers interesting possibilities for the analysis of the origin of such differences. Thus a biological or hereditary determination of sex differences would imply the existence of a *universal pattern* of male and female behavior. If sex differences in behavior are environmentally determined, on the other hand, we should expect the traditional behavior characteristics of each sex to vary from one culture to another. Data on this question are still relatively meager. Psychologists have generally neglected the wealth of information offered by the comparative study of behavior phenomena in different cultural milieux.

Certain observations reported by anthropologists, however, offer suggestive material on this problem. In the course of her investigations conducted on the island of Manus in New Guinea, Mead found that when wooden figurines were offered to the children for the first time, it was the boys rather than the girls who accepted them as dolls, crooning lullabies to them and displaying typical parental behavior.[30] Owing to the traditional division of labor in this group, the women are busy with their various duties throughout the day, while the men have more leisure time between their activities of hunting and fishing. As a result, the father rather than the mother usually attends to the children and plays with them. This socially established differentiation of behavior was reflected in the play responses of the boys and girls.

A vivid demonstration of the cultural determination of sex differences is furnished by a more recent study by Mead, in which she observed the traditional emotional characteristics of men and women in three primitive societies.[31] Each of these groups presents a different pattern of male and female personality. Among the *Arapesh,* both men and women display emotional characteristics which in our society would be considered distinctly feminine. In this group, both sexes are trained to be cooperative, unaggressive, gentle, noncompetitive, and responsive to the needs of others. Among the *Mundugumur,* on the other hand, both men and women are violent, aggressive, ruthless, and competitive. Both sexes take great pleasure in action and in fighting. Perhaps the most interesting pattern is presented by the *Tchambuli,* among whom there is a genuine reversal of the sex-attitude of our culture. In this group the women are impersonal, practical, and efficient. The men are artistic, graceful, emotionally subservient, timid, sensitive to the opinions of others, and throughout their lives dependent upon the security afforded to them by the women. A clue to the understanding of these widely differing patterns of male and female behavior was furnished by the social and economic organizations and other cultural traditions of the three groups.

"Racial" and National Differences

The Concept and Criteria of Race.—The classification of men into racial groups is essentially a biological one and corresponds to such divisions as breed, stock, and strain in infrahuman organisms. In its simplest terms, any definition of race implies a certain community of physical characteristics based primarily upon a common heredity. The task of classifying individuals into races is far more difficult and complex than would appear from the glibness with which individuals are commonly assigned to one group or another. The essential problem in the classification of racial groups consists in the identification of inheritable physical characteristics which differ clearly from one group to another and which may thus serve as *criteria* of race. A wide variety of such criteria have been proposed and investigated by anthropologists, including skin color, pigmentation of the eyes, hair color and texture, gross bodily dimensions, facial and cranial measures and indices, blood groupings, endocrine activity, and constitutional type.

In the application of any of these racial criteria, a number of difficulties are encountered. In the first place, wide *variability* exists within any one racial group in any of these characteristics. Closely related to this is the extensive *overlapping* between different groups in any of the proposed criteria. A third difficulty is the *inconsistency* which is frequently found when more than one criterion is employed. An individual might thus have the coloring of one racial group, the cephalic index * of a second, and the stature of a third. Finally, it should be noted that many of the alleged racial characteristics which

---

* The cephalic index is one of the most common indices of race and is found by dividing head width by head length and multiplying the quotient by 100.

were formerly accepted as innate have proved to be *unstable* and susceptible to environmental influences. Even such apparently "hereditary" traits as body height, skull shape, and facial conformation have been shown to be dependent in part upon stimulating conditions in early childhood.[32]

It should thus be borne in mind that at best any racial classification is approximate. No sharp line of demarcation can be established between groups, nor can any individual be unequivocally assigned to one particular group. The classification which is most widely accepted at present is one which is based upon a combination of criteria, chief among which are cephalic index, hair quality, hairiness on the body, facial conformation, and bodily proportions. The major racial divisions in this classification are as follows: (1) Caucasian, including Nordic, Alpine, and Mediterranean; (2) Mongoloid, including Mongolian, Malaysian, and American Indian; (3) Negroid, including Negro, Melanesian, and dwarf blacks; and (4) Doubtful, including a number of small, scattered groups which cannot be assigned to any of the three major divisions.[33]

The discussion of race differences is further complicated by the common confusion of racial categories with *nationality* and with *linguistic groupings,* such as "Latin" or "Aryan." The extensive amount of *race mixture* which has gone on for many generations also adds to the difficulty of classifying the individual into a particular racial group. Psychological investigators, furthermore, have often chosen their subjects on the basis of accessibility, and have only infrequently attempted a systematic classification into racial categories. In the sections which follow, some of the most representative findings will be reported for each of the three major racial groups.

The Negroid.—The large majority of investigations on the negroid race have employed the American Negro. On most intelligence scales, Negroes have generally obtained lower average scores than whites. This difference is larger in speed than in other aspects of performance,[34] and greater in the verbal than in the performance type of test. Thus in one investigation [35] on 907 white and Negro school children in three Virginia cities, the whites were markedly superior in analogies and sentence completion; the Negroes were slightly more accurate but slower in a stylus maze; and there were no significant or consistent differences in cancellation.

In any attempt to arrive at an estimate of the performance of Negroes on intelligence scales, we are immediately confronted with large regional differences in average score. In the army testing during the World War, for example, this variation was so large as to reverse completely the white-Negro relationship when certain specific groups were compared. Thus on the Army Alpha Examination, the Negro draft from New York, Illinois, and Ohio obtained higher average scores than the white draft from Mississippi, Kentucky, and Arkansas.[36] Similar results have been obtained in studies on Negro school children in northern and southern states.[37] In certain localities, the Negro child's performance shows no inferiority to that of the white child; in others, the difference between the two groups is very striking.

Especially clear-cut are the differences between northern and southern Negroes. On the Army Alpha, the median scores obtained by the white, northern Negro, and southern Negro draft, respectively, were 58.9, 38.6, and 12.4. The corresponding medians of those who took the Army Beta were 43.4, 32.5, and 19.8. In reference to Negro children, the average IQ's found by one writer by combining the results of several studies were 86.3 for northern Negroes and 79.6 for southern Negroes. That these differences are the result not of selective migration but of the difference in environmental stimulation to which northern and southern Negroes are exposed was indicated in a series of investigations by Klineberg.[38] In the first place, southern Negro children who had migrated to the north with their families were found not to have been above average in their scholastic achievement in southern schools before migration. In the second place, the comparison of average intelligence-test scores of Negro children who had lived in New York City for varying periods of time showed a progressive increase with length of residence in New York.

In regard to *"nonintellectual" traits*, no reliable differences have been established between Negro and white groups. The groups tested in such studies have usually been small and often highly selected. In certain cases, the conditions under which the tests were administered were not comparable for white and Negro groups. It appears to have been fairly conclusively shown, however, that there is no basis to the popular belief that the Negro has an "innately superior musical sense." The application of the Seashore tests of musical aptitude has revealed no consistent or significant differences.

The Mongoloid.—Investigations [39] on American Indians, both in the United States and Canada, indicate the poorer performance of the Indian child in general on such verbal tests as the Otis and the National Intelligence Test. This inferiority is less marked on the nonlanguage and performance scales, but it is still clearly apparent whenever speed plays an important part in determining the score. As has been reported above, clear-cut differences are found in the test performance of monoglots and bilinguals. A fairly close relationship has also been established between socio-economic level and average test score of various Indian groups.[40]

In an extensive investigation on American-born Japanese children, 570 Japanese children between the ages of 10 and 15 were given the Stanford-Binet and the Army Beta, as well as tests of school achievement.[41] On both scales, the Japanese children seem to be superior to the white children in those tests which involved sustained attention and visual perception. Thus on the Army Beta, there was a statistically significant difference in favor of the Japanese children in digit-symbol substitution and in number comparisons, and a smaller difference in the same direction in cube analysis and geometric construction. The picture completion test, which is obviously dependent upon environmental background, was the only test in the scale in which the Japanese children were reliably inferior. On the Stanford-Binet, the Japanese children were reliably superior in four tests: Induction, paper cutting, enclosed boxes, and code. Their inferiority on the verbal tests was sufficient, however, to pull down their total score, the median IQ of the Japanese children being 10 points lower than that of white children in the same districts. In an investigation in which the Pintner-Paterson Performance Scale was administered to 500 Japanese and Chinese children in the public schools of Vancouver, both groups obtained a higher average IQ than white children, the Japanese obtaining a higher average than the Chinese children.[42] One could easily speculate upon the special traditions and cultural factors which might account for the superiority of these Oriental groups in certain types of tests.

The Caucasian.—Psychological investigations on racial subgroups within the Caucasian division have been conducted largely with immigrants in the United States, and are therefore limited in the scope of their findings. In addition to the operation of selective factors, which have been discussed above, the adjustment to life in a new culture, with its attendant shift of standards and bilingualism, introduces many complicating factors. The frequent confusion of racial and national groups in such studies further confuses the issue.

A particularly fruitful approach is to be found in the *cross-comparison* of national and racial groups within the same sampling. Race is a biological classification, nationality a cultural one. Such cross-comparisons can thus afford an index of the relative contribution of these two classes of factors in the production of behavioral differences. This approach is illustrated in an investigation conducted on 10- to 12-year-old boys in rural sections of Germany, France, and Italy.[43] Each of these countries includes more than one of the Caucasian subgroups within its population. In Germany, Nordic and Alpine samplings were obtained; in France, Nordic, Alpine, and Mediterranean; in Italy, Alpine and Mediterranean. The subjects were selected from those geographical areas in which pure types of each race were most likely to be found. Only children who had themselves and whose parents had been born in each particular area were included in the study. The subjects were further selected on the basis of eye color, hair color, and cephalic index so as to fall within the specified limits of the given racial group.

Each subject was examined individually with six of the tests in the Pintner-Paterson Performance Scale, brief oral directions being given in the subject's own language. When the subjects were classified into racial groups, no reliable difference in average score was obtained. The differences among the three national groups, on the other hand, were larger and more nearly reliable. Marked variation was found, furthermore, within the sampling of a single racial group from one nation to another. The difference between one Nordic group and another, for example, was larger than that between the Nordic and Mediterranean groups as a whole. Such data suggest that there is no basis for an intellectual hierarchy in terms of race, but that cultural factors play the major role in the production of group differences.

The Multiple Group Concept of Individuality

Nature of a Psychological Group.—Psychologically the individual belongs to every group with which he shares behavior. From this point of view, group membership is to be defined in terms of stimulational value rather than biological categories. The effective grouping is not based upon the individual's race or sex or physical characteristics, but upon his experiential background. Thus if the individual is reared as a member of a certain national group with its own traditions and cultural background and its own peculiar complex of stimulating conditions, he will display the behavioral characteristics of that group regardless of his racial origin. It should be understood, of course, that mere physical presence does not constitute group membership in a psychological sense. Thus if a Negro child were brought up in a community composed exclusively of whites, he would not necessarily receive the same social stimulation as a white child.

Multiplicity of Overlapping Groups.—It follows from such a concept of a psychological group that any one individual is effectively a member of a large and varied set of groups. A multiplicity of behavioral groups, large and small, cut across each other in the individual's experiential background. The individual is born into a broad cultural division such as, for example, "western civilization," with its characteristic sources of stimulation. He will develop certain intellectual aptitudes, emotional traits, attitudes, and beliefs as a result of his affiliation with this group. He is also a member of a given national group with its more specific ways of acting.

If the individual displays certain physical characteristics, such as a particular skin color, facial conformation, or body build, he may be classified as a member of a given "racial" group which occupies a distinct position within the broader national division. In so far as his racial background leads to certain social distinctions and culturally imposed differentiations of behavior, it will indirectly produce an effective grouping. The same may be said of sex. If within a given society traditional beliefs in regard to sex differences exist so that the sexes are exposed to dissimilar psychological stimulation, then the individual's sex will in part indirectly determine his behavioral characterstics.

There are a number of other less clearly defined behavioral groupings which may be very important factors in the individual's development. Whether the individual was reared in the city or the country, the particular state or province in which he spent most of his life, and even the specific neighborhood in which he lives, will significantly affect his emotional and intellectual development. Other groups with which the individual identifies himself behaviorally are his occupational class, his religious sect, his political party, his club, his educational institutions, his family, his generation and age group, and his recreational group, such as persons sharing a certain hobby. These groups influence the individual's behavior in two essential ways. First, they directly stimulate and foster certain ways of acting. Secondly, the reactions of other people to the individual are affected by his group affiliation. The social attitudes and "social expectancy" which the individual encounters as a result of this group membership will in turn influence his behavior.

The Nature of Individuality.—The individual may be regarded as partly a resultant of his multiple group memberships. To be sure, each individual also undergoes experiences which are absolutely unique to himself. Such experiences are probably less significant, however, in shaping the more basic aspects of his personality than is his shared behavior. The types of experiences which are common to a group of individuals have a certain degree of permanence in the sense that they will tend to be repeated more often and to be corroborated or reënforced by other similar experiences. In general, the more highly organized the group, the more consistent and systematic will be the experiences which its members undergo. This will tend to make the shared experiences on the whole more effective than the purely individual ones.

In view of the pronounced effect of such shared or common behavior upon the individual's development, it may appear surprising that individuals are no more alike in their behavior repertory than we ordinarily find them to be. The extent of individual differences within any one group is extremely large. In fact, the variations among individuals have always proved to be more marked than the differences from one group to another. How can the complete "individuality" of each person be explained in terms of his shared experiential background?

The key to this problem seems to lie in the *multiplicity* of overlapping groups with which the individual may be behaviorally identified. The number of such groups is so great that the *specific combination* is unique for each individual. Not only will this furnish an experiential basis for the existence of wide individual differences, but it also suggests a mechanism whereby the individual may "rise above" his group. There are many examples of individuals who have broken away from the customs and traditions of their group. Through such situations, the modification of the group itself may be effected.

In these cases the individual is not reacting contrary to his past experience, as might at first appear. This would be psychologically impossible. His behavior is the result of psychological membership in various conflicting groups. Many group memberships can exist side by side in a composite behavioral adjustment. But in certain cases two or more groups may foster different ways of reacting to the same situation. This enables the individual to become aware of the arbitrariness of the restrictions and traditions of each group, to become critical of them, and to regard them more "objectively." Membership in many unlike groups frees the individual from the intellectual and other limitations of each group and makes possible the fullest development of "individuality."

REFERENCES

Anastasi, A. *Differential Psychology.* New York: The Macmillan Company, 1937.

Boas, F. *The Mind of Primitive Man.* New York: The Macmillan Company, 1938.

Freeman, F. N. *Individual Differences*. New York: Henry Holt and Company, 1934.

Garth, T. R. *Race Psychology*. New York: McGraw-Hill Book Company, Inc., 1931.

Gilliland, A. R., and Clark, E. L. *Psychology of Individual Differences*. New York: Prentice-Hall, Inc., 1939.

Huxley, J. S., and Haddon, A. C. *We Europeans: A Survey of "Racial" Problems*. London: Jonathan Cape, 1935.

Klineberg, O. *Race Differences*. New York: Harper and Brothers, 1935.

Lincoln, E. A. *Sex Differences in the Growth of American School Children*. Baltimore: Warwick and York, 1927.

Mead, M. *Sex and Temperament in Three Primitive Societies*. New York: William Morrow and Company, Inc., 1935.

Terman, L. M., and Miles, C. C. *Sex and Personality*. New York: McGraw-Hill Book Company, Inc., 1936.

Wellman, B. L. Sex differences, in Murchison's *Handbook of Child Psychology*. Worcester: Clark University Press, 1933, Ch. 15.

CHAPTER XIV

EDUCATIONAL PSYCHOLOGY

By HORACE B. ENGLISH, *The Ohio State University*

Educational Psychology at First the Handmaiden of Educational Reform.—From the beginning of the modern period there has been a close connection between psychology and education. The early educational reformers appealed to psychological principles in support of their proposals—as indeed they do today. We must note, however, that all too often the appeal was to a psychology specially tailored to fit the theory. Strongly convinced that they had a vast improvement to make in education, Komensky, Pestalozzi, Rousseau, and other great prophets of educational advance looked about them for the facts which would support their beloved projects.

And here became manifest the almost fatal limitation of all armchair theorizing—one can find support for almost any theory if one is allowed to select the facts. If one sincerely believes, for example, in the unspoiled innocence of the child, as did Rousseau, one experiences no difficulty in gathering instances which confirm his faith. Those who believe in original sin and the depravity of the natural man are equally untroubled for evidence. We find what we hope to find.

None the less, the reformers' appeal to the facts of child nature and learning was healthy. Bias in favor of a theory could not wholly conceal the facts even when the facts worked against it. Little by little a truly impartial psychology of childhood began to emerge. Partly under the impetus provided by the doctrine of evolution, people began to study children not merely to provide the underpinning of an educational theory, but in order to learn what children are really like.

The Application of General Psychology to Education.—Meanwhile, an independent science of psychology was gradually developing out of the matrix of philosophy. As much as a hundred years ago, Herbart attempted to draw from this new science whatever principles seemed likely to serve the schools. Here for the first time was an attempt—at least the first systematic attempt—to get the psychological facts and principles first and then from them derive the educational application, instead of following the reverse direction by seeking to justify a program already chosen by the appeal to psychology.*

Herbart's attempt was brilliantly successful. Few except the special student realize how much even today the framework of educational practice owes him. And with the growth of psychology during the intervening century, education has continued to draw upon it for sustenance.

There has thus grown up a considerable body of facts and principles, drawn from the several fields of psychology, which seem to have direct bearing on school practice. Many scholars still think of educational psychology as such a collection of borrowings from other branches of the science.

The Direct Psychological Attack on Educational Problems.—But it is much more than this. The educational psychologist of today does not wait until useful principles emerge from studies pursued for other ends. Instead, he investigates independently the psychological aspects of all educational problems. In doing so, he does indeed bring to bear any principles and any methods of investigation elaborated elsewhere in the science of psychology if these bid fair to serve his purpose, but he does not hesitate to modify them or to develop new ones as needed. A very real contribution to psychological methods as well as important facts and conclusions have resulted from this vigorous, direct attack upon the practical problems of education.

Consider the origin of intelligence tests. Early in the century the Paris school system became aware of a practical problem of some importance: Were the laggards in school unable to learn, or merely unwilling, or badly taught? They turned to a celebrated French psychologist, Alfred Binet. Could he devise a way to tell? He could and did.

---

* Great psychologist that he was (and great educator, also), Herbart, none the less, failed to realize the extent to which the school was a magnificent laboratory in which to test the truth or error of the psychology.

Now it is true that for some years Binet had been studying the higher thought processes and that the Binet scale shows the clear influence of the earlier experiments. And of course Binet's approach was through and through psychological. Yet essentially, intelligence testing began with a direct attempt to solve an educational problem. Today by far the greatest part of educational psychology does not consist in borrowings from general psychology but of principles and facts independently developed in this practical but thoroughly scientific fashion. The result is a discipline, less tidy and systematic, perhaps, than might be desired, but one which is thoroughly useful and functional for the teacher.*

The Expanding Field of Education.—The orientation of educational psychology toward practical educational issues imposes one important, though temporary, limitation upon it. It has hitherto been largely concerned with formal schooling and with children— for it was so in the main that we conceived education. But a broader conception of education is winning its way. The out-of-school life of the child is being recognized as a part of his education, more important in most respects than the comparatively few hours spent in class. Our treatment of educational psychology will attempt to reflect this new emphasis.[1]

In a still more important direction, however, our conception of education has recently been expanding. A truly adult education is beginning to emerge. No longer is education considered a matter of the school years and of formal instruction. We are learning to think of education as all of those deliberate efforts to alter the individual to the end of his own greater happiness and of his usefulness to society. Thus conceived, agencies, hitherto unrecognized as part of education must be accepted as such.

Thus the library has for decades been recognized as an important instrumentality for public enlightenment and the diffusion of "Culture." We need, however, to see its function more broadly in terms

---

* The same evolution seems to be taking place in other parts of applied psychology. The earlier dependence of applied psychology upon general theory is greatly lessened. The relationship between general and applied psychology will, to be sure, always remain intimate, but the day is not far distant, apparently, when a major task of general psychology will be to correlate and assimilate the facts discovered in the several applied fields.

of the human needs which may be satisfied in a library, the growth in personality which may be subserved through its instrumentality—and we need, of course, research designed to reveal how this can best be accomplished.

That the public library is fully cognizant of its opportunity and its responsibility in fostering adult learning and growth is indicated by the rapid development of the readers' advisory service. Many large libraries make definite provision for meeting the educational needs of individual readers by a series of personal consultations carried on over an extended period by specially equipped personnel. Leaders such as Alvin Johnson are now advancing the thesis that the true function of the public library in a democracy should be that of a people's university, broadly conceived to include all activities essential to a full-bodied program of adult education. Playgrounds, recreation "field houses," and other similar institutions must also be seen as integral parts of public education, as must, of course, the C.C.C. and the activities of the N.Y.A.*

Correlative with the changed outlook on education must go a new orientation in educational psychology. We must give consideration to the psychological development of the adult years and must place even more emphasis on the nonintellectual forms of development. A promising beginning has been made in this field and significant findings have already appeared.

Today, however, it cannot be denied that the vast majority of research studies in educational psychology concern the school years and deal with education conceived primarily in terms of schooling. Fortunately, many of the principles adduced from a study of children seem to apply fairly well to adults, though it is unsafe to assume such application without empirical verifications. Since we desire to keep close to verifiable fact, we shall perforce give major emphasis to the educational psychology of the young.

Even this, however, is of course far too ambitious a project for one chapter. We have preferred in what follows to deal with certain sample topics fully enough that the reader may see a little

* C.C.C. stands for Civilian Conservation Corps, and N.Y.A. stands for National Youth Administration.

of the outlook of educational psychology—or at least of one educational psychologist. No attempt at all is made to survey the field as a whole.

Child Nature in Relation to the Education Process

Suppose one is a teacher facing for the first time a class of boys and girls. What would one *most* seek to know? Surely one would not ask the fairy godmother first for knowledge of the subject matter to be imparted nor yet of the methods of teaching it. Neither would one seek first a more consistent philosophy of education, important as that may be. Surely first of all, one would seek to know more about the twenty or thirty or fifty young individuals who sit more or less restless in their appointed places.

Some doubt has been raised as to whether such understanding of the individual can come from scientific psychology. That which is unique necessarily eludes scientific study, we are told, yet it is the unique person who is, without question, the true object of education. Psychology may deal with individual differences but the *individual* remains the forgotten man—or child.

Every Individual Is Unique.—Even if this is admitted—and there are influential psychologists who refuse to admit it—it would still remain true that the unique person can only be understood as a member of a group of other individuals whom he resembles and from whom he differs in myriad ways. A scientific study of individual differences may not be able to grasp the inner secret of individuality; but it is at least a solid basis for understanding the individual, and a necessary basis.

We shall, in what follows, therefore, proceed by analysis of different qualities and processes. Thus in the account of development which immediately follows, we shall consider various of its aspects in separate sections. Yet because these qualities and processes are essentially those of a single person, they are interrelated in complex ways. It must, indeed, never be forgotten that growth in height or in numerical skills or in emotional maturity or in character are interrelated aspects of the developing person who is Jimmie Randolph or Betty Bruce.

Physical Growth and Development.—This is immediately apparent when we consider physical growth, for this is of interest to the psychologist as such only in its bearings on other aspects. But the "only" here may be said to include practically the whole of educational psychology. There is no aspect of a child's behavior which is not influenced greatly by the child's size and strength, and by the attitudes which children take towards this kind of growth.

As Pressey puts it, " for the child, the fact that he is constantly growing is not simply a fact; it is an experience, presenting to him very difficult problems." [2]

The Case of the Oversized Child.—At seven K. M. was as big as most girls of ten and looked the part. When she played with the neighbors' baby they expected her to show the discretion of her apparent age and expressed disgruntled surprize that a "big girl like you should show such poor judgment." Throughout her childhood she was constantly being held to the standards of her size rather than of her social or intellectual maturity. She grew into a petulant young woman who had a sense of always being picked on.

With puberty the problem changed but not for the better. Since she was a good half-head taller than any of her classmates in the rather small high school she attended, to dance with her was literally difficult, and to associate with her socially was for most boys of her age humiliating. During her junior and senior years, she began to associate with college men. This again put upon her the necessity for adjusting to problems beyond her level of social maturity.

Because the men she was associating with were just a little ashamed of "cradle snatching" and also because their intellectual interests were in advance of hers, the relationship was restricted even more than usual to the sole basis of the physical. As a result, K was both bewildered and overstimulated. Only very careful treatment kept her from a career of sex delinquency. Today she looks back to a childhood and adolescence in which she was deprived of experiences necessary for a well-rounded development—deprived of these experiences as truly by her unusual size as another might be by poverty, an inadequate home, or disease.

The Effects of Illness and Disease.—The mention of disease may lead us to consider how this also may be related to behavior. That a seriously sick child cannot learn so well as a normal child is perhaps not so axiomatic as it seems; there are too many examples of invalids who have achieved great things, in and out of school. But the effect of illness upon conduct rather than capacity is surely obvious. Nervousness, crankiness and ill-temper, loss of self-control and a host of other behavior problems are often traceable directly to ill-health. Hardy's study, however, warns us of the complexity of the problem.[3] She found, as might be expected, that children with an excessive amount of illness were more often behavior problems, though the difference was not so great as might have been anticipated. But, short of such extreme cases, even a great deal of illness in childhood does not seem to be correlated very highly with maladjustment in adolescence or early maturity.*

Even without this study, however, we might realize the complexity of the relation when we recall that one and the same illness will make one child fretful and another resigned and "easy to deal with." The effect of health on conduct clearly depends on the co-action of other experiences and on the previous personality of the invalid.

The Effects of Sensory Defect.—A single illustration from the field of sensory defect will help further to make clear the interrelation of physical development with other aspects of growth. Consider the child with severe myopia or short-sightedness. At school, reading is likely to be retarded. He is often unable to see what the teacher puts on the board and is thus retarded in learning. His visual deficiency has generally kept him from exercising his curiosity upon visual forms, hence even when he can see them, he is apt to pay little heed to the differences between *b* and *d* or *p* and *q* or *m* and *n*. (We adults are apt to forget how minor and how intrinsically uninteresting the shapes of letters are to any child, let alone to the handicapped.) And the precise discriminations required for reading, especially in the earlier years, inevitably slow down the person with poor vision.

---

* In passing one may notice that Dr. Hardy found that recollections and school attendance records are but poor guides to the amount of actual illness.

Now reading, being *the* instrument of intellectual progress in school—as doubtless it will continue to be despite the inroads of the "activity movement,"—the next effect of poor eyesight we must take into account is a general lowering of achievement in academic subjects.

The statistics which from time to time purport to show that there is no relation between visual deficiency and school marks are unconvincing when critically examined. Evidence that there is almost no correlation between excellence of vision and marks is irrelevant: Fair, good, and excellent eyes may be substantially alike in serving academic achievement, but our question concerns the effect of drastically poor eyes. As we shall presently note, moreover, those with poor eyesight are not infrequently thrown back upon reading as a substitute for other play and eventually as a sort of compensation they attain higher academic levels. But in the earlier school years the depressing effect of very poor vision is clearly manifest.

We have begun this survey of the effects of poor eyes in typical schoolmasterish fashion by considering "school work." But the child's personality has been developing for six years before he presents himself at the door of the school. What has his defect been doing to this development? And what does it do through the school years?

Consider first the necessity of caution in movement. Parental teaching and a school of literal hard knocks early teach the half-blind child that the impetuous, carefree romping of his comrades is for him full of danger. Glasses, though they help him to see, make only another ground for an unchildlike wariness. Play is restricted in scope and especially in success. The give-and-take of childhood play, the habit of successful and happy competition are held to a minimum. Then, too, the social status of one who cannot play well is seriously impaired. From this comes loss of self-confidence and initiative, and therewith a further impairment in social acceptability.

A more subtle effect concerns the education in emotional language. It is well established that most of our emotional expressions are conventional; both to express and to understand the expressions of others by facial and postural gestures is a thing which must be learned.

Learned, of course, by seeing the subtle play of expression in the faces and bodies of those about us. The blind and the near-blind are shut off from observing these fleeting responses of their associates. If, for example, their talk is tedious, they are oblivious to the warning signals of boredom in their listeners. Nor do they so easily learn by imitation to convey in face and voice the finer shadings of emotional expression. Once more, social acceptability is restricted.

All of these influences tend in the direction of what is called the introverted personality. They tend to shut the handicapped out of the social life of childhood, back upon himself and his own inner resources. And even though one reads but slowly, the *book* then becomes the easiest source of experience and delight; for here are no complicated problems of eye-motor adjustment to unseen flying missiles or obstacles, no comrades who jeer one's failure to "hit it on the nose." Play with others being difficult and all too often humiliatingly unsatisfactory, retreat to the inner world of fantasy and daydreams is an ever-present temptation.

Now none of this, of course, is an inevitable result of severe visual handicap. Other influences may counterbalance or prevail over the push towards an unhealthy kind of introversion which the handicap imposes.

But these counter influences must not be left to chance. It is too much to expect the visually handicapped child of eight to find adequate play substitutes for baseball, too much to expect him to collect the playfellows who will share his own more restricted play interests and skills. Parents and teachers must be alert to discover and make possible for the child adequate outlets—and must do this, if possible, without the appearance of special treatment.

We have treated the case of a single sensory defect at this length, not only because of its intrinsic interest, but because it brings out a number of important general principles. And specifically what we have just stated is the line of attack upon any kind of social maladjustment. Social contacts *can* be fostered, a healthy play life *can* be encouraged and made possible; but only by adults who clearly see the problem. The child who cannot make friends easily, by the very definition of the problem, faces difficulties beyond his unaided power to surmount—this is true no matter whether his friendlessness is due to physical handicap, or to shyness, to poverty or to any other cause. If he is to make progress, the social situation must be simplified for him somehow, or otherwise made easier, until a level is reached where he can successfully cope with his problem. This, as we shall see in a later section, is the essence of all teaching; and social adjustment, no less than geography, presents a problem of teaching.

Factors in Leadership.—The positive side of the medal is no less important if we are to understand child growth. In the life of a child, large-muscle play is so predominant that size, weight, and strength largely determine social status and leadership.

One September morning the writer was watching a third-grade group at play. An enterprizing youngster improvised a typical eight-year-old game. Folding his arms across his chest, he would sneak up behind a playfellow and give him a stiff shove to the sing-song chant: "He who crosses my path gets himself bumped.". The game was gradually taken up by boy after boy till only one was left. This lad was spun helplessly around again and again with mounting pain and dismay. At last, however, he began to understand the game. Then, indeed, the picture changed. To judge by his behavior, he was a rather dull boy, but he was bigger and heavier than any of the others. When he bumped, he bumped solidly. In a very short time, he had assumed a position of unquestioned dominance in the play of the group, and with this dominance a measure of respect. Height and weight had prevailed over alertness as a determiner of social position.

The effects, moreover, of social leadership in childhood play are not lost. Leadership seems compounded in about equal parts of the desire to lead and a knowledge of the necessary techniques. Both are gained more readily by the child with a high size-energy-health index, as is brought out in Cabot's studies of the relation between physique and personality trends.[4] The child who is excluded from leadership in childhood by a frail physique may compensate for a late start, but one may doubt whether his leadership is ever so serene and wholly "natural" a performance as it is in the case of those who learned to lead in the games of childhood.

One more reminder of the complex interrelations with which we are dealing. A child small for his age may play predominantly with younger children and may lead or even tyrannize over them by virtue of his greater intellectual maturity. And all these and similar considerations cut across considerations of environmental opportunity.

These few concrete examples must suffice to illustrate something of the nature of the relationship between physical development and the development of behavior and personality. The examples are admittedly somewhat extreme, yet, paradoxically, they bring out clearly the general principles which pervade the whole topic. They show how unevenness of development imposes strain upon the growing organism. They point to the critical influence of physical status on social acceptability and social development. And, most important, they indicate the possibility of preventing, by taking thought, many or even most of the untoward effects of uneven development.

Intellectual Development.—We have begun our survey of development with the physical aspects because childhood is a time of gross bodily activity and because physical play is the school of personality. Yet it may be questioned whether in the long run these obvious effects of physical status are more important than those which depend upon differences in intelligence. (In any case, we must remember that the two influences interlock.) Especially in adult years, intelligence not only very largely influences success; it very largely determines a whole way of life. In the school years, also, it is a more potent determiner of the child's whole development than is commonly realized.

That it is extremely important in considering academic success almost goes without saying, but there are other and in the end probably more significant correlates of intelligence.

The Case of the Overly Bright Child.—Marian was the youngest of five children. Her intelligence was such as is attained by only one in about ten thousand—not miraculous at all, but distinctly high. Long before she went to school she practically taught herself to read—with a little help from her older sister. Entering school at six, she at once became a serious social problem. Her superiority over the others in the class was evident to her teacher, her classmates, and herself. She was impatient with those who could not do things as well as she and constantly sought permission to recite or otherwise take over the performance at the first sign of others stumbling. Despite tactful handling by the teacher, the other pupils came to resent her "butting in all the time." Conscious of her own rectitude and superiority, Marian reacted by alternate sulkiness and rather spiteful attempts to show the other children up. The suggestion that she be transferred to the second grade met the astonishing objection from the school that this might hinder her social development! It ought surely to have been obvious that her social development was being seriously distorted where she was; it was primarily to obviate this that assignment to a higher grade was sought. The event justified the prognosis. Jumped to the second grade, Marian's conduct became more in accord with what was to be expected from her excellent home. Although she still led the class in academic studies, she found it impossible to lord it over the somewhat older and bigger children; and to maintain her cherished superiority she was compelled to adopt more tactful manners.

Ralph's case is quite parallel. The son of a high school teacher, he was brought to the Psychological Clinic as a behavior problem. At life age $10\frac{1}{2}$ he was apparently already a little bit advanced in the 6th grade. But on the Stanford-Binet test (Form L) he obtained a score equal to that of the average child of 15. On a performance scale (Grace Arthur), he did even better, indicating that his intellectual development was not of a purely verbal type. On a test of academic proficiency he reached the tenth-grade level. No wonder the boy found school deadly dull! No wonder that he thought people did not appreciate him as they ought (they didn't!), that he indulged in fantasies of running away, that he made no friends in this elementary school to which he had just transferred from another town.* No amount of extra promotion would actually solve this problem,

---

* From his replies to the Brown Personality Inventory—a series of questions designed to help a psychological examiner to discover the symptoms of maladjustment. Less than one child in a hundred shows as many signs of strain and unhappiness as did Ralph.

of course. Ralph would be equally maladjusted at 10½ in either sixth or tenth grade. But promotion to the junior high school with a more varied and flexible program gave more scope to his intellectual gifts and did a great deal to help his morale. The full story of Ralph however, cannot be told here. Although his superior intelligence and the failure to give it opportunity to function at school was basic, around this basic difficulty a number of other factors were grouped. Indeed it may be put down as an almost invariable fact that psychological troubles do not come singly.

Is Intelligence Inherited or Acquired?—This question is a hardy perennial which bobs up in every discussion of the subject. The only sensible answer, however, is that it is clearly *both*. No competent authority today questions that differences in environment affect the level of intelligence achieved. It is equally certain that hereditary factors have considerable influence. Despite a great deal of interesting research, it is still too early to say in general how much is attributable to inheritance and how much to environment. And even if we knew the general answer, there would still be individual variations.

It is possible, however, to rephrase the question in more practical terms. First, granted run-of-the-mine conditions of life, how much do people change in relative intelligence? Apparently, rather little. Thus somewhat less than half of the children who are carefully reëxamined show a change of five points or more in the so-called intelligence quotient (when based on the 1916 Stanford Revision of the Binet test).[5] There is thus a very real possibility of predicting the progress in intelligence and of all that depends upon it from a well-conducted examination for intelligence. This is not quite the same thing as underwriting a prediction made by a half-trained person who has administered a "mental test" in routine fashion. For worthwhile results there must be expert testing and even more expert interpretation of test results. Follow-up studies over many years by Gesell and his associates at Yale show, however, surprisingly few deviations from the duly recorded predictions of the line of development made in their clinic.

Like any other prediction, however, prediction of intellectual development is subject to error. Even under what seem to be quite "ordinary" conditions, very considerable fluctuations ·in relative intelligence do turn up occasionally to plague the psychological examiner. And under especially favorable or adverse conditions, still greater changes take place.

Our second question, then, is : What are these favorable or adverse conditions? Reluctantly we must confess our very great, though not complete, ignorance. As might also be expected, the cultural, educational, financial, and social status of the home all have a bearing on development.

But their influence is irregular. The same home which causes, apparently, a marked increase in the intellectual level of one orphan, seems to do little or nothing to the intelligence of another. About all we can say at present is that superior homes are *likely* to harbor the conditions which favor the growth of intelligence; but what, in more detail, these conditions are, is still to be discovered. Only two general principles seem fairly certain: The homes or schools which keep the child happily busy at tasks and activities commensurate with the ability level already attained are those most likely to aid in the further development of ability. And the earlier in life the favorable influences act, the greater their effect; the critical years for determining relative standing in intelligence are those before the child goes to school. Thereafter, all children gain of course; but they seldom change places; the relatively dull remain dull and the relatively bright remain bright.

Practical Uses of Intelligence Testing.—From a practical standpoint all this adds up to the conclusion that the school can place considerable reliance upon the careful intelligence-test result. It measures only one factor in behavior, to be sure, but it measures that factor fairly reliably.

This gives us much greater control over the educative process. It is possible, for example, to judge much more safely whether a child is intellectually old enough to begin school or to carry on the work of a given grade. If he is failing, it helps us to narrow the range of possible causes of failure. And because, by the time a boy or girl enters high school, little change in relative ability can be expected, it is possible to rest educational or vocational guidance upon a fairly secure, even if quite incomplete, base.*

It is now possible, furthermore, to determine the level of intellectual maturity at which certain kinds of learning are possible, as well as whether a given child has reached that level. Thus it has been established that a very great deal of character education misses its goal because it mistakenly assumes a capacity to deal with abstractions about virtuous conduct of which the average child under ten is incapable. Both the curriculum and general program of the school and the judicious treatment of the individual are dependent upon our knowledge of intelligence and the relative constancy with which it develops.

Other Aspects of Intellectual Development

It is difficult, we have seen, to modify a person's relative standing in general intelligence partly because it depends upon such a large number of conditions, many of them very little understood. This is less true, however, of more specific kinds of intellectual development. Growth in numerical skill, for example, depends to a high degree upon specific teaching and other opportunities for learning. Thus, while the prospects of altering the relative intelligence of a child are not, in general, very good, it is entirely possible deliberately to induce growth in number of concepts and arithmetical skills, in handwriting, in knowledge of geography, and—we believe—in pleasingness of personality and in character.

Even here, however, one must reckon with the personal equation. Good teaching and bad teaching alike act on individuals of widely different inherent abilities. It is true that general intelligence is, as we have just seen, partly acquired. But when a fifth grade teacher faces the problem of teaching Joseph arithmetic, his intelligence operates for her as a "given," as something inherent in Joseph. Only

---

*In some quarters this is dubbed a fatalistic doctrine, and one inimical to democracy. We fail to see, however, anything undemocratic in the attempt to find the kind of education or the kind of job which is best suited to a person's capacity.

There is an issue for democracy, however, though of quite a different character, tied up with the matter of intelligence tests. Half of the high school graduates who have the intellectual capacity for college work are denied the opportunity, chiefly because of lack of money. This is stultifying to both the principles and the prospects of real democracy.

in very exceptional cases will Joe's "IQ" change fast enough for the change to affect, during a particular school year, his ability to absorb arithmetic.

Relation of Intelligence to School Success.—Common experience, of course, fully confirms the theoretical expectation that there is a relation between intelligence and the learning of school subjects. It is more difficult than might be anticipated, however, to state exactly how close the relation is. Under ordinary school conditions intelligence correlates about .50 or .60 with scholastic achievement. This means that about a third of the differences between pupils is attributable to intelligence. But this relation holds only under the above mentioned "ordinary school conditions"; it is subject to very considerable change with every change in the circumstances. If all the pupils are very much alike in intelligence, the differences found will be nearly all attributable to "other factors" and the resulting correlation between intelligence and achievement will be low. If, on the other hand, the pupils tested differ very greatly in intelligence, then intelligence will account for much more of the difference in achievement; and the correlation will be high. A blanket statement about the "true" relation of intelligence to achievement is simply impossible.*

Should Pupils Be Grouped According to Ability?—It is considerations of this sort which lend an air of unreality to most discussions of "homogeneous grouping." There is at least an initial plausibility in the idea that pupils should be divided for teaching purposes into groups of approximately equal ability. The proposal to do so (on the basis, in early days, solely of intelligence tests) met both enthusiastic welcome and heated protest. The plan was characterized on the one hand as violently undemocratic and on the other as the salvation of democracy. And elaborate statistics were prepared showing how much more (or less) was learned under homogeneous than under heterogeneous grouping.

---

* That is, in the absence of a true zero point in the measurement of both intelligence and achievement. Our statement is an elaboration of the practical deduction to be made from the acknowledged relativity of measurement in these fields.

Apparently it did not occur to most of the contestants in either camp to notice that any system of dividing pupils by grades is already a form of "homogeneous grouping," and that what was being debated was merely a question of how much further to carry the grouping. The answer, moreover, is clear: *Other things being equal*, the more nearly pupils are equal in ability, the more nearly they will profit equally from the same instruction.

Unfortunately for simplicity, other things never are equal. Complex problems of motivation present themselves: Will the dull be better motivated if grouped with others of like intellect or be stimulated by the performance of the superior children? (The former, apparently.) What is the effect on personality? Are children thus made too acutely aware of intellectual differences with resulting conceit or shame respectively? (That depends very largely on how the system is handled; in general, segregation apparently tells the children nothing they haven't long guessed about their own abilities, but it sometimes gives openings for opprobrious remarks about the inferior.) Should not social development be a factor in grouping? (Without question; probably it is the first thing to be considered. But we cannot tell in general which makes more social maladjustment: To be schooled with those who are decidedly inferior intellectually so that one gets into all manner of bad attitudes; or to be grouped with those physically and perhaps socially more mature. Compare the cases of Marian and Ralph in the preceding section. The question as to where the child is most likely well adjusted must be raised in each individual case on its own merits.)

And so one might go on. Obviously the proper placement of a child in school is to be decided on the basis of all his characteristics, not just on his intelligence. We try to put him in the group where he will show the greatest all-round development. At most, we can say that intelligence is the leading determiner in individual cases more often than any other quality.

Special Talents and Defects.—It may be urged, however, that achievement in arithmetic or music or languages is determined more by special talents than by general intelligence. The question of the very existence of special talents is a thorny one. Some psychologists seem to deny them altogether, others to minimize their effect. Of one thing we may be quite sure: It is in the last degree unlikely that we are born with special talents corresponding at all closely with the highly artificial and conventional divisions of school subject matter. The boy or girl "just naturally" good at figures was not really "born that way"; his special flair is acquired.

Even so, for a particular teacher special talent and, more pressingly, special disability are like intelligence, somewhat in the nature of a "given"; in one short year, the teacher cannot hope to make up *all* the deficiencies of previous environment and training. Struggling with the reasonably intelligent girl who repeatedly confuses the imperfect with the imperative, the teacher may be excused if he concludes that "the gift of language was just left out of Amy's make-up."

Careful investigations, however, clearly indicate that school failure is rarely if ever due to such specific and irremediable defect. Amy's dullness in French, Carl's stupidity in history, and Marylyn's failure at contract bridge are all found to be due to a subtle interplay between interests, early training, and present motivation. The situation can always be modified by effective teaching aware of the individual factors operating in each case. Whether in a given case it is worth the effort, whether for example it is worth while to struggle with Amy's French, depends upon the values put upon a particular subject of study *for a particular child*. At any rate, the pupil's present intellectual status is less useful as a fatalistic determiner of what can possibly be learned than as a guide to where and how to set about the educative process.

The Development of Personality

Without explicitly saying so, we have discussed the growth of personality while considering physical and intellectual growth. A brief specific treatment of the development of personality, however, would seem to be in order. Unfortunately it is beset with grave difficulties.

In the first place, although there is a very real sense in which we may speak of the unity of personality, the development of personality must be considered as proceeding along many relatively distinct lines —even more so than in the case of physical or intellectual development. The trouble is that we do not know just what the basic lines of development are. This gives rise to difficulties which are by no means purely academic.

Likable Personalities.—Let us take a simple example. Since personality is primarily a matter of emotional and social adjustment, it seems not unreasonable to consider "likability" as one of its components, and growth in likability as a goal of educational effort. Well, here are two children, both rather disinclined to talk very much. In other respects, however, they are very different; they belong, as we sometimes say, to different types. It is clearly conceivable, therefore, that the training which increases talkativeness may make one child more likable, the other much less. We succeed in being likable, in other words, by so many different means that no single training formula is of much value.*

Neglect of such considerations is a prime error in the mail order courses which promise to develop in everyone a radiant personality. The sovereign remedies, the little tricks which take no account of basic factors—it is folly to think of applying these mechanically to all and sundry. The small good they do in a few cases is more than offset by the harm done in the vast majority of cases by raising unfounded hopes and by encouraging people to depend upon essentially magical procedures instead of rationally directed effort.

The commercial success—for their sponsors—of such courses should, however, be a source of shame to psychologists. It points to a need for a sound program which we are as yet ill-equipped to supply. Indeed the success—again for the salesman—of quack schemes for improving oneself or one's condition "in twelve easy lessons" is a challenge to all educators. And the educational psychologist might well ask, in the cant phrase of the day, "What do these quacks have that we don't have?" that they are so successful in peddling their wares.

---

* The difficulty is not lessened by the fact that all personality traits are to some extent relative to the observer. Not only does each one attain likability in different ways; one's likability is a different thing for different people.

Maturity of Personality.—Another difficulty faces us when we seek to improve personality—certainly not one which troubles the "get-rich-in-personality-quick experts" but does perplex the real educator. In the case of physical and intellectual growth, we have little doubt as to the value of reaching a mature level, and small doubt as to what maturity is. True, when we look upon a young and altogether delightful babe or small child we are often tempted to wish that it might remain in this immature condition, but we really know better. True, also, that not many years ago there were men who frankly avowed their desire to have women remain intellectually undeveloped; but this again is an outworn attitude. The desirability of a mature development in these areas is unquestioned.

When we turn to social or emotional maturity, however, we do not know just what it is or just what kinds of maturity in personality are desirable and should be sought in education. Growing up, in this field, seems somehow intimately related to the culture in which a child lives. In our culture, for example, growing up involves coming to terms with competition between persons. To become an adult thus means learning how to compete successfully. But as Margaret Mead [6] has shown us, among the Arapeshes of New Guinea there is no need to develop aggressiveness or competitiveness, and growing up does not in that tribe involve development along these lines.

Now of course we are engaged in educating young Americans, not young Arapeshes, and we should, reasonably, prepare them for the society in which they are to live. Society, however, is not static but eternally changing; and education, is, or should be, a prime agency in such change. Perhaps we have too much competition in our social life; in that case education should discourage competitiveness. Eventually it might be possible to develop a social order in which competitiveness might seem, not adult but childish.

At least for the present, however, it is clear that education will be some kind of a compromise. Children will have to learn to adjust themselves to a world in which competition is a fact and maturity will therefore involve learning how to compete. But they may also learn that there are many values in life, some of which are really antagonistic to competitiveness; and they may learn to work toward a form of society in which aggressive competitiveness shall be at least minimized.

The example shows how complex is the problem of attempting to chart progress toward the goal of mature personality, when we aren't sure just what maturity means. It would be misleading, however, to emphasize our ignorance at this point unduly. We certainly cannot say that extroverts are more mature than introverts; but we can describe forms of both extroverted and introverted behavior which are more mature than certain other forms of extroversion and introversion. We can certainly declare that the modulation of emotional response, its nice gradation to suit the objective requirements of the situation, is more mature than the explosive, all-or-none response which is so commonly exhibited by the child.

Maturity of Interests.—In the field of interests, also, very significant studies have been made which show that growth toward maturity takes certain characteristic directions—at least in our present society.

Thus one has only to examine surveys of childhood interests (or indeed to recall his own development) to discover that not only do interests change markedly, but that there is a fairly consistent pattern and direction to that change. From simple five-year-old games of tag, playing house, or playing with blocks the development is rapid through active sports and games at ten, more complexly organized sports at 15, and a rapid turning to social interests—dancing, cards, etc.—during adolescence. Girls give up their dolls for more adult interests, for dates. Boys gradually discard their marbles and kites and turn to the sex-social sports of swimming and tennis, which in the 'teens become popular with both sexes. In short, play tends to increase in complexity and vigor with physical and mental growth, and the recreational situation becomes increasingly dominated by sex-social interests. At first recreational interests are not distinguishable from the vocational; as the years slip by into adolescence, vocational interests become more serious, better related to the workaday world if not always to the youth's capacities.

Now deviation from the normal interest development in any one respect need not be serious, though it is usually significant. It would be a mistake to consider an adolescent girl abnormal if she found great pleasure in dressing dolls; it would be equally a mistake to ignore such a deviation from the usual. Behavior of this sort needs to be understood in relation to the whole personality. And a picture of the normal development in many interests does enable us to check up on an individual case, to see where the child is falling behind his fellows to a crippling extent, and particularly to note those cases where interests remain impoverished and juvenile.* A mere statistical concept of what is mature often proves distinctly useful.

Signs of Unwholesome Development.—Nor is this all. Even if we cannot say that this or that line of development is more mature and therefore more desirable than another, there are certain other kinds of development which we can say are definitely unwholesome or dangerous. Not, however, that even these are obvious. In principle, to be sure, we should all agree that any kind of development which pointed toward mental disorder or criminality was most undesirable, but a long line of investigators have shown that parents and teachers do not recognize the signs of incipient unwholesome development. They tend to be more exercised when a child exhibits troublesome or bothersome behavior than when he acts in mentally unhealthy ways. Recently there have been indications that more attention is being given to wholesomeness of personality; apparently emphasis upon the mental-hygiene point of view is producing some results. But the change is not yet great even as a matter of accepted point of view; and one strongly suspects that the change in practice is even less.

One does not wish to close this very brief survey of the development of personal quality on too negative a note. Scientific study of personality has barely begun, yet much has already been accomplished. Studies have shown how readily children's attitudes may be changed by movies, the radio, drama, and the arts. They have shown, too, something of the limitations of moralizing instruction and have suggested some of the reasons for its failure in most cases. The very valuable studies of *Character Education Inquiry* [7] have at least shown

---

* For adults, of course, a certain restriction of interest range becomes a necessity of effective work. But a child or adolescent needs many and varied interests, both because life is pleasanter and because an exploration of future possibilities is desirable.

us some of the ways in which character does *not* develop, and have thus laid the basis for a constructive approach. Even now, educational psychology is rich with many, if somewhat isolated, suggestions for those whose privilege it is to assist children in developing fine personality and character; the near future should see extraordinary progress in this field.

THE PROBLEM OF LEARNING

How a person shall develop, we have been insisting, is largely a result of learning. How, then, does this learning take place, under what sorts of favorable or unfavorable conditions? This is obviously a very important, practical question.

Or is it just one question? Is there just one process of learning or are there many? This is not merely an academic issue. For if there are several different processes by which we learn, the favorable conditions for learning may be for each process quite different. We do not expect to train runners for short distances and for long distances by the same training regime, although we may speak of training for running-speed in both cases. We recognize that sprinting and distance running are largely different processes despite the identity of the *word* running applied to both. Surely, then, we ought not to let the identity of the word learning mislead us into an oversimplified picture of the processes by which we *learn*.

Memory and Habit Formation.—As a matter of fact, the older psychologies did make distinction between memory, as a sort of "higher" learning, and habit-forming. Memory was primarily (or exclusively) human, habit was part of our animal inheritance. Even William James, who theoretically challenged the distinction, treated memory and habit in widely separated chapters.

As the doctrine of evolution began to take hold in psychology, however, this view was bound to be called in question. For evolution means—or was thought to mean—a persistent effort to explain human behavior in terms applicable also to lower animals and to explain the higher functions of man in terms of lower functions. Memory was thus to be considered only a more complex habit.

A half-century of active experimentation and no less active theorizing have made abundantly clear that in fact memory and habit are fundamentally very similar, perhaps quite identical. Nor is there a competent psychologist alive today who would seek to make a sharp distinction between the learning of animals and of man. The present writer believes, even so, that the rich tangle of facts brought to light by a half-century of research can only be put in order by giving up the idea of a single fundamental learning process. The old distinction between memory and habit does not hold; but it does not follow that we have no other distinctions in kinds of learning.

Many Varieties of Learning.—It is only fair to warn the reader that this view is somewhat heretical. And it is very difficult to support it in brief compass without being unfair to opponents. Note how we closed the previous paragraph. The final statement is a bit of quite unassailable logic—which means, of course, that no intelligent person challenges it. Why then do we trouble to print it? Because it is really a necessary starting point in our thinking. But there is always danger in a brief statement addressed to persons not familiar with the topic that the very printing will seem to imply that our opponents deny the logic. Of course they do not; they merely insist that we show evidence that the processes by which we learn *are* really multiple.

We then support our position by pointing to sound experiments leading to apparently contradictory conclusions. This, we argue, can be most readily explained if we recognize that there is more than one kind of learning. A conclusion valid for one kind might easily be inapplicable to another. We should have to admit, however, that there are other possible explanations of the discrepancies. Again, in a brief statement, it is difficult enough to be fair to one's own position, let alone to one's opponent's.

It is safe to assert, at any rate, that there is no agreement as to whether the learning process is single or multiple, or as to just what it is. A general theory of learning which would cover all cases is still somewhat premature. This is regrettable; a sound general theory of learning would be very useful. But the lack of such theory need not—and has not—kept us from finding empirically and experimentally principles of great practical value. Much of the best work in educational psychology today is devoted to the elucidation of relatively detailed practical rules.

A Definition of Learning.—There is little that unifies these detailed principles or rules; a fact which does not make easier the task of one who must survey the field in half a chapter. But there is this common element: All are concerned with the way the organism, be it human or other animal, improves as the result of experience or training. This in fact is the best we can do in the way of a brief definition of learning.

The definition ignores rather than denies the cooperative role of heredity. We have earlier insisted that it is impossible to conceive of change except in terms of *both* hereditary and environmental influences. We attribute to learning that aspect of the change which is consequent upon the latter.

This is a matter of definition and for our general orientation. In specific studies, however, it is generally necessary to take full account of maturation (which is the result of the convergence of hereditary and *prior* learning influences) as well as of the present environment factors.

Learning as Activity.—Learning is not passive absorption but an active response made when the learner experiences a need. Indeed the learning is effective in proportion as the goal is specific and well-defined. We must not overemphasize a conscious understanding of this goal, though that may be useful. What is necessary is that the target be specific, that there be activity and that it be directed at the target.

It may be theoretically possible to learn wholly unintentionally; there is a considerable amount of not very convincing evidence on this point. It is unnecessary, of course, for the learner to say to himself, "Now I want to remember this"; that may even act as a distraction.* But for effective learning (most investigators believe for any learning at all) it is necessary that the response to be learned

---

* None the less, a certain conscious realization of what one is trying to do is a help. A whole series of experiments show how little is learned unless there is *intent to learn*. Unfortunately intent to learn is not enough!

have definite relation to a goal, that the learner be actively attacking a problem or problematic situation.

This necessity for activity has in theory long been recognized. Without activity there is no learning. Hence the old so-called "Law of Use or of Exercise" (which held that learning is proportionate to exercise or repetition) and the emphasis in school upon drill, however mechanical. We now realize, however, that the activity must be activity directed toward a goal, fulfilling a need.

More Than Activity Is Necessary.—In a long series of experiments, Thorndike who first clearly formulated the "Law of Use," himself has shown its limitations. What happens, he asked, when a person is frequently confronted by a situation, or when he acts many times in the same way in the presence of a situation, without realizing the relation of the act to the situation. Results were quite unequivocal. Repetition of a situation in and of itself confers no learning. Reacting in the same way to a situation with no realization of the relationship the act has to the situation does not necessarily lead to a strong habit. There are many illustrations of this in everyday life. Consider that "you practically always raise the body and bend it back after tying your shoes, and so have the sensations of bending the body back as a sequent to those of tying your shoes. You have done this from 10,000 to 40,000 times—but the experience of tying your shoes has probably never called to mind any sensation—of the backward body-bending." Thorndike concludes, "All educational doctrines which attach value to experience or activity as such, irrespective of the direction of the experience or activity and of its consequences, are made less acceptable than before. Experience, in the sense of merely confronting and responding to the situations of life, can hardly be a powerful agent for either good or harm when several thousand repetitions of such an experience do so little." [8]

Exercise or activity must be supplemented, then, according to Thorndike, by a realization of its "Belongingness." When we learn a motor skill—riding a bicycle, for example—it is rare that its personal significance escapes us. We know what we are trying to do, even though the relation of subordinate part-skills to the whole is not always grasped. When it comes to knowledge or "book learning," however, it is quite clear that all too often the material offered the child has no relation, which the child can see, to his personal goals or needs.

Now in proportion as it lacks such relation, the material offered is uninteresting or meaningless. And a long series of experiments have made clear that learning is efficient almost in proportion to the extent that what is learned possesses meaning.[9]

Indeed, were it not for the kind of learning which finds its clearest expression in the conditioned response, we should be tempted to suppose that meaningfulness is an absolute prerequisite to learning. But there is too much evidence which seems to show that there is learning of a sort at least partly independent of meaning, that almost meaningless material can be learned (and of course thereby take on meaning). English and his coworkers, in an extended series of experiments, have put to the test a reformulation of an earlier hypothesis: That there are two sorts of learning, one which is like the conditioned response, is uninfluenced by meaning, and depends primarily upon frequency of repetition; and another which is directly dependent on meaningfulness (and probably independent of repetition.)[10] These two processes, however, are never found apart, though their respective contributions to a given bit of learning may vary.

While a considerable body of experimental fact from various sources seems to support this hypothesis, the issue is far from clear. For one thing, meaningfulness is an attribute of the learning task whereas the learning process must ultimately be characterized in terms of some activity of the learner. "Insight," "belongingness," and "reorganization" have been suggested as better descriptions partly for this reason.*

In any case the statement stands that meaningfulness makes for efficiency. To establish what is properly called a conditioned response (in which meaning is apparently all but ruled out) requires many repetitions and such highly special conditions of isolation of the animal from all competing stimuli that it cannot be considered effi-

---

* There may seem to be a perplexing variety of terms used to express the fact that activity alone is not enough. The diversity is not due to inability to agree on words; it is due to the fact that the "something other than activity" is as yet not accurately isolated and identified, hence can be only approximately named. But there is energetic experimentation which should shortly remedy this defect.

cient—except in the sense that we can by this means learn what cannot, apparently, otherwise be learned at all. And when we turn to classroom conditions the superiority of that which the individual learner finds meaningful is beyond all question.

Interest and Learning.—The doctrine of interest in education, as set forth by John Dewey, finds here much of its validation. Dewey's position, though stated with great clearness, has often been grossly misinterpreted. The teacher was expected to trick the child into learning by dressing things up in an "interesting" dress—which was to run the risk that only the interesting concomitants would be learned.

Interest Depends on Meaning or Significance.—It would probably be much better if teachers were not told that they should interest the child. "Interest" is only indirectly a cause or a favoring factor in learning. Instead, let this be firmly realized: The child finds interesting that which is significant or meaningful for him, that which evokes in him purposeful striving. And it is under these conditions also that he learns. But the feeling of interest is obviously not so much a *cause* of learning as a *sign* that the effective conditions of learning —namely significance or meaningfulness—are present. Interest is a guide, not a goal of teaching.

The practical difference is very great. The teacher is led to be concerned not to see that things are made "interesting" but that they are made significant, and hence learnable. He must insure that what is offered for learning will be seen as relevant to the goals and purposes which are alive for the learner.

It is probable that Dewey's position was misunderstood at least in part because of a confusion between the "feeling of interest" and "interests." Of course these are related terms but they are not the same. The feeling of interest is part of the response we make to anything significant; our interests, on the other hand, are merely another name for the above-mentioned living goals and purposes which must be "tapped" if learning is to proceed. The one is a symptom, the other a necessary condition. It seems to the writer much safer therefore if we usually avoid speaking of interest and think rather in terms of the significant or the meaningful, of that which is relevant to purposes.

Even so, we cannot evade the question whether we do not imply a curriculum built around the necessarily immature purposes (or "interests") of the child. How, one may well ask, is society to progress if education must be guided by the evanescent whims or transient enthusiasms of the child? In one form or another, this question is raised in every class in teacher training, year after year.

Now of course the answer is that only very superficial followers of the doctrine of interest propose to identify the goals of education with the child's goals or interests. We do indeed propose to build the curriculum about the child's present interests—that is, about the goals or purposes which are real for him—but we do so in such a way that his interests will expand and develop in an intelligent and adult direction. Not present purposes alone but purposes as they may become is the concern of education.

Motivation and Learning.—It is sometimes said that if we can only link learning activities to the urgently felt needs of the pupil, there is no problem of motivation. We should not, however, allow our sense of the dramatic to run away with us. Thrilling purposes and pressing needs are colorful and obvious; but the greater part of a person's learning goes on in quieter fashion when meeting less dramatic crises or solving more humdrum problems. Under favorable circumstances a relatively weak purpose can be the occasion of most valuable learning, and fortunately so.

We must not forget, however, that a person is the focus of many needs of differing strengths, and that the respective responses to these needs are sometimes mutually incompatible. Some of our needs, therefore, may fail to give rise to learning activity unless the relatively weak purpose is somehow strengthened. Such strengthening of the relatively weaker purpose is what we mean by motivation.*

Now it seems to be the typical school learning situation to require some degree of motivation. Relatively seldom, whether he likes it or not, can the teacher establish a direct relation between a powerful

---

* We are not for present purposes making a sharp distinction between incentive and motivation.

purpose in the pupil and the learning activities that we wish.* A major responsibility is to get pupils to learn many things for which, to put it mildly, they have no great yearning.

There is thus a real problem of motivation. Many psychologists, however, have come to believe, on the basis of extensive experimentation, that motivation has no direct effect on learning. This sounds pretty serious until we ask what motivation does do. Its function, we learn, is to stimulate activity or performance. Now activity, as we saw in an earlier section, does not necessarily lead to learning; but there is no learning without it.† Hence motivation may by stimulating activity, indirectly enable us to promote learning and especially to guide learning in appropriate directions.

An obvious caution is, however, suggested. Since mere activity is insufficient, there still remains with the teacher the duty of rendering what is to be learned not only attractive but intelligible. And we must not expect to find any direct proportional relation between the intensity of motivation and the amount of learning.‡

Socialization.—As a schoolroom device for motivation, socializing the learning period is one of the most interesting and useful. One can easily think up a number of reasons why children learn better when working by themselves. The experimentally demonstrated fact is, however, that efficiency is decidedly increased by a large amount of social activity in learning. (Of course there is also need for a great amount of strictly individual studying.)

---

* The last phrase reveals the writer's educational philosophy that society may legitimately impose upon the child certain ultimate objectives, such objectives as skill in the use of language, adequate arithmetic, graceful and healthful posture, honesty, love of country.

The whole confused issue of propaganda in education is, of course, involved. Let us merely record our judgment that the school cannot escape the task of selecting objectives for the pupils. One primary objective—still selected by adults for the pupil—may well be that the pupil shall develop intelligence enough ultimately to choose for himself; but even this does not enable the school to avoid intermediate guidance. Those who hold otherwise seem not to understand the implications of their words.

† Sometimes we seem to get such a direct relation; every increase in motivation is paralleled by an increase in learning. But in other carefully controlled experiments this is not the case. Leuba gives an illuminating discussion.[11]

‡ There is a sense, of course, in which whatever we do leads to a change—and this may be called learning if one wishes. More often, however, we think of learning as a *progressive* change or improvement. And activity certainly does not guarantee, but is necessary for, improvement.

Thus certain German psychologists as early as the beginning of the century found performance notably improved under social conditions. They found homework less accurate and less rapid than work done under such social conditions as a study hall provides. Many laboratory studies, both there and in this country, were later carried out in which the mere presence of other persons seemed (in general) to improve performance.[12]

More important for school practice is the series of experiments on the *cooperating* social group. The experimental work on this subject, both in the laboratory and in the classroom, has been well summarized by the Murphys.[13] Not quite all the results are consistent, though the trend in favor of group study and discussion as compared with more individualized procedures is fairly clear. The following are, perhaps, typical. Barton[14] found that four days of group discussion of algebra problems produced a large and reliable superiority in achievement over the method of individual assignment, initial ability and training being carefully balanced. Bane[15] found discussion particularly helpful for long-time retention—probably because discussion insured more active participation and an attempt to understand interrelations.

Most impressive of all is Collings'[16] four-year comparison of a highly socialized with a more conventional school program. A number of other factors in addition to socialization doubtless played their part, so the experiment cannot be regarded as very conclusive. But we can hardly ignore a program in which the socialized groups did 38 per cent better in school subject matter than did the comparison groups from the same county.

It is worth noting that the pupils were also learning how to cooperate as well as learning subject matter better. Collings reports also marked superiority for other desirable learnings in the school which socialized its program.

Coming at the problem from a very different angle, Lewin and his associates have shown that the cooperative situation is decidedly more favorable to the development of personality (which after all is also a matter of learning) than individualistic procedures.[17] All in all, the argument for cooperative or socialized situations is too strong to be ignored—though whether it is strong enough to overcome the inertia which protects traditional practice is another matter.

Competition and Rivalry.—This is, of course, the commonest device to stimulate individuals to learning activity. Its influence was eliminated with difficulty from most of the studies made of the effect of socialization. Is it effective in increasing performance or activity? Undoubtedly. Whether competition or any other motivation produces learning rather than mere activity is, as we have insisted all along, dependent upon other factors.

Certainly children who would never for a moment have done certain things necessary for learning have been aroused by competition, by rivalry, to intense activity. All too often, however, the feverish activity fails to lead to learning or to the learning desired. Emphasis upon competition may result primarily in learning how to compete. Whether this seems a desirable outcome depends partly on one's social philosophy and very much upon the personality of the learner—most of us, apparently, need to learn how to cooperate far more than we need to learn how to compete.

Much experimental ingenuity has been expended in the attempt to discover the relative potency of various kinds of competition. Thus Maller,[18] working with higher elementary school classes found the motives studied to be effective in the following order: (1) Work for one's own sex; (2) work for oneself; (3) work for one's team (constituted by pupil choice); (4) work for one's school class; (5) work for an arbitrary group assigned by the teacher.

It must be noted, in the first place, however, that these are only group differences. For a given child one of the motives which is generally weaker may be very much the stronger. Psychologists and educators, though they talk much of individual differences, have yet to learn to take them seriously. Whenever, therefore, we are presented with an average we should at once reply: "Interesting and useful but what about individuals?"

In the second place, apparently very slight changes in circumstances modify the result. Thus the frequency with which the children were shifted from one motivation to the other affected the differences in performance. Obviously the situation is extremely complex and description in terms of "self-competition versus group competition" is only a very crude first approximation to a careful analysis.*

Finally we must note again that Maller was measuring the effect of competition on *performance,* not directly on learning. It is certainly easily possible, even probable, that self-competition is more *likely* to result in a meaningful performance than group-competition. Working, that is to say, against one's own record, one is more likely to ask what it is all about.† In any case, we must always be alert to ask ourselves *what* is being learned as a result of the activity induced by the competition. The writer, for one, admits his inability to say by sheer deduction what are the personality and character effects of self-competition or whether they are better or worse than those of group-competition. Yet such learnings are obviously of more critical importance than learning the location of Danzig and its relation to Polish commerce—significant as the latter is to one's world outlook. A more mature educational psychology such as is beginning to emerge will not leave such questions to speculation.

Reward and Punishment.—Another familiar motivation is the giving or promising to give rewards, the inflicting or threatening to inflict punishment or pain. In view of the conflicting experimental evidence, the naïve confidence of most parents and teachers in these modes of motivation is most curious. Almost certainly the problem is not even properly stated in terms of "reward" and "punishment"— almost certainly, that is to say, there is no one kind of thing which happens to a person, no one process which goes on inside him, when he is "rewarded." And it is still less likely that "punishment" can thus be regarded as a unitary variable. It is therefore hardly reasonable to expect to find any consistent relation between punishment and either learning or performance.

A parallel may help us to see what is meant here. On this hot sticky evening the writer will abandon all scientific caution and admit his

---

* That is, experimental results and theoretical analysis alike suggest that competition is not a unified variable at all but only the name of a *group* of influences which may affect performance in differing ways.

† If, however, group-competition is associated with discussion, self-competition may lose its advantage.

belief that climate affects, let us say sweetness of disposition. Today the temperature happens to have reached 90° F. with a relative humidity of 92 per cent. Now in spite of the "bromide," it is not only the heat but the humidity; both must be considered. Why not get a "climatic index" by adding degrees of temperature to percentage of humidity?

A "climatic index" of 182, that is, of 90 + 92 would be "something" however obtained, but we can see how meaningless the device is if we take an index of say 95. This might be a temperature of 90° F. and humidity of only 5 per cent (the Sahara Desert) or it might be 40° F. and 45 per cent humidity—surely two radically different climates. We would hardly expect a "climatic index," thus calculated, to show a consistent relation with anything. It is suggested that the case may not be greatly different with "punishment" as defined either in school or in most psychological experiments. Very severe punishment (paralleling the "climatic index" of 182) fairly consistently disorganizes the recipient and interferes with adjusted response and with learning. But milder punishment sometimes seems to help, sometimes to hinder—presumably because such mild punishment may represent "different climates." And what constitutes mild or severe punishment is almost impossible of general definition.

It seems hardly worth while, therefore, to review the experimental literature dealing with this subject. Most of it is designed to throw light on a complex theoretical issue which remains completely unsettled. The practical question, however, remains: Should the school use punishment and reward, either or both?

It is necessary at this point to make a distinction between the strictly disciplinary use of punishment and the use of punishment for the promotion of learning. And we need spend very little time here over the former, though it constitutes a fascinating chapter in educational psychology by itself. There is reasonable ground for difference of opinion as to how much discipline, and what kind, is needed in the school, but there is no question that it is needed. Among other things, discipline implies constraint and inhibition of pupil action. There are various ways of securing such inhibition—punishment is one. Punishment is a way of stopping a child from doing something.

Now in a particular case, inhibitions may or may not be necessary or valuable, depending on a variety of considerations. It may even have a relation to learning. Punishment may be necessary—or at least the only thing a harassed teacher can think of—to keep one child from disrupting the classroom and thus preventing *other pupils* from learning. It is even possible to use punishment *to keep a child* himself from learning bad habits. But it does so, not by acting directly on the learning process, but by stopping the activity from being exercised.

Obviously such a use of punishment involves, if it is to be effective, very close supervision over the whole life of the pupil and is generally quite impracticable. A teacher might, by very severe punishment, prevent pupils from practicing during school hours an undesirable speech form: say the double negative "haven't got no." But the teacher controls only a small part of the pupil's day. He may prevent practice of "haven't got no" ten times a day while forty other times it goes unprevented. If the punishment is unusually effective, the specific speech habit may even be completely inhibited *in the classroom* but it usually remains undiminished elsewhere. The purely disciplinary use of punishment is too negative to be of much use in learning.

But is the disciplinary value the only use of punishment? Is there not a "Law of Effect" which states that the painful or the unsatisfactory effect of an action causes it to be unlearned? The answer, apparently must be in the negative, both on grounds of theory and everyday experience. The punishment of a rat every time he takes the wrong pathway in a maze experiment serves eventually to compel the rat to take the *right* path—he has nothing else to do. And the learning comes from what the rat does, not from what it does not do. But punishing a child for an error in grammar or in morals is quite different from punishing the rat in a maze; it still leaves him with an infinitude of other errors to make. Under ordinary conditions, punishing a mistake is obviously less than half the battle.

If Tuckman's [19] experiments are to stand, punishment is indeed less than half the battle in teaching to eliminate habitual error. In his experiments, children seemed to learn to repeat their mistakes even though they were punished for them. Apparently, punishment or no punishment, we do not learn *from* our mistakes as much as we learn to make them again. And indeed a candid examination of the human scene must convince anyone of the persistence of error despite the clearest indication that the error leads to ill effects.

None of this, of course, calls into question the fact that men or children sometimes deliberately and rationally refrain from doing things because of the fear of consequences. If we are not as rational as we like to think, it cannot be doubted that we are occasionally able to rise above the level of immediate impulse. Punishment and reward may therefore play their part as *guides* to learning, as signals to the learner as to what he is to try to learn. As such their consideration belongs in the next section. But there is very inadequate evidence for the common belief that either punishment or reward has a direct effect on the processes of learning. Like other incentives, they may redirect *activity*—which may or may not lead to learning, or to the learning desired.

This brings us once more to point out the danger inherent in the use of incentives. In one sense it is highly unlikely, of course, that the child who is rewarded learns *nothing*; the trouble is that he is too likely to learn merely to seek the reward. Thus in school, marks may become the end sought instead of skills, knowledge, and character. It is equally unlikely that the punished child learns absolutely nothing. But since we learn only what we do, the child's learning is all too likely to be limited to hating or fearing the adult who is chastizing him. The emotionally charged atmosphere of punishment and conflict is certainly tremendously unfavorable to learning anything else. To use punishment, therefore, as an emergency measure of discipline to put an end then and there to serious or dangerous misconduct may well be defended; but those who use it as a way to promote learning must reckon with its purely negative and highly ineffective nature.

Guidance in Learning.—All education may be thought of as an attempt to guide the learning process. Yet how surprisingly little we know about the intimate details involved. When should we help a pupil—if at all—when should we let him work at his problems by himself? And by what techniques shall we proceed? One of the earliest techniques studied scientifically is also one of the oldest as a teaching device. The pupil is physically constrained in some fashion or other while performing the act to be learned. The hand of the little child is held and guided as he forms "his letters" or the letter to be formed is grooved and the pencil traces in the groove.

The chief defect of this technique is that the child does not learn the right activity. Tracing letters is just not writing. Learning to be sensitive to the pressures of the teacher's restraining fingers when one's movements go astray is of little help when the teacher's hand is no longer there.

Mechanical Guidance.—Mechanical aids to learning have therefore come into marked disfavor—and rightly so if they cause the learner to develop dependence upon the device. This need not be the case, however; indeed the exact opposite effect may be secured. Thus during the World War the writer and two associates [20] developed a device which demonstrated to the inexpert rifleman that he was not "squeezing the rifle stock" hard enough in the process of firing. The device permitted, indeed almost compelled, the learner to get the "feel" of a proper squeeze; and it set up a standard by which he could tell when that proper "feel" had been attained. The device was amazingly successful in the teaching of men given up as hopeless by their company officers. [21]

How does this differ from teaching children to write by tracing in a groove? Clearly in this: That the learner is not taught dependence upon any cue to correct performance which he cannot have in ordinary practice. Rather the device served chiefly to turn the learner's attention to precisely that guide to correctness which he must in this action always use. Even in seemingly routine skills there must be a sort of "understanding" or insight, though that understanding may be sensory rather than intellectual; and any guidance given must have as its purpose to promote this grasp of what is to be done. Guidance by mechanical means thus differs only in unimportant detail from guidance by explanation and direction in words.

It is probable, however, that in nonverbal performances guidance may be very much more effective. The traditional verbal directions for the "trigger squeeze" are simple, clear, and vivid—but they work badly for many recruits all the same. "Is *that* what the lieutenant meant?" was their characteristic comment when once they got the "feel," the kinesthetic cue, to the correct movement. Both school and industry need to give increased attention, in the writer's judgment, to the possibilities of nonverbal guidance for motor skills. Only—the guidance must promote, not hinder, the learner's acquisition of insight into the essentials of his performance.

Guidance by demonstration, depending on the learner's imitation of correct performance, is another established procedure. Indeed in many learning situations it seems almost indispensable. All too often, however, demonstration, like mechanical aids, fails to convey to the learner what he needs to do. Nearly everyone has tried to teach a dog or a cat by this means—and failed. Apparent success usually comes when the animal is about to perform the act in question anyway. The case with children is not greatly different. Almost we can say that demonstration works only for those who have already "got the right idea"—that is, for those who have already surmounted the highest hurdle in learning.

Verbal Guidance.—For most persons, teaching is taken to be nearly equivalent to verbal guidance. It is actually so much more than that! Yet though teaching is so much more, we must not undervalue in theory—there is small danger that we will in practice—verbal exposition, that most characteristically human method of inducing learning. Most primitive is the method of description and direct injunction. The method is valuable, as Davis [22] says in an excellent summary of this topic, "because it can be adapted to individual needs and repeated in various ways until the learner has a thorough comprehension of every part of the process. It is probable that no other form of guidance is complete unless accompanied by explanation and direction. Think, for example, of the difficulty in teaching deaf-mutes, and you will renew your faith in verbal instruction, despite attacks upon its excessive use.

Yet as every teacher knows, explanation may be utterly ineffective. As every preacher must confess, exhortation all too often fails to promote the development of character or the learning of virtue. Here we must revert to the principle earlier propounded that one learns only as one reacts. So often verbal guidance does not cause the pupil to act at all or to act in the desired way. There is some reason to think that explanation has its chief value early in the learning period; later it is only a distraction.[23] Indeed this is almost certainly true of complex motor skills when considered as a whole. Yet even in the later stages of learning to play golf, for example, there is a place for the careful analysis of particular errors which really means, probably, that the learning is in an early stage for these errors.

Knowledge of Results.—The mention of error leads, naturally, to our next topic. Theoretically—and most practically, too—it should be the purpose of teaching to prevent the learner from making errors. But so long as teaching remains a human and therefore imperfect activity, so long will errors be committed by pupils. A large part of guidance must consist in informing the learner that he has made an error.

There is an enormous body of experimental work which shows that knowledge of results is an aid—perhaps an indispensable aid— to learning. Most of the experiments intended to show the effect of praise or blame or of reward and punishment, may be more simply interpreted as tests of the effect of informing the learner as to how he is doing. Marks for excellence in school work are justifiable in proportion as they inform the pupil about his progress—their value as incentives is clearly less important.

The experimental work is on the whole remarkably concordant. Knowledge of results facilitates learning in virtually all circumstances but it is effective in proportion as it is (1) *prompt* and (2) *specific*.

The first requirement really is promptness. Ten seconds after the reaction is really too long; a tenth of a second is better. How different this is from much of our testing work in school. A teacher who returns pupil exercises the next day is a veritable paragon of promptness. Only when we can somehow reinstate the original learning activity does the delayed information have its full effect.

There are numerous devices intended to inform the learner promptly as to his success. Pressey [24] has devised a number of machines which score the "new type" examination in the classroom almost as fast as the test can be taken. And the Petersons [25] have worked out in their "Chemotester" a device which reveals to the pupil whether he is right or wrong as soon as he puts his mark on the test paper. Both plans have proved useful in practice. They are, however, a little bothersome for the teacher and different, hence have not been widely adopted.

And then specific information. A grade of "C" may be as just and fair as you like, but it falls far short of telling a pupil precisely what it was that was wrongly done, or was well done. Even such a comment as "awkward sentences" or "poor organization of ideas" falls far short of being really specific.

Experimental studies in the laboratory (even studies with white rats!) and studies under school conditions show almost complete agreement. Let the learner know exactly where and how much he went astray if he is to improve.* Nowhere, however, is the gap between our actual practice and our best knowledge of how to teach more shockingly obvious.

Tests in the Improvement of Learning.—What is the reason for this neglect of sound practice? Undoubtedly one reason is that it is not easy for the teacher to know *specifically* just what the forty or more pupils are doing. How, then, can he inform them specifically? It is at this point that we touch once more upon a major activity of educational psychology—the improvement of our means of appraising pupil progress.

Too often the devising and giving of tests seems like an end in itself. Actually, however, tests are merely means for accurately determining just what a pupil has learned and what he has mislearned, to the end that the teacher may guide him rightly.

Not all tests need be of the "new type." There is a worthy place in education for essay examinations and for informal oral quizzing as well as the more recently developed "objective tests." There is

---

* Even if the evidence is of humiliating failure? Of course! Only—the failure should not be allowed to seem humiliating. It is not knowledge of success and failure which is in question here but other and far-reaching considerations of the total learning situation. It is not a quibble to insist, however, that when the learner really understands the situation, information as to wherein he has erred will not seem either humiliating or discouraging.

room, nay there is imperative need, for teacher-made tests and for standard tests. There is need for tests of subject matter; but also of attitudes, of personality, of character—in short, for tests of everything which is to be learned or otherwise developed in school.

The testing movement, however, in its contemporary form at least, is new, and has led to a great deal of very shoddy work. There is much valid criticism of tests and of specific testing activity. Particularly valid is the criticism that too many of our tests fail to measure the kind of learnings which it should be the primary aim of the school to promote. Nor is the criticism less valid because the critics seem to have no alternative but rest with a purely negative— not to say negativistic—attack on the "narrowness" of tests. The challenge remains: If we are to guide learning—*any* kind of learning —we must discover ways of promptly appraising just where the learner is going and thus of informing him promptly and specifically of his progress and of his straying from the true path.

Individualizing Teaching.—Guidance, however, does not consist wholly in knowing how to correct the learning process. Quite as important and indeed logically prior to such corrective teaching is the discovery of just what is to be learned.

When children first come to school, for example, they have an extraordinary variety of understanding of arithmetical concepts. In a large scale investigation at Cincinnati, MacLatchy [26] found that almost no child knew all the basic concepts necessary for effective beginning work in arithmetic and there was no one concept known to all. Before beginning to teach arithmetic, therefore, a teacher should find out specifically just which concepts each particular child lacks.

This sort of situation is not limited to the first grade. Perhaps school tends to make children more alike—certainly our promotion plans are designed for that purpose. But we don't succeed. In every subject from "arithmetic" through "politeness" to "zoology," individual differences at the beginning of a study are the invariable rule. In a course in educational psychology (preceded by a prerequisite course in general psychology) half the class knew more when the course began than the poorest did when it ended. Nearly ten per cent achieved the passing grade before the course started! [27]

How is one to determine what specifically to teach these students without an accurate and detailed appraisal of their individual achievements? Topic by topic throughout the course, some of the students are enduring "Twice Told Tales"—or worse, with a corresponding waste of learning time.

It is not only—or even mainly—the bright and the well prepared who suffer. At every level it is indeed a rare teacher who does not teach over the heads of most pupils upon occasion. And educational diagnosis (by means of tests and measurements of some sort or other) reveals how extraordinarily individual deficiencies may be. Three children in elementary school were equally bad in reading. According to the older attitude of fundamental thoroughness, all three needed to be "drilled in fundamentals." One of these children, however, read words well enough but did not know that their position on the page or line mattered. The second just wasn't interested in reading—all he wanted to do was to draw. The third was failing because she lacked vocabulary. Effective teaching of course had here three radically distinct tasks. To have put these three children through the same first-grade reading routine would have been educational malpractice.[28]

Finally it is only by adequate—and continuous!—appraisal that we can discover the level of insight and understanding achieved by each pupil and thus know for what new educative experiences he is ready. To send out teachers who are unskilled in the use of the tests and other modern methods of relatively objective appraisal is comparable to sending out physicians untrained in the use of laboratory diagnoses, unskilled even in the use of clinical thermometers.

Retention and the Results of Schooling.—Obviously it is not enough to learn something; the result of learning must be available when we need it later for the solution of our problems—whether the result be a bit of information, a new skill, reorganized thinking, or reconstructed personality. If these be transient, the learning is of little avail. How then can we maintain the gains made?

Overlearning.—Laboratory studies of learning have shown clearly the value of what is called—or rather miscalled—"overlearning," as a means of making learning permanent. To study something to the point where one can just barely repeat it is to run the risk that it will be promptly forgotten. This is clearly true of all those forms of everyday learning which are parallel with the "by-heart" learning of laboratory experiments. Formulas, dates, telephone numbers, and definitions, all these are more permanently learned if study for the sake of learning is continued well beyond the just-learned point.

The writer's own experiments, already referred to, make it somewhat doubtful, however, that memory for the substance of a passage is really helped by overlearning. Certainly frequency of repetition plays here a less important role. When the learning task is to discover new relations, to reorganize one's thinking (or one's conduct?), it does not seem necessary to repeat a successful performance in order to insure its permanence.

Yet even here, we must not minimize the effect of repetition. What we call logical or substance learning certainly includes, and depends on, a great deal of sheer by-heart knowledge and skill. Moreover, the first flash of insight, the first discovery is seldom complete. When we re-study something carefully, we nearly always discover new aspects, gain new understandings. And these new understandings come to the aid of the earlier ones and are supported by them. It is sound pedagogy, therefore, on many grounds, to urge that we carry the studying or the repetition forward beyond minimum limits.

Review.—Another principle derived from laboratory studies of memory has been found to be of prime importance in school learning. Forgetting is greatly retarded, learning is much more enduring if there is an almost immediate "review" or "recitation." Learning consists in achieving a new level of performance. But this new level is often lost if the new concept learned is not almost immediately put to work.[29]

Now the simplest way to put it to work is to try it out. If it is a bit of information, use it in answering a question. If no one asks a question calling for that information, ask yourself one. If you have gained a new understanding of certain concepts, try solving a problem by means of the new concept. If you cannot do it any other way,

you can help to make the new insight permanent by restating it in
your own words. Even a formal test has been shown—in experiment
after experiment—to be an excellent *learning* device and one which
very favorably influences permanence of learning. This is, apparently,
independent of the already discussed advantage to be gained from
knowledge of results. In practice, however, the two advantages combine to make a very strong argument for repeated appraisal.

But not exclusively by the teacher! Not even mainly. Pupils
must learn to check their own learning, step by step. In careful study
or where the material is especially difficult, it is probably wise for
the student to review his learning after every paragraph, certainly
after every section, and again at the conclusion of larger units. This
constant checking up on themselves is one of the outstanding ways
in which good students differ from poor ones in their study habits.

The Strategic Spacing of Study Periods.—Laboratory experimentation yields us another principle of some direct, practical importance concerning the "distribution of practice." Where something has to be learned "by heart," enduring retention is most economically attained if the repetitions are spread out over a considerable time. Cramming for examinations is thus certainly inefficient
if any long-time learning is the criterion. For "permanent" learning,
short intensive reviews at increasing intervals are most effective.
Indeed it is likely that nothing is very permanently learned unless
such review or practice is in some way or other provided by the circumstances of one's life.

True, many psychologists hold that when a thing is once learned,
it is never forgotten unless interfered with. According to their view,
which is supported by much evidence, the function of reviews is
actually to ward off interfering associations. This theoretical position has the merit of explaining the persistence of "buried memories"
—they are isolated from interference. The practical conclusion for
ordinary learnings is, however, the same—spaced reviews or repetitions of the desired learning.

The principle of distributed practice is sometimes invoked to
prove that three-day-a-week classes are better than five-day-a-week.
Here, however, we meet a whole flock of confusions. In the first

place, distributed practice has not been shown to favor "logical" or "substance" learning; the slight evidence is even adverse. More important is the fact—too often ignored by teachers—that not all of a student's learning is done in class or is closely paced by the class meetings. Finally, most of the study is not repetition or review but the acquisition of new insights.

The problem of the best spacing of class meetings, like most other complex educational problems, is thus more profitably attacked by direct experiment in the practical situation rather than by dependence upon general principles derived from much simpler situations. Not that we should be so naïve as merely to measure the amount of learning in three-a-week and five-a-week classes! For it is well known in college circles that instructors increase assignments in the former so that one does about the same amount of studying for a three- as for a five-hour course. The moral, one is sorry to say, is rather too clear to Mr. Average Student. The result is a still further complication of the comparison by the fact that three-hour courses are more likely to be elected by superior students. Direct experiment in complex practical situations is thus not easy; but when it is carefully and critically done, it yields conclusions much more safely applied.

The Results of Schooling.—A proper application of the principles just briefly reviewed and of others would doubtless work a very considerable improvement in the retention of school achievement. Investigation certainly seems to indicate that improvement is needed: A twenty-five per cent loss in grade school history in a little over a year. A thirty per cent loss in high school chemistry in two years, and a fifty per cent loss in college botany. College students, business men, and statesmen who cannot spell as well as sixth graders (this is not actually proved as the other figures are) and college professors who have forgotten how to do square roots. The Carnegie Foundation [30] survey of the effect of college study—or rather of college attendance—yields a gloomy picture of the educative process.

Before we get too discouraged, however, one question may be asked: Is it clear that we really want or need to retain much of what we learn in school or college? Frequent review—and use, we noted, is the best kind of review—is a splendid means to enduring retention. Does not the fact that we forget so much of what we studied in school rather argue that we use it little? Critical examination of some of the items in school examinations inclines one to blame the unrealistic character of a curriculum out of touch with modern needs for the poor retention disclosed quite as much as the teaching or the learning. Who cares that we have forgotten how to extract cube root?

Perhaps, in other words, the meager results of schooling are due to too exclusive attention to only one kind of result. We have already admitted—or insisted—that our intellectual advancement is dependent upon acquiring and retaining unchanged certain skills or certain items of information. But surely this is only a small part. In the writer's experiments [31] it was found that pupils can often answer a larger percentage of questions dealing with the "substance" of a passage after a month than they could immediately after it was studied. Instead of forgetting there is what is technically called reminiscence. Indeed even 90 days later, forgetting and reminiscence practically balance one another..

In similar fashion, Tyler [32] found that while factual tests in zoology showed losses of 20 to 70 per cent in fifteen months, ability to apply zoological principles to new situations showed no net loss at all. The rather considerable permanence of attitude changes as a result of seeing just one motion picture may be in part a similar phenomenon. [33]

What we need, apparently, is to conceive of learning and education in somewhat less rigid terms. Certainly Bartlett's [34] interesting experiments show that memory is not the static phenomenon it has usually been considered. We do not so much *retain* experience as *reconstruct* it. It becomes, with the passage of time, simpler, neater, more compact, more significant—and more usable. And speaking more generally, in the education of the near future we shall less frequently ask what a person has got out of his education; rather we shall ask, how has he changed as a result of education.*

* We shall not be content, however, as some are today who accept this view, to guess at these changes; we shall insist that they be measured. For only in this way can we be assured that they have occurred.

Transfer of Training.—With this last statement we have opened up the thorny question of the transfer of training. In effect we have asserted that the meaning of education is this: That we train a man in one situation so that he improves in his behavior in some other situation.

In this very broad sense, transfer of training becomes almost synonymous with education; for the purpose of education, as Pressey says, "is to prepare for meeting situations which must inevitably differ in many respects from the educational situation in which the preparation was acquired." And there is very real reason for keeping in mind this wider meaning. But historically, the problem of transfer grew up with a narrower connotation to which we may give some attention. Can a person gain a sort of general mental discipline from the study of certain subjects like Latin or mathematics or from a special kind of training in fortitude as in initiations? Does the study of Latin tend to give a person increased sensitivity to literary and esthetic values, help him to think more clearly or express himself with greater vigor? Or do athletics build character in participants which carries over to everyday life? Or for that matter, does the study of educational psychology help to make one a better teacher?

The problem of transfer is particularly acute in the case of Latin because, of course, save for a very tiny minority, Latin has no direct value; it must justify itself in the curriculum in terms of its transfer value. It should be recognized, however, that only in degree is this more true of Latin. Latin is carrying the ball for the whole team of traditional school subjects. Latin is not spoken today. But the average student of high school French or Spanish meets no practical demand to speak the language he so painfully studies for three years —thank the merciful heavens! Navigators must know spherical geometry; do any of the rest of us need it? Is it not just as much a "dead language" as Latin? Civics, of course, is directly practical —in intent. But is there evidence that its study actually makes anyone a better citizen? Indeed if Latin has *no* "disciplinary value," all education is in a bad way.

The Real Problems of Transfer.—What we need is to put the question in quite a different way. We need not ask whether any subject has "transfer value." Of course it has, since any experience one lives through changes one's nature, for better or worse. We can ask, however, (a) specifically what does one do better or worse as a result of a particular course of training or study; (b) whether this course helps (or hinders) more than others; and most important and usually neglected, (c) how can one best increase the spread or transfer effect?

Perhaps we have more data for the answer of such questions if we take as an example the effect of a study of Latin on ability in English. Specifically, we may ask whether Latin increases the student's English vocabulary? (Question (a) above). Are there other subjects which affect vocabulary more? (Question (b).) Can one teach Latin so as to increase the transfer to English vocabulary? (Question (c).)

A number of experimental precautions must be observed in seeking the answer to these questions. Most of the older investigations, having neglected these precautions, are very unreliable. But Thorndike and Ruger [35] showed quite clearly that Latin does influence the English vocabulary. After a year's study of Latin, there was a gain of 22 per cent on a brief but fairly reliable test of words of Latin derivation. Non-Latin students who were otherwise comparable showed a gain of only 8 per cent. On words of non-Latin derivation, however, the students not studying Latin were slightly superior.

The last result strengthens our belief that the superiority first mentioned is really due to Latin study. It also shows just what the study of Latin does and does not do for English vocabulary. The study of Latin does not develop some mysterious "language sense." It increases the grasp of words derived from Latin but not of other words.

But how about the second question? Is this gain from Latin any greater than might be derived by other means? Sometimes, certainly. One investigation [36] even showed that Latin did *slightly* more for vocabulary than the regular English class.

And this brings us clearly to the third question. Can transfer be increased by a shift in the teaching emphasis? Apparently, yes! For both English and Latin did more for English vocabulary where there was emphasis upon word study. It may seem at first that this is not a question of transfer at all. The pupils merely learned words because they were taught words. This is not quite the case, however. The gains were for words not specifically taught in the Latin course in the form actually tested. When one learns to recognize the word *reducible* from a study of *re-ducere,* there is really some transfer.

Other investigations bring out the fact that the transfer is greater when the pupils are taught to analyze both Latin and English words, get some idea of how words are formed, and are alert to the possibilities of detecting the Latin in the English word. Transfer, in short, seems to depend upon a kind of generalization, upon knowing how to apply general principles.

How Transfer Is Obtained.—There are many ways to secure generalization, and they are not equally efficacious. Overman's [37] study of transfer in arithmetic is illuminating at this point. The experimentation was very carefully controlled to test the respective merits of four methods of teaching the addition of two-place numbers in the second grade. The four methods may be briefly described as follows: (I) Demonstration: The children were simply shown how to do the additions and given practice. (II) Generalization of Procedure: The pupils were helped to formulate general rules of procedure, such as the keeping of columns straight, and these rules were constantly referred to during practice. (III) Rationalization: The pupils were given reasons and principles, such as that it is not possible to add one's and ten's, but the practical application of this in the "rule of straight columns" was not drawn. If a pupil did not keep a straight column, he was asked to straighten it up, not because "columns should be kept straight" but because "you can't add ten's and one's." (IV) Generalization and Rationalization: This combines the methods of (II) and (III) ; both rules and principles were discussed. Of course an equal amount of total time was given to each method. Transfer was tested by the addition of three-place numbers.

After what has been said about the dependence of transfer on generalization, we should expect the first method to be the poorest and so it was. But which of the other three is best? All three certainly illustrate the principle of generalization. It must be confessed that the present writer expected that the fourth, or combined, method would be best. In fact the second was measurably better. The percentage increases in transfer over Method I were as follows: for Generalization of Procedures 45 per cent; for Rationalization 15 per cent; for the Combined Method 37 per cent. Evidently, these second graders were rather ill-prepared to understand even the simple rational principles given them. Perhaps they needed more basic training in certain number concepts before attempting two-place additions. But taking them as they are, one gets better transfer by the simpler sort of "generalization" of Method II than by the more fundamental generalization of Method III.

Formal Discipline.—Were we to stop here, we should give a distinctly erroneous impression of the experimental investigations of transfer. It has been shown that transfer exists, and that one kind of subject matter transfers better than another. But these are precisely the contentions of the traditionalist, of the believer in formal discipline. Nor is he disturbed by the further finding that the amount of transfer is greatly dependent on teaching methods; he might even claim with some plausibility that the teachers of disciplinary subjects are more likely to teach for transfer, to strive for generalization from the disciplinary subject to life situations. Our discussion of the experimental facts thus seems to favor the contentions of the classicist.

Yet as a matter of actual fact, the trend of investigation is quite distinctly adverse to the traditional claims for formal discipline. For the values obtained, though real, are invariably small. Latin does help one to learn French, but not nearly so much as the same effort spent on French itself; and similarly all along the line. Nowhere is the value of quantitative measurement more strikingly evident. Every contention of the traditionalist is qualitatively justified and quantitatively revealed as unimpressive.

Space, of course, does not permit us to cite all the evidence for this rather sweeping generalization. The evidence is very considerable and not to be brushed aside merely because one does not like it. Until other evidence is produced to the contrary, we may fairly conclude that no subject can justify its place in the curriculum in terms of its transfer value alone—transfer being taken in the narrower sense just discussed.

Applicational Transfer.—There is, however, another aspect of the transfer problem—one which ought to trouble the advocates of "practical" subjects as well as the classicist. Can we get people to carry over what they have studied in school into everyday life? Will the study of hygiene—or even the dramatic toothbrush drill—cause children to brush their teeth at home more regularly? Will study about the devastations of forest fires lessen the number of fires due to human carelessness and thoughtlessness? Will the more favorable attitude toward a minority group which results from a motion picture result in actually more understanding of one's neighbors? Here again the question is not so much, "Does transfer exist?" but, "How can we make transfer greater?"

Experimentation in this field has barely been begun; one predicts that twenty years hence the techniques of securing applicational transfer will occupy the central place in any discussion of educational psychology. What data we have indicate that the principles of transfer from subject to subject hold for transfer from the classroom and the study to practical life. Transfer depends upon intelligent effort directed to that end. Transfer depends on teaching for transfer. This means that the opportunities to use what is being learned must be specifically and fully considered. The teacher must forget his "ivory tower" and direct his efforts to the improvement of pupil behavior in the whole sweep of life activities.

OMITTED TOPICS

A Concluding Section.—This volume is intended to help orient the student to the multifarious activities of contemporary psychology. As one looks back at this chapter now that it is written, one has a renewed sense of its many omissions. Whole areas of educational psychology to which scholars are devoting their lives are not even mentioned or are treated only by implication. It has seemed worth while, therefore, to bring together here a list—just a bare list with almost no attempt at system—of topics which the interested student will find treated in textbooks of educational psychology, some in one, others in other texts. Even this list is, of course, very incomplete.

There is first a cluster of topics about the general subject of individual differences and the problem of treating pupils differently in the light of their differing natures: Special abilities and disabilities, exceptional children (the unusually bright or dull, the delinquent, the emotionally unstable, the crippled, etc.) ; the problems of teaching and of educational and vocational guidance in relation to differences —in interests, attitudes, ideals, sentiments, and aptitudes.

Then there is a cluster of topics concerning primarily the teacher's, activities: Authority and discipline, the mental hygiene of the school-room, the maintenance of effective general conditions for learning, and the social psychology of the classroom.

Lastly, there is a group of topics concerning the outcomes of schooling: The whole range of problems involved in educational measurements and the appraisal of progress ; the psychology of learning as applied to specific subjects ; motor and manual skills, creative activities, thinking, character, the prevention of personality maladjustment and the promotion of happy personal living.

REFERENCES

Davis, R. A. *Psychology of Learning.* New York: McGraw-Hill Book Company, Inc., 1935.

Eurich, A., and Carroll, R. *Educational Psychology.* New York: D. C. Heath and Company, 1935.

Griffith, C. R. *Introduction to Educational Psychology.* New York: Farrar and Rinehart, Inc., 1935.

Jordan, A. M. *Educational Psychology.* New York: Henry Holt and Company, 1934.

Mursell, J. L. *Psychology of Secondary School Teaching.* New York: W. W. Norton and Company, Inc., 1932.

Pressey, S. L. *Psychology and the New Education.* New York: Harper and Brothers, 1933.

Skinner, C. E., et al. *Educational Psychology.* New York: Prentice-Hall, Inc., 1936.

CHAPTER XV

CLINICAL PSYCHOLOGY

By C. M. Louttit, *Indiana University*

Psychology, as the reader is aware, is the science which studies those natural phenomena concerned with the behavior of living organisms in the complexities of their environments. Much of this science is concerned with the behavior of man. Like any other scientific material the data and methods of psychology find a useful application in the practical problems of man's everyday affairs and in other chapters of this book such applications will be discussed. It is the task of this chapter to consider one specific sort of application, namely, to problems of individual adjustment.

CLINICAL PROBLEMS

Diagnosis.—In the records of a psychological clinic may be found cases of many sorts, for example the child whose ability is so inadequate that he is called feebleminded, the girl who has serious difficulty in learning to read, the boy who steals, the shy child who cries on the slightest provocation, the child who exhibits temper or who is afraid of many common things, the adolescent who is concerned about what his vocational future should be, married adults who are having difficulties in marital adjustment, adults who want advice on occupational adjustment, children for whom special types of foster or adoptive homes are sought, and so on. It is evident that most of these problems involve some sort of inadequate adaptation, that is, the persons have some difficulty in behaving in ways that are acceptable either to themselves or to society. The primary aim of clinical psychology is to help each individual client so to change his behavior that it becomes more satisfying or more socially acceptable. In order to do this it is first of all necessary to understand in specific detail the nature of the behavior difficulty and to discover the important etiological (causative) factors which have resulted in this behavior. The investigation of an individual's problem behavior, including an unbiased description of the behavior, significant facts in the person's experiential history, his physical and mental condition, and other pertinent facts, constitute the field of psychological diagnosis. Logically, diagnosis leading to intelligent understanding of a problem is the first concern of the psychoclinician; unfortunately diagnosis is often his chief interest.

Treatment.—If, however, the ultimate aim of clinical psychology, that is, helping the individual to readjust, is to be successful, the psychologist must go further than diagnosis alone, and must either carry out or plan some sort of corrective measures or treatment. The feebleminded child may need custodial care; the child who cannot read must have special teaching; the delinquent child may stop his stealing if he is given a better environment in which to learn more socially acceptable behavior, or, in another case, stealing will stop if personality difficulties are corrected; the shy, timid child must be taught self-confidence; and the aggressive extrovert must learn about the rights of others. An exact program to be tried for a given individual can be known only when we understand his behavior and the circumstances of its development. Frequently, in fact in most cases, any plan of treatment requires the cooperation of other people —it cannot be carried out by the psychologist alone.

Medical and Social Aspects.—The need for cooperation is evident in all psychoclinical work. In diagnosis the physical examination must be contributed by the physician and most of the social history by the social worker. Plans of treatment require even more cooperation for parents must change their attitudes and behavior; social workers must often find new homes and supervise old ones; the psychiatrist or psychologist sometimes carry on technical psychotherapy; the school teacher may have to give special attention to a child or revise her attitudes; club leaders may be pressed into service; recreational opportunities may have to be specially planned; the physician may be needed for medical and surgical care, or attention may have to be paid to poor eyesight or hearing. Thus we see that clinical psychology has very definite relations to many fields, especially to education, social work, and medicine.

Even this brief discussion may lead the reader to ask whether the work of the clinical psychologist is strictly psychological. Such a question cannot be answered decisively yes or no. Like any other attempt to deal with practical human affairs by applying scientific knowledge, it is necessary to integrate material from several sciences. While the clinical psychologist is trained to take, and should maintain, an objective psychological point of view, it is necessary for him to use material from other fields, for example, sociology, education, or the medical sciences, to help in solving the problems he meets. In this chapter we shall be more concerned with the psychological contributions to the study of behavior problems, but necessary cooperation among different professional groups must not be lost sight of.

METHODS

Diagnostic Methods.—The essential aim of psychological diagnostic methods is an understanding of the child's present behavioral condition and the possible reasons for this condition. In order to realize this aim, information, more or less complete depending upon the case, must be secured in the following six areas:

(1) Present behavior picture.
(2) Physical condition.
(3) Psychobiological development.
(4) Socio-economic condition.
(5) Psychosocial history.
(6) Performance ability.

The amount of information or the degree of its completeness required in each of these areas will vary from case to case depending upon its nature. For example, idiocy may be diagnosed on the basis of present behavior picture alone, although some measure of performance ability may be desired, and a physical or medical history may be useful in discovering causes. Again, school retardation may be explained completely on the basis of measures of performance ability. On the other hand very complete materials may be necessary in all the areas in order to understand the nonspecific symptoms of a serious personality disorder.

In this place we can do little more than suggest the nature and significance of the information desired in these six areas. For more extensive details the reader is referred to the books listed at the end of the chapter, especially Kanner, Louttit, and that from the Institute of Juvenile Research.

(1) *Present Behavior Picture.*—The obvious starting point in any diagnostic study is the complaint. Why did this individual come to the clinic, or for what reason was he referred to it by a parent, teacher, social worker, physician, court official, or some one else? The reason given for referral, that is, the complaint, may not adequately represent the real problem. Thus "not doing well in school" may be described in many ways. The child may be two or three years over age for his grade; he may be in the proper grade, but getting low marks; his marks may be average, but the teacher complains of his lack of application; the parents may have set high standards of A or B grades, and the presence of C's on his report card may be the basis for the complaint. "Lying" may represent a real attempt to avoid issues or it may be a term applied by parents or teachers to purely imaginative tales which the child fully recognizes are not true. Thus we could offer many other illustrations and from such examples might generalize that every complaint should be substantiated by specific examples of behavior.

Does the complained-of behavior occur in all situations or only at home, only in school, or only elsewhere? Does the child steal only money, or food, or both? Does he have difficulty only with reading, or with arithmetic? Does he play only with younger children? Does he bully the younger children, but avoid older ones? What are some specific examples of his disobedience? These questions illustrate the sort of details that must be known in order to secure a description of present behavior uncomplicated by the mother's or teacher's bias. Sometimes actual observation of the child by the examiner in different situations is necessary because the referrant's complaint is inaccurate or deliberately misleading. For example Dr. Esther L. Richards reports a case of a young boy whose mother's account of his behavior minimized its inadequacy and indicated a perfect developmental history. However, observation of the child's behavior in Dr. Richard's office showed quite clearly that he was seriously subnormal.

(2) *Physical Condition.*—Psychological behavior is the behavior of a biological organism. Therefore, the physical condition of the organism is always a possible reason for behavior difficulty. In every diagnostic study it is necessary to take the physical conditions into account. Of course the medical examination which is necessary to determine physical condition is exclusively the task of the physician. While the psychologist need not be a physician himself, he should be sufficiently acquainted with medical matters to integrate intelligently the physician's findings into the total case history.

While any physical illness has its psychological implication, there are certain areas which are of peculiar importance. One of these areas is general vitality, that is, the adequacy of general physical status. Malnutrition, tuberculosis, cardiac conditions are in point here because they reduce the subject's activity and effort. In turn his achievement and the adjustments dependent upon it are decreased. Crippled conditions—whether due to neural, muscular, or bone and joint pathologies—disturb the normality of action and in this way directly affect the patient's behavior and attitudes. Neurological pathologies are traditionally thought to be uniquely related to behavior pathologies. There is no very good evidence that this unique relation is true, but there can be no doubt that such physical disorders play a significant part in the individual's behavior. Endocrine disorders are also important to behavior. The cretin, with his extreme hypothyroidism, is usually feebleminded; and there is some evidence that the mongolian (usually an imbecile) exhibits a glandular pathology. On the other hand, the hyperthyroid individual is more active and more irritable than the normal. Lastly, sensory defects, especially in vision and hearing, are important causes of poor school adjustment in children, and of occupational difficulties in adults.

In order to understand an individual's problem, his physical status must be taken into account. If the medical examination shows an abnormal condition, this must be corrected before further efforts are made to adjust his behavior. If the physical disorder cannot be corrected, then it constitutes a known factor which must be included in any plans for psychological treatment.

(3) *Psychobiological Development.*—Certain items of behavior depend upon a sufficient degree of physical maturation before they can develop. Thus the appearance of such activities as walking, talking, control of elimination, self-feeding, and so on, is in part dependent upon sufficient biological maturity and in part upon training or experience. Because of relative uniformity of biological development and the relative constancy of infant-training procedures in our culture, there are established certain normative ages at which these acts appear.

The following list includes the more important behavior events appearing in infancy and indicates the approximate range of ages within which their appearance is considered normal:

Bowel control	12-18 months
Bladder control, daytime	15-20 months
Bladder control, night	30-36 months
Sitting alone momentarily	6 - 8 months
Crawling	7-10 months
Standing alone	12-16 months
Walking alone	12-18 months
Talking, 2 words	11-13 months
Talking, sentences	22-26 months

When the appearance of these behavior patterns varies widely either above or below the norms, there must always be a reason, and this may be important in interpreting the subject's behavior. If the majority of the behavior patterns occur at a late age one is immediately suspicious of a general behavioral retardation, indicating feeblemindedness or borderline ability. Inconsistency in retardation may reflect parental attitudes or abilities. For example, late establishment of elimination control may mean that the mother made no effort to train the child because of her fear of tiring him, or because of ignorance or lack of interest in establishing such control. In some cases a child fails to walk or talk because of an inhibiting event; thus at the first attempt to walk the child falls and hurts himself, and then makes no further efforts for several months. In one case a child of two and a half years had started to talk normally, but following a fire in the house in which an older brother was burned to death with a consequent emotional disturbance of the whole family, the child made no further effort to speak for three years.

(4) *Socio-Economic Condition.*—The patterns of behavior, the attitude, the outlook on life of every individual are specifically determined by the interactions of that individual with his environmental conditions. This is, therefore, another large area that we must know about before we can understand the person's behavior. Every individual interacts with a variety of environmental social groups and inanimate physical conditions. In infancy and early childhood the family is the most important of such groups; with increasing age the neighborhood, school, gangs, occupational and recreation groups and so on, become increasingly important. Depending upon the age of the client and the nature of his problem, information in some or all of these directions is necessary.

For children, who constitute the greater share of the psychologist's clientele, the family is the fundamental social group. At the time he is being studied, each child (excluding for the moment children in institutions) is a member of a family. The family is, however, not merely the father, mother, and siblings, but psychologically must include the emotional and intellectual attachments and relations between them; that is, the family is a dynamic, not a static, body. The child is affected by the attitudes and behavior of his parents toward each other and toward him, but no less are the parents affected by the child and his relations to his siblings. Therefore, we must know not only who are members of the family group (not forgetting relatives or servants who live in intimate contact with the home), but also we must secure some idea of the relations among them. For example, do parents love and respect each other? Does one dominate the other? What are their attitudes toward all the children or toward this particular child? Is he favored or neglected? Are his siblings older or younger? What are their ages and sex? How do the children react to one another? A host of such questions immediately spring to mind. the answers to which are necessary to a full understanding of the child.

The economic condition of the family and the physical nature of the client's home may be indicative. The stealing of a boy who comes from a poverty-stricken home is an entirely different problem, even a different kind of behavior, from that of the spoiled son of wealth. Economic inadequacy means greater worry and greater strain which colors all the family relations. On the other hand, economic plenty may mean an overabundance which stifles independence and resourcefulness. There is evidence to show that among the poor, behavior problems more frequently are of the conduct type, that is, they tend to be socially disturbing, while among more wealthy families the problems are of the personality type, that is, they are inhibiting to the development of full maturity.

With increasing age the other aspects of the environment assume greater importance. From the preschool child's first excursion a block away from home and his meeting with other children, to his death, the requirements of the 'neighborhood and community, physical and social, constantly make demands upon the individual. The child in school has adjustments to make to the school regulations, the teacher, and other children. The adolescent must not only adjust himself to the school and college, but there are also group pressures from his gang or crowd. The adult has his particular problems at his work, in his church or club, with his neighbors and so on. In each case the static, physical nature of the environment is of importance. But of greater consequence are the dynamic relations between the individual and the group. Does the teacher like or dislike the child? Does the child play agreeably with the other children? Is this adolescent accepted by his group? Does this adult complain about his boss or fellow-workers? Here again are a host of questions that must be answered if we are to gain an adequate conception of the factors that may be influencing the client's behavior.

(5) *Psychosocial History.*—While the present social situation in which the client is living is important to his behavior, the influences of his past social interactions are of greater cumulative significance. For this reason information concerning experiential history or reactional biography is necessary. Ideally we would like to have a detailed day-by-day account of the client's experiences. This is, of

course, impossible, but records of specific events and relations will be helpful.

A few paragraphs above we called attention to the importance of the conditions in the child's home. While the home situation at the time of examination is important, the cumulative effect of past conditions is probably of even greater significance. For example, the way the child was treated in infancy may be reflected in his present feeling of security or insecurity. Serious changes in the dynamics of the family—a new sibling, death of a father or mother, divorce, or the introduction of a step-parent—may have had a serious influence on the subject's attitudes and behavior. Emotion-provoking situations, such as a frightening experience or the constant thwarting of desires giving rise to anger, may now be forgotten, but their influence remains evident in behavior patterns.

In the direction of academic or vocational achievement, the effects of formal educational experiences are important. It is necessary to know about the child's school history—including not only formal achievement records but also his success in adjusting to the teachers and other children. For adolescents and adults an account of vocational experiences will be significant. In short no item of the subject's life experience is entirely foreign to our needs.

While a bare recital of informational items in the experiential history would become tiresome, a general principle will suggest its own details. Each subject is a biological organism in constant interaction with its environment. The cumulative effect of inter-actions determines the nature of his behavior patterns. Sometimes the interactions directly produce behavior as when a person learns a foreign language or learns to steal. On the other hand the demands of the immediate situation may conflict with previously learned behavior or attitudes, or they lead to taboo behavior. In such cases there is emotional conflict and the subject exhibits behavior which is symptomatic of the conflict—he may try to run away from it; he may compensate for it; he may repress it, and so on. In any case it is necessary to learn the factors in the reactional biography which are of possible significance in the development of the behavior about which we are concerned.

As we can never know *a priori* what experiences are of particular importance in a specific case, it is a fundamental diagnostic problem to discover many experiences. Those of infancy and early childhood in the home are always important; at later ages the experiences in school, with other children or adults, recreational and vocational events, all should be investigated. Environmental pressures lasting over long periods are probably of greater significance than unique events; however, the latter should not be neglected. From an extensive record of life experiences the various items must be evaluated in connection with the special problem of the specific individual.

(6) *Performance Ability.*—At least half of the cases seen in psychological clinics present problems associated with lack of ability to do certain things, or with an apparent superiority in ability, hence there is the need to know what the subject can do. It is in connection with problems of this sort that psychology has developed special techniques in the form of testing instruments. Unfortunately it is commonly believed that clinical psychology and mental testing are the same. From our preceding discussion of diagnostic methods it is evident that clinical psychology is more extensive than mental testing alone. On the other hand psychometrics, or mental testing, is more extensive than its special clinical use. For our present purposes we have to consider those aspects of psychological testing which are significant in the diagnostic study of a particular problem. More extensive information on testing in general may be found in the books listed at the end of this chapter, especially those of Garrett and Schneck, and Symonds.

The purpose of clinical psychometrics is to evaluate the performance ability of the subject, and on the basis of the discovered facts to predict probable future achievement. For measuring performance ability a wide variety of tests is available. The type most frequently thought of is the intelligence test. It is unnecessary here to discuss the nature of intelligence; for our purpose we can take it to be composed of those abilities which are measured by certain tests.

All intelligence tests present certain tasks to the subject. He is required to do as many tasks as well as he can. The tasks may require understanding and use of language as in the well-known Binet [1] test, or they may require manual performance based upon insight into the task as in form boards, picture-completion tests, and mazes.[2] Regardless of the kind of performance required, the subject's success is compared with norms based upon the results from large unselected groups of children or adults. The scores on the tests are computed on all-or-none passes and failures, time, errors, or according to a point system. As children have been the most frequently examined subjects, the scores on the tests are usually expressed as a performance age or mental age. This means that if the child has a mental age of seven years, his performance is equivalent to the average performance of seven-year-olds. This mental age in itself is not very meaningful unless we know how old our subject is. For example, a performance age of seven years would mean entirely different things in a five-year-old, a seven-year-old, or a twenty-year-old. In order to express this relation easily, the ratio between the two values, that is,

$$\frac{MA}{CA} \times 100 = IQ,$$

has been widely used. It is evident from this formula that the intelligence quotient, IQ, is the percentage of the expected performance that the child actually earns.

During the past twenty years the IQ has become a common term in the English language. This is unfortunate because it implies a significance which the ratio does not actually possess. In the first place IQ's or the performance ages from two or three different tests may be numerically quite different and have different meanings. Furthermore, the obtained IQ may have been influenced by conditions of the subject or the examiner purely extraneous to the subject's performance ability. Poor health, emotional disturbances, fear of the examiner, carelessness on the part of the examiner, and many other things may operate to lower the performance score. The IQ's are not foolproof values, and are meaningful only when interpreted cautiously in the light of all information available.

If one keeps in mind that IQ's, or other expressions of test performance, are not absolute measures, they may be extremely valuable. Experience and experiments have shown that there is a significant relationship between performance on a test like the Binet and school achievement. Therefore, low test performance may explain poor achievement and give some basis for prediction of future school and even occupational achievement. A comparison of the performances on language and manipulative tests may indicate strengths and weaknesses in ability. In brief, intelligence-test results may eliminate or establish poor abilities as causative factors in many types of behavior problems.

In addition to the several types of so-called intelligence tests a number of other measuring instruments have been devised. A very important class is achievement tests. These amount to standardized examinations in particular subject matters of the school curriculum. They are available for all subjects of the elementary grades and for most high school subjects. Their value for the psychoclinician lies in the opportunity offered to measure the child's school achievement, uncomplicated by the question of the teacher's bias.

Aptitude tests, by sampling performance in areas significant to a certain kind of task, for example, mechanical, musical, artistic, or clerical, give some indication of a subject's possible success in those fields. In nature they are similar to both intelligence and achievement tests and may be used in the clinic to secure information on abilities in specialized fields.

The three types of tests mentioned above do not exhaust the tools of psychometrics. Frequently used in clinical work are instruments for measuring or indicating personality adjustments, emotional stability, motor coordination, sensory acuity, social maturity, economic status, and so on. In the short space available we cannot describe each of these. In his diagnostic investigation the psychologist must be able to use these various instruments; above all he must be able to interpret apparently contradictory findings on various tests; and further he must be able to integrate the test results with all of the other information available on the subject.

Methods of Treatment.—While the methods of diagnosis used by the psychoclinician are basically the same for every case, this is not true of methods of treatment. Therefore, it is not possible to set forth therapeutic plans that can be easily adapted to the

requirements of each new case. As in any sort of therapy, the first
need is to have some insight into the causes of the problem. Therapy
is directed primarily at the removal of the causes. It is important
to keep this in mind because a certain form of undesirable behavior,
for example, truancy, may be due to different reasons in different
children. To treat truancy *per se* would be treatment of symptoms and
would fail to solve the child's real problem.

The mother of a ten-year-old girl complained first of the child's
enuresis and then of her disobedience and forwardness. Investigation of the problem revealed that a five-year-old brother received most
of the attention from both parents. Without paying specific attention
to either the enuresis or disobedience, the parents were advised to
plan the children's bedtime so that the girl would have a half hour
alone with the parents. In two weeks the father voluntarily reported
that the girl's whole attitude had changed and that there were definite
signs of improvement as regards the enuresis. In this case nothing
was done about the problems as such, but an effort was made to relieve the tension surrounding the girl's feeling of neglect. With
correction of the cause the symptoms disappeared.

Corrective Programs.—For convenience in discussion we may
describe three types of treatment or corrective measures used by
psychologists. The first of these, and probably the most frequently
used, is some planned program which requires someone other than
the psychologist to take direct responsibility for carrying it out.
This does not mean that the psychologist has no part in the treatment;
his function is primarily directive and supervisory. In as much as the
behavior of the individual is determined primarily by the environmental forces in which he lives, some attack on the undesirable factors
is always indicated. Frequently the program involves changing
parental attitudes and methods of dealing with the child, as in the
case mentioned earlier. In such instances it is the parent who must
carry out the details of the corrective program. The parents must
assume some responsibilities in many other cases in which the school
or persons outside the school are primary factors. If the parents
cannot or will not cooperate, or if one or both are dead, the problem
may involve finding a suitable foster home. In such cases the co-

operation of social workers or child-placing agencies must be secured. When the behavior problem, or an academic-adjustment problem is associated with the school the corrective program must be in that direction. It may mean reassignment to grade or classroom, irregularity in curriculum, change of school, and so on. Here the teachers and school administration must assume responsibility for carrying out the program under supervision of the psychoclinician. For feebleminded subjects and certain other behavior groups institutional care and training may be indicated. The theory underlying this type of treatment procedure is that as the child's behavior is the resultant of environmental forces, and as the child's behavior is constantly developing, a change in the environmental forces will result in changed behavior. We may call this type of treatment environmental manipulation.

Reëducation.—The remaining two kinds of corrective procedures are directed at the client himself. The first of these is reëducation in a narrow sense. In cases of speech difficulty, poor motor skills, special subject disabilities, and the like, the treatment is primarily a special teaching program. Children of very low ability and sensitive children of especially high ability may need an individual program of teaching. This is sometimes carried on by the psychologist himself and sometimes by a specially trained teacher. The theory underlying treatment of this sort is that defects in certain special types of behavior may be overcome by specific training.

Psychotherapy.—The third general type of treatment is so-called psychotherapy or therapeutic interviewing. Here the psychoclinician plays a very definite role, because the whole value of this type of corrective measure depends upon how well the clinician can guide or help the client in talking about himself and his problem. The practice of Christian Science, the confessional, and psychoanalysis are all special types of psychotherapy. Without necessarily accepting the special tenets upon which these rest, it cannot be denied that in some cases they have a real therapeutic value. Psychotherapy is perhaps most useful in dealing with adolescents or adults. In children a present effect may often be changed by merely changing the environment. If, however, the same forces persist and no change is made by adolescence, the behavior becomes well established. Usually the conditioning factors are no longer evident; they are forgotten. Changing the environment now no longer works. However, if it were possible to have the patient recall the earlier etiologically significant events and then help him reinterpret them in an objective way, the effect would be similar to that of changing his environment at a younger age. The basic method and purpose of all psychotherapy is to force the patient to recall and to objectify forgotten experiences or even very recent experiences which he has been refusing to accept. Of all the therapeutic methods this one requires the most specific skill and, if incorrectly used, may do more harm than good. Traditionally it is a method reserved for psychiatrists, but its successful use depends more upon sympathetic interviewing than upon formal training.

TYPES OF PROBLEMS

Mental Deficiency.—In Chapter XII on differential psychology the distribution of ability levels is discussed. Those persons whose behavior places them at the lowest end of this distribution are commonly spoken of as feebleminded or mentally deficient. Because of their limitations academically, occupationally, and socially, the feebleminded are all psychological problems. It is with this group that clinical psychology has made some of its most useful contributions.

Mental-Test Criterion of Deficiency.—While feeblemindedness has been defined in terms of test performance, for example, Terman says that a Stanford-Binet IQ less than 70 designates feeblemindedness—it is dangerous to depend upon this criterion alone. It is well known that performance on the Binet or other test may be affected by purely temporary factors and that the scores are seldom exactly the same from test to test. Therefore, if a child gets an IQ of 72 on one examination, he would not according to Terman's criterion be feebleminded. A year later, however, when his Binet performance results in a perfectly reasonable drop of five or more points he would suddenly be regarded as feebleminded. Also scores on tests similar to the Binet, in that they require language ability, may be quite different. Subjects who are very poor in language may be average or better on nonlanguage tests. Therefore, the psychometrician's criterion of feeblemindedness on the basis of test performance alone is essentially useless.

Social Criteria of Deficiency.—If we attempt to delimit feeblemindedness by actual observation of defective people, we find that a social criterion is the most useful one. The British Mental Deficiency Committee defines feeblemindedness as "a condition of incomplete development of mind of such a degree or kind as to render the individual incapable of adjusting himself to his social environment in a reasonably efficient and harmonious manner and to necessitate external care, supervision, or control." This definition is the prototype of all those based on a social criterion which is now recognized as the best by clinical psychologists.

Low-Grade Defectives.—In as much as feeblemindedness is not defined in terms of so-called intelligence alone, the psychologist has a very definite diagnostic task. The diagnostic problem of the two lowest grades of feeblemindedness, that is, idiocy and imbecility, is not usually difficult and an adequate conclusion can be drawn on the basis of test performance where the IQ is consistently below 20 for the lower category and 40 for the higher. Comparison of nonstandardized behavior, for example, play with children of younger ages, may indicate the behavior level of the subject. In short, the lowest levels of feeblemindedness are not difficult to recognize. It is also important to note that the lowest levels do not constitute very serious social problems because of their small number and entirely inadequate capabilities; at most they require custodial care throughout their lives, which is, however, an economic loss.

High-Grade Defectives.—The highest grades of feeblemindedness, that is, the moron and the borderline, constitute the majority of all the mentally deficient and they are of high enough ability that they are able to remain at large in the community and frequently engage in antisocial behavior. It is these highest groups which present the most serious social problems and also the more difficult diagnostic problems. As the most serviceable distinction between the feeble·

minded and the not-feebleminded must be based upon social adapta-
bility, diagnosis must establish the probability of the subject's making
a social adjustment, albeit at a low level. While performance in the
neighborhood of 60 per cent on a variety of tests and at different
times is a good starting point, a final conclusion can be drawn only by
knowing other facts: Has the subject's behavioral development shown
retardation? How well has he adapted previously to social requirements? Has he exhibited delinquent or impulsive behavior? What
are the details concerning his school achievement? These are examples of questions which should be answered.

Two cases will make clear the contrast between the feebleminded
and the not-feebleminded when both have shown similar test performances. One man of 25 has a mental age of 8.5 years (IQ about
60) on the Binet; he left school at 16, having reached only the
fourth grade, but it is reported that he always seemed eager to learn
and worked hard; after leaving school he obtained a job in a garage
as a chore boy and in a few years had learned something about auto
mechanics; he is now working steadily, is considered a good workman
though a little slow. The second case is that of a girl of 18 with a
mental age of 10.5 years (IQ about 75); she left school at the age
of 16 when in the 6th grade; her teacher reports that she was
promoted because of her size rather than her work; she was always
a trouble-maker and in conflict with both teacher and parents; at the
time she was seen she had been arrested for solicitation; she did not
mind going to a penal institution and promised to "go back on the
streets" when released. While these cases are very brief, they do indicate the dangers of accepting test results at face value. The man
apparently has a higher ability in manual skill which he is able to
use in making a vocational adjustment at a relatively high level.
In spite of his low test score he can hardly be called feebleminded.
On the other hand, the girl does not use her ability to its best advantage and seems unable to make an adequate social adjustment. To
call her feebleminded does no violence to the facts.

School Problems.—As the clientele of present psychological
clinics is predominately school-age children, it is evident that school
problems would be very frequent. Children are referred to clinics

because of generally poor school work and retardation, because of disabilities in specific subjects, and because of social and personal adjustment difficulties. The last of these, we shall consider later.

Low General Level of Ability.—There is no doubt that most children who are retarded in their grade placement are below average in ability. In the smaller proportion of cases their ability may be low enough to be considered feebleminded. In a much larger proportion of cases, perhaps fifteen per cent of all school children, the mental level is higher than feebleminded but lower than average. The task of the psychologist in these cases is to evaluate the evidences of mental level and advise the teacher what she may expect from this child.

Nonintellectual Factors.—While low ability is certainly a reason for retardation and poor school work, it is not the only reason. The classroom teacher is perhaps a little too inclined to decide that a child is stupid because he is retarded or because his work is poor. It is a task of the school psychologist to determine the real reasons for the child's poor work. Apart from low ability, we find that children may be retarded because of poor physical condition, inadequate visual or auditory acuity, emotional and personality disturbances, poor work habits, irregular school attendance including absences and changing schools, personal attitudes of discouragement and inadequacy, parental attitudes stimulating the child against school, special difficulties in one subject, and many other less common ones. Evidently the discovery of reasons for poor work will require careful clinical study of the child and his history—it is very definitely a purely psycho-clinical problem.

Special Deficiencies.—Special disabilities in school subjects, mentioned above as a reason for retardation, are rather frequent academic problems. A child may be doing well in all of his work except one subject such as reading, history, algebra, or language. Quite evidently such a special deficiency will reduce the general average of his work and in certain cases will be a reason for poor achievement in much of his subsequent study. In the primary grades attention is devoted primarily to those subjects—reading, writing, spelling, arithmetic, language—which are the necessary tools for all academic work. The work of higher grade levels includes subjects, for example, history, geography, and science, the content of which is most important. All of these obviously require skills in the tool subjects, and inadequacies in the content subjects are usually based on lack of the tool skills, inadequate preparation, lack of motivation, or social or personality difficulties which interfere with many adjustments.

Because of the primary importance of the tool subjects, we shall specifically consider them. Spelling and handwriting we can dismiss with a word. The need for accurate spelling and for legible handwriting cannot be denied. Because of the essential nonphonetic spelling of English, disabilities are frequent; however, modern emphasis on a limited list of necessary words and attention to specific types of errors in regular spelling classwork has reduced the need for much special attention. Similarly with handwriting, changes in the aims and ideals of teaching the subject have automatically solved many of the problems.

Reading Skill.—Reading is a skill necessary for all academic achievement. Therefore, the child who does not learn to read adequately is under a serious handicap. For the measurement of reading ability there are available a number of tests which indicate gross achievement and which analyze the reading into such factors as speed, vocabulary, comprehension, etc. By using such tests it is possible to determine the degree of reading retardation and also the relative influence of various factors. Even with a measure of reading skill it is necessary to discover the reason for the observed disabilities. Among the common etiologic factors are poor visual or auditory acuity, poor preparation in earlier steps, emotional and personality inhibitions, inefficient eye movements, and of course low intelligence. The psychoclinical task is to separate the possible reasons for the poor reading and then suggest a program which will correct these. Visual correction, training in eye movement, vocabulary drill, training for reading speed are some examples of aids that may be necessary.

Arithmetic.—Next to reading, arithmetic is probably the most important tool subject. In this subject there is a sequence from enumeration or counting to computation (addition, subtraction, multiplication, and division), and finally to problem solving. Low intelligence is perhaps of greater significance in limiting achievement in the last of these than in the first two. Factors such as sensory defects, emotional attitudes, and so on are of importance here as well as in reading. In this subject adequate preparation in the lower steps is of great value in learning the subsequent ones. One cannot add when he cannot count, and he cannot solve problems if he cannot do all of the four processes. Therefore, attention in diagnosis must be directed to the adequacy of preparation in all steps, and where any are weak there must be a program of special training.

Speech Defects.—A special disability which is not specifically related to the school is in speech. Speech defects of various sorts are widely prevalent, and they have occasioned enough interest to call for a special professional group of speech pathologists and speech correctionists. As with the other problems we have discussed, speech defects are psychological in nature. There are two large classes: (1) The articulatory defects which are poor sound formations due to lack of training, abnormal training, or organic or structural defects; and (2) stuttering or disorders of rhythm, which may be due to bad habit, but which are more usually considered as symptomatic of a more general personality disturbance. In either case any program of corrective exercises must be based on knowledge of the subject's abilities and personality make-up. The psychologist has the task of examining the child in order to analyze the behavior in the same way that he does for any problem. He also frequently carries out therapeutic training himself.

Superior Mental Ability.—The clinical psychologist is frequently asked to examine children of superior ability, that is, those children whose IQ is at least greater than 110, or more usually greater than 120. Psychoclinical study may be desired to establish the degree of superiority and to plan a program of education and living so that the best advantage may be taken of the superiority. The need for such planning is evident when it is realized that groups of such children, when taught in special classes have been found rather consistently to advance in academic fields much faster than normal groups. This does not mean that such superior children must be accelerated in school, but it does mean that their programs should be enriched and made broader.

Superior children are not always referred to psychological clinics for the pleasant task of helping them to take advantage of their ability. As a matter of fact they are referred because of practically every problem that is ever seen in a clinic—conduct and personality problems, special subject disabilities or even school retardation. Indeed about the only thing I have not personally experienced is the reference of a superior child with a complaint of feeblemindedness, but I expect that even this is not impossible.

Problems Arising from Superior Ability.—There is, of course, no reason why a superior child should not exhibit a conduct or personality problem, be retarded generally in school or in a specific subject sometimes for the same reasons that these things occur in any other child. In addition, the child's superiority itself, especially when it is not recognized by the teacher, may be the very reason why problems occur. A child whose mental level is considerably above that necessary to do the classroom work is going to find little to keep him stimulated and busy. Unless he has out-of-school guidance, he may develop lazy habits, or at least may direct his energies into nonscholastic channels and of course soon begins to fail. Or the extra time and energy are directed into behavior unacceptable to the school, and he becomes a disciplinary or conduct problem. Furthermore, because of his superiority, he may find it difficult to meet his classmates at their own level; in turn they reject him, and the stage is set for the development of personality difficulties.

Behavior problems such as these enumerated have been found again and again in children with unrecognized superiority. Experience in dealing with such children has also frequently shown that their interest in new tasks and new fields may be easily aroused. As a result of increased interest and activity in new directions, the secondary problems of behavior begin to disappear.

Behavior Problems.—Probably the difficulties most frequent in general child-guidance clinics are those commonly called primary behavior problems. These include habitual patterns of behavior, not due directly to physical or mental disabilities, which are either socially disturbing or which interfere with the individual's own personal adjustment. The former types are usually called conduct problems, and the latter personality problems. This simple dichotomy has its uses, but extensive clinical experience shows its weakness. As we cannot attempt here to show its inadequacy, we shall use it as a convenient way of dividing the problems into groups for discussion.

What Is a Behavior Problem?—Although we speak of problem behavior, we must realize in the very beginning that there can be no precise designation of what kind of behavior is a problem. We know by observing how a person behaves, and we can know his thoughts, beliefs, ideals, attitudes, and other such implicit behavior only by observing what the individual overtly does in various situations or by observing what he says. This is true of any sort of behavior. If what he does or says violates standards, ideals, or rules of the social group, we immediately consider it problem behavior. Thus the child who swears is frowned upon; the thief is pursued; the child who will not eat worries his mother; the temper tantrum disrupts the household. All these types of behavior and many more are considered problems because they are socially disturbing. This much is clear.

If we look a bit further however we find that the swearing child's parents do not object; the policeman is not concerned about temper tantrums on his beat; and the underworld praises the thief. Thus the same behavior pattern is a problem to one social group but not to another. The conclusion must be that problem behavior can be so judged only in the light of social norms. Exactly the same things are true concerning that behavior which is not socially disturbing, for example, withdrawing, fear, or jealousy. The shy, timid, quiet child is welcomed by some teachers because he causes no trouble, and there are parents who actively foster such behavior in their children. Here the norms which are violated are mental-hygiene ideals which, unfortunately, are not widely known outside of persons professionally interested and trained. Such persons recognize this behavior as of equal, or probably even greater, seriousness than actively disturbing behavior.

Behavior that Violates Social Ideals.—There is much evidence that social or personal ideals govern the designation of what behavior will be considered a problem. Wickman's well-known study indicated that teachers considered that behavior which was most contrary to personal ideals or school regulations as more serious. On the other hand, professional mental-hygiene workers rated the nondisturbing, withdrawing behavior as more serious. Tilson, reporting data from preschool clinics, to which referrals were usually made by parents, showed that of 903 problems treated only 249 had been included in the reasons for the referral—the rest were discovered by the clinics.[3] Thus we see that the behavior for which children are referred to clinics is determined by the ideals of the referrants; the behavior may disturb them, or they may be concerned over the child's well-being.

It is true, of course, that certain behavior such as stealing violates social norms, and although the family group or the immediate neighborhood may not object, society as a whole does. Therefore, there are certain kinds of behavior which are generally regarded as undesirable. On the other hand, a mother or teacher may object to behavior which is a problem to her alone. Thus one teacher in Wickman's study held gum-chewing and failure to stand when speaking in the classroom as almost heinous reactions, and many mothers are greatly worried at the terrible behavior of their ten-year-old boys when they fail to wash cleanly behind their ears. If we keep clearly in mind the tenuous nature of the definition of primary behavior problems, we may now turn to a brief discussion of their nature.

A Classification of Problems.—From the foregoing it is evident that behavior which is socially disturbing—the so-called conduct problems—would be more frequently the basis for referral to a behavior clinic. Considering the complaints alone we find a wide variety of problems, in fact each case is almost unique. However, it is possible roughly to group the problems into classes, and to arrange these in order of increasing social seriousness. As it will be impossible to discuss each specific problem in detail, a brief catalogue will give

the reader an idea of the nature of the problems with which the
clinic must deal. Among the behavior difficulties causing concern in
the home the following are most frequent:

Feeding difficulties: poor appetite, food fads, excessive appetite.
Elimination problems: enuresis, soiling, constipation.
Sleep disturbances: wakefulness, nightmares and night terrors,
    drowsiness.
Sex problems: masturbation, excessive modesty, sex curiosity,
    sex acts.
Emotional problems: temper, excitability, overactivity.
Temperamental problems: disobedience, carelessness, untidiness.

Another group of problems are of consequence in the home, and
also to people outside of the home, in the school and community.
These include lying, swearing, vulgar and obscene language, fighting,
destructiveness, incorrigibility, teasing, cruelty, etc. The problems of
wider social significance are, of course, those which are considered
legally as delinquencies. While these have significance in the smaller
social groups already mentioned, they are perhaps of greater importance to the whole of society. Delinquencies include stealing,
truancy, begging and vagrancy, injury to persons, murder, arson,
injury to property, etc.

Personality Problems.—The problems which are not socially disturbing—the so-called personality problems — also show a sequence
from the relatively mild to the very severe. In general the less obvious personality problems are characterized by submissive, withdrawing behavior; more specifically we can list inferiority feelings,
seclusiveness, bashfulness, dependency, self-accusation, etc. Among
other types of problems of this class that are somewhat more evident
to observation are:

Self-centeredness, including boasting, egotism, showing-off.
Jealousy.
Fear: cowardice, anxiety, worry.
Daydreaming and absent-mindedness.
Negativism: reject affection, shirking.
Suspiciousness and feeling slighted.
Listlessness, laziness, lack of ambition.

Essentially similar in general nature to these milder personality disorders, but more severe in degree, are the conventionally accepted mental disorders, that is, the psychoneuroses and psychoses.

The enumeration given in the last few paragraphs indicates the nature of problems which are dealt with in the behavior clinic. It must be kept very clearly in mind, however, that the clinic does not deal with a problem, but with a child or adult who exhibits a problem or a whole constellation of them. We are frequently asked, "What can I do with my ten-year-old son who has no ambition and is lazy?" That question cannot be answered until we have some knowledge of probable reasons why the child is lazy and lacks ambition. It is in the effort of trying to understand a particular child and his problem behavior that we need the information discussed in the beginning of this chapter.

A Study of Causes Is Imperative.—The need of knowing the causes of a particular problem in a particular child may best be shown by two cases, in both of which the complained-of behavior is similar, but which from the point of view of etiology are quite different. In both of these cases the referrant was disturbed because the children lacked confidence, withdrew from usual contact with other children, and exhibited fear. In both cases the problem was evident in school adjustments. On the basis of the behavior alone both would have to be classed in the submissive, withdrawing group. Information concerning the history of the two children clearly showed the differences between them. One case, a nine-year-old boy, comes from an economically and socially superior home. The father, however, is extremely timid, both in his own behavior and in his expression of concern over his son. The boy is not allowed to play with other boys unless he is being supervised by the mother or father. Even then no rough play is permitted. Both parents constantly caution the boy against getting hurt and they encourage him in his overcautious attitudes. With this sort of environmental influence it is little wonder that the boy lacks confidence and avoids close contact with his classmates.

The contrasting case is a high school girl who comes from an immigrant home of low economic and social level. The parents speak only the foreign tongue of their homeland. The girl speaks the foreign language also, but earlier in her life had learned English as spoken in her own foreign community and with a very pronounced accent. About the time she was to start high school the family moved from the foreign neighborhood so that the girl had to attend high school with children who did not speak her sort of foreign-accent English. The other school children teased her and did not accept her. Her reaction to this environmental influence was to avoid the other children. She withdrew from contacts, lost confidence in herself, became fearful of association with the other children. In both of these cases the net result in observable behavior was essentially similar. However, it is quite evident that they are entirely different problems. Without a very careful investigation of the children's histories, only the most significant points of which are briefly related here, it would have been impossible even to begin planning a method of helping them.

Vocational Guidance.—In Chapter XVII there is an extended discussion of vocational guidance. However, we may mention here the part that clinical psychology plays. Essentially the task of vocational guidance is to discover the capabilities and aptitudes of an individual and then to help that individual to find the sort of occupation in which he can make the most fruitful use of those abilities. On the one hand the vocational counselor must have knowledge of occupations, analyses of specific jobs, and be familiar with community resources in the way of possible positions and of training facilities. These aspects of the counselor's task are not particularly psychological.

On the other hand vocational guidance requires knowledge about the individual to be guided. It is in this connection that the clinical psychologist plays a part. With his available testing tools the psychologist appraises the subject's ability, skills, aptitude, and achievements. On the basis of quantitative scores from a variety of tests and from a qualitative interpretation of the subject's behavior on the tests he can make suggestions as to the kind of work for which he is probably best fitted. This can be done only in a general way. For example, even after a very extensive examination we cannot predict whether the individual should be a pattern-maker, or a tinsmith, but the results would probably indicate that some such manipulative, mechanical trade would suit him best. The psychologist must, however, do more than make the appraisal we have mentioned. While all evidence may indicate that the person has the skills and aptitudes for a particular occupation, he may not be successful in such a direction because of personality difficulties or habit patterns which would interfere with successful adaptation. Therefore, the clinical psychologist must evaluate these aspects of the individual and integrate both sets of findings before he can honestly make suggestions for the individual. From this discussion it is evident that anyone who does vocational counselling should have adequate preparation in clinical psychology as well as in the general field of occupations.

Adult Problems.—In our discussion so far we have continually spoken of children. The history of clinical psychology shows that most work in this field has been done with subjects in the lower age levels. However, it is evident that many of the techniques we have described and most of the problems we have mentioned may apply also to adults. Therefore, it is only reasonable to expect that clinical psychologists would direct their attention to the problems of this older-age group. That they have done so has been increasingly true in the last decade or so. Psychologists working with children have always had occasional adult problems brought to their professional attention, and among those working with the feebleminded the adult group was large. However, it is only relatively recently that clinics have been organized, and individual psychologists have devoted themselves especially to the clinical problems of adults. We can do little more here than to call attention briefly to some of the activities that have been carried out in this direction.

The Criminal Adult.—Clinical psychology in the broad sense has been directed to the study and rehabilitation of criminals. Sociologists, psychologists, and psychiatrists interested in criminology have been working ever since the first behavior clinic was established at Sing Sing Prison in 1918 on the problems of why men are criminals. We know now that criminals are products of their environments and are not so born. With this fact well established there is greater point to efforts at rehabilitation instead of punishment. But rehabilitation can come about only when we understand in some detail the reasons why a particular man or woman has committed this crime or these crimes. It is just the discovery of such reasons and attempts to correct them that is the task of clinical psychology.

Vocational Adjustment.—Associated with the idea of vocational guidance is the plan of fitting the best man to the job and of keeping the worker adjusted so that industrial efficiency is maintained. Viteles has long been applying clinical psychology to the problems of industrial personnel. Not alone in relation to his job, but in his everyday adjustment as well, the adult may have difficulties as well as the child. Therefore, we find efforts being directed at personal guidance of the adult, to the end of helping him find greater happiness and greater efficiency. In recent years this effort has been especially directed toward the aged, who as a group present a very special set of problems.

Problems in Marriage.—Among the endless adjustments that adults must make those of marriage are perhaps the most pressing. Apart from all questions of sexual, economic, intellectual, or other adjustments, when a man and woman marry, they are undertaking to bring two different personalities into continuous, intimate relation. If the personalities of the two parties are similar or even complementary, the adjustment is usually satisfactorily made. If they are opposite and clashing, then troubles almost inevitably develop. The clashes of personality, the inability of one partner to accept what he considers the other's "faults," the strains produced by financial worries and sexual incompatability, the conflicts of intellectual and social interests all result in the dissolution of the marital partnership and, therefore, of the integrated, harmonious home. Very often this final result of a broken home is not necessary if the partners can be helped in making the necessary adjustments to each other. Psychologists and sociologists interested in the family have established clinical centers where married couples may secure help and guidance. As in all other kinds of psychoclinical activity the tasks revolve around securing information about the persons involved and on the basis of such information planning a program designed to eliminate the disturbing elements.

PSYCHOLOGICAL CLINICS

The origin of the type of work that we have been describing and the term clinical psychology are to be found in the work of Lightner Witmer, who first proposed the possibilities of this sort of psychological application at the University of Pennsylvania in 1896. During the subsequent quarter of a century there was a very slow, but constant growth. Clinics were started in connection with universities, school systems, and institutions, some of them coming more or less directly from Witmer through his students, others independent of Witmer's influence. In 1916 with the publication of the first Stanford Revision of the Binet test there was a greatly accelerated spread of psychological study of individual children. The demonstrated value of the psychological examining of soldiers during the World War gave further impetus to applied psychology. These two events emphasized mental testing and had the unfortunate result of causing neglect of Witmer's fundamental clinical principles in favor of rather formal testing. The real clinical point of view, while never absolutely lost, was reintroduced by way of the psychiatric child guidance clinic during the 1920's. At the present time psychological clinics and clinical psychologists in other sorts of clinics are increasing in number. It is true that there are still many unsolved problems concerning the relations of the various professional groups, but none of these problems are crucial to the contribution of clinical psychology.

A question frequently asked by students is "Where does the psychologist do the sort of work you have described?" We can answer that only briefly by calling attention to several types of organizations in which psychologists have been found valuable. In the first place we must repeat that at present clinical psychology is more frequently interested in children than adults. This being so we should expect to find psychologists more frequently in children's agencies. From the very beginning clinical psychology has been associated with education. Most present-day psychological clinics are operated by universities, schools of education, public or private schools, or school systems. University clinics are usually for the primary purpose of training psychologists, and thus service work is secondary. The psychologist in the school system, however, has a very definite function. It is his responsibility to examine and recommend treatment for the whole array of problems in which the child's school adjustments are concerned. In some large school systems as New York, Chicago, and Cleveland, the psychological departments are very extensive parts of the school organization.

Child-guidance clinics, which we have already mentioned, were started under the auspices of the National Committee for Mental Hygiene. During a five-year experiment with several trial clinics financed by the Commonwealth Fund there was developed a standard organization for such clinics. In brief, this organization established the cooperation of the psychiatrist, psychologist, and psychiatric social worker. Ideally these three professional groups, with the assistance at times of the teacher, recreation worker, and others, pool their professional knowledge of the child and together plan a therapeutic program for him. Usually the psychiatrist has final responsibility, although there are excellent clinics with a psychologist in administrative charge. In any case the contribution of the psychologist is very definitely recognized. At the present time there are between two and three hundred child guidance clinics of various sizes operating in this country.

Other children's agencies have also found the psychologist's service of value, but perhaps not so frequently as they will in the future. Child-placing agencies, children's homes, children's hospitals, juvenile courts, and juvenile correctional institutions are examples of auspices under which psychologists work. Institutions for the feebleminded have long had psychologists on their staffs for work with both children and adults.

Other than in institutions for the feebleminded, clinical psychological work with adults has been slow in developing. However, it has increased a great deal in the last ten years and gives promise of greater increase in the future. Work with psychotic patients, both within the institution and outside, has been primarily the concern of the psychiatrist. However, there is a growing recognition that the psychologist has a valuable contribution to make which is evident in the increasing employment of psychologists in institutions and outpatient clinics for psychotic and psychoneurotic adults. In the penal systems of the Federal government, of New Jersey and Indiana, to mention some outstanding examples, psychology is in practical use in the classification and subsequent treatment of prisoners. Social agencies, especially those devoted to family welfare, and some group-work agencies have found the psychologist's services of value. In connection with such organizations, and sometimes independently, the psychologist may help with problems of marital adjustment, vocational fitness, personal sufficiency and so on.

In everything said so far there has been the implication that the psychologist is hired by some agency. Like the teacher, the psychologist must usually enter the employ of someone else. However, there are a few men and women successfully carrying on a private consulting practice in some of the larger urban centers. Such consultants are usually the best trained and most capable people. Their activities may include any of the tasks we have earlier mentioned, or they may specialize in children's, industrial, educational, marital, or other problems.

REFERENCES

Bronner, A. F., Healy, W., Lowe, G. M., and Shimberg, M. E. *A Manual of Individual Mental Tests and Testing.* Boston: Little, Brown and Company, 1937.

Garrett, H. E., and Schneck, M. R. *Psychological Tests, Methods, and Results.* New York: Harper and Brothers, 1933.

Institute for Juvenile Research, *Child Guidance Procedures.* New York: D. Appleton-Century Company, Inc., 1937.

Kanner, L. *Child Psychiatry.* Springfield, Illinois: Charles C. Thomas, 1935.

Louttit, C. M. *Clinical Psychology.* New York: Harper and Brothers, 1936.

Symonds, P. M. *Diagnosing Personality and Conduct.* New York: D. Appleton-Century Company, Inc., 1931.

Terman, L. M., and Merrill, M. A. *Measuring Intelligence.* Boston: Houghton Mifflin Company, 1937.

CHAPTER XVI

INDIVIDUAL MENTAL EFFICIENCY

By Douglas Fryer, *New York University*

Developing and maintaining mental efficiency should be of interest to everyone, whether child or adult, in realizing his potential value, both because he wishes to be more of an individual and because he desires to be a better citizen. Education has this as its purpose. Through general education, habits unfold in the use of mental tools and in the application of mathematical, scientific, and philosophical concepts. In specialized education, skillful patterns of performance and logical ways of thinking are formed as they are to be used in the work of the occupations. Each science has its technical language; each profession and each business has its field of knowledge; all work has its specialized habits. Whether general or special, education should develop and maintain efficiency in the individual.

True education is what the individual seeks for himself. It cannot be forced upon him, but he can be guided, if he will, by information about methods for the development of personal efficiency, and by information concerning channels of advancement and progress in attaining knowledge and skills. To give this information is the purpose of vocational and educational guidance as it is furnished by counselors and teachers in school systems and social agencies. Its use is left to the individual and the value of the guidance is determined by the direction he takes in his development.

Educators believe that maximum efficiency brings the greatest satisfaction for the individual, that all should strive for this goal with the best direction available, that personal adjustment in life comes from the greatest individual efficiency in mental and physical work. Whether it is true that greatest happiness is determined by maximum individual efficiency has yet to be proved and there are, to the contrary, many anecdotes of the satisfied Robinson Crusoe and the happy moron. But this is, in any case, the philosophy of many civilized peoples.

Psychology has accumulated facts and methods of mental activity which can be used by the individual in directing his development toward greatest efficiency. This chapter assembles the information on the growth of individual mental efficiency and on the influences that may affect it.

LEARNING AND WORK

Learning is the acquisition of knowledge and skill. It is the formation of work habits. But learning may continue in any task long after acceptance of the individual as an artisan. Work is the exercise of mental and physical habits of varying degrees of efficiency. Accordingly, learning, from its initial acquisition, is work. But by definition learning is the development of habits to an accepted criterion of work.

Learning.—All learning progresses in a characteristic manner whether it be the learning of languages, occupational skills, or professional knowledge. Progress is similar for various tasks, but the number of learning periods depends upon the difficulty of the task. Generally, acquisition is greater during the early stages of the learning; it becomes less and less as the learning progresses toward perfection. But if the material to be learned is essentially new, acquisition may be increasingly greater during the very early stages of the learning. This is due to the initial difficulty of any new tasks. A fuller description of learning will be found in Chapter XIV of this volume.

Learning Curves.—Progress in learning can be plotted as a curve on cross-section paper with the number of trials on the abscissa, or X-axis, and the amount of acquisition on the ordinate, or Y-axis. The general form of the learning curve will be noted in Fig. 20. Various features of learning curves have been described as initial spurt, end-spurt, plateau, insight, positive and negative acceleration. The initial spurt is said to represent transfer from previous learning. An end-spurt represents final motivation to achieve the goal. If an end-spurt appears in a learning curve it is followed by the usual end-plateau, which is said to represent the 'physiological limit' of learning. The plateau, which is a flat place appearing at various parts of the curve, may represent a constant obstacle in acquisition which must be overcome before progress can continue. Insight is defined, often, as a rapid rise in the learning curve. It appears frequently in curves of learning of complex materials and is essentially an instantaneous solution of a necessary part of the task. By definition, the end-plateau in the learning curve is the beginning of the work curve.

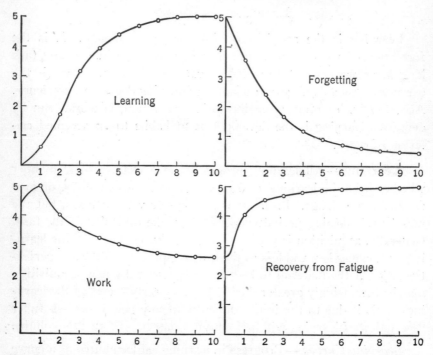

FIG. 20.—HYPOTHETICAL CURVES OF PERFORMANCE ILLUSTRATING LEARNING, FORGETTING, WORK, AND RECOVERY FROM FATIGUE (TESTS OF PERFORMANCE ON ABSCISSA; AMOUNT OF PERFORMANCE ON ORDINATE).

Positive acceleration in learning curves indicates learning of increasingly greater and greater amount, and it is found only in curves derived with essentially new material and then in their early stages. Most curves are negatively accelerated throughout, thus representing ever decreasing acquisition. Learning is usually influenced by previous learning. However, the generalized curve adopted to represent all learning from its beginnings is positively accelerated in its early stages and negatively accelerated in its later stages. It is S-shaped, as illustrated in Fig. 20.

Individual Differences.—Individual learners vary from the average of learners in a task as is represented in the generalized learning curve. Progress all along the way from the initial trial to the end-plateau may differ for individuals. There are 'poor' and 'good' learners for any task in education or industry.

These differences are often due to previous training in tasks which are prerequisites of the learning. "Background," as it is called, determines the goodness or poorness of the individual's efficiency in specific learning situations. Learning efficiency in any task, whether it be Latin in college or machine operation in the vestibule school, is based on prerequisite training. But most obvious differences in learning are evident when intellectual capacity varies widely between individuals, such as might exist if the average marine engineman and the average tool-and-die maker were set the task of learning certain processes of mechanical engineering. Such individuals, who differ in general intelligence-test scores, also usually differ in inherent capacity to learn in many specialized tasks.

Forgetting.—Forgetting is at least in part a process of inhibition of formerly learned habits by new learning. The curve of forgetting, which was plotted by Ebbinghaus, falls rapidly at first and its slope becomes more and more gradual with time. It is negatively accelerated, as in Fig. 20. The steepness of the slope is in inverse proportion to the amount of overlearning. Forgetting of language and of motor learning follows exactly the same course and duplicate curves result if the criteria of the learning are the same.

Work.—Under ideal conditions, efficiency in work should continue uniformly at the level of the physiological limit of the learning. According to this idea, the curve of work would be a straight line parallel to the abscissa at the height of the end-plateau of the learning curve. That this is not the case is evident to all. Working efficiency depends upon many influences other than the degree of learning. Curves of work fluctuate irregularly. They show a general decrement of fatigue over a long period of time. There are varied and numerous influences determining efficiency in mental and physical work.

Work Curves.—Measures of work are plotted in a manner similar to those of learning, with the periods of work on the abscissa and the amount on the ordinate. Curves may be prepared to indicate efficiency over periods of years as well as a few hours or minutes. Work curves in industry show daily, weekly, and seasonal fluctuations. Individual curves for experimental periods of work may show initial spurt, end-spurt, warming-up and practice, rhythmical or "chance" variations during the work period, and the fatigue decrement. The general form of the work curve is illustrated in Fig. 20.

The curve of work was first established in 1889 for a work period of one hour by Axel Oehrn,[1] a pupil of Kraepelin, upon 10 professors and graduate students, with various kinds of materials. While rising at the very first, due to practice, the curve of work falls gradually, due to fatigue, almost from the beginning to the end of the work period. The length and height of the initial rise varies with the kind of task and with the individual subjects. Oehrn established the point of maximum efficiency, which is the point where the fatigue effect begins to overbalance the practice effect, as 24 minutes in learning nonsense syllables, 26 minutes in writing from dictation, 28 minutes in addition, 38 minutes in reading, 39 minutes in counting letters one by one, 59 minutes in counting them 3 by 3, and 60 minutes in learning numbers.

Initial Spurt.—The initial spurt takes place only during the first few minutes of a work period. Kraepelin noted its presence and it has been established by numerous investigations with various kinds of work. The initial spurt usually is completed somewhat before the end of the first five minutes. It is explained as due to the removal of associative interference. It will be recalled that in learning, the initial spurt was explained as an effect of transfer and these two activities are similar.

End-Spurt.—An end-spurt may be expected if the worker is aware that the end of the work period is near. It is explained as due to a change in conscious motivation. Some investigators have reported end-spurts when the end of the work period was not known, but probably these are not true end-spurts, as rhythmical or "chance" variations may occur at any point in the work curve.

Learning in Work.—Learning continues in all work. It seems impossible to achieve maximum learning in any task however automatic. Old end-plateaus are passed and new end-plateaus at higher levels in the learning curve take their place. Where fatigue effects are eliminated, learning curves and work curves differ only in the amount of acquisition involved. This is because work curves represent psychological activity nearer perfection than learning curves.

Learning effects are most evident, of course, in the early part of work curves. Oehrn used the following formula to distinguish the practice effect in work curves:

$$\frac{(M - m') \times 100}{M}$$

where M is the point of maximum efficiency and m' is a point of minimum efficiency which will be found prior to that of maximum efficiency. By this formula it is possible to compare learning effects in work curves of different maximal levels.

Warming-up and *practice* are now distinguished as separate learning effects in work curves. Warming-up is defined as immediate improvement following the initial spurt of adaptation of the work period. Practice is permanent or persistent acquisition which is measurable after rest. Warming-up is a measure of learning as it takes place.

Robinson and Heron [2] argue that any absence of warming-up in work curves, as variously reported, is due to fatigue, for warming-up is present always in curves of discontinuous work. These investigators introduced rests to remove the effects of fatigue in continuous work and found warming-up. In one experiment, 3 conditions were used in reciting the alphabet backwards: (I) Continuous work for 20 minutes; (II) In thirty-second periods with rests of 15 seconds for 20 minutes of actual recitation; and (III) In thirty-second periods with rests of 30 seconds for 20 minutes of actual recitation. The curves for Condition I, where the work was continuous, showed little or no warming-up. But those for Conditions II and III which included rests showed definite effects of warming-up.

Fatigue nullifies the warming-up effects in continuous work curves and the fatigue decrement may be present almost from the beginning of the work period, as it was under Condition I of Robinson and Heron's experiment. But even under conditions where any effect of warming-up is absent in the work curve there is likely to be a measurable learning effect after rest.

FATIGUE

Mental and physical activities are distinguished as two kinds of work. But both mental and physical work involve neuromuscular . organization and the only valid physiological distinction, which is one of degree, is according to the exercise of small or large muscle groups. Also, fatigue has been distinguished as mental, muscular, physiological, and sensory—likewise an arbitrary classification.

Measures of Fatigue.—Fatigue measurements are made of:

    (1) Feelings of fatigue (subjective fatigue).
    (2) Physiological changes in tissues during work
        (physiological fatigue).
    (3) Decrement in performance (objective fatigue).

There is little correlation between these "kinds" of fatigue and they will be considered separately.

Feelings of Fatigue.—Feelings of fatigue are referred to as subjective fatigue. They are measured by the psychometric method of single stimuli with estimates at various times during work on a scale of possibly as many as 10 units ranging from pleasantness or satisfaction in the work to unpleasantness or dissatisfaction. The usual curve of subjective fatigue for a repetitive mental task drops rapidly with negative acceleration from the very beginning to the end of the work period (see Fig. 21). But there are wide individual differences in susceptibility to feelings of fatigue and the slope of the curve will vary with the task.

The form of the curve was originally suggested by Thorndike,[3] as based on the work of 29 adults for 2 hours in grading printed compositions. Average ratings of "satisfyingness" secured every 20 minutes on a ten-point scale follow: 4.4, 4.0, 3.6, 3.4, 2.8, 2.6. For 5 individuals performing the same task for a four-hour period, the average ratings of "satisfyingness" taken every 20 minutes were 6.0, 5.7, 5.2, 5.0, 4.6, 4.3, 3.6, 3.3, 2.8, 2.4, 2.5, 2.2. Muscio,[4] in England, secured a similar curve of subjective fatigue for work performed by medical students and by typists with ratings at various hours of a day's work on a scale of (4) fit, (3) fairly fit, (2) a little tired, and, (1) very tired.

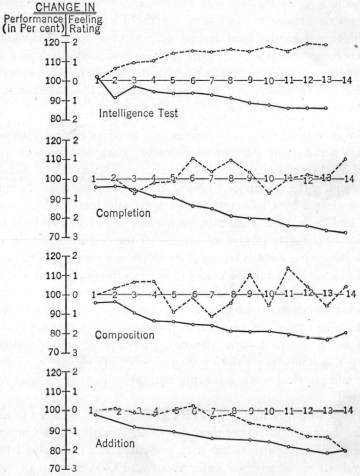

FIG. 21.—CURVES OF CHANGE IN RATING OF "FEELINGS OF FATIGUE" (CONTINUOUS LINE) AND PER CENT CHANGE IN PERFORMANCE (BROKEN LINE) IN FOUR TASKS. (AFTER POFFENBERGER.)

It would be expected that the conditions of the work would influence the slope of the curve of feelings of fatigue. Poffenberger[5] has established this as a fact. Curves of feelings of fatigue for four tasks, based on averages for 10 to 13 subjects working about

5 hours, as reported in Poffenberger's study, are shown in Fig. 21, in which the measures are the amounts of feeling change on a seven-point scale from the first records. Curves of performance are included in Fig. 21 for purposes of comparison. The usual curves of feelings of fatigue are indicated for the 4 kinds of work, but for intelligence tests the total feeling decrement is only 1.3, while for sentence completion it is 2.7, for judging compositions it is 2.3 and for addition it is 2.2. For these subjects, work such as performing intelligence tests involved less unpleasantness than automatic performance such as addition.

Physiological Fatigue.—Nerves and muscles exhibit fatigue, although nerve tissue fatigues very slowly. Fatigue of nerves is indicated by the presence of carbon dioxide (CO_2) and heat following work and by the absorption of Nissl substance of the cells. In muscles it is indicated by a reduction in glycogen, and increased presence of CO_2 and lactic acid. However, such measures give very little information of the state of general fatigue of the organism during work, while indicating what is taking place in the metabolism of cells.

Pulse, or heart rate, increases in any new mental or physical work when compared with a preliminary period of complete relaxation. This is the only undisputed conclusion upon the physiology of mental work. The pattern of respiration usually changes, but its character does not conform to any standard. Results of investigations of changes in temperature during mental work are equivocal. Reaction time and physical work following mental work may or may not be affected.

But it would seem that general metabolism is influenced in mental work. In a careful experiment in 1909, Benedict and Carpenter [6] came to this conclusion, but they presented it tentatively, from an analysis of elimination of water vapor and CO_2, amount of oxygen absorbed and heat given off during 4 hours of mental work as compared with 4 hours of rest. Various other investigators have reported increased CO_2 elimination and oxygen consumption and in a check experiment in 1930 Benedict and Benedict [7] have verified this result. But the amounts were slight and the increase from rest was not cumulative. These investigators have computed the extra caloric demands of intensive mental work for one hour as being met by eating one oyster cracker or one-half of a salted peanut!

Investigations of physiological changes have contributed very little to our knowledge of the effect of mental work in fatigue. Varied organic changes accompany mental work, but they are all slight and seemingly unimportant losses of energy. Either the nature of the loss of energy which is mental fatigue is as yet unmeasurable or the degree of loss now measurable is the necessary amount for maintenance of efficient mental work. Further investigations into physiological fatigue are needed.

Fatigue Decrement in Performance.—Fatigue decrement is noted in a comparison of the first and last halves of work curves. The fatigue decrement may be measured by (1) the continuous work method, or (2) the interpolated task method. In the interpolated method, standard tasks are introduced at regular intervals during any work and the tested loss is considered to be the fatigue decrement in that work. This method is recommended only with highly heterogeneous work, for the influence of the different materials of the test on the measurement of fatigue in the work is uncontrolled.

The continuous method is generally used where the work is homogeneous and allows for frequent measures of efficiency, as in the addition or multiplication of problems of equal difficulty. Oehrn's formula for fatigue effect, comparable to his formula for practice effect given on page 403, is as follows:

$$\frac{(M - m) \times 100}{M}$$

where M is the point of maximum efficiency and m is a second point of minimum efficiency which will be found following the point of maximum efficiency in the work curve.

But such formulas can be used only if the work is highly practiced. By substituting for the beginning measure of maximum efficiency a measure of performance in the same task after rest, or at the beginning of the next work period, the effect of practice during the work period is included. Arai [8] reports 93.2 per cent decrement for an eleven-hour work period where the measure of maximum efficiency was taken at the beginning of the work period and 106.1 per cent decrement where it was taken as the beginning of the next work period after rest. It is evident that learning continues in work even after the task is highly practiced, as this was. Efficiency measured after rest following the work period is considered to be the most accurate indicator of performance without fatigue for it includes the practice effect of the work period.

Fatigue decrement in performance varies with individuals, with length of the work period, and with the working materials. Hylan and Kraepelin [9] found that an appreciable amount of fatigue developed within five minutes in work of addition of one-place numbers. Oehrn reported fatigue decrements for various tasks during one-hour work periods as follows:

Reading 5.9%	Counting letters one by one........ 6.2%
Writing 8.4%	Counting letters three by three 6.9%
Addition....15.4%	Memory for numbers 22.3%

For two-hour periods of mental multiplication of two-place numbers, Arai reported a fatigue decrement of 24.2 per cent, but with wide individual differences between subjects. The fatigue decrement for 11 hours of continuous work of mental multiplication of four-place numbers was 93.2 per cent. This result is for one subject, and daily variations for eleven-hour periods of continuous work on 4 days were as follows: (1) 111.9, (2) 91.3, (3) 91.4, (4) 78.3. The fatigue decrement is correlated roughly with length of period of work, increasing (in time taken to do a unit of work) from approximately 5 per cent for one hour to 100 per cent for 11 hours of continuous work.

An investigation by Poffenberger [10] clearly demonstrates the differential effects of varied tasks upon fatigue. Performance curves are shown in Fig. 21 for four tasks (along with curves of feelings of fatigue) for about five-hour periods of continuous work, in which the measures of work are given in terms of per cent of the initial record. For addition, the fatigue decrement was 20 per cent. In judging compositions upon the Hillegas Composition Scale and the completion of sentences there was little change in the level of performance and the curve for performance of intelligence tests shows an increment of 20 per cent. Learning must be taken into consideration in any interpretation of the curves of the more complicated tasks as in this experiment. Only in the first two tasks was there preliminary practice. The curve of work for intelligence tests is a typical learning curve. But the important point here is the different effects of various tasks on fatigue in performance. Fatigue decrement is determined by the kind of work.

Correlation with Feelings of Fatigue.—A comparison of the curves in Fig. 21 for feelings of fatigue and performance shows lack of correspondence. This fact has been noted by several investigators. In Thorndike's investigation performance for two-hour and four-hour periods remained substantially the same whereas feelings of fatigue increased steadily.

Recovery from Fatigue.—Curves of recovery from fatigue vary with individuals, the extent of the work period, and the nature of the task, to an even greater extent than do fatigue curves. But any curve of recovery will probably show rapid recovery at first and negative acceleration in returning to normal.

Poffenberger's study[11] indicates recovery after 10 minutes of rest in feelings of fatigue of 77 per cent for intelligence tests, 68 per cent for judging compositions, 48 per cent for addition, and 37 per cent for completion of sentences. It is evident that substantial recovery of normal feeling is rapid and that it varies in time with the task.

No curve of recovery from the fatigue decrement of mental performance has been published. But Manzer[12] has reported the average recovery for various muscle groups exhausted on the ergograph of 82 per cent after 5 minutes, 90 per cent after 10 minutes, and 95 per cent after 20 minutes. Arai[13] reported the average recovery from 10 minutes rest after 2 hours of continuous mental multiplication of two-place numbers of 74 per cent of the fatigue decrement. Twenty-one per cent of the fatigue decrement existed after 60 minutes rest, which suggests the form of the recovery curve. Poffenberger[14] found only 40 per cent recovery of the fatigue decrement from 10 minutes rest after 5 hours of addition. From this and other evidence it would appear that the curve for recovery from the fatigue decrement in mental performance will be negatively accelerated, which will have a large proportion of the recovery for short spells of work taking place within 10 minutes—possibly a recovery of 75 per cent of initial mental efficiency. A hypothetical curve of recovery from the fatigue decrement in mental performance is shown in Fig. 20.

REST

Rest is regarded as the antithesis of work or as the inhibition of psychological activity. Physiologically, it is a period of metabolic recuperation. In terms of mental measurement it is a state of recovering from feelings of fatigue or from fatigue decrement in performance. It is accomplished by a change in activity or by relaxation or sleep.

Rest-Pauses.—Interpolated periods of relaxation in spells of work are called rest-pauses. Generally speaking, they have a beneficial effect upon the continued exercise of any mental or physical activity. Both learning and work are influenced by them.

During Learning.—The fact that interpolated rest-pauses during the learning period have a beneficial effect on the learning has been called the "Law of distributed practice." The influence of rest-pauses was noted in the early research of Ebbinghaus in the learning of nonsense syllables. Various investigators of both verbal and motor learning have indicated their beneficial effects. If plateaus in learning curves may be considered as resulting from fatigue counteracting practice, as they may well be, rest-pauses cause recovery from fatigue for they remove the plateaus. Rest is an important factor in efficient learning.

Distributed practice affects immediate and delayed recall differently. Austin [15] reports the interesting result that 5 readings of logical material (history and economics) distributed over 5 days was 3 times as efficient as 5 readings in one period for free recall 2 weeks or 1 month later. But they were equally efficient when tested for immediate recall. The application of this result to study for permanent retention will be evident.

Optimum intervals for practice and number of trials per practice period have been determined for various materials. For example, Hardy [16] established a four-day interval for 3 trials a day as superior to shorter intervals of 12 hours, or of 1, 2, and 3 days, in learning a stylus maze. Lashley [17] found that an equal amount of practice of archery distributed in 5 or 12 trials a day was more beneficial in the learning than when distributed in 20, 40, or 60 trials a day.

The kind of activity composing the rest-pause has an important influence upon the learning. Robinson [18] has demonstrated that activities of the rest period affect later recall of the learning the least that are similar or dissimilar, and that between these two extremes there is the greatest retroactive inhibition. It is generally accepted that complete relaxation is most beneficial as a rest-pause. Jenkins and Dallenbach [19] have shown that about twice as many nonsense syllables are recalled after various hours of sleep as compared with similar waking intervals.

Rest-Pauses in Industry.—A vast literature has been accumulated upon the effect of rest-pauses in industrial processes, a topic surveyed in Chapter XVIII. The general benefits from adequate rest for maximum production are clearly appreciated in personnel administration. Investigators of the Industrial Health Research Board of Great Britain have found that unauthorized resting time among industrial workers is 10 or more minutes an hour, which indicates the necessary time of desirable rest-pauses. The voluntary rest-pause is more beneficial than that imposed by the conditions of the work. Various kinds of work require a different distribution and length of rest-pauses. It is likely that rest-pauses will benefit more the less efficient workers. Industrial work of a monotonous character, or work requiring constant attention and judgment, or heavy work, or work requiring continuous sitting and standing, or repetitive work generally, benefits from rest-pauses. The beneficial effect is noted in the decrease in feelings of fatigue, and in increased production. The expected increase in production for repetitive work, according to Wyatt,[20] the outstanding English authority in this field, is between 2 and 5 per cent. Wyatt states that a rest-pause should be introduced at the time when output is shown on the curve of work to be at its maximum.

Mental Work.—No operation can be maintained at maximum efficiency unbroken by rest for any length of time even under the strongest motivation. This has been indicated in the discussion of fatigue. Also, it has been shown that a 75 per cent recovery may be expected after short spells of mental work from a rest-pause of 10 minutes, but full recovery requires a much longer time, possibly hours.

Most of the investigations into the effects of rest-pauses on mental work have been with continuous or repetitive performance. Hylan and Kraepelin [21] found that the benefit of rest in addition work is not proportional to its length. Graf [22] tried single rest-pauses of ½, 2, and 5 minutes duration in one-hour work periods of simple addition. He found that the two-minute length showed the greatest benefit, and for single rest-pauses of 1, 3, 5, and 10 minutes duration in two-hour work periods, he found that the five-minute length was the most efficient. He established the best time for the single rest-pause as being at the end of the second third of the work spell, or at 40 minutes and 80 minutes, respectively. As the number of rest-pauses is increased in a period of work, their length should be decreased to achieve maximum efficiency. It is to be expected that optimum length and distribution of rest-pauses will vary with individual workers and with the nature of the task.

In mental work, as in learning, the activities of the rest-pause will affect efficiency. Wyatt [23] reports results of an unpublished study by Jackson in which the gain in performance, when a rest-pause of 15 minutes was included in the middle of a two-hour period of simple addition, was measured for different ways of spending the rest-pause, as follows:

Nature of Rest	Per Cent Gain
Complete relaxation in a chair	9.3
Uncontrolled rest	8.3
Music	3.9
Tea	3.4
Walk	1.5

Miles and Skilbeck [24] found that output in an industrial process was increased 14.2 per cent by a fifteen-minute change of work twice a day. A change in activity, which establishes a new mental set, often has a beneficial effect upon mental performance.

Two essential conclusions can be drawn from the investigation of rest-pauses, first, that they are beneficial for efficiency and happiness in all work, including learning, and second, that the conditions of their use depend upon the character of the task and the capacity and personality of individual workers. The conditions of their use must be determined for each working situation.

Sleep.—Sleep is an extreme condition of relaxation or rest and of lowered physiological activity. Studies with animals indicate that sleep is essential to life. Ten puppies kept awake artificially died within a week. The necessary hours of sleep to maintain normal efficiency among human beings have not been determined. Evidently there are wide individual differences in this requirement. It is possible that some adults can maintain a high degree of working efficiency on 5 hours of sleep in 24 while some require 9 or 10 hours. The normal sleeping time is thought of as one-third of the twenty-four-hour day, or 8 hours.

Sleep and Learning.—Loss of sleep is detrimental to learning and sleep is beneficial to retention. Weiskotten [25] showed an average increase in time of learning nonsense syllables of 57 per cent during a period of sleeplessness extending from 16 to 58 hours with an average increase in relearning time of 102 per cent. In the study by Jenkins and Dallenbach,[26] the retention of nonsense syllables after various intervals of sleeping and waking was as follows:

Hours Between Learning and Recall	Per Cent Recalled After Interval of	
	Sleeping	Waking
1	71	46
2	54	31
4	56	23
8	57	9

We forget because of the inhibition of previously learned material by waking activity. Sleep is advantageous to retention, and sleep just after learning is most beneficial.

Loss of Sleep and Work.—Probably the chief effect of loss of sleep is one of reduced motivation or the ability to apply oneself to the performance of a task. But individuals rise to the occasion under adequate motivation and loss of considerable sleep may not affect performance. There is the condition known as mental 'second breath' where the individual feels 'inspired,' sleep seems unnecessary, and quality, and possibly quantity, of accomplishment is on an extraordinarily high level. The individual may make demands upon himself beyond those of normal function for periods of days and weeks. The human organism is a most adaptable machine.

After loss of sleep, individuals report increased irritability, nervousness, and lack of control. Speech becomes tangled and lapses occur. Distractors are more disturbing. Sustained attention seems more difficult. Feelings of fatigue are materially affected by loss of sleep.

Results of research upon the effect of loss of sleep on performance are contradictory. Robinson and Hermann [27] have reported no decrease in efficiency of performance in such tests as strength of grip, tapping, aiming, reading letters of the alphabet, and mental multiplication for subjects without sleep for 60 to 65 hours. On the other hand, Lashlett [28] has reported reduced efficiency of 10.7 per cent in code writing, 13.8 per cent in addition, 8.8 per cent in pursuit meter readings, 33.8 and 51.8 per cent in ataxiameter measures, and 24.5 per cent in the Thorndike intelligence examination with loss of sleep of 72 hours. It seems probable that mental efficiency will be reduced by any amount of deviation from normal sleeping time providing motivation is not developed to overcome an anticipated loss in ability to work.

MOTIVATION TO WORK AND TO LEARN

Psychologists generally have thought of the causes of psychological activity as originating in and genetically traceable to the tissue needs of the body. At the beginning of human life, motivation is observed largely in the stimulation of internal receptors, such as the pressures and pains of hunger, defecation, thirst, and urination. But certain external stimuli will affect the organism, such as loud sounds, bright lights, absence of support, and temperature changes. Environmental changes that are ineffective as stimuli, are associated with these adequate stimuli and provide additional motivation, such as those that determine eating at certain hours or the various discriminations established among people and objects. And proprioceptive stimuli are conditioned in a similar manner, developing postural activity. Motivation in the indivdual has some such origin as this. An extensive survey of its development will be found in a book by Young listed at the end of this chapter.

Conscious differentiation of stimuli is a part of the developmental process. Overt motor activity is inhibited and verbal discriminations are made. These also are inhibited and conscious choice takes place in thought. Early motivation becomes social, as when the child learns to evacuate only under approved conditions. Such socialized motivation as prestige, wealth, authority, appearance, cooperation and so on, develops in response to specific stimulation. Here the genetic history of motivation is vague, while in theory every stimulus is said to motivate activity because of its relation to the original tissue needs of the human body. The hierarchy of specific motives of the adult is the result of a development from general to special forms of behavior in a complex environment.

Psychological stimulation is not a specific change in the environment of a worker as usually defined in objective experiment. It is the total 'mass' of changes affecting the individual at any one moment. These changes may be studied in the environment, in awareness, and in physiological activity. Motivation is 'mass stimulation.'

Motivation to learn and to work at adolescent and adult levels is studied as:

(1) Conscious motivation, observed in intention and mental set.
(2) Rhythms, noting the influence on work of repeated regular patterns of stimuli.
(3) Distractors, in which the influences of noise and irregular stimuli are considered.
(4) Incentives, measuring the effects in performance of such stimuli as reward and competition.

(5) Atmospheric conditions, noting the general influences of the environment, such as temperature, humidity, and lighting in work.
(6) Drugs, in which the effects on efficiency of stimulants, depressants, and smoking are determined.

Conscious Motivation.—Scientifically speaking, conscious motivation is intention or *Aufgabe,* which is the goal and plan of work, and mental set or *Einstellung* or determining tendency, which is activity in process that is known to the worker.

Mental Set.—The standing broad jumper who is set for a spring is in a state of readiness. This is the motor aspect of mental set which in successive performance is a state of continual preparedness. The adjustment is automatic according to the degree of exercise of the activity. After acceptance of intention, mental set is conscious only in the 'knowing' of its presence or in reëstablishing it by intention from the vagueness of temporary relaxation.

Müller and Schumann [29] reported the first experiment on mental set in 1889, which is a classic in the study of motivation. They found that after an individual had compared a heavier weight with a standard weight he was predisposed to underestimate a lighter weight when compared with the same standard. This was explained as being due to the presence of a strong *Einstellung* which had developed as the result of previous exercise with the heavier weight. From this it becomes evident that normal sets are necessary for the act of comparing, and the conditions of the set determine the resulting performance. Steffens [30] demonstrated that established sets are not transferred from one muscle group to another, such as the left to the right hand. Müller and Schumann believed that the operation of the set depended upon the worker's awareness of its existence and Strohal [31] showed this to be true. He found by introspective study that the operation of a particular mental set was paralleled in consciousness by an "impalpable knowing" which continued unchanged as long as the set persisted, and changed as soon as a new set was taken. Thus a characteristic dynamic awareness is necessary to performance and it is expected that performance will continue unimpeded under the motivation of mental set according to the degree of automaticity of the task.

Intent.—But for tasks of a low degree of automaticity or in learning tasks or where a frequent shift of set is required, greater conscious specificity of stimulation is necessary for performance. Motivation involving considerable conscious detail is called intention or *Aufgabe*. No change in performance, no learning, no observation, nothing, except unconscious inertia, ever takes place in psychological activity unless initiated in conscious intention. This is theory but the bulk of psychological research supports it. Automatic performance proceeds under the motivation of set, but to change the set requires intention to do so.

Külpe [32] investigated the relative value in learning of general and specific intention. Groups of nonsense syllables in different colors, projected on a screen, were learned with 4 specific intentions to observe parts of the material and a general intent to observe all. The amount of specific material learned with intention to observe it was about twice as much as that learned with general intention to observe all, and the amount of other specific material learned was equal. It was evident that the specificity or clearness of intention determined observation and learning.

A series of recent experiments by Moore [33] will illustrate this important point. In one experiment the material to be observed was a selection known as the "Marble Statue" which consisted of 166 words and 67 ideas. Such observation is similar to the reading of literature in college. Subjects tested were formed into comparable groups. Group A intended to observe the ideas; Group B intended to count the words; and Group C, the control group, intended just to read the passage. All were tested for recall of ideas and differences between groups were statistically reliable. Group A, which specifically intended to observe the ideas, recalled 13 per cent more on the average than Group C, which intended to read the passage, and 630 per cent more than Group B, which intended to do something else, while Group C recalled 442 per cent more than Group B. A repetition of this experiment with nonsense syllables, showed a greater advantage for Group A, which intended specifically to learn, of 68 per cent over Group C which intended only to read. The difference between the results of the two experiments is due evidently to the nature of the task. In another experiment with colored geometrical forms, Group A, which intended to observe geometrical form, was tested for recall of color; Group B, intending to observe color, was tested for form; and Group C, intending to observe both color and form, was tested for both. The superiority of Group C over A and B was 68 and 43 per cent, respectively, which were statistically reliable differences. A fourth experiment verified these results with colored pictures in which Group A intended to observe pictures and was tested for colors, Group B intended to observe colors and was tested for pictures, and Group C intended to observe both and was so tested. Differences between groups were statistically reliable and Group C recalled 81 per cent more than A and 33 per cent more than B.

Intention is necessary to observation and intention to observe specific material results in improved observation for that material without impairment of general observation. These conclusions are particularly important for mental efficiency. But to read, not knowing what specific matter should be remembered, would be far better than to search for nonessential information. To read with intention to note the specific information related to the problem of study brings far the best results for the same expenditure of time.

Intention and Performance.—Changes go on in the environment about us (concrete stimuli) and instruction may be given to us (verbal stimuli), but they do not affect our performance unless they are accepted in the development of intention. This refers, of course, to unforced and unfatigued activity, where there is freedom for the course of action to be determined within the individual.

The initiation of psychological stimulation is in conscious intention. This is demonstrated in a series of experiments by Fryer [34] which showed that performance was more closely allied to conscious intention than to environmental stimulation such as verbal instructions. In one experiment, intention was developed to add columns of figures at a uniform rate. But contradictory advice and inviting suggestions were introduced, which disturbed this conscious stimulation. Always, intentions developed to support the established set and 85 per cent of the resulting changes in performance corresponded with the new intentions. These changes were frequently in the opposite direction to that expected from the environmental stimulation. In another experiment, it was found that rate of performance did not vary more than 5 per cent when workers intended to add sums at a comfortable working speed. This is the extent of individual variability that may be expected among routine mental workers who do not intend to change an established working set. But with workers trained to work with intention not to change rate such variations were as low as 2 per cent. This implies that variation in rate is due to the absence of uniform intention to maintain an unchanging rate. Any significant change in performance is intended and automatic activity will continue at about the same rate unless there is intention to change it.

The Golden Rule in Mental Efficiency.—Observation, thought, and action are directed by intention and the clearer the intention the more efficient the performance. But the foundations of motivation in all mental activity are in mental set which is the product of the past, influencing the present.

Working Rhythm and Distractors

Rhythm is regarded as having a facilitating effect on work, either in feelings or performance, while distractors are regarded as inhibitory. They are extraneous environmental stimuli as far as the working situation is concerned, which have an effect in learning or in performance only because of their integration in the "mass" stimulation affecting the worker. Rhythm is distinguished as regular and distractors as irregular stimuli. They may be visual or auditory stimuli or stimuli of any sense department, such as breezes of a fan on the pressure spots, which are regarded often by workers as distractors. But the usual rhythms and distractors are auditory, and these will be considered here.

Auditory Rhythm.—Auditory rhythm is defined as repeated temporal patterns which may vary within themselves in timing, intensity, or pitch. But the temporal patterns are not necessary to the sense of rhythm. Sensitivity of rhythm is determined by the individual. Highly rhythmic stimulation may not be observed as rhythm at all and any regularly repeated stimulus, such as the noise of the wheels of a railroad train, may assume various rhythmic patterns according to the individual's training in rhythmic combinations. It was Pavlov's belief that rhythm has its foundation in intervals of time which are fractioned by the pulse waves. But no acceptable explanation of the sense of rhythm has been established.

Rhythm and Performance.—Environmental stimuli become working rhythms only when accepted by the worker as a part of a working situation, such as in the addition of a column of figures or the assembling of a unit of a machine. As Fryer [35] has shown, workers perform at their intended rate regardless of the rate of an accompanying rhythm unless they intentionally make it a part of the conscious working situation. This is unusual. When observers intended to add columns of figures at a comfortable rate, no relation existed between their working rate and the rhythm rate (average of correlations of —0.07). But when workers intended to coordinate the adding rate and the rhythm rate, it was done perfectly by those with sufficient rhythmic sense. Any coordination that occurred was intended. When guided by an external rhythm some workers performed at rates as high as they could under conditions where they established their own motivation. But the temporal coordination and the adding remained as distinct awarenesses. This implies that neither the performance nor the coordination can be too difficult or the integration, which depends upon an oscillation of attention, will break down. At difficult rates performance in the experiment depended upon the stronger intention, which determined whether the worker disregarded the rhythm and finished the performance or made incomplete additions in time with the rhythm.

Optimum Rate of Working Rhythm.—Evidently there is an optimum rate or natural working rhythm in both immediate and delayed reproduction of temporal intervals. But research is uncertain upon this point. There are wide individual differences in rhythmic sense and some individuals are unable to reproduce temporal intervals at all while others do so in varying degrees of accuracy. But it appears that most individuals can coordinate performance with a temporal pattern according to a minimum criterion of accuracy.

Preference for temporal rates of regular clicks was determined by Harrell [36] for 27 adults and he found that the preferred rate was 5.08 clicks per second with a mean variation of 2.49 clicks indicating wide individual differences. In direct reproduction of rhythmic patterns by beating with a baton, Gault and Goodfellow [37] found that training improved accuracy. Jersild and Bienstock [38] showed that adolescents (ages 13-17) kept time better to music played at faster than at slower rates. What are fast and slow rates depends, of course upon the kind of performance.

Auditory Distractors.—Irregular extraneous stimuli, called distractors, may facilitate or inhibit activity and these effects are due to intention developing when the worker becomes aware of the distractor. A distractor may stimulate one person to greater and another to reduced effort. The distracting stimulus is equivocal in its effect on any performance.

Noise.—Noise abatement commissions have been appointed in numerous cities all over the world for the purpose of regulating excessive noise on the theory that noise is detrimental to human welfare. But if we are to believe the results of numerous studies, any usual amount of noise produces little effect upon immediate efficiency. Morgan [39] tested the effect of various distractors, such as gongs, buzzers, and music, upon a complicated coded task where the reaction was to press the correct telegraph key. The effect of the distractor was a slight decrease in rate of initial performance which was followed by a later increase over the normal rate. With the removal of the distractor there was a decrease in rate of performance to the normal rate. A series of experiments by Pollack and Bartlett [40] leads to similar conclusions that on the average a slight initial decrease is followed by a slight permanent increase in performance with distractors. But the effect of distractors on efficiency is unimportant.

Introspections of the workers in Pollack and Bartlett's study indicated that an adaptation in attitude took place in order that the intended performance might be maintained. Baker [41] reports that efficiency in performance depends upon whether or not the worker takes the initial attitude that extraneous distractors have a detrimental effect or that they have a facilitating effect or that distractors first hinder and later facilitate performance. Different groups were shown fictitious graphs of performance where these effects were present in order to create the initial attitudes. These attitudes predetermined the performance in each case. When the worker believed that noise hindered, efficiency dropped upon its introduction. When the worker believed that noise facilitated, efficiency increased when noise was present. Evidently attitude to maintain expected performance will determine the result in any experiment on efficiency with distractors.

The workers in various investigations of noise-effects report that work with distractors is uncomfortable and unpleasant. Noise is irritating and it produces an attitude of dissatisfaction. There is little experimental evidence upon this point. But Bartlett, [42] the English authority in this field, believes that the summed effects of distractors, industrially and socially, may be of great significance in spite of the evidence that noise has but a small effect on efficiency. Noise is irritating, aggravating, and causes individual and social unhappiness. It belongs to that large class of unpleasant stimuli, such as putrid odors, light glare, and high temperatures, to which the normal person can adjust and maintain efficiency. But it is a cause of dissatisfaction which people will not endure except under the requirements of necessity.

INCENTIVES TO WORK

Any extraneous stimulus of which the worker is aware may have a facilitating or inhibiting effect in psychological activity, such as learning, thinking, and performance generally. Environmental stimuli are never expected to hold a one-to-one relation with reaction, or anything approaching perfect correlation. However, by controlling the varied influences on the work of the individual it is possible to distinguish one environmental factor and measure its effect in motivation. In this manner, 'mass' stimulation is broken up for study and 'unitary' incentives are segregated.

Such incentives as have been investigated with human beings will be classified here according to popular nomenclature, as follows: (1) Knowledge of results (K of R), (2) rewards, (3) punishments, (4) praises, (5) reproofs, (6) social facilitation, (7) competition, and (8) cooperation.

K of R—"Knowledge of results" is information given the learner or worker of his performance. In certain learning experiments by Thorndike and his coworkers, right-wrong statements are made following performance, "right" being regarded as "reward" and "wrong" as "punishment." Used in this sense, reward strengthens the learning connections and punishment weakens them, which is the expected effect of K of R. When punishment strengthens the learning, as is frequently observed, it may be because of the temporal relation of the "punished" connections to the "rewarded" connections. Thorndike [43] has shown that "punished" connections nearest the "rewarded" connections are strengthened most and those farthest away least. An experiment by Book and Norvell [44] shows how work progresses when K of R is given and withheld. Making small letter a's was one task, crossing out letters in Spanish words was another, translating digits according to a code into letters, was a third, and the final task was multiplication. Performance was increased with K of R and reduced when it was withheld in all 4 tasks and in making small letter a's the results were as follows:

	Men	Women
Per cent gain when K of R was given following performance without K of R	15.67	12.03
Per cent loss when K of R was removed following performance with K of R	12.18	15.08

The total per cent gain when performance with K of R followed performance without K of R was 46.82 for men and 42.27 for women. But when performance without K of R followed performance with it, the total per cent gain was 35.38 for men and 33.34 for women, implying that K of R has a differential temporal effect as a motivating stimulus.

Numerous experiments have indicated the effects of K of R upon learning and work with various tasks, such as learning nonsense syllables, making change in money, perception of length of lines, lifting weights, and reaction time. Various kinds of K of R have been used, such as the presentation of work sheets, progress curves, stars for credit, partial and complete information, and general and special knowledge. Knowledge of results increases personal efficiency generally, and in degrees according to the completeness, exactness, and clearness with which the K of R is related in intention to the details of the performance.

Individual Rewards, Punishments, Praises, and Reproofs. —The effect of electric shock on an individual in the laboratory is not the same as that observed when he is repairing a fuse box at home. "Standing in the corner" is not the same punishment for a child of 12 as for one of 6, or for a girl as for a boy, or for pupils in a private school as for those in a public school, and so on. Any specific punishment for an employee does not have the same effect as for a prisoner. Punishment is not a "unitary" cause of behavior. There are many punishments, and many rewards; various praises and reproofs. Each incentive will differ in kind and is determined by the individual.

Educational theorists from Herbart to John Dewey have advocated the educational principle that reward and praise are stronger motivating forces in life than punishment and reproof. Yet there is not the dichotomy of stimulation that is implied in this educational theory. Among those confined to penal institutions little can be accomplished in determining behavior without at least the threat of punishment and every mother knows how often she uses reproof or punishment so that her child may conform to accepted forms of social behavior.

Punishment.—The type of punishment will, of course, determine its motivation. Electric shock applied as a punishment has been found generally to increase efficiency in learning and reaction. In

Johanson's experiment,[45] electric shock decreased reaction time 15 per cent and more than twice as much as K of R, which lowered it 6 per cent. But various experiments have indicated that electric shock may vary in its effect according to its intensity. Vaughn and Diserens [46] reported that fewest trials, least errors, and lowest total time were required in learning a stylus maze pattern with slight shock when none, slight, moderate, and intense electric shocks were administered for errors in the learning. Efficiency decreased with increased shock. According to Rexroad,[47] the effect of the same electric shock may vary with the individual. It may have an "instructive" effect, as with K of R, it may have an "incentive" effect as shown in greater care to avoid errors, and it may have a "disruptive" emotional effect. Results with other "punishments," such as bells, pressures, unpleasant tastes, loss of a desired object, closely parallel those with electric shock and lead to the same conclusions. As a general rule, "punishments" are incentives to learn and to work, but always there are wide individual differences in the effects of the punishments.

Rewards.—Few specific rewards have been studied as human incentives. Different foods are found to have an individual effect upon different animals. Industrial studies have indicated the different effects of various systems of remuneration, which are reviewed in Chapter XVIII. Chase [48] offered children of ages 2 to 8 a gold star on a record card as a reward for work on a modified dynamometer. With this reward, performance increased, but the improvement was not statistically significant over work with K of R. Leuba [49] reported a statistically reliable increase in multiplication by 11-year-old children with the reward of a chocolate bar. Undoubtedly, there are many rewards that will affect the efficiency of performance by people of all ages and levels of training.

Praises and Reproofs.—No line of demarcation exists between rewards and punishments on the one hand and praises and reproofs on the other. But variability in motivating effects would be expected to be greater with praises and reproofs perhaps because of their greater differences in social implication. The related effects of praises and reproofs can be judged from a glance at the assembled results from studies comparing them: [50]

Investigator	Subjects	In Ascendency	Reliable Difference
Chase	Young children	Reproof	No
Gilchrist	College students	Praise	Not reported
Gates and Rissland	College students	{ Praise { Reproof	Not reported
Hurlock	School children	{ Reproof { Praise	No (initial measure) Yes (continuous measure)

In these studies both praises and reproofs usually increased performance. This was true in Chase's investigation of performance on the dynamometer. Gilchrist reports an increase of 79 per cent with praise in work in the Courtis English Test but there was no increase with reproof. According to Gates and Rissland both praise and reproof increased performance but slightly in motor coordinations and color naming. Hurlock reports that initial increases were made by 52 per cent of the control group, 79 per cent of the praised group, and 80 per cent of the reproved group. But the average increase of the reproved group on the fifth day over the first day was 16 per cent and of the praised group it was 79 per cent, indicating the more permanent motivating effect of praise upon school children. Other studies show the same trend that praises and reproofs generally are incentives to work. But praises are more likely to have the greater motivating effect, particularly over a long period of time.

Some interesting results indicating the influence of differences between the sexes in social training are reported by Eaton [51] who found that praise decreased steadiness in men and increased steadiness in women and that the steadiness decrease in men with praise was equal to that caused by a short period of exercise in basketball. Likewise, reproof increased steadiness in men and decreased steadiness in women.

Social Incentives.—K of R and even the rhythms and distractors have their social implications in conscious integration of "mass" stimulation. Also, the rewards, punishments, praises and reproofs are motivating stimuli largely because of their social significance. But certain patterns of environmental stimuli are regarded as social stimulation and belong to social psychology. Social facilitation, competition, and cooperation are of this kind.

Social Facilitation.—Social facilitation has been defined as the incentive effect of the sight or sound of others performing in similar manner. It was investigated first by Mayer,[52] about 1900 in Germany, with mental tasks performed by school boys and various instructions were found to be more effective in group work without competition than in individual work. Allport [53] found that associations increased while individuals were working in groups; 65 to 95 per cent of the individual workers in a series of experiments produced more controlled associations while working in groups than alone. On the other hand, arguments against selected passages of philosophical writings were greater in number when individuals were working alone. The more intellectual the task, the less likely will group work facilitate performance. Also, the group serves as a distractor when the worker is socially handicapped in the task. Travis [54] selected stutterers for a typical experiment in social facilitation. Instead of 80 per cent of the workers producing more associations in group work, as is reported by Allport, 80 per cent of the stutterers produced more associations when working alone. Thus, a social group may have either a facilitating or an inhibiting effect upon mental efficiency. Which it is will be determined by the attitude or mental set of the worker.

Competition.—Competition may exist when individuals work alone or in groups. Triplett [55] measured its motivating effect by experiment over 40 years ago and concluded that competition has a definite dynomogenic effect, liberating latent energy not usually available. An experiment by Greenberg [56] indicates how competition develops in children of ages 2 to 7 years. Two children were seated opposite at a table and took blocks from the same pile for their work of block building. No competition existed at 2 years of age and the children were between 4 and 5 years of age before half of them exhibited any competitive behavior. But in about 90 per cent of the 6-year-olds, competition was well developed.

Competition and Reward.—The experiment by Leuba [57] compares the effect of competition with that of reward in doing arithmetical problems among school children. Competition was motivated by public ranking according to performance and reward by a chocolate bar for having accomplished a set task. The average number of multiplications were as follows:

	Competi-tion Alone	Reward Alone	Competi-tion and Reward Combined
Mean performance with incentive	34.6	32.9	38.9
Difference from performance with no incentive	11.0	12.3	15.3
PE of difference	1.7	1.4	1.4

All differences are statistically significant. To secure a chocolate bar the children exceed their "no incentive" record by 42 per cent. The competition alone increased performance 48 per cent. The competition and reward combined increased performance 66 per cent. Thus, this competition was a slightly stronger incentive than the reward of a chocolate bar.

Competition and Cooperation.—There is a vast literature upon competition and cooperation because of the social import of the subject. Cooperation is interpreted usually as working for the good of a group in competition with other groups. Maller [58] compared individual and group competition for their incentive effects, using tests of addition performed by 814 children in grades 5 to 8 in the New York City school system. Average performance in work for self was superior to work for the group and the difference was decidedly reliable. Work for the group was twice as variable and decreased in amount while work for self was consistently high over a long period of time. When allowed to choose test scores to apply to group-or self-records, poorer work was given to the group. Similar results have been found in hand printing, in the dynamometer squeeze, and in substituting numbers for letters according to a code, and with workers of various ages and training. All experiments indicate the same general conclusion that the incentive to work for self has a greater and more permanent motivating effect than the incentive to work for a group.

Cooperation.—But Maller found that both working for self and working for the group were superior incentives to ordinary practice work or work with no specific incentive. Usually cooperation is an

incentive to work. Hurlock [59] studied the effect of cooperation among
school children in grades IV and VI. The average gain was 41 per
cent for group competition (cooperation) over the practice effect as
measured in the control group. Hurlock reports that all forms of
group rivalry were stimulated by discussion and publicity of the
group's achievement, indicating the basis of cooperation in group
competition.

Individual Differences in Effects of Incentives.—Wide individual differences in effects of incentives are evident in all group
investigations. The older children in a group do not respond to the
incentive of competition as do the younger children; nor do the
brighter respond in the same manner when competing with duller
children of the same age; nor do boys when competing with girls.
In the study of Leuba [60] the slower multipliers improved far more
than the faster in the group of school children. Divided into quarters the increases from the no incentive situation to that of the
incentive situation were as follows:

	Individual Competition	Reward	Reward and Competition
Lowest quarter	71 per cent	92 per cent	139 per cent
Highest quarter	34 per cent	32 per cent	36 per cent

The same appeal affects workers differently in various industries,
plants, labor unions, school years, religions, nationalities, races, and
so on.

Social "background" is responsible for differences in the motivating effect of incentives. Each individual responds according to
the social implication of an incentive for him. If an appeal to cooperation has a consistent effect upon group accomplishment, it is
because the individuals forming the group have had similar training.
All environmental changes affecting the individual, such as noise,
rhythms, honors, praises, rewards, and so on, are integrated with
the psychological influences of the individual's past. Homogeneity
of group training results in similarity of response; heterogeneity
causes individual differences in motivation. The individual behavior
may deviate little or much from a group norm.

Atmospheric Conditions

Until about 25 years ago it was thought that the reduction in oxygen or the increase of carbon dioxide (CO_2) in air was responsible for the ill effects of poor ventilation. Now we know that air from which dirt and odors have been removed causes no bad results in feelings, health, or efficiency, providing adequate temperature and humidity are maintained. An excellent survey of the research in this field will be found in two papers by Burnham listed at the end of this chapter. The oxygen content of air is never decreased or the CO_2 content increased to a point affecting the human organism under conditions of the worst ventilation.

The chemical constituents of air are unimportant, but adequate temperature and humidity are of great importance. This is illustrated in an early attempt to understand the situation by Paul,[61] who confined himself in a small glass cabinet for 4 hours, breathing the same air over and over again. As long as the temperature was not over 60° F. (and the humidity not more than 72 per cent of saturation) he was without discomfort. With a rise in temperature of 68° to 86° (humidity 72 to 92 per cent) serious symptoms resulted. That these symptoms were not due to lack of oxygen was evident because no beneficial effects resulted from breathing air outside the cabinet. Also, a man outside the cabinet breathed the air within with no ill effects. Similar results were obtained in an experiment conducted by the New York State Commission on Ventilation.[62] It was found that any change in the air that increased the radiation of heat from the body, such as an air current stirred by a fan, was advantageous in high temperature. The ill effects attributed to bad ventilation are due to the inability of the organism to eliminate its own heat owing to high temperature and high humidity.

Temperature.—High external temperature increases metabolism, which will raise efficiency. But when the oxidation and elimination processes of the body are insufficient to carry off its waste products, fatigue will result from their accumulation. This is what takes place under conditions of prolonged high external temperature with its detrimental effect on efficiency. The relation of high external temperature to fatigue is a fact of common observation. Also, a low external temperature causes an increase in metabolic activity in order to maintain normal bodily temperature, with similar effects in increased consumption of energy, accumulation of waste and fatigue.

Apparently there is an optimum temperature for all forms of activity in the various occupations. Huntington [63] concluded that outdoor temperatures affected indoor working efficiency. He found that the optimum outdoor temperature for physical work was 60° F. and for mental work 40° F. This effect of outside temperature on indoor work may be the result of radiation from the walls of the building. The optimum temperature for mental work, that is, the temperature of the room in which one is working, appears to be about 68° F. with a relative humidity of 50 per cent. But excessive temperature (within a range of 68° to 86° F.) has not been found to affect efficiency in mental performance so long as adequate motivation can be maintained.[64] It has a marked influence on comfort, however, and under ordinary conditions high temperatures are expected to lower motivation and thus decrease efficiency.

Humidity.—It is necessary that superfluous heat be eliminated from the body at all times, and humidity, as well as temperature, influences this activity. Increased humidity reduces evaporation and augments the conduction of heat by the air. Thus it has two opposing effects on body temperature: One of increasing the elimination of body heat because of the improved conductivity of the air; and the other of decreasing this elimination due to slower evaporation of perspiration. Which effect will dominate depends upon temperature. With temperatures below 60° F., where perspiration is at a minimum, high humidity has a cooling effect. With temperatures above 70° F., high humidity checks the evaporation of perspiration (and also the elimination of water vapor from the lungs), which has a warming effect on the body. A neutral zone for effects of humidity on the body exists at temperatures of 68° to 70° F.

Investigations show surprisingly little effect of different humidities, as with different temperatures, on mental work. Any bad effects of ventilation are upon mental attitude in the form of discomfort which affects motivation to work. Very high humidity with low temperature makes one feel chilly, and high humidity with high temperature causes oppressive feelings of heat.

Illumination.—The essential requirement of good illumination for mental or physical work is an even distribution of light, such as is gained in indirect lighting. As the eyes seldom maintain focus within the field of work it is of advantage from the point of view of minimum fatigue that the total visual environment be of approximately the same intensity of illumination. Intensity of illumination within wide limits is relatively unimportant. This is explained by the fact that the eye has great power of adaptation, with a ratio of 1 to 10,000 at threshold. The important point in good lighting is to reduce the frequency of necessary adaptation. But there are minimum and maximum intensities of illumination for greatest efficiency and least fatigue in different occupational tasks, as would be expected. The main disturbing factor to vision, as measured in loss of efficiency and fatigue, is glare and contrasting light intensities over the field of work. These factors are avoided by using uniform artificial or natural illumination.

Drugs, Stimulants, and Smoking

Questions about the effect of drugs and stimulants upon efficiency have engaged the attention of most every person at some time. Extensive propaganda and widespread partisanship exist concerning the moral, mental, and physiological influences of alcohol, tobacco, caffeine, strychnine, and other drugs. The actual effects of drugs and stimulants can be determined only by scientific experiment. But investigation is exceedingly difficult. Suggestion must be controlled, for the subject in an experiment will have any expected effect if he knows he is taking a drug or smoking tobacco. The drug must be disguised, neutral substances of the same taste and odor must be substituted as controls, smoking tobacco must be checked against smoking hot air of the same taste and odor, and so on, if results approaching the truth are to be expected.

All of this has been done and yet it is difficult to establish reliable effects. Motivation may change in an experiment in which a subject knows that he is ingesting an experimental substance. The human organism will adjust to any ordinary conditions and perform normally if at all possible. Yet from the confusion of results of experiments, certain tentative conclusions can be drawn concerning the effects of drugs, stimulants and the smoking of tobacco upon individual efficiency.

Strychnine.—It is popularly believed that strychnine is a stimulant, but any stimulating effects of strychnine are due probably to the selective action of a poison. The effects on the body are confined largely to the lower nerve centers and it is said that strychnine lowers resistance at the synapse. Undoubtedly, suggestion plays a part in any influence credited to small doses of strychnine in the facilitation of performance.

Caffeine.—Caffeine is a true stimulant, which is not cumulative in its effect, nor is the stimulation followed by a depression. The effect of caffeine is of special interest because it is present in coffee, tea, and various soda fountain drinks. The usual large cup of coffee or of strong tea contains about 2.5 grains of caffeine, which is a small dose as measured in its effects upon efficiency.

Hollingworth's study of caffeine [65] is a classic in the field and it indicates the effects of various doses of the drug ranging from 2 to 6 grains over 72 hours of tests. Caffeine was found to be a stimulant to speed of movement and this effect appeared within one hour and lasted from one to 4 hours according to the size of the dose. Even small doses caused a slight loss of muscular steadiness, but with a dose of 6 grains this effect was tremendous (583 per cent) and increased over a period of several hours. It was greater than that resulting from a large dose of alcohol. In tests of naming colors, naming opposites, and simple addition, all doses acted as approximately equal stimuli to performance, lasting from 3 to 7 hours. In tests of speed of perception, speed of cancellation, and speed of discrimination (reaction time) the larger doses acted as a stimulant after 2 hours which lasted until the following day. For most of the 16 subjects tested by Hollingworth, doses of one to 4 grains did not affect sleep at all but with a dose of 6 grains the sleep of practically all was disturbed. Taken on an empty stomach, the drug had the greatest influence. Subjects of lightest body weight were affected most with headaches, dizziness, feverishness, irritability, and so on, when the doses were larger than 4 grains.

Such results imply that caffeine acts as a long-period stimulant upon most performance and the stimulation varies according to the size of the dose and with the individual. One or more cups of coffee are as effective in dispelling a headache as headache powders which consist essentially of caffeine. The popular notion that an after-dinner cup of coffee will cause insomnia is evidently erroneous and the reason for sleeplessness on such an occasion is not because of the small amount of caffeine consumed, but rather the excitement of the evening or the suggestion that one cannot go to sleep after drinking coffee.

Smoking Tobacco.—Nicotine is popularly assumed to be the drug present in tobacco smoke, but it is doubtful if it exists in smoke at all except possibly from a rapidly smoked cigarette. Busch[66] has shown that a large number of toxic substances may be present in tobacco smoke and it is possible that pyridine, which was found by Busch in all tobacco smoke tested, may be its principal toxic substance. Blood pressure is increased and heart rate is stimulated uniformly by tobacco smoking. Digestive secretions are stimulated. Habitual users do not establish a physiological tolerance for it.

Tests of Motor Function.—Hull's experimental technique[67] is interesting in view of the experimental difficulties of disguising tobacco smoking for control tests. He used a pipe heated by an electric coil for the control smoke. The subjects, divided equally between nonsmokers and habitual smokers, were blindfolded during the smoking and smoked a tobacco loaded pipe, or the control pipe, for 25 minutes on alternate days without inhaling. A complete series of tests of various physical and mental functions was administered prior to the smoking and repeated 3 times with intervening rest periods of 5 minutes following the smoking. Results were compared for the tobacco smoking days and nontobacco smoking days for nonsmokers and habitual smokers. No significant difference in rate of tapping was found by Hull following the smoking of tobacco, which agrees with results from other investigators. But steadiness was significantly decreased by smoking both for habitual smokers and for nonsmokers, which again is in agreement with conclusions from other investigators that smoking decreases precision of voluntary movement. This is the only unquestioned effect of smoking on motor activity. Habituation increased the initial detrimental effect of smoking on steadiness.

Statistical Studies of Efficiency.—Statistical studies, of which there have been many reporting differences in academic standing, intelligence, learning capacity, athletic prowess, weight, height, death rate, lung capacity and so on, between smokers and nonsmokers of tobacco, are subject to the errors of sampling. For this reason the conclusions drawn from most of them are open to question. Always it must be borne in mind that smoking may be a symptom of other conditions responsible for the difference reported. The same may be said of statistical studies of users and nonusers of alcohol and drugs. While it is reported, for example, that nonsmokers are superior to smokers in scholarship among college students, this is merely a correlation and not an indication of a cause. Low academic standing likewise is related to greater social activities.

While it is generally agreed that smoking retards development and is injurious to the health of adolescents, proof of this is lacking. Pearl [68] has shown that the death rate for various ages is definitely higher for heavy smokers and it is not significantly different for moderate smokers when compared with nonsmokers, but here the samples for the age groups are small. Pack [69] studied 248 football men in 14 institutions, defining smokers as "habitual user when not in training," and he found that smokers of the same age and averaging 3.3 pounds heavier had a lung capacity of 7.3 per cent below that of nonsmokers. Excessive smoking may reduce lung capacity, explaining the shortness of breath of the habitual smoker. It is interesting that among college populations generally, smokers exceed nonsmokers in physical measures which may be because they are older or because those who smoke are more likely to engage in developmental physical exercise.

Smoking and Mental Performance.—Smoking has little effect upon mental performance, with the possible exception of repetitive activity, such as addition. In Hull's study,[70] speed of adding was decreased significantly in all tests for nonsmokers and increased significantly for habitual smokers. The per cent losses for nonsmokers were 2.48 (after 4.5 minutes), 3.18 (after 39.5 minutes), and 2.61 (after 1 hour and 14.5 minutes). For habitual smokers the per cent gains were 3.47, 5.03, and 7.19, respectively. Accuracy seemed not to be affected materially by smoking among either the habitual smokers or the nonsmokers. This is an interesting result which is in agreement generally with other investigations. While the experimental evidence favors a slight improvement in rate of ordinary routine mental performance when the smoker is accustomed to smoking, where new associations are concerned, as in learning, there is probably a slight inhibition on mental activity following smoking even by habitual smokers.

The Motivation for Smoking and Drinking. —Janet,[71] the eminent French psychopathologist, says that the inebriate drinks alcohol because of the need to face the realities of life. In psychoanalytical theory, alcohol is desired because it removes inhibitions and destroys sublimations—it is a submerger of life's conflicts. Juliusberger [72] gave this as the explanation for the frequent relation found between alcoholism and sex exhibitionism, homosexuality, incest, abuse, crime, etc. Such theories have been derived from a study of mental abnormalities. Smoking and drinking alcoholic beverages are common social phenomena, existing world-wide and among both primitive and civilized peoples. People drink alcohol to remove feelings of fatigue, to intensify conscious states, to forget the hectic business problems of the day, to gain social ease, to enjoy better a meal, to be exciting in conversation, to go to sleep easily, and because they "like the feel of it." Similarly, people smoke tobacco because it aids digestion, brings the social group into greater *rapport*, gives a mental lift, and provides the atmosphere for contemplation. Patrick [73] says that drinking alcohol is a means of achieving relaxation in a complex social environment, which is as satisfactory a general theory for smoking and drinking as can be given. But there are many motives for different individuals to drink or to smoke, as there are for most expressions of human behavior.

Alcohol and Performance.—Experimentation into the effects of alcohol upon mental and motor efficiency generally leaves no doubt that alcohol is a physiological and psychological depressant. Heart action and respiration are increased, and alcohol must be excreted from the body, as are other poisonous drugs, with the exception of about 2 oz. daily which are oxidized similar to starches and sugars. Work appears to be performed with greater ease, but the objective record indicates a decrease in efficiency. These are the conclusions of research from its very beginning. Kraepelin [74] reported that large doses caused both an immediate and long period decrease of efficiency in the mental processes of apprehension, memory and judgment. Rivers [75] reported decreased efficiency in operations such as typewriting and mental multiplication. While early workers had suggested an initial stimulation of mental and motor activity by alcohol, this is explained as an incentive effect from expectation.

Dodge and Benedict [76] have reported from extensive research into the physiological and psychological effects of alcohol that latency of reaction in the knee-jerk increased 10 per cent and muscular thickening decreased 46 per cent following a dose of 30 c.c. of alcohol. In the protective eyelid reflex, latency was increased 7 per cent and extent of movement was decreased 19 per cent. Sensory and motor measures were decreased in efficiency with the same dose as follows:

Sensory threshold to electric stimuli ....14 per cent
Speed of eye movements ....11 per cent
Finger movement (tapping) .... 9 per cent
Eye reaction-time .... 5 per cent
Speech reaction-time .... 3 per cent

Memory and free association were only slightly affected in the direction of decreased efficiency with a dose of 30 c.c. Nowhere in all of the functions tested by Dodge and Benedict was there a facilitation of performance with either a dose of 30 c.c. or 45 c.c.

Hollingworth [77] has extended the study of the effects of alcohol among mental activities. Likewise, he finds no facilitation of performance with various doses of alcohol. His technique is interesting. Beer was administered in doses of 3 to 4 bottles, 5 to 6 bottles, and 6 to 9 bottles, and the alcohol was extracted from the beer for the control period. A bottle of beer contained 13.14 c.c. or 10.37 grams of alcohol and so Hollingworth's doses were larger than those used by Dodge and Benedict. Six tests of various functions were administered during a three-hour period of work in the morning and 6 during a similar period in the afternoon following the administering of the beer at noon. Results for various tests are given below in terms of per cent loss for the afternoon of the morning performance:

| | No. of Bottles of Beer | | |
	3—4	5—6	6—9
Steadiness of hand	—68	—241	—370
Tapping (speed)	— 7	— 13	— 14
Coordination of eye and hand	— 6	— 10	— 20
Color naming (Woodworth-Wells)	— 2	— 7	— 12
Opposites (logical relations)	— 5	— 12	— 23
Adding	—10	— 15	— 16
Substitution (Woodworth-Wells)	— 4	— 9	— 6
Memory for paired associates	—21	——	— 60

The effect of small doses on the associative processes had disappeared by the last test 3 hours after administration of the dose. But in the case of such motor processes as tapping, steadiness, and coordination, recovery was slower even with the smallest doses.

The loss in efficiency usually is correlated with the amount of alcohol in the system. As concluded by Dodge and Benedict similar functions are similarly affected. Reflex activity and motor activity appear to be detrimentally affected in greater degrees by the doses used than the higher mental activities. The recovery of reflex activities was found to be most rapid by Dodge and Benedict. Recovery of motor activities generally was found by Hollingworth to be slower than intellectual activities. It is interesting that steadiness is detrimentally affected the most by all drugs including smoking. Then, there are wide individual differences in the effects of all drugs, stimulants, and the smoking of tobacco.

. Efficiency and Morale

Morale is the supreme standard of living according to G. Stanley Hall.[78] It is the synthesis of efficiency, adjustment, and mental health. All standardized psychological tests indicating efficiency of performance are prognostic of morale. We think of the interest inventory, measuring interests in the occupations; the attitude scale, measuring emotional set in controversial problems; and the mental-hygiene inventory, measuring abnormal reactions and complexes in various physical and social situations, as indicating feeling and emotional adjustments that are symptomatic of morale. Likewise, morale depends upon individual efficiency. This is an opinion held by the productive workers of the world in both the manual and mental occupations.

William H. Burnham,[79] a pioneer mental hygienist of the past generation, believed that the essential conditions for the development of normal mental activity in the individual are a task, a plan, and freedom—freedom to choose one's tasks in life and to plan their development. Morale depends on this, and it is the purpose of education to provide the tasks which can be accomplished by the individual, and the purpose of educational guidance to offer the stimulation for their choice and development. The individual must have freedom of choice if he is to avoid the disturbing inhibition of abnormal mental activity. This is what a democratic education means.

Psychological activity is performed with the various tools of human expression, with motor tools of skillful coordination as in the manual occupations, with verbal tools of linguistic and mathematical habits as in speaking and lecturing, and with imagery and symbols as in thinking and mental work generally. But in all work, mental set contributes the determination from earlier training. Thinking is directed or planned awareness and performance is planned motor or verbal reaction. These activities stem from the same source and differ only in the tools of their expression. Efficiency results from the perfection of mental set in all activities and morale from its adjustment to life.

To know that one can do a task and to do it with superior advantage among one's fellows is accompanied by the social poise of orderly mental activity and the self-control of purposeful inhibition. Often it is not necessary that what one does be acceptable to the social group as long as self-recognition of its importance exists. But this is borderline territory where only the genius can avoid being regarded as abnormal. The adjustment necessary to high individual morale usually involves both self-recognition and group recognition of personal efficiency.

Mental activity in individuals of high personal efficiency is easy flowing—whether in thinking or performance. The tools function smoothly. The activity is directed toward a goal, which is carried in conscious intention or mental set according to the degree of automaticity of the activity. Inhibition or interference is exceptional. Haste is habitually avoided, as is waste. Periods of rest or relaxation to offset fatigue are interpolated with the task. A program or routine of considerable regularity is recognized as desirable. In this manner we observe the social poise of orderly mental activity in learning and work. Such a development is as preventive of mental disturbance as it is sustaining of morale.

The purposeful inhibition in self-control is a positive function. Inhibitions accompany high personal efficiency. They are the interference of directed activity upon other activity. Fatigue, which inhibits efficiency, is inhibited by rest. Reaction to the ever-present inhibits dreaming. Bursts of anger and fear are inhibited by efficient coordination. The energy of emotion is given direction by a goal. Courage may be regarded as behavior trained in a certain direction. Positive thought and action are without cowardice. To kick at nothing is wrenching and in mental activity, responding inadequately is just as disturbing. So with negative inhibition, which is the interference of other activity upon that intended. In all fear or inferiority or fatigue there is lack of adequacy of expression as evidenced by abortive reaction and imaginary evils which never exist in coordinated behavior. Efficiency, which is free from the handicap of negative inhibition avoids the dilemma of maladjustment. Upon such efficiency depends individual morale.

REFERENCES

Aveling, F. *Directing Mental Energy*. New York: George H. Doran Company, 1927.

Bills, A. G. *General Experimental Psychology*. New York: Longmans, Green and Company, Inc., 1935.

Burnham, W. H. The optimum temperature for mental work. *Ped. Sem.*, 1917, 24, 53-71.

Burnham, W. H.   The optimum humidity for mental work.   *Ped. Sem.*, 1919, 26, 311-329.

Burnham, W. H.   *The Normal Mind*.   New York: D. Appleton-Century Company, Inc., 1924.

Crane, G. W.   *Psychology Applied*.   Chicago: Northwestern University Press, 1937.

Hall, G. S.   *Morale, The Supreme Standard of Life and Conduct*.   New York: D. Appleton-Century Company, Inc., 1920.

Moore, B. V.   *Conditions of Efficient Work*.   Ch. 23, pp. 711-750 in Skinner, C. E., *Readings in Psychology*.   New York: Farrar and Rinehart, Inc., 1935.

Poffenberger, A. T.   *Applied Psychology*.   New York: D. Appleton-Century Company, Inc., 1930.

Young, P. T.   *Motivation of Behavior*.   New York: John Wiley and Sons, Inc., 1936.

CHAPTER XVII

VOCATIONAL PSYCHOLOGY (FITTING THE WORKER TO THE JOB)

By MORRIS S. VITELES, *University of Pennsylvania*

The Objectives of Vocational Psychology.—In its vocational applications, psychology seeks (1) to increase industrial efficiency; (2) to promote the adjustment of the worker[1]; (3) to further industrial stability by eliminating sources of grievances and misunderstandings between workers and employers.[2]

MATCHING MEN AND OCCUPATIONS

The Scope of Vocational Guidance and of Vocational Selection.—These objectives are achieved, in part, by the application of psychological methods in *fitting workers to jobs* through (1) *vocational guidance* and (2) *vocational selection*.

The aim in vocational guidance is to discover the most suitable occupation for a given individual. In vocational selection, the objective is to choose the most suitable individual for an available job. Although there are differences between the immediate objectives of vocational guidance and vocational selection, the two frequently overlap. In a plant where many varied jobs are available, the process of placing an applicant on the job for which he is best adapted may take on some of the characteristics of guidance. In an area where there are only a few industries and few distinctive occupations, vocational guidance consists largely of informing the young man whether he is better fitted for one or another of these restricted occupational opportunities.

An illustration of the parallel functions of vocational guidance and vocational selection is found in the experience of the United States Employment Service. Between July 1, 1933, and June 30, 1938, over 33 million individuals seeking work registered at its offices. Of these, approximately one-fourth were young people between the ages of 16 and 25 who had little or no work experience.

Another larger group consisted of older workers displaced from occupations and industries in which there was no current demand or prospect of employment. In the case of both groups, it becomes necessary for the Employment Service to make a thoroughgoing analysis of the aptitudes, interests, and other characteristics of the applicants to facilitate placement in occupations for which they are adapted. The problem here is essentially one of guidance, rather than the narrower one of helping employers to select competent workers originally conceived to be the function of an Employment Service.

Technical Aspects of Vocational Guidance and of Vocational Selection.—Not only is there overlapping in the scope of vocational guidance and selection, but there' is marked similarity in the techniques employed by both. Each profits from the experience of the other, especially in so far as the improvement of techniques is concerned. In both, the application of psychology in the improvement of techniques takes the same form, namely: (1) The development of better methods of occupational analysis; (2) the preparation of better techniques for the analysis of the individual; and (3) the formulation of sound methods for integrating the information about occupations with the information on the individual with the view of effecting a satisfactory adjustment between the demands of the job and the qualifications of the individuals.

PSYCHOLOGICAL METHODS IN OCCUPATIONAL ANALYSIS

The satisfactory adjustment of an individual to a job requires a consideration of its requirements in the way of physique, health, aptitudes, interests, education, skills, temperament, character, and other important characteristics. Knowledge of these requirements is obtained by *job analysis*, which is the study of the job designed to reveal its duties, conditions of work, and the qualifications that a worker should have for efficient performance and adjustment on the job. Facts uncovered in the job analysis are generally embodied in a *job specification*, such as that illustrated in Fig. 22.

The Psychological Approach in Job Analysis. —The chief contribution of psychology to job analysis consists of techniques for the determination of the traits required by the job and for describing them in specific, objective, and quantitative terms. The traditional job specification is largely confined to a statement on duties, tools, methods, and working conditions, supplemented by a brief description of such personal requirements as age, sex, health, education, and perhaps specialized skills. For vocational guidance and selection

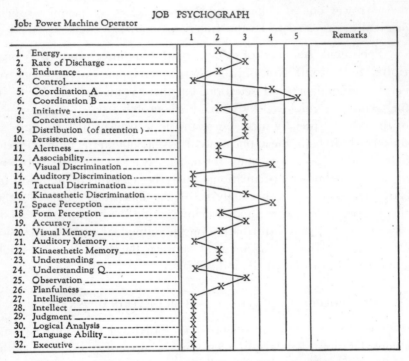

JOB PSYCHOGRAPH

Job: Power Machine Operator

FIG. 22.—JOB SPECIFICATION FOR POWER MACHINE OPERATOR.
(From Otis and Smith.)

there is needed a full description of the aptitudes and other characteristics which underlie skill, satisfaction, and success on the job.

At times, a description of such traits is included in the job specification, but, generally, when included, there is no exact definition of the traits or statement of the extent to which each is necessary for job success. For instance, in describing the qualifications of street car motormen and conductors one study [3] states that they should be "mentally alert," but no attempt is made to define the nature of mental alertness or to indicate the amount required. "Good disposition" is given as another qualification of the motorman and conductor, but just what this trait means, and how it can be measured are not indicated. "Motormen and conductors," it is added, "must be level headed, cool and resourceful," but it is left entirely to the fancy of the reader to determine what is meant by these traits.

Classification of Occupations by General Intelligence Levels.—An example of the psychological approach in describing job requirements is found in the classification of occupations in terms of general intelligence levels. A portion of such a classification, prepared by Fryer and Sparling, is presented in Table I.[4] The basic data for this are taken, in the main, from distributions collected in the U. S. Army during the last war when various intelligence tests, including the historically famous Alpha, were given to nearly two million civilian draftees drawn from a large variety of occupations. As in the original study, the range of the middle 50 per cent of mental ages of each occupational group is used in establishing desirable limits of general intelligence for the occupation.

This classification satisfies the minimum requirements for scientific occupational analysis from the psychological point of view, in that:

(1) *The nature of the trait under consideration is immediately apparent,* since it is generally agreed that general intelligence coincides with "educability"—with learning ability as ordinarily displayed in progress in the school situation, which also affects occupational progress to the extent that the latter depends upon learning material or tasks similar to those included in the school curriculum.

(2) *The amount of the trait required for "reasonable assurance" of success in each occupation is stated in terms of a standard point of reference*—in this case, mental age.

(3) *The trait is one which is measurable by available instruments,* such as the various revisions of the Binet-Simon Scale, the Army Alpha, and numerous other standard written and verbal tests of general intelligence.

TABLE I.—CLASSIFICATION OF OCCUPATIONS BY INTELLIGENCE LEVELS *

Corresponding Intelligence—Achievement Values

Intelligence Groups	C Average 13.0 to 14.9 Mental Age (Estimated Average Mental Age: 13.75)	

	GENERAL	Intelligence for routine and skilled mechanical work Rarely capable of complicated abstract detailed work *Skilled occupational level*

	EDUCATIONAL	Ability for elementary school graduation and some secondary school training

ACHIEVEMENT LEVELS — **OCCUPATIONAL (EXPECTED SUCCESS AS)**

Engineman (Locomotive)	Lathe hand (Production)	Shop mechanic (Railroad)	Horse trainer
Farrier	Auto mechanic (General)	Printer	Cobbler
Telephone operator	Auto chauffeur	Carpenter (General)	Engineman (Stationary)
Stock checker	Tailor	Motorman (Street car)	Barber
Handyman (General mechanic)	Dressmaker	Conductor (Street car)	Hairdresser
Policeman	Milliner	Baker	Sales clerk
Auto assembler	Lineman	Cook	Horse hostler
Engineman (Marine)	Machinist (General)	Mine drill runner	Horse shoer
Riveter (Hand)	Motorcyclist	Painter	Storekeeper (Factory)
Tool and die maker	Brakeman (R.R.)	Concrete worker	Aeroplane worker
Auto engine mechanic	Actor (Vaudeville)	Farmer	Boilermaker (General)
Laundryman	Butcher	Auto truck chauffeur	Rigger
Gunsmith	Fireman (Locomotive)	Bricklayer	Teamster
Plumber	Blacksmith (General)	Caterer	Miner (General)
Pipefitter			Waiter
			Station agent (General)

* From Fryer and Sparling.

(4) *The statement of requirements is based upon an experimental study* of the distribution of general intelligence among those actually working in the occupation under consideration.

"Family" Groupings by Intelligence.—An important feature of the classification of occupations by general intelligence levels is that it groups occupations into "families" which have a common denominator in terms of the required level of intelligence. Such a classification shows that most people, so far as general intelligence is concerned, are capable of successful achievement in a wide range of occupations. This is apparent in Table I which shows, for example, that even within the narrow range of mental ages 13 to 14.9 are found 50 per cent of workers in occupations so diverse as auto assembler, street car conductor, tailor, milliner, salesclerk, hairdresser, horseshoer, bricklayer, and so on.

Limitations of Occupational Classifications by Intelligence Level.—Although such a classification into families is important, its practical significance is limited by the wide range of general intelligence characterizing almost every occupational group. For example, although 50 per cent of the workers named in the occupations above have mental ages of 13 to 14.9, an additional 25 per cent have mental ages about 14.9, ranging to the very top of the mental-age scale, and 25 per cent have mental ages below 13, ranging in some instances to close to the bottom of the scale. Moreover, there is much overlapping from level to level, so that one finds some unskilled workers exhibiting the same degree of general intelligence as some of the less alert in professional ranks, and many semiskilled and skilled workers possessing general intelligence equal to that of the most alert professional man.

Such facts clearly limit the significance of general intelligence, as expressed in mental age, for vocational guidance and selection. Moreover, there are relatively few instances of close relation between amount of general intelligence and degree of proficiency or success in particular jobs. For example, the range of mental ages of the middle 50 per cent of speckers in the textile industry was found by the author to be from 10.3 to 14 years. There was no tendency for those in the upper end of the range to work faster or to turn out a better product than those in the middle or at the lower end of the total range. In other words, the percentage of good speckers among girls with mental ages above 14 years and among those with mental ages below 10.3 years was as high as the proportion within the middle 50 per cent.

Similar facts have been uncovered in the study of many other occupations, such as street car motormen, compositors, inspectors, assemblers, and others, particularly at the semiskilled level. As a matter of fact, it is only rarely that a close relation is found between degree of job success and general intelligence level over the entire range of the scale, although occasionally, as in clerical work, where rate of promotion has been shown to depend somewhat upon mental age, and in "higher grade" jobs, there does appear a relation between amounts of general intelligence and degrees of job proficiency.

Minimum Mental-Age Requirements.—While, in general, little significance can be attached to the entire range of mental ages, minimum requirements in the way of general intelligence are frequently significant in determining qualification for work. This is particularly true at the professional and semiprofessional levels and, to some extent, in major executive and sales-managerial jobs. Minimum critical mental-age levels have also been established for advanced types of clerical and secretarial work, and, to some extent, for highly skilled trades. However, to be useful, minimum critical general intelligence test scores or mental ages must be experimentally established for each occupation and for individual plants by a direct comparison between performance on the job and general intelligence test scores.

Minimum standards of general intelligence are also useful in the guidance and placement of subnormals. For productive work in industry, even of the unskilled type, a minimum age of 5 to 6 is apparently needed. Burr, of the Vocational Adjustment Bureau of New York City, has shown that for packing small articles, such as powderpuffs, a minimum mental age of 7 or 8 is required; for crude hand sewing, packing difficult articles, etc., a minimum mental age of 9 or 10; for stock-keeping, winding cotton and wool braid, a minimum mental age of 10 or 11, and so on.

Maximum Intelligence Levels May Be Significant.—Studies also show that for certain jobs maximum mental-age levels may be significant. Among department-store cashiers, for example, the author has found excessive turnover among employees with higher mental ages. There is evidence that excessive feelings of monotony, dissatisfaction with occupational prestige, social position and progress, lack of interest and motivation and waste of abilities may follow from the placement of a highly intelligent individual into a repetitive or "low grade" job.

In Summary.—In general, it may be said that general intelligence level is a particularly significant item in the statement of occupational qualifications at the professional and semiprofessional level. It also has significance at the level of the skilled trade and in directing workers toward clerical occupations. The importance of the general intelligence specification rapidly diminishes as occupations approach the semiskilled levels and practically disappears, except for a lower minimum, at the level of unskilled work. Moreover, at all levels, the statement of requirement in terms of general intelligence must be supplemented by a detailed analysis and description of the special aptitudes, temperamental and other characteristics which, along with and generally to a greater extent than general intelligence, determine occupational success or failure.

Viteles Job Psychographic Method.—Among procedures used in analyzing and recording such specialized requirements for occupational success is the *Viteles Job Psychographic Method*. This starts with a list of 32 "abilities" (shown on page 444) each carefully defined to indicate its scope of function in occupational activity. The following is a typical definition:

COORDINATION (B). *This refers to the harmonious combination of visual and muscular functions on the job. It is movement controlled by sight. It is important, for example, in such a job as telephone operating, in which the operator is required to place a plug into a hole of small diameter, the location of which is perceived through vision. At the other extreme is that of selling life insurance, in which Coordination B is a negligible factor.*

The psychographic method also provides a standard 5-point scale for rating the *importance of each ability on the job*. The units in this scale are: (1) *Negligible*, (2) *barely significant*, (3) *significant*, (4) *of great importance*, (5) *of utmost importance*.

Ratings are graphically recorded on a form such as that shown on page 444, as part of the job specification for "power machine operator," to produce a job psychograph which shows at a glance the abilities that are most essential to success and their general relation to each other and to less important abilities. There are indicated on such a job psychograph the keystone specific abilities which must be particularly considered and objectively measured in vocational guidance and selection. The preparation of the job psychograph, as the compilation of other facts about the job, requires intensive study of the job by trained observers, supplemented by the judgment of workers, supervisors, and others thoroughly familiar with the job.

An important feature of the job psychographic method is that it facilitates a preliminary grouping of jobs with similar patterns of abilities into families of occupations which are alike in mental requirements, although diverse in terms of specific tasks performed and even of material handled. For example, a study of clerical jobs by the author in 1922 revealed that the same job psychograph could be employed as a basis for hiring for seven distinct jobs because of the similarity in the underlying pattern of abilities required for success in all. The importance of such grouping becomes strikingly apparent when it is recalled that there are probably 20,000 separate occupations. Until these are classified in terms of common aptitudes and other characteristics, job seekers cannot be considered for the full range of opportunities matching their specific characteristics.

Recent Adaptations of the Job Psychographic Method.— Variations of the job psychographic method developed by other investigators have been widely used in European countries. In this country, the United States Employment Service is using a modification of the Viteles Job Psychographic Method in studying occupational requirements. The terms originally used by the author are replaced by descriptive phrases such as:

1. *Work rapidly for long periods.*
14. *Perceive form of objects.*
33. *Attention to many items.*
36. *Tact in dealing with people.*

The number of traits listed on the U. S. Employment Service *Occupational Characteristic Check List* has been extended to 45, including a few traits of temperament or personality as well as "abilities" to which the job psychograph was originally confined. More important still is a modification of the rating system which requires analysts to indicate the *amount of each characteristic demanded of the worker* in order to do the job satisfactorily, the amount required being defined as follows:

(A) A very great amount of the trait, such as would be possessed by not more than 2 per cent of the general population.

(B) A distinctly above-average amount of the trait, such as would be possessed by the highest 30 per cent of the general population, but less than the amount designated by A.

(C) An amount of the trait less than that possessed by the highest 30 per cent of the general population.

Advances in Grouping Occupations into "Families."—In addition to gathering data on several thousand occupations, the United States Employment Service has made use of these results in setting up families of occupations—each family having common denominators in terms of skill, abilities, temperamental, and other characteristics. One such "family," for example, consists of 22 occupations, in 4 industries, which are alike in requiring *strength, dexterity,* and *coordination* in "B" amounts and in that *none has a formal education requirement.* Preliminary groupings of this kind reveal marked possibilities for setting up more comprehensive families to be used not alone for placement and guidance, but for curriculum planning in schools, so that training can be given for families of similar occupations, thus enlarging the future chances for the employment of the student.

The Test Method in Occupational Analysis.—Job psychographic methods involve primarily a subjective analysis and rating of the requirements of a job. This has been supplemented by the more objective technique of describing job qualifications in terms of the psychological tests used in forecasting occupational proficiency. When this method, early advocated by Link, is employed, requirements for the job are actually stated in terms of critical scores on tests which have been experimentally validated as "predictors" of proficiency on the job. This is essentially what happens when tests to be used in selecting workers for specific occupations are prepared, since the passing score on the test battery becomes, in practice, the stated qualification for employment.

Occupational Ability Patterns.—The test technique for stating the mental requirements has been employed by Trabue in the development of occupational ability patterns. Such a pattern presents graphically the average scores made on a selected group of tests by a relatively homogeneous group of workers employed in an occupation, in comparison with the distribution for a random population. The tests used for this purpose by Trabue include a measure of educational achievement, the Minnesota Clerical Test—Numbers, the Minnesota Clerical Test—Names, the Tweezer Dexterity Test, the Minnesota Manual Dexterity Test, Strength of Right Hand, Strength of Left Hand, Bernreuter Personality Inventory.

The occupational ability pattern or profile presumably gives a picture of the range and pattern of measured aptitude and personality traits which distinguish each job. The assumption is that for purposes of vocational guidance and selection the *individual profile* obtained by giving the same tests can be compared with the occupational ability pattern in determining suitability for the job. It is also assumed that by observation, patterns can be matched to arrive at families of occupations which are alike in terms of fundamental requirements.

In fact, the method is far less objective and exact than it appears to be on the surface. Subjective judgment is involved in making the comparison of an individual's profile of scores with the occupational ability patterns. In practice, there has been a tendency to overemphasize the correspondence between the shape of the individual profile and an occupational ability pattern. This is a particularly serious danger because while only the average score of each occupational group is shown in the profile, the scores are actually widely distributed. Moreover, although the significance of individual tests undoubtedly varies from job to job, no data on such differences are given. This means that the assignment of relative weights becomes a matter of judgment.[5]

In general, in spite of the use of test scores as a basis for the graphic presentation of occupational requirements, the occupational ability pattern essentially possesses the same disadvantage of subjectivity as do the job psychographic methods described above. In addition, it is more susceptible to abuse, oversimplification, and misinterpretation by untrained and uncritical observers. At the same time it is considerably more cumbersome, time-consuming, and costly than the job psychographic methods.

Hull's Proposal for a Universal Aptitude Battery.—A more exacting approach to the use of test techniques is found in a plan elaborated by Hull, of Yale University. He looks forward to the time when there will be a single universal battery of 30 or 40 tests which will sample all important traits. As the outcome of suitable experimental investigations there would be developed 40 or 50 different equations, each weighting the tests in the battery in a different way so as to make the best possible prediction of success in each of 40 or 50 occupations. Occupational qualifications would be stated in terms of mathematical formulas very much like those used in designating chemical combinations, the elements being the tests used in measuring mental traits.[6]

This program for using tests in job analysis perhaps represents the ideal toward which the psychologist should strive in matching men and occupations. However, at the present time there are relatively few jobs for which adequate test batteries have been developed and in the case of which an objective statement of mental requirements in terms of test scores can be made. For the time being, a systematic subjective analysis and statement of occupational qualifications in psychographic form remain as probably the most helpful psychological procedures in occupational analysis.

Factorial Analysis in the Study of Occupational Qualifications.—In the study of occupational requirements, as in other fields of psychology, use is being made of statistical procedures, such as multiple factor analysis, which facilitate the discovery of basic factors underlying occupational proficiency. Alexander, employing the Thurstone technique, has found that shop achievement of boys in a technical school could be accounted for in terms of four factors, each contributing to achievement to the extent indicated below: [7]

g (Spearman's general factor)	10 per cent
f (practical factor found particularly in performance tests)	13 " "
x (temperamental factor—"the will to succeed")	43 " "
z (undefined)	34 " "

In Summary.—This is an illustration of the mathematical exactitude with which it may be possible, in the future, to determine the factors entering into occupational activities. Unfortunately, little progress has been made in the formulation of occupational requirements in such exact terms. Moreover, much remains to be done in analyzing jobs from the viewpoint of temperamental requirements and social relations and in supplementing the "atomistic" approach with an emphasis upon the "total job pattern." [8] However, in spite of these deficiencies, psychological techniques for analyzing occupational requirements at least represent an important advance beyond the vague, ill-defined procedures of the so-called practical vocational counselor and industrial personnel worker.

ANALYSIS OF THE INDIVIDUAL
EVALUATION OF TRADITIONAL TECHNIQUES

Progress in vocational guidance and vocational selection also calls for a supply of adequate techniques for analyzing the individual. This involves: (1) An evaluation of techniques commonly used in guidance and selection and, (2) the development of improved tools and procedures to supplement or supplant those which are found to be inadequate or unsatisfactory.

Experimental Studies of the Application Blank.—An excellent illustration of the psychological approach in evaluating techniques commonly used in matching men and occupations is to be found in experimental studies of the application blank. In employment practice, an over-all judgment of the fitness of the applicant is made from the examination of this blank, without any attempt to determine the differential significance of individual items. Psychological studies show that some items may be absolutely worthless in determining fitness for work while others may be highly valuable in predicting performance on the job. For example, an investigation by the author, in 1926, revealed that 7 application-blank items—age, nationality, marital status, number of children, number of dependents, weight, and previous occupation—were of significance in predicting the sales performance of taxicab drivers, employed by the Yellow Cab Company of Philadelphia, operating on a commission basis. No other items on the application blank were of any value for this purpose.

A preliminary study showed that by weighting and combining scores on these items it was possible to eliminate 60 per cent of the poorest earners, that is, those falling in the lowest 25 per cent in terms of sales performance, while rejecting from employment only 22 per cent of the best and only 18 per cent of the average earners. The use of this scoring method in hiring has brought satisfactory results in differentiating between men who produce a gross revenue inadequate to pay the fixed charges and overhead on the taxicab supplied to them and those whose sales performance is satisfactory.

In this study the author made use of a method for weighting application blank items originally developed by Russell and Cope for use by the Phoenix Mutual Life Insurance Company in selecting salesmen. On the basis of experiments extending over a period of almost 20 years, this company reports a marked improvement in sales and decrease in turnover among insurance salesmen from the use of weighted application item scores.[9]

Bridgman has shown that scholarship ratings, achievement, and age of graduation are much more significant than other items in predicting the success of college graduates in the Bell Telephone

System.[10] From a study by Uhrbrock and Richardson [11] it appears that in the plants of the Procter and Gamble Company the satisfactory supervisors are men with 9 or more years of schooling, between 25 and 39 years of age, with military service, who are confident of their ability to read blueprints.

Such findings are important not only in themselves but in demonstrating the possibility of transforming a procedure which ordinarily has little merit into one that really helps in hiring qualified workers.

The Value of Photographs in Estimating Fitness for Work.—The photograph of an applicant is frequently used in gauging "intelligence," "trustworthiness," "character," "sociability," "aggressiveness," and other qualifications. Experimental studies by Anderson, McCabe, Husband,[12] and others show clearly that photographs give neither reliable nor valid clues to vocationally significant aptitudes and temperamental characteristics.

In most such experiments observers without experience in employment or counseling are used. Viteles and Smith [13] presented to 24 members of a metropolitan personnel association, including mainly employment managers and vocational counselors, 2 photographs of 5 *successful* and 5 *unsuccessful* men in each of the fields of law, medicine, education, and engineering. One photograph of each man was taken at the time of graduation from college (younger group); the second 25 years later (older group). Ratings on vocational success were made by Landis and Phelps, who supplied the material for the experiment, from biographies appearing in a yearbook published on the 25th anniversary of the graduation of 850 men from a large Eastern university.

Each observer, without being told that the photographs were of the same men, was asked to indicate, for the "older" group, whether it was the picture of a "successful" or "unsuccessful" man and the occupation in which he was employed. In the case of the younger group, judgment was in the form of prediction as to whether he would be "successful" or "unsuccessful," and guidance as to which of each of the four occupations he should enter. In addition, each observer was asked to estimate the per cent certainty of his judgment and the basis of judgment, for example, shape of face, height of forehead, position of eyes, etc.

Results were compared with those obtained by Landis and Phelps using college students as observers. Personnel workers made correct judgments in 52.8 per cent of the cases while college students were correct in 51.3 per cent of the cases. Both would have done just as well by tossing coins and recording, without looking at the photographs, a success judgment for every head and a failure judgment for every tail. With respect to certainty of judgment, the average "per cent of certainty" for personnel workers was 55 and for college students 34.8, in spite of the fact that the accuracy of judgment in both cases was no better than chance. In matching photographs and careers, there was likewise not even an approximation of accuracy. "General impression" and "facial expression" were reported by the personnel men as their basis for judgment in over 50 per cent of the cases.

It is apparent from such experiments that no dependence can be placed on the photograph as a tool for estimating fitness for work. The functions of the photograph must be limited to gathering preliminary impressions on appearance and to the identification of applicants and employees.

"Character-Analysis" Systems.—The continued use of photographs in judging the qualifications of applicants reflects in part the faith placed in formal systems of character analysis. Shape of head and face; color of hair, eyes and skin; texture of hair and skin; skull dimensions; formation of teeth are among the physical signs which, according to the exponents of such systems, are dependable in diagnosing occupationally significant traits.

None of these character-analysis systems has withstood the test of experimental investigation. Characteristic of such studies is that of Cleeton and Knight [14] who, using calipers, tapes, head squares and other especially designed instruments, with 28 college students as subjects, made careful measurements of physical characteristics claimed to be diagnostic of "judgment," "intellectual capacity," "frankness," and 5 other traits. These were correlated with ratings on the traits made independently by close associates and by 70 observers experienced in handling men who had no previous acquaintance with the subjects. The highest correlation proved to be .32, or approximately 5 per cent better than chance, and almost half of the correlations were negative. No agreement was found among different physical factors described by character analysis as diagnostic of the same traits. The average correlation of 201 pairs of factors proved to be zero.

Other investigators, using both these and other evaluation methods, have likewise failed to confirm the claims of the character analysts.[15] Even when the latter cooperate, as did the exponents of "Vitosophy" in an experiment by Ford,[16] the correlations obtained between trait measurements and character-analysis readings turn out to be like those obtained by random drawings from a lottery box.

Graphological Systems of Character Analysis.—A number of character-analysis systems depend upon psychophysiological rather than upon physiognomic or other physical signs. Chief among these are graphological systems which make handwriting the basis of judgment. Starting with an early investigation by Binet, there has been a series of studies designed to test the validity of such systems. Typical is an experiment by Brown, who, applying procedures earlier employed by Hull and Montgomery, asked 30 subjects to copy a piece of prose under identical conditions. The samples of handwriting were then submitted to microscopic examination and the measurements correlated with ratings on personality traits provided on one another by the subjects whose long mutual association gave each a fairly reliable knowledge of the character of the others. Susceptibility to objective measurement of the handwriting signs and agreement among graphologists with respect to their significance were the criteria employed in selecting the traits to be studied. The results, given in Table II, show consistently low correlations between handwriting signs and their supposedly associated personality traits. In some cases the direction of the correlation is actually opposite to that claimed by the graphologists.

Such studies have been criticized by professional graphologists who claim that accurate graphological diagnosis calls for a consideration of the general features of script and their interrelation or "global pattern" rather than the microscopic study of detailed elements or signs. Moreover, from the laboratories of such graphologists come findings which, at least on the surface, appear to be highly favorable to graphology. Saudek [17] examined 73 specimens of handwriting submitted by 18 business firms and interpreted 19 of them as belonging to dishonest people and 54 to honest individuals. The firms confirmed the accuracy of his diagnosis in 14 out of 19 cases of dishonesty. In no case was an honest person diagnosed as dishonest. Kügelgen, Seesemann, Klages, and others have reported similarly favorable results.

TABLE II.—SHOWING COEFFICIENTS OF CORRELATION BETWEEN TRAITS OF HANDWRITING AND VARIOUS TRAITS OF PERSONALITY

(Computations based on data of Lois E. Brown)*

Personality Trait	Handwriting Trait	Correlation Coefficient (r)
Bashfulness	Width of down strokes	.11
Ambition	Tendency to upward slope as line crosses page	.23
Persistence	Width of down strokes	—.05
Persistence	Disconnected writing—per cent of breaks of line within words	—.03
Personal neatness	Neatness in appearance of writing	.23
Personal individuality	Individuality in appearance of writing	.15

* From C. L. Hull, *Aptitude Testing*. Yonkers-on-the-Hudson: World Book Company, 1928, 150.

Powers,[18] of Dartmouth College, has applied the global approach in an experiment in which personality sketches of 10 subjects were matched with their handwriting samples by 123 male undergraduates, 25 faculty members, and 17 professional graphologists. On the basis of chance the number of correct matchings should be 1 out of 10. The average number of correct matchings was 1.77 for the student group, 1.80 for the faculty group, and 2.41 for the graphologists. It is evident that handwritings evidently indicate even to untrained judges definite personality traits. Graphologists, on the other hand, give better judgments and make more correct matchings than do untrained persons.

Disagreements in the findings of experimental studies of graphology are paralleled by differences of opinion among psychologists on the significance of handwriting as a diagnostic tool. At one extreme is the position of Symonds, of Columbia University, who includes graphology among systems supported by charlatans and urges that there be no acceptance of claims made by graphologists. At the other extreme are Roback, who finds graphology one of the most promising of "psychodiagnostic" systems, and Allport and Vernon, who feel that "on *a priori* grounds handwriting, which may be considered as "crystallized gesture," should be expected to furnish a valuable though intricate index to the patterns of personality." [19] However, regardless of what future promise there may be in handwriting as a clue to personality, in *terms of everyday practice in vocational selection and guidance, there is still no justification for the use of handwriting in predicting fitness for work,* particularly since the degree of accuracy in prediction in even experiments favorable to graphology is far below the level reached by most psychological tests.

Evaluation of the Interview.—Among traditional methods of vocational selection and guidance the interview probably represents the one which is most consistently employed and is given the greatest weight. Experimental studies have led to the conclusion that the interview, as ordinarily conducted, fails to furnish valid and reliable information as to aptitudes, temperamental characteristics, attitudes, and other traits of the individual. In an early study by Scott, Bingham and Whipple, 20 salesmanagers and 3 investigators of problems in selecting salesmen interviewed 24 applicants for sales positions and rated them in order of suitability as salesmen. In practically every case range of opinion covered almost the entire order-of-merit scale. Most applicants were rated as belonging in the best half of the group as frequently as they were placed in the worst half of the group. A later study of the same type by Hollingworth [20] produced similar evidence of disagreement among interviewers.

In an experiment by Scott, estimates on the sales ability of 12 applicants were made by 13 salesmanagers and later compared with the actual sales records. Results showed considerable disagreement among interviewers. In addition, most of the estimates showed no relation to actual sales performance. Even when the estimates of all 13 were pooled, the prediction of sales performance was less than 25 per cent better than chance. However, results showed that a few of the interviewers made more valid judgments than did others and that the opinions of certain interviewers agree better with the pooled judgment of the group than do those of others.

Improving the Interview.—The failure to define terms; varying conditions in the interview; individual differences in the capacity and training of interviewers constitute major sources of error in the interview. The influence of these and other sources of error can be reduced by appropriate modification of interviewing techniques and conditions. For example, in an English study [21] it was found that (1) by selecting and carefully finding the traits to be observed in an interview, and (2) by providing a standard method for the expression of judgment in the form of a rating scale, it is possible to arrive at an estimate of certain traits—particularly temperament and character—that are as reliable and valid as the results of psychological tests now commonly used for measuring these traits. With the traditional, unimproved method of interviewing, coefficients of reliability for estimates on selected personality traits averaged .31, while validity coefficients were approximately .22. By introducing the changes noted above, the correlation of 2 independent observers for "simple" traits, such as cheerfulness, curiosity and assertiveness, reached an average of .60; for more "complex" qualities such as initiative, industry, cooperation with equals, an average of .55. Correlations between the estimates of acquaintances and strangers ran as high as .58 for the "simple" qualities and .46 for the more complex qualities.

O'Rourke,[22] of the U. S. Civil Service Commission, has found that while there is considerable disagreement among untrained interviewers, the use of a standard interview and training in interviewing techniques results in a marked increase in the uniformity of ratings. In an extensive program sponsored by the Employment Board, Department of Public Assistance, Commonwealth of Pennsylvania, numerous examining boards, including a total of about 800 examiners, were trained in the use of a rating scale for recording estimates on personality traits made during oral examinations given in establishing eligibility lists for about 5,000 vacancies. According to Bingham, interview ratings provided reliable estimates since, in sample studies, among ratings given by several members of the inter-viewing board there is seldom "a rating on any trait which diverges more than one-fifth of the scale length from the average of the rating on that trait given to that candidate by the other examiners," and "the average deviation from the consensus is about one-ninth of the scale." [23]

Unfortunately, although these ratings may be reliable, a later investigation, supervised by the author, shows that they had no practical significance in selection since (1) only approximately 10 per cent of the candidates were eliminated from further consideration on the basis of the oral interview ratings, and (2) in a sample of 251 Junior Visitors in 18 counties, there were no diagnostic differ-ences in oral interview scores among those considered, appointed, and not appointed.

Although uncritical observers tend to be overly optimistic, the sum total of evidence on the interview suggests that it is possible to obtain important data on fitness for work from properly conducted interviews. However, considerable experimentation in improving the content and method of oral interviewing is needed if the interview is to be made a really effective and dependable technique in vocational guidance and selection.

PSYCHOLOGICAL TESTS IN INDIVIDUAL ANALYSIS

From this review of traditional methods it is apparent that certain of them, in improved form, have a legitimate place in a scientific program of selection and vocational guidance. It is also clear that the provision of more dependable objective techniques for measuring vocationally significant traits is still a major need in matching men and occupations.

There is considerable evidence that the psychological test repre-sents the best available tool for measuring such traits. This state-ment refers, of course, only to reliable tests which are properly designed, adequately standardized, and fully validated. It implies also (1) that the test, like diagnostic tools in other fields, will be used by trained persons capable of interpreting test results, and (2) that it will be employed only in combination with other sources of information to arrive at a balanced "global" view of all the factors which affect occupational adjustment. Under such conditions the forecasting efficiency of the psychological test tends to be considerably higher than that of other techniques now at the disposal of the guidance agency and of the employment office for analyzing the individual.

Varieties of Tests Used in Vocational Guidance and Vocational Selection.—The tests most frequently used in vocational guidance and selection include measures of (a) *proficiency*, (b) *aptitude*, (c) *interest*, (d) *temperament and character*, and (e) *attitudes*.

Proficiency Tests.—Proficiency tests are used to measure the acquired achievements and skills of an applicant for placement or guidance. These include tests of *educational achievement* and *trade tests*.

Trade tests are particularly useful in selection because (a) applicants at times claim skill in occupations with which they have only superficial familiarity, and because (b) previous employment experience cannot be relied upon to provide an adequate index of occupational skill.

A study in Minneapolis, for example, shows that applicants with less than a year of experience as typists do almost as well on standard typing tests as those who claim five or more years of experience. In a study by the Employment Stabilization Research Institute of the University of Minnesota, tests of trade knowledge, adapted from the Army Trade Tests, were administered to 126 applicants for such jobs as welders, interior wiremen, sheet-metal workers, etc. Of these, 26 who claimed to be journeymen or experts were reclassified by the tests as novices or apprentices.[24] Such facts show the reason for using measures which establish more objectively and dependably an applicant's readiness to do a job than does a record of experience.

Aptitude Tests.—Aptitude may be defined as a condition or set of characteristics regarded as symptomatic of an individual's ability to acquire with training some "usually specific" knowledge, skill, or set of responses. Vocational aptitude tests are designed to measure those capacities or abilities which enable an individual to profit from training and experience on the job and to develop into a satisfactory worker. They are of particular value as "predictors" in forecasting the productive efficiency of individuals who have had no training or experience in the occupation under consideration.

Interest Tests.—Interest is commonly defined as a tendency to give attention to, to be attracted by, to like and find satisfaction in an activity, object, or person. Tests of vocational interest concern themselves primarily with the degree of intensity of interest in an occupation and with predicting the permanence of that interest. The measurement of interest is of value, particularly in vocational guidance, to indicate (1) whether an individual will like the actual work of the occupation he is considering well enough to become absorbed in it and to remain on it; (2) whether he will find himself among congenial associates, with interests similar to his own; (3) to suggest alternate fields of occupation which may not yet have been seriously considered.

The interest measure may perhaps, in certain instances, also be used in predicting the degree of success in the occupation, but, on the basis of available evidence, and pending the accumulation of further evidence, it seems well to assign to interest tests the responsibility of predicting "satisfaction" rather than degree of productive success on the job.

Tests of Temperament and Character.—Temperament and character, according to Roback, refer to the affective and conative aspects of personality, temperament being essentially the sum total or blend of one's affective qualities as they influence others; character referring to the volitional and inhibitory phases of behavior.

Bevington,[25] on the basis of a study designed to establish the relative importance of intellectual, temperamental, economic, and social factors in the success of London working-boys concluded that temperamental factors and character are of much greater importance than intellectual, economic, or social factors in determining a lad's industrial success. Actually the importance of such factors probably varies from job to job. However, there is no doubt that in the case of practically all jobs a worker must not only have competency; he must get along with people and have certain character qualities of regularity, thoroughness, persistence, honesty, sociability, and the like. There is need for an ever-increasing emphasis upon the objective measurement of such traits in vocational guidance and vocational selection.

Attitude Tests.—In the measurement of attitudes, the vocational psychologist is primarily concerned with emotional predisposition or set toward general ideas and concepts expressive of the complexities of personnel relations in industry. Attitudes toward unions, systems of wage payments, general conditions of work, are among those which have been considered in the measurement of employee attitudes.

Tests of attitudes have so far been used very sparingly in guidance and selection, but recent investigations indicate a growing recognition of their importance in adjustment to work which may well lead to an extension of attitude measurement in matching men and occupations, quite apart from the measurement of attitudes of employed workers, discussed in Chapter XVIII.

THE USE OF TESTS IN VOCATIONAL SELECTION

It is quite impossible, within the limitations of this text, to describe or even list the great number of tests which have been used in measuring vocationally significant traits. A report by the Adjustment Service [26] of New York City names 25 tests, apart from trade tests, used in examining the first 10,000 cases handled by that agency. Pallister [27] sent a questionnaire to 74 American psychologists asking an opinion on the efficiency of 53 vocational tests. Twenty-three tests are "rated" as efficient by 75 per cent or more of those who expressed a judgment on each.

Such lists represent, of course, only the best opinion of psychologists who have concerned themselves with problems of vocational guidance and selection. In practice, no test has a place in a scientific program of vocational adjustment until its dependability and forecasting efficiency have been objectively determined by means of appropriate experimental procedures.[28] Applying these procedures, psychologists have standardized and validated tests for a large variety of occupational tasks. Below are a few illustrations of progress in this direction.

Tests for Manual Occupations.—Representative of tests for manual occupations is a battery developed by the author for the selection and placement of *electric-substation operators*.[29] Following a comprehensive job analysis of the job, 84 electric-substation operators, including all operators with less than 10 years and more than one year of service, employed by the Philadelphia Electric Company, were classified into *poorest*, *average*, and *best* operators, on the basis of ratings by 13 supervisors and a study of operating errors. An analysis showed that during the period January 1, 1926, to September 30, 1928, the *poorest* group averaged 7.5 times as many errors as the *best,* and 2.5 times as many errors as the *average* group. The *average* group averaged 3 times as many errors as the *best* group.

On the basis of the job analysis, there was developed a battery of tests designed to measure the abilities required for accurate operation, that is, for avoiding errors in operation. These included the *Pursuit Test* and the *Location Test* taken from the MacQuarrie Tests of Mechanical Aptitude, a *Directions Test*, developed by the author, a *Learning Test,* adapted from a laboratory instrument used in experiments on serial response, and 6 other tests. On this battery the average score of *best* operators proved to be 81.4, of *average* operators 69.2, of *poorest* operators 53.5. Moreover, 70.6 per cent of the *best*, 31.5 per cent of the *average*, and only 7.7 per cent of the *poorest* operators had scores above a critical score of 75 set as the passing score in hiring new men.

For the years 1926 to 1928 inclusive, substation operating errors in the metropolitan area of the Philadelphia Electric Company System had averaged *35* per year. The tests were installed for use in hiring new men and in reassigning experienced men on the basis of aptitude in 1928. Operating errors dropped to *20* in 1929; to *18* in 1930; to *12* in 1931. Between 1932 and 1938 inclusive the average number of operating errors per year has been 5 and there is no year in which there has been more than 8 operating errors. The improvement subsequent to 1932 may be partly credited to programs for retraining experienced operators. However, there is evidence that the use of the tests in selecting and reassigning operators has been the major factor in decreasing the number of operating errors.

The U. S. Employment Service has recently investigated the validity of a test battery in forecasting the efficiency of power-sewing-machine operators in the garment industry. With a criterion of vocational accomplishment computed from the ratio of earned hours to clock hours of work, the validity of the test battery proved to be .66 for single-needle operators, .56 for double-needle operators, and .40 for a preliminary sample of 23 operators.

According to a recent report,[30] of 222 men hired by the New York Telephone Company as panel dial switchmen, 126 obtained a score of 50 and above on a selected battery of tests and 96 obtained scores below 50. Of the former, 9 or 7.1 per cent failed on the job in contrast with 34 or 33.5 per cent of the latter group.

In England, the National Institute of Industrial Psychology has devised a series of analogous tests, simulating types of work performed by process workers, for use in hiring employees for a dyestuff plant. Ratings on temperamental reactions during the test performance, noted and recorded in accordance with a standard method, were weighted with objective test scores in selection. Of 97 men hired during a 2-year period, not one has had to be dismissed as unsuitable.[31]

Tests for Transportation Workers.—Considerable progress has been made in the development of dependable tests for the selection of transportation workers. The Milwaukee Electric Railway and Light Company reports a reduction in the percentage of men discharged because of accidents from 14.1 per cent to 0.6 per cent following the introduction of the *Viteles Motorman Selection Test* in hiring motormen.[32]

Tests for selecting street car and autobus operators were introduced by the Paris Combined Transport Services in 1921, and by 1924 the system was in full working order. The number of motor vehicles operating in Paris and its surrounding area showed an increase of 218 per cent between the years 1923 and 1933, and the number of vehicular accidents increased 155 per cent. During the same period there was an increase of 30 per cent in the number of buses and street cars, while accidents involving these were reduced by 37 per cent. The average number of accidents per operator was reduced from 1.53 in 1923 to 0.27 in 1933. These accomplishments have led to a wide extension of the testing program to include conductors, machinist apprentices, dispatchers, etc. Since July 1, 1924, 8,000 applicants for such jobs have been examined annually.[33]

On the basis of test results 198 signalmen on a French railway were divided into five classes, A, B, C, D, and E; classes D and E being judged as unlikely to be successful. Of 92 signalmen considered "satisfactory," 82.6 per cent fell into class A, B, or C, as against only 6.6 per cent of the 102 considered "unsatisfactory." [34]

Similar results are reported for other occupations by laboratories attached to French railways. In England, Germany, U.S.S.R., and other European countries, selection tests are widely used for many classes of occupations in the transportation industry.

Selection of Clerical Workers.—Clerical occupations have received considerable attention in the occupational testing program. Bills and Pond, in parallel but independent studies carried on in the offices of a life insurance company and of a brass manufacturing plant respectively, using Bureau Test VI, have found "a definite and consistent relationship between intelligence test scores and advancement in clerical work." [35]

A more recent study of 250 employees of 6 companies, in service between 5 and 10 years, by a committee of the Life Office Management Association, confirmed the usefulness of Bureau Test VI in predicting promotability and revealed the possibility of eliminating 2 parts of the test with resulting increase in efficiency of administration and ease of scoring, and with practically no loss in the efficiency of the test as a selection instrument. Findings with the new test show, for example, that an individual with a score of 80 has 4 chances out of 10 of being promoted to the so-called second level of clerical jobs (involving "complicated clerical work"), and no chance at all of promotion to the third level ("decision-making jobs").* With a score above 141, the employee has no chance of remaining in lowest level, that is in jobs involving "simple clerical work"; 4 chances out of 10 of reaching the second level, and 6 out

---

* For the purposes of this study jobs were classified into 3 levels: I, simple clerical work; II, complicated clerical work; III, decision-making jobs.

of 10 for reaching the third level of clerical work at the end of 5 to 10 years.[36]

In a recent study by the U. S. Employment Service, test scores were correlated with average hourly production of 67 key-punch operators. Amount of education, Taylor Number Test, and Minnesota Clerical Test (numbers only) gave a multiple correlation of .50 with the criterion. The Minnesota Clerical Tests (both names and numbers) and the Taylor Number Test yielded a multiple correlation of .48. The criterion yielded a reliability of .90 when the production records of alternate weeks were correlated.[37]

An interesting feature of investigations by the U. S. Employment Service is an attempt to supplement prediction for specific clerical occupations by an analysis of the usefulness of tests in measuring qualifications for the general field of clerical work—particularly for machine clerical tasks. This involves essentially the technique of combining into a single general battery those items which are common to specific job batteries. Such an analysis, for example, has been made of data for 562 workers, including samples of coding clerks, card-punch-machine operators, hand transcribers, adding-machine operators, bookkeeping-machine operators, calculating-machine operators, and comptometer operators. Criterion data for each group consisted of either production records or work samples, test items being included in the general battery when they consistently differentiated between the highest, middle, and lowest-third groups of subjects in each group.

Tests for Sales and Allied Occupations.—Recent years have witnessed much progress in the development of tests for predicting success in sales and service occupations. Considerable research in measuring competency for department-store selling is being carried on by the U. S. Employment Service. Particularly significant in this, as in other studies by this group, are (1) the attention given to the development of reliable and valid criteria of job performance, and (2) the validation of test items on independent groups. Employing a battery including 66 interest items, 10 personal data items, and 21 personality items, relationships such as shown in Table III were obtained from 3 independent samples totalling 497 salespersons.

Follow-up on a group of contingents yielded further encouraging results. This has led to additional experimentation which, it is hoped, will yield a department-store-salesperson test battery valid for use over wide geographical areas.

TABLE III.—PER CENT OF THE HIGHEST, MIDDLE, AND LOWEST-THIRD GROUPS OF SALESPERSONS, ACCORDING TO BATTERY SCORES, WHO ARE IN THE HIGHEST, MIDDLE, AND LOWEST-THIRD GROUPS ON THE CRITERION SCORES

(Department-Store-Salesperson Studies—497 Subjects)*

Battery Score Group	Per Cent of Subjects in Criterion Score Group		
	Lowest Third	Middle Third	Highest Third
Highest Third ...	20 per cent	28 per cent	52 per cent
Middle Third	28 per cent	39 per cent	33 per cent
Lowest Third	52 per cent	32 per cent	16 per cent

* From data supplied by U. S. Employment Service.

In a study on the relation between scores on the Strong Vocational Interest Blank, data were collected from several life insurance companies using this interest inventory in selecting salesmen. Successful life insurance agents scored higher in life insurance interest than unsuccessful agents and than men in general. Though many men with low life insurance interest scores entered the business, few remained in it, and still fewer wrote a satisfactory volume.

It was also found that 85 per cent of agents with an A interest rating wrote $100,000 or more of insurance a year, in contrast with 51 per cent of B-plus men, 44 per cent of B men, 25 per cent of C men. In terms of an average volume of paid-for-insurance of $150,000, 67 per cent of A men were successful in contrast to 43 per cent of B plus men, 21 per cent of B men and 6 per cent of C men. These data are interpreted by Strong as indicating the fact of genuine relationship between interest and ability, but are described as inadequate for determining the exact degree of relationship.[38]

Lovett and Richardson, in a study involving 650 men in the Procter and Gamble sales force, have investigated the validity of diverse items, such as mental alertness, business information, dominance-submission, interest, etc., in predicting sales and sales-managerial success. From their findings the authors concluded that (1) items of mental alertness should have a prominent place in selecting for promotion; less for routine sales; (2) personality items should have a prominent place in selecting for sales success; less for sales managerial success; (3) homemade items deserve a try-out; (4) routine salesmen tend to be more conventional in responses on social-attitude items than are "promotion" men; (5) sales and sales-managerial ability are fairly distinct and independent.[39]

In England, in an attempt to devise means of selecting potential salesmanagers from the general sales staff, a battery of 6 tests, including measures of intelligence, vocabulary, and temperamental traits, selected by experiment from a greater number, was applied to 42 salesmanagers and to 120 salesmen. The fact that the mean total score of the salesmen was 107, and that of the salesmanagers 141, the maximum scores being 159 and 240, respectively, was interpreted as evidence that the battery could be used in differentiating between sales and sales-managerial ability. As an additional check, the tests were applied to a group of 34 London supervisors. The scores of supervisors, who represent a junior managerial grade between salesman and salesmanager, fell between those of salesmen and managers, leading to the practical use of the tests for promotion purposes.[40]

EVALUATION OF PSYCHOLOGICAL TESTS IN VOCATIONAL GUIDANCE

Integration of Experiments in Vocational Guidance and Vocational Selection.—Largely because of the greater complexity of the problem, the experimental validation of tests and allied psychological techniques has not proceeded so far in the field of vocational guidance as in that of vocational selection. However, a few significant studies are available.

In England, Farmer and Chambers, of the Industrial Health Research Board, have attempted an integration of the two fields of research through the intensive analysis of a series of vocational experiments.[41] Each experiment in vocational selection, they point out, may be made to serve a wider purpose if it is compared with other similar experiments, especially if the same tests were used in each of several experiments. In comparing results in such a way the value of particular tests for vocational guidance as well as for vocational selection can be considerably increased.

Starting with these premises, tests of various types were given to 2,731 males aged from 14-38, engaged in occupations of all degrees of skill, from highly skilled to routine manual work. Test results were correlated with measures of practical proficiency in each occupation. The investigation served to confirm the usefulness of intelligence and mechanical aptitude tests in measuring fitness for skilled trades while showing the relative ineffectiveness of sensorimotor tests for this purpose. Tests of intelligence and of aesthetokinetic coordination prove to be useful in guiding those with only an elementary education into semiskilled occupations. The results suggest that good results are not likely to be obtained by using tests in placing men in unskilled work. Of particular significance for vocational guidance is the finding that psychological tests correlate more closely with occupational proficiency when maturity has been reached than with proficiency immediately at the end of training.

Evaluation of the "Total Situation" in Vocational Guidance.—So far, the discussion has been limited to the experimental evaluation of individual specific tools in gauging fitness for work. It is seldom, however, that the interview or the psychological test or some other tool is used as the sole basis for vocational guidance and selection. For this reason, investigators have turned to the study of the "total situation"—to inquiries designed to compare results obtained when only usual methods are employed with those achieved when traditional techniques are supplemented by psychological procedures.

The Main London Experiment.—This has been the aim of a series of English experiments. In one of these,[42] conducted in London during the years 1925-29 inclusive, 1200 pupils about to leave elementary school were divided by chance into two groups. Children in the *control* group were given vocational guidance at school or "choice of employment" conferences in the ordinary way, while in counseling the *tested* group, dependence was placed upon the results of a psychological test supplemented by an improved interview, a careful analysis and evaluation of school records, medical records, social findings, etc.

For a period of between two-and-a-half and four years regular inquiries were made into the vocational progress of children in both groups. Many interesting facts were revealed by this follow-up. For example, of *tested* children who entered clerical work upon recommendation by the psychologists, 75 per cent retained their first posts. The corresponding figure for those who took up clerical work when it was not recommended was 35 per cent. In the *control* group, only 44 per cent of the children who entered clerical work on the advice of the school conference retained their first jobs, while of those who entered this work against the advice of the conference approximately the same percentage, 43 per cent, made no change of job.

In analyzing employers' reports, it was found that as the jobs occupied by the children in the *tested* group became more and more unlike the jobs recommended, the percentages of good reports tended to decrease regularly. In the *control* group this relation was less well defined. Reports from children showed that those entering fields of work recommended to them seemed generally more satisfied with their work. This was particularly true of children in the *tested* group. In general, the inquiry findings showed *first, that vocational advising is feasible, the young people whose occupations are the most similar to those advised tending to be most successful;* and *secondly,* that *the newer psychological technique of vocational guidance is distinctly more dependable than the ordinary procedure followed by the school conference.*

The Birmingham Experiment.—In a later experiment,[43] in Birmingham, 328 children, divided by chance into *control* and *tested* groups, were treated in much the same way as in the main London experiment and followed up for 2 years subsequent to graduation from the elementary school. Here two investigators cooperated closely in advising the children—one a vocational psychologist, the other an assistant organizer in the Juvenile Employment Department who had received special training in psychological methods. Each child in the *tested* group was examined by both investigators. Both investigators also took part in counseling every child in the *control* group, making such recommendations as they could without the aid of special psychological methods. Consequently, any superiority in the adjustment of the *tested* children can be regarded as probably due to the greater dependability of the psychological method of advising and not to the superior qualifications of the persons employing that method.

From whatever angle the data of this investigation are studied, the same indications appear clearly, namely, that *tested* children show more satisfactory occupational adjustment than do children from the *control group*. Considered as a whole, the results of these experiments suggest even more strongly than those of the London investigation that the ordinary methods of advising children on the choice of work are definitely inferior to those practiced by psychologists.

The Clinical Approach in Vocational Guidance.—Similar experiments at Fife and at the Wormwood Scrubs Boys' Prison [44] have produced additional evidence of the value of the psychological examination in guidance.

In considering these investigations, it is important to note that they represent not an evaluation of traditional methods in comparison with psychological tests, but an evaluation of the ordinary method with what the English call the method of the "psychological examination," known in this country as the "clinical method" in psychological practice. In this clinical approach, early advocated by the author, use is made of psychological tests and other objective techniques, but the emphasis is upon the complete study of the individual—an individual looked upon as an integrated organization of behavior patterns—as a "whole" personality against a background of social and economic factors affecting vocational adjustment.[45]

Contrasts with the "Thorndike" Study.—In this and other respects the English studies differ markedly from a recent ill-conceived attempt by Thorndike and his associates [46] to determine the value of psychological tests in vocational guidance by studying the progress of children to whom no advice had been given, but who had each taken an intelligence test, a test of "mechanical ability," and a test of "clerical capacity." This investigation started with 2,225 children, 14 years of age, tested in 1921-22. Eight or more years later the educational and work histories of these children were studied in order to determine the relationship of school record and test results to (1) educational progress, and (2) success in clerical, mechanical, and professional work, respectively.

The study involved a detailed analysis, by correlation and other techniques, of interrelationships among these variables. The outcome includes essentially a long series of zero correlations and the conclusions that the results do not support "the opinions of those enthusiasts for vocational guidance who assume that an examination of a boy or girl of 14 and a study of his school record will enable a counselor to estimate his fitness to succeed in this, that, and the other sort of work."

This study has been legitimately criticized on many grounds. The experimental situation failed to duplicate the actual guidance situation, where test results are used only in combination with other data as a basis for individual guidance by a competent counselor. There is serious question as to whether the tests employed are valid measures of the aptitudes considered in the investigation. The possible influence of differential training was entirely neglected. The failure to use control groups of untested individuals, as a way of comparing the "psychological" with the "traditional" method of guidance, greatly detracts from the significance and value of the sweeping conclusions drawn from the data by those who collaborated in the investigation. With these defects stands the inadequacy of the criteria of vocational success employed by the investigator.

The results obtained by vocational psychologists must depend upon the suitability of their techniques. Starting with unsuitable techniques and inadequate criteria for follow-up, Thorndike has obtained results which *can* be interpreted as demonstrating the unsuitability of *his* methods, but *not* the impracticability of scientific vocational guidance. More thoughtful investigators, selecting more suitable tests and allied techniques, have demonstrated clearly that both guidance and selection based on the application of improved psychological methods are both practical and productive in promoting vocational adjustment.

RESEARCH AND PRACTICE IN MATCHING MEN AND OCCUPATIONS

Investigations described above are chiefly concerned with specific contributions in the way of improved tools and procedures for use in vocational guidance and vocational selection. It must be recalled that these are largely the outcome of extensive research on fundamental psychological problems involved in mental measurement and individual differentiation.

For example, results on the Strong Vocational Interest Blank have value only when considered in relation to information on the nature of occupational interests; the relation between interest and success; the genesis and permanence of interest; the relation between interest and aptitude; the effect of vocational information upon vocational interest, and similar data made available as the result of extensive experimentation by Hubbard, Freyd, Strong, Fryer, and many others.

The improvement of techniques for measuring mechanical aptitudes has been facilitated by the early experimental studies of Muscio, Perrin, and others on the nature and interrelations of motor ability, mechanical aptitude, and mechanical intelligence, and by the more recent work of R. H. Seashore, Paterson and his associates, Earle, Gaw, Cox, and other investigators.

The entire problem of the "uniqueness" of traits and of basic factors of personality considered, for example, by Hull, Thurstone, Alexander, and Kelley, has tremendous import for vocational psychology.

In Conclusion.—There is no space, in a short chapter, to discuss the significance of these and other basic problems. The reader must look elsewhere in this book and to more detailed texts in vocational and industrial psychology for a fuller treatment of these theoretical backgrounds of vocational psychology. In this chapter it has been possible to consider only the more immediate practical accomplishments of vocational psychology in fitting workers to jobs as one step in promoting the efficiency and adjustment of people at work.

REFERENCES

Bingham, W. V. *Aptitudes and Aptitude Testing.* New York: Harper and Brothers, 1937.

Burtt, H. E. *Principles of Employment Psychology.* New York: Houghton Mifflin Company, 1926.

Earle, F. M., et al. *Methods of Choosing a Career.* London: George G. Harrap and Company, 1931.

Hollingworth, H. L. *Vocational Psychology and Character Analysis.* New York: D. Appleton-Century Company, Inc., 1929.

Hull, C. L. *Aptitude Testing.* Yonkers-On-Hudson: World Book Company, 1928.

Keller, F. J., and Viteles, M. S. *Vocational Guidance Throughout the World.* New York: W. W. Norton and Company, Inc., 1937.

Macrae, A. *Talents and Temperaments.* New York: D. Appleton-Century Company, Inc., 1933.

Morton, N. W. *Individual Diagnosis: A Manual for the Employment Office.* Montreal, Canada: McGill University Press, 1937.

Paterson, D. G., (Editor). Analysis of the individual, *Occupations,* April 1934, 12, 1-91.

Stead, W. H., Shartle, C. L. and Associates. *Occupational Counseling Techniques.* New York: American Book Company, 1940.

Thorndike, E. L., et al. *The Prediction of Vocational Success.* New York: Commonwealth Fund, 1934.

Viteles, M. S. *Industrial Psychology.* New York: W. W. Norton and Company, Inc., 1932.

Viteles, M. S., (Editor). Analysis of occupations, *Occupations,* June 1934, 12, 1-85.

Viteles, M. S. *Science of Work.* New York: W. W. Norton and Company, Inc., 1934.

CHAPTER XVIII

VOCATIONAL PSYCHOLOGY (MAINTAINING FITNESS AT WORK)

By Morris S. Viteles, *University of Pennsylvania*

The selection and placement of competent workers, discussed in the preceding chapter, represents only the first step in insuring efficiency and adjustment on the job. After the worker is employed, much remains to be done to make sure that he will fully use his capacity under conditions favorable to ease, safety, and satisfaction at work.

Psychology and Industrial Training

Adequate training is the first essential in accomplishing these objectives. An individual who is fully qualified for the job may become an inefficient worker because he has not been properly trained. The recognition of the importance of training is leading industry to substitute systematic programs of training for the traditional procedure of "breaking-in" a new worker, in which instruction was largely left to the caprice of the foreman or of some other minor official.

Concentrated versus Distributed Learning in the Acquisition of Industrial Skills.—This improvement or "rationalization" of the training program calls for the application of principles of learning, developed originally in laboratory investigations of the type described in Chapter XIV, which prove to be of great significance for the development of industrial skills. So, for example, findings from experiments on *concentrated* versus *distributed* learning suggest that wherever feasible, intensive training programs with long practice periods should be replaced by programs calling for shorter practice periods distributed over a longer time.

In learning industrial skills, as in acquiring other skills, there is a point beyond which further practice during one time-interval pro-

478

duces no effective return. Because distributed practice provides more opportunity for the consolidation and organization of the patterns of muscular response characterizing industrial skill, its beneficial effect may continue for long periods, while prolonged practice periods may actually be harmful.

The practical implications of this principle appear in an experiment by Henshaw and Holman [1] who made use of 3 groups of 30 subjects in studying the influence of varying distributions of practice upon learning a chain-assembly operation. Each group worked 80 minutes each morning on this task. During the afternoon Group I spent an additional 80 minutes in assembling chains; Group II spent the time in cartridge filling; and Group III remained unemployed. After 2 weeks of work the performance on chain assembly of the 3 groups was found to be practically identical in spite of the fact that Group I had actually twice as much practice on chain assembly as Groups II and III. After a lapse of a few months, 5 subjects from Groups II and III were again employed at chain assembly for 80 minutes each morning for an additional 2 weeks. After an initial drop in amount of work done, due to the interruption of practice, this group continued to improve to the point where the rate of output was considerably above that of Group I after the same total time had been spent in practice.

The results show that the lengthening of the daily training period beyond a certain point, in the case of this task, had no beneficial effect on learning. Such results, as well as those obtained by others, indicate the importance of determining the optimum arrangement or distribution of training time for each industrial operation.

Overlearning in Industry.—The experimental study of learning by psychological methods is of value not only in determining the optimum arrangement of training period but also the optimum length of the total time to be devoted to training in a specific industrial task. Meyer,[2] for example, examined the practice curves of 3 workers on 3 machine operations. On one, production time per unit decreased to approximately 65 per cent of the initial time by the end of 30 days, beyond which no further improvement appeared. On the second, the integration of response at a fixed level did not appear until approximately the 40th day of work and reached a consistent plateau level only after 50 days of work, when production time was decreased to approximately 60 per cent of that required at the beginning of the work period. On the third operation, involving more complex machine work, there was no sign of levelling-off of production at the end of approximately 45 days, when observations were discontinued, in spite of the fact that production time per unit had decreased to approximately 38 per cent of the initial time.

Experiments by Engel [3] and others also indicate that in the acquisition of industrial skills, as in other instances of learning, waste may ensue from excessive overlearning. In practical terms, such experiments have suggested the desirability of establishing experimentally the optimum total training time for each job * at that point beyond which further training, under given incentives and conditions of work, will produce no significant increase in rate of work or improvement in quality of work.

Industrial Application of the Practice Curve.—It is to be observed that the practice curve, and more particularly the plateau, is used as a criterion in determining when the effect of practice has decreased to the point where, for all practical purposes, training may be discontinued. Observations of the plateau effect have also been used in determining the point in the training program at which incentives, financial or other, should be introduced to prevent the consolidation of performance at a rate markedly below the limit of improvement. Kitson,[4] for example, has demonstrated the existence of arrested progress in learning in an experiment involving 40 experienced hand compositors with an average experience of 8 years. The institution of a wage incentive plan resulted in a doubling of production within a period of a year and a half. According to Kitson, the incentive provoked spurts of learning, leading to settlement at a higher plateau level which, it is conceivable, might be raised still further with further changes in motivation or conditions of work.†

The implications for industrial training of the influence of incen-

---

* And for the individual where selection fails to provide a group that is relatively homogeneous from the viewpoint of "educability" in the task.

† See pages 399 f.

tives upon learning have recently been considered by Mace [5] in experiments, involving 88 university students learning complicated arithmetical operations, designed, in part, to compare rates of improvement (a) when the subject attempted to meet a specified "absolute" standard of performance; and (b) when the subject undertook to improve upon his previous performance, etc. From these experiments Mace concludes that best results in learning are obtained when (1) the beginnner is provided with a standard well within his capacity; and (2) subsequent standards are adjusted to the performance of the worker so that continued progress may be added to the consciousness of initial achievement. The superior performance of subjects learning under such conditions, according to Mace, is due in lesser part to the intensification of the will-to-work and in larger part to the prolongation of this will-to-work throughout the practice period. These findings and conclusions, it may be noted, are in harmony with those which might be expected from the operation of the "level of aspiration" postulated by Hoppe.[6]

It is apparent that practice curves, properly employed, can furnish invaluable aid in promoting the acquisition of industrial skill. They may perhaps also be used to supplement selection techniques in predicting from the character of the curve at an early stage of practice the ultimate performance of the new worker. Poppelreuter,[7] of Germany, has urged this procedure as preferable to short psychological tests of the analytic type in forecasting ultimate performance. Although there is some question as to the validity of this technique [8] and many difficulties of a practical and theoretical nature to be considered before it can be widely used, there is evidence that practice curves can be useful for this purpose. Apart from its other functions in industry, the practice curve furnishes a record of improvement which can be used in supplying learners with the *knowledge of results* useful in furthering continued improvement with practice.

Whole versus Part Method in Acquiring Industrial Skill. —Experiments on the *whole* versus the *part method* of learning find their application in industry in determining whether a learner should be taught a new job as a whole or whether various parts should be learned separately and then fitted together. Exponents of the part method, such as Berling [9] of Germany, Gastev [10] of U.S.S.R., insist that a learner be required to practice the separate operations of a task before attempting to do the task as a whole. So, for example, the machinist apprentice practices filing on a special device which provides a graphic record of movement, pressure exerted, and "levelness." He then goes on to develop accuracy in hammering by aiming at points placed on a lead block. Following this he proceeds to practice on micrometer readings, and so on. Only after the required level of efficiency has been reached on each separate operation is the apprentice given an opportunity to coordinate these skills by work on the kind of material ordinarily used by the machinist and on the whole task of transforming this material into a useful object or tool.

In contrast is the more common "modified whole" method of machinist apprentice training which puts the apprentice to work on the whole process of filing and hammering and measuring a piece of metal to produce a useful tool or object. In this training system, the complexity of the task is increased with the years of apprenticeship, but each task is performed as a whole, all of the constituent skills being practiced in proper sequence.

Experimental Studies of Whole and Part Methods of Training.— Experimental studies of this problem include an investigation by Beeby [11] who measured the effectiveness of training by whole and parts by the method of *simultaneous combination*, where the right hand and left hand, having been separately trained in tracing squares on the right and left side of the apparatus respectively, were forced to perform these movements together, and by *simultaneous division*, in which the hands having been trained to perform the movements together were required to perform them separately. From his findings Beeby concludes that the "whole" method of learning a muscular habit is preferable to the "part" method, although he also points to the need of further research in order to determine the degree of complexity of movement at which the disadvantages of the "whole" method outweigh its advantages.

Typical of experiments in industry is a study by Dilger [12] who compared two methods of instruction in the use of the file. One group of 15 subjects practiced filing for one half-hour each day, 2 times a day, for a period of 16 days, under the ordinary conditions of production, in preparing metal pieces of standard thickness with flat surfaces free from irregularities. The second group, matched with the first on the basis of psychological test scores, alternated practice on filing on a special apparatus with practice on measuring.

At the end of 16 days each worker was given 2 work problems requiring from 3 to 8 hours for completion. The performance of the first group proved to be superior to that of the second, leading to the conclusion that the most desirable training program is that which promptly gives the worker practical "whole" tasks of progressive difficulty to be done under direct supervision, supplemented from time to time by test problems.

On the basis of laboratory and industrial studies there appears reason for questioning the usefulness of the part method in industry. A modified whole method may be preferable to the whole method where the task is very complex but even in such instances, as Link has pointed out, "it is best to give an individual an idea of the process as a whole, even if it is only a superficial idea." [13] After this, if necessary, the task can be split into "natural subdivisions," each subdivision being kept, however, as large as possible in order to take advantage of the associations between movements inherent in the task as a whole.

Practice in the "Best Method of Work."—Regardless of whether the whole or part method of learning is employed; whether training is concentrated or distributed in the development of industrial skill, workers must be taught and must practice only good methods of work. Left to their own resources, or given only casual training, workers may as readily adopt a relatively difficult, wasteful method of work as choose a method designed to promote efficiency, ease, and safety at work. For example, among "speckers" in the textile industry the author observed 3 distinct methods of manipulating tweezers in the removal of small specks of foreign matter from finished flannel cloth. Most of the girls, who had been given little guidance in learning the job, had "hit upon" a tapping wrist movement which was fatiguing, time-consuming, and detrimental to quality of production. Few in the group employed a rolling movement of the wrist, which represents the "best method" of work for this task.

The significance of such differences in working methods becomes apparent when it is found, as Barnes [14] has recently demonstrated, that the time required for grasping a small object, such as a thin steel washer frequently used in industrial operations, as a preliminary to picking it up and carrying it, may be 20 or 30 times as long as that required for grasping when the same object is to be moved by sliding. In an experimental study of an assembly task, in which a lock washer, a steel washer, and a rubber washer were assembled onto a bolt $\frac{3}{8}$ inch in diameter and one inch long, the combined time for "grasp and carry" was twice as great as that for "grasp and slide."

The problem in planning correct methods of work, in the interest of safety as well as efficiency, [15] is to select the "best way" of performing each task. This problem is discussed on pages 502 f., which also refer to the controversy between industrial engineers and psychologists with respect to the *"one best way* of work." For the purposes of this section it need merely be noted that the development of work habits to provide economy of effort and time, and to promote safety at work, involves not restrictive and rigid requirements as to methods of work, but reasonable conformity to a standard method designed in accordance with the principles listed on pages 503 f.

Transfer Effects in Industrial Training.—A not uncommon practice in industry is to employ practice on miniature models of equipment or on analogous tasks in training workers. Miniature models of a locomotive and a train of cars have been employed in instructing railroad engineers how to apply brakes to avoid both excessive jolting and accident. In training electric substation operators, miniature boards have been constructed in the belief that by practising on these the operator will acquire skill in the manipulation of the actual switches and other apparatus found in the electric substation. In training bill sorters, an attempt has been made to facilitate learning by practice on the analogous task of sorting cards with different designs. Exponents of a so-called "functional method" of training in U.S.S.R. provide practice on cancellation tests and substitution tests of increasing difficulty in order to develop speed and accuracy in inspecting overshoes. Practice on "judgment" tests is given to electric substation operators in training them to solve problems arising in the course of their work.

The usual assumption in such training is that the effect of practice in one specific activity may be transferred to another activity of the same kind, even to one involving the use of different materials. Laboratory investigations on transfer of the type described elsewhere in this text * have been supplemented by studies involving industrial tasks. In one experiment, by Langdon and Yates,[16] 32 subjects spent 80 minutes each morning and afternoon for 2 weeks on assembling bicycle chains. Before training was started and at the end of the 2 weeks each subject in this *experimental group* was given a series of 9 motor tests involving match insertion, threading links, placing rings on a rod, etc.

The same tests were given in the same order and at the same intervals to a *control group* of 28 subjects who had received no training on bicycle chain assembly. The experimental group showed no greater improvement on the allied tasks, that is, the transfer tests, than did the control group. Similar results on another experiment, involving the estimation of the size of steel balls lifted on a spoon, supported further the conclusions reached by these investigators that the effect of training in manual dexterity is specific and that there is no transfer from repetitive practice in one specialized task to another. Such findings and conclusions suggest that training on the task itself, under actual conditions of work, is the only certain method of promoting the integration of skills necessary for the successful performance of a task.

Transfer Effects in Attitudes and Methods of Work.—From experiments involving the assembly and wiring of an electric lamp-holder, Cox also concludes that "skill, developed by the mere repetition of one manual operation, confers little advantage on the performance of other operations that may be subsequently undertaken." [17] On the other hand, Cox found that systematic training in the general principles underlying manual control, illustrated by spe-

---

* See pages 361-365.

cific examples from manual operations, tends to improve performance over a wide range of manual activity. There is apparent here, even in simple manual tasks, transfer effects in terms of "ideas" and "attitudes," such as have appeared in experimental investigations in other fields, and which may have a wide application in "breaking-in" new employees and in the development of good work-habits in young people.

Shaw has applied such findings in the development of a preliminary training course on principles and methods of work (general motion study) given to all apprentices and to new female operatives employed by the Metropolitan Vickers Electric Company (Manchester, England).[18] It is also possible that beneficial results reported for the so-called "functional method of training" in U.S.S.R. reflect a gain in the way of attitudes of carefulness and precision transferred from practice on operations somewhat analogous to the work for which "technically illiterate" Russian workers, without experience in handling modern equipment or tools, were being trained.

Transfer Effects and Technological Change.—The general problem of transfer is of particular interest to the vocational psychologist because of the increasing flexibility demanded of workers in a changing industrial civilization. It is quite probable, as Koepke[19] has suggested, that the most immediate need in training for industry is the development of "bimanufiability," or skill in the simultaneous use of the two hands, to facilitate adjustment to a variety of semiskilled jobs in industry and easy transfer and adaptation to new tasks, new machines, new methods of work associated with rapid technological advances in industry. Training of this kind would emphasize or develop a "general skill," useful in many semiskilled jobs, which would make the services of an individual more marketable than they are under a system of vocational education which stresses expertness in a single specific task or job. Further research on this problem is needed as a preliminary to the formulation of an adequate philosophy and suitable methods of vocational training and reëducation as aids in promoting individual adjustment to work in the face of technological and other changes.

In Summary.—Training methods in industry have been improved by the application of principles of learning developed on the basis of psychological experimentation. In many diverse industries significant gains in efficiency have followed from the rationalization of the training program, including reductions in time taken to pack chocolates; increased production in roughing silverware and in the output of coal; decrease in time required for training machinist apprentices, electric linemen, and other workers,[20] etc. Such material gains have been accompanied by increased ease of work and improved individual adjustment to the job.

PSYCHOLOGICAL TECHNIQUES IN ACCIDENT PREVENTION

In 1938, in American industry, there were approximately 16,500 fatal accidents and over 1,350,000 nonfatal injuries. It is estimated that approximately 90 per cent of these resulted from failure of the human element. Motor vehicles, operated for business and pleasure, accounted for approximately 39,600 deaths, 1,150,000 personal injuries, and an economic loss of $1,500,000,000.[21] It is generally conceded that only about 5 per cent of motor vehicle accidents result from mechanical failures; 95 per cent being attributable to inadequacies of the man operating the machine!

In reducing the number of accidents caused by human failures, the organized safety movement has resorted largely to educational campaigns, competitions, posters, and other forms of mass propaganda. These have been effective in lowering both the frequency and severity of accidents in industry. However, psychological experimentation indicates very definitely that mass propaganda must be supplemented by a more individualized approach if accidents are to be reduced to a minimum.

Individual Differences in "Accident Proneness."—This conclusion is based on experimental findings which show that accidents do not distribute themselves by chance, but that they happen frequently to some men and infrequently to others. Studies in diverse industries have revealed the existence in some individuals of a heightened susceptibility to accident, or "accident-proneness" from which others are relatively free.

Greenwood and Woods,[22] of the Industrial Fatigue Research Board of Great Britain, were among the first to study these individual differences in accident susceptibility. They started their investigations with three hypotheses:

(1) *A hypothesis of simple chance distribution,* which assumes that inequality in accident rates is due to a chance distribution and that it is purely a matter of "accident," in the proper sense of the word.

(2) *A hypothesis of biased distribution,* which assumes that having one accident alters the chance of the same individual having another accident by either lessening or increasing his susceptibility to accident.

(3) *A distribution of unequal liability hypothesis,* which assumes that some individuals are more liable to accidents than others under equal conditions of exposure to risk, whether or not they have sustained any previous accident. This presupposes that there is something in the individual quite apart from any accidents he may have had that makes him more liable than others to sustain accidents.

A comparison of distributions of industrial accidents with theoretical distributions showed that the first hypothesis failed to account for the observed distributions of accidents. The theoretical distributions of the other two hypotheses coincided fairly well with the actual distributions of accidents in industry but, on the whole, the assumption of unequal liability was superior to the other.

Early Experimental Data on Accident-Proneness.—In order further to test this finding, accidents sustained by individuals in one period were compared with accidents sustained by the same individuals in another period. If involvement in accidents is wholly a matter of "chance," the number of accidents sustained by individuals in one period should be altogether independent of the number sustained by them in another period. Examining the records of 411 workers employed in the same location between 1913 and 1924, Newbold, another English investigator, actually found that those involved in 1 or 0 accidents during the first 6 years of employment averaged 0.32 accidents during the second 6 years, while employees with 2 or more accidents during the first 6 years averaged 1.06 accidents during the second 6 years of employment.[23]

Approaching the problem from the same point of view, Marbe, a German psychologist, examined the accident records of officers in the German army who had carried insurance for a period of 10 years. Those with no accidents during the first 5 years of this insurance period averaged 0.52 accidents during the second 5 years. Officers with 1 accident during the first 5-year period averaged 0.91 accidents during the second 5-year period; those with 2 or more accidents during the first 5 years averaged 1.34 accidents during the second 5 years.[24]

TABLE IV.—ACCIDENT RATES IN TWO SUCCESSIVE PERIODS
OF 3 YEARS EACH *

Accident-Group 1931-33 Accidents Per Driver	Same Groups 1934-36 Accidents Per Driver
0	0.101
1	0.199
2	0.300
3	0.484
4	0.700

* From *The Accident-Prone Driver, House Document No. 462, Part 6*, Washington, U. S. Govt. Printing Office, 1938.

Accident-Proneness in the Operation of Motor Vehicles.—Studies of motor vehicle operators have furnished particularly useful data on accident-proneness. In Connecticut,[25] the accident records of a random sampling of 29,531 drivers were investigated for the 6-year period 1931-1936, inclusive. Table IV shows the accident rate of these drivers during two successive periods of 3 years. It is apparent that those having multiple accidents in the first half of the 6-year period tended to repeat again in the second half, in accordance with the expectations inherent in the hypothesis involving a distribution of unequal liability.

Accident-Prone Individuals Have More Accidents.—The existence of accident-proneness reveals itself not only in the fact that the same drivers repeatedly have accidents, but in the related fact that such drivers pile up a tremendously greater number of accidents during any one period than do those who are not susceptible to accidents. So, for example, in the Connecticut sampling, it was found that accident repeaters, who constituted 4 per cent of the total drivers and 20 per cent of those who had accidents, were involved in 36 per cent of all of the accidents during the 6-year period.

Industrial studies have furnished striking examples of this situation. A study of 553 accidents sustained during a 3-year period by 321 drivers employed by the Socony-Vacuum Oil Co. (Philadelphia Division) showed that 14 per cent of the driving force was responsible for 47 per cent of all the accidents, 25 men having incurred 211 accidents in 3 years' time.[26]

Another investigation, covering 1871 accidents reported by a group of companies employing 1294 taxicab drivers, revealed that 20 per cent of the drivers were responsible for about 51 per cent of all the accidents. One-half the men were responsible for about 82 per cent of all the accidents. Approximately 25 per cent had no accidents at all during the period covered by the reports. Since these drivers operate similar equipment under the same conditions, the higher frequency of accidents in the case of the accident repeaters cannot be attributed to chance, but to habits, or attitudes, or psychomotor dispositions that make each man in the group peculiarly susceptible to accidents.[27] Similar facts and conclusions appear in a study, by the Sub-Committee on Commercial Drivers of the Committee on the Psychology of the Highway, Division of Anthropology and Psychology, National Research Council, covering accident records for the years 1933-35 of 4 companies operating large fleets of motor vehicles and employing some 1400 drivers.[28]

Discovery and Treatment of Accident-Prone Individuals. —The question which arises from this discovery that some men are more susceptible to accident than others is how to detect and how to treat the accident-prone individual. There is evidence, in studies by Farmer and Chambers,[29] that psychological tests can be used in the detection of accident-prone individuals. One such investigation, involving 1800 subjects employed in diverse occupations, showed that the accident rate of the 25 per cent with the lowest scores on a weighted battery of intelligence and aesthetokinetic tests was about 2.5 times as great as that of the remaining 75 per cent. Further follow-up for periods of from 1 to 4 years revealed an increasing relationship between test scores and accident incidence. This suggests that the tests measured an important and relatively stable factor in accident causation whose effect makes itself felt with increased exposure to the conditions of the working situation. This study also showed that there is a definite relationship between capacity for work and safety in work, in as much as those who made higher scores on the tests proved in general to be the more proficient workers.

Detection of accident-proneness prior to employment is particularly important in the case of applicants for employment in the transportation industry, where the liability to accident is high because of the very nature of the job. Reduction in the frequency of accidents following from the application of tests in selection, such as reported for the Milwaukee Electric Railway and Light Company, the Paris Combined Transport Services, and other organizations, on pages 467 f., again shows that accident-proneness can be detected in advance of employment.

Clinical Methods in the Treatment of Accident-Proneness.— Tests do not eliminate all accident-prone individuals. Moreover, there is evidence that individuals who are essentially accident-free may develop heightened accident-susceptibility subsequent to employment as the end-effect of ill health, emotional disturbances, difficulties in the home or in the plant, the development of bad work habits, and so on. Accident records of such individuals can be improved by *clinical study* designed to determine the causes of accidents in the individual case, followed by suitable treatment.

The character of the treatment depends upon the diagnosis. It may take the form of systematic instruction to replace faulty habits of operation where these seem to be involved in the accidents. In other instances medical treatment, discipline, encouragement, or supervisory follow-up may be used in rehabilitating the accident-prone employee. Treatment is differential in character. It is based on the recognition that there are many different causes of accidents, that these may be combined in different patterns in different individuals, and that the remedy must be adapted to the cause.

Between January 1, 1929, and January 1, 1930, 154 accident repeaters were studied and treated in an "accident clinic" maintained by The Milwaukee Electric Railway and Light Company.[30] These men showed an 81.5 per cent reduction in accidents as compared with a 25 per cent reduction for the system as a whole. The average accident per man in this accident-prone group was reduced from 2.8 to .51, a figure well below the average for the entire system. Moreover, of the men handled in the "accident clinic" only 3 were recommended for discharge. The Cleveland Railway Company reports equally favorable results from its program of accident prevention through individual case study.[31] An elaborate program of individual study and treatment of accident-prone drivers was undertaken in 1927 by the Boston Elevated Railway Company. As a result of the application of appropriate procedures, the actual net savings in the cost of injuries and damages in 1929 as compared with 1928 amounted to $300,670.73.[32]

The Noncommercial Driver and Highway Accidents.—The successful application of psychological methods in decreasing the incidence of motor vehicle accidents in the transportation industry has led to the application of the same methods in the attempt to reduce accidents among the operators of private automobiles. So, for example, extensive experiments have been conducted at Iowa State College,[33] at Harvard University, and in London, under the auspices of the National Institute of Industrial Psychology of Great Britain, to isolate the traits characteristic of "accident repeaters" as contrasted with safe drivers.

For this purpose elaborate apparatus has been constructed, including measures of vigilance, speed estimation, glare, traffic-light color discrimination, depth perception, etc. These have been applied on a large scale throughout the United States and elsewhere through the efforts of automobile clubs, insurance companies, and other organizations interested in motor vehicle accident prevention. In taking these tests people have been led to believe that deficiencies in their performance indicate deficiencies in driving ability which may seriously handicap them as safe drivers.

Unfortunately, a careful study of the elaborate data published by DeSilva and others [34] who are inclined to place great reliance upon such tests in dealing with the driver of the private automobile shows practically no significant relationship between individual performance on these tests and individual safety on the road. As valuable as such instruments may be in experimental work, "we have not yet reached the point where the apparatus can distinguish the repeater from the normal driver or predict that the deficient person will have accidents." This statement, quoted from a letter by an investigator formerly attached to the staff of the Harvard Traffic Bureau, more correctly summarizes the actual status of the widely commercialized "tests of driving ability" than do many of the published statements.

Difficulties in Standardizing General Tests of Driving Ability.— There are many possible reasons for the failure of tests applied to private drivers to produce favorable results comparable to those obtained through the administration of tests to applicants for driving jobs in the transportation industry. It may be that the tests developed in the university research laboratories are not as adequate as those developed by psychologists working in the industrial situation. A perhaps more reasonable explanation is to be found in the fact that experimental groups and accident records are much better controlled in the industrial situation and therefore give more valid findings. The incompetent private driver, too, is in a position to compensate for his deficiencies to an extent impossible in the industrial situation, where schedules must be maintained, cars operated in all kinds of weather, and so on. This gives a better discrimination between "safe" and "unsafe" drivers in the transporation industry than can be obtained in samplings of private automobile operators.

Another important limitation is the fact that the so-called "tests of driving ability" make an attempt to reproduce conditions on the road, but do not and perhaps cannot actually succeed in doing so. So, for example, in the laboratory tests of reaction time, the driver's attention is concentrated on one point, while on the road the field of attention must be kept broad.[35] There are cues on the road not present in the laboratory test. These and other factors all contribute to detract from the validity of tests of the type developed by Lauer, DeSilva and others.

Training Drivers.—Considerations such as those discussed above, and the fact that "nonaccident-prone" drivers, involved in occasional accidents, contribute so largely to the annual total of accidents, suggest the desirability of focusing less attention upon a laboratory testing program and more attention upon other techniques in reducing accidents among operators of private automobiles. Among the most important of these are adequate training programs which will promote the development of safe driving habits and attitudes conducive to safe operation.[36]

Systematic courses in motor vehicle operation for high school students, of the type developed by Neyhart, of Penn State, probably represent a psychologically sound advance although, as Toops and Haven point out, considerably more research is needed to determine the exact value of this approach.[37] Training for new drivers should probably be supplemented by periodic reëxaminations, under standard road conditions, of experienced drivers, particularly of accident repeaters, with suitable re-instruction when needed. A periodic checking of driving habits by each driver, of the type suggested by Toops and Haven,[38] and other procedures will also find a place in a well-rounded program of preventing highway accidents attributable to the human element.

Specific Factors in Accident Causation.—Investigations of accident susceptibility and programs for detecting and treating accident-proneness have been supplemented by studies of the influence of specific factors upon the incidence of accidents. These show that accidents are more numerous among young and inexperienced workers than among the old, although they tend to be of greater severity among the latter. Training in safe methods of work serves to prevent accidents. Accidents are more frequent in the extremes of heat and cold than at a moderate temperature. The number is increased under unfavorable lighting conditions. The accident rate is adversely affected by fatigue; speed-up of production; by the week-end's cessation from work. Accident frequency does not increase with night work although the causes of accidents vary with the shift. Accidents are more numerous among the unhealthy than among the healthy, and possibly number more among the industrially inefficient than the efficient.[39]

In the transporation industry the author has investigated the influence of sex upon safety by comparing the accident rate of 2000 male taxicab drivers with that of 40 women taxicab drivers operating under exactly the same conditions, both representing the complete complement employed by two companies in Philadelphia. Over an 11-month period male taxicab drivers were responsible for 0.257 accidents per thousand miles in operation, while women, carefully selected and trained so that they represented a sampling of superior female drivers, were responsible for 0.722 accidents per thousand miles, or approximately three times as many as the men. The same ratio applied to accidents per thousand dollars of revenue.[40]

Designing Machines for Accident Prevention.—Attention has recently been directed to the consideration of differences in the "accident liability" of various jobs. Because of the very nature of the tasks and machines involved, the job of comptometer-operating has a much lower accident liability than does the job of operating a street car or an electric switchboard. It has been suggested that much can be done to reduce the accident liability of jobs such as the latter by considering psychological factors in the design, construction, and installation of machines and tools.

Making Automobiles Safe.—According to Henderson, many of the seemingly inexplicable cases of cars going out of control are due to the 'self-righting reflex.' [41] By the operation of this reflex, the driver responds automatically to any sudden severe disturbance of equilibrium by gripping the wheel to steady himself and forcing his legs forward and his feet down on the accelerator pedal in the typical "extensor thrust." It is suggested that there should be another pedal for the left foot, at the place where it usually rests when not on the clutch, and that heavy pressure on this pedal should either close the throttle or cut off the power. A violent forward thrust of the legs would then slow down the car, instead of causing it to accelerate out of control.

As Dunlap [42] points out, body designs of up-to-date cars introduce needless hazards. The driver who fails to keep over to his side of the road may be merely "hoggish," but in many cases it is because he cannot see where his wheels are. Placing windows lower, setting the radiator and hood down, giving greater breadth to the windshield, would help to make driving safer by increasing the range of vision.

Apart from the changes in the car itself, accident liability in the operation of a motor vehicle can be reduced if colors most quickly discernible to all drivers were used in traffic lights. The importance of size, shape, and color of road markers and signs has been emphasized by Toops and Haven. They have also pointed out items in car construction which tend to increase accident liability, such as dash lights which contrast brilliantly with darkness outside of the car; lights which fail to pierce fog; glaring headlights; 6-inch front corner posts which make the automobile "just as potentially dangerous on the road as if all its metal parts were made of pewter instead of the finest tool steel." [43]

Designing Electric Substation Equipment for Safety.—The author has recently considered this problem from the viewpoint of electric substation operation,[44] particularly in terms of applying to the design of equipment and markers the principles of attention developed from laboratory studies and investigations in the psychology of advertising.

Observations in substations show, for example, that there has been a failure to capitalize upon differences in *form* or *shape* as a way of keeping an operator accurately oriented with respect to equipment under his charge. On most systems it is the practice to identify different electric buses * with markers of the same size and shape, labeled No. 1 Bus and No. 2 Bus, respectively. It is suggested that the danger of confusing buses, with all the hazards attached thereto, could be more easily avoided if markers of different shapes were used in identifying the buses, so that, for example, Bus No. 1 would invariably, in the mind of the operator, be the bus with the square marker, and Bus No. 2 that with the octagonal or perhaps circular marker. With differences in the shapes of markers could also be

---

* Main copper conductors.

combined differences in color, so that Bus No. 1 would invariably be thought of as the bus with the red-and-white square marker, and Bus No. 2 as that with the octagonal or circular yellow and black marker.

In the construction of switchboard panels it is common practice to depend solely upon the color of identically shaped indicating lights, generally red and green, to indicate the set-up as the operator "sizes up" the situation before proceeding with his work. The effectiveness of the indication, from the viewpoint of attracting and controlling attention, could be considerably improved if a direction clue were added to that of color. If this were done, an illuminated red bar in line with the bus might be chosen as the universal symbol for a closed circuit breaker; an illuminated green bar at right angles to the bus as the symbol for an open circuit breaker, thereby capitalizing upon the principle of *direction* in guiding attention to the operation to be performed.

The principles of *accommodation of attention* and of *motion*; the *square root law of effect*; findings of studies on *color contrast* effects and *legibility* of print are other examples of psychological data which have wide application in designing electric substation equipment so as to decrease the probability of "mental lapses" and the dangers of accidents and errors in its operation.

In Summary.—It is apparent that the psychological approach to the study of accidents has already produced a wealth of data of extreme significance in the elimination of this source of waste within and outside of industry. Perhaps more important than the facts and methods is the change in the underlying philosophy of accident prevention—the substitution of the principle of "causation" for the earlier philosophy of "fault"—the replacement of a fatalistic doctrine of "chance" by a dynamic policy of individual mental hygiene in accident prevention.

FATIGUE IN INDUSTRIAL WORK

Fatigue Indications.—The reduction of unnecessary fatigue represents an important step in maintaining fitness for work and in promoting the efficiency and the adjustment of the individual worker and the stability of the industrial system. Fatigue is characterized by (1) a decreased capacity for work, known as *work decrement;* (2) *modifications in the physiological state* of the individual; and (3) a *feeling of weariness.**

Fatigue and Production.—Decreased production and a lowering of the quality of production represent the most easily observed signs of fatigue in industry. Changes in output occurring as a result of fatigue are graphically presented in Fig. 23 which represents a typical daily production curve, showing the sluggish start while the worker is warming up; the sharp rise as he gets into his stride; a period of high production; followed by a decline in output toward the end of the working spell.

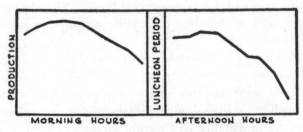

FIG. 23.—TYPICAL DAILY PRODUCTION CURVE.
(After Burtt, "Psychology and Industrial Efficiency," by permission of D. Appleton-Century Company, Inc.)

The shape of the work curve varies with the type of work, but that reproduced in Fig. 23 is the one most frequently observed. The objectives in fatigue reduction, in so far as industrial output is concerned, are to prevent the decline at the end of the working period, to raise the general level of production, and to eliminate excessive variations which frequently appear in the process of production within the working spell.

Physiological Changes in Fatigue.—Fatigue is marked not only by decreased output but by changes in the physiological balance of the body involving the respiratory system, digestive system, nervous

* See pages 404-409.

system, endocrine glands, transformations in blood cells and chemistry, body secretions, etc., and other modifications in metabolism.*

The Feeling of Fatigue.—Fatigue is also accompanied by a feeling of weariness which appears with prolonged work.† This is the subjective sign of deep-seated bodily changes and decreased capacity for work which characterize fatigue. The feeling of fatigue may be accompanied by irritability, anxiety, excessive worry, disturbed emotional states of all kinds which lead to disturbances in social relationships both inside and outside of the plant. Unfortunately, laboratory studies of the type early reported by Poffenberger [45] show that there is no consistent relationship between decrease in output, changes in physiological state, and the feeling of fatigue. Because of this it has been found impracticable in laboratory and industrial experiments to employ the feeling of fatigue as an index of fatigue. However, particularly in English experiments, and to some extent in experiments recently conducted in U.S.S.R., this factor in industrial adjustment has been assigned its proper weight by the use of introspective reports along with measures of energy expenditure and changes in output in evaluating the fatigue status of the individual worker.

The Psychological versus the Economic Concept of Efficiency.—This emphasis upon the feeling of fatigue and upon physiological factors distinguishes the psychological approach in fatigue reduction from that of the industrial engineer. The latter has been inclined to treat efficiency as a purely economic concept, defined entirely in terms of changes in quantity and quality of output produced by variations in methods or conditions of work. In contrast, is the insistence of the psychologist that the term "efficient" should be restricted to that method or condition of work which makes possible maximum production and quality of work at the least physiological cost to the worker and which reduces to the minimum the feeling of fatigue and dissatisfaction experienced by the worker at his task. Viewed in this way one measure of efficiency is the relationship between energy input and output, that is, the proportion of the

* See pages 406 f.
† See pages 404-406.

energy that is usefully expended. Another criterion, as Thorndike has suggested, is the degree of satisfaction derived from the task "measured by the tendency of the individual to relax or abandon the action in question in spite of the fact that the work can be maintained at a constant level of production." [46]

The Elimination of Unnecessary Fatigue.

—A certain degree of fatigue is a normal result of activity. Fatigue becomes harmful if carried to the point where *recovery* is not adequate, where recuperation does not take place after a reasonable period of rest. The objective of fatigue study is to eliminate unnecessary fatigue produced by unsatisfactory conditions or methods of work, unsuitability for the job, and so on. This involves a consideration of the influence upon fatigue of (1) the *time element,* (2) the *work element,* (3) the *environmental element,* and (4) the *personal element.*[47]

The Time Element in Fatigue Reduction: *Hours of Work.*

—The number of hours spent at work has a definite relationship to fatigue. Industry's initial opposition to reducing hours of work has been largely overcome by the finding that production is not adversely affected and is frequently increased by shortening the working day and the length of the working week. For example, a reduction of hours from 58.2 to 50.6 per week in an English munitions plant was followed by a 39 per cent increase in average hourly output and a 21 per cent increase in average weekly production. Shortening the working week from 66 to 48.6 hours brought a 68 per cent increase in average hourly output and a 15 per cent increase in the average weekly production of women engaged in turning out fuse bodies. Such results have contributed to the progressive reduction of hours of work to a point, at least in the United States, where large returns in fatigue reduction are to be sought not primarily in curtailing hours of work, but in improving methods and conditions of work.

Rest-Pauses.—Although, in general, hours of work in American industry are not excessive, the fatigue produced by exertion during these hours can be decreased by the introduction of rest-pauses at periodic intervals. Vernon and Bedford,[48] of Great Britain, report an average increase of 6.2 per cent in production on 8 varied jobs from the introduction of 7- to 10-minute rest-pauses in the morning spell of work. In a plant manufacturing airplanes and airplane parts, the introduction of suitable rest-pauses by investigators attached to the Obucha Institute of Occupational Diseases, in Moscow, resulted in a 10 per cent increase in output with a pronounced reduction in fatigue as measured by performance on psychological tests.[49]

Equally striking results are reported by the Moscow Institute for the Organization, Hygiene and Economics of Labour. A "complex brigade" of scientists from this Institute, including an engineer, a time-study man, two physiologists, three psychologists, and a physical culture instructor, studied the effect of varied *régimes* (distribution of work time) upon the production of overshoe inspectors working on conveyor belts. A comparison of 6 *régimes,* differing in the lengths of alternating work and rest-pauses, showed marked variations in terms of effect upon output, quality of work and fatigue, as measured by standard psychological tests and by changes in sensory thresholds.

The selection of the optimum *régime* was followed by well-marked increases in output and ease of work, as measured in terms of the worker's feeling of comfort. This investigation is of interest in illustrating (1) the influence of changes in conditions of work upon fatigue in terms of psychological and physiological effects as well as in terms of production; and (2) a procedure of joint investigation by psychologists, physiologists, and industrial engineers, first employed in Great Britain, which can be beneficially applied in research on problems of industrial fatigue.

Findings from studies on the effect of rest-pauses include the demonstration that (1) the optimum length and location of the rest-pause vary from job to job; (2) the best time for introducing a rest-pause is immediately before the decline in rate of production; (3) the beneficial effects of rest-pauses increase with time, etc. In general these investigations have given support to the conclusion that *recovery* from fatigue is facilitated by rest-pauses, and to the principle that in industry "more output can be achieved by applying oneself steadily for short periods, and then resting, than by applying oneself less steadily and having no rest periods."

The Work Element in Fatigue Reduction.—Inefficient working methods and badly designed machines and tools are responsible for a tremendous waste of human effort at work.

Efficient Methods of Work.—One important step in eliminating such waste is to find the easiest and most economical way of doing the task. This need was early recognized by Frederick W. Taylor, the pioneering spirit in scientific management, who actually employed the practice of isolating and timing the constituent operations of a job in determining the "quickest and best" motions to be used by the worker.

Formal procedures for this purpose were first developed by F. B. and L. M. Gilbreth.[50] These include (1) a classification of movements into 17 fundamental elements, such as search, grasp, assemble, etc., each known as a *therblig;* (2) graphic methods for recording and charting the sequence of movements on a task; and (3) apparatus for photographing and timing motions. The analysis of charts and models prepared through the application of such *time and motion study* techniques leads to elimination of unnecessary movements and the combination of remaining motions into a standard method of work designated as the *one-best-way* of work. In this are combined the best elements observed in the study of different workers performing the same task.

Time and motion study procedures have been widely applied in all types of industry. Through their application Gilbreth succeeded in reducing the number of movements required for laying a brick from 18 to 5, and demonstrated that the number laid per hour could be increased from 120 to 350. In certain jobs in the paper industry production has been increased 100 per cent; in packing cloth about 150 per cent; in riveting 69 per cent, in part, by improving methods of work following a time and motion study analysis of each job.

Unfortunately, in most instances it is impossible to determine exactly the extent to which increased production depends upon the improvement of working methods because, in practice, variations in working methods have ordinarily been accompanied by the introduction of new systems of wage payments and other modifications in conditions of work. Moreover, there has generally been a failure to measure the influence of changes in working methods upon the energy consumption and feelings of the workers. For these and other reasons, psychologists, although recognizing the inherent soundness and value of time and motion study analysis, have been hesitant to approve whole-heartedly results obtained through its use in industry.

The "One-Best-Way" of Work.—In particular, serious questions have been raised concerning the concept of "one-best-way" of work. It is pointed out, for example, that the fastest motion, frequently included in the final series, may not be the best from the viewpoint of fatigue. There is objection to the practice of arriving at a uniform, standard method of work by building-up a composite of the seemingly "best" ways in which various expert workers do separate parts or elements of the job, since these "little best ways" may be far more effective and energy-saving for some workers than for others.[51] In general, there is evidence of neglect of individual differences in musculature, in leverage, in other aspects of physical, physiological, and mental make-up. The existence of such differences makes it highly questionable whether one set of movements, however good they may be, can be regarded as the best movements for every worker.

The Characteristics of Good Work Movements.—Such criticism does not represent a denial of the importance of discovering easy and economical methods of work. However, reasonable rather than too rigid requirements as to the best methods of work seem desirable. Principles for evaluating work movements and for selecting methods which will reduce fatigue and promote satisfaction while increasing output have been outlined by Myers,[52] founder of the National Institute of Industrial Psychology of Great Britain, as follows:

(1) Successive movements should be so related that one movement passes easily into that which follows, each ending in a position favorable for the beginning of the next movement.

(2) The order of movements should be so arranged that little direct attention is needed for passage from one to another.

(3) The sequence of movements should be so framed that an easy rhythm can be established in the automatic performance of the various elements of the operation.

(4) Continuous movements are preferable to angular movements which involve sudden changes in the direction of movement.

(5) The number of movements should be reduced as far as possible within the scope of limitations suggested above.

(6) Simultaneous use of both hands should be encouraged.

(7) When a forcible stroke is required, the direction of movement and placement of material should be so arranged that, so far as practicable, the stroke is delivered when the movement has reached its greatest momentum.

The application of such principles should result in a series of standard operations to be used in training workers and to which, in general, each worker should be required to conform. This does not imply that industry should expect absolute slavish and drill-like similarity of movements on the part of the workers. Individual modifications which creep in after initial training, so long as they do not affect quality or quantity of production or safety of work, must be allowed. However, where modification results in a reduction of output or quality of work, in increased fatigue or increased danger of accidents, steps must be taken to retrain the worker to the use of the standard method of work which, if properly formulated, represents a powerful safeguard of both individual welfare and industrial efficiency.

Posture and Distribution of Load.—The posture adopted during work, the weight of the load carried, and the distribution of load are important factors in inducing fatigue. Bedale, of the Industrial Health Research Board, has demonstrated that energy cost per unit of work remains lowest when there is least departure from normal, erect posture in handling loads. From studies by Cathcart and others the conclusion has been reached that loads carried should not exceed 40 per cent of the body weight of the worker for continuous work or be greater than 50 per cent for intermittent carrying. Experiments with various ways of loading and wheeling barrows showed that less energy is used, as measured by oxygen consumption, when barrows are properly loaded and are wheeled at a normal, brisk, walking pace without extra stops.[53]

Design and Speed of Machines.—The avoidance of unnecessary fatigue calls for a study of machine design as a basis for eliminating unnecessary movements and awkward postures. Studies of type-writers, of laundry machines, leather working machines, boring machines, ironing machines and other industrial equipment have led to changes in the interest of ease and economy of effort at work.[54]

Speed and *rhythm* are important considerations in fatigue elimination. There is evidence, for example, that work with machines and moving belts is facilitated by the regular and rhythmic character of activity as contrasted with the irregular and sporadic nature of movement of manual work when the tempo is under the control of the worker. However, for every type of work and also for the individual worker there is an optimum speed or rhythm which makes it possible to gain maximum production with the least expenditure of energy and with improved feelings of ease, comfort, and satisfaction.

These conclusions are supported by the findings of a recent English plant and laboratory investigation of machine-feeding processes.[55] These show that efficiency and satisfaction in machine feeding are largely dependent on the relation between the speed of the machine and the capacity of the operator. If the former exceeds the latter, the result is an irregular rate of working conducive to strain and fatigue. In such cases a reduction in the speed of the machine brings increased output and pleasure in work. If the speed is much below the capacity of the worker, the conditions are distasteful and conducive to boredom. If the speed of the machine is adjusted to the average capacity of a selected group of workers, it is too fast for some and too slow for others, so that output and comfort may be increased by adjusting the speed of each machine to the capacity of the individual concerned. A closer adjustment may be effected by the use of a variable speed device which makes it possible to adapt the speed to the changing capacity of the worker during the day.

The Environmental Element in Fatigue Elimination.— The conditions under which work is done, including illumination, ventilation, plant lay-out, and so on, are important factors in fatigue.

Illumination.—Laboratory experiments reported by Luckiesh and Moss show that energy expenditure, as measured by (1) pressure of the finger on a key while reading and (2) rate of heartbeat, is greater when reading is done under low illumination than under high.[56] Production can be considerably increased and fatigue reduced by providing adequate illumination and through the elimination of glare, shadow effects, and so on.

In one investigation, by Hess and Harrison, differences in output of roller-bearing inspectors were found to vary directly with changes in illumination, increasing to 12.5 per cent above the base with an increase of illumination from 5 to 20 foot candles. A study by the Industrial Health Research Board showed that only when the intensity of artificial illumination approached 24 foot candles did the efficiency of typesetting, as judged by the number of errors, turned letters, and total output, approximate the efficiency in good daylight lighting. When illumination was only 2 foot candles, one quarter of the possible output was lost, the mistakes more than doubled, and the fatigue experienced by the compositor materially increased.

Ventilation.—Atmospheric conditions exert a profound influence on the production and well-being of workers. In the plant of the Eastman Kodak Company an improvement in ventilating workrooms was followed by a 4 per cent increase in output and a 50 per cent reduction in illness. Studies by the Philadelphia Electric Company show that the introduction of air conditioning into offices was followed by a 45 per cent reduction in loss of time because of illness among employees. The following are typical findings from studies by the Industrial Health Research Board on the effects of atmospheric conditions: [57]

(1) Using involuntary rest-pauses as measures of fatigue, it was found that miners usually rested about 7 minutes per hour under good conditions. In hot damp air and little air movement they took off 22 minutes per hour, and their rate of production fell off 41 per cent.

(2) In weaving, high temperatures and humidity cause fewer breakages of threads but more fatigue to workers. Raising the air-

movement velocity to 147 feet per minute increased the comfort and efficiency of workers without adversely affecting breakages.

(3) Older men (50 or more) are more affected by heat than younger men (30 to 39).

Noise.—Excessive noise adversely affects industrial output and fatigue. Laboratory experiments by Morgan,[58] Laird,[59] and others show that work in noisy surroundings is actually costlier, in terms of energy consumption, than work under quiet conditions. In Laird's experiment introspective observations indicate the presence of a feeling of annoyance during noisy conditions of work.

English experiments show that, in a weaving shed, production was increased 3 per cent and personal efficiency 7½ per cent through the use of "ear defenders" which reduced noise intensity by about 50 per cent and simultaneously increased the feeling of well-being.[60] Similar improvements in proofreading, typing, and other forms of industrial work give further evidence of the importance of reducing the unfavorable effect of this environmental element upon fatigue.

The Personal Element in Fatigue Reduction.—The clothing worn by the worker, his diet, habits of sleep, and home conditions help to determine how quickly the worker will tire on the job. Haggard and Greenberg, on the basis of experiments in the physiological laboratory and in a tennis-shoe factory, recommend that the number of meals should be raised to 5 or 6 a day as a means of reducing industrial fatigue.[61] Proper shoes for meter readers, policemen, and others who do considerable walking on the job have been helpful in making work easier. Workmen whose physical condition is impaired by poor health are more susceptible to fatigue than are healthy individuals. The cooperation of the physician and physiologist is required in eliminating such sources of unnecessary fatigue and, in particular, in selecting men who are physically fit for the job.

Of particular interest to the psychologist, in so far as the personal element in fatigue reduction is concerned, is the relation between suitability for the job and fatiguability. There is some evidence that there is such a relationship, that the more competent workers resist fatigue more easily than do those who are essentially unqualified for the work. However, difficulties in isolating the variable of fatigue from other factors which influence total production, and in developing adequate tests of fatiguability, have retarded the accumulation of unequivocal data to be used in reaching conclusions with respect to the actual relation between "suitability" and "fatiguability."

BOREDOM AT WORK

Closely allied to the feeling of fatigue is the feeling of boredom, or *monotony,* which appears to be associated with repetitive work in industry. Restlessness, yawning, loss of interest, growing difficulty in keeping at the task, an increase in the effort required to maintain efficiency are some of the many overt symptoms of monotony. Less evident on the surface, but repeatedly demonstrated in both laboratory and industrial investigations, is the inclination toward the overestimation of time intervals.

The Monotony Curve.—Another important symptom of monotony is the characteristic nature of the progress of work during the day as reflected in the daily working curve. One feature of monotony in work is the tendency for production to *fall* instead of to rise during the middle of the working spell.[62] Apparently, as Myers [63] has explained, the worker comes to his work feeling ready to go ahead with it, slows up in the middle of the spell as he becomes bored with the work, and speeds up at the end of the day in anticipation of its end. He thus produces a curve inverse in shape to that of the usual production curve.* Associated with this change in the shape of the curve is the marked irregularity in production from period to period. Boredom causes a more variable rate of working, characterized by repeated fluctuations in the time taken to complete consecutive units of output.

These characteristics of production in monotonous work are well illustrated in Fig. 24, showing the production of girls engaged in the manufacture of electric lamps, whose feelings of boredom were noted introspectively. The curves representing the average rate of work during 5-minute periods of a composite day are shown by the broken lines whereas the general tendency is represented by the heavy black lines.

---

* See page 498.

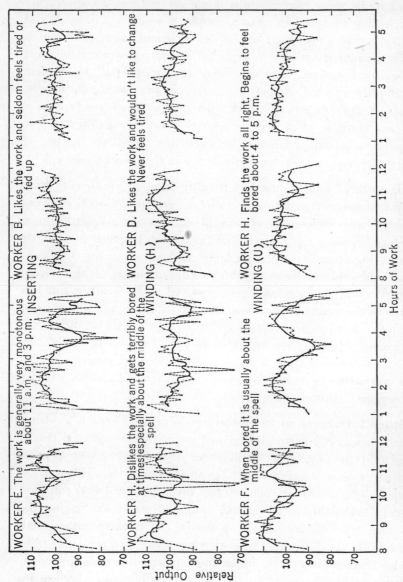

FIG. 24. Output curves obtained when boredom was experienced (left half) and almost absent (right half) in different industrial processes. (From Wyatt, Fraser, and Stock, "Effects of Monotony in Work." London: Ind. Fat. Res. Bd. Report No. 56, 1929, by permission of Controller of His Britannic Majesty's Stationery Office.)

Individual Differences in Susceptibility to Monotony.— Investigations show that all individuals are not equally susceptible to the feeling of boredom. For example, a recent study by Wyatt and Langdon [64] shows that of 355 experienced unmarried female workers employed on simple types of repetitive work who were assessed for boredom, 3 per cent were *hardly affected,* 33 per cent were *slightly affected,* 38 per cent *experienced a moderate degree,* 23 per cent *suffered severely,* and 3 per cent were *seldom free* from boredom. Here, as in earlier studies, wide individual differences in susceptibility appear. Moreover, workers for whom the feeling of boredom represents a serious problem are in the distinct minority.

Monotony and General Intelligence.—Experiments have clearly demonstrated that differences in susceptibility to monotony are associated with differences in general intelligence. Wyatt, Fraser, and Stock [65] gave intelligence tests to operators engaged in winding and inserting filaments in electric lamps, in soap wrapping, in chocolate packing, and in tobacco weighing. Output curves obtained from the workers of inferior intelligence proved to be steadier and less affected by the midspell depression than those of the more intelligent operatives. Introspective reports indicated that, on the whole, workers of inferior intelligence appeared to like the repetitive processes and seldom suffered from boredom, while those of superior intelligence seemed to be industrial misfits and would have been better employed on less repetitive jobs.

Other Influences in Monotonous Work.—There is evidence that whether or not an individual will experience boredom depends, in part, on traits other than intelligence. That temperament plays an important role is suggested in laboratory studies by Thompson,[66] Wunderlich,[67] Winkler,[68] and in the investigation by Wyatt and Langdon.[69] Inability to mechanize simple motor tasks; having the mind free for "daydreaming"; a desire for creative rather than routine work, also influence the worker's reaction to a repetitive task.

Such findings indicate the importance, in avoiding maladjustment, of fitting to highly repetitive tasks those individuals who are by disposition and temperament especially adapted to it. As Wyatt and

Langdon point out, "in selecting operatives for repetitive work relative immunity from influences which prevent the worker from making full use of potential ability should be taken into account," especially since it has been found that "(a) boredom lowers the rate of work; (b) workers of inferior ability tend to work more closely to their maximum than those of superior capacity; and (c) the rate of work when learning an industrial process is reduced by boredom." [70]

The Effect of Uniformity and Variety in Work upon Monotony.—Uniformity in work seems to be one of the constants in the monotony-producing situation. The insistence upon uniformity, upon specialization, is based upon the belief that keeping the worker at one task favors production, whereas variation of any kind from task to task interferes with industrial efficiency. This belief has been investigated in a number of laboratory and plant studies.

In one of these, Wyatt and Fraser [71] examined the effect of variety as compared with uniformity of work in soap wrapping, tobacco weighing, handkerchief folding, and other repetitive tasks. The results of the investigation indicate that, in many instances, complete uniformity in manual repetitive work may be less productive and lead to greater irregularity in the rate of working than a reasonable degree of variety. The latter is also preferred by the workers. The effect seems to depend partly on the nature of the process and partly on the individual operative. Furthermore, while frequent changes are definitely detrimental to production, there is some evidence that from the point of view of production and of satisfaction the best results are attained when the form of activity is changed after $1\frac{1}{2}$ hours of unvaried work.

Other Antidotes to Repetitive Work.—Another method of overcoming adverse effects of monotony is suggested by the finding that piece-rate systems of payment seem less conducive to the feeling of boredom than the time-rate systems. The possibility of greater earnings, the competitive feature, seem to induce interest, to set up a goal which counterbalances the effect of boredom or perhaps compensates for the "set" or attitude toward monotony on the part of the worker. Rest-pauses properly spaced do much toward changing the shape of the production curve in a repetitive job and toward decreasing the expressed discontent. Short pauses for conversation and the development of group morale are other devices for overcoming boredom at work. Recent studies by Wyatt and Langdon suggest that music, played at intervals during the working day, is an effective antidote to boredom.

General Aspects of Monotony.—There has been much general discussion of the effect of repetitive work upon the well-being of the worker and the stability of our industrial civilization. An illustration of one point of view in the discussion of this subject is Marot's [72] insistence that the assignment of highly specialized repetitive tasks to individual workers induces a thwarting of the creative impulse and a resulting disturbance in the adjustment of the individual worker. To the boring effect of monotony, to the thwarting of the creative impulse in the ceaseless and meaningless turning of the same screw day after day, she ascribes the strife and disgruntlement which display themselves in periodic conflicts in American industry today.

Somewhat the same attitude, although oriented in terms of the individual worker rather than from the viewpoint of industrial strife, is reflected in Mayo's [73] insistence that monotony induces pessimistic reveries, an obsessional concern on the part of the worker with his difficulties and disappointments which ultimately result in complete maladjustment.

Such generalizations, when examined, appear to grow more out of the free play of poetic imagination than from the controlled and scientific study of the problem. Complaints from bored workers, it is true, appear to be more frequent than those from the less bored. That boredom seems to increase sensitivity to certain features of the environment and is therefore of importance in relation to dissatisfaction and unrest is one of the conclusions drawn by Wyatt and Langdon as the result of their exhaustive experiment. [74] However, an examination of the many studies in this field shows clearly that much of the blame levelled against repetitive work is wrongly directed. They indicate, for example, that machine work, repetitive work at an imposed speed and rhythm, are not invariably accompanied by an overwhelming and depressing feeling of monotony.

There seems to be no universal, deep-seated conflict with an instinct of workmanship. As a matter of fact, there are many who prefer routine work, who like automatized tasks which leave the mind free for more pleasurable activities. There are others, apparently a smaller number, who rebel against uniform, specialized work, but even in their case, adaptation is not so difficult as is suggested by the protagonists of the "creative" instinct and by critics of the "machine age."

INDUSTRIAL INCENTIVES

The output of an industrial worker depends partly upon conditions which are external to himself and in part upon internal conditions. The former include temperature, lighting, ventilation, construction and speed of machinery, and so on. Among internal conditions may be distinguished two sets of factors loosely designated as the *capacity-to-work* and the *will-to-work*.

Capacity-to-Work versus Will-to-Work.—Efficiency in industry is determined to a large degree by the willingness of the worker to use the capacity at his disposal. As Strong points out, one has only to know what is happening in the way of restriction of output among organized and unorganized workers "to realize that few, if any, employees are working up to their capacity. Instead of output representing capacity, it represents what employees believe to be sufficient to hold their jobs, to guard against future wage cuts, to be looked upon with favor by their associates." [75]

Financial Incentives.—The practical problem in industry is to develop devices for stimulating inclination to work. Wage incentives are generally employed for this purpose, on the theory that earnings are of tremendous and immediate interest to the worker. In the United States, a survey by the National Industrial Conference Board [76] of 631 companies employing 700,699 wage earners, showed that, in 1935, approximately 50 per cent of these were paid under some form of wage incentive plan including bonuses, premiums, straight piece rates, multiple time and piece rates, and diverse other systems.

Experimental Evaluation of Wage Incentives.—Although great effort and enormous sums have been devoted to devising, installing, and administering various wage incentive plans, little has been done to determine how well they work. Such evaluation is made difficult because, in practice, the introduction of a new wage plan is generally accompanied by modifications in method and conditions of work. Moreover, there is evidence that any change, whether it be in schedule of hours, conditions of work, wage plan, etc. affects production by directing the active attention of the worker to the task.[77] For these and other reasons there are few unequivocal facts on the general value of financial incentives and on the merit of particular plans.

Typical of data obtained under relatively controlled conditions are those reported by Wyatt, Frost, and Stock,[78] from a comparison of the effects of *time rate, bonus systems,* and *piece rates* on the output and feelings of workers engaged in the repetitive tasks of wrapping, packing, weighing, etc. The substitution of a bonus rate for time rate increased output 46 per cent. A further increase of 30 per cent in production was obtained when a bonus system was replaced by a piece rate. Moreover, the piece rate and bonus systems were not only more productive than a time rate (in the order stated) but results showed in general, that (1) workers preferred both the latter to the time rate and that (2) the higher output obtained by the payment by results system could in no sense be said to have been obtained at the expense of the workers' well-being or happiness.

Nonfinancial Incentives.—Such findings, and more particularly day-to-day observations in industry, show that incentive wage-payment plans, properly devised and administered, are of great importance in furthering achievement at work. However, there is also growing realization that an incentive "wage-payment plan, in itself, is but one factor and a comparatively minor one" [79] in motivating workers and that increasing reliance must be placed upon so-called *nonfinancial incentives* in promoting the full use of workers' co-operation. Wyatt, Frost, and Stock, for example, in the study cited above, conclude that "there can be no doubt that payment systems are of the greatest importance in stimulating the 'will-to-work,' but they are not, in themselves, sufficient to produce it. If an operation is regarded as totally aimless and futile, the strongest monetary incentive may have no effect." [80]

The basis for this conclusion is illustrated in Fig. 25, showing the relative output in successive weeks in different processes under 3 systems of wage payment. The order of popularity of different

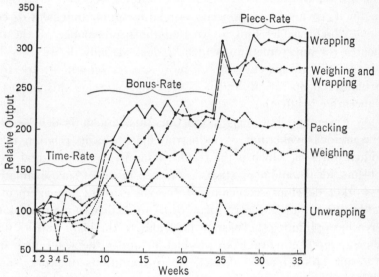

FIG. 25.—RELATIVE OUTPUT IN SUCCESSIVE WEEKS IN DIFFERENT PROCESSES UNDER THE INFLUENCE OF VARIOUS WAGE-PAYMENT PLANS.

(After Wyatt, Frost, and Stock, "Incentives in Repetitive Work." London: Ind. Health Res. Bd. Report No. 69, 1934, by permission of Controller of His Britannic Majesty's Stationery Office.)

operations, as developed from controlled interviews with workers, was *wrapping*—1; *packing*—2; *weighing and wrapping*—3; *weighing*—4; *unwrapping*—5. It can be seen that the effect of the wage incentive plan is most marked in the operations which arouse the more favorable feeling tones and is completely absent in the least popular processes. In the most popular operation, wrapping, the rate of output was almost trebled by the end of the experiment, while production on the least popular operation, which involved very similar movements, but which appeared to be futile to the workers, showed no improvement.

Restrictive Practices and "Intent."—The limitations of financial incentives are also indicated in industrial surveys [81] which show a tremendous amount of voluntary restriction of output by both organized and unorganized workers. Such restrictive practices, as well as other difficulties with wage plans, are the outcome of the failure of wage incentive plans to promote *intent* favorable to production.* "The worker who has no desire to perform a given industrial operation for its own sake is induced to do so by an arrangement of conditions which enables him to see that the performance of the task procures for him something which he does actually desire. . . . The desire for the reward engenders a more *specific intention* to perform the industrial operation, and it is only in so far as this is so that the incentive is effective." [82]

As Fryer and Hiester [83] point out, this "intent is developed in the conscious evaluation of industrial incentives in relation to individual purpose, which is the result of family, economic, and social problems, ideals, and aspirations." If, as a result of such evaluation, the worker develops suspicions of the sincerity of management in establishing a wage incentive plan, or of its ability to maintain rates, or reaches opinions otherwise unfavorable to the plant and its management, *intent* favorable to production under the wage plan may not result. As a matter of fact, where conditions of work, supervision, and general personnel policies or practices are questioned by the worker, the introduction of a new wage incentive plan may release energies in a direction unfavorable to performance on the tasks leading ultimately, in some instances, to misunderstanding and strife between management and employees.

Social Motives in Work.—Such considerations have led many to question the emphasis upon financial incentives by industrial engineers who have been so largely responsible for the development of elaborate systems of wage payment. Whitehead, of Harvard University, has gone so far as to insist that the basic psychological generalization of economics, as applied in industry, "has exhausted much of its usefulness at the present time" and "has become a positive danger to our social and economic structure. . . . By postulating men

---

* See page 514.

and women as actuated in their economic activities solely by a desire for personal gain," he writes, "attention has been so far diverted from a due consideration of the *social* motives involved that these are being systematically thwarted in our present economic civilization. . . . We need," he adds, "to develop an organic conception of society in which economic activities take their place as one important aspect of the whole social process." [84]

The Hawthorne Study.—Whitehead's conclusions follow, in the main, from an evaluation of an extensive investigation, initiated by Mayo, at the Hawthorne plant of the Western Electric Company, of 5 young women engaged in independent but similar tasks of relay assembly. Started in 1927, the study represents 12 years of work, including 5 years of continuous and controlled observation of the effect of changes in number and distribution of hours of work, rest-pauses, wage-payment plans, etc., introduced into 23 experimental periods of unequal length. The remaining time has been largely devoted to an exhaustive analysis and interpretation of the data.[85]

The major conclusion from this exhaustive study is that the true motivating factor in industrial production is the social situation. While the widely-used incentive wage plans assume that the worker is primarily motivated by economic interest, this study shows that social considerations outweigh economic ones. Modifications of physical circumstances, it is claimed, are effective only when the social situation is appreciably altered. Factors which cause the rate of output to vary include leadership, "unconscious" rivalry, imitation, and financial incentives. However, financial incentives are responded to only in so far as they minister to the individual's own social situation. When financial incentives are opposed to the trend of the stable social organization characterizing a group of workers, they lose their power to motivate. The influence of one worker, or the group, on another worker was found to take various forms and to take place in different time spans.

Other Influences in Motivating Workers.—There seems much justification, from the consideration of experiments in other fields, for Whitehead's insistence upon the force of the social situation in creating intent to work. At the same time, a careful examination of his data, involving, it should be noted, only five cases, reveals a consistent neglect of the significance of other factors and an evident bias in the handling of his data to support his main thesis. This becomes particularly obvious when it is recalled, that interpreting the data at the end of two years of observation, Mayo, with Putnam and Pennock, reached the conclusion that "the mental attitude of the operator toward the supervisor and working and home conditions is probably the largest single factor governing the employees' efficiency." [86]

It is clear, from other studies, that specific factors have a much more direct influence upon the will-to-work than is suggested in Whitehead's interpretation of the Hawthorne data. These include prestige, recreational facilities, recognition of worth,[87] identification with the work process,[88] and others. The influence of such specific nonfinancial incentives is well illustrated in a study reported by Feldman,[89] showing the effect in changes of supervision upon production. Among the employees of an insurance company were approximately 1,000 clerks, divided into 22 sections. In 1933, a new wage plan providing group incentives for the 22 sections was inaugurated. Costs for each section for the previous 12 months were computed and each was allowed a group bonus on the savings it could effect over the cost for that period. All members of a section, including the supervisor, shared in these savings monthly on the basis of salaries, no change being made either in the basic salary or in established policies with respect to salary increases. At the end of 1933 every section showed some improvement, but the extent of improvement for the sections ranged from 2 per cent to 12 per cent, with an average of 8 per cent.

In 1934, management effected a general shift of all section heads, with the general aim of putting those who had been in charge of above-the-average bonus groups into those less-than-the-average sections. One objective in this was to determine whether differences in results were related primarily to differences in supervision or to differences in personnel or conditions of work. An analysis of production at the beginning of 1935 showed increases in production in all sections, ranging from 6 per cent to 18 per cent. The order-of-merit of supervisors remained practically the same as in the study made at the end of 1933. In spite of the reassignment to new sections, those whose units stood high at the end of the first year were at the top of the list during the second year and vice versa. Changes in relative order were limited to 3 cases of supervisors who had moved a step or two.

Early in 1935, the management again shifted by lot, 20 of the 22 supervisors. Although they were reassigned by chance, the listing at the end of the year showed the surprising result that in progress made the same general order of supervisors again prevailed. Moreover, an analysis of errors in terms of 1935 and 1936 earning records showed perfect correlation between the standing of the accuracy record of the work of each section under a supervisor and the standing on the earning record.

The Measurement of Employee Attitudes

The Objectives of Attitude Measurement in Industry.— The determination of the best kind of nonfinancial incentives as well as of the value of financial incentives as such involves a study of employee attitudes toward incentives. If management can determine the true nature, extent, and cause of dissatisfaction with particular incentives, constructive corrections can be made which will increase the value of these devices for stimulating the will-to-work.

Such studies are needed, not only to determine attitudes toward financial and other incentives, but also to find out how particular policies and practices are affecting the personnel relations of the plant and through it the stability of the industry and of our industrial civilization. As Uhrbrock points out, "if carefully planned studies of employees' attitudes are made from time to time, employers should be able to gauge their progress in eliminating points of irritation in the work situation. By means of the attitude measurement technique workers may safely express their opinions about working conditions, pay, and hours. Employers, on the other hand, may keep themselves informed of changes in workers' attitudes and modify company practices so as to insure mutual harmony and good-will.[90]

An Illustration of Employee-Attitude Measurement in One Plant.
—Interview and questionnaire techniques, developed by psychologists
for measuring attitudes, have been adapted to industry and have been
applied in a number of companies. Bergen,[91] for example, reports
on the use of a questionnaire involving a combination of an "attitude
scale" with questions of the multiple type employed in measuring the
"morale" and reactions to particular policies of 1,000 employees from
selected office and factory departments of a manufacturing company.
Typical items from such a scale and the value assigned to each are
presented in Table V.

TABLE V.—REPRESENTATIVE ITEMS FROM AN ATTITUDE SCALE
FOR MEASURING EMPLOYE ATTITUDES *

Attitude Statement	Scale Value (Factor 10)
I am made to feel that I am really a part of this organization ..	9.72
I can feel reasonably sure of holding my job as long as I do good work	8.33
On the whole, the company treats us about as well as we deserve	6.60
I have never understood just what the company's personnel policy is	4.06
In my job, I don't get any chance to use my experience	3.18
A large number of the employees would leave here if they could get as good jobs elsewhere	1.67
I think the company's policy is to pay employees just as little as it can get away with	0.80

* (From Industrial Conference Board Management Record, April, 1939.)
The range of values in the attitude scale, while statistically reliable, must
be recognized as arbitrary. For the purpose of interpreting results, therefore, it
will help to multiply each scale value by 10 and to think of the possible scores as
ranging roughly from 0 to 100.

Results showed a range in average departmental morale score
from 45.9 to 69.4, with an average of 57.1 for all employees. A
further analysis revealed that these variations in morale were due
largely to differences in supervision and leadership.

The average morale score of all salaried employees was 57.5 and
of the hourly workers 56.0. Average morale of male employees
proved somewhat higher than that of the women, and the scores of

female employees with over 7 years' service, employed in the general offices of the company, were especially low. Male employees with from 2 to 7 years' service had a lower morale score than those with greater or less service. This suggested the possibility that men who entered the company during the depression had fared worse than those hired earlier or later.

In addition to calculating general "morale scores," certain of the statements in the attitude scale were used to measure employee attitude toward specific items in the personnel policy. Among some of the more significant findings of this analysis are the following:

(1) Approximately one-half of the factory workers were dissatisfied with the wage incentive plan, suggesting the need for employee participation in the determination of job standards and piece rates.

(2) Seventy per cent of the hourly workers felt that there should be work sharing before lay-offs, and more than one-half of these workers felt that recent lay-offs had been handled fairly.

(3) There was considerable dissatisfaction among the salaried group with respect to the fairness of promotion policies and practices.

(4) A close relationship appeared between departmental morale and attitudes toward supervision and leadership.

Attitudes Toward Lay-Off.—In addition to general studies of attitudes there are instances of attempts to measure the attitude of employees with respect to single items of policy. An investigation of this type is reported by McGregor [92] who, in February, 1938, during a series of lay-offs that eventually affected nearly 30 per cent of the 7,000 hourly employees of a New England manufacturing plant, made a questionnaire survey of the attitudes of the workers toward various aspects of the lay-off problem.

Replies from a sample of 550 individuals showed, among other findings, that (a) 8 different policies were favored by groups ranging from 5 per cent to 25 per cent of the total; (b) employees with considerable seniority tend to favor a policy stressing seniority; those with many dependents tend to favor a policy stressing need; (c) although 90 per cent of the employees of this company were mem-

bers of a C. I. O. union, there did not appear to be a strong desire to
have the union usurp what is normally considered to be the prerogative
of management, *viz.*, the administration of the lay-off policy; (d)
97 per cent of the group favored some form of work-sharing.

Workers' Attitudes Toward Unions.—The study of attitudes of
workers in single plants has been supplemented by the attempt to
measure the attitudes of workers as a group in particular situations. Such, for example, was the aim of Chamberlin,[93] who *interviewed* 200 men employed in textile mills in Massachusetts—100
union members and 100 nonunion members. Their answer to his
inquiries indicated that 90 per cent of union members and only 38
per cent of nonunion members believed that the unions get results.

To a request for reasons for which they would join the union,
nonunion men gave the following in the orders noted: (1) because
fellow workers had joined; (2) a feeling of greater security; (3)
because a union is the only way that the working man can get results;
(4) a liking for such organizations.

The principal objection of nonunion men to unions was the
union's failure to get results (45 per cent), with the type of leader
running a close second, (41 per cent).

Both union members and nonunion members showed remarkably
emphatic agreement that the strike is not the only way workers can
get results, 87 per cent of union members and 100 per cent nonunion
members answering "no" to the question on this item. However,
there is close agreement between union members and nonunion
members that bankers and inventions are the causes of depression.
Moreover, 88 per cent of union members and 65 per cent of nonunion
members agree that mill owners do not treat the working man like
a human being.

The Place of the Psychologist in Modern Industry.—
There is no place to cite additional examples of what has been done
and what remains undone in analyzing the will-to-work, the general
nature of satisfaction at work,[94] and similar factors which are basic
to mutual understanding between labor and management. The import
of this discussion is doubtless clear. Among the few great questions

of our age is that which asks what modern industry means to the individual worker in terms of his satisfaction and fullness of life. The accumulation of evidence and the formulation of adequate procedures for promoting both efficiency and satisfaction at work present a continuing challenge to the industrial psychologist, to labor, and to management.

The psychologist is in a particularly happy position as the active agent in cooperative effort in meeting this challenge. In spite of the suspicion with which the psychologist is occasionally viewed both by management and labor, his is primarily an impartial outlook—the attitude of the observer who is basically interested in human beings and in their social adjustment.

As Harding [95] points out, "to tell an employer that the workers' complete health, physical and mental, is one of the industrial psychologist's ultimate criteria, may provoke him to reply either that he is not a philanthropist or that he has no use for cranks. And the employee who hears that industrial psychology increases the efficiency of his firm may inquire suspiciously, 'At whose expense is efficiency increased?' These attitudes—mistaken attitudes—can be met only by pointing out that the industrial psychologist is not thinking in terms of 'employer' or 'employee,' but rather concerns himself with 'workers,' in whichever category these may be found."

"Industrial psychology," adds Harding, "is impersonal, impartial, and independent of political structures. Its origins and applications are found not in the industrial system, but in the very nature of work itself. It should be thought of "as the psychology of work." And "so long as people have to work (or want to), psychology will continue to offer its contribution towards insuring the efficiency of their work, towards helping them to achieve their ends with the least misdirection of effort."

REFERENCES

Burtt, H. E. *Psychology and Industrial Efficiency.* New York: D. Appleton-Century Company, Inc. 1929.

Crowden, G. P. *Muscular Work, Fatigue and Recovery.* London: Sir Isaac Pitman and Sons, Ltd., 1932.

Farmer, E. *The Causes of Accidents.* London: Sir Isaac Pitman and Sons, Ltd., 1932.

Hall, P., and Locke, R. W. *Incentives and Contentment.* London: Sir Isaac Pitman and Sons, Ltd., 1938.

Hoppock, R. H. *Job Satisfaction.* New York: Harper and Brothers, 1935.

Moore, B. V., and Hartmann, G. W. *Readings in Industrial Psychology.* New York: D. Appleton-Century Company, Inc. 1932.

Viteles, M. S. *Industrial Psychology.* New York: W. W. Norton and Company, Inc., 1932.

Viteles, M. S. *Science of Work.* New York: W. W. Norton and Company, Inc., 1934.

Welch, H. J., and Miles, G. H. *Industrial Psychology in Practice.* London: Sir Isaac Pitman and Sons, Ltd., 1932.

CHAPTER XIX

PROFESSIONAL PSYCHOLOGY *

By Douglas Fryer, *New York University*

The professional psychologist deals with the problems of human adjustment which are brought to his attention privately, or in the school, the factory, and social institution. He applies the knowledge gained throughout almost 100 years of psychological experimentation. He seeks to understand various mental relations for the value this may have for others. As consultant, he recognizes the symptoms of mal-training and endeavors to correct them. His task is similar to that of the educator but he works in a more specialized capacity of guidance in the mental problems of a complex society.

In this chapter are considered the varied fields of professional psychology not included in other chapters in this volume which are concerned with its highly developed branches of educational psychology, clinical psychology, and industrial or vocational psychology. Applied knowledge has accumulated in psychology useful to the lawyer—sometimes referred to as legal psychology, to the advertiser—sometimes referred to as consumer psychology, to the personnel officer of college and professional school, and to the musician, artist, and other social groups. This chapter discusses these contributions.

College Personnel

In the educational tradition developing out of the middle ages the function of the academic college was to furnish intellectual stimulation to a select few who were particularly able to profit by knowledge interpreted in the classroom. This view has been modified in the American system of education. The academic college is a continuation of the secondary school for large numbers of youth who have demonstrated superior ability. Its function is the development of these young people for an important place in society.

---

* Exclusive of its specialized branches of Educational, Clinical, Industrial, and Vocational Psychology.

With this purpose the college personnel program is concerned with the adjustment of the student as a step in life's adjustment. Selection of those qualified to enter college—their guidance into college—is its first task, but this is only the beginning. Group and individual guidance is offered in planning study programs for cultural and professional development. Help is given in learning how to perform mental work efficiently. Personal problems are discussed as they arise. Guidance is offered generally in the problems of dormitory, fraternity, and sorority living, in campus organizations, social functions, publications, glee clubs, orchestras, bands and sports. This guidance leaves the initiative and motivation with the individual student. Its goal is to offer full information about all problems of college life.

Psychological research has contributed extensively to an understanding of the intellectual problems of college adjustment. College aptitude tests have passed their 20th birthday of recognized usefulness and they have radically improved the college classroom by reducing the number of those of low intellectual ability entering and staying in college. Comparatively recently attention has centered on the influences of varied individual student problems, such as parental attitudes, college roommates, and the effect of the personalities of teachers upon classroom achievement. Illustrative of the broader problems of student guidance, 73 freshmen in one college reported 5959 difficulties in which they required guidance, but of these only 714 or 12 per cent were related to courses of instruction.[1] No student enters college without some problem arising which seemingly is far removed from the intellectual activities of the college but which limits his adjustment to them.

Testing Intellectual Adjustment.—The testing of college students to guide them in their mental adjustment had its beginnings with J. McKeen Cattell, as early as 1890, in the study of individual differences at the University of Pennsylvania. The tests used by Cattell were of sensory and motor functions. But gradually tests of distinctly mental function were developed. Correlation coefficients between tests of mental functions and academic grades have indicated the usefulness of such tests in predicting success in college. The average (median) of the coefficients for eight investigations prior to 1918 was .34. This was a pioneer period in college aptitude testing.

Use of the General Intelligence Test.—The general intelligence examination was developed for group testing during the World War (1917-18) upon the principle of measurement by sampling abstract and symbolic mental activities. The Army Alpha Examination, with its five alternate forms, was adopted in the personnel program of many colleges and it was used widely for several years as an aptitude examination prognostic of educational development. Many regarded the general intelligence examination as a solution of student selection problems and much higher relationships were expected between intelligence scores and college grades than have been found to exist. Segal[2] has assembled coefficients reported in numerous studies and he computed an average (median) of sixteen correlation coefficients between Army Alpha and college grades of .44, with the range of the middle 50 per cent of these coefficients from .40 to .50. The general intelligence examination is predictive of academic success, but not with a high degree of individual accuracy.

Introduction of the College Aptitude Test.—The college aptitude or scholastic aptitude test is a development of the general intelligence test. It consists of problems of greater difficulty and measures only at the superior level of intellectual activities. But it is based on the same principle of measurement by sampling all symbolic mental functions.

Various colleges developed their own college aptitude tests in the early twenties and college associations have issued yearly forms for their constituent colleges. Columbia College probably inaugurated the first plan of admissions in which a general aptitude test was used as a criterion of selection. This test, which then was called the Thorndike College Entrance Examination for High School Graduates, is known now as the CAVD Test (completion, arithmetic, vocabulary and directions), and it is issued yearly in alternative forms for use by various colleges. The American Council on Education has maintained an examination service for over 15 years under the direction of L. L. Thurstone and it supplies yearly as many as 300 colleges with the American Council on Education Psychological Examination. In this examination are included various sub-tests of symbolic thinking, for example, a completion test of word usage, an artificial language test of translation, an analogies test of relationships between figures and forms, a same-opposite test of related meaning of words, and a test of arithmetical reasoning. Practically all colleges now administer a general aptitude test as a part of their admissions program. But probably no college uses such a test as the sole criterion for the selection of its students.

Relation between General College Aptitude and Scholarship.— Literally hundreds of studies have reported upon the validity of the general college aptitude test in predicting college scholarship. The American Council Psychological Examination is typical of the college aptitude tests and Segal reports an average (median) for 34 correlation coefficients of .48 with college grades. The range of the middle 50 per cent of the coefficients is from .40 to .55. Investigations of the Thorndike and other college aptitude tests report similar validity coefficients. So the general college aptitude test is a slight improvement over the general intelligence test, as represented by Army Alpha, in the prediction of college scholarship.

Other Measures for Prediction of Scholarship.—General achievement examinations, testing knowledge of secondary school subjects, have been developed for the prediction of college scholarship and secondary school grades always have been used, of course, for this purpose. Special aptitude tests for most college subjects have been tried at various times. But seldom are the coefficients reported between them and scholarship in their special subject higher than for a general aptitude test. In fact the rule is the reverse and often a special aptitude test in one subject will predict grades in another subject better than in the subject for which it was prepared.

Predictive Value of Secondary School Grades.—Segal and Wagner [2] have assembled separately from 50 to 100 correlation coefficients reported in investigations of the validity of secondary school grades in predicting college grades and agree on an average coefficient of about .55, with a range of the middle 50 per cent of the coefficients from .50 to .65. Secondary school grades are the best single criterion for prediction of college scholarship where they are appropriately weighted and interpreted. But enormous differences exist in the grading systems of secondary schools, which makes it difficult to use this criterion effectively in selecting students for college where they are assembled from various parts of the country. The secondary school grade is a less stable measure, and less easily handled, than test results. The use of tests of both general college aptitude and general educational achievement is increasing because of their practical efficiency.

The Achievement Test.—The College Entrance Examination Board test is representative of general educational achievement tests and the average correlation coefficient with college scholarship, as reported by Segal, is .46. Correlation coefficients with college scholarship for other general achievement examinations, such as the New York State Regents Examination and the Iowa Placement Tests, are somewhat higher than this. It may be that the general achievement examination of secondary school subjects is a slightly better predictive measure of college scholarship than the general college aptitude test. But it is not used so widely because it duplicates in large degree a measure of scholarship already available in secondary school grades. Achievement tests in special subjects form parts of the general achievement examination, of course, and tests in special subjects, such as mathematics and English, are often included in the examination program for admission to college as an aid in sectioning of classes or guidance in preparing study programs.

Combination of Measures for Predicting College Success.— The degree of the prediction of scholarship from two or more measures is indicated by the multiple correlation coefficient. Segal and Wagner [2] agree in reporting an average multiple correlation coefficient of combinations of tests used by numerous investigators in predicting college scholarship of about .65, with the range of the middle 50 per cent of the coefficients that have been reported from .60 to .70. There is little likelihood that prediction of college scholarship can be made with greater accuracy than this, as it depends in part upon the reliability of the college grading system. Instructors vary in their grading, and predictive measures will not correlate higher with college grades than the grades correlate with themselves. While the reliability of grading varies for different colleges, it is usually not higher than the coefficient given above for combined predictive measures of scholarship.

Other measures for prediction of college scholarship besides those already mentioned include reading test scores, character ratings, psychoneurotic inventory scores, attitude and interest scores. Naturally, all measures are not equally valid in prediction of college scholarship. At present, equations weighting various measures according to their contribution are being investigated in an endeavor to predict college success more accurately. This method allows one to use items for prediction from the personal history, such as age, time spent in study, and ratios of relatives graduating from college. Segal and Proffitt [3] have assembled results of studies in three universities showing an average correlation coefficient of —.28 between age of entrance into college and scholarship. But students who spend a few years between secondary school and college make better grades, on the average, than do students entering immediately after graduation from secondary school. The tendency is to use as many measures as possible in the intellectual guidance of the student into college and throughout his college career.

The Personal Problems of the College Student.—After college entrance, emphasis in guidance is more upon the personal problems of the student. It is the purpose of the Dean's office or Personnel Office to deal systematically with personal difficulties which are reflective of maladjustment. Through interviews, the student's problems are understood and factual information is placed before him that may assist him in learning how to live in a college community. Mental hygiene problems often are handled by a psychiatrist with office hours at the University, as are general medical problems by a physician. Certain large universities maintain a staff of trained counselors who have their regular student clientele with files summarizing the problems of individual students and their solution.

The Search for Causes of Maladjustment.—The college probation system is supposed to provide the motivation for "catching up" when behind in study. An analysis of the probation system in one college by Henry [4] shows that it does not do so. Only about one-fifth of freshmen probationers and about half of the later ones finally graduate. Yet Henry shows that these probationers do not differ from the average student in general intelligence, in secondary school grades, in regents examination grades, in age, number of high school units, subjects liked best and least, weight, height, etc., etc. The causes are to be found elsewhere in college life.

In the study by Emme, referred to earlier, the student consultant classified the 5,959 adjustment problems of the college freshmen into 19 areas of difficulties in order to indicate whether (1) low intelligence, as measured by the American Council Psychological Examination, (2) high neurotic tendencies, as measured by the Thurstone Personality Schedule, or (3) low socio-economic status, as measured by the Sims Inventory, Form C, accompanied any of these groups of problems. Low intelligence accompanied the problems of only three of the groups, that is, educational guidance problems, economic problems, and relations with teachers outside the classroom. High neurotic tendencies accompanied the problems of six groups, that is, in the use of the library, classroom problems with teachers, problems related to other groups of people, personal student relations, religious problems, and problems related to administrative officers. Low socio-economic status accompanied the problems of seven of the groups, that is, economic difficulties, educational guidance problems, health problems, religious problems, library problems, vocational problems, and relations with teachers outside the classroom. The importance of low socio-economic status and high neurotic tendencies in college adjustment is supported by the similar findings of other investigators. It is evident that they are the causes of many difficulties arising in college life and have an indirect effect upon classroom work.

Concluding Statement on College Personnel.—Academic colleges differ in their specific functions in education and in the cultural and intellectual levels of their student populations. In a list assembled by Pintner,[5] the intelligence-test averages (medians) for different colleges have a range of more than forty Army Alpha points. Less tangible but just as real are their differences in social standards. Their curriculum is indicative of their function. But all of them fit into the mold of American education in which the purpose of the college is conceived as training for life and its task that of individual student guidance.

With this essential goal, psychological and personnel research has contributed to an understanding of intellectual adjustment and has had some measure of success in indicating the varied and related problems of this adjustment. This contribution to the college personnel activities.has been but briefly reviewed here. The statistical methods of prediction, the interpretation of knowledge gained through research, and the guidance techniques of college personnel form a field of work which is a profession in itself and the student who wishes further information of it may consult selected references (Bennett; and Paterson, et al)[6] at the end of this chapter.

PROFESSIONAL PERSONNEL

In its contribution to personnel work, psychology has everywhere stressed the importance of differences between individuals. Measurements of these differences have been developed and used with fully as much emphasis among professional schools as among the academic colleges. This is equally true for professional schools which require a college education for admission as for those based on the secondary school and comparable with the academic college.

Special Professional Aptitude.—From a descriptive picture of the different professions one might think that there existed tasks performed by several which distinguish them definitely in their mental requirements. For example, one might conclude that to be successful in dentistry one must have special aptitude in making fine discriminations of color and brightness of teeth, odor of decay, form of cavity reflected in a mirror, and in particular, in the performance of minute coordinations and skillful movements of the hand. In fact, in the battery of psychological tests, administered to all persons wishing to prepare for dentistry in Germany (1932)[7]—tests sponsored by the National Association of Dentists of Germany—special aptitude tests for such qualities as these are included with general abstract and mechanical intelligence tests, but the value of the special aptitude tests for prediction has not been determined.

It is important to know whether or not special aptitude exists for the various professional tasks. A trial of special aptitude tests for dentists, where their predictive value of success in professional training has been carefully evaluated, may be considered typical of similar experimental programs for the measurement of special aptitude in any of the professions. Harris,[8] used several mechanical aptitude tests, a general intelligence test, and college grades to predict success in dental college. The Wiggly Block Test, Finger Dexterity Test, and the Tweezer Dexterity Test (O'Connor), a Hand Steadiness Test, and a Cube Carving Test were used as the mechanical aptitude tests; the Otis Self-Administering Test of Mental Ability, Higher Examination (Form B), was the measure of general intelligence; and total predental average and science predental average in college were the scholarship measures. First-year average grades and four-year average grades in dental college were the validity criteria. The predental total averages and the predental science averages correlated with the first-year averages in dental college with coefficients of .44 and .41 and with the four-year averages with coefficients of .53 and .59. The general intelligence test correlated .55 with the first year averages and .36 with the four-year averages. These are expected relationships. But none of the mechanical aptitude tests correlated with the two validity criteria with coefficients higher than .15 and the reliability of each coefficient was unsatisfactory.

Special aptitude tests are of less value for predicting success in any of the professions than a general aptitude or general intelligence test. Aptitude is not regarded as specific for a given profession. Assuming the intellectual qualifications for professional training, success in a profession depends upon a variety of intangible mental and social qualifications which are little understood and are measured but inadequately at present.

Testing General Professional Aptitude.—The general aptitude test in the various professions is similar to the college aptitude test, but usually its problems are clothed in the terminology of the profession. The assumption at its basis is the same as that of the general intelligence test. It samples symbolic mental operations, but the problems are of an order of difficulty comparable to the intellectual level of the professional school. More and more psychologists have realized, as experience has been accumulated in mental measurement, that uniform individual motivation or cooperation is absolutely essential to a group-testing program and it is believed that this is accomplished best in a profession through the use of the problems, ideas, and language of that profession as the materials of the test.

Professional aptitude examinations are administered in schools of medicine, law, engineering, education, dentistry, commerce, nursing, etc., and in the various departments of graduate schools. The professional aptitude tests correlate with scholarship in professional school with coefficients between .40 and .70, and perhaps with an average higher than .50, but the validation results of professional aptitude tests are usually retained as confidential information of professional organizations.

Often, a general aptitude test is used by teachers' colleges as a criterion for certification as well as for guidance into teaching. The Coxe-Orleans Prognostic Test of Teaching Ability, which is one of the standardized tests for teachers' colleges, measures the applicant's observation of teaching practices, his ability to understand educational subject matter and to analyze educational problems. Coefficients in ten normal schools between scores and freshmen grades are reported as having a range from .53 to .84. Aptitude for teaching is distinguished from aptitude for scholarship and correlation coefficients between estimates of teaching ability and aptitude tests are not nearly as high as between tests and grades.

Aptitude measurement on the part of medical schools is organized for accredited schools by the Association of American Medical Colleges with its Committee on Aptitude Tests so that students planning to enter medical training are examined at the same time in their separate colleges and the tests are scored at headquarters and distributed to the medical schools of the United States. The Medical Aptitude Test (Moss) measures comprehension, memory, logical reasoning, and scientific vocabulary and understanding, and its problems are stated in the form of a medical diagnosis. This test has been in continued use in alternate forms since 1930 by about 90 per cent of the medical schools of the United States.

The content of law aptitude tests usually is pertinent to the legal profession and includes mental problems involving legal reasoning without legal knowledge, but the same abilities are measured as in other professional aptitude tests. The Ferson and Stoddard Law Aptitude Examination measures accurate recall, comprehension, and reasoning by analogy, analysis and logic, and it is used by a number of law schools, but various others have developed their own professional aptitude examination. One leading law school uses a power examination of general mental ability.

Mechanical aptitude is considered to be a prerequisite of the engineering profession and high ratings in mechanical aptitude tests, of which there are a large variety, are thought to be indicative of professional success. But here as elsewhere in the professions, the general aptitude test correlates higher with college work in engineering than any test of mechanical aptitude. The engineering college aims to furnish a broad symbolic education in the mechanical activities of a modern civilization, while its specializations may lead into such fields as hydraulics, aeronautics, sanitation, mining, and so on.

Concluding Statement on Professional Personnel.—A personnel program will be found in most professional schools similar to that of the academic college. The general aptitude test, of the professional school, with its material in the language of the profession, is equally valuable to that of the college in predicting scholarship. It is possible that college grades correlate higher with professional school scholarship than do secondary school grades with college scholarship. But an insufficient number of studies have been reported to establish this point.

Many other indicators of professional development besides the general professional aptitude test and preprofessional scholarship are available. The Strong Vocational Interest Blank, with forms for both men and women, will show how fully the individual's feeling life has absorbed the likes and dislikes of the profession of his choice as well as of other professions. Professional units for which scoring keys are available for men follow : Architect, chemist, dentist, engineer, farmer, mathematician, physician, physicist, psychologist, lawyer, minister, musician, city school superintendent, teacher, and artist. Those which are available for women follow: Lawyer, librarian, nurse, physician, teachers of English, of mathematics and physical sciences, of social sciences, artist, author, dentist, and social worker. For a more extensive discussion of aptitudes and their measurement in the professions one may refer to Bingham's book.[9]

The professions as a group are at the top of the occupational ladder in intellectual qualifications. There are differences in the average intelligence of professional groups, but distributions overlap to a high degree and critical ratios for these differences are probably not significant for many of the professions. Students of medicine, law, and engineering rank highest in average intelligence scores. Those in education and agriculture are somewhat lower and those in dentistry, pharmacy, and nursing are lowest of all. The engineering college equals the academic college in intellectual level, with teachers' colleges slightly lower. Schools of the same profession in different parts of the country differ considerably in intellectual qualifications, as do the academic colleges.

The professions rank highest of all occupations in social prestige. The following order among the professions is established from the rankings secured by Hartmann[10] among persons of varied socio-economic levels: Doctor, lawyer, engineer and teacher, with college professor of equal status with lawyer, and clergyman and dentist ranking above or equal with the teacher. The public school teacher ranked lower than the high school teacher and principal or superinendent. The nurse ranked lowest, and the public school teacher second lowest, in prestige among the professional occupations, but both were above the large body of business and commercial occupations which ranked next as a group among the occupations generally.

CONTRIBUTIONS TO THE PROFESSIONS

Facts and methods of the scientific laboratory have wide application generally in the problems of the various professions. Suggestion plays an important role in inducing and exaggerating the symptoms of disease and the physician must distinguish what is organic from what is psychological. Human motives determine whether a person ignores an important symptom of disease which should have immediate treatment or if he visits several specialists for examination because of "normal feelings." The study of psychology is useful in any profession that is concerned with the efficiency and happiness of human beings.

A Few Specific Contributions to the Professions.—Knowledge of the functional effects in vision of such factors as convergence, accommodation, two-point discrimination, stereoscopy, constancy of size, and the equivocalness of visual stimuli generally, which is gained in laboratory experimentation, has a specific bearing on the work of the oculist, optometrist, and the specialist in stage and office lighting. Similarly, the experimental facts of audition, smell, taste, and the other senses serve a useful purpose. The criteria of visual space which we learn through years of experience are turned back on us by the artist in portraying depth, size, and movement on the canvas. Knowledge of odor compensations, mixtures, and variability in fatigue should be useful information in the preparation of acceptable diets and perfumes, and psychometric scaling methods are available to determine their degree of acceptance. Any theory of acoustics cannot violate the facts of binaural intensity and time differences; nor can a program of animal training ignore the conditioned reaction formula which has been worked out with such exactness in animal psychology. Innumerable facts of the laboratory are useful to the professional specialist. Such knowledge gradually filters into common usage as a free scientific contribution to human welfare.

Analytic Contributions.—A scientist often sets out to solve a particular problem the solution of which will be of inestimable value to society. Such an investigation in psychology usually starts with an analysis of the factors involved in the activity and it may entail, and usually does, research extending over years. Alfred Binet of France at the turn of the century and until his death, and then Lewis Terman of the United States, with a host of collaborators, developed our modern measures of general intelligence, first, by an analysis of mental capacities and, later, through the standardization of the tests. This is an old story which is told more fully elsewhere. The intelligence measure is an outstanding contribution to human welfare and it is a useful tool for all professions, although its administration and particularly its interpretation require the training of the specialist.

Similarly, Strong, along with other collaborators, has contributed a measure of human interests indicating the direction of occupational development giving the greatest individual pleasure. This is an extremely useful measure for the vocational counselor. Also, Thurstone has established a technique which indicates the degree of radical or conservative thinking upon any problem, making possible a measure of attitude. Such measures are particularly useful to personnel officers in industry and to government officials.

From the laboratory comes the knowledge that discrimination of temporal intervals has the lowest threshold for pressure. Fifteen hundred per second can be distinguished on the most sensitive cutaneous surface while in vision separate stimuli fuse into continuous or moving stimulation at about 24 per second. Temporal discrimination of pressure is the basis of the vibratory sense, and Gault has developed a language in vibrations for the use of the deaf-blind. Seashore has analyzed the factors involved in musical talent over years of painstaking investigation and he has prepared phonograph records measuring the basic sensory discriminations involved in musical talent. These are used widely by teachers of music as tests of musical aptitude.

Other similar analytical contributions might be mentioned, but these illustrate the manner in which the psychologist approaches a problem necessary for solution in the interest of social welfare. All important contributions of this kind have been made in the 20th century. Psychology is indeed a young science.

Concluding Statement on Professional Contributions.—Perhaps of greatest value to other professions of all that has been contributed by psychology are the methods that have been developed to secure an exact statement of fact or opinion from another person, where it is impossible for the examiner to determine otherwise the accuracy of what he learns. This is, of course, the scientific method as applied to the study of conscious activity. Medical diagnosis is based in part upon the statement of the patient. The lawyer examines a witness to determine the accuracy of his report. The politician checks to find out if expressed opinion of his program is representative. It is essential in all professional work to determine the validity or correctness of personal statements irrespective of belief as to their truth or falsity.

Notable advances have been made in the laboratory in securing an exact report of conscious activity. The descriptive introspection is used to outline the factors involved in any such activity. Psychophysics offers controlled techniques where magnitude of stimulus is related to quantity of sensitivity as in determining the size of a letter that is normally visible. The psychometric scaling methods determine relative magnitude of feeling preferences and of sense discriminations. Through their use knowledge is gained of the relative values of simple and complex stimuli in everyday life, such as colors, odors, pains, textures, wall paper, house paint, textile designs, advertising copy, etc. These are definitely laboratory methods. Precision in their use is necessary for observer as well as experimenter. But through their study the conditions for accuracy of the psychological report are established.

Contact between the professional specialist and his client is of the nature of an interview, and industrial and clinical psychologists in particular have developed the interview as a quantitative tool in a manner similar to a standardized psychological test. The response to a question, where the variability of response is known, is of the nature of an item in a test. Interview questions can be prepared for various situations on short notice. But the interview is less formal and forbidding than a test. As frequently used it consists of questioning by an experienced examiner who does not know the answers to his questions but who can judge their accuracy through their possibilities of accuracy and who, through check questions, can establish the reliability of the answers.

LEGAL PSYCHOLOGY

Legal psychology is that branch of professional psychology which is concerned with unsocial motivation, the mentality of the delinquent and criminal, and with the methods for the detection of crime and the determination of the accuracy of testimony.

The Accuracy of Testimony.—Reference has been made to the accuracy of the psychological report. Research has indicated numerous errors of sensitivity from which inaccuracies in the report may arise, as in the localization of a sound or the color of an object under varying intensities of illumination. Estimations of time vary according to the events encompassed in a temporal interval and they differ enormously between individuals even for the unusual situation where there is intention to observe duration. This is likewise true of estimates of rates of movement which are offered in testimony of the speed of an automobile involved in an accident. Errors of memory, which increase with elapsed time and with the greater inaccuracies for events observed only once, add to the difficulties of securing accurate testimony. Intentionally observed events are remembered better than casually observed events, but the report of a witness is seldom based on the intention to observe and to remember. Accuracy in casual observation of events concerned with people is vastly greater than of events concerned with things. Suggestion influences the report of a witness and in this instance the methods of questioning may determine the nature of the report, as is recognized in court procedure.

Various laboratory experiments have been performed upon the accuracy of testimony, which indicate that the methods of securing evidence influence its reliability. Marston [11] tested the reliability of the free recital, the direct examination, and the cross-examination. The direct examination secured 31 per cent of 150 items into which the event was analyzed, and the cross-examination secured 29 per cent, and the free recital 23 per cent. But 94 per cent of the items actually reported in the free recital were accurate, while only 83 per cent were accurate in the direct examination and 76 per cent in the cross-examination. The oath reduces errors in testimony; sworn testimony is more accurate, but it is less complete. Trained observers, such as journalists and detectives, are more accurate in the reporting of events, as might be expected.

Detection of Crime.—Münsterberg of Harvard University was an American pioneer in the application of psychology to useful purposes. Early in this century he suggested word associations, breathing, circulatory changes, and involuntary movements as symptomatic of deception, and their measurement as useful in the detection of crime. Many of the measures used today for this purpose were first worked out in his laboratory.

The measurement of deception is a different problem from that of the determination of the accuracy of testimony or of the psychological report. In deception there is intention to deceive while in testimony there is intention to tell the truth—the witness believes he is telling the truth. This is the ideal, of course, with much deviation in actual practice. Measures of deception are based on the hypothesis that in avoidance of a true response or accurate statement, where a question must be answered or an act performed that is related to a crime, there will be a disturbance of normal verbal or physiological functions.

"The Lie Detector."—Any set-up of apparatus arranged to measure symptoms of deception may be called a "Lie Detector." The cardiograph, measuring heart action, the pneumograph, measuring breathing, the sphygmometer, measuring blood pressure, the chronoscope, measuring reaction time, the galvanometer, measuring strength of electric current, and other apparatus, are instruments often applied in lie detection. The name of "Lie Detector" was ascribed by a newspaper reporter to Marston's experimental set-up for testing deception in Münsterberg's laboratory at Harvard in 1915. This set-up included a chronoscope and voice key, a pneumograph and kymograph, a sphygmometer and stethoscope. Various combinations of apparatus and techniques are called lie detectors today.

Essential to lie detection is the determination of the validity and reliability of the techniques used in its measurement. The four leading ones in use today follow: (1) The free-association reaction test, (2) I/E Ratio test of inspiration-expiration, (3) the psychogalvanic reaction test, and (4) the blood pressure test. Their validation will be discussed below. As suggested by Münsterberg, diffused movements increase in deception to such a degree that they are measurable.

It is possible that facts known about muscle reading, eye movements, and facial expressions may be applicable in measuring deception at some future date.

Free-Association Reaction Test.—The free-association reaction technique, which was developed by Jung, was the first scientific method to be tried in determining the truth of a report. It consists of the presentation of a series of words with instructions to respond as rapidly as possible to the stimulus word. Two kinds of stimulus words, called crucial and noncrucial words, are distributed in the list, with the crucial words related to the crime. Through the use of a voice key and reaction-time apparatus the time of the reaction may be recorded in milliseconds. The associated word is noted for analysis of its significance. The assumption of the measurement is that the guilty person will inhibit his associations to words related to the crime, thus increasing his reaction-time, and that he will respond with unusual or stereotyped words. The average "times" of the crucial and noncrucial words are computed as a quantitative indicator of disturbance of free associations and the response words are studied for suggestions of suppression of knowledge or greater knowledge than should exist.

Numerous laboratory studies of artificial crime situations have been made by means of this technique with considerable success in the detection of the guilty party. Crosland [12] describes its use in the determination of guilt among members of college fraternities where actual thefts had occurred. There were seven crimes and about ten suspects were examined for each crime. The guilty persons for six of the seven crimes were indicated correctly by the test according to later confessions and recovery of the stolen articles. But practical applications of the technique in crime detection are not numerous. This is due to the difficulty of securing a list of crucial words stimulating disturbances in the responses of the guilty party and not of other suspects, for most of the details of a crime are publicized generally.

The I/E Ratio.—A breathing test of deception has been devised by Benussi,[13] an Italian psychologist, following his discovery that the ratio of the time of inspiration to that of expiration was greater before truth-telling than before lying; and with the inverse holding true after the statement is made. This measure is called the I/E Ratio. The technique includes the use of a pneumograph and tambour contacts recording on a kymograph. A question is asked the subject who is required to wait several seconds before replying in order that the emotional effect may be recorded in the breathing. Laboratory trials of this technique have been singularly successful, but the method is extremely laborious because numerous measures and mathematical computations are required, which is the reason why the I/E Ratio is not used in actual criminal detection. But breathing records are taken, often, for the suggestions they may contain.

The Psychogalvanic Reaction Test.—The psychogalvanic reaction test is a measure of changes in resistance to insensitive electrical current through the skin surface, usually at the hand where perspiration is more likely to decrease resistance. Extensive research in the study of emotions with this technique has not led to any definite conclusions, since galvanic readings are related to almost any change in the human subject, such as movements of muscles and conscious ideas, as well as emotional disturbances. Ruckmick [14] has experimented extensively with this technique in the laboratory and believes that it may prove valuable in crime detection. Summers [15] has reported a few cases in actual practice. But the method is probably the least valuable of the four leading techniques.

Systolic Blood Pressure.—While working in Münsterberg's laboratory at Harvard, Marston [16] found that a record of systolic blood pressure showed changes that were symptomatic of deception. This is a most useful discovery because it can be applied to the investigation of deception in actual criminal cases. Marston has told his story of crime detection in a recent publication. [17] A discontinuous record of blood pressure is taken, as is done by the medical doctor, with a sphygmometer. The rubber sleeve is bound around the upper arm and inflated, checking the flow of blood. Then pressure is reduced until the first pulse beat is felt at the wrist. The reading of blood pressure is taken as the amount of pressure in the bag that is overcome by the pressure in the arteries. A continuous record can be taken and recorded on a polygraph with a low degree of pressure in the bag of the sphygmometer.

In Marston's original laboratory experiment the subject was given two accounts of a crime implicating a friend, one furnishing him an alibi and the other including evidence against him. He defended this friend in cross-examination on two occasions, once with the alibi and again by lying out of the evidence against him. The differences between the lying and truth-telling accounts were convincingly indicated by differences in blood pressure. Other laboratory studies showed the method to be singularly successful in separating the false and true report.

Marston continued to develop the discontinuous blood pressure technique during the world war and Larson carried on investigations in the police departments of Berkeley and Los Angeles using the continuous method and combining it with breathing records. Marston [17] reports that Larson tested 861 suspects, clearing 310 from suspicion and securing 182 confessions in this work. Larson [18] concluded that the technique was extremely useful in eliminating suspects and suggesting clues. Marston says that to date (1938) more than 100 police departments now practice scientific lie detection, that this record is admitted into trial courts in at least four states, and that probably over 25,000 cases have been examined which are validating lie detection in practice. He quotes a report of the chief of police of Wichita, Kansas, revealing the administration of 1684 deception tests to 672 suspects in 1935 with 220 recorded deceptions and 85 confessions.

Commercial Lie Detectors.—Most commercial lie detectors include both a continuous blood pressure record and a breathing record, as in the Berkeley Psychograph and the Keeler Polygraph. The Darrow Photopolygraph combines a record of blood pressure, respiration, reaction time, psychogalvanic reaction, and tremor of hands, that is to say, all four and more of the essential techniques that have been discussed.

Concluding Statement on Legal Psychology.—A fuller discussion of legal psychology will be found in a volume by Burtt.[19] A wealth of knowledge of the workings of the human mind has been accumulated which is useful in establishing the validity of testimony, but few of the techniques concerned with psychological reporting have been applied to the actual examination of witnesses. Developments along this line should be forthcoming in the future. Deception can be determined by several methods in the laboratory, but the measurement of systolic blood pressure under cross-examination has proved to be the most successful indicator of veracity in criminal investigation. The commercial lie detector of today usually combines a continuous record on a polygraph of systolic blood pressure and breathing, while other measures are sometimes included.

Legal psychology deals with the causes of crime and delinquency as well as with the specific problems discussed here. It is concerned with the criminal as a socially unadjusted person. If the causes of unsocial acts are mental disease or mental deficiency, in so far as the law defines the terms, clinical diagnosis determines the treatment. Such problems are discussed in the chapters on abnormal and clinical psychology. Mental disturbance leads to unsocial acts and in our worst crimes occasionally there exist extreme forms of delusions, as in dementia praecox where social responsibility is lost. It is believed by some psychiatrists that all criminal acts are the product of a mentally disturbed if not a diseased mind. Low grade defectives— imbeciles and idiots—lack responsibility for their acts and may commit serious crimes. About 20 per cent of the delinquent and criminal population are mentally defective as contrasted with one per cent for the general population. The mentally disordered and low grade defective, who have lost or who never have attained responsibility for social living, are all potential criminals and require institutional care.

If the causes of unsocial acts are not shown to be due to mental disease or mental defect, legal practice considers that the individual is fully responsible for his behavior. However, sociologists have indicated the effect upon crime and delinquency of living in the low privileged areas of large cities. Studies of murderers and other criminals lead to the conclusion that in attitude all feel justified in their ways of living. They believe they are oppressed and hence form their own social code. Specialists of all kinds, working with criminals and delinquents, are unanimous in concluding that most unsocial acts are the product of wrong motivation, improper direction of goals, and the influence of undesirable social suggestion, all of which have their roots in early life and are determined by environment. Prevention can result only from correct education. Treatment of offenders is a clinical problem and reëducation in institutions within the terms of legal punishment may return the offender to society better trained for social living.

Consumer Psychology

The branch of professional psychology that is concerned with human motivation in marketing relations is called consumer psychology or the psychology of advertising and selling. Consumer psychology contributes both general principles of human behavior and methods and facts of the consumer's marketing activities. By its methods it measures and predicts consumer response—to radio, magazine, and billboard advertising, or to specialized sales programs. All men are consumers and its principles are those of general psychology applied to man in his consumer relations.

Principles of Consumer Psychology.—Man as a consumer is motivated, just as is the "organism" of laboratory experiment, by metabolic activity affecting internal receptors. His tissue needs are the original determiners of his "desire to purchase." They give rise to the drives known as hunger, thirst, cold and warmth, sex excitation, the various pressures of fatigue, exhilaration, and so on. It is considered good consumer psychology to keep these primitive forces in mind while planning the manufacture and selling of produce.

But most of the desires of the consumer as expressed in the market are highly artificial wants. They have developed with civilized living. The original drives of life are given direction in relation to the many and varied objects of the external world. Stimuli affecting external receptors become the originators of activity. A certain breakfast food or a certain soft drink or cocktail is preferred to another, not because of its satisfaction of thirst or hunger but because of the prestige of its name. Because of this, good will may be expressed to Pepsodent toothpaste, feathers in a hat, Co-op peaches, and resistance to Kolynos toothpaste, high crowns in a hat, and Premiere canned peaches, or any such set of comparisons which are determined in the habitual social patterns of man's behavior. It is often the table linen and not the food with which fault is found in a restaurant, or the name on the wrapper and not the vermicelli it contains. Habits and attitudes of consumption, and their development, are the immediate concern of advertiser and seller.

The Psychology of Personal Selling.—An ingratiating but corpulent business man selling an electric fan to an unsuspecting Eskimo is the "good salesman" of past generations. Personal selling has its share of "fly by night" ventures even today. But generally speaking, advertising and selling serve the consumer with ideals of truth and honesty in the giving of information.

Personal selling is concerned with the attractive presentation of information about products for sale just as is advertising, but through personal contact. The psychological factors are the same. Only the medium changes. Little is known exactly or scientifically of personal selling procedures. Kitson [20] has summarized what psychology contributes by way of general principles. He discusses the stream of mental activity of the consumer in six stages from initial attention to final satisfaction: Attention is gained for a product through varied stimuli and their repetition; interest, or feeling, follows attention and is developed by information and activity aroused toward the product; the next step, desire, comes when the consumer seeks the product by actual or incipient behavior; confidence is present when habits of good will are developed; the "psychological moment" of decision and action arrives when instinctive needs and familiar habits are met and rational questions are answered; and the final stage, satisfaction, results in the purchase.

The Sales Interview.—The sales interview is a highly variable method of consumer contact and it may always remain so; the salesman changes his sales methods with the product and with the customer, and these in turn change with the salesman. But there is in development a standardized sales interview. Only recently McKinney [21] subjected the sales interview to psychological measurement and Mitchell and Burtt [22] have attempted to validate current techniques of sales interviewing.

Laboratory investigations such as these are highly suggestive of valid field procedures.

Four pairs of contrasting methods were studied by Mitchell and Burtt: (1) Demonstration versus oral elaboration, (2) presentation of facts (long-circuit) versus short-circuit appeals, (3) breezy versus dignified approach, (4) domineering versus friendly approach. A salestalk was delivered according to each of these eight approaches by a trained salesman to forty college students who were asked to rate the salestalk on a five-point graphic scale. Results indicated that the demonstration method was considerably superior to elaboration. Presentation of facts was better than the short circuit method. The friendly approach was favored over the domineering approach. The average differences in ratings between these paired methods were statistically significant. Some of the 40 "prospects" favored the breezy approach and some the dignified approach, which suggests that here we have a question of individual preference.

Psychology of Advertising.—Advertising receives an enormous amount of study to determine its value as a medium of contact with the consumer. Appeal value is measured in attention, recognition, recall, brand of last purchase, and so on. Measurement may be by either laboratory or field investigations. Through field study the final effect of all advertising on the consumer is determined. Laboratory studies are particularly useful in suggesting the value of related content and form of advertisements in advance of launching an advertising campaign with its accompanying cost. From the study of past advertising information is gained of existing procedures.

Historical Method.—Early investigators measured the amount and size of advertising in various media. For example, Scott and Starch [23] found that the size of advertisements in the Century Magazine—as indicated by the number of agate lines—increased steadily and more than fourfold from 1872 to 1913. Gaudet and Zients [24] showed that the use of the full-page advertisement in the Literary Digest increased rapidly from 1910 to 1918 and thereafter remained stable until 1932 at about 50 per cent of the total advertising. These results may be evidences of business competition and are of little if any value in determining the psychological factors operating in advertising.

Psychological Methods of Investigating Advertising.— Methods in present use of investigating the psychological influences of advertising include (1) the psychometric scaling methods for measurement of the attention value of advertising copy, (2) recall and recognition tests of its memory value, (3) field questionnaires or inventories, and (4) consumer interviewing.

*The Psychometric Scaling Methods.—*The three psychometric scaling methods of the laboratory—the *order-of-merit method,* the *method of single stimuli,* and the *method of paired comparisons*—are used in the estimation of the appeal of advertising where comparisons can be made between separate advertisements. These three methods have been examined for their relative merits. Barrett [25] reported an average correlation of .987 between the order-of-merit method and the method of paired comparisons for judgments of weights, specimens of handwriting, and propositions of belief. The two methods give equal results and the order-of-merit method is far less time-consuming, which accounts for the neglect of the method of paired comparisons in the estimation of advertising. After reporting a correlation of .55 between the method of single stimuli and the order-of-merit method in the judgment of jokes, Conklin and Sutherland [26] concluded that the method of single stimuli secured the more direct estimates of preference. Circumstances will determine which method shall be used in the investigation of advertising appeal, but the method of single stimuli has the widest application in all practical problems of psychology, including those of advertising.

*Measuring the Memory Value of Advertising.—*Recall and recognition tests correlate with very low coefficients. Achilles [27] reported an average correlation for adult groups of .23 and for child groups of .21 between tests of recognition and of recall. Recall and recognition have distinct uses in marketing and they must be investigated separately.

Likewise, measures of aided recall, where the method of paired associates is used, and of unaided (pure) recall, where advertisements are reproduced without assistance, do not correlate highly. Brandt [28] compared the memory value for trade names by these two methods and reported a coefficient of .53. Memory for advertising will differ according to the form of its expression.

In tests of recall by the method of paired associates the kind of the product is given and the company name of its advertisement must be supplied, for example, vacuum cleaner—Hoover. The method of paired associates has been developed by Link [29] so that two associates may be presented and the subject is tested for a third, which Link calls the "method of triple associates." He believes that this form of testing aided recall has practical advantages, because of the use in advertising of vehicles or themes to carry an idea of the utility or attractiveness of the product, for example, the theme of Texaco gasoline is "Firechief."

The Field Questionnaire.—Consumer questionnaires consist of carefully worded questions upon radio programs, packages or containers, the product and its vehicles of advertising, which are framed in a manner to interest the consumer and elicit if possible the information desired. Various forms of recall and recognition tests may be included in a questionnaire. Return coupons attached to advertisements, often have questions of the sales program as their purpose. The questionnaire is mailed to a sample group of consumers which is selected to represent a certain territory or economic level of the population. Returns are usually unsatisfactory, which reduces the reliability of results. Generally speaking, the questionnaire is not a highly effective method in consumer psychology. But questionnaires of political polls have been very successful in accurately indicating political opinion. This is because of more representative returns, which are probably due to the public interest in the results of the political poll.

The Consumer Interview.—Consumer interviewing is an improved technique for field studies where trained interviewers telephone or visit the consumer and secure similar information to that usually requested in the questionnaire. While the method involves a greater initial expense than the questionnaire, it determines with a high degree of exactness the effect of advertising when adequate sampling is provided.

Results of Laboratory Studies of Advertising. —Numerous dimensions or cues in sensitivity have been investigated to determine their influence upon the appeal or memory value of advertising copy, such as color, size, repetition, motion, isolation, brightness, contrast, and so on. Some of the results of laboratory investigations concerned with these factors will be reviewed here. Such investigations offer the information necessary for selection of content and form in the make-up of advertising. But they do not predict the final effect on the consumer where the advertising is in relation to all other influences affecting him.

Attention value does not increase proportionately with size or space. Rather, attention values conform to a square-root relationship for different areas. Nixon [30] measured attention value as the time spent in visual fixation of half- and full-page advertisements. The attention value of the half-page to the full-page was 75 per cent, which is very close to the value for the square-root relationship between these areas. Similar results are reported by other investigators, but there has been some controversy over this point. While large sizes have greater attention value, additional area alone does not compensate for increased cost.

Likewise, laboratory studies of color in advertising do not indicate that color alone has as great attention value as has been attributed to it. Also, color preferences are highly variable and there are no colors that are universally preferred to the extent necessary that they and not others be included in advertising.

Contrast of color brightness and saturation between foreground and background in advertising is more important for attention value. Likewise with size contrast. Pedestrians will pause more frequently before a highly illuminated show window than one less illuminated. Motion in window display increases the number stopping to look.

Familiar contrasts are often less effective in any form of stunt advertising. In habitual activities, however, this is not true, as is illustrated in an experiment by Paterson and Tinker [31] who measured the effect in speed of reading upon reversing the familiar contrast of black on white of the printed page. Black on white was more legible than white on black and the investigators advise that whenever white on black is used as a device to attract attention in advertising the amount of reading text be limited to a minimum.

Habitual behavior is always an influence to be taken into consideration. The attention value of the upper left corner of the flat page is greatest; and right pages are superior to left pages for advertising because of habitual reactions in reading. Preferred pages are near the beginning and the end of advertising sections of magazines. It is interesting in this connection to find that advertising of competing products does not decrease the attention value of them in related space.

The conditions under which advertising is read should determine its make-up. Lucas [32] shows that length of headlines does not influence their recall when read at the person's own rate, but when the reader is pushed for time their length does determine their recall. It might be concluded from this that advertising in magazines and papers read at leisure could make use of much longer headlines than those read in the rush hours of the day.

Specific determiners of appeal value are not the rule in advertising, as has been indicated. Pictures, color, size, type, and so on, may be important, but their relationships are more influential in determining the appeal and memory value of an advertisement. Strong [33] shows that attention value increases more rapidly than the additional cost of the increase when white space is added up to 60 per cent of the total advertisement, but thereafter white space is relatively less important. Just as these factors in advertising make-up are mutually dependent in determining appeal and memory value, so it is to be expected that any advertisement or advertising will be influenced by its surroundings. Only field studies can determine the ultimate effect on the consumer.

Laboratory Studies of Radio Advertising.—Radio advertising differs from magazine and newspaper advertising because of its medium of auditory presentation and because of the related memory value of the accompanying program. For this reason radio advertising is a distinct problem for both laboratory and field study. Stanton [34] has measured the relative effectiveness of auditory and visual media by presenting fictitious advertising statements, consisting of 75 words for each advertisement, to be read (visual presentation) and listened to from a loud speaker (auditory presentation). Separate groups were tested for trade names given in the copy after one day, seven days, and twenty-one days. The auditory presentation was significantly superior when measured both by unaided recall and aided recall. The peak of superiority for the auditory presentation was on the seventh day. For recognition, however, there were no significant differences between the two forms of presentation, although the tests on all days were slightly in favor of the auditory presentation.

Here are positive results favoring the auditory presentation of the radio for recall of the advertising. But there exists a great deal of conflicting evidence upon the relative effectiveness of the auditory and visual presentation in the educational classroom. The usual conclusion is that children learn best from auditory instruction and adults from visual instruction. Undoubtedly the radio situation differs in its motivation from that of the classroom. Any conclusion upon this point at present must be considered tentative.

Results of Field Studies of Advertising.—Differential effects of advertising are demonstrated over and over again by field studies. Link [29] has reported the results of an extensive field study conducted by the representatives of the Psychological Corporation throughout the United States. Housewives in 14 cities were interviewed by the triple associates method to determine the recall value of advertising. Twenty-seven firms were distributed in these results from 69.1 per cent for Chase and Sanborn, in answer to the question, "What coffee advertises: 'Look for the Date on the Can'?", to 3.8 per cent for Johns-Manville, in answer to the question, "What building company advertises, 'I smell smoke'?" Repeating the test on various dates gave results for Chase and Sanborn, as follows:

Date	Mar. '32	Sept. '32	Oct. '32	Dec. '32	Feb. '33
No. of Cities	14	18	47	43	39
No. of Housewives..	1578	541	1445	1956	1399
Per Cent Correct ...	69.1	66.8	71.0	75.6	74.1

The increase at December '32 coincided with the introduction of a leading performer in the radio program of this company.

Radio Advertising.—The entertainment program of the radio has association value for the product advertised and field studies of radio advertising are concerned with its appeal as well as that of the advertising accompanying it. An investigation reported by Gaskill and Holcomb [35] illustrates a technique for establishing the validity of field measures of radio advertising. These investigators distributed a questionnaire to a sample of listeners of sponsored broadcasts consisting of a specially prepared recognition test of the multiple choice variety and including ten questions upon each broadcast but with five of these questions on the advertising and five on the program. (Two alternate forms of the test gave split-half reliability coefficients on 350 cases of .89 and .70.)

Scores in this test were computed as the per cent correct response for program and for advertising, thus giving two scores for each broadcast. Corrections for relative amount of time spent on the air were applied by dividing the average score for program and for advertising by the number of quarter hours of the weekly broadcast. Corrections for the relative amounts of time consumed by the advertising part of the program for the separate broadcasts—assuming that effectiveness of advertising is directly proportional to the time spent in presentation of the advertising—were made by dividing the advertising scores by this time. Corrections for influence of amount of newspaper and magazine advertising—on the assumption that this is an unequal influence upon the memory value of the advertising—were made by dividing the advertising scores of the broadcasts by the amounts of such advertising computed for a definite period. Program and advertising scores were equated for comparison of total broadcasts by setting the highest average score for program and for advertising at 100 per cent and multiplying the average scores of the other broadcasts by $\dfrac{100}{x}$, where "x" is the average score of the broadcast adopted as 100 per cent.

In this manner, Gaskill and Holcomb compared five national sponsored broadcasts, each advertising one product, for the State of Iowa.

Results showed that the average memory value of the program content was higher than that of the advertising. There was no relation between the amount of time used in presentation of the advertising and its memory value. But its memory value was affected by ingenious "sandwiching in" of advertising announcements. The complete isolation from the program of the advertising announcement as

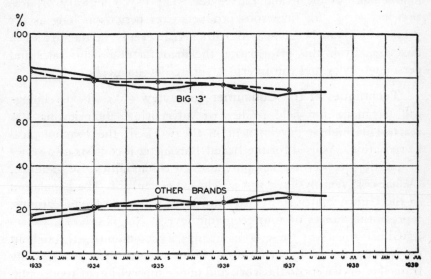

FIG. 26.—COMPARISON OF TRENDS OF CIGARETTE BRAND BAROMETER AND ANNUAL CIGARETTE SALES FOR THE BIG '3,' CONSISTING OF CAMELS, CHESTERFIELDS, AND LUCKY STRIKES, AND OTHER BRANDS.

Continuous line represents moving percentage averages of bimonthly interviews and broken line annual percentage totals of sales. (Courtesy of Psychological Corporation.)

an introduction or conclusion had low memory value. Amount of newspaper and magazine advertising had a negligible influence on memory of the broadcasted advertising.

"Psychological Brand Barometer."—The "Psychological Brand Barometer" was established in 1932 by Link and the Psychological Corporation as a continuous field study by interview, measuring the number of people buying advertised products or the percentage of customers. Its practical value lies in its prediction of what will appear in the sales records of retail stores shortly, in distributors records

somewhat later, and in manufacturer's records after a considerable delay. Fig. 26 shows a comparison of barometer percentages and annual sales of cigarettes, indicating the high degree of exactness of sales prediction well in advance of any knowledge the company has of its own sales. Brand Barometer readings are reported as having an accuracy within one per cent. Business firms contribute to the maintenance of the Brand Barometer. The Psychological Corporation has curves for numerous products over periods as long as six years which can be compared with actual events in the life of a business. From this information the manufacturer plans sales and personnel policy and can interpret future developments.

Techniques of the Consumer Interview.—As a psychological technique for field studies of advertising, interviewing has reached its highest development in the work of the Psychological Corporation. As used for the Brand Barometer it consists of a series of questions concerning last purchases of commodities, for example, "What cold remedy have you purchased recently?" The population of the United States is divided into A, B, C, and D buying groups, representing homes of four economic levels. Neighborhoods are selected as samples of these home-groups in communities throughout the country for the interviewing of housewives at their doors. Only trained interviewers do the work and under supervision of representatives of the Psychological Corporation. A sufficient number of interviews is scheduled in each survey to represent the community, and a sufficient number of communities to represent the corresponding economic class, so that the sample for each survey is representative of the buying habits of the country. Recently the Psychological Corporation has reported a reliable sample of 4000 homes of the B economic group as accurately responsive to advertising influences.

Interview Reliability.—Jenkins [36] has measured the reliability of the interview of last purchase for 19 products over 48 hours by a repeat interview on the excuse that the interviewer of the previous day had lost his records. A reliability index of 90 per cent was reported, with an average deviation of 1.8 per cent for the 19 commodities, showing uniformity between products. Considering that some individuals in the sample might have made purchases of different brands during the time elapsing between the two interviews, 90 per cent reliability of the consumer interview may be considered as exceedingly high.

Interview Validity.—Likewise Jenkins and Corbin [37] have measured the validity of the interview of last purchase for thirteen products by asking the interviewee to give the store of purchase and verifying it. A validity index of 77.5 per cent with an average deviation of 10.4 per cent was reported for the thirteen products. This validity index means that the interviewee named as his most recent purchase the brand of the product actually shown on the sales slip of the store in which he said he purchased it. Probably this estimate is reduced by housewives having made their most recent purchase at a store other than the one indicated—an error in naming the correct store. But this measured validity of the interview is judged to be satisfactory for practical purposes although it varies considerably for different products.

Concluding Statement on Consumer Psychology.—The foregoing discussion provides a limited introduction to consumer psychology. More complete surveys will be found in books on this subject.[38] From these it will be noted that the literature of the field is contributed by both the applied psychologist and advertising specialist. This literature includes various and sundry investigations, into the effect of such specific factors as repetition of runs of advertising, size and kind of type, the use of humor, drawings, photography, curved lines, various geometrical figures, and so on—all from the point of view of their value in attracting attention or their appeal in informing the consumer. On the other hand, the "new" psychology of selling and advertising [39] emphasizes measurement of the ultimate effect in consumer response by means of the field investigation.

Trade marks, trade names, and slogans are used quite generally in advertising. They differ in appeal and memory value, both of which are subject to measurement. Certain perfumes and cigarettes are preferred over others because of their trade name rather than because of any observable difference in value. Questions of trade-mark infringement are borderline territory between legal psychology and consumer psychology in which the degree of normal confusion between trade names is measured by recognition tests. For example, Paynter [40] studied the confusion existing between Coco Cola and Cheero Cola. Results of this study, which showed 40 per cent confusion, were used in a legal case between the Coco Cola and Cheero Cola Companies. Also, Paynter compared the confusion of nine similar worded trade marks that had been the subject of adjudication of infringement or noninfringement. He found the highest confusion (48 per cent) to be for a noninfringement case. Noninfringement cases had an average of 32.5 per cent confusion and infringement cases 33.2 per cent confusion, thus indicating that legal action has little relation to degree of actual confusion in advertising recognition.

REFERENCES

Bennett, M. E. *College and Life.* New York: McGraw-Hill Book Company, Inc., 1933.

Bingham, W. V. *Aptitudes and Aptitude Testing.* New York: Harper and Brothers, 1937, 166-205.

Burtt, H. E. *Legal Psychology.* New York: Prentice-Hall, Inc., 1931.

Burtt, H. E. *Psychology of Advertising.* Cambridge: Houghton Mifflin Company, 1938.

Link, H. C. *The New Psychology of Selling and Advertising.* New York: The Macmillan Company, 1932.

Marston, W. M. *The Lie Detector Test.* New York: R. R. Smith, 1938.

Paterson, D. G., Schneidler, G. G., and Williamson, E. G. *Student Guidance Techniques.* New York: McGraw-Hill Book Company, Inc., 1938.

Poffenberger, A. T. *Psychology in Advertising.* New York: McGraw-Hill Book Company, Inc., 1932.

CHAPTER XX

PHYSIOLOGICAL PSYCHOLOGY

By G. L. Freeman, *Northwestern University*

General Orientation

Psychology, in most of its branches, studies the activities of human (and subhuman) beings as *total* organisms. Occasionally behavior is analyzed into some simple components, such as reflexes, but attention is generally centered on the person as a whole—a compact, integrated biological unit reacting to its external environment in various ways. Useful as these total appraisals may be, we also need to know how particular parts of the body function in behavior. Students of medicine and other biological sciences, who are especially interested in this question, turn for an answer to *physiological psychology, a field which takes as its problem the relationship of integrated behavior to the various bodily mechanisms.*

The anatomy and physiology of sense organs, nerves, glands, and muscles contribute to an understanding of man-as-a-whole, since breakdown of a total function is almost invariably due to breakdown in the action of some part. Behind the relatively simple front of each overt action lies a background of great complexity. The attempts of the physiological psychologist to unravel the mysteries of this background can be compared with the efforts of a mechanically-minded individual to understand the workings of an automobile. In each case much has to be mastered that is only indirectly related to the action of the total machine. One must be able to appreciate the principles of internal gas combustion, gear reduction, and friction loss before the workings of the automobile become clear. So the physiological psychologist needs to attain a thorough understanding of bodily structures and functions before attempting his examination of behavior mechanisms. But this is not the full extent of his task. Knowledge which comes from the study of body parts in isolation does not satisfactorily explain the more complicated forms of behavior. The facts and theories developed from such work must be tested experimentally for their application to the operation of the intact organism. And, since parts often act differently together than when taken apart, *integration* becomes the major problem of physiological psychology.

Psychological Function and Bodily Structure.—No exact correspondence may be expected between psychological function and bodily structure. There are several reasons for this. In the first place, a psychological function always involves a number of bodily parts, and even such a relatively simple act as seeing a green light depends upon an elaborate chain of events in the retina, the brain, and the eye muscles. In the second place, a given bodily part is capable of contributing to several different psychological activities, as when the arm muscles respond reflexly to a painful stimulus or contract slightly when the person imagines he is hammering a nail; and, while certain structures are more important to one type of activity than are others, to speak of the brain as the 'seat of consciousness' and of the glands as the 'basis of emotion' is an unwarranted simplification of the idea. Finally, a number of bodily structures are yet without well-defined functions, and many psychological disorders have no known organic basis.

Fully aware of these limitations, the physiological psychologist leaves the writing of a definitive physiology of emotion, learning, and other activities until such time as their psychological analyses are more adequate and the methods of bodily correlation are more refined. By setting out first to understand the bodily mechanisms themselves and second to apply that knowledge to activities of the total organism, he is more likely to arrive at basic principles than if he begins with psychological functions first and proceeds to hypothetical, unsubstantiated, and inept physiological explanations. It is very significant that so many positive statements made about the bodily mechanisms involved in performance have turned out to be untrue! Consequently we are here concerned mainly with certain physiological processes known to govern integrated behavior and with the contributions of different bodily structures to these processes.

The Energetics of Activity.—The human organism may be regarded as an engine specifically designed for changing energy from one form to another. Energy is received from the foods that we eat and from the stimuli that fall upon our sense organs. Energy is released in our performances, which vary all the way from involuntary startle to a noise, to solving a problem in higher mathematics. The energy transformation or turnover that takes place when we react to stimuli is known as work, and our efficiency, like that of other machines, can be measured by dividing our work output by our energy input.

Why is it that energy is received by the human machine in two different forms and given out in only one? Or, to state the question another way, if all energy outgo involves reactions to incoming stimulus energies, what is the function of food? To understand this we must realize that the human organism is not a truly inert machine, to be set into motion by the application of energy sources distinct from itself. External stimuli, such as the air vibrations producing hearing, serve mainly as 'trigger charges' to release food energies already stored in the bodily tissues. The economy of the human body is organized around two complementary systems: (a) The digestive-circulatory system, and (b) the neuromuscular system. As indicated in Fig. 27, food energies are changed by the digestive system into a concentrated type of fuel which is made easily available by the circulatory system to tissues of the neuromuscular system; the external-stimulus source touches off the fuels stored in the neuromuscular system and a response is made.

Since these two systems tend to act as a unit, the key to the *why* of organic response is to be found more in the complicated energy exchanges going on within the body tissues than in the work of outside stimulus energies acting upon them. The sight of water does not lead a man to drink unless he is thirsty, and a certain physiological state must be operating before the mere presence of a mate leads an animal to make sexual advances. It is a fundamental biological fact that the behavior of all living organisms tends to be self-regulatory and not that of a robot, controlled by the external promptings of a fortuitous and changing environment. This self-regulation involves (1) basic tissue conditions which upon reaching states of excess or deficiency give rise to internal stimulations and so excite the organism to general activity, and (2) mechanisms of overt reaction which are potentially able to secure stimuli which will return the internal tissue conditions to a more 'normal' state and hence restore the equilibrium of the entire apparatus. In the absence of food or mate, activities appear which tend to provide them. Such reactions

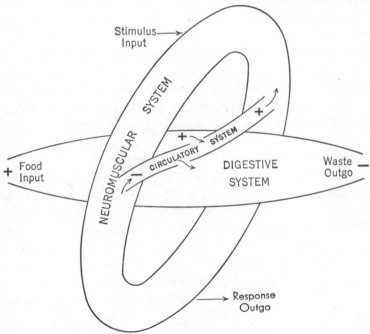

Fig. 27.—The Plan of the Body.

are of direct and immediate value to the organism as equilibration of basic inner tensions. So too are the more remotely conditioned outlets in which much apparently purposeless activity in children eventually finds specific expression.

The physiological psychologist's interest in the energetics of activity builds around the question of *energy sources* and of *control mechanisms* which direct the spontaneous activity thereby aroused. Studies showing that 'hunger' contractions of the stomach coincide with periods of heightened general activity have indicated the importance of the digestive-circulatory system as a source of energy; and experimental removal and implantation of the several endocrine glands have contributed greatly to our knowledge of more diffuse energizing phenomena—in which the tissue "need" does not lead so directly to overt behavior, but manifests itself mainly in raised metabolism and reactivity of other bodily tissues. In the matter of control mechanisms, it is fairly certain that the "spontaneous" activities aroused by tissue demands are rather nonspecific, being supplied with a minimum of internal "steer" or direction. The digestive-circulatory system is much better adapted for conserving existing bodily energies than for acquiring or avoiding new stimulus energies which are beneficial or harmful to continued organic function. The latter need is supplied by the neuromuscular overlay apparatus, whose chief characteristic is a maximum capacity for change or modification of behavior in the most appropriate direction. Thus, whenever the digestive-circulatory system is disturbed or forced into a state of disequilibrium through the absence of basic tissue needs, such as the need for food, it sets up a nonspecific compulsion of the superposed neuromuscular system to so adjust the organism in the environment as to acquire stimuli which have the capacity to produce more or less adequate readjustment in the basic system. Since environment is ever-changing, it is obvious that great functional plasticity must be the chief characteristic of the neuromuscular apparatus.

The Neuromuscular Apparatus.—The neuromuscular apparatus is not a homogeneous affair, but is organized in relation to a threefold plan; these divisions are the *sensory receptors,* the *central (brain) adjustors*, and the *motor effectors* (see Fig. 28).

External stimuli act on receptor organs; the energy released by these structures supplies the charge which excites the central adjusting neurones; and these nerve cells, in turn, discharge upon some motor outlet or effector organ which develops the overt response. A cross-sectional view of the neuromuscular apparatus at any moment would show a vast number of nerve discharges passing from receptors of the eye, ear, and skin to the brain and spinal centers of the central nervous system, and an equally vast number of discharges passing from these adjustor nerves to the effector organs, the muscles and glands. These nerve discharges are electrochemical phenomena which accompany energy transformation in nerve cells, and their detection by delicate electrical amplifying devices serves to tell us what parts of the neuromuscular apparatus are doing work. Nerve discharges of external origin are not generally chained directly through a stereo-

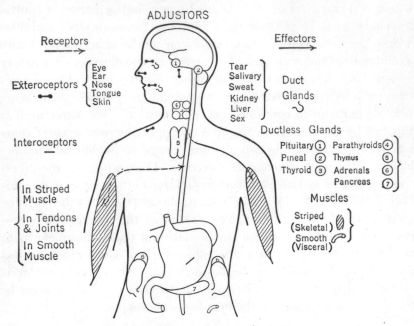

FIG. 28.—NEUROMUSCULAR APPARATUS.

Different symbols are used for each type of organ to indicate its approximate location. Only the ductless glands are numbered for specific identification. Glands are properly classed along with muscles as effector organs because of their motor functions.

typed circuit to a particular motor outlet. Instead, such discharges on reaching the adjustor centers have to be integrated or made to fit with excitation of internal origin before the discharge leading to appropriate motor response is released. In this way the integrity of the total apparatus is preserved; and much incongruous and harmful behavior is avoided, such as removing an irritating stimulus from the back of the neck when one's arms are already engaged in keeping the body from falling out of a tree.

Methods of Investigation.—Many different techniques are used by physiological psychologists in the study of behavior mechanisms. Where the problem is largely that of determining the functional contributions made by some particular part of the neuromuscular apparatus, that part may be removed and behavior changes after extirpation compared with those which held prior to the lesion; or the part may be *stimulated* electrically and concomitant changes in behavior noted. Sometimes the problem is to find the major adjustor centers involved in a given performance, and here the activity in question is initiated while various brain structures are explored for *electrical signs of heightened activity*. These three methods are largely limited to animal experimentation; and many difficulties arise from trying to "homologize" or relate the connections found between structure and function with analogous activity in man. Correlations between behavior changes and *pathological lesions* are often helpful, as in the connection between speech loss, or aphasia, and the locus of brain tumors. An even more fruitful method takes various *peripheral indicators of central function* such as blood pressure, galvanic skin resistance, or electrical "waves" from the brain, and studies changes occurring in them during performance of the intact human organism. Since such physiological reactions are extremely sensitive and not under voluntary control, they are of great diagnostic value, as with the use of blood-pressure changes in the detection of guilt or brain-wave records to warn of impending epileptic seizures.

From this brief overview, it appears that physiological psychology has important practical bearings and is, at the same time, a very complicated field of study. Those specializing in it must be rather versatile persons, mastering many difficult techniques and having a considerable background of anatomical and physiological detail in order to interpret their results. In the sections which follow we shall see specific applications of the various methods to the study of the gross divisions of the neuromuscular apparatus.

SENSORY FUNCTIONS

By virtue of the place which they hold in the threefold plan of neuromuscular action, *receptor mechanisms are primarily concerned with the initiation of behavior.* With the exception of the cases of muscle and gland excitation by *autocoid* substances in the blood stream, man reacts only to energy changes affecting his sense organs. These influences or stimuli give qualitatively different effects, such as red, green, pressure and pain, and quantitative changes such as in intensity and in duration. The physiological psychologist is especially interested in how these two different aspects of sensory function are related to the activity of the receptor organs. These structures are specifically differentiated cells with low thresholds of excitation for certain kinds of stimuli (called "adequate") and high thresholds for all other energy manifestations. They either exist as more or less independent units distributed throughout body tissues, as in the skin, or are collected together in elaborate sense organs, which possess in addition to the specially sensitized tissue a number of accessory parts adapted to concentrate particular kinds of stimulus energy thereon, as in the eye and the ear. Receptors are divided into two great classes, depending upon their adequate stimuli. (1) The *exteroceptors* are a part of the body surface; they include the eye, ear, nose, tongue, and skin, and react to stimuli in the external environment. (2) The *interoceptors* are embedded in the inner body tissues, especially the muscles and digestive organs, and react to pressure stimuli arising from the activity of these parts, that is, the internal environment.

Qualitative Variations.—Much speculation has been aroused concerning the relationship between the various receptor structures and the different qualitative experiences or sensations. According to a now discarded view, nerves from the eye, ear, etc., carried a different type of discharge or specific nerve energy. We know today that all nerves that convey excitation from receptors to the central nervous system behave in approximately the same manner, and the fact that each sensory nerve arouses a special type of response is determined largely by the kind of tissue with which that nerve connects. This means that if it were possible to attach the optic nerve to the ear and the auditory nerve to the eye, we might be able, as has been said, "to see the thunder and hear the lightning."

Search for the origin of the various sensory qualities in the terminal receptor and brain cells of the sensory circuit has given rise to a controversy of wide implication. The most common view supposes that specialized receptor structures exist for each quality in a given sense modality, and that the analysis is, therefore, *peripheral.* An alternative notion is that the receptor structures in a given sense organ, such as the eye, are largely alike, and that the total pattern of stimulation is sent forward to the brain for *"central"* analysis. The classic example of the specialized receptor theory is one which suggests that the different receptor structures in the skin respond exclusively to one type of stimulus—one for warm, another for cold, etc. Direct correlation studies have shown, however, no specialized receptors under any warm or cold spots of the skin—only free nerve endings and afferent fibers in blood vessels; and recent work on the differential effect of warm and cold stimuli upon these undifferentiated end organs suggests the importance of central brain processes in the analysis of sensation. In the field of hearing, where the specialized receptor theories are also more traditional, study of the electrical responses of the auditory nerve lends some support to a theory of central analysis. Even in the field of vision, where either specialized structures or qualitatively different photochemical substances in the eye have always been proposed as the basis for the sensations of red, green, etc., the importance of central brain factors begins to be recognized. It is, of course, too early to state in any one of these fields the relative importance of receptor and brain cells in the qualitative analysis of sensory functions; but it is certain that this domain should provide a veritable bonanza for any research worker with a fruitful imagination and equipment for refined physiological investigation.

Quantitative Variations.—Much more is known concerning quantitative variations in sensory functions. These have to do with the amount of inertia of the receptor and time relations in the associated nerve discharge. According to the *all-or-nothing law,* each receptor has a quantity of energy ready for discharge, and any stimulus that is of sufficient intensity to overcome the "threshold" inertia of the receptor and touch off that energy, discharges the whole of it. Increments in stimulus intensity, if registered in the brain, would, therefore, represent the involvement of more receptors. There would also be increased frequency of discharge for each receptor, since stronger stimuli excite the nerve earlier in its resting or refractory period.

Since the number of receptors in any given sense organ is limited, the questions of gradations in response becomes an important one. From the time of Weber and Fechner it has been known that the minimum increase in stimulus intensity necessary to be sensed as just perceptible, becomes progressively greater as one proceeds from low to high intensity. The logarithmic increase in the frequency of nervous discharge found to accompany equal stimulus increments correlates with the first observation, and means that most of our receptors are sensitized to respond to the lower range of intensities. When the stimulus is more intense the receptive apparatus is relatively unresponsive, having few units which remain to be discharged by the added increment.

The duration of a stimulus as well as its intensity affects the receptor mechanism, and under prolonged activation the receptor loses its excitability. This is known as *sensory adaptation* and depends upon the fact that receptors and their associated nerve fibers respond at different rates to the same external energy charge. The receptor loses its excitability very slowly, while the associated nerve responds, rests, and responds again many times before the receptor itself rests. The receptor thus operates after the fashion of an electrical interrupter in changing a continuous stimulus into a series of discontinuous nerve discharges, between the passage of which the nerve cell is able to recover its excitability. Of course if the nerve cell were stimulated sufficiently long, it would be excited earlier and earlier in the *refractory period* when it is supposed to rest, and would ultimately be entirely exhausted. But before this great physiological impairment occurs, the receptor will itself have become inactive and no further stimulus effect will be transmitted to the sensory nerve and other parts of the central nervous system. This buffer action of the receptor in sensory adaptation actually protects the brain cells from possible fatigue effects brought on by prolonged external stimulation.

MOTOR FUNCTIONS

Effector structures are specialized types of cells that react in specific ways to nerve discharges conveyed by receptor and adjustor units. All have a relation to the general function of motility. The *striped* or skeletal muscles move the body framework about in the environmental field. The *smooth* muscles of the hollow viscera (stomach, intestines, blood vessels) contract and relax to maintain the steady flow of fuel energies throughout the body and the *duct glands* (tear, salivary, sweat) provide essential substances for the same end. Secretions of the *ductless* or endocrine glands pass directly through the gland cell walls into the blood stream, where they are carried to other parts of the body, raising and lowering their activity. Physiological psychology has two general problems connected with the action of these effector mechanisms, the muscles and glands. One is to classify all the specific mechanisms of overt adjustments. The other is to determine what backlash influence effector activities have upon other parts of the neuromuscular apparatus.

We have already seen that man is no mere touch-and-go mechanism, turning external "stimuli" into external "responses." Muscles and glands, besides serving to effect specific adjustments which will favorably modify the organism's relation to the external environment, act to sustain and energize the rest of the reaction apparatus. For purposes of discussion, we shall classify functions of the first type as *phasic reactions,* and functions of the second type as *tonic reactions.* The phasic response is of short duration and usually represents a temporary adjustment to some momentary and fleeting stimulus, as in the reflex withdrawal of the hand from a heated object. The tonic response represents a more enduring but less specific adjustment calculated to sustain a certain continuity in the organism's conduct by supporting appropriate phasic responses, as in the general postural alertness which accompanies unexpected contact with a harmful environmental stimulus. Phasic acts of a voluntary or reflex nature occur only when the muscles are in a state of slight tension, and these same tonic activities by supplying a major share of backlash excitation to the brain cells are largely responsible for their lowered thresholds to sensory excitation during waking activity. Since practically all effector organs have both phasic and tonic functions, it is hard to assign each type of reaction exclusively to a given class of effectors. On the other hand, it can be said that tonic bodily trends of alertness or lassitude are largely influenced by the activity of the ductless or endocrine glands and by the maintained states of slight muscular tension, while the more intense and shortlived contractions of skeletal muscle and the secretions of the duct glands contribute little to tonic functions. Attempts at more precise distinctions stress the evidence for two different kinds of muscle tissue, differences in central adjustor control, and differences in sources of sensory stimulation. But until there is more general agreement on these points, we may think of all effector mechanisms as potentially capable of phasic and tonic reaction. And while it is often difficult to segregate the two, every motor adjustment gives some indication of the mutual contributions of activity specifically directed toward the source of stimulation and of widespread supporting postural adjustments.

Phasic Reactions.—Qualitatively different phasic reactions, including the many exact adjustment mechanisms for maintaining balance, grasping objects, or rejecting harmful substances from the digestive tract, cannot be adequately surveyed in our limited space. Instead we will confine ourselves to certain quantitative variations common in all such responses. When a muscle or gland is stimulated by a mass discharge of energy over its associated motor nerves, it reacts suddenly, thereby causing an overt movement, or secretion of some glandular product. In the case of muscles, at least, response is roughly graded to stimulus intensity in accordance with the all-or-nothing law. If the stimulation is continued for a long time, progressive decrements in response appear. This is usually referred to as fatigue, though an equally appropriate term would be *motor adaptation*. The primary cause for the loss of muscular responsiveness is the rapid accumulation of split waste products, especially at the point of junction between nerve and muscle. Like all cells of the body, muscle fibers are able to carry on work by burning up certain fuels, which they manufacture from foods carried to them by the blood. When motor activity occurs too frequently, as in continued electrical stimulation of a frog's muscle over its associated motor nerve, the rate at which fuel molecules are split up by the activity exceeds the rate at which they are burned by the oxygen of the blood stream, and the toxic substances resulting from this partial combustion accumulate on the muscle and literally foul its connection with the central nervous system. This "fuse plug" arrangement operates to cut off the stimulus to continued action before the muscle fibers are seriously impaired and, during rest, when waste products are being removed and new fuels supplied, the muscle recovers its irritability.

Because much of man's work also shows decreased output with time, many psychologists have tried to explain this phenomenon on the same basis as the fatigue effects found in the nerve-muscle experiment with the frog. It is known, however, that in such work as prolonged mathematical activity, a man may show decreased output without true motor fatigue, and that true fatigue is often present without decrement of output. The latter situation is especially true when one applies progressively stronger inner stimulation to get through some arduous and monotonous task, when renewed command of the motor apparatus is apparent. Actually, both motor and sensory adaptation act to protect the central nervous system from impairment; only the fact that the central adjustors can command new sources of stimulation from the backlash of tonic reactions enables the organism to break through these barriers when necessary and compensate for loss of phasic responsiveness.

Tonic Reactions.—We have already indicated that phasic reaction to stimulation is of necessity superposed upon tonic bodily trends. A vast array of motor processes comprise this organic excitation background, acting to direct sensory stimulation into specifically prepared channels of overt response and sustaining elaborate patterns of central adjustor activity. Most obvious and well-known for their energizing effect on phasic reaction are the processes of skeletal muscle tension; we often find them compensating for the deleterious influence of sleep loss and in work under distraction. Less thoroughly understood but of recognized importance are the visceral tensions and the postural changes in smooth muscle tissue; these often carry for long times the residual effects of frustration due to a deflection of the central excitation pattern from the thwarted overt activity. Most obscure of all factors and probably most vital to a thorough understanding of an individual's general reactivity level are the secretions of endocrine glands, called autocoids; these are poured directly into the blood stream, some secretions called *hormones* serve to excite while other substances called *chalones* serve to depress the activity of other glands and bodily tissues. Thus, the pituitary gland is known as the "motor" of the gonads and certain of its hormones are in-

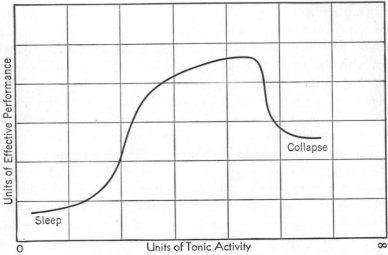

FIG. 29.—THEORETICAL RELATION OF SUPPORTING TONIC ACTIVITY TO THE EFFECTIVENESS OF PHASIC PERFORMANCE.

jected artificially to raise and lower sexual vitality. Another instance is seen in the favorable effect of the thyroid hormone on the general "drive" of patients with low metabolism.

As with our discussion of phasic reactions, we cannot treat here exhaustively the many qualitative variations in tonic activity, but shall mention only certain questions of operation which apply to all these processes. The first and most important concerns the relationship of quantity of tonic activity to the vigilance of the central nervous system. When is the brain "asleep," we may ask, and when is it in the state of excitability that is known to us as consciousness? Repeated demonstration of the relativity of so-called mental effort and tonic motor activity leads us to assume that backlash excitation from these processes supplies a major portion of stimulation necessary for brain activity during waking hours. While final confirmation is far from complete, we may think of muscular tension and related tonic processes as supporting increasingly effective performance up to a certain point, after which more excessive reactivity is accompanied by performance of decreased effectiveness. As indicated in Fig. 29, performance levels sustained by a low degree of tonic activity would be akin to sleep, whereas the upper limits of reactivity would be accompanied by the collapse of integrated behavior.

It is also known that when overt phasic activity is blocked short of its goal, the supporting tonic processes tend to persist as a heightened reactivity level and so develop an excitation pattern which exerts a more or less constant pressure to be relieved. Experiments have shown that the more successful the overt reaction to a stimulus situation, the less the residual tensions. In this direction, possibly, lies new light on the ever-baffling problems of the neuroses, and it is proof of yet untouched areas, that physiological psychology is just beginning to become aware of its potential contributions to psychiatry.

Brain and Behavior

Having taken into account the operation of both receptors and effectors, we are now left with the adjustor mechanisms that intervene. The primary function of these mechanisms is to integrate the various excitations coming from the receptors and to direct the effector responses with reference to stimulus conditions. In spite of their recognized importance, the control mechanisms in the brain and spinal cord are the most imperfectly known link in the total receptor-adjustor-effector sequence. Many elaborate theories of how these centers function in specific types of behavior rest upon assumed properties of nerve cells which have no basis in physiological experiment. The starting point for most of these accounts has been either the theory, dating from the phrenologist, Gall, that psychological activities are localized within minute brain areas, or the associated notion that all integrated activity is patterned after the spinal reflex. Neither of these theories is correct in fact. Gall's doctrine of localization gains support from results showing definite impairment upon destruction of certain brain areas, but does not take into account many negative instances of vicarious function and gives no answer to the all-important question of how different areas exercise their functions or influence each other. Extension of the theory of reflex integration to this problem is also unwarranted; for while many spinal reactions such as the knee jerk may be explained by the conduction of impulses from receptors to effectors over inherently restricted pathways, greater plasticity of central connection is necessary to explain the more complicated behavior patterns. No amount of subsidiary theorizing in the form of allied reflex arcs or the interplay of facilitative and inhibitory neural circuits alters the fundamentally weak assumption that particular reactions are restricted to connections of lower "resistance" between individual nerve cells.

Experimental evidence on the localization of brain function involves two types of research. Each of these has contributed a somewhat different answer to the problem. The traditional approach consists in removal or stimulation of some general area correlated with such changes in effector or receptor activity as may be noticed. But dealing thus with a brain part in isolation is, in a sense, an artifact, and consequently the newer approach consists in taking some well-defined behavior pattern, such as a learned reaction, and correlating the different amounts of brain tissue removed with functional loss. The first approach gives a view of the special functional contributions made to the total behavior flux by grossly different anatomical structures; the second approach shows us that similar anatomical units within these gross structures are largely equipotential, that is, capable of being used in many different functional acts.

Structural Organization of Reaction Levels.—The gross divisions of the adjustor apparatus are responsible for the general form that the response takes. The same effector and receptor mechanisms function in many different types of behavior; but the structural arrangement of the central nervous system makes it an organization of levels, so that certain parts of it may dominate behavior at a given instant. For explanatory purposes a rough comparison may be drawn between this neural organization and that of a commercial agency engaged in providing appropriate answers to an almost inconceivable variety of questions. In the interest of efficiency, simple and urgent messages are responded to on the ground floor level, the receiving clerks connecting directly with the sending clerks, and the news that a response has been made reverberating to offices on higher floors. If, however, an automatic response is not immediately forthcoming, or if the response made is not entirely appropriate, the higher offices take up the task of directing the sending end of the concern. The more complicated the problem, the more work will be put upon fashioning the response. The news will be transmitted upward from floor to floor, each department supplying whatever information it can give upon the topic. The nature of the message and the ability of a department to answer it will determine where the dominant direction occurs. Only those messages that cannot be answered appropriately at the lower levels are passed to a higher floor for decision. If they do reach so far, this office is in command of all the information which has been collected by those departments below it. In the central nervous system, the cerebral hemispheres represent the highest floor, the spinal cord the lowest floor, and other brain centers the intermediate floors. Nervous impulses developed by the receptor mechanisms may thus pass through different adjustor centers to effect motor responses, and the particular loop-line connection used determines the dominant center for integration.

Fig. 30 indicates the major features in the structural organization of reaction levels. The *spinal cord* carries integrating centers for local "reflex" response to local stimulation and is, in addition, the grand artery for entrance and exit of nerve discharges to and from other adjustor centers. A structuro-functional division of each of the spinal segments enables us to recognize nerve fibers entering the back, or dorsal, side of the cord as sensory and those on the front, or ventral, side as motor. Running parallel to the segments of the spinal cord are the *autonomic nerve chains* or ganglia which act as relay stations and independent correlation centers for smooth muscles and glands. The divisions of this part of the nervous system have opposed functions; the *sympathetic ganglia* serve to inhibit digestive actions and to mobilize bodily energies for emergency adjustments,

as in fight or flight; and the *parasympathetic* division controls the
bodily energies for appetitive or vegetative reactions.

The brain has three divisions: (1) the hindbrain, which comprises
the medulla oblongata and the cerebellum, (2) the midbrain, and (3)
the forebrain, which comprises the thalamus and the cerebral hemis-

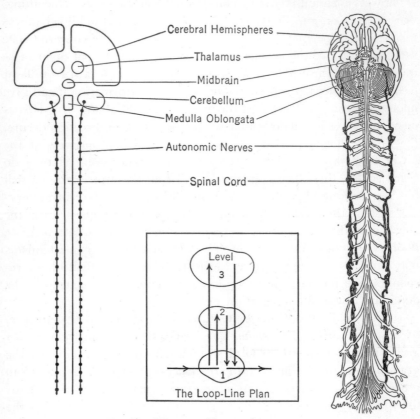

Cerebral Hemispheres

Thalamus

Midbrain

Cerebellum

Medulla Oblongata

Autonomic Nerves

Spinal Cord

Level 3

2

1

The Loop-Line Plan

FIG. 30.—LEVELS OF NEURAL INTEGRATION.

pheres. The *medulla oblongata* carries control centers for respiration
and circulation—automatic reactions necessary to the continuance
of life. The *cerebellum* and the *midbrain* are two great coordinating
centers for muscular responses, especially those of the tonic type. The
thalamus is the vestibule by which sensory stimulation enters the
cerebral hemispheres and is also a motor center for the regulation of

certain bodily activities involved in the emergency emotions. The *cerebral hemispheres* serve to coordinate the activity in lower centers, and specialize in directing the most complicated neuromuscular reaction patterns. These various brain parts have been successively superposed upon the spinal cord. As each new structure has developed, it has established connection with the lower and more primitive centers and taken over a portion of their function. In man, the cerebral hemispheres have grown so enormously that the outer layer or *cortex* is folded upon itself, forming many convolutions. This

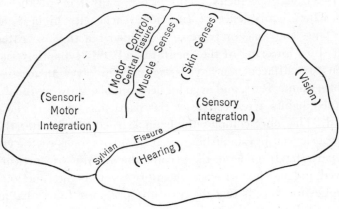

FIG. 31.—CORTICAL LOCALIZATION OF FUNCTION.

structural growth is paralleled by a degree of functional dominance over the rest of the adjustor apparatus which exists in no other species.

Certain areas of the cerebral cortex show a considerable degree of specialization, while equally large groups of cells seem to have more general facilitating and inhibiting functions. Fig. 31 shows the localizations roughly. The primary centers of motor control are located in front of the central fissure; at the lower end of the fissure is one of the centers of speech control and any lesion here will cause speech loss, or aphasia. The primary reception centers for stimulation from muscles and other internal tissues are in the parietal lobe, set in appropriate relation to the motor centers corresponding to these parts. The special senses also have well-defined reception areas—vision on the medial side of the occipital lobe, and hearing in the temporal lobe below the Sylvian fissure. The remaining areas, including the frontal lobe, as indicated, are general integrating centers. The fact that these parts of the cerebral cortex are most adaptable and labile prevents the harmful stereotypy of behavior and has done much to make man ascendant over all other animals.

Mass Action within the Cerebral Cortex.—While various neural strata dominate different types of reactions, it is not to be inferred that individual nerve cells within a given brain part have exact functional specificity. This is especially true of the cerebral cortex, where equivalence of function reaches its highest development. The "engram" or trace of a learned reaction, so often "explained" by a lowering of the "neural bond" or "synaptic resistance" between two adjacent nerve cells, actually involves an area of considerable extent. Rats, and even higher animals, show residual effects of learned habits irrespective of the particular part of the cortex removed. The more complex the habit learned, the greater the difficulty experienced in establishing even the gross locus of the essential neural pattern. In general, the greater the amount of cortical tissue destroyed, independent of place, the more severe is the functional loss. The suggestion here is that the traces of previous functional activity are not laid down on the brain surface according to a strictly spatial plan, but exist as ratios of excitability involving a wide cortical territory and capable of being reorganized in the parts remaining after brain lesion. This relatively nonspecific response of cortical cells in the control of complicated discriminative behavior is known as *mass action,* and it is probable that upon complete removal of the cerebral hemispheres or the relative functional decortication produced by a startling stimulus, the thalamic centers act somewhat similarly in fashioning the emotional type of display. It is, of course, hard to estimate the extent to which results obtained on the brains of the animals apply to man. In so far as quality of tissue is concerned, the results are comparable; and aside from the primary sensory reception and motor projection areas, the cortical tissue of man seems to be generally capable of mass action and equipotential function. Cases have been reported of patients who recovered from complete removal of the frontal lobe without serious impairment to their intellectual processes.

BODILY MECHANISMS AND PERSONALITY

The notion that personality traits are intimately related to structural differences of individuals has had a long and unjustified vogue. Such pseudoscientific approaches as phrenology and physiognomy are still practiced upon the unwary public, and there is much talk among certain psychiatrists of the characteristic mental disorders of special body "types."

Before we examine the evidence on this problem, it is well to recognize that psychological tests are only beginning to give us valid and reliable criteria for detection of different aspects or traits of personality. Until fairly recently, estimates of relative intellectual ability rested upon nothing more substantial than the opinions of the persons making the concomitant structural measurements; and even now we find gross system-classifications of abnormal behavior substituted for continuously graded tests of the emotional or nonintellectual aspects of personality. With this state of affairs on the psychological side, and with the difficulty of making complete anatomical and physiological assays on a sufficiently large sample of the population, it is small wonder that few definite relationships have been found. The balance of evidence is definitely negative with reference to an intimate connection between physique and personality, but a few suggestive reports show that more subtle physiological variations may be involved.

The Psychoanatomy of Types.—The psychoanatomy of types assumes that men can be pigeonholed into several rough divisions according to their general structural development and that these divisions will correspond, also roughly, to fundamental differences in temperament and intelligence. This notion can be traced as far back as Hippocrates, and contributions since that time have been chiefly the substitution of more exact physical measurements without a corresponding increase in their significance. Height, weight, carpal development, height-weight ratios, head shape, and relation of limb to trunk development have all been tried and found wanting. For example, the correlations between height-weight ratios and tested intelligence on the average are so small (+.28) that normal individuals of extreme limits in size may show almost any degree of intelligence from high to low; and the slight relation reported between body type and emotional disorders provides no basis for individual prediction. We can see, therefore, that the only possible connection between physique and personality would have to come from some common determining factor, such as the endocrine glands; and only in extreme cases, as in the thyroid deficiency of cretins, could we expect an obvious relation. It is difficult to see why in the face of such low correlations as have been found, the psychoanatomy of types is still so well received. The automobile mechanic is not misled even by a high apparent correlation between body build and engine power, but directs his attention to the essential physical correlates of power. It would be sensible to adopt a similar attitude with reference to man.

Neuroanatomical Differentiation.—Numerous attempts have been made to correlate the intellectual aspects of personality with differences in neural structure; but no post-mortem method of assorting brains on the basis of weight, size, number of convolutions, or thickness of the cortical layer has yet served to classify them as to previous functional capacity. The six-per-cent difference in brain-weight between men and women disappears when corrected for the proportionally heavier bodyweight of men and so constitutes no evidence of superior function. Widely quoted surveys of the brains of "geniuses" have little or no statistical reliability. While absence of large amounts of cortical tissue certainly lessens capacity to learn, the brains of superior human beings probably have not only an extensive mass of tissue but are also very highly organized. A complicating factor in all of these studies is the uncertainty as to what part of a given brain was once functionally active, and what portion was inactive tissue, serving merely to support and protect the active parts. There is great need for more delicate and refined techniques of differentiating brains, and it is here that brain chemistry—with its assay of the products of cell activity—may prove very useful. At present we can only surmise that it is neither the amount of cortical tissue nor the quantity of energy available which alone accounts for the abilities of man, but rather differences in the capacity of brain structures to make efficient use of the bodily energies as well.

Physiological Differentiation.—For many aspects of personality, especially the so-called temperamental traits, it now seems that such bodily bases as exist are more likely to be revealed by physiological analysis of behavior than by attempted correlations with either gross or microscopic anatomical structures. Measurable variations that are probably important to this problem include metabolic rate, blood pressure, and electrical skin resistance, muscular tension and the acidity of the blood, urine, and saliva. Differences in the hormone content of the blood undoubtedly have even greater significance, but biochemical assay is not yet ready for such a complicated field of research.

It is difficult, as yet, to say exactly what these various physiological measures indicate in terms of general organic reactivity or of differential body chemistry. Individuals rated as "neurotic" or "lacking in emotional stability" show high variability and slow recovery of equilibrium in galvanic skin measurements taken during displacing stimulation. On the other hand, attempts to relate such results to specific glandular or muscular conditions have not been generally successful. In the absence of adequate information it is easy to be led into abortive speculations. Thus, one writer foretells the day when "the physician will have bottled hormones labeled 'happiness,' etc." Such a seductive verbalism minimizes the tremendous obstacles which are yet to be surmounted and actually hampers study of the precise relationships between endocrine activity and total behavior.

Conclusion.—One cannot review the problems of physiological psychology without being impressed by the magnitude of the task remaining to be accomplished. Much of the work mentioned in this chapter has been negative, serving mainly to sweep away old and false notions. On the other hand, the new lines of attack which are developing hold tremendous promise for the more refined prediction and control of human behavior. Students interested in detailed information on the topics covered should consult the selected references given below. From such books, even more than from this introductory account, the inseparable linkage of psychology and physiology becomes increasingly clear. For example, gastric ulcers are now seen as related to frustrations of behavior, while surgical removal and glandular treatment are being successfully prescribed for disorders which would formerly have received only a "mental" treatment. The psychosomatic approach to abnormal behavior is one of the most promising frontiers of present-day science. Its development is ready and open to laboratory and clinical workers who are trained conjointly in psychology and physiology.

REFERENCES

Adrian, E. D. *The Basis of Sensation.* New York: W. W. Norton and Company, Inc., 1928.

Adrian, E. D. *The Mechanism of Nervous Action.* Philadelphia: University of Pennsylvania Press, 1932.

Boring, E. G. *The Physical Dimensions of Consciousness.* New York: D. Appleton-Century Company, Inc., 1933.

Cannon, W. B. *The Wisdom of the Body.* New York: W. W. Norton and Company, Inc., 1932.

Cannon, W. B., and A. Rosenblueth. *Autonomic Neuroeffector Systems.* New York: The Macmillan Company, 1937.

Child, C. M., *Physiological Foundations of Behavior.* New York: Henry Holt and Company, 1924.

Coghill, G. E. *Anatomy and the Problem of Behavior.* Cambridge, England: University Press, 1929.

Creed, R. S., et al. *Reflex Activity of the Spinal Cord.* Oxford, England: Clarendon Press, 1932.

Dodge, R. *Conditions and Consequences of Human Variability.* New Haven: Yale University Press, 1931.

Freeman, G. L. *Introduction to Physiological Psychology.* New York: The Ronald Press Company, 1934.

Hill, A. V. *Muscular Activity.* Baltimore: Williams and Wilkins Company, 1926.

Hoskins, R. G. *The Tides of Life.* New York: W. W. Norton and Company, Inc., 1933.

Jacobson, E. *Progressive Relaxation.* Chicago: University of Chicago Press, 1938.

Kempf, E. J. *The Autonomic Functions and the Personality.* Washington: Nervous and Mental Diseases Publishing Company, 1921.

Lashley, K. S. *Brain Mechanisms and Intelligence.* Chicago: University of Chicago Press, 1929.

Paterson, D. G. *Physique and Intellect.* New York: D. Appleton-Century Company, Inc., 1930.

Sherrington, C. S. *The Integrative Action of the Nervous System.* New Haven: Yale University Press, 1926.

CHAPTER XXI

AESTHETICS

By Kate Hevner, *Indiana University*

Introduction

The Problem.—With the first intimation that there is to be a scientific analysis of art and beauty, the romantic and tenderminded aesthete will perhaps take a hostile attitude. Such an attitude would be regrettable, for the appreciation and understanding of beauty is a skill which requires a great deal of practice and experience, and with the great complexity and specialization of modern life, we should no more expect the layman to acquire this skill in appreciation without systematic instruction than we would expect him to acquire proficiency in French simply by listening whenever possible to the French language, or by spending some time in a French city.

The particular problem for the psychologist in the field of art is a complete description of the experience of beauty. He cannot, as does the philosopher, discuss the nature of art, nor its relation to goodness, to truth, or other values of life. He must leave to the historian and anthropologist the problem of the origin and development of art forms, and to the sociologist the interactions between art and society. But the psychologist must frankly analyze; he must leave not one sensation or perception upon another. He must discern in the aesthetic experience each one of the component parts and trace its source in the stimulus (music, poem, or painting) which has aroused the reaction.

The Justification for the Scientific Approach.—Contrary to popular notion, this is good, not bad, psychology, and for several reasons:

(1) If we have no words, no concepts for these details, they will not be noticed or perceived. The details into which we analyze a

painting—pattern, balance, rhythm, perspective, chiaroscuro, etc.
—cannot be perceived if they cannot be named.[1] If our vocabularies fall short of complete description, our mental reaction and
manipulation of them will also fall short of the process of real appreciation.

(2) The study of each separate part of the experience does not
necessarily obscure the whole; in fact, if the whole is not perceived
as a compound of many interacting parts it will seem too simple to
hold the attention long enough for real appreciation.

(3) Acquiring the skill of appreciating is comparable to any
other kind of learning. There are the simpler and more fundamental
reactions to be acquired, and from these we proceed to the manipulation of higher units. The skillful rider and jumper will disdain the
restricted ring where the beginners are practicing mounting and trot-
ting, but no one would deny that these are necessary preliminaries.
Too exhaustive an analysis of one poem may destroy forever its
aesthetic quality but the process will enhance the poetic quality of
verses encountered in the future.

(4) There is a popular misconception that the aesthetic experience is a kind of miracle which stabs the heart, and shakes the soul,
and takes the breath away. It is felt by those who "possess the organ
by which poetry is perceived." It would be as ridiculous to speak
of those who "have the organ with which tennis is played." If one
has the leisure, the opportunity, the interest, either can be acquired,
and there is no evidence that more special talent is required for one
than for the other.

(5) There are certain kinds of art forms which depend for their
effectiveness on a very slight or subtle suggestion. A simile must
not be pushed to the last detail; the unspoken word may be the most
poignant. For this one type only, analysis would be likely to endanger
appreciation.

(6) Finally, if analysis destroys our pleasure in certain outworn
art objects, there is no cause for alarm. To maintain our aesthetic
skills, in a dynamic society such as ours, taste must be continually
changing and growing. To be dissatisfied with our earlier enthusiasms is one of the best signs of aesthetic health.

The Aesthetic Experience

General Characteristics.—The beauties of today—music, painting, literature, drama, sports, nature—are so different one from the other, and the ways of enjoying them are also so many and so varied that the psychologist who tries to describe *the* aesthetic experience faces almost as impossible a task as a doctor who might try to prescribe one single remedy for all kinds of diseases. Nevertheless it is important to have a clear analysis of this kind of experience for every amateur has need of it in understanding and developing his artistic enthusiasms. For this description the psychologist must draw not only upon the facts and theories of psychology in general, and upon the large body of experimental data in the psychology of art, but also upon the records of the poets and painters themselves. In fact, biography, criticism, and miscellaneous evidences of the artist's methods of working are sometimes of more value than carefully laid out experiments even though it is difficult to transform ecstasy, inspiration, and genius into terms which square with the facts and theories of modern and scientific psychology.

Let us first answer the question: What *is* the aesthetic experience? What does it feel like to be having it, and how can you tell when you are in the midst of it? At the outset we must make clear that the aesthetic experience is a very complex function rather than one single category of activity exclusive of all others. That is to say, it is in a class with such activities as playing bridge or tennis, debating a political problem, shopping for a new wardrobe, rather than *one* limited psychological function such as thinking, memorizing, perceiving, each of which has its distinctive and mutually exclusive character, even though it rarely or never occurs in a pure state. The aesthetic experience is rather a blend, a complex, which borrows from practically every one of the other functions, and derives its unity from the subjective aspects and diffuse bodily responses rather than from the compact means-to-end objective set that organizes most of the other complex activity of everyday life. It is usually an experience with a pleasant affective tone, although not necessarily so (for example, it may be ugly, or tragic), and it stands out a little from the general flow of neutral activity with a certain dignity, intensity, and unity so that one may recall it later as a definite experience. One turns back to the more common attitudes of daily life with a distinct feeling of having made a transition.

The aesthetic experience is complex in the same way that driving a car is complex. We might say that the activity of driving a car is composed of sensations of pressure on the accelerator foot, of tensions or readiness in the arm muscles, of wind on the face, together with a definite set of the head and eyes, with attention on the road and its signs, a feeling of or drive toward a purpose or goal (destination) and perhaps some slight emotional activity either of fear, or exhilaration. But it might also include such extraneous activity as smoking a cigarette, or carrying on a conversation, the making of judgments, experimenting with the mechanism, etc. A symposium or round table of psychologists to discover the "essence" of driving, would bring out as many different viewpoints and theories as we find in the history of aesthetics, and for the same reasons.

It is customary to speak of persons as having "talent" for art, or an artistic temperament, but a more precise description would state that certain individuals are in the habit of taking an aesthetic attitude toward their experiences. They have a certain way of looking for certain values and making certain judgments, rather than others. They look for broad meanings, for generalizations, for abstract qualities, for patterns and rhythms. Their habitual standards of reference are beauty, ugliness. We may discern other and different habitual attitudes among individuals of our acquaintance—a sentimental attitude which calls for the more romantic view of life, with a ready tear and a lush complacency; or the argumentative attitude, with a brittle skepticism toward men and motives; or a consistently optimistic or nonchalant and objective attitude. These become habitual ways of reacting, not absolutely fixed and continuous but frequent enough to be commonly recognized.

An Active and Attentive State.—The aesthetic experience is always an active, an intensely active, state of mind and body, not at all the passive acquiescence which appearances sometimes seem to imply. To be sure we sit at leisure to enjoy our music, we pause inactive to gaze at a picture, and many of our aesthetic experiences take place while we are in the more quiet bodily attitudes. The amateur has therefore often believed that we must be relaxed and limp, drained of our own initiative and energy so that the reaction from the aesthetic object may flow over us unresisted. Such figurative language has thwarted perhaps the attempts of many a novitiate who has tried to penetrate the mystery of appreciation by this method. No attitude could be more inauspicious. Appreciation requires alertness of mind and body. Attention must be directed wholeheartedly toward the objective stimulus and "attention" means that a state of readiness, of partial contraction, is being maintained by the muscles of the body, that the eyes are turned toward the stimulus and actively focussed there, that the ears are catching every detail of sound, that the mind follows the senses to supplement and interpret. It means also that the musculature is not occupied with any other activity, that it is free to respond to the movement and the rhythm of the stimulus, that it is actively seeking to follow every suggestion, to emphasize the experience at every point. Relaxation is lassitude and finally oblivion and sleep. Appreciation is muscle tonus, muscle coordination; it is activity, tensions, responses. It is awareness, alertness, animation, energy.

Sensory and Perceptual Activity.—Sensations themselves claim much more of the attention in this attitude than in other attitudes of life. Because of the economy demanded in our ordinary attitudes we pay the minimum of attention to our sensations, using them only as cues from which to catch the significance for further reaction. The sound of the clock enters consciousness only as an indication of lunch time; the sight of the clouds serves only to set in motion the business of closing the windows against the storm. In such cases we react to our sensations strictly in terms of their meaning. But in the aesthetic attitude we linger over the sensations as pure sensations, following the reverberations of the sounds, inhaling deeply of the aroma, tracing the movements, and feeling the brightnesses. We dwell on the qualities and intensities of the colors, the shapes, the sizes, the blends, the richness, the extensity and intensity, experiencing them not only with their proper sense organs but with the whole body. We follow outlines and surfaces with eye movements and muscular tensions, interpreting one sense by means of another and translating sounds and sights into kinaesthetic experiences, the better to apprehend them and to enhance and intensify the original sensations.

Along with this keen attention to the qualities of the sensations, the relations or patterns among the sensations themselves must also be noticed. The succession of separate tones becomes a melody, the combination of certain lines becomes a "figure" upon a "background," and our attention is held by these various forms. All the elements in a musical composition must be organized and reorganized into still larger units until the process of perceiving the piece as a unified whole is an immediate and effortless achievement. There is a melody in the bass which must be discerned and the progress of the harmony must be followed, first independently and then in relation to the various other melodies. The separate phrases of the melody must be identified so that they may be recognized when the composer uses them in different fashions. We must hear the repetitions and the contrasts, be alert to variation, elaboration, ornament. We must concentrate our attention first on one element and then on another, devoting all our bodily energy first to the pulse of the rhythm and next to the developing and expanding of the harmony and then to the echoes and extensions of the melody, returning to this element or that until the whole becomes not one thin and simple unit of perception, but a rich and vivid experience, crowded with sense impression and quickened with muscular tensions.

In the graphic arts there are the same possibilities for enriching and enlivening the original experience, for emphasizing and relating the various parts. Take occasion to notice, for example, the pattern of one of the colors in some familiar picture. Locate all the separate bits of it and see them as one pattern. Find all the lines which turn in one direction. Observe them as a unit and feel the pull of them. Look for the different planes and distances, the nearest one, and the farthest one. Notice the brightnesses and dullnesses, the lights and shadows, and organize them into a pattern. Look at the picture with half shut eyes and see the parts that stand out from it. Relax the whole body and let the eye wander over the picture lazily, observing the progress of the eye movements. Walk away and come upon it suddenly from a different angle. Look at it in a mirror and continue the search for new patterns. Try to memorize it, to imagine it different.

Of course by the end of such an exercise the observer will be utterly and indescribably bored with the picture, completely impatient and exasperated with the music. He will resent them as bitterly as the child resents his piano scales and his problems in long division. But we must remember that the objective was not the appreciation and enjoyment of the picture, but the building up of habits of observation; the awakening of the senses and the training of the perception so that the apprehension of the details will be ready and nimble. For if the skill in perception is slow and awkward, if the mere task of comprehending the form demands all the attention, there will be no time or energy left for the enjoyment of it. The pleasure of the total effect would be lost, just as the smack of a French epigram is lost to a beginner whose French is so poor that he must decipher each syllable with painstaking care. To achieve any pleasure in art, as in language, the facility must be so ready that as the sentence proceeds (or as the music proceeds) one is aware of the trend of the ideas and approaches the end with a certain foresight. Then the conclusion will be important as a fulfillment and it will be rich with satisfaction because it was wanted and needed. The moment for its enjoyment, however, must always be free. For the inexpert, the effort and confusion and uncertainty will crowd out the pleasure, and the experience cannot be crowned with success.

The process of acquiring this skill, however, is itself an aesthetic process, for each newly discovered pattern or insight brings an increment of enjoyment. So long as the last bit of the music can catch our wayward attention, we shall find it absorbing and beautiful. It is like the child's pleasure in the hundredth telling of the fairy tale. He can anticipate each detail of it as it unfolds itself in the telling, but he could not recall it of his own volition. He cannot foresee the end from the beginning nor yet from the middle—in fact not until that very last penultimate detail is set in place for him. When the music is completely known to us, when there is no slightest detail of it that escapes our anticipation, when memory serves all too well, and curiosity is entirely dead, then it requires an effort to hold our attention upon it, and with that the pleasure is gone and we find the music wholly trite and thoroughly objectionable. The life of a popular song is said to be approximately three months.

The Role of Empathy.—In the apprehension of the beautiful stimulus, a process called empathy (German: Einfühling, or "feeling into") was first recognized by Theodor Lipps as playing a significant part. In empathy we project our own states of being into inanimate objects, and attribute to them the activities which we ourselves are experiencing. The sensations of strain and movement from our own muscles and joints, induced directly by the stimulus, are not perceived as our own sensations, but are projected into the stimulus, and thus give it greater significance. Modern experiments have shown that actual *movements* can be detected during the process of perception. These often do not come to consciousness as sensations of our own movements. If they do, and if we are self-conscious to the extent of experiencing them as our own sensations, to that extent we have lost our aesthetic attitude because our attention is no longer upon the art object but upon ourselves. Schoen [2] has pointed out, however, that empathy is not limited to the aesthetic experience but is a psychological principle of the source of all meaning. All significant experience is an instance of empathy. Inner strains, incipient movements and stresses are phases of all perception and not at all limited to aesthetic perception. Philosophers and critics of the end of the 19th century greatly overworked the concept of empathy when they made it the sole basis for a theory of aesthetics.

Meanings in Aesthetic Activity.—In seeking the meaning of the sensations and perceptions the aesthetic attitude is again contrasted with the usual daily reaction in that it turns away from the useful, the personal, and the concrete toward the fanciful, the impersonal, and the abstract. It is not that we are never occupied in our daily routine with abstractions, for in solving any simple, practical problem we make use of such abstractions as the state of our health, our financial standing, our knowledge of chemistry, or economics, etc., and to bring these necessary concepts to mind, we engage in activities which we call reflecting, summarizing, evaluating. But in the aesthetic attitude these concepts and references are not so immediate and personal. To put it more succinctly, when the meanings are abstract, far removed, nonpractical and impersonal we find in them an aesthetic quality. Because the adequate conception of them demands more of the effortful mental activities—recalling, summarizing, evaluating—they are characterized by a breadth, distance, largeness which gives them that sense of importance and mastery characteristic of the aesthetic moment. It is their infrequency and unusualness and difficulty that sets them apart and enshrines them, placing them a little above the plane of daily achievement. That is why the ugly— death, horror, deceit, angry passion—acquire so readily the aesthetic quality. In so far as these concepts are abstractions, unusual, and impersonal, their representation in consciousness requires effortful summarizing and evaluating which brings with it the largeness and breadth of the aesthetic moment. When vivid sense impression and emotional toning are also added—and these are very likely to arise— the experiencing of these ugly realities has all the qualities to make it an aesthetic experience par excellence.

This sense of mastery, this insight, this consciousness of difficulty overcome is the invariable accompaniment, perhaps even the sine qua non, of the aesthetic experience. Insight is the sudden comprehension of the relation of the details of a certain experience which gives it a wholeness and fixes it definitely and completely into place among other concepts. We use the word "sudden" because this wholeness can come only while all the numerous details are fresh in the memory so that their integration seems important, while the effort, the puzzling, and the straining to organize them is vividly present. Without the felt effort and the remembered disorganization the significance of even the most profound utterance becomes utterly trite and empty. The aesthetic moment is the realization of the felt want completely fulfilled. The deeper the want, the harder the struggle to fulfill it, the more mental and bodily activity involved, the greater will be the satisfaction.

The Role of Emotion.—The aesthetic experience also has an emotional accompaniment, which helps to give the other activities their importance and significance. The art object always has a moving effect. It appeals, as William James would say, to the bodily sounding board. A genuine emotion, a physical response of more or less violence, with clenched fists, shaking knees, flushed face and fast, deep breathing, with visceral reactions and that familiar all-gone feeling in the pit of the stomach—such a stirred-up state of the whole organism is of course never present in the aesthetic experience. An experience of such violence would completely absorb all of the attention and there would be no awareness of the other necessary components, the sensations, perceptions, and ideational activities. The emotional content of the aesthetic moment must rather be in the nature of a mood which we define as qualitatively like an emotion but a much paler and more diluted emotional state. It may be sustained over a much longer period of time and needs only a few of the characteristic bodily components to make itself felt. The gentlest stab of visceral reaction, the slight lifting of the head or the faint tightening of the throat may be sufficient to throw the glamour of emotion over an experience, to give it color and poignancy. A gesture or an attitude copied from an art object, a suggestion, conscious or unconscious, which finds its answer in a muscular or visceral response will serve to emotionalize the whole experience. Even the bodily symptoms derived from a totally different source may lend their effects to a neutral stimulus, making it seem for a time a beautiful thing, as when the effects of certain drugs enhance all sensation and perception for short periods of time, giving all experience an aesthetic quality. The effects of the sex hormones likewise produce periods of heightened sensitivity and an emotional toning wherein otherwise drab personalities, objects, and experiences are transposed into the realm of the aesthetic.

Important Criteria of the Aesthetic Experience.—Along with this general description we will further differentiate two specific criteria of the genuinely aesthetic experience, which, to be sure, have already been mentioned in passing—(1) the attention must be centered on the beautiful object, and (2) there must be the feeling of insight, of comprehension, of significance, mastery.

If these criteria are correct, then this would mean that the truly aesthetic experience cannot be of long duration for the constant shifting is the prime characteristic of attention and when the shift is toward practical matters, to the feelings or mood, to anything of a personal nature, the attitude is for the moment lost. Likewise when the beholder is consciously reasoning, studying, and evaluating the material, experiencing the effort and strain, the struggle, the defeat, his experience is not aesthetic. The true "appreciation" then, the authentic experience of aesthetic enjoyment is a period of constant shifting from one attitude to another and the aesthetic moment is more vivid, in fact is only possible in contrast to the alternate periods of effort and of self-consciousness which are interspersed with it. As the attention fluctuates from one aspect of experience to the other, the aesthetic attitude comes and goes. It is therefore possible to spend an evening listening to a concert or reading a novel and to have a continuously growing experience. One may become more and more absorbed in the music so that the periods of aesthetic attitude are of longer and longer duration. The bodily responses are more and more intense and unified in tone, the sensations organize themselves more and more readily, the insight covers more and more of the details of the music structure. The personal and self-conscious attitudes are pushed farther and farther into the background.

Different schools and creeds may variously describe this occurrence as detachment, or disinterestedness, or repose in the object of beauty, or objectified pleasure; they may center the process around catharsis or significant form or empathy or distance or even intuition or social expression. Each of these theories emphasizes certain aspects of the experience of beauty and if their protagonists should attempt a subjective analysis, using exclusively modern psychological terminology, many of the above paragraphs would undoubtedly be duplicated.

Individual Differences in the Aesthetic Experience.— —In our discussion we have not only assumed an aesthetic experience occasioned by some of the standard objects of beauty, but we have assumed a typical, complete, and well-rounded experience, common to the more or less cultivated individual. Obviously the experience may be something different, something better or something rather less than the standard product we have described above. These variations, the individual differences always expected in psychology, we conceive as quantitative rather than qualitative differences. They are differences in degree, in intensity—permutations and combinations of the various components of the experience. Some of these expected differences we will outline briefly.

(1) Essentially, as already indicated, appreciation is a moment of fulfillment when the importance, the significance, of our present experience is uppermost in our minds and when our attention is on the objective stimulus which has occasioned the experience. The significance may arise, however, from a number of different sources, from the emotional thrill which shoots through the whole body, from the meaning, the ideology which has such a strong pull on our own lines of thought, from the intensity and keenness of our sensations, or from our concentrated struggle to discern the pattern or meanings. The specific avenue of approach varies from time to time and from person to person.

(2) Individual differences in capacity for the aesthetic experience as well as in the acquisition of skill in appreciation are of course to be expected—the usual differences in talent and in training. Some enjoy music rather than the visual arts, some find depth rather than frequency of experience. Others seem to enjoy in all directions and still others in none. Certainly there are large differences in sensory endowment which must show up in important ways. Ease and rapidity in the flow of ideas and associations must also have their effect, and the quickness and acuteness of the bodily responses in the affective life. The degree of muscle tonus, the glandular secretions and hormones, the body chemistry in general must also play a large part in the readiness to respond and in the susceptibility to the stimulus of the beautiful.

(3) The genesis of this particular kind of experience—the aesthetic—is as yet an unexplored process and a study of its development might fail to disclose the usual progress from simple to complex, from easy to difficult, from the rudimentary to the richly complete. The history of the aesthetic experience from infancy to adulthood may show on the contrary a disappearing function. In its earlier stages it may be a continuous unembarrassed forthright enjoyment of the sensuous and affective life, crowded with significant and im-

portant experiences and insights, which gradually gives way to the self-conscious and the practical, to the restrained and colorless round of ordinary adult activities.

The Aesthetic Object

The Problem of Form.—In the study of the aesthetic object the problem which is central and important for psychology is the problem of *form:* What is form, what is good form, and what part does it play in the aesthetic experience? Form in art is always contrasted with meaning or subject matter. In painting, the form lies in the shapes, colors, lines, and patterns rather than the recognizable objects, the pictured scene, or the story which it tells.

Form in Poetry.—In poetry the form in contrast to the meaning is the sounds of the vowels and consonants, the patterns of rhythms, rhymes, and accents. The form of a poem is exactly what one would hear if he listened to the reading of a poem in a foreign language which he did not understand. It is exceedingly difficult for the casual listener to divorce the sounds of words from their meanings and it is therefore difficult for us in America to "hear" the poetry of a poem in the English language. As a consequence psychologists who have wished to experiment with form in poetry have found it necessary to manufacture their own poetry, selecting a certain stanza length, meter and rhyme scheme, with various alliterative patterns, and then fitting nonsense syllables into this framework. If a bona fide poet should undertake to "manufacture" such poetry, unhampered by the necessity of choosing the words for their meanings, he could produce stanzas which for sheer beauty of form would far surpass the meaningful verses which he ordinarily creates.

The average student is familiar with the more obvious kinds of poetic form, the lyric, the elegy, the sonnet, etc., each calling for a distinctive pattern of meter, rhyme, stanza length, etc. Familiar too, are the most common meters and line lengths, iambic pentameter, spondees, anapests, etc. But there are more important and more subtle elements of form, details by which one author may be distinguished from another even though both are writing in the same meter and stanza form. These more subtle elements, though appreciated by critics and connoisseurs, have only recently been isolated for scientific study by objective experimental methods. In prose style,[3] for example, counts can be made of the numbers and proportions of monosyllable, two-syllable, three-syllable, polysyllable words, the proportion of adjectives to nouns ("adjective quotient"), proportion of nouns to verbs, proportions of dependent clauses, periodic sentences, words of Latin or Anglo-Saxon origin, etc. Graphs can be made to portray these quantitative studies more effectively. For poetic style, a long series of experimental studies by means of voice records has shown that the true form of poetic line is not the set meter,

$$\smile \ — \ \smile \ — \ \smile \ — \ \smile \ — \ \smile \ —$$

The curfew tolls the knell of parting day

but a changing distribution of normal, strong, and weak accents or stresses, together with longer and shorter pauses and a rising and falling in the pitch of the voice. In other words, each verse should be written out as a line of music, with whole, half, quarter, and eighth notes to indicate the rhythm, and with a melodic line adjusted to the speaking of the separate words and to the meaning of the line. Such quantitative and objective studies of poetic form will bring out the variations in rhythms, or cadences, and inflections of pitch characteristic of each individual poet.[4] Scarcely any line of poetry will scan perfectly, and *it is these variations from the set meter rather than the meter itself that constitutes the beauty of poetic form.*

Expressiveness of Form: Unity between Form and Content.—In music, the form is more readily abstracted from its meaning by the layman. In fact, form is so predominant in our experience of this most formal of the arts that very often music is apprehended as pure form, and the meaning or program is negligible or entirely absent. We listen only for sensuous and perceptual experience, rather than for meanings. Because of this characteristic of music, the most extensive experiments in the function of form have been carried on in music rather than in painting or literature. Let us suppose, for example, that a composer has undertaken the task of setting to music a spirited ballad of adventure. He creates a piece of music which fits

FIG. 32.—PORTRAIT A. CURVES.

the length, the rhythms, and the meter of the poetry, and with a melody and a harmonic scheme which seem to him suitable for the ideas and the story. He might play his music (without the words) to an audience ignorant of its purpose, and ask them to report to him the moods and feelings which they absorbed from it, or in other words, the expressiveness which it has for them. If they should report that the music seems vigorous, strong, restless, exciting, he could feel reassured that his music is complementing and enhancing the effect of the words. More technically we would say that there was a unity between the form and the content of the song, and we should expect that it would be particularly effective as an art form.

Expressiveness of Lines.—Such unity between form and the content in painting has often been pointed out by critics. It has been said that Botticelli and his pupils must have understood the effect of certain lines on mood to judge from the clever way they arranged the hair in their portraits.[5] In one certain portrait the hair has the form of restless waves, with a heavy braid hanging down on one side. The face is full of animation and restlessness, and the hair seems to be appropriate for the temperament of the girl. In another portrait representing a woman in a pensive quiet mood, the hair is brushed straight back from the face with only one strand escaping.

Psychologists have explored the expressiveness of lines both by requesting their subjects to draw lines which seemed to be expressive of certain feelings or moods, and by asking them to match certain given lines with adjectives. In one such experiment five hundred subjects were asked to choose the appropriate type of line for each of thirteen different feelings.[6] The eighteen ready-made lines from which they chose included wavy lines with small, medium, and large curves, and angular lines with the same variations. They found that quiet gentleness was indicated by wide curves in horizontal position, agitation by small angles running upward from left to right, etc. The reader may judge for himself the effectiveness of line quality by turning to the two outline sketches of a seated figure on pages 598 and 600. From the circle of adjectives representing eight different moods or feelings (see Fig. 34), he may check all the adjectives which might be used to describe the person who is represented in Fig. 32, Portrait

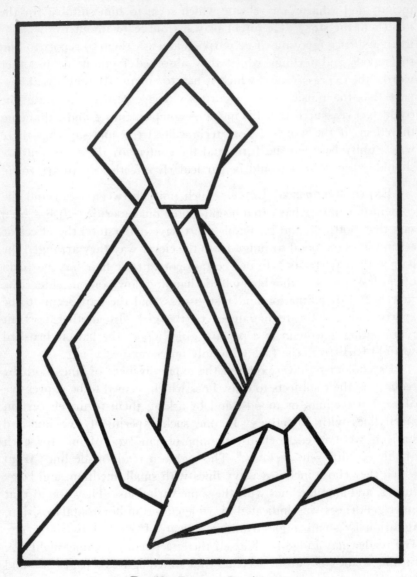

FIG. 33.—PORTRAIT B. ANGLES.

A, and Fig. 33, Portrait B. The graphs which represent the characteristics attributed to each figure by fifty observers are presented in Fig. 35 and since the postures and the designs are the same for both

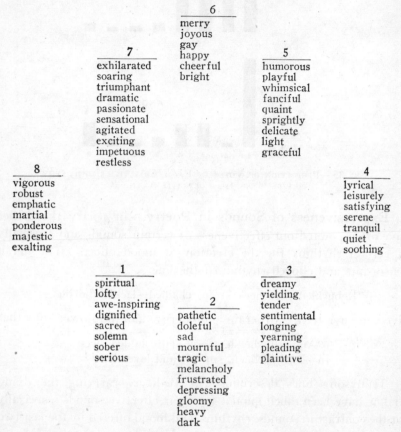

<u>6</u>
merry
joyous
gay
happy
<u>7</u>   cheerful   <u>5</u>
exhilarated bright   humorous
soaring   playful
triumphant   whimsical
dramatic   fanciful
passionate   quaint
sensational   sprightly
agitated   delicate
exciting   light
impetuous   graceful
restless

<u>8</u>
vigorous   <u>4</u>
robust   lyrical
emphatic   leisurely
martial   satisfying
ponderous   serene
majestic   tranquil
exalting   quiet
              soothing

<u>1</u>   <u>3</u>
spiritual   dreamy
lofty   yielding
awe-inspiring <u>2</u>   tender
dignified pathetic sentimental
sacred   doleful longing
solemn   sad   yearning
sober   mournful pleading
serious   tragic   plaintive
         melancholy
         frustrated
         depressing
         gloomy
         heavy
         dark

FIG. 34.—CONVENIENT ARRANGEMENT OF ADJECTIVES FOR RECORDING THE MOOD EFFECT OF MUSIC, OF POETIC SOUNDS, COLOR AND DESIGN IN ART, ETC.

Contrasting moods are represented opposite each other on the circle, and a complete circuit carries one through all the most common affective states. Observers check as few or as many adjectives as they like.

figures, the differences in the characteristics must be attributed to the qualities of the lines.[7] It is obvious that the successful portrait painter can indicate the personality of his subject through his choice of color, line, and texture as well as by the pose and facial expression.

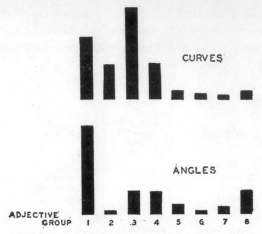

FIG. 35.—PROPORTION OF VOTES IN EACH ADJECTIVE GROUP, FROM
50 OBSERVERS, FOR PORTRAITS A AND B.

Expressiveness of Sounds in Poetry.—In poetry the critics
have often pointed out effectiveness of certain sounds and especially
of certain rhythms for the creation of mood effects. The harsh
consonants and clipped rhythm of the line

"Rebuckled the cheek strap, chained slacker the bit"

give a greater feeling of strain and energy than the slower smoother

"And still she slept and azure lidded sleep
In blanched linen, smooth and lavendar'd."

Tennyson's lines describing Sir Bedivere carrying the dying
Arthur have been much quoted for their effective sounds, especially
for the contrast in sounds, rhythms, and mood offered by the last two
lines.

"Dry clash'd his harness in the icy caves
And barren chasms, and all to left and right
The bare, black cliff clanged round him, as he based
His feet on juts of slippery crag that rang
Sharp smitten with the dint of armed heels—

And on a sudden, lo! the level lake
And the long glories of the winter moon."

Experiments have been devised whereby subjects have been asked to change the meaning of nonsense syllables in a certain direction by altering one sound.[8] Or the observer is asked to decide which of two syllables seemed smaller, for example, sost or dost, dost or dist, doosh or deesh, etc. Again, experimental "poems" have been "manufactured" containing a predominance of long open vowel sounds such as ōō, à and ō, and soft, round, pleasing consonant sounds such as r, l, m, rd, ld, rl, etc., to be contrasted with high thin vowels ēē, ī, ā, and harsh consonants z, ch, k, st, g, etc. Verses were also written of two and of three syllable meters and of various patterns of voice inflections. The effects of these variables were studied by checking adjectives from given lists.[9] Rhythms were found to be much more effective in expressing the mood than any other element, with voice patterns second, consonant sounds third, and vowel sounds of much less importance. Harsh consonants are more gay and humorous, and the deeper open vowels more dignified and powerful.

Expressiveness of Music.—In the earliest experiments on the meaning of music the psychologist asked his subjects to listen to phonograph recordings of musical compositions and to record his thoughts and feelings. It was discovered that there were large individual differences in the interpretations, according to the temperament and experience of the listener, his sophistication in musical matters, his physiological well-being, immediately previous experience, etc. Musicians steeped in their own musical traditions were nonplussed when they discovered that for the layman selections in the minor key were not always sad, and that listeners who were asked to match a list of titles with a series of musical compositions made many "mistakes." But continued analysis and experimentation brought about more precise formulation of the problems and many refinements in method.

Modern experimenters are aware that music for such experimentation must be carefully chosen since some music is not meant to have a meaning or program and such music excites little affective tone in its hearers. In certain compositions there are several well-defined moods in the various sections of the piece which have caused conflicting reports in conscientious observers. Psychologists have sometimes been too eager to simplify the materials for their experiments in order to eliminate sources of error, and they have found that when the stimuli are restricted to simple tone qualities, as for example isolated tones produced by a singer,[10] or even chords quite different in structure produced on the piano,[11] there is no distinctive affective character attached to them. Listeners do not agree in their interpretation of such musical sounds in isolation, and only experts who can first identify the structure of the chord will perceive the sadness of the minor or the brightness of the major chord.

Likewise it has become apparent that music arouses not a genuine knee-shaking emotional state, but rather its paler, and gentler replica which we call mood or affective tone.[12] It is a more generalized and somewhat more stable and lasting state and is best indicated not by descriptions of bodily states, accounts of imagery, or daydreams—since these are supplied by the listener's own imagination rather than by the music itself—but more accurately and more satisfactorily by checking quickly, while the music is still a present stimulus, a few adjectives from a conveniently arranged list. If the list is long enough to cover the most common affective states—dignity, sorrow, yearning, tenderness, calm, brightness, gayety, excitement, vigor, etc.,—varied enough to allow for individual differences, and arranged conveniently so that the exact meaning may be quickly located, data may be collected from many listeners and many compositions and may be converted very readily into quantitative records of affective reactions. Experiments of this kind show that average listeners are in very general agreement on the meaning of musical compositions, and that they follow quite accurately the intentions of the composer in so far as these may be determined.

Knowing that the meaning of music is readily discernible to the listener, it is natural to question by what means, musically speaking, he is made aware of these meanings, by the tunes or melodies, by the rhythm, or the harmony, or by other elements in the musical structure. One experimenter studied this problem by gathering together for study a number of songs, known to have one and the same well-defined interpretation or meaning, and searching among them for common elements of structure.[13] Gundlach assembled a number of American Indian songs used in tribal ceremonies, and contrasted the group of war songs with the healing songs of the medicine men, and with the love songs. He found that the most striking differences between the groups were in the rhythms, a fact which might be interpreted as giving rhythm the place of most importance in expressiveness. War songs were faster, and lower in pitch than the love songs, and had larger ranges of tone than the healing songs.

In another series of experiments [14] the effectiveness of six musical elements—mode, rhythm, tempo, pitch, melody, harmony—was explored by writing two musical compositions which differed in only one respect, for example, in harmony, or in mode, etc. Two different audiences heard the two versions and recorded their reactions, by checking adjectives appropriate to the music. Differences in the two versions must be attributed solely to the one element which was modified since all the other elements in the two compositions were held constant in every way. Of all the factors studied tempo plays the largest part, is effective on most groups, and gives the most clear-cut and consistent results. Modality is perhaps second in importance although it has not the general usefulness of tempo since its effects are severely limited to happy-sad and humorous-sentimental contrasts. Pitch should probably be rated as third in importance—high pitches are sparkling, playful, and low pitches sad, dignified, vigorous. Harmony and rhythm are on the whole less effective than these first three, for they show smaller majorities and cover a more restricted range of feeling tone. Simple harmonies are more happy, graceful, serene, and sentimental than complex modern harmonies. Flowing rhythms are happy, graceful, sentimental; firm rhythms give strength and dignity. The ascending or descending quality of melody, the only aspect of melody studied, proved to be of practically no importance in carrying the meaning.

Function of Form.—We have said that the problem of form in art is the central problem for psychologists, and we have discussed both the more obvious and the more subtle details of form in poetry, music, and visual art. Let us inquire next into the function of form in the aesthetic experience.[15] The formal elements are without question the ABC of art, and the beginner, the amateur, should devote his first lessons to the understanding of them. Indeed there are certain schools of thought (usually referred to as Formalists) who *identify* the formal with the aesthetic. The more impersonal and nonrepresentative the art work, the more aesthetic they find it, and they tend to stress the intellectual at the expense of affective or emotional qualities.

The first function of form is to insure that the attention of the observer is fixed upon the art object. There must be a complete absorption, a concentration of attention. This will take place the more readily as more of the motor and muscular activities are aroused to activity by the form, as for example if bodily rhythms follow the pulse of the music or poetry, if by means of empathy the musculature is drawn to follow the pose of the portrait, the imagery of the verse, or the successive stresses of the harmony. We may notice poetic forms, especially, performing this function in such works as Coleridge's *Kubla Kahn*, in Blake and Swinburne, and in Shakespeare's songs. One critic describes this class of poetry as the "spell weaving," [16] because its form has an almost hypnotic effect on its hearers.

Form will also help the observer to comprehend or perceive the art work as one unit in all its completeness. This function is not peculiar to aesthetic experience, for order and organization and pattern are necessary for all comprehension, whether of a picture, a college course, or a practical problem. Space patterns, repetitions, and rhythms help the observer to perceive, assimilate, and remember, and form therefore is a potent force in heightening the effect of mastery, of complete mastery over difficult and widespread elements.

Form will also help to create the illusion of "distance" [17] in the aesthetic experience, by emphasizing the pattern, by conventionalizing materials that might otherwise seem too personal or realistic or trivial. It is the sonnet form that brings into the realm of poetry such lowly forms of life as the grasshopper and the cricket. The personal and prosaic statement "I am mentally depressed and ill" becomes in rhythmic form, at the same time more dignified and more poignant:

> "My heart aches, and a drowsy numbness pains
> My sense, as though of hemlock I had drunk."

But the final justification for form in art is in its function as the carrier of feeling, as the vehicle for mood and affective tone. Largely by means of suggested movement, by empathy, by the appeal to the bodily sounding board, the patterns and rhythms and repetitions give the emotional toning without which experience is flat and colorless, and bring about that heightening and broadening of awareness which is the especial characteristic of the aesthetic moment.

STUDIES OF PLEASANTNESS

Color and Form.—There have been many experiments and studies in the pleasantness or unpleasantness of various colors and sounds,[18] but few of them have had any great significance for the psychology of beauty, because of the fact that the aesthetic quality of a musical composition or painting depends upon something other than the simple pleasantness of single colors or tones. Preferences for colors and combinations of colors depend largely upon the setting in which they are perceived, and upon qualities such as saturation, contrast, size, lighting, etc. Judgments are not stable or constant. The famous studies of the pioneer experimenter Gustav Fechner in his search for preferred dimensions of rectangles have also very little significance for the psychology of beauty. The proportions of the "golden section," the 5 : 3 rectangle, have shown much variation under different environmental conditions.

Sounds and Tones.—Studies of the consonance of tone combinations and the closely related problems of the theory of chords and chord progressions are more important. The history of music shows many series of changes in the "rules" of harmony, melody, and rhythm from the earliest times to the present day. Acceptable forms in music are different in each century. Sociologists[19] and musicians[20] have been making attempts to relate the popularity of certain composers and forms to concurrent historical events and circumstances. Psychologists have devoted much effort to the analysis of the phenomena of consonance, and its pleasantness has been variously attributed to fusion, smoothness, simplicity, etc. Moore's[21] theory that consonance is a matter of habituation and practice derives support not only from the history of music, but also from laboratory experiment. At the end of short training periods during which they had practice in hearing certain chords, the listeners preferred passages containing these chords rather than others. Farnsworth [22] has also shown that preference for endings in melodies is highly subject to training. The dissonance of one generation becomes the consonance of the next.

STUDIES IN ARTISTIC SINGING AND PLAYING

Psychologists have also contributed much to the understanding of the problems of learning in music by their analysis of the various techniques. The earliest study of this kind was made by Whipple, [23] and it was nothing more than a measure by measure comparison of two player piano rolls of the same composition played by two famous piano artists. The problem of interpretation yielded for the first time to analytic and objective methods. "His performance was finely poetic and subtlely nuanced," writes the critic of Paderewski. "The legato passages were caressingly played, and his touch reveals the same marvelous temperament as of yore." Such eulogies are of little help to the piano student who is struggling to acquire the "marvelous temperament," but the mechanical piano rolls record the exact intensity and timing of the artist and the student may compare them with the original music as the composer wrote it. Of course any great pianist takes liberties with the music. One holds a grace note five times as long as the score indicates, and connects two succeeding measures very carefully with a smooth even tone. Another pauses carefully between the same two measures and emphasizes the pause by a staccato touch. Their styles are analyzed just as the slow-motion movies disclose the techniques of the tennis and golf stars. Subsequent studies by Ortmann [24] with a time and intensity recording device showed that all the effects "expressivo," "ritardando," etc., practiced by accomplished pianists are merely variations of these two factors. The Iowa Piano Camera [25] gives a photographic record of the beginning, duration, moment of ending, and relative intensity of each note played, and by means of it students are enabled to study the objective record of their own performance. At Iowa phonophotographic studies have been made of the violin playing and the singing of concert artists,[26] especially of their vibrato. The results are proving very useful in the mastery of technical difficulties of tone production.

STUDIES OF ARTISTIC CREATION

The process of artistic creation so important from psychology's point of view has not received the attention it merits because of the great difficulty of getting the artist or composer or poet into the laboratory where he might be set to work under the experimenter's direction! Biography and especially the accounts of some artists who are adept at introspective analysis have been helpful.[27] Evidence leads us to believe that among artists there are as many different techniques and temperaments as among bankers, professors, or any other class of society. A study of student poets and nonpoets by means of a number of tests,[28] showed fewer differences than might be expected between the two groups. The poets had larger vocabularies, a more versatile imagery, greater facility at finding rhymes, and much more ability in devising figures of speech. Extensive studies of the growth of artistic development in children, and elaborate case studies of gifted children are providing insight into the creative process and temperament.[29]

The classic notebooks of Leonardo da Vinci are valuable data on the methods of the artist. The much corrected manuscripts of Beethoven provide insight into that master's painstaking correcting and altering of his work. Occasional examples may be found in successive published editions, of changes and revisions made by poets 'n their original verses. Psychologically speaking, the most important study of the process of creation has been made by Lowes in his tracing of the sources of *The Ancient Mariner* [30] through the personal history and the notebooks of Coleridge. The deliberate stocking of the mind with information and details of observation and the continuous experimenting with rhymes and meters occupied a great part of the poet's daily life. The ultimate poem is created, not at one stroke and out of nothing, but from the reading and experience of many years. Scattered through Coleridge's notebooks are ideas and observations, often the very phrases used in the published stanzas. Wordsworth.

in his preface to *We Are Seven* describes the motive for the writing, and the poet's developing plans for the poem.

A most enlightening contrast in the creative process and its results may be found in two poems, *Kubla Khan* of Coleridge, and a stanza written by a woman patient of Dr. Morton Prince.[31] In both cases, the author was ambitious to write verse, and had been filling his mind with techniques of meter and rhyme. In both cases the theme was one which had been dominating the thoughts and feelings, and the actual composition was done outside the normal consciousness, that is, in a dream and with vivid visual imagery. *Kubla Khan* is a perfection of musical and imaginative beauties. The other verses are sincere and dignified, but commonplace in ideas and phraseology. This striking difference in the quality of the verses is the difference between the stored minds and the experiences in poetic techniques of the two authors. The creative process is psychologically the same.

PSYCHOLOGICAL TESTING IN THE FIELD OF AESTHETICS

Psychologists have developed some very useful and excellent tests in the field of art, and by means of them have made some important discoveries and helped in the solution of many problems, although as in other fields of psychological testing the music tests have been somewhat abused. They have often suffered particularly by being overrated. The layman has expected the tests to work magic, and has been disappointed and resentful when they produce controversial evidence in certain instances. Psychological testing caught the popular fancy, and its techniques could be handled (although not mastered) more readily than many other experimental techniques. Therefore in the psychology of music and art, there is a preponderance of testing studies, and many problems which could have been better studied by other methods have been attacked only by the testing method.

There are three different kinds of tests in the aesthetic field: (1) Those designed to measure original native talent or propensity for artistic success; (2) those which measure specific achievement, or progress in artistic training; and (3) those which measure appreciation in general. There is no strict line of demarcation between these various kinds of tests, but for convenience in discussing them, we will try to distinguish between them.

Tests to Detect Talent.—Tests which could detect original talent would be particularly useful for vocational advice. If we could distinguish at the age of 8 to 10 years the children who can best profit by musical or artistic training, or if we could designate in each freshman class at any music conservatory those who will fail to win success in music, tests of the first type would be especially welcome.[32] With such aims in view the Seashore tests were devised in 1919 [33] to measure such things as fine discriminations in pitch and loudness, and in rhythm and tempo. They measured also the span of memory for tonal patterns and the discrimination of degrees of consonance. These tests have been very widely used, and have thrown some light especially on such problems as differences in social culture and training, and, in so far as these differences can ever be separated from environment, on differences between races. If all the factors which enter into a successful musical career are to be measured, there must be included tests for motor coordination and speed, and in this field there are many different tests available. Tests for certain personality traits, for perseverance, temperament, etc., would also be called for, as well as measures of creative imagination, and of inventive ingenuity.

Tests for specific achievement in music and art have been devised and standardized. They measure ability of school children to read and write music, to sing accurately, to play certain instruments, and to transpose and to work out other exercises in music theory. By means of these tests children may be placed in classes appropriate to their development, and standards may be set up for the teaching of music as for teaching arithmetic or geography. There are similar tests for achievement in art, in drawing and designing. With these there are also objective tests for knowledge of technical terms, for the history and work of great artists, and for identifying selections in music, or in art.

Tests for Appreciation.—Tests for appreciation in general are somewhat different from the achievement tests, in the same way that tests for general intelligence are different from objective tests in history or geography or arithmetic. These appreciation tests attempt to measure the ability to comprehend and discriminate in poetry, art, or music. They assume that acceptable taste in art develops from ability, interest, opportunity, and experience in art just as, let us say, sagacity or reasoning ability grows out of native endowment plus specific training and practice. By means of adequate tests for appreciations of various kinds, there are psychological, educational, and sociological problems which may be explored. Sex differences may be discovered and the relative success of teaching devices may be measured. Culture patterns may be better evaluated and more accurate descriptions of individuals and of personalities may be set up.

In making these appreciation tests the psychologist has one problem which no other maker of objective or psychological tests encounters, namely the difficulty in finding a standard for what is beautiful. For standards in art forms change from one age to another and from one culture to another, and even in one age and one environment it would be impossible to find complete agreement on the criteria of the beautiful, or on the relative degrees or steps in the scale from the ugly to the beautiful. There are no "facts" or logical "standards" in the field of art as there are in arithmetic, geography, or engineering.

There are, however, several methods of solving the practical problem of making a useful test.[35] One method is to offer the subject two compositions, one of them by a successful artist, poet or composer, and the other by a layman, or an amateur, and if the subject states that he prefers the work of the artist, he may be given credit for a "right" choice. In order to eliminate as many as possible of the irrelevant factors which enter into such a judgment, the compositions should be on the same subject, for example, two landscapes, or two sonnets, or two minuets, and in the same manner, that is, the classic or the romantic, the futuristic, etc. Or if the psychologist constructing the test should himself manufacture a poem, or a picture, or a piano piece which is a parody of the original, in which he tries deliberately to produce a composition of inferior quality, the standard of good and bad becomes even more stable. In some cases, the psychologist has tried to do even more than this; he has made mutilations of original compositions by altering some one quality such as the rhythm, the spatial or harmonic form, the melody (in music), or the thought (of a poem). The Oregon Music Discrimination

Test,[36] for example, consists of forty-eight very short compositions played in pairs on the piano. The subject hears the original as it was written by Mozart, Bach, Debussy, etc., and another version in which one of four elements is mutilated—the melody, harmony, rhythm, or form. If he repeatedly chooses the original when the form or the melody is spoiled, but makes many errors in the rhythmic and harmonic items, the psychologist may diagnose him as below or above the average for his age (according as his score is high or low), but may also state that his perception of musical pattern in form and melody is well developed but his ear for subtleties of harmony and his feeling for rhythms needs to be improved.

The pioneer experimenting of this kind was done in the field of poetry. Abbott and Trabue [37] devised a test consisting of twenty-six short poems, each with three new versions, one, the metric in which the movement is rendered either entirely awkward or less fine and subtle than the original; a second, the sentimental in which the emotion is falsified by introducing silly, gushy, affected or otherwise insincere feelings; and a third, the prosaic, in which the poet's imagery is reduced to a more pedestrian and commonplace level. From these four poems, the subject chose the best and the worst version. This excellent and carefully standardized test was given by the authors to hundreds of subjects in schools and colleges, and has proved to be very useful in a number of respects. They (and the similar tests for music and art) have a large usefulness in high school and college classes for the information they furnish the teacher regarding the taste of the individual pupils and the general level of the class. They also separate fairly well the adequately prepared teacher of English from the teacher whose standards in poetry are no better than those of his students. The authors learned from this test, moreover, that children prefer verses without subtlety, objective in mood, easy to understand, and in simple strongly marked rhythms, whereas poetry written expressly for children sometimes wins recognition from adults rather than from children. Sentiment in poetry is demanded by adolescents and reaches its peak in the high school years, although a liking for it often continues well into college. Recognizing that it is in the nature of adolescence to prefer exaggeration to restraint, to express their emotions overintensely, teachers may capitalize on this fact and provide for them poetry of a vigorous, unrestrained, and emotional type, but with its source always in genuine feeling, not affectation.

In all tests of this kind it must of course be understood that high scores mean simply conformity with current art standards. As civilizations and cultures change, the ideals of beauty in music, art, and poetry will also change, nevertheless these changes are so slow that the standards from one school to another or from one generation to another are relatively stable. New tests would have to be devised perhaps after several decades, but in the meantime, the present tests may serve many practical purposes. Whenever it is necessary to secure ratings from large groups, at short notice, and especially when group comparisons are to be made, tests are found to be very convenient. Not the least of their practical usefulness is their value as teaching devices, because they force the observer to concentrate his attention on the objective form, and afford him opportunity to notice details of form which he might otherwise never clearly perceive. For this purpose, the poetry test, the Oregon music test, and the Meier-Seashore Art Judgment Test [38] are particularly valuable. This latter test, composed of 125 pairs of pictures, of all genres, and of many degrees of complexity and difficulty is a self-administering exercise which would be a most enlightening experience for any observer.[39]

REFERENCES

Chandler, A. R. *Beauty and Human Nature.* New York: D. Appleton-Century Company, Inc., 1934.

Cheney, S. *Expressionism in Art.* New York: Boni and Liveright, 1934.

Gordon, K. *Esthetics.* New York: Henry Holt and Company, 1909.

Langfeld, H. S. *The Aesthetic Attitude.* New York: Harcourt, Brace and Company, 1920.

Lanz, H. *The Physical Basis of Rime.* Stanford: Stanford University Press, 1931.

Ogden, R. M. *The Psychology of Art.* New York: Charles Scribner's Sons, 1938.

Schoen, M. *Art and Beauty.* New York: The Macmillan Company. 1932.

Seashore, C. E. *Psychology of Music.* New York: McGraw-Hill Book Company, Inc., 1938.

CHAPTER XXII

POINTS OF VIEW

By MILTON METFESSEL, *The University of Southern California*

In the foregoing pages of this volume you have been introduced to the vast area of human knowledge covered by the several fields of psychology. We may now view the fields together, and look for problems common to all of them. Is there a system of thought which can be found to organize the facts and ideas of the separate fields into a consistent whole?

Psychologists in the past have been motivated to attempt an answer to such a question. Many problems have been encountered, with the result that different solutions have been presented. It is our task in this chapter to examine the outstanding attempts to characterize and organize psychology as a whole. Each proposed thought system represents a different point of view. Systematic points of view generally are referred to as *schools of psychology,* of which the most important go by such names as *existential, functional, behavioristic, psychoanalytic, gestalt,* and *hormic.*

The various points of view have been developed by many psychologists. Our presentation of their work is of necessity limited, and so it is impossible to do full justice to the splendid contributions of a large number. For purposes of simplicity, then, one or two men have been singled out as representative of a system of thought.* Another limitation which we impose on ourselves can be found in our emphasis on the positive aspects of each point of view. To be sure, there are many salient differences between the various schools, but they become a matter of greater interest as one progresses in the study of psychology.

VIEW OF SIMPLE EXISTENCES

Edward Bradford Titchener, the great American psychologist who spent most of his productive years at Cornell University, was

---

* The historical background of each viewpoint would fill volumes if treated in adequate detail. Here we can present only a few important highlights.

interested in psychology as the science of such experiences as images, sensations, emotions, and thought processes. He was a man of unusual interests, one of the few who wanted to know the nature of mental processes in and of themselves. He was more intrigued with knowing what perceptions, emotions, and thoughts *are*, than in knowing the relations they have to everyday experience.

He regarded all mental processes as existences. He did not think that *mind*, in the common-sense meaning of the term, was immaterial and spaceless, subject to laws of its own which are different from other laws of nature. The common-sense view of mind is illustrated in the following example: A woman comes to a physician and complains of an illness. The good doctor gives her all the tests known to medical science, and finally tells her, "There's nothing wrong with you. It's all in your mind." In order to understand what Titchener meant by mind, we shall turn to the ideas of Ernst Mach, a respected Viennese physicist of the last century.

Science and the World of Experience: Mach's View.— Mach stated that all the sciences have the same subject matter, the world of experience. The physicist's instrument, the biologist's organism, the botanist's plant, and the psychologist's self are experiences. All objects, bodies, and selves are complexes of simple existences, or what Mach called "sensations." They are colors, spaces, times, heats, sounds, and the like. Sometimes these "sensations" are connected in semipermanent forms which common sense regards as objects, bodies, and selves. Mach drew a picture of himself in his study, as the scene appeared with his right eye closed. He pictured part of his nose, his moustache, arms, legs, and trunk in the setting of tables and bookshelves. Mach regarded all information he had of the *self* as the same kind of information he had of objects, namely, the information of sensations. Common sense distinguishes between objects and selves by different relationships of the sensations comprising them, and not by the sensory elements themselves. These sensory elements are the same for physics, biology, and psychology.

Becoming One with Subject Matter.—The simple existences, which are the data for all sciences, are meaningless. There are examples in the literature of primitive peoples who sit for hours, wide awake, yet passively living their environment. Perhaps you have been at a river's bank, and you became so absorbed in your surroundings that you forgot your self, and you were no longer aware that there were things called trees and rocks. You became one with your environment in a wordless, objectless, meaningless existence. Your experience was one of sensations without any reference, according to Mach's view, and you were in the realm of *existential experience*.

Psychology as a Separate Science.—If the data of all science consist of these meaningless separate existences, what then distinguishes the objects of physics and the objects of psychology? Consider another example. Suppose that you wrote a description of the scene at the river's bank. You would not have written it in terms of the simplest existences, but rather of objects and events. You might have mentioned green trees, the multicolored water, the sunlight shimmering on the eddies, the little whirlpool over at the left, and the white spray as the water dashed against the rock. You might have recounted the stirring of the wind above you, the roar of the rushing stream, and the discordant blast from an automobile hidden by the trees of the other side. From such a description, it is apparent that you were thinking of objects and events separate from yourself. Nevertheless, your direct information was from your experience of visual and auditory sensations. A tree was experienced after light waves from the sun were reflected to your eye, and nerve currents carried energy to your brain. A tree is a physical object when you regard your experience of it as dependent upon the sunlight, and it is a psychological object when you think that it is dependent upon the activity of the nervous system. As Titchener points out, an object is physical or psychological according to your point of view.

Titchener's definition of psychology thus became "the science of existential experience regarded as functionally or logically dependent upon the nervous system (or its biological equivalent)." [1] By "functionally dependent" he meant that the experience varies when the activity of the nervous system varies. In some psychological laboratories, there are devices which record the activity of the brain, by means of electrodes placed on different parts of the scalp. The recording needle writes a different kind of a pattern for an image of a beautiful sunset, an auditory impression of a symphony, an emotion of fear, and thought process in solving a mathematical problem. When the activity of the nervous system changes, the experience changes.

As Titchener conceives it, the subject matter of psychology is not the activity of the nervous system, but the experience which is dependent upon it. Mind is the sum-total of all the experiences so regarded. Consciousness is a cross section of mind, at any given moment.

Description in Simplest Possible Terms.—The first task of an existential psychologist is to describe experiences in the simplest possible terms. Such a description is called an *introspection*. There must be a sampling of all manner of experiences, from sensations to higher thought processes. Can a thought process be reduced to simpler mental processes? Titchener's answer is in the affirmative, for his analysis showed that the thought process is made up in part of images. Thus numerous experiences are worked over introspectively, splitting them up into component parts until further analysis is impossible. When a mental process cannot be further divided, it is an elementary mental process.

At best introspection is an arduous and difficult task. Living as we do continually in a world of objects, there is always the danger of referring the experience to a physical object. If a student is asked to analyze the contents of his thoughts into simple existences, he is quite likely to state *what* he was thinking of: A trip to Europe, or a good night's sleep. An existential psychologist wants to know the mental processes that went into the thought trip-to-Europe: Visual images, muscular sensations, and so on.

Analysis of an Emotional Experience.—Titchener has given us the following example of how an experience can be divided into various mental processes:

Suppose that you are sitting at your desk, busy in your regular way, and obscurely conscious of a rumble of a car that is passing down the street; and suppose that the rumble is suddenly interrupted by a shrill scream. You leap up, as if the scream were a personal signal that you had been expecting; you dash out of doors, as if your presence on the street were a matter of imperative necessity. As you run, you have fragmentary ideas: 'a child,' perhaps, in internal speech; a visual flash of some previous accident; a scrap of kinesthesis that carries your whole attitude to the city car-system. But you have, also, a mass of insistent organic sensation: you choke, you draw your breath in gasps, for all the hurry you are in a cold sweat, you have a horrible nausea; and yet, in spite of the intense unpleasantness that floods your consciousness, you have no choice but to go on . . . the mental processes that we have just described make up the emotion of horror.[2]

There were perceptions of various phases of the whole situation, ideas, memory, attitude, kinesthetic sensation, organic sensation, and unpleasantness. Which of these can be reduced further? Titchener suggested that attitude was made up of kinesthesis, or muscular sensation; that memory of a previous accident was a visual flash; and that the idea was made up of the combined muscular sensations and auditory images of a word, *child*.

The Simplest Psychological Existences.—From many such experiences, Titchener drew the conclusion that there were three classes of elementary mental processes: Sensations, images, and affections. These are the simplest items in the existential world regarded as dependent upon the nervous system. Titchener found that he could describe every perception of meaningful sights and sounds as groupings of simpler meaningless mental processes of sensation. Sensations were therefore the characteristic elements of perceptions. In every idea which he analyzed, he always came across a process called an image; and in every emotion, he found pleasantness and unpleasantness, which taken together he called affection. He found that any given moment of experience was an exceedingly complex array of mental processes. Even perceptions, ideas, and emotions have to be singled out from each other in the total experience, before their own nature can be examined, and an analysis made into sensations, images, and affections.

Classification of Mental Elements.—A science not only describes, but in order to organize it must classify. Someone told Titchener that if he reduced all mental life to simple existences, it would be impossible to classify them. Titchener replied that, although the mental elements are simple, they are still actual processes, and as such, they have various aspects or attributes. A sensation can be defined as a mental element with at least five attributes: Quality, intensity, clearness, duration and extent. Sensations can be grouped on the basis of these attributes. *Quality* is that attribute by which one sensation is distinguished from another. For example, a violin tone is distinguished from the sight of the violin and musician by quality of sensation. Another attribute is *intensity*. One sensation is greater-than, or more-than another sensation. A third attribute is clearness. In a given experience, some sensations are vivid, others vague. A fourth attribute, *duration,* is the basis for an analysis of the variations of a sensation in the passage of time. The attribute of *extent* is the basis for the size of things, in fact, for all space perception.

Titchener also classified experience with reference to parts of the body, such as muscular sensations from the vocal organs, or from the eye. Another means of classifying uses the stimulus as a reference point.

Existential System of Thought.—Existential psychology emphasizes the organization which lies submerged in our workaday world. Science can know no other world than the world of experience, and psychology shares that world with other sciences. Psychology, however, is concerned only with those experiences which are immediately dependent for their nature upon the nervous system. Pure science describes in the simplest possible terms, and considers each item as isolated, and therefore meaningless. One cannot describe the nature of any object or event if ulterior objects and processes enter into the description. The simplest possible terms in which existential psychological experience can be described are sensations, images, and affections. These are the elements into which all mental furniture can be divided. They can be classified according to their attributes, by reference to parts of the body, or by their stimuli.

View of Adaptation to Environment

The idea of evolution, originating in biology, was carried over into psychology. Whereas biology was interested primarily in the relation of bodily features to the preservation of life, psychology inquired into the role of consciousness in adaptation to environment. Sense organs, muscles, nerves, and glands contributed to the continuation of life, but did not conscious processes provide important means to the same end?

The Adjustment of Inner to Outer Relations: Spencer's View.—This viewpoint came to be known as functional psychology, since the whole field was organized in terms of the ways in which consciousness functioned for the welfare of the living being. Herbert Spencer, an Englishman, was one of the first to lay the foundation for such an organization. He thought that our understanding of psychology was not a matter of what went on in consciousness alone, but that the environment had to be taken into consideration. All events inside the organism, or internal relations as he called them, were in some way connected with external relations, or the environment. Mental life, no less than bodily life, was a continual adjustment of the internal relations to the external relations.

Environmental Demands as Met by Reflex and Automatic Acts.—Human beings are equipped by heredity to make certain adjustments to the environment without a long process of learning. One of the simplest examples of the adaptive process is the eye-wink reflex. If an object is thrown toward your eye, in a split second the lid closes as a protective gesture. Then there is the reflex which automatically makes possible adaptation to strong light by shutting out some of it, and to weak light by admitting more.

Automatic acts, such as walking, talking, writing, and driving an automobile, when learned, at first occupy a considerable portion of attention. We are conscious of the acts themselves as we learn them. It is fortunate that we do not have to devote as much attention to these acts all through our lives. Having learned to go through the movements of typewriting, we no longer pay any attention to those movements, and we are left free to concentrate on the thought of what we are writing.

Consciousness as a Part of the Adjustive Processes of an Organism: Angell's View.—Much of what we do day in and day out is of a routine nature. Consciousness steps out of the picture when its function is no longer needed. James Rowland Angell, for many years President of Yale University, pointed out that consciousness becomes a "master device" in adjusting to the environment, when hereditary acts or learned automatisms fail us. Nature did not make of man a creature adapted to all possible environments. If you are driving your automobile, the shifting of gears, turning of the wheel, and foot action on the accelerator are a complicated coordination of movements, which you leave to your nervous system for successful operation. While driving in situations which are not dangerous, you may lose yourself in thoughts and forget that you are driving an automobile. If, however, another car looms up unexpectedly, you quickly become aware of your driving and consciousness comes to your aid to help you out of the situation.

Since we never reach a complete and final adjustment until death, we have a recurrent series of one adjusting process after another. As a result our conscious processes are frequently called into use to assist in making adjustments. Both bodily and mental life cooperate —the entire organism is involved.

What Does Consciousness Do?—Whereas Titchener and the existential psychologists were interested in analyzing experience into simple mental processes, functional psychologists such as James Rowland Angell and John Dewey held that mental processes should be described in terms of how they function in achieving successful adjustments to life situations. The nature of a sensation, for example, is determined by the way in which the entire activity of the organism is being used. One of the functions of sensation is that it leads to movements, and the neural process is one complete act from the time the sense organ is stimulated until muscles respond. The sensation cannot be freed from the entire process, and so its nature depends upon the activity. The example Angell uses in this connection is a disagreeable odor. Such a sensation not only produces a quality of odor, but choking and retreating movements, the consciousness of which greatly changes the odor quality.

Sensation, Perception, and Attention in Adjustment.— We use the data of our senses as the raw material of the life situations we have to face. The value of sensation in adjustment is apparent when we consider the difficulties of the blind and the deaf. In a hostile environment, these people would not survive. The sense of pain has a definite protective value in our lives, warning us of bodily dangers. Human beings make much less use of smell and taste in adjusting than do many animals.

When we perceive, we are given the actual objects with which we deal, buildings, automobiles, sidewalks, and people. Perception serves to organize the sensations of things and people into units. If such an organization of sensations did not occur, we could not cope with situations. In the difficulty called word-blindness, people so afflicted have sensations of sound but they cannot organize them into perceptions as we do.

Before we can adjust to a situation, we must attend to it. Attention is an activity in which numerous muscular adjustments are made in order to perceive a situation. Our eye muscles adjust themselves, we hold our breath, and the like. Because it is in the nature of attention that we perceive first one part and next another part of a situation, attention makes it possible for us to group numerous perceptions into a comprehensible whole. It also helps us to achieve an organized response.

Serviceable Memory and Imagination.—Memories permit us to draw on our past experience to help us face the situation now before us. What we do now can be determined by what we remember as having been of value to us in previous similar situations. Where past experience is not sufficient, we can call upon imagination. Both memory and imagination make use of images, and frequently we work out one set of images after another until we hit upon those which reveal an appropriate form of action.

Uses of Emotion and Feeling.—Darwin made exhaustive observations of various emotional attitudes in men and animals, and tried to trace the value in adjustment of screams, growls, tense postures, and erection of dermal appendages such as hair and feathers. An animal's strong and harsh cry of rage had a possible value of frightening an adversary. In civilized man, the value of such emotional expressions is probably less than in animals.

Intense anger and fear do serve us, as Angell points out. They represent a compelling break in the continuity of our mental life, and make us acutely aware of a crisis and the necessity for an adjustment to it. Angell's idea was that a strong emotion appeared when there was a conflict between normal impulses arising out of special situations.

The feelings of pleasure and displeasure connected with emotional life are by nature tied up to the purposes of the organism. According to one view, if our mental activities move along unimpeded toward a given end, we feel pleasant. If, for any reason, there appears a thwarting of progress toward that goal, we feel unpleasant.

Summary.—Functional psychologists split up consciousness into sensory processes, acts of memory, imaginings, reasonings, feelings, and the like. The nature of these processes, however, is influenced by the neural activities as a whole. Consciousness should be understood as one of the devices by which man adapts to his environment, cooperating with bodily life when nonconscious activities fail. Conscious processes are organized with reference to adaptation to the environment.

VIEW OF STIMULI AND RESPONSES

We have seen that existential psychology is limited to our "internal" experience, although it uses the "external" world for purposes of classification. Functional psychology is colored throughout by the adjustive relationship of consciousness to the environment. A third view leaves out all reference to experience or consciousness, and confines itself to a study of the relationship of various stimuli which impinge on an organism to the responses made by that organism. It is known as behavioristic psychology.

Animal Learning: Thorndike's View.—At the beginning of this century, some of our psychologists were occupied in researches on instinct and learning. They found that they could control their experimental situations much better with animals than with human beings. Edward L. Thorndike, the famous Columbia University psychologist, was one of the early experimenters on animals. His classical experiment with a kitten learning to escape from a box is a good example of stimulus-response psychology. The stimulus for the animal was a box with a door which could be opened to get a piece of fish. The response necessary to solve the problem was turning a button. The kitten made a large number of movements with paws, mouth, and other parts of his body. Most of them were useless movements. Some of the promiscuous movements were made at the button, and the door opened. The next time the kitten was put in the cage, he did not go immediately to the button, but repeated his first performance of useless movements. However, some of the useless movements were eliminated, since the kitten took a shorter time to get out. As the trials were repeated, more useless movements were dropped out. The connection of the appropriate response to the confinement stimulus was gradually strengthened, or in Thorndike's words, stamped in.

Conditioned Reflex: Pavlov's View.—A Russian experimenter, I. P. Pavlov, arrived at the notion of the conditioned reflex from his experimentation on dogs. The salivary reflex is a natural reflex for which the adequate stimulus is food in the mouth. A bell is not a natural stimulus for its occurrence. By presenting repeatedly the sound of a bell shortly before the dog was given food, he found that the bell did become a stimulus for the salivary flow. Any reflex is called *conditioned* when a biologically inadequate stimulus is substituted for the biologically adequate stimulus. Pavlov found in this a cue for the years of experiments which he later performed on brain activities, such as learning, sleep, and neuroses.

Subject Matter of Animal Psychology Cannot Be Revealed by Internal Observation.—It is obvious that an animal cannot make observations of his experience, and report them to a scientist. Thorndike and Pavlov had to speak of learning objectively in terms of stimulus and response, whereas previously it had been described as subjective association of ideas. The techniques which the animal experimenters used were as adequate in revealing the nature of learning as were subjective procedures.

Psychology Studied in Other Persons: Meyer's View.— Since the methods of animal psychology were so successful, they were applied to human beings. In a book entitled *Psychology of the Other One*, Max Meyer contended that the study of psychology would be more objective and scientific if the psychologist left himself out of the subject matter. Besides believing that the consciousness of the psychologist should be eliminated from the study, he doubted that consciousness could be studied in other people, because he considered it to be a personal matter. He suggested that the whole of our psychology could be written without any recourse to consciousness. For instance, in place of thought, we can study language; for the symbols of thought are subjective and personal, while those of language are objective and social. Likewise, it is unnecessary to say that an animal moves about in search of food because he is hungry, since the word *hunger* refers to an animal's conscious state. Meyer states that it is more consistent to say that such an animal moves about because there is no food in the digestive cavity. The movements, food, and digestive apparatus all belong to the same category of objective realities. This attitude may be clearer if we consider our objections to stating that a plant grows roots into the ground because it is hungry.

Measurement of Responses.—Meyer pointed out that the great discoveries of science have been made when the scientist restricted his descriptions to that which he could measure. When we measure, we use sense organs, primarily our eyes. As far as is known, our sense organs cannot receive our conscious experiences, and consciousness is not directly measurable. With responses, however, behaviorists tell us that it is different. We can measure the action of muscles and glands, and later determine their significance to us.

Sufficiency of Response Information.—Although a muscular response is a result of a stimulus, it is not an immediate result. Before a muscular response can take place, nervous excitations have to travel from sense organs to the nervous system and then to the muscles. In the solution of many psychological problems, however, it is possible to disregard the intermediate nervous excitations. One example is to be found in the relation of reaction time to traffic accidents. One of the first things studied with accident-prone drivers is the time it takes for them to push down on a brake pedal after a stimulus has been given. If a driver shows that he is slow compared to others, or that he is highly variable, fast at one time and slow at another, it is not necessary to find out what went on in the sensory and motor impulses of his nervous system.

We have often heard the phrase, "We learn by doing." The behavioristic view is limited to what a person does. In life situations, it is our actual output that counts for us. We may have excellent intentions, but unless they find some outward expression they are a matter of individual interest only.

The Stimulus-Response Formula of Watson.—John Broadus Watson is the psychologist who is most often associated with the behavioristic viewpoint. His keynote for psychology is, "Given a stimulus, to predict a response." Throughout all his writings he stresses those aspects of psychology which can be of practical service to man. In many of the applications to psychology, it is interesting to notice that little emphasis is placed on man's consciousness and great emphasis is placed on man's behavior. An advertiser need not be concerned with more than the stimuli he can fashion, and the increase in sales because of those stimuli. If the company's profits increase, it is not necessary to know what people thought when they bought more goods.

Prediction of Response from Stimulus.—Man's actions occur in a world of law and order. It is admitted generally that what any given individual does can be traced to preceding conditions in his life. It is from these preceding stimuli that we can predict some human behaviors with sufficient certainty even by common sense. To be sure, our predictions are not perfect, but we rely on them. The President of the United States can predict that millions will listen to his fireside chat. A bank cashier predicts that the loans he makes will be repaid. A personnel manager predicts that individuals of his choice will be successful in the places to which he assigns them. As we become closer acquainted with a friend, we can better map out in advance what he will do in any given situation.

Society's Control of Man's Behavior by Stimuli.—Education, religion, laws, and advertisements each represent a complex of stimuli which have proven to be controls for the behavior of men. Behavioristic psychology has in recent years entered each of these fields, trying out one situation after another and studying the responses which take place. In many of these studies, psychologists have elaborated the stimulus-response formula, and have delved into brain action, gland secretion, and the basic drives which motivate man. The psychological interest is not in brain action or drives for themselves, but rather in their relationship to the understanding and prediction of behavior. Thus advertisers are guided by basic drives, such as sex, hunger, superiority, and protection, in determining what stimuli they will present.

An Application of Behavior Measurements.—When you take an intelligence test, you are measured by the number of correct answers you can give to certain situations which are presented to you on the test paper. Alfred Binet, the French psychologist, devised intelligence tests by trying out one question after another on children of various ages, computing how many of a given age would answer it correctly. If a question were answered correctly by 66 per cent to 75 per cent of the children of a given age, it was regarded as an item for that age. One item for age five, for example, was the successful behavior of a child in repeating the stimulus of a sentence with ten syllables. Sometimes a five-year child could respond correctly to a stimulus in the nine-year classification. From cues such as these, Binet evolved an objective scale for measurement of mental age. In no instance was it necessary for the child to observe his experience and report on it. The practical value of intelligence tests lies in its measure of what an individual actually does.

Summary.—The behavioristic viewpoint emphasizes the study of measurable movements of an organism in relation to the stimuli preceding those movements. The subject matter of psychology consists of activities, and those activities can be organized according to the formula: Given a stimulus, to predict a response. Behaviorists hold that the facts of psychology can be ascertained in objective terms, and that a description of consciousness is not essential.

VIEW OF UNCONSCIOUS PROCESSES

A group of European scientists, dealing with the troubles of people, found that many of the strange and irrational occurrences in the lives of unfortunate people could not be explained along the rational lines of existential, functional, and behavioristic psychology. They looked for explanations in what they sometimes referred to as the subconscious, which contained those events which never reached the surface of consciousness, but which influenced conscious life to a considerable extent. They probed into the not-at-all calm and serene emotional depths of their patients' lives.

Hysteria: Charcot's View.—A celebrated French neurologist, T. M. Charcot, made extended studies of people who were paralyzed in their legs, who could see only one word at a time, who had distortions of their faces, who had loss of sensations in their hands, and who complained of strange pains in different parts of their bodies. As a result of this work, he learned to distinguish between paralyses which had some physical basis, and those which did not. It is primarily to Charcot that we are indebted for a searching of psychological facts to account for hysterical symptoms of paralyses, anesthesias, contractures, and the like. Before the days of Charcot, tongue muscles were incised as a cure for stuttering, operations were performed on the neck to eliminate stiffness, and in other ways surgery was resorted to in an attempt to relieve what Charcot found to be psychological.

Dissociation of Consciousness: Janet's View.—One of Charcot's students, Pierre Janet, Professor of Psychology in the College de France, has given an interesting account of a hysterical case. A thirty-two-year-old man was confined in a hospital bed. because he could not move either of his legs, when he was awake and conscious. At night, however, when he was asleep, he jumped with agility out of bed at times, grabbed a pillow, and spoke to it as though it were his child whom he was protecting from his mother-in-law. He then fled out of the room with the pillow, went to the top of the hospital building, running at an unusual speed. The attendants had to exercise great care in catching him, since when he was awak·

ened, both of his legs again were paralyzed. When informed of the episode, after he was carried back to bed, he could not believe that such an experience happened to him. All those events did not exist in his conscious life, but while running in his somnambulistic state, he evidently was guided by sensations of doors, hallways, the pillow, and the roof of the hospital.

Janet tells of other hysterical cases: Those who had double existences, at one time being one personality, and at another time, being an entirely different person; those who forgot who they were and awakened in a strange place; those who lacked sensitivities in hands or entire arms; and those who saw only a small central part of the field of vision, since called "tunnel vision." He came to the conclusion that in each of these instances there was a restriction of consciousness. He decided that in hysteria the patient had a lowered psychic energy, and as a result of the exhaustion some part of his consciousness was broken off from the totality. Under certain conditions, that part broken off would function, as in the case of the paralyzed man who fled with the pillow, but at that time only those perceptions and ideas which related to the dissociated part would be reacted to by the patient.

Neuroses and Sex.—Charcot had noticed that persons suffering from neuroses generally had some difficulty in their sexual life, which sooner or later revealed itself. However, it was Sigmund Freud, another of his students, who saw the significance of Charcot's observation. He proceeded to make use of the relation of neuroses to sexual difficulties in his treatments. He found that the patients were ashamed to discuss these troubles, but that once they could be brought to recall their past experiences along this line, a sort of mental catharsis took place, and the neurosis was relieved.

Freud found that the recollection of these troublesome experiences was an exceedingly difficult task. He became convinced that his patients had actually forgotten the original sexual episodes. He also was satisfied that it was those forgotten experiences that somehow were the cause of the neuroses. What was the process by which these vivid emotional experiences were forgotten? How did they possess a strange power to change an entire personality?

In building a psychological system to answer these preliminary questions, Freud adopted a picturesque terminology. He conceived of the personality, or psyche, as being partly conscious, and partly unconscious. We are aware of the external world and certain aspects of ourselves, but we are ignorant of the deeper and more powerful forces of our personalities. That great region of activity within us of which we are not aware is the unconscious. A patient who forgot a crucial incident in his life, Freud decided, had driven it from his conscious system, which permits of ready recall, into his unconscious. Freud called this *repression*.

Id, Ego and Superego.—In order to explain repression, Freud made use of three agents of the psyche, which he termed the id, the ego, and the superego. The id, or it, is the unconscious home of the instinctive impulses. It strives powerfully to find expression in some form, but by itself it is primitive and unorganized, and cannot determine the manner of its expression. It is the ego, which is the organized part of the psyche, which guides the particular outlets of the forces of the id. The ego depends for its existence upon the perceptual system, by means of which we are conscious of the external world and ourselves. The superego is that part of the psyche which harbors ideals of conduct, somewhat similar to the conscience. These are the three players in Freud's drama of life, and the setting is one that spells battle.

The Ego and Conflicts.—The ego is the buffer between forces of the id and the superego. The ego controls all forces which enter consciousness and which lead to action. It makes an attempt to remain peaceful and organized in the conflict between the id and the superego. It is the ego which accounts for the repression of instinctive strivings in conformity with the dictates of the superego. The phenomenon of repression reveals the relationships of the ego and the id. Although in some instances the ego and the id are distinctly separable, it remains that the ego developed out of the id. Not all of the ego is conscious. Freud found that many patients were not aware that they had repressed any vivid experience. That aspect of the ego which functions in repression is therefore sometimes unconscious.

It would seem that the ego possesses power in its own right, if it can conquer an instinctive impulse by repressing it. Freud explains that repression actually reveals a weakness of the ego. The forces in the id, baffled by the ego in their attempts at expression, are not content to remain idle and defeated. The repressed process appears in the form of a neurotic symptom, and enjoys a gloating existence outside of the ego-organization. For instance, one person may develop a compulsion to wash his hands, and during the course of a day, he may repeat the process many times, even though his hands are clean. Compulsive handwashing to Freud is a neurotic symptom which defeats in a way some prior repression by the ego.

The Pleasure Principle and the Reality Principle.—As Freud describes it, the id is dominated by the pleasure principle, which is that force in the individual that attempts to secure immediate gratification of instinctive cravings. The id, because it is unconscious and unorganized, cannot become aware of dire consequences which may result from gratification. It is the ego, possessed of a knowledge of social precepts and future consequences of many kinds, called the reality principle, which acts as a temporary check upon the forces of the id.

Anxiety and the Pleasure Principle.—Returning to the individual who washes his hands without an apparent reason, Freud stated that, if he restrains himself from such an irrational act, he is thrown into a state of unpleasant anxiety. Vague anxieties are characteristic of neuroses. Freud found in these anxieties the secret of the seeming power of the ego.

By itself, the ego is often in a state of helplessness, particularly in the face of danger. It may experience danger either from some external object, or from some forces in the id. When some repressed instinctive power seeks expression, the ego feels afraid but does not know of what it is afraid. Thus arises the feeling of anxiety, which seems meaningless or irrational but none the less real. Freud says that the anxiety states are distress signals sent out by the ego to the all-powerful pleasure principle. The pleasure principle cooperates with the ego by leaving that particular force of the id as such under ego-repression, but forces it out in some queer behavior, uncontrolled by the ego. In the case of handwashers, the feeling of vague anxiety calls forth cleansing the hands, which is pleasant, and both the danger and anxiety disappear for a time. Handwashing does not bring out a conflict with the superego, which the direct action of the id's impulse would have done.

Motivation from Within the Individual.—It is apparent that much emphasis is placed by Freud upon the driving forces submerged in the unconscious. In the *id* Freud originally proposed two distinct tendencies, sexual instincts and ego instincts. The latter primarily were the instincts of self-preservation. The sex instincts were always directed toward a particular object. When a particular attachment to a certain object was repressed, the sexual impulse or *libido* transferred itself to another object. Thus arose the principle of *transference*. When he found that many individuals turned their love to themselves (*narcism* *), he argued that the libido had then found its love object in the ego.

Life Instincts and Death Instincts.—For this reason he could not find a conflict between the ego instincts and the sex instincts, since the ego instincts sometimes became servants of the libido. He then combined the instincts of self-preservation and species-preservation into the single concept of *Eros*. He did find, however, that there was an instinct separate from Eros, and he called this the death or destruction instinct, which operated in silence. Eros and the death instinct work in opposition to each other, forming a psychic polarity in the unconscious.

The death instinct accounts for tendencies to suicide in some individuals, and *sadism* (the torturing of a loved one) in others. All impulses tending to destruction and hate fall into this category.

Infantile Sexuality.—All the time Freud was evolving the concepts of id, ego, superego, repression, transference, Eros, and death instincts, he was utilizing these concepts in his work with neurotic patients, which involved first of all the recall of the experiences that had been repressed. He applied many methods in his attempt to overcome the resistance of the ego. He used hypnosis, which Janet

---

* Old spelling *narcissism.*

had used with some success. He had his patients talk for hours, over periods of time, limiting what they said to matters pertaining to their unhappiness. One procedure, for which Freud became famous, was his interpretation of dreams. During dream states, he thought, the repressed desires appeared in strange guises. Out of this work there came a study of symbolism, in which objects and events in dreams were understood to stand for sexual events or objects. He also studied lapses of memory, slips of the tongue, and queer mistakes people made which they could not understand, but which Freud interpreted as a disguised expression of a repressed force in the id.

By these methods, Freud frequently was successful in reviving an experience which he determined to his satisfaction was connected with the neurosis. However, one repressed experience, when brought into consciousness, gave evidence of another such experience farther back, and Freud had to continue his probing into the unconscious. He would usually wind up in experiences dating back to infancy. Libido finds its earliest expression, according to Freud, through oral and anal stimulation. Later it moves outward and becomes attached to persons and objects. The persons involved, in his theory, are generally the parents of the child. Love of boy for mother, and girl for father, give rise to the Oedipus complex, and the Electra complex, respectively. The child realizes he cannot become a substitute for the parent, and a conflict ensues which results in repression. Throughout infancy all efforts at libido expression are met with, first, an outer, and second, an inner resistance. These experiences Freud found to be the original source of the trouble.

Summary.—Freudian psychology, concentrating on the relationship between conscious and unconscious processes, divides the psyche into three interacting entities, the id, the ego, and the superego. The id is the unconscious part of the psyche, and contains two warring instincts, the life instinct at one pole and the death instinct at the other. Dominated by the pleasure principle, it lacks the organization to determine the specific outlets for the impulses. Those outlets are primarily a function of the ego, which grows out of the id, and in its organized part, has a separate existence from the id. The ego strives to keep the conscious life of an individual organized. Growing out of the ego, because of early sexual repressions, is the superego, somewhat akin to conscience.

View of Organized Experiences

In Titchener's view of existential experience, our everyday world is reducible to three simple, ultimate existences: Sensations, images, and affections. In Germany, a group of psychologists, most prominent among whom were Max Wertheimer, Wolfgang Köhler, Kurt Koffka, and Kurt Lewin, came to regard introspectively analyzed sensations, images, and affections as artificial. We should study our experiences, they say, but we should recognize the natural patterns into which our experiences fall, and then we should determine the conditions under which the natural patterns appear.

Experiences of the All of Objects and Events.—Think for a moment of your experience of this page of print. You can analyze it into sensations of blackness, whiteness, pressure, and the like, if you are a good introspectionist. Nevertheless, before and after the analysis, your experience is an organized totality, for you then are not aware of elementary mental processes. You are experiencing a page of print in its entirety. A perception of *all* of it, as such, possesses for you a strong reality. This book we regard as something which does not depend upon us for its existence. We can leave the room, and believe that the book is still here. We can find it when we return. We open it, close it, put it on the shelf, walk away from it, and it remains the same book to us.

Objective and Subjective Experience.—Köhler called those experiences of the *all* of objects and events, which appear as actualities outside of us and independent of us, *objective experiences*. There are other experiences which we do not refer to the outside, but which we regard as personal and inside. We have experiences of muscular strain, emotions, and memories. They are our *subjective experiences*.

We can come to regard outside objects as experiences within us, as Titchener did, but Köhler reminds us that our ordinary experiences of things and movements have a strong and natural objectivity. The allness and the externality of chairs, books, and even sounds have been present to us from early childhood. A case in point: A physicist tells of an experience of his five-year-old son, at the time of an earache. "Can't you hear that ringing sound?" the boy asked his father. It was difficult for the child to understand that the ringing came from processes in his ear and not from some external source, since sounds which he had heard in the past could be heard by other people and were not a personal affair with him. It is still another step removed from naïve experience to think that sounds which can be heard by others, that is, external sounds, are also processes inside one's head.

Although most of the work of Köhler to date has consisted of studies of objective experience, he recognizes the place of subjective experiences in psychology. Instead of analyzing objective and subjective experiences into sensations, images, and affections, Köhler believes that the task of psychology is to study the patterning of all experiences. He saw an outstanding characteristic of experience in its organization into wholes. The view which emphasizes the organized wholes of our experience has been called the *gestalt* view. The nearest English words to *gestalt* are *configuration* and *pattern*, but they do not carry the precise meaning, so the word *gestalt* has become a part of our English psychological terminology.

The Whole Is More than the Sum of Its Parts: von Ehrenfels' View.—Christian von Ehrenfels, an Austrian philosopher, was one of the men whose works form the background of the gestalt view. von Ehrenfels was interested in music. The idea current at his time was that a melody was a sum-total of the notes comprising it. He wondered why a melody played in one key remained the same when played in another key. When transposed, the sensory parts comprising the melody, that is, the notes, were all changed. The melody, he concluded, was a quality of the whole sequence. von Ehrenfels' idea was that experiences had many qualities as-a-whole, and such qualities disappeared when those experiences were broken up into parts. Likewise, he believed that, when we add together the parts of an experience, we do not arrive at whole-qualities. The whole-qualities are independent of the parts, in as much as the parts may be changed and the whole-qualities still remain identical.

However, von Ehrenfels regarded the whole-qualities, such as melodies, as new elements added to the sensations of the notes making up the musical composition. We have both the sensory elements and the whole-qualities, which are added by thought processes. Köhler and other gestalt psychologists later came to the opposite conclusion that wholes were the primary and immediate sensory data and that elements, such as simple sensations, were products of abstract thought that came afterward. This view can be traced to the interpretations which Wertheimer gave to his famous experiments on the perception of movement.

When you see motion pictures, there is no movement on the screen. If Irene Dunne seems to walk from a chair to a table, the pictures which are thrown on the screen in rapid succession to produce the action do not in themselves have that movement. The pictures are still photographs of successive positions. Why, then, do we see movement? For experimental purposes, we can illustrate what happens by arranging a situation which involves two alternately flashing lights. There is no light in the space between them, but under stipulated conditions a brief flash of one followed by a flash of the other will appear as a light moving. If the conditions are proper, there will be a perception not of two lights, but of one light in motion. This is called the *phi phenomenon*. It is obvious that the movement cannot be described as two elementary sensations of light. The movement is not in the lights. According to gestalt theory, the movement involves the same organized brain processes which are occasioned if a light moves in space

Just as Isaac Newton is said to have thought of the law of gravitation by watching an insignificant apple fall from a tree, so Max Wertheimer saw in the phi phenomenon a new principle in psychology. It was an organized experience, divorced in nature from any elementary sensations. The organization occurred because of dynamic brain processes, forces interacting with each other and forming unitary experiences. Wertheimer believed that what was true of the phi phenomenon was also characteristic of other varieties of experience.

Segregated Wholes.—If we perceive wholes, you may ask: "Why do I have in my total visual field separated objects, this book, my hand, my pencil, paper, and a table? Are they not parts of my visual field?"

Gestalt psychologists would welcome your question, since the *parts* which you mention are recognized as genuine to them. Köhler calls such parts *segregated wholes*. A book is not to a visual field what an abstract sensation is to a book, for in direct objective experience we have a visual field and a book, but no segregation into different sensations. The "parts" which are acceptable to gestalt psychologists are those which are segregated in ordinary perception.

Gestalt psychologists have shown great interest in their studies as to why vision and other sensory fields are organized into a number of units. They rejected the theory that books, tables, and pencils have acquired meanings because of the use to which we put them, and thus come to exist as units. Köhler vigorously defends the theory that from the beginning of experience, objects as such are segregated naturally in the visual field, although as time goes on these segregated objects are given names and take on meanings. Thus a mother's face is perceived by a baby as an organized unit without name or any other reference. In support of natural segregation, Köhler points to adult experience, in which an unknown object looms up in mist or darkness. Although it is immediately perceived as a single entity, its meaning or use does not appear immediately.

Conditions of Sensory Organization.—Objects of man's construction and of nature become separated entities because, for one reason, within the outline of the object there is a closed area with similar surface properties, different from the surfaces just outside the boundary of the object. Our perception of an object as such can be destroyed under some conditions if the surface properties are altered to blend with the surrounding areas. A warship, painted with an irregular series of lines, presents at a distance isolated patches similar to those presented by sea and sky.

Sensory organization does not stop with closed areas. We have a powerful tendency to organize objects which are separated in space and independent of each other into larger wholes. Wertheimer made exhaustive studies of the conditions under which groupings of this kind occur. Although he resorted to nonsense visual forms in order to eliminate meaning as an explanation, one of the conditions he mentioned may be illustrated from a possible daily-life occurrence. If you are looking at six automobiles parked in line next to a curb, and some police officers walk between them from the sidewalk into the open street, the cars would fall into one group and the police officers into another. If, in anticipation of a parade, one officer should take a station in front of each automobile, you could have a new grouping, consisting of a series of six similar, separate units, each with a car and an officer. The conditions of groupings of this order may be generalized as our tendency to group similar items separately from the dissimilar items in the rest of the field.

At this point, suppose that the owner of the third car appears. After talking excitedly to the officer next to his car, the officer gets in and the two drive off together. Another grouping occurs, with two car-officer units as parts of one larger group, and three car-officer units as parts of another. In the new grouping, there is a new condition involved, which may be called *proximity*. It can be described as the tendency to group like units which have the least distance between them. *Similarity* and *proximity* are the two simplest conditions under which groupings occur.

Physical objects in the same positions may be grouped in numerous ways in direct experience. In the illustration used above, it would be possible to maintain the grouping of the officers into one unit and cars into another unit through all the changes which occurred. However, this would be a departure from natural sensory organization, occasioned by a special attitude.

The organization in the sensory field, considered by the Gestalt psychologists as the result of interacting forces in the brain, applies to the segregated wholes of single things, as well as to groupings of those things. Köhler does not believe that the waves of light from a book, for example, bring the book as a gestalt to the nervous system. In his view, the light waves from the parts of the book are as independent of each other as light waves from any other surfaces in the environment; there is an unorganized mass of waves. Our eyes are so constructed that rays of light from a point in the outside world are brought together on one retinal point, with the geometrical relations of the outside world for the most part intact. Nevertheless, what occurs at each point of the retina still is independent of occurrences at the other points. According to Köhler, there are no segregated wholes on the retina. If we think that a picture of a book on the retina is a whole, we are committing the *experience error,* which means that we think of the sensory experience we have of that retinal area and not of what occurs in the retinal area itself.

Constancy of Size.—Thus, as Köhler conceives it, stimulation is not organized dynamically, but the nervous system organizes segregated wholes in accord with the world of physical objects. Consider the fact that an object remains the same size to us, even though we change our distance from it. In order for you to see this book, there must be light reflected from it to your eyes. There is an image of it on your retina. If you hold it one foot or two feet away from your eyes, it appears to be the same-sized book. Nevertheless, on your retina it is twice as large at one foot as it is at two feet. Although your experience of the book must come from that retinal stimulation, your perception of the size of the book does not correspond to it, but rather to the actuality in the outside world—the book measures the same whether it is one foot or two feet from your eye. It is possible to think that the book remains the same because the total organization in the brain remains the same, even though the sensory stimulation from the book is changed.

The Gestalt Formula.—Köhler elaborates the stimulus-response formula for psychology into: *Constellation of stimuli* ⟶ *Organization* ⟶ *Reaction to the results of organization.* Thus far in this discussion we have concentrated upon the first and second terms of the formula. The gestalt psychologists have contributed to numerous fields of psychology, including that of reaction and behavior. The behavior of another person is regarded as a segregated whole of the sensory field, primarily visual, in the objective experience of an observer. Köhler cites many examples in which there are similarities in organization of the subjective and objective experience of the same behavior. One instance which he mentions is the behavior of a pianist playing a sonata. The organization of the sonata is present in the subjective experience of the pianist, such as a *crescendo* followed by a *ritardando*. The activity of his muscles in playing conforms to the organization. The resulting sound waves are grouped in the objective experience of a listener in a similar manner to the grouping in the subjective experience of the pianist. In crescendo, the subjective and objective experience of the behavior both have a whole-quality of *swelling*.

It is not implied that the precise elements in the subjective experience of another individual are revealed by behavior observation. Köhler is speaking of the whole-qualities, which gestalt psychologists say can have varying or interchangeable elements.

Köhler's Study of the Behavior of Apes.—The gestalt psychologists have found evidences for their view in numerous experiments on perception, learning, memory processes, and emotions. One of Köhler's famous studies on the mentality of apes is a sample of the kind of experiments performed. The tests had many variations, but in one instance Köhler suspended a banana above the reach of the apes. Near by, but not directly under the banana, was a box. Six apes were placed in the room, and at first they attempted the impossible task of reaching the banana by jumping. One of the apes, named Sultan, ceased jumping and paced about the room. Suddenly, he stopped next to the box, pushed it to a spot sufficiently near the banana so that, by a leap, he was able to grasp his reward. Only a few seconds after Sultan stopped near the box, he had secured the banana. None of the other apes had noticed the box. From Sultan's behavior, Köhler concluded that the ape had surveyed the situation as a whole. Suddenly, he saw the connection between the box, jumping, and the banana, and the problem was solved. Insight is the term Köhler applies to the experience of the solution of a problem when there is reference to the whole situation. In this sense, Sultan had insight. Köhler does not regard insight as a mystical faculty leading to marvelous accomplishments. It is simply a term to mean that, in the experience of a total field, a pattern appears in which certain parts are felt as dependent upon other parts.

Recapitulation.—Gestalt psychology emphasizes the organized wholes of experience, which have properties not contained in the sum total of the parts. The nature of the parts is dependent upon the whole. The formula for psychology, according to Köhler, is *Constellation of stimuli→Organization→Reaction to results of organization.* Light waves and sound waves striking the eye and ear are not dynamically organized into segregated wholes. Such an organization takes place in the nervous system, which reconstructs the units of the physical world, after their unitary nature has been temporarily lost en route. To a whole of experience there corresponds a functional whole in brain processes.

VIEW OF PURPOSES

It would seem to be a simple statement of fact that as we go about our daily tasks we are guided by purposes. You may be walking along the street, and a friend may ask, "What are you doing?" You reply, "I am going to get something to eat." Your behavior of walking is related to a future goal, and in that sense your actions are purposeful.

Hormic Energy.—The late William McDougall of Duke University organized psychology around the concept of purpose. According to McDougall, living beings are distinguished by the presence of a kind of force which is never found in lifeless materials. If a stone moves, we look to some cause which preceded the motion, but when a human being moves, the crux of an understanding of that movement lies in what it is that the human being wants. In other words, a human being is moved by energy which is characterized by purpose. McDougall is even more explicit: The energy from which human action springs always is related to some future event. Such energy is called *hormic* energy. The word *hormic* is derived from a Greek word meaning "directed toward a goal." Hormic energy is present only where there is life.*

Purposive Causation.—McDougall states that physical science explains present physical events in terms of past events, or present

---

* This may be classed as one of the many forms of vitalism, all of which postulate forces which are distinct from physical forces. In its most extreme form, vitalism explains life on the basis of a "vital principle," which must be understood as a nonmaterial force.

effects as due to antecedent causes. Organisms, however, have two peculiarities which he finds cannot be accounted for as present effects determined entirely by past causes. The first peculiarity he ascribes to some, and possibly all, organisms is conscious activity. The second is that there is to be found in organisms a goal-seeking characteristic. When an animal moves about in search of food, he goes through many varied actions as a means of securing it. The antecedent cause may be described as hunger, or lack of food in the stomach, but from McDougall's point of view the actions may be accounted for in terms of the goal—a future attainment of food. There are thus two types of causation, mechanistic and purposive.

Goal-Striving.—When we examine our own experience, Mc-Dougall tells us that we find, to a lesser or greater degree, a conscious striving toward some goal. We have a certain understanding of what we do when we consider the future event toward which we are aiming our behavior. By keeping that goal steadily before us, our activities are organized with respect to it.

McDougall believes that the goals toward which we strive are ends in themselves. He cites concrete, practical objectives such as food, shelter, rest, and victory, and abstract future achievements like honor, virtue, and the solution of mathematical problems. We strive toward these objectives as ends in themselves, because they are worth while to us, and not because their achievement gives pleasure to us. Although he recognizes that pleasure often accompanies the reaching of a goal, he cites instances of self-sacrifice in which the specific goal of an individual is known to be painful, but the individual proceeds toward it because he believes that it is intrinsically good.

The Inherited Propensities of Man.—If we accept the contention that the knowledge of a goal toward which we are striving explains many of our actions, the question arises, why do we seek goals? To this question McDougall answers, "Man is so constituted that, like animals of other species, he desires and, under appropriate circumstances, strives to attain certain great natural goals, food, shelter, companions, a mate, knowledge, and so forth." [3] In simpler terms, we are "made that way." McDougall believes that each organism possesses by nature certain needs and, in addition, inherited propensities to satisfy those needs by the achievement of goals which correspond to them. Sometimes we substitute means, such as money, by which we can achieve natural goals, for the goals themselves. In that case the money becomes a goal.

McDougall offers tentatively the following list of inherited propensities of man: Food-seeking, disgust, sex, fear, curiosity, protective or parental, gregarious, self-assertive, submissive, anger, appeal, constructive, acquisitive, laughter, comfort, rest or sleep, migratory, and other simple propensities like coughing and sneezing. These propensities are somehow activated by hormic energy. Whether each propensity draws its energy from one general source, or whether each propensity has its own supply of energy, cannot be determined at the present time.

Survey of the View of Purposes.—The activities of men and animals exhibit a characteristic not found in the world of physics. Physical events can be explained by other physical events preceding them (mechanistic causes). The activities of organisms have a peculiarity which may be described as reference to a future event, or goal, Since those activities may be better understood when their goals are known, they may be explained in terms of future events (purposive causation). McDougall finds goal-seeking characteristic of both conscious activities and behavior.

A Closing Word

One concludes writing a chapter such as this one with many regrets. The various schools of thought in psychology are highly abstract, and to give them a minimum of abstractness and a maximum of concreteness adjusted to students newly ushered into a study of psychology, leaves much unsaid. If, however, it has been made clear that each point of view has one main emphasis, and the system of thought of each is organized about that emphasis, the limited goal of the chapter has been reached. Titchener's existential view of psychology is centered around analysis of experience into sensations, images, and affections. Angell's functional view emphasizes the rofe of conscious processes in the adaptation of man to his environment. Watson's behavioristic view organizes psychology around stimuli and responses, with studies of consciousness unnecessary. Köhler's gestalt view places emphasis on the wholes of objective and subjective experience, with the primary task of psychology stated as the determination of the conditions under which natural patterns appear in experience. McDougall's purposive view holds that the distinguishing characteristic of organisms, compared to inorganic material, is the presence of hormic energy, or energy directed toward a goal. A more recent view, championed by Edward C. Tolman of the University of California, has been omitted with many misgivings. In time, Tolman's view of purposive behaviorism may become very important, integrating as it does many of the views presented above. The highly technical language necessary to present it faithfully leaves no alternative but to recommend its merits to more advanced students of psychology.

REFERENCES

Angell, J. R. *Psychology.* New York: Henry Holt and Company, 1908.

Freud, S. *The Problem of Anxiety.* New York: The Psychoanalytic Quarterly Press and W. W. Norton Company, Inc., 1936.

Heidbreder, E. *Seven Psychologies.* New York: D. Appleton-Century Company, Inc., 1933.

Keller, F. S. *The Definition of Psychology.* New York: D. Appleton-Century Company, Inc., 1937.

Köhler, W. *Gestalt Psychology.* New York: Horace Liveright, 1929.

McDougall, W. *The Energies of Men.* New York: Charles Scribner's Sons, 1933.

Meyer, M. F. *Psychology of the Other One.* Columbia, Missouri: The Missouri Book Company, 1921.

Titchener, E. B. *Systematic Psychology: Prolegomena.* New York: The Macmillan Company, 1929.

Tolman, E. C. *Purposive Behavior in Animals and Men.* New York: D. Appleton-Century Company, Inc., 1932.

Watson, J. B. *Psychology, from the Standpoint of a Behaviorist.* Philadelphia: J. B. Lippincott Company, 1919.

Woodworth, R. S. *Contemporary Schools of Psychology.* New York: The Ronald Press Company, 1931.

LITERATURE CITED

Chapter II

1. C. J. Warden, *A Short Outline of Comparative Psychology*. New York: W. W. Norton and Company, Inc., 1927.
2. Warden, *Op. cit.* C. J. Warden and L. H. Warner, The development of animal psychology in the United States during the past three decades, *Psychol. Rev.*, 1927, 34, 196-205.
3. G. J. Romanes, *Animal Intelligence*. London: K. Paul, 1881.
4. C. J. Warden, T. N. Jenkins, and L. H. Warner, *Comparative Psychology, Vol. I, Principles and Methods*. New York: The Ronald Press Company, 1935. Warden and Warner, *Op. cit.*
5. H. S. Jennings, *Behavior of the Lower Organisms*. New York: Columbia University Press, 1906.
6. Warden, Jenkins, and Warner, *Op. cit.* Warden and Warner *Op. cit.*
7. Jennings, *Op. cit.*
8. Warden and Warner, *Op. cit.*
9. J. B. Watson, *Behavior: An Introduction to Comparative Psychology*. New York: Henry Holt and Company, 1914.
10. Warden, Jenkins, and Warner, *Op. cit.*

Chapter III

1. C. J. Warden, T. N. Jenkins, and L. H. Warner, *Introduction to Comparative Psychology*. New York: The Ronald Press Company, 1934. *Comparative Psychology*. New York: The Ronald Press Company, 1936, *Vol. III, Vertebrates*.
2. C. J. Warden, T. N. Jenkins, and L. H. Warner, *Comparative Psychology, Vol. I, Principles and Methods*. New York: The Ronald Press Company, 1935, 167-183.
3. Warden, Jenkins, and Warner, *Comparative Psychology, Op. cit.*, 193-213.
4. Warden, Jenkins, and Warner, *Introduction to Comparative Psychology, Op. cit. Comparative Psychology, Op. cit.*
5. Warden, Jenkins, and Warner, *Comparative Psychology, Op. cit.*, 219-232.
6. C. J. Warden, *Animal Motivation: Experimental Studies on the Albino Rat*. New York: Columbia University Press, 1931, 375.
7. C. J. Warden, The relative strength of the primary drives in the white rat, *J. Genet. Psychol.*, 1932, 41, 16-35.

8. C. P. Richter, Animal behavior and internal drives, *Quart. Rev. Biol.*, 1927, 2, 307-343.

9. L. H. Warner, and C. J. Warden, The development of a standardized animal maze, *Arch. Psychol.*, 1927, No. 93.

10. Warden, Jenkins, and Warner, *Comparative Psychology, Op. cit.,* 232-244.

11. N. L. Munn, *An Introduction to Animal Psychology: The Behavior of the Rat.* Boston: Houghton Mifflin Company, 1933.

12. Warden, Jenkins, and Warner, *Comparative Psychology, Op. cit.,* 249-272.

13. Warden, Jenkins, and Warner, *Comparative Psychology, Op. cit.,* 267-270.

Chapter V

1. H. M. Skeels, R. Updegraf, B. L. Wellman, and H. M. Williams, A study of environmental stimulation, *Univ. of Iowa Studies in Child Welfare*, 1938, 15.

2. K. Lewin, *Topological Psychology.* New York: McGraw-Hill Book Company, Inc., 1936, 45.

3. R. Barker, T. Dembo, and K. Lewin, Experiments on frustration and regression in children, *Psychol. Bull.,* 1937, 34, 754 f.

4. H. A. Murray, *Explorations in Personality.* New York: Oxford University Press, 1938.

5. Developed by Walter Dyk at the Harvard Psychological Clinic.

6. Erik H. Erikson developed this method for use with college students at the Harvard Psychological Clinic. He is now applying it to school-age children at the Institute of Child Welfare, University of California.

7. D. M. Levy, Primary affect hunger, *Amer. J. Psychiat.*, 1937, 94, 643-652.

8. H. L. Witmer, et al., The outcome of treatment of children rejected by their mothers, *Smith Coll. Stud. Soc. Work*, 1938, 8, 187-234.

9. G. Murphy, L. B. Murphy, and T. M. Newcomb, *Experimental Social Psychology.* New York: Harper and Brothers, 1937.

10. M. M. Shirley, *The First Two Years, III. Personality Manifestations.* Minneapolis: University of Minnesota Press, 1933.

11. Murphy, Murphy, and Newcomb, *Op. cit.,* 289-297.

12. G. W. Allport, *Personality: A Psychological Interpretation.* New York: Henry Holt and Company, 1937, 126 f.

13. M. M. Shirley, *Op. cit.* The observations on 10-year-olds have not been published.

Chapter VI

1. C. H. Cooley, *Social Organization*. New York: Charles Scribner's Sons, 1909.
2. F. H. Allport, *Institutional Behavior*. Chapel Hill: University of North Carolina Press, 1933.
3. D. Katz, and R. L. Schanck, *Social Psychology*. New York: John Wiley and Sons, Inc., 1938.
4. M. Ginsberg, *Sociology*. London: Methuen, 1934.
5. N. Bukharin, *Historical Materialism*. New York: International Publishers, 1925.
6. Katz and Schanck, *Op. cit.*
7. J. Dollard, L. W. Doob, N. E. Miller, O. H. Mowrer, et al., *Frustration and Aggression*. New Haven: Yale University Press, 1939.
8. M. Mead, *Cooperation and Competition Among Primitive Peoples*. New York: McGraw-Hill Book Company, Inc., 1937.
9. F. H. Allport, *Social Psychology*. Cambridge: Houghton Mifflin Company, 1924.
10. E. A. Ross, *Social Psychology*. New York: The Macmillan Company, 1908. G. Tarde, *The Laws of Imitation*. New York: Henry Holt and Company, 1903.
11. E. B. Holt, *Animal Drive and the Learning Process*. New York: Henry Holt and Company, 1931.
12. R. Messerschmidt, The suggestibility of boys and girls between the ages of six and sixteen years, *J. Genet. Psychol.*, 1933, 43, 422-437.
13. H. T. Moore, The comparative influence of majority and expert opinion, *Amer. J. Psychol.*, 1921, 32, 16-20.
14. C. E. Smith, A study of the autonomic excitation resulting from the interaction of individual opinion and group opinion, *J. Abn. and Soc. Psychol.*, 1936, 31, 138-164.
15. Allport, *Social Psychology, Op. cit.*
16. H. Cantril, Experimental studies of prestige suggestion, *Psychol. Bull.*, 1937, 34, 528.
17. A. O. Bowden, F. F. Caldwell, and G. A. West, Halo prestige, *J. Abn. and Soc. Psychol.*, 1934, 28, 400-406.
18. D. Katz, and H. Cantril., An analysis of attitudes toward communism and fascism, *J. Abn. and Soc. Psychol.*, 1940, 35.
19. S. Freud, *Group Psychology and the Analysis of the Ego*. New York: Boni and Liveright, 1921.
20. R. E. Horowitz, Racial aspects of self-identification in nursery school children, *J. Psychol.*, 1939, 7, 91-99.

21. J. F. Dashiell, An experimental analysis of some group effects, *J. Abn. and Soc. Psychol.*, 1930, 25, 190-199.
22. I. Child, An experimental investigation of "taboo" formation in a group of monkeys, *Psychol. Bull.*, 1938, 35, 705.
23. F. H. Allport, The J-curve hypothesis of conforming behavior, *J. Soc. Psychol.*, 1934, 5, 141-183.
24. L. M. Terman, and others, *Psychological Factors in Marital Happiness.* New York: McGraw-Hill Book Company, Inc., 1938.
25. H. L. Hollingworth, Review of psychological factors in marital happiness, *Psychol. Bull.*, 1939, 36, 191-197.
26. J. F. Brown, *Psychology and the Social Order.* New York: McGraw-Hill Book Company, Inc., 1936.
27. M. Opler, An interpretation of ambivalence of two American Indian tribes, *J. Soc. Psychol.*, 1936, 7, 82-116.
28. D. Katz, and H. Cantril, Public opinion polls, *Sociometry*, 1937, 1, 155-179.

Chapter VII

1. G. Le Bon, *The Crowd.* London: R. F. Unwin, 1917.
2. F. H. Allport, *Social Psychology.* Cambridge: Houghton Mifflin Company, 1924. E. D. Martin, *The Behavior of Crowds.* New York: Harper and Brothers, 1920.
3. C. H. Woolbert, The audience, *Psychol. Monog.*, 1916, 21, No. 92.
4. H. Gurnee, *Elements of Social Psychology.* New York: Farrar and Rinehart, Inc., 1936.
5. Allport, *Op. cit.*, 301 f.
6. Allport, *Op. cit.*, 305 f.
7. Allport, *Op. cit.*, 294.
8. Allport, *Op. cit.*, 312 f.
9. Martin, *Op. cit.*

Chapter VIII

1. C. J. H. Hayes, *Essays on Nationalism.* New York: The Macmillan Company, 1926.
2. P. Radin, *The Racial Myth.* New York: McGraw-Hill Book Company, Inc., 1934.
3. H. D. Lasswell, *World Politics and Personal Insecurity.* New York: McGraw-Hill Book Company, Inc., 1935.
4. J. Dollard, L. W. Doob, N. E. Miller, O. H. Mowrer, et al. *Frustration and Aggression.* New Haven: Yale University Press, 1939.

5. F. H. Allport, *Institutional Behavior*. Chapel Hill: University of North Carolina Press, 1933.
6. A. A. Goldenweiser, *Early Civilization*. New York: Alfred A. Knopf, Inc., 1922.
7. E. D. Martin, *The Mystery of Religion*. New York: Harper and Brothers, 1924.
8. Hayes, *Op. cit.*, 72 f.
9. F. Oppenheimer, *The State*. Indianapolis: Bobbs-Merrill, 1914.
10. Oppenheimer, *Op. cit.*, 13.
11. E. B. Holt, The whimsical condition of social psychology, and of mankind, in *American Philosophy Today and Tomorrow*. New York: Lee Furman, 1935, 171-202.
12. J. F. Brown, *Psychology and the Social Order*. New York: Mc-Graw-Hill Book Company, Inc., 1936.
13. O. H. Mowrer, Authoritarianism versus self-government in the management of children's aggressive reactions as preparation for citizenship in democracy, *J. Soc. Psychol.*, 1939, 10, 121-126.
14. K. Lewin, and R. Lippitt, An experimental approach to the study of autocracy and democracy, *Sociometry*, 1938, 1, 293-300.

Chapter X

1. J. W. Carter, Jr., A case of reactional dissociation (hysterical paralysis), *Amer. J. Orthopsychiat.*, 1937, 7, 219-224.
2. P. Janet, *The Major Symptoms of Hysteria*. New York: The Macmillan Company, 1907, 29-31.
3. C. C. Wholey, A case of multiple personality, *Amer. J. Psychiat.*, 1933, 12, 653-687.
4. W. H. R. Rivers, A case of claustrophobia, *Lancet*, 1917, II, 237-240.
5. Case cited by E. Bagby, *The Psychology of Personality*. New York: Henry Holt and Company, 1928, 219-223.
6. T. A. Ross, *The Common Neuroses*. London: Arnold, 1923, Ch. 14.

Chapter XII

1. G. H. S. Razran, Conditioned responses in animals other than dogs, *Psychol. Bull.*, 1933, 30, 261-324.
2. H. A. Fjeld, The limits of learning ability in rhesus monkeys, *Genet. Psychol. Monog.*, 1934, 15, 369-537. A. M. Koch, The limits of learning ability in cebus monkeys, *Genet. Psychol. Monog.*, 1935, 17, 165-234.

3. M. A. Hoge, The influence of temperature on the development of a Mendelian character, *J. Exper. Zool.*, 1915, 18, 241-285.

4. C. R. Stockard, *The Physical Basis of Personality*. New York: W. W. Norton and Company, Inc., 1931, Chs. VI and VII.

5. B. S. Sanders, *Environment and Growth*. Baltimore: Warwick and York, 1934.

6. E. Conradi, Song and call-notes of English sparrows when reared by canaries, *Amer. J. Psychol.*, 1905, 16, 190-199. W. E. D. Scott, Data on song in birds, *Science,* 1901, N. S. 14, 522-526.

7. W. Craig, The stimulation and inhibition of ovulation in birds and mammals, *J. An. Beh.*, 1913, 3, 215-221. W. Craig, Male doves reared in isolation, *J. An. Beh.*, 1914, 4, 121-133. J. P. Foley, Jr., First year development of a rhesus monkey (Macaca mulatta) reared in isolation, *J. Genet. Psychol.*, 1934, 45, 39-105. J. P. Foley, Jr., Second year development of a rhesus monkey (Macaca mulatta) reared in isolation during the first eighteen months, *J. Genet. Psychol.*, 1935, 47, 73-97.

8. W. N. Kellogg, and L. A. Kellogg, *The Ape and the Child*. New York: McGraw-Hill Book Company, Inc., 1933.

9. J. M. G. Itard, *The Wild Boy of Aveyron,* (transl. by G. and M. Humphrey). New York: D. Appleton-Century Company, Inc., 1932.

10. P. C. Squires, Wolf children of India, *Amer. J. Psychol.*, 1927, 38, 313-315. W. N. Kellogg, A further note on the "wolf children" of India, *Amer. J. Psychol.*, 1934, 46, 149 f.

11. A. F. Tredgold, *Mental Deficiency*. New York: William Wood, 1929, 290-292.

12. G. M. Stratton, Jungle children, *Psychol. Bull.*, 1934, 31, 596 f.

13. H. Gordon, *Mental and Scholastic Tests Among Retarded Children*. London: Board of Education, Educ. Pamphlet No. 44, 1923.

14. E. J. Asher, The inadequacy of current intelligence tests for testing Kentucky mountain children, *J. Genet. Psychol.*, 1935, 46, 480-486. B. T. Baldwin, E. A. Fillmore, and L. Hadley, *Farm Children*. New York: D. Appleton-Century Company, Inc., 1930. N. D. M. Hirsch, An experimental study of the east Kentucky mountaineers, *Genet. Psychol. Monog.*, 1928, 3, 183-244. M. Sherman, and C. B. Key, The intelligence of isolated mountain children, *Child Development,* 1932, 3, 279-290.

15. Sherman and Key, *Op. cit.,* 287.

16. F. Galton, *Hereditary Genius*. London: The Macmillan Company, 1914.

17. For a survey of these studies, cf. A. Anastasi, *Differential Psychology*. New York: The Macmillan Company, 1937, Ch. XIII.

18. R. L. Dugdale, *The Jukes: A Study in Crime, Pauperism, Disease, and Heredity.* New York: G. P. Putnam's Sons, 1910.

19. H. H. Goddard, *The Kallikak Family: A Study in the Heredity of Feeblemindedness.* New York: The Macmillan Company, 1921.

20. For a survey of these studies, cf. Anastasi, *Op. cit.,* Ch. IV.

21. F. N. Freeman, K. J. Holzinger, and B. C. Mitchell, The influence of environment on the intelligence, school achievement, and conduct of foster children, *27th Yearbook, Nat. Soc. Stud. Educ.,* 1928, Part I, 103-217.

22. H. H. Newman, F. N. Freeman, and K. J. Holzinger, *Twins: A Study of Heredity and Environment.* Chicago: University of Chicago Press, 1937, 187-195.

23. F. M. Teagarden, A study of the upper limits of the development of intelligence, *Teachers College, Columbia Univ. Contrib. to Educ.,* 1924. E. L. Thorndike, On the improvement in intelligence scores from thirteen to nineteen, *J. Educ. Psychol.,* 1926, 17, 73-76.

24. H. E. Jones, and H. S. Conrad, The growth and decline of intelligence, *Genet. Psychol. Monog.,* 1933, 13, 223-298. C. C. Miles, and W. R. Miles, The correlation of intelligence scores and chronological age from early to late maturity, *Amer. J. Psychol.,* 1932, 44, 44-78. R. R. Willoughby, Family similarities in mental test abilities, *Genet. Psychol. Monog.,* 1927, 2, 235-277.

25. Miles and Miles, *Op. cit.*

26. E. L. Thorndike, et al., *Adult Learning.* New York: The Macmillan Company, 1928.

27. F. M. Ruch, Adult learning, *Psychol. Bull.,* 1933, 30, 387-414; also The differentiative effects of age upon human learning, *J. Gen. Psychol.,* 1934, 11, 261-286.

28. K. B. Greene, The influence of specialized training on tests of general intelligence, *27th Yearbook, Nat. Soc. Stud. Educ.,* 1928, Part I, 421-428.

29. For a survey of these studies, cf. A. Anastasi, Practice and variability: a study in psychological method, *Psychol. Monog.,* 1934, 45.

30. E. Kretschmer, *Physique and Character* (transl. from 2nd ed. by W. J. H. Sprott). New York: Harcourt, Brace and Company, 1925.

31. C. G. Jung, *Psychological Types* (transl. by H. G. Baynes). New York: Harcourt, Brace and Company, 1924.

32. E. L. Thorndike, et al., *The Measurement of Intelligence.* New York: Teachers College, Columbia Univ. Bur. Pub., 1926.

33. E. Heidbreder, Measuring introversion and extroversion, *J. Abn. and Soc. Psychol.,* 1926, 21, 120-134.
34. For a survey of these studies up to 1930, cf. D. G. Paterson, *Physique and Intellect.* New York: D. Appleton-Century Company, Inc., 1930.
35. R. Pintner, *Intelligence Testing: Methods and Results.* New York: Henry Holt and Company, 1931, Chs. XVIII and XIX.
36. Cf. e.g., C. L. Hull, *Aptitude Testing.* Yonkers-on-Hudson: World Book Company, 1928, Ch. IV, Paterson, *Op. cit.*
37. E. Heidbreder, Intelligence and the height-weight ratio, *J. Appl. Psychol.,* 1926, 10, 52-62.
38. W. H. Sheldon, Morphologic types and mental ability, *J. Pers. Res.,* 1927, 5, 447-451.
39. W. H. Sheldon, Social traits and morphologic types, *J. Pers. Res.,* 1927, 6, 47-55.
40. C. R. Garvey, Comparative body build of manic-depressive and schizophrenic patients, *Psychol. Bull.,* 1933, 30, 567 f., 739.
41. For a survey of these studies, cf. A. Anastasi, *Differential Psychology, Op. cit.,* Ch. IX.
42. Tredgold, *Op. cit.,* Ch. XIV.
43. C. L. Hull, Variability in amount of different traits possessed by the individual, *J. Educ. Psychol.,* 1927, 18, 97-104.
44. J. C. DeVoss, Specialization in the abilities of gifted children, in Terman's *Genetic Studies of Genius, Vol. I,* Ch. XII. Stanford: Stanford University Press, 1925.
45. L. M. Terman, The vocabulary test as a measure of intelligence, *J. Educ. Psychol.,* 1938, 9, 452-456.
46. J. P. Guilford, *Psychometric Methods.* New York: McGraw-Hill Book Company, Inc., 1936, Ch. XIV. T. L. Kelley, *Essential Traits of Mental Life.* Cambridge: Harvard University Press, 1935. L. L. Thurstone, *Vectors of Mind.* Chicago: University of Chicago Press, 1935.
47. S. E. Asch, A study of change in mental organization, *Arch. Psychol.,* 1936, No. 195. H. E. Garrett, A. I. Bryan, and R. E. Perl, The age factor in mental organization, *Arch. Psychol.,* 1935, No. 176.
48. A. Anastasi, The influence of specific experience upon mental organization, *Genet. Psychol. Monog.,* 1936, 18, No. 4, 245-355.

Chapter XIII

1. L. C. Pressey, Sex differences shown by 2544 school children on a group scale of intelligence, with special reference to variability, *J. Appl. Psychol.,* 1918, 2, 323-340.

2. W. F. Book, and J. L. Meadows, Sex differences in 5925 high. school seniors in ten psychological tests, *J. Appl. Psychol.*, 1928, 12, 56-81.

3. L. S. Hollingworth, Differential action upon the sexes of forces which tend to segregate the feebleminded, *J. Abn. Psychol.*, 1922, 17, 35-37.

4. For a survey of many of these results, cf. E. A. Lincoln, *Sex Differences in the Growth of American School Children.* Baltimore: Warwick and York, 1927.

5. See Ch. XIII.

6. A. H. Arlitt, On the need for caution in establishing race norms, *J. Appl. Psychol.*, 1921, 5, 179-183.

7. G. O. Ferguson, The psychology of the negro, *Arch. Psychol.*, 1916, No. 36.

8. S. D. Porteus, *The Psychology of a Primitive People.* New York: Longmans, Green and Company, 1931, 308 f.

9. O. Klineberg, *Race Differences.* New York: Harper and Brothers, 1935, 155.

10. O. Klineberg, An experimental study of speed and other factors in "racial" differences, *Arch. Psychol.*, 1928, No. 93.

11. W. Goodsell, *The Education of Women.* New York: The Macmillan Company, 1923.

12. Arlitt, *Op. cit.*

13. E. Jamieson, and P. Sandiford, The mental capacity of southern Ontario Indians, *J. Educ. Psychol.*, 1928, 19, 536-551.

14. T. R. Garth, A comparison of the intelligence of Mexican and mixed and full blood Indian children, *Psychol. Rev.*, 1923, 30, 388-401.

15. R. Pintner, and R. Keller, Intelligence tests for foreign children, *J. Educ. Psychol.*, 1922, 13, 214-222.

16. R. Pintner, Comparison of American and foreign children on intelligence tests, *J. Educ. Psychol.*, 1923, 14, 292-295.

17. Jamieson and Sandiford, *Op. cit.*

18. M. L. Darsie, Mental capacity of American-born Japanese children, *Comp. Psychol. Monog.*, 1926, 15, No. 3, 1-89.

19. Porteus, *Op. cit.*

20. F. L. Goodenough, The consistency of sex differences in mental traits at various ages, *Psychol. Rev.*, 1927, 34, 440-462. S. D. Porteus, The measurement of intelligence: 643 children examined by the Binet and Porteus tests, *J. Educ. Psychol.*, 1918, 9, 13-31.

21. L. M. Terman, et al., *The Stanford Revision and Extension of the Binet-Simon Scale for Measuring Intelligence.* Baltimore: Warwick and York, 1917.

22. G. M. Whipple, Sex differences in Army Alpha score in the second-ary school., *J. Educ. Res.,* 1928, 15, 269-275.
23. C. C. Brigham, *A Study of Error.* New York: College Entrance Exam. Board, 1932, 373.
24. D. McCarthy, Language development, in Murchison's *Handbook of Child Psychology.* Worcester: Clark University Press, 1933, Ch. VIII.
25. A. Anastasi, *Differential Psychology.* New York: The Macmillan Company, 1937, Ch. XV, for fuller discussion of these results.
26. E. Heidbreder, Introversion and extroversion in men and women, *J. Abn. and Soc. Psychol.,* 1927, 22, 52-61.
27. H. Hartshorne, and M. A. May, *Studies in the Nature of Character: Vol. I, Studies in Deceit;* and *Vol. II, Studies in Service and Self-Control* (with J. B. Maller). New York: The Macmillan Company, 1928, 1929.
28. G. W. Allport, and P. E. Vernon, A test for personal values, *J. Abn. and Soc. Psychol.,* 1931, 26, 231-248.
29. L. M. Terman, and C. C. Miles, *Sex and Personality.* New York: McGraw-Hill Book Company, Inc., 1936.
30. M. Mead, *Growing Up in New Guinea.* New York: William Morrow and Company, Inc., 1930.
31. M. Mead, *Sex and Temperament in Three Primitive Societies.* New York: William Morrow and Company, Inc., 1935.
32. For a summary of these data, cf. Anastasi, *Op. cit.,* 458-461.
33. A. L. Kroeber, *Anthropology.* New York: Harcourt, Brace and Company, 1923.
34. Klineberg, *Op. cit.,* section on "Problems of Measurement."
35. Ferguson, *Op. cit.*
36. R. M. Yerkes, (editor), Psychological examining in the United States Army, *Mem. Nat. Acad. Sci.,* 1921, 15.
37. W. W. Clark, Los Angeles negro children, *Educ. Res. Bull., Los Angeles City Schools,* 1923, 3, No. 2, 1 f. J. Peterson, and L. H. Lanier, Studies in the comparative abilities of whites and negroes, *Ment. Meas. Monog.,* No. 5, 1929.
38. O. Klineberg, *Negro Intelligence and Selective Migration.* New York: Columbia University Press, 1935.
39. T. R. Garth, *Race Psychology.* New York: McGraw-Hill Book Company, Inc., 1931. W. S. Hunter, and E. Sommermier, The relation of degree of Indian blood to score on the Otis Intelligence Test, *J. Comp. Psychol.,* 1922, 2, 257-277. Jamieson and Sandiford, *Op. cit.*
40. T. R. Garth, A comparison of the intelligence of Mexican and mixed and full blood Indian children, *Op. cit.*

41. Darsie, *Op. cit.*
42. P. Sandiford, and R. Kerr, Intelligence in Chinese and Japanese children, *J. Educ. Psychol.*, 1926, 17, 361-367.
43. O. Klineberg, A study of psychological differences between "racial" and national groups in Europe, *Arch. Psychol.*, 1931, No. 132.

Chapter XIV

1. S. L. Pressey, J. E. Janney, and R. G. Kuhlen, *Life—A Psychological Survey.* New York: Harper and Brothers, 1939.
2. S. L. Pressey, *Psychology and the New Education.* New York: Harper and Brothers, 1933, 9.
3. M. C. Hardy, Some evidence of an inverse relation between health history and behavior adjustment during childhood, *J. Abn. and Soc. Psychol.*, 1937, 31, 406-417; Adjustment scores of adolescents having a history of frequent illness during childhood, *Amer. J. Orthopsychiat.*, 1937, 7, 204-209.
4. P. S. de Q. Cabot, The relationship between characteristics of personality and physique in adolescents, *Genet. Psychol. Monog.*, 1938, 20, 3-120.
5. H. B. English and C. D. Killian, The constancy of the IQ at different age levels, *J. Consult. Psychol.*, 1939, 3, 30-32.
6. M. Mead, *Sex and Temperament in Three Primitive Societies.* New York: William Morrow and Company, Inc., 1935.
7. H. Hartshorne and M. A. May, general editions of *Studies in the Nature of Character,* New York: The Macmillan Company. 3 Vols.: Vol. 1, H. Hartshorne and M. A. May, *Studies in Deceit,* 1928; Vol. 2, H. Hartshorne, M. A. May and J. B. Maller, *Studies in Service and Self-Control,* 1929; Vol. 3, H. Hartshorne, M. A. May and F. K. Shuttleworth, *Studies in the Organization of Character,* 1930.
8. E. L. Thorndike, *Human Learning.* New York: D. Appleton-Century Company, Inc., 1931, 15, 19.
9. J. A. McGeoch, The influence of associative value upon the difficulty of nonsense-syllable lists. *J. Gen. Psychol.*, 1930, 37, 421-426; E. L. Welborn and H. B. English, Logical Learning and Retention: A Review of Experiments with Meaningful Verbal Materials, *Psychol. Bull.*, 1937, 34, 1-20.
10. H. B. English and A. L. Edwards, Reminiscence, substance learning, and initial difficulty—A methodological study, *Psychol. Rev.*, 1939, 46, 253-263.
11. C. J. Leuba, A preliminary experiment to quantify an incentive and its effects. *J. Abn. and Soc. Psychol.*, 1930, 25, 275-288.

12. F. H. Allport, The influence of the group upon association and thought, *J. Exper. Psychol.*, 1920, 3, 159-172; S. B. Weston and H. B. English, The influence of the group on psychological test scores, *Amer. J. Psychol.*, 1926, 37, 600-601; P. R. Farnsworth, Concerning so-called group effects, *J. Genet. Psychol.*, 1928, 35, 587-594.

13. G. Murphy and L. B. Murphy, *Experimental Social Psychology*. N. Y.: Harper and Brothers, 1931, Ch. IX or the revised edition (1937, with T. M. Newcomb as added author), Chs. VII, VIII.

14. W. A. Barton, Jr., The effect of group activity and individual effort in developing ability to solve problems in first year algebra. *Educ. Adm. and Super.*, 1926, 12, 512-518.

15. C. L. Bane, The lecture versus class-discussion method of college teaching, *School and Society*, 1925, 21, 300-302.

16. E. Collings, *An Experiment With A Project Curriculum*. New York: The Macmillan Company, 1923.

17. K. Lewin, R. Lippitt and R. K. White, Patterns of aggressive behavior in experimentally created "Social Climates," *J. Soc. Psychol.*, *S.P.S.S.I. Bull.*, 1939, 10, 271-299.

18. J. B. Maller, *Cooperation and Competition, an Experimental Study in Motivation*. New York: Columbia University Press, 1929.

19. J. Tuckman, *The Influence of Varying Amounts of Punishment on Mental Connections*. New York: Teacher's College Bureau of Publications, Columbia University, 1933.

20. A. Kohlstad and W. S. Heller.

21. *Memoirs of the National Academy of Sciences,* 1921, XV, 118 f.

22. R. A. Davis, *The Psychology of Learning*. New York: McGraw-Hill Book Company, Inc., 1935, 312.

23. T. L. Wang, The influence of tuition in the acquisition of skill, *Psychol. Rev. Monog.*, 1925, 34, No. 154.

24. S. L. Pressey, Third and fourth contributions toward the coming industrial revolution in education. *School and Society*, 1932, 36, 668-672.

25. J. C. Peterson and H. J. Peterson, Reducing the costs of tests without impairment of their value. *Trans. Kans. Acad. Sci.*, 1932, 35, 132-140.

26. J. MacLatchy, A phase of first-grade readiness. *Ed. Res. Bull.*, 1931, 10, 377-380.

27. S. L. Pressey, *Psychology and the New Education, Op. cit.* 363-365.

28. S. L. Pressey, *Op. cit.*, 366 f.

29. H. E. Jones, Experimental studies of college teaching; the effect of examination on permanence of learning. *Arch. Psychol.*, 1923, No. 68; A. L. Edwards and H. B. English, Studies in substance

learning and retention: XII. The effect of the immediate test on verbatim and summary retention. *Amer. J. Psychol.*, 1939, 52, 372-375.

30. W. S. Learned and B. D. Wood, *The Student and His Knowledge.* New York: The Carnegie Foundation for the Advancement of Teaching, 1938.

31. H. B. English, E. L. Welborn and C. D. Killian, Studies in substance memorization, *J. Gen. Psychol.*, 1934, 11, 233-260.

32. R. W. Tyler, Permanence of learning, *J. Higher Ed.*, 1933, 4, 203 f.

33. R. C. Peterson and L. L. Thurstone, *Motion Pictures and the Social Attitudes of Children.* New York: The Macmillan Company, 1933.

34. F. C. Bartlett, *Remembering, a study in experimental and social psychology,* Cambridge Univ. Press, 1932.

35. E. L. Thorndike and G. J. Ruger, The effect of first-year Latin upon knowledge of English words of Latin derivation. *School & Society,* 1923, 18, 260-270, 417 f.

36. R. I. Haskell, quoted by S. L. Pressey, *Psychology and the New Education, Op. cit.,* 529.

37. J. R. Overman, An experimental study of the effect of the method of instruction on transfer in arithmetic. *Elem. Sch. J.,* 1930, 31, 183-190.

CHAPTER XV

1. L. M. Terman, and M. A. Merrill, *Measuring Intelligence.* Boston: Houghton Mifflin Company, 1937.

2. A. F. Bronner, W. Healy, G. M. Lowe, and M. E. Shimberg, *A Manual of Individual Tests and Testing.* Boston: Little, Brown and Company, 1937.

3. E. K. Wickman, *Children's Behavior and Teachers' Attitudes.* New York: Commonwealth Fund, 1938. M. A. Tilson, *Problems of Preschool Children.* New York: Teacher's College Contr. to Educ., Columbia University Press, 1929, No. 356.

CHAPTER XVI

1. A. Oehrn, Experimentelle studien zur individual psychologie. *Psychol. Arbeit.,* 1895, I, 92-151.

2. E. S. Robinson and W. T. Heron, The warming-up effect. *J. Exper. Psychol.,* 1924, 7, 81-97.

3. E. L. Thorndike, Curve of work and the curve of satisfyingness. *J. Appl. Psychol.*, 1917, I, 265-267.

4. B. Muscio, Feeling-tone in industry, *Brit. J. Psychol.*, 1921-22, XII, 150-162.

5. A. T. Poffenberger, The effect of continuous work on output and feeling, *J. Appl. Psychol.*, 1928, 12, 459-467.

6. F. G. Benedict and B. S. Carpenter, Influence of muscular and mental work on metabolism and the efficiency of the human body as a machine, *U. S. Dept. of Agr. Exper. Stat. Bull.*, 1909, No. 208.

7. F. G. Benedict and C. G. Benedict, The energy requirements of intense mental effort, *Science,* 1930, 71, 567.

8. T. Arai, Mental Fatigue, *T. C. Columbia, Contrib. to Educ.*, 1912, 54, pp. 115.

9. J. P. Hylan and E. Kraepelin, Ueber die wirkung kurzer arbeitszeiten, *Psychol. Arbeit.*, 4, 454-495.

10. A. T. Poffenberger, The effects of continuous mental work, *Amer. J. Psychol.*, 1927, 39 (Washburn Commemorative Volume) 283-296.

11. *Op. cit.* The effect of continuous work on output and feeling.

12. C. W. Manzer, An experimental investigation of rest pauses, *Arch. Psychol.*, 1927, 90, pp. 84.

13. *Op. cit.*

14. *Op. cit.* The effect of continuous mental work.

15. S. D. M. Austin, A study of logical memory, *Amer. J. Psychol.*, 1921, 32, 370-403.

16. M. C. Hardy, The effect of distribution of practice in learning a stylus maze, *J. Comp. Psychol.*, 1930, 10, 85-96.

17. K. S. Lashley, The acquisition of skill in archery, *Carnegie Inst. of Wash.*, 1915, No. 211, 105-128.

18. E. S. Robinson, The "similarity" factor in retroaction, *Amer. J. Psychol.*, 1927, 39 (Washburn Commemorative Volume) 297-312.

19. J. G. Jenkins and K. M. Dallenbach, Obliviscence during sleep and waking, *Amer. J. Psychol.*, 1924, 35, 605-612.

20. S. Wyatt, Rest-pauses in industry, *Indust. Health Res. Bd.*, Report No. 42, 1927, pp. 24.

21. *Op. cit.*

22. O. Graf, Uber lohnendste arbeitspausen bei geistiger arbeit., *Psychol. Arbeit.*, 1925, 7, pp. 548.

23. *Op. cit.*

24. G. H. Miles and O. Skilbeck, An experiment on change of work, *J. Nat. Instit. Indus. Psychol.*, 1923, I, 236-239.

25. T. F. Weiskotten, On the effects of the loss of sleep, *J. Exper. Psychol.,* 1925, 8, 363-380.

26. *Op. cit.*

27. E. S. Robinson and S. O. Hermann, Effects of loss of sleep, *J. Exper. Psychol.,* 1922, 5, 19-32.

28. H. R. Lashlett, Experiments on the effect of the loss of sleep, *J. Exper. Psychol.,* 1928, 11, 370-396.

29. G. E. Müller and Fr. Schumann, Ueber die psychologischen grundlagen der vergleichung gehobener gewichte, *Arch. f. d. ges. physiol.,* 1889, 45, 37-112.

30. L. Steffens, Ueber die motorische einstellung. Experimentelle beitrage, *Zsch. f. psychol. u. physiol. der sinnesorgane,* 1900, 23, 240-308.

31. R. Strohal, Untersuchungen zur deskriptiven psychologie der einstellung, *Zsch. f. psychol.,* 1933, 130, 1-27.

32. O. Külpe, Versuche uber abstraktion, Berickt uber den I. *Kongress fur exper. Psychol.,* Leipzig, 1904, 56-68.

33. J. H. Moore, The role of determining tendencies in learning, *Amer. J. Psychol.,* 1936, 48, 559-571.

34. D. Fryer, A genetic study of motivation under changing auditory situations, *Brit. J. Psychol.,* 1934, 24, 408-433; Variability in automatic mental performance with uniform intent, *J. Appl. Psychol.,* 1937, 21, 528-545; Specific conscious intent and its correlates in performance, *Brit. J. Psychol.,* 1937, 27, 364-393.

35. D. Fryer, Motivation effects of auditory timing upon repetitive mental work, *Brit. J. Psychol.,* 1934, 25, 140-169; Conscious activity in coordination of repetitive mental work and rhythmic timing, *Brit. J. Psychol.,* 1937, 28, 150-166.

36. T. W. Harrell, Factors influencing preferences and memory for auditory rhythm, *J. Gen. Psychol.,* 1937, 17, 63-103.

37. R. H. Gault and L. D. Goodfellow, An empirical comparison of audition, vision, and touch in the discrimination of temporal patterns and ability to reproduce them, *J. Gen. Psychol.,* 1938, 18, 41-48.

38. A. T. Jersild and S. Bienstock, Development of rhythm in young children, *T. C. Columbia, Contrib. to Educ.,* 1935, 22.

39. J. J. B. Morgan, The overcoming of distraction and other resistances, *Arch. Psychol.,* 1916, No. 35, pp. 84.

40. K. G. Pollack and F. C. Bartlett, Psychological experiments on the effects of noise, *Indust. Health Res. Bd.,* Report No. 65, 1932, pp. 37.

41. K. H. Baker, Pre-experimental set in distraction experiments, *J. Gen. Psychol.,* 1937, 16, 471-488.

42. F. C. Bartlett, *The Problem of Noise*. New York: The Macmillan Company, 1934.

43. E. L. Thorndike, An experimental study of rewards, 1933, *T. C. Columbia, Contrib. to Educ.*, No. 580, pp. 72.

44. W. F. Book and L. Norvell, The will to learn. An experimental study of learning incentives, *Ped. Sem.*, 1922, 29, 305-362.

45. A. M. Johanson, The influence of incentive and punishment upon reaction-time, *Arch. Psychol.*, 1922, No. 54, pp. 53.

46. J. Vaughn and C. M. Diserens, The relative effect of various intensities of punishment on learning and efficiency, *J. Comp. Psychol.*, 1930, 10, 55-66.

47. C. N. Rexroad, Administering electric shock for inaccuracy in multiple choice reactions, *J. Exper. Psychol.*, 1926, 9, 1-18.

48. L. Chase, Motivation of young children. An experimental study of the influence of certain types of external incentives upon the performance of a task, *U. of Iowa Stud. Child Welfare*, 1932, 5, pp. 119.

49. C. J. Leuba, A preliminary experiment to qualify an incentive and its effects, *J. Abn. and Soc. Psychol.*, 1930-31, 25, 275-288.

50. L. Chase, *Op. cit.*; E. P. Gilchrist, The extent to which praise and reproof affect a pupil's work, *Sch. and Soc.*, 1916, 4, 872-874; G. S. Gates and L. Q. Rissland, The effect of encouragement and of discouragement upon performance, *J. Educ. Psychol.*, 1923, 14, 21-26; E. B. Hurlock, The value of praise and reproof as incentives for children, *Arch. Psychol.*, 1924, 71, pp. 78; E. B. Hurlock, An evaluation of certain incentives used in school work, *J. Educ. Psychol.*, 1925, 16, 145-159.

51. M. T. Eaton, The effect of praise, reproof and exercise upon muscular steadiness, *J. Exper. Educ.*, 1933, 2, 44-59.

52. A. Mayer, Ueber einzel und gesamtleistung des schulkindes, *Arch. f. d. Gesamte Psychol.*, 1903, I, 276-416.

53. F. H. Allport, The influence of the group upon association and thought, *J. Exper. Psychol.*, 1920, 3, 159-178.

54. L. E. Travis, The influence of the group upon the stutterer's speed in free association, *J. Abn. and Soc. Psychol.*, 1928-29, 23, 45-51.

55. N. Triplett, The dynamogenic factors in pacemaking and competition, *Amer. J. Psychol.*, 1897, 9, 507-533.

56. P. J. Greenberg, Competition in children: An experimental study, *Amer. J. Psychol.*, 1932, 44, 221-248.

57. *Op. cit.*

58. J. B. Maller, Cooperation and competition, An experimental study of motivation, *T. C., Columbia Contrib. to Educ.*, 1929, No. 384, pp. 176.

59. E. B. Hurlock, The use of group rivalry as a school incentive, *J. Abn. and Soc. Psychol.*, 1927-28, 22, 278-290.

60. *Op. cit.*

61. L. Paul, Die wirkungen der luft bewohnter raume, *Zeit. f. Hyg. u. Infectionsk,* 1905, 49, 405-432.

62. *Ventilation, Report of the New York State Commission on Ventilation.* New York: E. P. Dutton and Co., 1923.

63. E. Huntington, *Civilization and Climate.* New Haven: Yale Univ. Press, 1924, (3rd Ed.), pp. 453.

64. E. L. Thorndike, W. A. McCall, and J. C. Chapman, Ventilation in relation to mental work, *T. C., Columbia, Contrib. to Educ.,* 1916, No. 78, pp. 83.

65. H. L. Hollingworth, The influence of caffeine on mental and motor efficiency, *Arch. Psychol.,* 1912, 22, pp. 166.

66. A. D. Busch, Tobacco smoking and mental efficiency, *N. Y. Med. J.,* 1914, 99, 519-527.

67. C. L. Hull, The influence of tobacco smoking on mental and motor efficiency, an experimental study, *Psychol. Mono.,* 1924, 33 (Whole Number 150) pp. 159.

68. R. Pearl, Tobacco smoking and longevity, *Science,* 1938, 87 (Jan.-June) 216-217.

69. F. J. Pack, Smoking and football men, *Pop. Sci. Mo.,* 1912, 81, 336-344.

70. *Op. cit.*

71. P. Janet, L'alcoholisme et la depression mentale, *Rev. Int'l. de Socio.,* 1915, 23, 476-485.

72. O. Juliusberger, Beitrag zur psychologie der soganante dipsomanie, *Zentralblatt f. Psychoanalyse,* 1912, 2, 551-557.

73. G. T, W. Patrick, *Psychology of Relaxation.* Boston: Houghton Mifflin and Company, 1916, pp. 278.

74. E. Kraepelin, *Ueber die beeinflussung einfacher psychische vorgange durch einige arzneimittel.* Fisher, 1892, pp. 258.

75. W. H. R. Rivers, *The Influence of Alcohol and Other Drugs on Fatigue.* London: Arnold, 1908, pp. 136.

76. R. Dodge and F. G. Benedict, *Psychological Effects of Alcohol.* Washington: Carnegie Inst. of Wash., 1915, pp. 281.

77. H. L. Hollingworth, The influence of alcohol, *J. Abn. and Soc. Psychol.,* 1923-24, 18, 204-237: 311-333.

78. G. S. Hall, *Morale, The Supreme Standard of Life and Conduct.* New York: D. Appleton-Century Company, Inc., 1920.

79. W. H. Burnham, The normal mind, *Ped. Sem.,* 1922, 29, 383-399.

CHAPTER XVII

1. R. Gregory, Science and social service, *Occup. Psychol.,* Spring 1938, 137.
2. J. H. Blaksley, Some problems of an industrial civilization, *Human Factor,* 1936, 10, 325.
3. *Street-Railway Transportation in Cincinnati.* Cincinnati, Ohio: Vocation Bureau, Cincinnati Public Schools, 1926.
4. D. Fryer, and E. J. Sparling, Intelligence and occupational adjustment, *Occupations,* June 1934, 12, 60.
5. M. R. Trabue, Graphic representation of measured characteristics of successful workers, *Occupations,* April 1934, 12, 40-45.
6. C. L. Hull, Aptitude test batteries, *Occupations,* April 1934, 12, 65-69.
7. W. P. Alexander, Research in guidance: a theoretical basis, *Occupations,* April 1934, 12, 75-91.
8. F. Baumgarten, New aspects of job analysis, *Occupations,* June 1934, 12, 79-85.
9. *Selecting the Successful Salesman.* The Phoenix Mutual Life Insurance Company, Hartford, Conn., 1937.
10. D. S. Bridgman, Success in college and business, *Pers. J.,* 1930, 9, 1-19.
11. R. S. Uhrbrock, and M. W. Richardson, Item analysis, the basis for constructing a test for forecasting supervisory ability, *Pers. J.,* 1933, 12, 141-54.
12. R. W. Husband, The photograph on the application blank, *Pers. J.,* 1934, 13, 69-72.
13. M. S. Viteles, and K. R. Smith, The prediction of vocational aptitude and success from photographs, *J. Exper. Psychol.,* 1932, 15, 615-629.
14. G. N. Cleeton, and F. B. Knight, Validity of character judgments based on external criteria, *J. Appl. Psychol.,* 1924, 8, 215-231.
15. D. G. Paterson, *Physique and Temperament,* New York: D. Appleton-Century Company, Inc., 1930.
16. A. Ford, A check on character analysis, *Pers. J.,* 1930, 9, 121-123.
17. R. Saudek, *Experiments with Handwriting.* London: George Allen and Unwin, Ltd., 1928.
18. Reported in G. W. Allport, and P. E. Vernon, *Studies in Expressive Movement.* New York: The Macmillan Company, 1933, 211.
19. *Op. cit.*
20. H. L. Hollingworth, *Judging Human Character.* New York: D. Appleton-Century Company, Inc., 1932, 61-67.

21. W. Spielman, and C. Burt, *The Estimation of Character Qualities in Vocational Guidance,* Ind. Fat. Res. Bd. Report No. 33, 1926, 57-72.

22. L. J. O'Rourke, A new emphasis on federal personnel research and administration, *Report of U. S. Civil Service Commission.* Washington, D. C.: 1930, 19-21.

23. W. V. Bingham, *Oral Examinations in Civil Service Recruitment.* Chicago: Civil Service Assembly, Pamphlet No. 13, 1939, 23.

24. G. L. Bergen, The practical use of tests in appraising occupational fitness, *Pers. J.,* 1934, 13, 74 f.

25. S. Bevington, *Occupational Misfits.* London: George Allen and Unwin, Ltd., 1933, 85.

26. G. L. Bergen, G. Schneidler, L. R. Sherman, *Use of Tests in the Adjustment Service.* New York: Amer. Ass'n for Adult Education, 1935.

27. H. Pallister, American psychologists judge fifty-three vocational tests, *J. Appl. Psychol.,* 1936, 20, 761-768.

28. For a description of such procedures see the texts by Bingham, Burtt, and Viteles listed under "References" at the end of this chapter.

29. M. S. Viteles, The human factor in substation operation, *Pers. J.,* 1929, 8, 81-113.

30. N. E. Rossett and P. Arakelian, A test battery for the selection of panel dial switchmen, *J. Appl. Psychol.,* 1939, 23, 358-366.

31. Some recent developments in the psychology of personnel management in Great Britain, in *Proceedings of the 7th International Management Conference, Personnel—General Management Papers.* Baltimore: Waverly Press, 1938, 84-86.

32. M. S. Viteles, Research in the selection of motormen, *J. Pers. Res.,* 1925, 4, 173-199. S. M. Shellow, Research in selection of motormen in Milwaukee, *J. Pers. Res.,* 1925, 4, 222-237.

33. Les efforts dans le domaine de la selection rationnelle des travailleurs, in *Proceedings of the 7th International Management Conference, Personnel—General Management Papers,* Baltimore: Waverly Press, 1938, 74-77.

34. J. M. Lahy, La selection professionnelle des aiguilleurs, *Trav. Hum.,* 1933, 2, 15-38.

35. M. A. Bills, and M. Pond, Intelligence and clerical jobs, *Pers. J.,* 1933, 12, 42 f.

36. From data supplied by M. A. Bills and C. M. Davidson, Aetna Life Insurance Company.

37. Data on the work of the U. S. Employment Service supplied by W. H. Stead, Associate Director, to the author as a member of the Technical Board of the U. S. Employment Service.

38. E. K. Strong, Jr., Interests and sales ability, *Pers. J.*, 1935, 13, 204-206.

39. R. F. Lovett, and M. W. Richardson, The significance of various types of test material, *Pers. J.*, 1934, 12, 248-253.

40. J. H. Mitchell, An experiment in the selection of sales managers, *Occup. Psychol.*, Summer 1938, 12, 314-315.

41. E. Farmer and E. G. Chambers, *The Prognostic Value of Some Psychological Tests.* London: Ind. Health Res. Bd. Report No. 74, 1936.

42. F. M. Earle, *Methods of Choosing a Career.* London: George G. Harrap Company, Ltd. 1931.

43. E. P. Allen, and P. Smith, *The Value of Vocational Tests as Aids to Choice of Employment.* Birmingham: The Birmingham Printers, 1932.

44. A. Rodger, *A Borstal Experiment in Vocational Guidance.* London: Ind. Health Res. Bd. Report No. 78, 1937.

45. M. S. Viteles, The clinical approach in vocational guidance, *Voc. Guid. Mag.*, 1928, 1-8.

46. E. L. Thorndike, et al. *Prediction of Vocational Success.* New York: Commonwealth Fund, 1934.

Chapter XVIII

1. E. M. Henshaw, and P. G. Holman, A Note on overtraining, *Brit. J. Psychol.*, 1930, 20, 333-335.

2. A. Meyer, Einfluss der übung auf die arbeitsgeschwindigkeit, *Indust. Psychot.*, 1930, 7, 53-55.

3. H. Engel, Einfluss der übung auf die arbeitsgeschwindigkeit, *Indust. Psychot.*, 1931, 8, 14-18.

4. H. D. Kitson, *Incentive Wage Plans from a Psychological Viewpoint.* New York: Bull. Am. Mgt. Assn.; Production Series No. 9, 1925.

5. C. A. Mace, Incentives—*Some Experimental Studies.* London: Ind. Health Res. Bd. Report No. 75, 1935.

6. F. Hoppe, Erfolg und miserfolg, *Psychol. Forsch.*, 1930, 14, 1-62.

7. W. Poppelreuter, Die arbeitskurve in der diagnostik von arbeitstypen, *Psychot. Zeitsch.*, 1928, 3, 35-51.

8. A. B. Blankenship, and H. R. Taylor, Prediction of vocational pro-- ficiency in three machine operations, *J. Appl. Psychol.*, 1938, 22, 518-526.

9. G. Berling, Planmässiges einführung des menschen in den indus- triellen arbeitsablauf, *Indust. Psychot.*, 1926, 3, 79-86.

10. M. S. Viteles, Industrial psychology in Russia, *Occup. Psychol.*, Spring, 1938, 7 f.

11. C. E. Beeby, An experimental investigation into the simultaneous constituents of an act of skill, *Brit. J. Psychol.*, 1930, 20, 336-353.

12. J. Dilger, Feilübungen am schraubstock und am anlergerät, *Indust. Psychot.*, 1929, 5, 369-374.

13. H. C. Link, *Education and Industry*. New York: The Macmillan Company, 1923, 134.

14. R. M. Barnes, Research in motion and time study, *Proceedings, 7th International Management Conference—Production Papers*. Baltimore: Waverly Press, 1938, 135 f.

15. F. M. Pepper, *Training from the Executive's Viewpoint,* Report, 22nd Annual Safety Congress. Chicago: National Safety Coun- cil, 1933, 396.

16. J. N. Langdon, and E. M. Yates, An experimental investigation into transfer of training in skilled performances, *Brit. J. Psychol.*, 1928, 18, 422-437.

17. J. W. Cox, Some experiments on formal training in the acquisition of skill, *Brit. J. Psychol.*, (Gen'l Section), 1933, 24, 68 87.

18. A. G. Shaw, Some developments in motion study training, *Pro- ceedings, 7th International Mgt. Conference*—Production Papers. Baltimore: Waverly Press, 1938, 124-128.

19. C. A. Koepke, A job analysis survey: its procedures and some of its results, *Occupations,* 1934, 12, 10, 15-34.

20. M. S. Viteles, *Science of Work*. New York: W. W. Norton and Company, Inc., 1934, 265-270.

21. *Accident Facts, 1939 Edition*. Chicago: National Safety Council, 1939.

22. M. Greenwood, and H. M. Woods, *The Incidence of Industrial Ac- cidents*. London: Ind. Fat. Res. Bd. Report No. 4, 1919.

23. E. M. Newbold, *A Contribution to the Study of the Human Factor in Accident Causation*. London: Ind. Fat. Res. Bd. Report No. 34, 1926.

24. K. Marbe, Uber unfällversicherung und psychotechnik, *Prakt. Psychol.*, 1923, 4, 257-264.

25. *The Accident-Prone Driver*, House Document No. 462, Part 6. Washington: U. S. Govt. Printing Office, 1938.

26. From data supplied to the author.

27. *Preventing Taxicab Accidents.* New York: Metropolitan Life Insurance Company, 1931.
28. H. M. Johnson, Born to crash, *Collier's,* 1936, 98, 4, 28.
29. E. Farmer, and E. G. Chambers, *A Study of Personal Qualities in Accident—Proneness and Proficiency.* London: Ind. Fat. Res. Bd. Report No. 55, 1929.
30. S. M. Shellow, The accident clinic; how it functions and what it accomplishes, *Pers. J.,* 1930, 3, 14.
31. *The Accident-Prone Employee.* New York: Metropolitan Life Insurance Company, 1930.
32. W. V. Bingham, Personality and Public Accidents, Transactions, 17th *Annual* Safety Congress, *New York,* 1928, 7 f.
33. A. P. Weiss, and A. R. Lauer, *Psychological Principles in Automotive Driving.* Columbus: Ohio State University, 1930; A. R. Lauer, *Methods of Measuring the Ability to Drive an Automobile.* Ames, Iowa: Iowa State College, 1936.
34. *Driver Testing Results.* Cambridge, Mass.: Harvard Traffic Bureau, 1937. A. R. Lauer, Facts and fancy regarding driver testing procedures, *J. Appl. Psychol.,* 1934, 31, 173-184.
35. R. S. Woodworth, *Experimental Psychology.* New York: Henry Holt and Company, 1938, 338 f.
36. M. S. Viteles, Bring your highway driving up to par, *Public Safety,* March, 1938, 22. See also T. W. Forbes, The normal automobile driver as a traffic problem, *J. Gen. Psychol.,* 1939, 20, 471-74. H. M. Johnson and P. W. Cobb, The educational value of drivers' clinics, *Psychol. Bull.,* 1938, 35, 758-766. H. R. De Silva, Automobile drivers can be improved, *Psychol. Bull.,* 1939, 36, 284 f. H. M. Johnson, Evidence for educational value in "driver's clinics," *Psychol. Bull.,* 1939, 36, 674 f.
37. H. A. Toops, and S. E. Haven, *Psychology and the Motorist.* Columbus: R. G. Adams and Company, 1938, 234-236.
38. *Ibid.,* 206 f.
39. E. Farmer, *The Causes of Accidents.* London: Sir Isaac Pitman and Sons, Ltd., 1932.
40. M. S. Viteles, and H. M. Gardner, Women taxicab drivers, *Pers. J.,* 1929, 7, 344-355.
41. Y. Henderson, How cars go out of control: Analysis of the driver's reflexes, *Science,* 1935, 82, 603-606.
42. K. Dunlap, Some problems of street and highway, *Scientific Monthly,* 1932, 28, 401-403.
43. *Op. cit.*
44. M. S. Viteles, Design of substations for accident prevention, *Edison Electric Institute Bulletin,* 1939, 101-106.

45. A. T. Poffenberger, *Applied Psychology*. New York: D. Appleton-Century Company, Inc., 1927, 134-35.

46. E. L. Thorndike, The curve of work and the curve of satisfyingness, *J. Appl. Psychol.*, 1917, 9, 266.

47. G. P. Crowden, *Muscular Work, Fatigue and Recovery*. London: Sir Isaac Pitman and Sons, 1932, 53 f.

48. H. M. Vernon, and T. Bedford, *The Influence of Rest Pauses in Light Industrial Work*. London: Ind. Fat. Res. Board Report No. 25, 1924.

49. F. B. Gilbreth, and L. M. Gilbreth, *Fatigue Study*. New York: Sturgis and Wollin Co., 1916.

50. *Op. cit.*

51. P. S. Achilles, Psychology in scientific management, *Wharton Review*, 1936, 4, 6.

52. C. S. Myers, *Industrial Psychology in Great Britain*. London: Jonathan Cape, 1926, 87 f.

53. G. P. Crowden, The practical value of psychology to industry, *Human Factor*, 1934, 8, 57-69.

54. I. L. Legros, and H. C. Weston, *On the Design of the Machine in Relation to the Operator*. London: Ind. Fat. Res. Bd. Report No. 36, 1926.

55. S. Wyatt, and J. N. Langdon, *The Machine and the Worker*. London: Ind. Health Res. Bd. Report No. 82, 1938.

56. M. Luckiesh, and F. K. Moss, Reflex effects and critical seeing, *Amer. J. Optham.*, 1935, 527-531.

57. Forty-four factors affecting efficiency, *Pers. J.*, Jan. 1939, Vol. 17, 7, 261. (Digest of 18th Annual Report Ind. Health Res. Bd. London.)

58. J. J. B. Morgan, The overcoming of distractions and other resistances, *Arch. Psychol.* 1916, 35, 84.

59. D. A. Laird, Experiments on the physiological cost of noise, *J. Nat'l Inst. Ind. Psych.*, 1929, 4, 251-258.

60. A. H. Davis, Some aspects of the problem of noise, *Occup. Psychol.*, 1938, 12, 45-47.

61. H. W. Haggard, and L. A. Greenberg, *Diet and Physical Efficiency*. London: Oxford University Press, 1935.

62. S. Wyatt, J. A. Fraser, and F. G. L. Stock, *Effects of Monotony in Work*. London: Ind. Fat. Res. Brd. Report 56, 1929.

63. C. S. Myers, *Industrial Psychology in Great Britain*. London: Jonathan Cape, 1926, 164.

64. S. Wyatt, and J. N. Langdon, *Fatigue and Boredom in Repetitive Work*. London: Ind. Health Res. Bd. Report No. 77, 1937.

65. *Op. cit.*

66. L. A. Thompson, Jr., Measuring Susceptibility to Monotony, *Pers. J.*, Vol. 8, 172-196, London, 1929.

67. H. Wunderlich, Die Einwirking einförmiger zeangsläufiger Arbeit auf die Persönlichkeistruktur, *Zeitschrift zur psychologische Berufswissens*, Vol. 21, 1925.

68. A. Winkler, Die Monotonie der Arbeit, *Zeitschrift zur psychologische Berufswissens*, Vol. 19, 1922.

69. *Op. cit.*

70. From S. Wyatt and J. N. Langdon, Fatigue and boredom in repetitive work, *The Human Factor*, 1937, 11, 198 f.

71. S. Wyatt, and J. A. Fraser, *The Comparative Effects of Variety and Uniformity in Work.* London: Ind. Fat. Res. Bd. Report No. 52, 1928.

72. H. Marot, *Creative Impulse in Industry.* New York: E. P. Dutton and Company, 1919.

73. E. Mayo, Basis of industrial psychology, *Bulletin of the Taylor Society*, 1924, 9, 249-59.

74. S. Wyatt, and J. N. Langdon, *Op. cit.*, 199.

75. E. K. Strong, Jr., Aptitudes versus attitudes in vocational guidance, *J. Appl. Psychol.*, 1934, 18, 515.

76. From Nat'l Ind. Conference Bd. Studies, *Financial Incentives.* New York: 1935.

77. D. Fryer, and O. Hiester, Why men work, *Wharton Review*, 1936, 9, 7.

78. S. Wyatt, L. Frost, and F. G. L. Stock, *Incentives in Repetitive Work.* London: Ind. Health Res. Bd. Report No. 69, 1934.

79. J. W. Riegel, Principles and methods of wage and salary, *Proceedings 7th Int. Mgt. Congress*—General Mgt. Papers. Baltimore: Waverly Press, 1938, 36.

80. *Op. cit.*

81. S. B. Mathewson, *Restriction and Output Among Unorganized Workers.* New York: Viking Press, 1931.

82. Mace, *Op. cit.*

83. *Op. cit.*

84. T. N. Whitehead, Social motives in economic activities, *Occup. Psychol.* 1938, 12, 273 f.

85. T. N. Whitehead, *The Industrial Worker.* Cambridge: Harvard University Press, 1938.

86. G. Pennock, Industrial research at Hawthorne, *Pers. J.*, 1930, 8, 311.

87. W. Williams, *Mainspring of Men.* New York: Charles Scribner's Sons, 1925.

88. L. Katin, Imagination and rationalization, *Human Factor*, 1932, 6, 184.

89. H. Feldman, *Problems in Labor Relations*. New York: The Macmillan Company, 1937.

90. R. S. Uhrbrock, Attitudes of 4430 employees, *J. Soc. Psychol.*, 1934, 5, 374.

91. H. B. Bergen, Finding out what employees are thinking, *Ind. Conference Bd. Mgt. Record*, April, 1939, 1-6.

92. D. McGregor, The attitude of workers toward lay-off policy, *J. Abn. and Soc. Psychol.*, 1939, 34, 179-199.

93. E. M. Chamberlin, What is labor thinking, *Pers. J.*, 1935, 14, 118.

94. R. Hoppock, *Job Satisfaction*. New York: Harper and Brothers, 1935.

95. D. W. Harding, Some social implications of industrial psychology, *Human Factor*, 10, 1936, 84.

Chapter XIX

1. E. E. Emme, The adjustment problems of college freshmen and contributory factors, *J. Appl. Psychol.*, 1936, 20, 60-76.

2. Two excellent summaries of the literature up to 1934 upon the prediction of college scholarship from various measures are available for the student as follows: D. Segal, Prediction of success in college, Washington: G. P. O., Bull., 1934, No. 15, Office of Education; M. E. Wagner, Prediction of college performance, *U. of Buf. Studies*, 1934, IX.

3. D. Segal and M. M. Proffitt, *Social Factors in Adjustment of College Students*, Washington: G. P. O., Bull., 1937, No. 12, Office of Education.

4. E. R. Henry, An analysis of probation students, *Report of the Fifth Annual Meeting of the American College Personnel Association*, 1938.

5. R. Pintner, *Intelligence Testing*. New York: Henry Holt and Company, 1931.

6. M. E. Bennett, *College and Life*. New York: McGraw-Hill Book Company, Inc., 1933; and D. G. Paterson, G. G. Schneidler and E. G. Williamson, *Student Guidance Techniques*. New York: McGraw-Hill Book Company, Inc., 1938.

7. H. Keller and C. O. Weber, Germany's elimination test for dentists, *J. Appl. Psychol.*, 16, 1932, 465-474.

8. A. J. Harris, The relative significance of measures of mechanical aptitude, intelligence, and previous scholarship for predicting achievement in dental school, *J. Appl. Psychol.*, 21, 1937, 513-521.

9. W. V. Bingham, *Aptitude and Aptitude Testing.* New York: Harper and Brothers, 1937, 166-205.

10. G. W. Hartmann, The prestige of occupations, *Pers. J.*, 13, 1934-35, 144-152.

11. W. M. Marston, Studies in testimony, *J. Am. Inst. of Criminal Law and Criminology*, 1924, 15, 5-31.

12. H. R. Crosland, The psychological methods of word association and reaction time as tests of deception, *Univ. of Oregon Pub., Psychol. Series*, 1929, I, No. 1, pp. 104.

13. V. Benussi, Die Atmungssymptome der Lüge, *Archiv. für die gesamte psychologie*, 1914, 31, 244-273.

14. C. A. Ruckmick, The truth about the lie detector, *J. Appl. Psychol.*, 1938, 22, 50-58.

15. W. G. Summers, A new psychogalvanometric technique in criminal investigation, *Psychol. Bull.*, 1937, 34, 551 f.

16. W. M. Marston, Systolic blood pressure symptoms of deception, *J. Exper. Psychol.*, 1917, 11, 117-163.

17. W. M. Marston, *The Lie Detector Test.* New York: R. R. Smith, 1938.

18. J. A. Larson, The cardio-pneumo-psychogram in deception, *J. Exper. Psychol.*, 1923, VI, 420-454.

19. H. E. Burtt, *Legal Psychology.* New York: Prentice-Hall, Inc., 1931.

20. H. D. Kitson, *The Mind of the Buyer.* New York: The Macmillan Company, 1921.

21. F. McKinney, An empirical method of analyzing a sales interview, *J. Appl. Psychol.*, 1937, 21, 280-299.

22. G. E. Mitchell and H. E. Burtt, Psychological factors in the sales interview, *J. Appl. Psychol.*, 1938, 22, 17-31.

23. Daniel Starch, *Principles of Advertising.* Chicago: A. W. Shaw Company, 1923, 539 f.

24. F. J. Gaudet and B. B. Zients, The history of full-page advertisements, *J. Appl. Psychol.*, 16, 1932, 512-514.

25. M. Barrett, A comparison of the order of merit method and the method of paired comparisons, *Psychol. Rev.*, XXI, 1914, 278-294.

26. E. S. Conklin and J. W. Sutherland, A comparison of the scale of values method with the order-of-merit method, *J. Exper. Psychol.*, VI, 1923, 44-57.

27. E. M. Achilles, Experimental studies in recall and recognition, *Arch. Psychol.*, No. 44, 1920.

28. E. R. Brandt, The memory value of advertisements with special reference to color, *Arch. Psychol.*, No. 79, 1925.

29. H. C. Link, A new method for testing advertising and a psychological sales barometer, *J. Appl. Psychol.*, 18, 1934, 1-26.
30. H. K. Nixon, Attention and interest in advertising, *Arch. Psychol.*, No. 72, 1923.
31. D. G. Paterson and M. A. Tinker, Black type versus white type, *J. Appl. Psychol.*, 1931, 15, 241-247.
32. D. B. Lucas, The optimum length of advertising headline, *J. Appl. Psychol.*, 1934, 18, 665-674.
33. E. K. Strong, Jr., Value of white space in advertising, *J. Appl. Psychol.*, 1926, 10, 107-116.
34. F. N. Stanton, Memory for advertising copy presented visually and orally, *J. Appl. Psychol.*, 1934, 18, 45-64.
35. H. V. Gaskill and R. L. Holcomb, The effectiveness of appeal in radio advertising: A technique with some typical results, *J. Appl. Psychol.*, 1936, 20, 325-339.
36. J. G. Jenkins, Dependability of psychological brand barometers: I. The problem of reliability, *J. Appl. Psychol.*, 1938, 22, 1-7.
37. J. G. Jenkins and H. H. Corbin, Jr., Dependability of psychological brand barometers. II. The problem of validity, *J. Appl. Psychol.*, 1938, 22, 252-260.
38. H. E. Burtt, *Psychology of Advertising.* Cambridge: Houghton Mifflin Company, 1938; A. T. Poffenberger, *Psychology in Advertising.* New York: McGraw-Hill Book Company, Inc., 1932.
39. H. C. Link, *The New Psychology of Selling and Advertising.* New York: The Macmillan Company, 1932.
40. R. H. Paynter, A psychological investigation of the likelihood of confusion between the words "Coco-Cola" and "Cheero-Cola," *J. Appl. Psychol.*, 1919, 3, 329-351.

Chapter XXI

1. A. E. Housman, *The Name and Nature of Poetry.* New York: The Macmillan Company, 1933, 18.
2. M. Schoen, *Art and Beauty.* New York: The Macmillan Company, 1932, 143 f.
3. E. Rickert, *New Methods for the Study of Literature.* Chicago: University of Chicago Press, 1927.
4. E. W. Scripture, The study of English speech by new methods of phonetic investigation, *Proceed. Brit. Acad.*, 1921-23, 10, 270-299. W. M. Patterson, *The Rhythm of Prose.* New York: Columbia University Press, 1916.
5. H. S. Langfeld, *The Aesthetic Attitude.* New York: Harcourt, Brace and Company, 1920, 154.

6. A. T. Poffenberger and B. E. Barrows, The feeling value of lines, *J. Appl. Psychol.*, 1924, 8, 187-205.

7. K. Hevner, An experimental study of the affective value of color and line, *J. Appl. Psychol.*, 1935, 19, 385-398.

8. E. Sapir, A study in phonetic symbolism, *J. Exper. Psychol.*, 1929, 12, 225-239.

9. K. Hevner, The affective value of sounds in poetry, *Amer. J. Psychol.*, 1937, 49, 419-434.

10. M. Sherman, Emotional character of the singing voice, *J. Exper. Psychol.*, 1928, 11, 495-497.

11. C. P. Heinlein, The affective character of the major and minor modes in music, *J. Comp. Psychol.*, 1928, 8, 101-141.

12. C. C. Pratt, *The Meaning of Music.* New York: McGraw-Hill Book Company, Inc., 1931, Chs. 9 and 10.

13. R. H. Gundlach, A quantitative analysis of Indian music, *Amer. J. Psychol.*, 1932, 44, 133-145.

14. K. Hevner, An experimental study of the affective value of pitch and tempo, *Amer. J. Psychol.*, 1937, 49, 621-630; and Experimental studies of expressiveness in music, *Amer. J. Psychol.*, 1936, 48, 246-268.

15. E. Murray, Some uses and misuses of the term 'aesthetic,' *Amer. J. Psychol.*, 1930, 42, 640-644.

16. E. D. Snyder, *Hypnotic Poetry.* Philadelphia: University of Pennsylvania Press, 1930.

17. E. Bullough, 'Psychical Distance' as a factor in art and an aesthetic principle, *Brit. J. Psychol.*, 1912, 5, 87-118.

18. A. R. Chandler, Recent experiments on visual aesthetics, *Psychol. Bull.*, 1928, 25, 720-732.

19. J. H. Mueller, Trends in musical taste, *New York Sunday Times*, Feb. 27, 1938.

20. O. Ortmann, In forty years, *Peabody Bulletin*, 1932, 29, 3-16.

21. H. T. Moore, The genetic aspect of consonance and dissonance, *Psychol. Monog.*, 1914, 17 (No. 73).

22. P. R. Farnsworth, Ending preferences in two musical situations, *Amer. J. Psychol.*, 1926, 37, 237-240; The effect of repetition on ending preferences in melodies, *Amer. J. Psychol.*, 1926, 37, 116-122.

23. G. M. Whipple, Analyzing musical style by means of reproducing piano, *J. Appl. Psychol.*, 1928, 12, 200-216. L. Skinner and C. E. Seashore, A musical pattern score of the first movement of the Beethoven Sonata, Op. 27, No. 2, *Iowa Studies in Music* IV, 1937, 263-280.

24. O. Ortmann, *The Physiological Mechanics of Piano Technique.* New York: Dutton, 1929.

25. From J. Tiffin, Phonophotographic apparatus, *Univ. Iowa Studies in the Psychol. Music,* 1932, 1, 118-133.

26. H. G. Seashore, An objective analysis of artistic singing, *Iowa St. Mus.,* 1935, 4, 12-157.

27. H. Cowell, The process of musical creation, *Amer. J. Psychol.,* 1926, 37, 233-236.

28. D. Stumberg, A study of poetic talent, *J. Exper. Psychol.,* 1928, 11, 219-234.

29. Especially at the University of Iowa under the direction of N. C. Meier.

30. J. L. Lowes, *The Road to Xanadu.* New York: Houghton Mifflin Company, 1930.

31. A. R. Chandler, *Beauty and Human Nature.* New York: D. Appleton-Century Company, Inc., 1934, Ch. 16.

32. H. M. Stanton, Prognosis of musical achievement, *Eastman School of Music Studies in Psychol.,* 1929, 1, No. 4, 1-89.

33. C. E. Seashore, *The Psychology of Musical Talent.* New York: Silver, Burdett Company, 1919.

34. P. R. Farnsworth, An historical, critical and experimental study of the Seashore-Kwalwasser Test Battery, *Gen. Psychol. Monog.,* 1931, 9, No. 5, 291-393.

35. K. Hevner, Appreciation of Music and Tests for Appreciation of Music, *University Oregon Pub.,* 1934, 4, 83-151.

36. Published by C. H. Stoelting Co., Chicago, 1932 Victor Phonograph Recording.

37. A. Abbott and M. R. Trabue, A measure of ability to judge poetry, *Teachers College Bull.,* 1922, 14th series, No. 2.

38. N. C. Meier, A measure of art talent, *Psychol. Monog.,* 1928, 39, 184-199.

39. See also M. McAdory, *The construction and validation of an art test.* Bureau of Publications, Teachers College, Columbia University, 1929.

Chapter XXII

1. E. B. Titchener, *Systematic Psychology: Prolegomena.* New York: The Macmillan Company, 1929, 142.

2. E. B. Titchener, *A Text-Book of Psychology.* New York: The Macmillan Company, 1919, 471.

3. W. McDougall, *The Energies of Men.* New York: Charles Scribner's Sons, 1933, 25.

INDEX OF NAMES

INDEX OF SUBJECT MATTER

RICHARD I. EVANS
DEPT OF Psychology